A

POLITICAL TEXT-BOOK

FOR 1860:

COMPRISING A BRIEF VIEW OF

PRESIDENTIAL NOMINATIONS AND ELECTIONS:

INCLUDING

ALL THE NATIONAL PLATFORMS EVER YET ADOPTED:

ALSO,

A HISTORY OF THE STRUGGLE

RESPECTING

SLAVERY IN THE TERRITORIES,

AND OF THE

ACTION OF CONGRESS AS TO THE

FREEDOM OF THE PUBLIC LANDS,

WITH

THE MOST NOTABLE SPEECHES AND LETTERS

OF

MESSRS. LINCOLN, DOUGLAS, BELL, CASS, SEWARD, EVERETT, BRECKINRIDGE,
H. V. JOHNSON, ETC., ETC., TOUCHING THE QUESTIONS OF THE DAY;

AND

RETURNS OF ALL PRESIDENTIAL ELECTIONS SINCE 1836.

COMPILED BY HORACE GREELEY AND JOHN F. CLEVELAND.

NEW-YORK:
PUBLISHED BY THE TRIBUNE ASSOCIATION,
154 NASSAU-STREET.
1860.

W. H. TINSON, Stereotyper.

ADVERTISEMENT.

The single end of this book is the presentation, in a compact and convenient form, of the more important facts, votes, resolves, letters, speeches, reports and other documents, which elucidate the political contest now agitating this country. It has been our aim to let every candidate and other important personage speak for himself, make his own platform, and vindicate (if he may) his own consistency and the soundness of his views on the great questions which underlie our current politics.

Of course, such a work can have but a comparative merit. Make it ever so large, and still many things must be omitted that the compiler would wish to insert; and every critic will plausibly ask, "Why insert this and omit that? Why give so much of A. and so little of B.?" Beside, it is not always possible to remember, or, if remembered, to find, all that would be valued in a work like this. We can only say that we have done our best: let him do better who can.

Inaccuracy of citation is one of the chief vices of our political discussions. You can hardly listen to a set speech, even from a well-informed and truthful canvasser, which is not marred by some misapprehension or unconscious misstatement of the position and views of this or that prominent statesman. Documents, heedlessly read and long since lost or mislaid, are quoted from with fluency and confidence, as though with indubitable accuracy, when the citations so made do gross injustice to their author, and tend to mislead the hearer. We believe the documents collected in this work are so printed that their general accuracy may be safely relied on.

By canvassers of all parties, we trust our Text-Book will be found convenient, not to say indispensable. But those who only listen, and read, and reflect, will also find it a manifest help to a clear understanding of the issues and contentions of the day. They will be interested in comparing the *actual* positions taken by Mr. Lincoln, or Mr. Douglas, or Gen. Cass, or Mr. Everett, as faithfully set forth in this work, with those confidently attributed to that statesman in the fluent harangue of some political opponent, who is intent on blazoning his inconsistency or proving his insincerity. To verify and correct the citations of a frothy declaimer is sometimes the easiest and most convincing refutation of his speech.

If a trace of partisan bias is betrayed in the thread of narrative which partially unites the successive reports, bills, votes, etc., presented in this work, the error is unintentional and regretted. Our purpose was to compile a record acceptable and convenient to men of all parties, and which might be consulted and trusted by all. Whatever is original herein is regarded as of no use or merit, save as a necessary elucidation of the residue. Without apology, therefore, or further explanation, the Text-Book is commended to the favor of the American public.

New-York, *August 1st,* 1860.

CONTENTS.

CONTENTS.

CONTENTS.

CONTENTS.

A POLITICAL TEXT-BOOK FOR 1860.

NATIONAL CAUCUSES, CONVENTIONS, AND PLATFORMS.

NATIONAL Conventions for the nomination of candidates are of comparatively recent origin. In the earlier political history of the United States, under the Federal Constitution, candidates for President and Vice-President were nominated by congressional and legislative caucuses. Washington was elected as first President under the Constitution, and reëlected for a second term by a unanimous, or nearly unanimous, concurrence of the American people; but an opposition party gradually grew up in Congress, which became formidable during his second term, and which ultimately crystalized into what was then called the Republican party. John Adams, of Massachusetts, was prominent among the leading Federalists, while Thomas Jefferson, of Virginia, was preëminently the author and oracle of the Republican party, and, by common consent, they were the opposing candidates for the Presidency, on Washington's retirement in 1796–7.

Mr. Adams was then chosen President, while Mr. Jefferson, having the largest electoral vote next to Mr. A., became Vice-President.

The first Congressional Caucus to nominate candidates for President and Vice-President, is said to have been held in Philadelphia in the year 1800, and to have nominated Mr. Jefferson for the first office, and Aaron Burr for the second. These candidates were elected after a desperate struggle, beating John Adams and Charles C. Pinckney, of South Carolina. In 1804, Mr. Jefferson was reëlected President, with George Clinton, of New-York, for Vice, encountering but slight opposition: Messrs. Charles C. Pinckney and Rufus King, the opposing candidates, receiving only 14 out of 176 Electoral Votes. We have been unable to find any record as to the manner of their nomination. In January, 1808, when Mr. Jefferson's second term was about to close, a Republican Congressional Caucus was held at Washington, to decide as to the relative claims of Madison and Monroe for the succession, the Legislature of Virginia, which had been said to exert a potent influence over such questions, being, on this occasion, unable to agree as to which of her favored sons should have the preference. Ninety-four of the 136 Republican members of Congress attended this caucus, and declared their preference of Mr. Madison, who received 83 votes, the remaining 11 being divided between Mr. Monroe and George Clinton. The Opposition supported Mr. Pinckney; but Mr. Madison was elected by a large majority.

Toward the close of Mr. Madison's earlier term, he was nominated for reëlection by a Congressional Caucus held at Washington, in May, 1812. In September of the same year, a convention of the Opposition, representing eleven States, was held in the city of New-York, which nominated De Witt Clinton, of New-York, for President. He was also put in nomination by the Republican Legislature of New-York. The ensuing canvass resulted in the reëlection of Mr. Madison, who received 128 electoral votes to 89 for De Witt Clinton.

In 1816, the Republican Congressional Caucus nominated James Monroe, who received, in the caucus, 65 votes to 54 for Wm. H. Crawford, of Georgia. The Opposition, or Federalists, named Rufus King, of New-York, who received only 34 electoral votes out of 217. There was no opposition to the reëlection of Mr. Monroe in 1820, a single (Republican) vote being cast against him, and for John Quincy Adams.

In 1824, the Republican party could not be induced to abide by the decision of a Congressional Caucus. A large majority of the Republican members formally refused to participate in such a gathering, or be governed by its decision; still, a Caucus was called and attended by the friends of Mr. Crawford alone. Of the 261 members of Congress at this time, 216 were Democrats or Republicans, yet only 66 responded to their names at roll-call, 64 of whom voted for Mr. Crawford as the Republican nominee for President. This nomination was very extensively repudiated throughout the country, and three competing Republican candidates were brought into the field through legislative and other machinery—viz., Andrew Jackson, Henry Clay, and John Quincy Adams. The result of this famous "scrub race" for the Presidency was, that no one was elected by the people, Gen. Jackson receiving 99 electoral votes, Mr. Adams 84, Mr. Crawford 41, and Mr. Clay 37. The election then devolved on the House of Representatives, where Mr. Adams was chosen, receiving the votes of 13 States, against 7 for Gen. Jackson, and 4 for Mr. Crawford. This was the end of "King Caucus." Gen. Jackson was immediately thereafter put in nomination for the ensuing term by the Legislature of Tennessee, having only Mr. Adams for an opponent in 1828, when he was elected by a decided majority, receiving 178 Electoral Votes to 83 for Mr. Adams. Mr. John C. Calhoun, who had at first aspired to the Presidency, in 1824, withdrew at an early stage from the canvass, and was thereupon chosen Vice-President by a very large electoral majority—Mr. Albert Gallatin, of Pennsylvania, (the caucus candidate on the Crawford ticket,) being his only serious competitor. In 1828, Mr. Calhoun was the candidate for Vice-President on the Jackson ticket, and of course reëlected. It was currently stated that the concentration of the Crawford and Calhoun strength on this ticket was mainly effected by Messrs. Martin Van Buren and Churchill C. Cambreleng, of New-York, during a southern tour made by them in 1827. In 1828, Richard Rush, of Pennsylvania, was the candidate for Vice-President on the Adams ticket.

U. S. ANTI-MASONIC CONVENTION—1830.

The first political National Convention in this country of which we have any record was held at Philadelphia in September, 1830, styled the United States Anti-Masonic Convention. It was composed of 96 delegates, representing the States of New-York, Massachusetts, Connecticut, Vermont, Rhode Island, Pennsylvania, New-Jersey, Delaware, Ohio, Maryland and the Territory of Michigan. Francis Granger of New-York presided; but no business was transacted beyond the adoption of the following resolution:

Resolved, That it is recommended to the people of the United States, opposed to secret societies, to meet in convention on Monday the 26th day of September, 1831, at the city of Baltimore, by delegates equal in number to their representatives in both houses of Congress, to make nominations of suitable candidates for the office of President and Vice-President, to be supported at the next election, and for the transaction of such other business as the cause of Anti-Masonry may require.

In compliance with the foregoing call, a National Anti-Masonic Convention was held at Baltimore, in September, 1831, which nominated William Wirt, of Maryland, for President, and Amos Ellmaker, of Pennsylvania, for Vice-President. The convention was attended by 112 delegates from the States of Maine, New-Hampshire, Vermont, Massachusetts, Rhode Island, Connecticut, New-York, New-Jersey, Pennsylvania, Ohio, Indiana, Delaware and Maryland —only Massachusetts, New-York and Pennsylvania being fully represented. John C. Spencer, of

New-York, presided over the deliberations of the Convention, and the nominees received each 108 votes. The candidates accepted the nomination and received the electoral vote of Vermont only. The Convention did not enunciate any distinct platform of principles, but appointed a committee to issue an Address to the people. In due time, the address was published. It is quite as prolix and verbose as modern political addresses; and, after stating at great length the necessary qualifications for the Chief of a great and free people, and presenting a searching criticism on the institution of free-masonry in its moral and political bearings, somewhat intensified from the excitement caused by the (then recent) alleged murder of William Morgan, for having revealed the secrets of the Masonic Order, the Address comes to the conclusion that, since the institution had become a political engine, political agencies must be used to avert its baneful effects—in other words, "that an enlightened exercise of the right of suffrage is the constitutional and equitable mode adopted by the Anti-Masons is necessary to remove the evil they suffer, and produce the reforms they seek."

DEMOCRATIC OR JACKSON NATIONAL CONVENTION—1832.

There was no open opposition in the Democratic party to the nomination of Gen. Jackson for a second term; but the party were not so well satisfied with Mr. Calhoun, the Vice-President; so a Convention was called to meet at Baltimore in May, 1832, to nominate a candidate for the second office. Delegates appeared and took their seats from the States of Maine, New-Hampshire, Vermont, Massachusetts, Connecticut, Rhode Island, New-York, New-Jersey, Pennsylvania, Delaware, Maryland, Virginia, North Carolina, South Carolina, Georgia, Alabama, Louisiana, Mississippi, Tennessee, Kentucky, Ohio, Indiana and Illinois.

Gen. Robert Lucas, of Ohio, presided, and the regular proceedings were commenced by the passage of the following resolution:

Resolved, That each State be entitled, in the nomination to be made for the Vice-Presidency, to a number of votes equal to the number to which they will be entitled in the electoral colleges, under the new apportionment, in voting for President and Vice-President; and that two-thirds of the whole number of the votes in the Convention shall be necessary to constitute a choice.

This seems to have been the origin of the famous "two-thirds" rule which has prevailed of late in Democratic National Conventions.

The Convention proceeded to ballot for a candidate for Vice-President, with the following result:

For Martin Van Buren: Connecticut, 8; Illinois, 2; Ohio, 21; Tennessee, 15; North Carolina, 9; Georgia, 11; Louisiana, 5; Pennsylvania, 30; Maryland, 7; New-Jersey, 8; Mississippi, 4; Rhode Island, 4; Maine, 10; Massachusetts, 14; Delaware, 3; New-Hampshire, 7; New-York, 42; Vermont, 7; Alabama, 1—Total, 208.

For Richard M. Johnson: Illinois, 2; Indiana, 9; Kentucky, 15—Total, 26.

For Philip P. Barbour: North Carolina, 6; Virginia, 23; Maryland, 3; South Carolina, 11; Alabama, 6—Total, 49.

Mr. Van Buren, having received more than two-thirds of all the votes cast, was declared duly nominated as the candidate of the party for Vice-President.

The Convention passed a resolution cordially concurring in the repeated nominations which Gen. Jackson had received in various parts of the country for reëlection as President.

Mr. Archer, of Virginia, from the committee appointed to prepare an address to the people, reported that

The committee, having interchanged opinions on the subject submitted to them, and agreeing fully in the principles and sentiments which they believe ought to be embodied in an address of this description, if such an address were to be made, nevertheless deem it advisable under existing circumstances, to recommend the adoption of the following resolution :

Resolved, That it be recommended to the several delegations in this Convention, in place of a General Address from this body to the people of the United States, to make such explanations by address, report, or otherwise, to their respective constituents, of the object, proceedings and result of the meeting, as they may deem expedient.

The result of this election was the choice of General Jackson, who received the electoral vote of the following States :

Maine. 10 ; New-Hampshire, 7 ; New-York, 42 ; New-Jersey, 8 ; Pennsylvania, 30 ; Maryland, 3 ; Virginia, 23 ; North Carolina, 15 ; Georgia, 11 ; Tennessee, 15 ; Ohio, 21 ; Louisiana, 5 ; Mississippi, 4 ; Indiana, 9 ; Illinois, 5 ; Alabama, 7 ; Missouri, 4—Total, 219.

For Mr. Clay : Massachusetts, 14 ; Rhode Island, 4 ; Connecticut, 8 ; Delaware, 3 ; Maryland, 5 ; Kentucky, 15—Total, 49.

For John Floyd, of Virginia : South Carolina, 11.

For William Wirt, of Maryland: Vermont, 7.

Mr. Van Buren received only 189 votes for Vice-President, Pennsylvania, which cast her vote for Jackson, having voted for William Wilkins of that State for Vice-President. John Sergeant, for Vice-President, received the same vote as Mr. Clay for President. South Carolina voted for Henry Lee of Massachusetts, for Vice-President.

NATIONAL REPUBLICAN CONVENTION—
1831.

The National Republicans met in convention at Baltimore, Dec. 12, 1831. Seventeen States and the District of Columbia were represented by 157 delegates, who cast a unanimous vote for Henry Clay, of Kentucky, for President, and John Sergeant, of Pennsylvania, for Vice-President. James Barbour, of Virginia, presided, and the States represented were : Maine, New-Hampshire, Massachusetts, Rhode Island, Connecticut, Vermont, New York, New Jersey, Pennsylvania, Delaware, Maryland, Virginia, North Carolina, Kentucky, Tennessee, Ohio, Louisiana and Indiana. The Convention adopted no formal platform of principles, but issued an Address, mainly devoted to a criticism on the Administration of Gen. Jackson, asserting, among other things, that—

The political history of the Union for the last three years exhibits a series of measures plainly dictated in all their principal features by blind cupidity or vindictive party spirit, marked throughout by a disregard of good policy, justice, and every high and generous sentiment, and, terminating in a dissolution of the Cabinet under circumstances more discreditable than any of the kind to be met with in the annals of the civilized world.

The address alludes to the charge of incapacity and corruption leveled against his imme-

diate predecessor (J. Q. Adams) by Gen. Jackson in his Inaugural Address, and adds :

The indecorum of this denunciation was hardly less glaring than its essential injustice, and can only be paralleled by that of the subsequent denunciation of the same Administration, on the same authority, to a foreign government.

Exception is taken to the indiscriminate removal of all officers within the reach of the President, who were not attached to his person or party. As illustrative of the extent to which this political proscription was carried, it is stated that, within a month after the inauguration of General Jackson, more persons were removed from office than during the whole 40 years that had previously elapsed since the adoption of the Constitution. Fault is also found with the Administration in its conduct of our foreign affairs. Again the Address **says** :

On the great subjects of internal policy, the course of the President has been so inconsistent and vacillating, that it is impossible for any party to place confidence in his character, or to consider him as a true and effective friend. By avowing his approbation of a judicious tariff, at the same time recommending to Congress precisely the same policy which had been adopted as the best plan of attack by the opponents of that measure ; by admitting the constitutionality and expediency of Internal Improvements of a National character, and at the same moment negativing the most important bills of this description which were presented to him by Congress, the President has shown that he is either a secret enemy to the system, or that he is willing to sacrifice the most important national objects in a vain attempt to conciliate the conflicting interests, or rather adverse party feeling and opinions of different sections of the country.

Objection is taken to Gen. Jackson's war on the United States Bank, and the necessity and usefulness of that institution are argued at considerable length. The outrageous and inhuman treatment of the Cherokee Indians by the State of Georgia, and the failure of the National Administration to protect them in their rights, acquired by treaty with the United States, is also the subject of animadversion in the the Address.

A resolve was adopted, recommending to the young men of the National Republican Party to hold a Convention in the city of Washington on the following May.

Such a Convention was accordingly held at the Capital on the 11th of May, 1832, over which William Cost Johnson, of Maryland, presided, and at which the following, among other resolves, were adopted :

Resolved, That an adequate Protection to American Industry is indispensable to the prosperity of the country ; and that an abandonment of the policy at this period would be attended with consequences ruinous to the best interests of the Nation.

Resolved, That a uniform system of Internal Improvements, sustained and supported by the General Government, is calculated to secure, in the highest degree, the harmony, the strength and the permanency of the Republic.

Resolved, That the indiscriminate removal of public officers, for a mere difference of political opinion, is a gross abuse of power ; and that the doctrine lately boldly preached in the United States Senate, that " to the victors belong the spoils of the vanquished," is detrimental to the interest, corrupting to the morals, and dangerous to the liberties of the people of this country.

DEMOCRATIC NATIONAL CONVENTION,
1835.

In May, 1835, a National Convention representing twenty-one States, assembled at Baltimore to nominate candidates for President and Vice-President. The Hon. Andrew Stevenson, of Virginia, was chosen president, with half a dozen vice-presidents and four secretaries. A rule was adopted that two-thirds of the whole number of votes should be necessary to make a nomination or to decide any question connected therewith. On the first ballot for President, Mr. Van Buren was nominated unanimously, receiving 265 votes. For Vice-President, Richard M. Johnson, of Kentucky, received 178, and William C. Rives, of Virginia, 87. Mr. Johnson, having received more than two-thirds of all the votes cast, was declared duly nominated as the candidate for Vice-President. This Convention adopted no platform.

THE OPPOSITION IN 1836.

In 1835, Gen. Wm. H. Harrison, of Ohio, was nominated for President, with Francis Granger, for Vice-President, by a Whig State Convention at Harrisburg, Pennsylvania, and also by a Democratic Anti-Masonic Convention held at the same place. A Whig State Convention in Maryland also nominated Gen. Harrison for President, with John Tyler, of Virginia, for Vice. Gen. H. also received nominations in New York, Ohio and other States.

Hugh L. White, of Tennessee was nominated by the Legislatures of Tennessee and Alabama, as the Opposition or Anti-Jackson candidate; while Mr. Webster was the favorite of the Opposition in Massachusetts, and Willie P. Mangum, of N. C. received the vote of S. C., 11. The result of the contest of 1836 was the election of Mr. Van Buren, who received the electoral votes of the States of

Maine, 10; New-Hampshire, 7; Rhode Island, 4; Connecticut, 8; New York, 42; Pennsylvania, 30; Virginia, 23; North Carolina, 15; Louisiana, 5; Mississippi, 4; Illinois, 5; Alabama, 7; Missouri, 4; Arkansas, 3; Michigan, 3—Total 170.

Gen. Harrison received the votes of

Vermont, 7; New-Jersey, 8; Delaware, 3; Maryland, 10; Kentucky, 15; Ohio, 21; and Indiana, 9—Total, 73.

Hugh L. White received the vote of Georgia, 11, and Tennessee, 15: total, 26. Mr. Webster received the vote of Massachusetts, 14.

WHIG NATIONAL CONVENTION,—1839.

A Whig National Convention representing twenty-one States met at Harrisburg, Pa., Dec. 4, 1839. James Barbour, of Virginia, presided, and the result of the first ballot was the nomination of Gen. William H. Harrison, of Ohio, who received 148 * votes to 90 for Henry Clay, and 16 for Gen. Winfield Scott. John Tyler, of Virginia, was unanimously nominated as the Whig candidate for Vice-President. The Convention adopted no platform of principles; but the party in conducting the memorable campaign of 1840, assailed the Administration of Mr. Van Buren for its general mismanagement of public affairs and its profligacy, and the

* Ballots were repeatedly taken *in committee* throughout two or three days; but as no candidate received a majority, it was only reported to the convention that the committee had not been able to agree on a candidate to be presented to the convention. Finally, the delegates from New-York and other States which had supported Gen. Scott, generally went over to Gen. Harrison, who thus received a majority, when the result was declared, as above.

result was the triumphant election of Harrison and Tyler, Van Buren receiving the electoral vote of only seven States; viz:

New-Hampshire, 7; Virginia, 23; South Carolina, 11; Illinois, 5; Alabama, 7; Missouri, 4; and Arkansas, 3—Total, 60.

South Carolina refused to vote for Richard M. Johnson for Vice-President, throwing away her 11 votes on Littleton W. Tazewell, of Virginia. Harrison and Tyler received the votes of the following States:

Maine, 10; Massachusetts, 14; Rhode Island, 4; Connecticut, 8; Vermont, 7; New-York 42; New-Jersey, 8; Pennsylvania, 30; Delaware, 3; Maryland, 10; North Carolina, 15; Georgia, 11; Kentucky, 15; Tennessee, 15; Ohio, 21; Louisiana, 5; Mississippi, 4; Indiana, 9; Michigan, 8—Total, 234.

ABOLITION CONVENTION,—1839.

A Convention of Abolitionists was held at Warsaw, N. Y., on the 13th of November, 1839, which adopted the following:

Resolved, That, in our judgment, every consideration of duty and expediency which ought to control the action of Christian freemen, requires of the Abolitionists of the U. S. to organize a distinct and independent political party, embracing all the necessary means for nominating candidates for office and sustaining them by public suffrage.

The Convention then nominated for President James G. Birney, of New York, and for Vice-President Francis J. Lemoyne, of Pennsylvania. These gentlemen subsequently declined the nomination. Nevertheless they received a total of 7,609 votes in various Free States.

DEMOCRATIC NATIONAL CONVENTION, 1840.

A Democratic National Convention met at Baltimore, May 5th, 1840, to nominate candidates for President and Vice-President. Delegates were present from the States of Maine, New-Hampshire, Vermont, Massachusetts, Rhode Island, New-York, New-Jersey, Pennsylvania, Maryland, North Carolina, Georgia, Kentucky, Tennessee, Ohio, Alabama, Mississippi, Louisiana, Indiana, Missouri, Michigan, and Arkansas. Gov. William Carroll, of Tennessee, presided, and the Convention, before proceeding to the nomination of candidates, adopted the following platform—viz.:

1. *Resolved,* That the Federal Government is one of limited powers, derived solely from the Constitution, and the grants of power shown therein ought to be strictly construed by all the departments and agents of the government, and that it is inexpedient and dangerous to exercise doubtful constitutional powers.

2. *Resolved,* That the Constitution does not confer upon the General Government the power to commence or carry on a general system of internal improvement.

3. *Resolved,* That the Constitution does not confer authority upon the Federal Government, directly or indirectly, to assume the debts of the several States, contracted for local internal improvements or other State purposes; nor would such assumption be just or expedient.

4. *Resolved,* That justice and sound policy forbid the Federal Government to foster one branch of industry to the detriment of another, or to cherish the interest of one portion to the injury of another portion of our common country—that every citizen and every section of the country has a right to demand and insist upon an equality of rights and privileges, and to complete and ample protection of persons and property from domestic violence or foreign aggression.

5. *Resolved*, That it is the duty of every branch of the government to enforce and practice the most rigid economy in conducting our public affairs, and that no more revenue ought to be raised than is required to defray the necessary expenses of the government.

6. *Resolved*, That Congress has no power to charter a United States Bank, that we believe such an institution one of deadly hostility to the best interests of the country, dangerous to our republican institutions and the liberties of the people, and calculated to place the business of the country within the control of a concentrated money power, and above the laws and the will of the people.

7. *Resolved*, That Congress has no power, under the Constitution, to interfere with or control the domestic institutions of the several States; and that such States are the sole and proper judges of everything pertaining to their own affairs, not prohibited by the Constitution; that all efforts, by abolitionists or others, made to induce Congress to interfere with questions of slavery, or to take incipient steps in relation thereto, are calculated to lead to the most alarming and dangerous consequences, and that all such efforts have an inevitable tendency to diminish the happiness of the people, and endanger the stability and permanency of the Union, and ought not to be countenanced by any friend to our Political Institutions.

8. *Resolved*, That the separation of the moneys of the government from banking institutions is indispensable for the safety of the funds of the government and the rights of the people.

9. *Resolved*, That the liberal principles embodied by Jefferson in the Declaration of Independence, and sanctioned in the Constitution, which makes ours the land of liberty and the asylum of the oppressed of every nation, have ever been cardinal principles in the Democratic faith; and every attempt to abridge the present privilege of becoming citizens, and the owners of soil among us, ought to be resisted with the same spirit which swept the Alien and Sedition Laws from our statute book.

The Convention then unanimously nominated Mr. Van Buren for reëlection as President; but, there being much diversity of opinion as to the proper man for Vice-President, the following preamble and resolution were adopted:

Whereas, Several of the States which have nominated Martin Van Buren as a candidate for the Presidency, have put in nomination different individuals as candidates for Vice-President, thus indicating a diversity of opinion as to the person best entitled to the nomination; and whereas some of the said States are not represented in this Convention, therefore,

Resolved, That the Convention deem it expedient at the present time not to choose between the individuals in nomination, but to leave the decision to their Republican fellow-citizens in the several States, trusting that before the election shall take place, their opinions will become so concentrated as to secure the choice of a Vice-President by the Electoral College.

WHIG NATIONAL CONVENTION, 1844.

A Whig National Convention assembled in Baltimore, on the 1st of May, 1844, in which every State in the Union was represented. Ambrose Spencer, of New-York, presided, and Mr. Clay was nominated for President by acclamation. For Vice-President, there was some diversity of preference, and Mr. Frelinghuysen, of N. J., was nominated on the third ballot as follows:

BALLOTS.			
	1st.	2d.	3rd.
T. Frelinghuysen, N. J.,	101	118	155
John Davis, Mass.,	83	74	79
Millard Fillmore, N. Y.,	53	51	40
John Sergeant, Pa.,	38	32 withdrawn.	
Total,	275	275	274

The principles of the party were briefly summed up in the following resolve, which was adopted by the Convention:

Resolved, That these principles may be summed as comprising a well regulated National currency—a Tariff for revenue to defray the necessary expenses of the Government, and discriminating with special reference to the Protection of the Domestic Labor of the country —the Distribution of the proceeds from the sales of the Public Lands—a single term for the Presidency—a reform of executive usurpations—and generally such an administration of the affairs of the country, as shall impart to every branch of the public service the greatest practicable efficiency, controlled by a well-regulated and wise economy.

The contest resulted in the choice of the Democratic candidates (Polk and Dallas,) who received 170 electoral votes as follows : Maine, 9; New-Hampshire, 6; New-York, 36; Pennsylvania, 26; Virginia, 17; South Carolina, 9; Georgia, 10; Alabama, 9; Mississippi, 6; Louisiana, 6; Indiana, 12; Illinois, 9; Missouri, 7; Arkansas, 3; Michigan, 5—170.

For Clay and Frelinghuysen: Vermont, 6; Massachusetts, 12; Rhode Island, 4; Connecticut, 6; New-Jersey, 7; Delaware, 3; Maryland, 8; North Carolina, 11; Tennessee, 13; Kentucky, 12; Ohio, 23—105.

DEMOCRATIC NATIONAL CONVENTION, 1844.

A Democratic National Convention assembled at Baltimore on the 27th May, 1844, adopted the two-third rule and, after a stormy session of three days, James K. Polk, of Tennessee, was nominated for President, and Silas Wright, of New York, for Vice-President. Mr. Wright declined the nomination, and George M. Dallas, of Pennsylvania, was subsequently selected to fill the second place on the ticket.

The ballotings for President were as follows :

BALLOTS.									
	1st.	2d.	3rd.	4th.	5th.	6th.	7th.	8th.	9th.
M. Van Buren	146	127	121	111	103	101	99	104	2
Lewis Cass	83	94	92	105	107	116	123	114	29
R. M. Johnson	29	33	38	32	26	25	21	—	—
James Buchanan	4	9	11	17	29	23	22	2	—
J. C. Calhoun	—	1	2	1	1	1	1	2	—
Levi Woodbury	—	—	2	—	—	—	—	—	—
Com. Stewart	—	1	—	—	—	—	—	—	—
James K. Polk	—	—	—	—	—	—	—	44	233

Mr. Van. Buren's name was withdrawn after the 8th ballot.

The platform adopted by the Convention was the same as that of 1840, with the following additions :

Resolved, That the proceeds of the Public Lands ought to be sacredly applied to the national objects specified in the Constitution, and that we are opposed to the laws lately adopted, and to any law for the Distribution of such proceeds among the States, as alike inexpedient in policy and repugnant to the Constitution.

Resolved, That we are decidedly opposed to taking from the President the qualified veto power by which he is enabled, under restrictions and responsibilities amply sufficient to guard the public interest, to suspend the passage of a bill, whose merits cannot secure the approval of two-thirds of the Senate and House of Representatives, until the judgment of the people can be obtained thereon, and which has thrice saved the American People from the corrupt and tyrannical domination of the Bank of the United States.

Resolved, That our title to the whole of the Territory of Oregon is clear and unquestionable; that no portion of the same ought to be ceded to England or any other power; and that the reoccupation of Oregon and the reannexation of Texas at the earliest practicable period are great American measures, which this Convention recommends to the cordial support of the Democracy of the Union.

LIBERTY PARTY NATIONAL CONVENTION, 1843.

The Liberty Party National Convention met at Buffalo, on the 30th of August. Leicester

King, of Ohio, presided, and James G. Birney, of Michigan, was unanimously nominated for President, with Thomas Morris, of Ohio, for Vice-President. Among the resolves adopted were the following :

Resolved, That human brotherhood is a cardinal principle of true Democracy, as well as of pure Christianity, which spurns all inconsistent limitations; and neither the political party which repudiates it, nor the political system which is not based upon it, can be truly Democratic or permanent.

Resolved, That the Liberty Party, placing itself upon this broad principle, will demand the absolute and unqualified divorce of the General Government from slavery, and also the restoration of equality of rights, among men, in every State where the party exists, or may exist.

Resolved, That the Liberty Party has not been organized for any temporary purpose by interested politicians, but has arisen from among the people in consequence of a conviction, hourly gaining ground, that no other party in the country represents the true principles of American liberty, or the true spirit of the Constitution of the United States.

Resolved, That the Liberty Party has not been organized merely for the overthrow of slavery; its first decided effort must, indeed, be directed against slaveholding as the grossest and most revolting manifestation of despotism, but it will also carry out the principle of equal rights into all its practical consequences and applications, and support every just measure conducive to individual and social freedom.

Resolved, That the Liberty Party is not a sectional party but a national party; was not originated in a desire to accomplish a single object, but in a comprehensive regard to the great interests of the whole country; is not a new party, nor a third party, but is the party of 1776, reviving the principles of that memorable era, and striving to carry them into practical application.

Resolved, That it was understood in the times of the Declaration and the Constitution, that the existence of slavery in some of the States, was in derogation of the principles of American Liberty, and a deep stain upon the character of the country, and the implied faith of the States and the Nation was pledged, that slavery should never be extended beyond its then existing limits, but should be gradually, and yet, at no distant day, wholly abolished by State authority.

Resolved, That the faith of the States and the Nation thus pledged, was most nobly redeemed by the voluntary Abolition of Slavery in several of the States, and by the adoption of the Ordinance of 1787, for the government of the Territory northwest of the river Ohio, then the only Territory in the United States, and consequently the only territory subject in this respect to the control of Congress by which Ordinance Slavery was forever excluded from the vast regions which now compose the States of Ohio, Indiana, Illinois, Michigan, and the Territory of Wisconsin, and an incapacity to bear up any other than freemen, was impressed on the soil itself.

Resolved, That the faith of the States and Nation thus pledged, has been shamefully violated by the omission on the part of many of the States, to take any measures whatever for the Abolition of Slavery within their respective limits; by the continuance of Slavery in the District of Columbia, and in the Territories of Louisiana and Florida; by the Legislation of Congress; by the protection afforded by national legislation and negotiation to slaveholding in American vessels, on the high seas, employed in the coastwise Slave Traffic; and by the extension of slavery far beyond its original limits, by acts of Congress, admitting new Slave States into the Union.

Resolved, That the fundamental truths of the Declaration of Independence, that all men are endowed by their Creator with certain inalienable rights, among which are life, liberty and the pursuit of happiness, was made the fundamental law of our National Government, by that amendment of the Constitution which declares that no person shall be deprived of life, liberty or property, without due process of law.

Resolved, That we recognize as sound, the doctrine maintained by slaveholding jurists, that slavery is against natural rights, and strictly local, and that its existence and continuance rests on no other support than State Legislation, and not on any authority of Congress.

Resolved, That the General Government has, under the Constitution, no power to establish or continue Slavery anywhere, and therefore that all treaties and acts of Congress establishing, continuing or favoring Slavery in the District of Columbia, in the Territory of Florida, or on the high seas, are unconstitutional, and all attempts to hold men as property within the limits of exclusive national jurisdiction, ought to be prohibited by law.

Resolved, That the provision of the Constitution of the United States, which confers extraordinary political powers on the owners of slaves, and thereby constituting the two hundred and fifty thousand slaveholders in the Slave States a privileged aristocracy; and the provision for the reclamation of fugitive slaves from service, are Anti-Republican in their character, dangerous to the liberties of the people, and ought to be abrogated.

Resolved, That the practical operation of the second of these provisions, is seen in the enactment of the act of Congress respecting persons escaping from their masters, which act, if the construction given to it by the Supreme Court of the United States in the case of Prigg *vs.* Pennsylvania be correct, nullifies the habeas corpus acts of all the States, takes away the whole legal security of personal freedom, and ought therefore to be immediately repealed.

Resolved, That the peculiar patronage and support hitherto extended to Slavery and Slaveholding, by the General Government, ought to be immediately withdrawn, and the example and influence of National authority ought to be arrayed on the side of Liberty and Free Labor.

Resolved, That the practice of the General Government, which prevails in the Slave States, of employing Slaves upon the public works, instead of free laborers, and paying aristocratic masters, with a view to secure or reward political services, is utterly indefensible and ought to be abandoned.

Resolved, That freedom of speech, and of the press, and the right of petition, and the right of trial by jury, are sacred and inviolable; and that all rules, regulations and laws, in derogation of either are oppressive, unconstitutional, and not to be endured by free people.

Resolved, That we regard voting in an eminent degree, as a moral and religious duty, which, when exercised, should be by voting for those who will do all in their power for Immediate Emancipation.

Resolved, That this Convention recommend to the friends of Liberty in all those Free States where any inequality of rights and privileges exists on account of color, to employ their utmost energies to remove all such remnants and effects of the Slave system.

Whereas, The Constitution of these United States is a series of agreements, covenants, or contracts between the people of the United States, each with all and all with each; and

Whereas, It is a principle of universal morality, that the moral laws of the Creator are paramount to all human laws; or, in the language of an Apostle, that "we ought to obey God rather than men;" and,

Whereas, The principle of common law—that any contract, covenant, or agreement, to do an act derogatory to natural right, is vitiated and annulled by its inherent immorality—has been recognized by one of the justices of the Supreme Court of the United States, who in a recent case expressly holds that "*any* contract that rests upon such a basis is *void*;" and,

Whereas, The third clause of the second section of the fourth article of the Constitution of the United States, when construed as providing for the surrender of a Fugitive Slave, *does* "rest upon such a basis," in that it is a contract to rob a man of a natural right—namely, his natural right to his own liberty; and is, therefore, absolutely *void*. Therefore,

Resolved, That we hereby give it to be distinctly understood by this nation and the world, that, as abolitionists, considering that the strength of our cause lies in its righteousness, and our hope for it in our conformity to the laws of God, and our respect for the RIGHTS OF MAN, we owe it to the Sovereign Ruler of the universe, as a proof of our allegiance to Him, in all our civil relations and offices, whether as private citizens or as public functionaries sworn to support the Constitution of the United States, to regard and to treat the third clause of the fourth article of that instrument, whenever applied to the case of a fugitive slave, as utterly null and void, and consequently as forming no part of the Constitution of the United States; whenever we are called upon or sworn to support it.

Resolved, That the power given to Congress by the Constitution, to provide for calling out the militia to suppress insurrection, does not make it the duty of the Government to maintain Slavery by military force, much less does it make it the duty of the citizens to form a part of such military force. When freemen unsheath the sword it should be to strike for Liberty, not for Despotism.

Resolved, That to preserve the peace of the citizens, and secure the blessings of freedom, the Legislature of each of the Free States ought to keep in force suitable statutes rendering it penal for any of its inhabitants to transport, or aid in transporting from such State, any person sought, to be thus transported, merely because subject to the slave laws of any other State; this remnant of independence being accorded to the Free States, by the decision of the Supreme Court, in the case of Prigg *vs.* the State of Pennsylvania.

WHIG NATIONAL CONVENTION, 1848.

A Whig National Convention met at Philadelphia, on the 7th of June, 1848, over which John M. Morehead, of North Carolina, presided. After a rather stormy session of three days, Gen. Zachary Taylor, of Louisiana, was nominated for President, and Millard Fillmore, of New-York, for Vice-President. Gen. Taylor was nominated on the fourth ballot, as follows:

BALLOTINGS.

	1st.	2d.	3d.	4th.
Taylor	111	118	133	171
Clay	97	86	74	32
Scott	43	49	54	63
Webster	22	22	17	13
Clayton	4	4	1	—
McLean	2	1	—	—
Total	279	280	279	279

Mr. Fillmore was nominated for Vice-President on the second ballot, by the following vote:

BALLOTINGS.

	1st.	2d.
M. Fillmore	115	173
Abbott Lawrence	109	83
Scattering	50	4
Total	274	260

Of the scattering vote cast on the first ballot, George Evans, of Maine, received 6; T. M. T. McKennen, of Pa., 13; Andrew Stewart, of Pa., 14; and John Sergeant, of Pa., 6.

The Convention adopted no Platform of Principles. After it had been organized, and a resolution offered to go into a ballot for candidates for President and Vice-President, Mr. Lewis D. Campbell, of Ohio, moved to amend as follows:

Resolved, That no candidate shall be entitled to receive the nomination of this Convention for President or Vice-President, unless he has given assurances that he will abide by and support the nomination; that if nominated he will accept the nomination; that he will consider himself the candidate of the Whigs, and use all proper influence to bring into practical operation the principles and measures of the Whig Party.

This resolution met with decided opposition, and the president ruled it out of order, from which decision Mr. Campbell appealed, and in a speech contended that it was strictly in order to define what sort of candidate should be voted for, and to declare that none but sound Whigs should receive important nominations at the hands of a Whig National Convention. The appeal was tabled.

Mr. Fuller, of New York, offered the following:

Resolved, That as the first duty of the representatives of the Whig Party is to preserve the principles and integrity of the party, the claims of no candidate can be considered by this Convention unless such candidate stands pledged to support, in good faith, the nominees, and to be the exponent of Whig Principles.

The president ruled this resolution out of order, and Mr. Fuller appealed, insisting that no true Whig could reasonably object to his proposition. This appeal was also laid on the table.

After Gen. Taylor had been nominated, Mr. Charles Allen, of Massachusetts, offered the following:

Resolved, That the Whig Party, through its representatives here, agrees to abide by the nomination of Gen. Zachary Taylor, on condition that he will accept the nomination as the candidate of the Whig Party, and adhere to its great fundamental principles—no extension of slave territory—no acquisition of foreign territory by conquest—protection to American industry, and opposition to Executive usurpation.

The president immediately decided the resolution out of order, and no further notice was taken of it.

After the nomination for Vice-President had been made, Mr. McCullough, of New-Jersey, offered the following:

Resolved, That Gen. Zachary Taylor, of Louisiana, and Millard Fillmore, of New-York, be, and they are hereby unanimously nominated as the Whig candidates for President and Vice-President of the United States.

Mr. D. R. Tilden, of Ohio, proposed the following, expressing the opinion that some such declaration by the Convention would be necessary, in order to secure the vote of Ohio for the nominee:

Resolved, That while all power is denied to Congress, under the Constitution, to control, or in any way interfere with the institution of Slavery within the several States of this Union, it nevertheless has the power and it is the duty of Congress to prohibit the introduction or existence of Slavery in any territory now possessed, or which may hereafter be acquired, by the United States.

This resolution, like all others affirming Whig or Anti-Slavery principles, was ruled out of order, and laid on the table. A motion was made to divide Mr. McCullough's resolve, so that the vote could be taken separately on President and on Vice-President, when, after discussion, the resolve was withdrawn.

Mr. Hilliard, of Alabama, offered a resolve indorsing Gen. Taylor's letter to Captain Allison, which, meeting opposition, was withdrawn; so the Convention adjourned without passing any resolves having reference to Whig principles, the issues before the country, or of concurrence in the nominations.

RATIFICATION MEETING AT PHILADELPHIA.

On the evening of the last day of the session (9th June), a ratification meeting was held at Philadelphia, at which Gov. Wm. F. Johnston, of Pa., presided, and at which speeches were delivered by Governor Morehead, Gen. Leslie Coombs, of Ky., and several others, and at which the following resolves, reported by W. S. Price, of Pennsylvania, were adopted:

1. *Resolved,* That the Whigs of the United States, here assembled by their Representatives, heartily ratify the nominations of Gen. Zachary Taylor as President, and Millard Fillmore as Vice-President of the United States, and pledge themselves to their support.

2. *Resolved,* That in the choice of Gen. Taylor as the Whig Candidate for President, we are glad to discover sympathy with a great popular sentiment throughout the nation—a sentiment which, having its origin in admiration of great military success, has been strengthened by the development, in every action and every word, of sound conservative opinions, and of true fidelity to the great example of former days, and to the principles of the Constitution as administered by its founders.

3. *Resolved,* That Gen. Taylor, in saying that, had he voted in 1844, he would have voted the Whig ticket,

gives us the assurance—and no better is needed from a consistent and truth-speaking man - that his heart was with us at the crisis of our political destiny, when Henry Clay was our candidate and when not only Whig principles were well defined and clearly asserted, but Whig measures depended on success. The heart that was with us then is with us now, and we have a soldier's word of honor, and a life of public and private virtue, as the security.

4. *Resolved*, That we look on Gen. Taylor's administration of the Government as one conducive of Peace, Prosperity and Union. Of Peace—because no one better knows, or has greater reason to deplore, what he has seen sadly on the field of victory, the horrors of war, and especially of a foreign and aggressive war. Of Prosperity—now more than ever needed to relieve the nation from a burden of debt, and restore industry—agricultural, manufacturing and commercial — to its accustomed and peaceful functions and influences. Of Union—because we have a candidate whose very position as a Southwestern man, reared on the banks of the great stream whose tributaries, natural and artificial, embrace the whole Union, renders the protection of the interests of the whole country his first trust, and whose varied duties in past life have been rendered, not on the soil, or under the flag of any State or section, but over the wide frontier, and under the broad banner of the Nation.

5. *Resolved*, That standing, as the Whig Party does, on the broad and firm platform of the Constitution, braced up by all its inviolable and sacred guarantees and compromises, and cherished in the affections because protective of the interests of the people, we are proud to have, as the exponent of our opinions, one who is pledged to construe it by the wise and generous rules which Washington applied to it, and who has said, (and no Whig desires any other assurance) that he will make Washington's Administration the model of his own.

6. *Resolved*, That as Whigs and Americans, we are proud to acknowledge our gratitude for the great military services which, beginning at Palo Alto, and ending at Buena Vista, first awakened the American people to a just estimate of him who is now our Whig Candidate. In the discharge of a painful duty—for his march into the enemy's country was a reluctant one; in the command of regulars at one time, and volunteers at another, and of both combined; in the decisive though punctual discipline of his camp, where all respected and beloved him; in the negotiation of terms for a dejected and desperate enemy; in the exigency of actual conflict, when the balance was perilously doubtful—we have found him the same—brave, distinguished and considerate, no heartless spectator of bloodshed, no trifler with human life or human happiness; and we do not know which to admire most, his heroism in withstanding the assaults of the enemy in the most hopeless fields of Buena Vista—mourning in generous sorrow over the graves of Ringgold, of Clay, or of Hardin—or in giving in the heat of battle terms of merciful capitulation to a vanquished foe at Monterey, and not being ashamed to avow that he did it to spare women and children, helpless infancy, and more helpless age, against whom no American soldier ever wars. Such a military man, whose triumphs are neither remote nor doubtful, whose virtues these trials have tested, we are proud to make our Candidate.

7. *Resolved*, That in support of such a nomination we ask our Whig friends throughout the nation to unite, to co-operate zealously, resolutely, with earnestness in behalf of our Candidate, whom calumny cannot reach, and with respectful demeanor to our adversaries, whose Candidates have yet to prove their claims on the gratitude of the nation.

This election resulted in the choice of the Whig Candidates, as follows:

Taylor and Fillmore—Vermont, 6; Massachusetts, 12; Rhode Island, 4; Connecticut, 6; New-York, 36; New-Jersey, 7; Pennsylvania, 26; Delaware, 3; Maryland, 8; North Carolina, 11; Georgia, 10; Lousiana, 6; Tennessee, 13; Kentucky, 12; Florida, 3—163.

Cass and Butler—Maine, 9; New-Hampshire, 6; Virginia, 17; South Carolina, 9; Alabama, 9; Mississippi, 6; Ohio, 23; Indiana, 12; Illinois, 9; Missouri, 7; Arkansas, 3; Michigan, 5; Texas, 4; Iowa, 4: Wisconsin, 4—127.

DEMOCRATIC CONVENTION, 1848.

The Democratic National Convention for 1848, assembled in Baltimore on the 22d of May. Andrew Stevenson of Va., presided. New-York had sent a double delegation: ("Barnburners" for Van Buren and Hunkers for Dickinson). The Convention decided to admit both delegations, which satisfied neither, and both declined to take part in the proceedings. The two-third rule was adopted, and Gen. Lewis Cass was nominated for President on the 4th ballot as follows: [170 votes necessary to a choice.]

	1st.	2d.	3d.	4th.
Cass	125	133	156	179
Woodbury of N. H.	53	56	53	38
Buchanan	55	54	40	33
Calhoun	9	—	—	—
Dallas	3	3	—	—
Worth	6	5	5	1
Butler of Ky	—	—	—	3

The first ballot for Vice-President resulted as follows:

William O. Butler	114	William R. King	29
John A. Quitman	74	James J. McKay	13
John Y. Mason	24	Jefferson Davis	1

No choice. Gen. Butler was unanimously nominated on the third ballot.

The Convention adopted the following platform:

1. *Resolved*, That the American Democracy place their trust in the intelligence, the patriotism, and the discriminating justice of the American people.

2. *Resolved*, That we regard this as a distinctive feature of our political creed, which we are proud to maintain before the world, as the great moral element in a form of government springing from and upheld by the popular will: and we contrast it with the creed and practice of federalism, under whatever name or form, which seeks to palsy the will of the constituent, and which conceives no imposture too monstrous for the popular credulity.

3. *Resolved*, Therefore, that, entertaining these views the Democratic party of this Union, through the delegates assembled in general convention of the States, coming together in a spirit of concord, of devotion to the doctrines and faith of a free representative government and appealing to their fellow-citizens for the rectitude of their intentions, renew and reassert before the American people, the declaration of principles avowed by them, on a former occasion, when in general convention, they presented their candidates for the popular suffrage.

Then follow resolutions 1, 2, 3, 4, of Platforms of 1840 and '44. The 5th resolution is that of 1840 with an addition about providing for war debts, and as amended, reads as follows:

Resolved, That it is the duty of every branch of the government to enforce and practice the most rigid economy in conducting our public affairs, and that no more revenue ought to be raised than is required to defray the necessary expenses of the government, and for the gradual but certain extinction of the debt created by the prosecution of a just and necessary war, after peaceful relations shall have been restored.

The next (Anti-National Bank and pro-Sub-Treasury) was amended by the addition of the following:

And that the results of Democratic Legislation, in this and all other financial measures upon which issues have been made between the two political parties of the country, have demonstrated to candid and practical men of all parties, their soundness, safety and utility in all business pursuits.

Here follow resolutions 7, 8, 9, of the platform of 1840, which we omit.

Resolved, That the proceeds of the Public Lands ought to be sacredly applied to the National objects specified in the Constitution; and that we are opposed to any law for the distribution of such proceeds among the States as alike inexpedient in policy and repugnant to the Constitution.

Resolved, That we are decidedly opposed to taking from the President the qualified veto power, by which he is enabled, under restrictions and responsibilities amply sufficient to guard the public interests, to suspend the passage of a bill whose merits cannot secure the approval of two-thirds of the Senate and House of Representatives until the judgment of the people can be obtained thereon, and which has saved the American people from the corrupt and tyrannical domination of the bank of the United States, and from a corrupting system of general internal improvements.

Resolved, that the war with Mexico, provoked on her part, by years of insult and injury, was commenced by her army crossing the Rio Grande, attacking the American troops and invading our sister State of Texas, and that upon all the principles of patriotism and the Laws of Nations, it is a just and necessary war on our part in which every American citizen should have shown himself on the side of his Country, and neither morally nor physically, by word or by deed, have given " aid and comfort to the enemy."

Resolved, That we would be rejoiced at the assurance of a peace with Mexico, founded on the just principles of indemnity for the past and security for the future; but that while the ratification of the liberal treaty offered to Mexico remains in doubt, it is the duty of the country to sustain the administration and to sustain the country in every measure necessary to provide for the vigorous prosecution of the war, should that treaty be rejected.

Resolved, That the officers and soldiers who have carried the arms of their country into Mexico, have crowned it with imperishable glory. Their unconquerable courage, their daring enterprise, their unfaltering perseverance and fortitude when assailed on all sides by innumerable foes and that more formidable enemy—the diseases of the climate—exalt their devoted patriotism into the highest heroism, and give them a right to the profound gratitude of their country, and the admiration of the world.

Resolved, That the Democratic National Convention of 30 States composing the American Republic tender their fraternal congratulations to the National Convention of the Republic of France, now assembled as the free-suffrage Representatives of the Sovereignty of thirty-five millions of Republicans to establish government on those eternal principles of equal rights for which their Lafayette and our Washington fought side by side in the struggle for our National Independence; and we would especially convey to them and to the whole people of France, our earnest wishes for the consolidation of their liberties, through the wisdom that shall guide their councils, on the basis of a Democratic Constitution, not derived from the grants or concessions of kings or dynasties, but originating from the only true source of political power recognized in the States of this Union; the inherent and inalienable right of the people, in their sovereign capacity, to make and to amend their forms of government in such manner as the welfare of the community may require.

Resolved, That the recent development of this grand political truth, of the sovereignty of the people and their capacity and power for self-government, which is prostrating thrones and erecting Republics on the ruins of despotism in the old world, we feel that a high and sacred duty is devolved, with increased responsibility, upon the Democratic party of this country, as the party of the people, to sustain and advance among us Constitutional Liberty, Equality and Fraternity, by continuing to resist all monopolies and exclusive legislation for the benefit of the few at the expense of the many, and by a vigilant and constant adherence to those principles and compromises of the Constitution which are broad enough and strong enough to embrace and uphold the Union as it was, the Union as it is, and the Union as it shall be in the full expansion of the energies and capacity of this great and progressive people.

Resolved, That a copy of these resolutions be forwarded through the American Minister at Paris, to the National Convention of the Republic of France.

Resolved, That the fruits of the great political triumph of 1844, which elected James K. Polk and George M. Dallas President and Vice-President of the United States, have fulfilled the hopes of the Democracy of the Union in defeating the declared purposes of their opponents in creating a National Bank, in preventing the corrupt and unconstitutional distribution of the Land Proceeds from the common treasury of the Union for local purposes, in protecting the Currency and Labor of the country from ruinous fluctuations; and guarding the money of the country for the use of the people by the establishment of the Constitutional treasury; in the noble impulse given to the cause of Free Trade by the repeal of the tariff of '42, and the creation of the more equal, honest, and productive tariff of 1846; and that, in our opinion, it would be a fatal error to weaken the bands of a political organization by which these great reforms have been achieved, and risk them in the hands of their known adversaries, with whatever delusive appeals they

may solicit our surrender of that vigilance which is the only safeguard of liberty.

Resolved, That the confidence of the Democracy of the Union, in the principles, capacity, firmness and integrity of James K. Polk, manifested by his nomination and election in 1844, has been signally justified by the strictness of his adherence to sound Democratic doctrines, by the purity of purpose, the energy and ability which have characterized his administration in all our affairs at home and abroad; that we tender to him our cordial congratulations upon the brilliant success which has hitherto crowned his patriotic efforts, and assure him in advance, that at the expiration of his Presidential term he will carry with him to his retirement, the esteem, respect, and admiration of a grateful country.

Resolved, That this Convention hereby present to the people of the United States, Lewis Cass, of Michigan, as the candidate of the Democratic party for the office of President, and William O. Butler of K y, for Vice-President of the U. S.

The following resolution was offered by Mr. Yancy, of Ala.

Resolved, That the doctrine of non-interference with the rights of property of any portion of the people of this Confederacy, be it in the States or Territories thereof, by any other than the parties interested in them, is the true Republican doctrine recognized by this body.

This resolution was rejected: Yeas, 36; nays, 216—the yeas being: Georgia, 9; South Carolina, 9; Alabama, 9; Arkansas, 3; Florida, 3; Maryland, 1; Kentucky, 1.

FREE DEMOCRATIC CONVENTION, 1848.

The Barnburners of New York, who were disgusted with the proceedings of the National Convention which had nominated Cass and Butler for President and Vice-President, met in Convention at Utica, on the 22d of June, 1848. Delegates were also present from Ohio, Wisconsin and Massachusetts. Col. Samuel Young presided over the deliberations of this Convention; and Martin Van Buren was nominated for President, with Henry Dodge, of Wisconsin, for Vice-President. Gen. Dodge subsequently declined.

On the 9th of August following, a Convention was held at Buffalo, which was attended by delegates from the States of Maine, New-Hampshire, Vermont, Massachusetts, Connecticut, Rhode Island, New-York, New-Jersey, Pennsylvania, Maryland, Delaware, Virginia, Illinois, Wisconsin, Michigan, Indiana, Iowa, and the District of Columbia. Charles Francis Adams, of Massachusetts, presided, and the Convention nominated Messrs. Van Buren and Adams as candidates for President and Vice-President, and adopted the following Resolves, since known as

THE BUFFALO PLATFORM.

Whereas, We have assembled in Convention, as a union of freemen, for the sake of freedom, forgetting all past political differences in a common resolve to maintain the rights of free labor against the aggressions of the Slave Power, and to secure free soil to a free people.

And Whereas, The political Conventions recently assembled at Baltimore and Philadelphia, the one stifling the voice of a great constituency, entitled to be heard in its deliberations, and the other abandoning its distinctive principles for mere availability, have dissolved the National party organizations heretofore existing, by nominating for the Chief Magistracy of the United States, under the slaveholding dictation, candidates, neither of whom can be supported by the opponents of Slavery Extension without a sacrifice of consistency, duty and self-respect;

And whereas, These nominations so made, furnish the occasion and demonstrate the necessity of the union of the people under the banner of Free Democracy, in a sol-

Pmn and formal declaration of their independence of the slave power, and of their fixed determination to rescue the Federal Government from its control;

Resolved, therefore, That we, the people here assembled, remembering the example of our fathers, in the days of the first Declaration of Independence, putting our trust in God for the triumph of our cause, and invoking his guidance in our endeavors to advance it, do now plant ourselves upon the National platform of Freedom in opposition to the sectional platform of Slavery.

Resolved, That Slavery in the several States of this Union which recognize its existence, depends upon State laws alone, which cannot be repealed or modified by the Federal Government, and for which laws that government is not responsible. We therefore propose no interference by Congress with Slavery within the limits of any State.

Resolved, That the Proviso of Jefferson, to prohibit the existence of Slavery after 1800, in all the Territories of the United States, Southern and Northern; the votes of six States and sixteen delegates, in the Congress of 1784, for the Proviso, to three States and seven delegates against it; the actual exclusion of Slavery from the Northwestern Territory, by the Ordinance of 1787, unanimously adopted by the States in Congress; and the entire history of that period, clearly show that it was the settled policy of the Nation not to extend, nationalize or encourage, but to limit, localize and discourage Slavery; and to this policy, which should never have been departed from, the Government ought to return.

Resolved, That our fathers ordained the Constitution of the United States, in order, among other great national objects, to establish justice, promote the general welfare, and secure the blessings of liberty; but expressly denied to the Federal Government, which they created, all constitutional power to deprive any person of life, liberty, or property, without due legal process.

Resolved, That in the judgment of this Convention, Congress has no more power to make a Slave than to make a King; no more power to institute or establish Slavery than to institute or establish a Monarchy: no such power can be found among those specifically conferred by the Constitution, or derived by just implication from them.

Resolved, That it is the duty of the Federal Government to relieve itself from all responsibility for the existence or continuance of slavery wherever the government possesses constitutional authority to legislate on that subject, and it is thus responsible for its existence.

Resolved, That the true, and in the judgment of this Convention, the only safe means of preventing the extension of Slavery into Territory now Free, is to prohibit its extension in all such Territory by an act of Congress.

Resolved, That we accept the issue which the Slave power has forced upon us; and to their demand for more Slave States, and more Slave Territory, our calm but final answer is, no more Slave States and no more Slave Territory. Let the soil of our extensive domains be kept free for the hardy pioneers of our own land, and the oppressed and banished of other lands, seeking homes of comfort and fields of enterprise in the new world.

Resolved, That the bill lately reported by the committee of eight in the Senate of the United States, was no compromise, but an absolute surrender of the rights of the Non-Slaveholders of all the States; and while we rejoice to know that a measure which, while opening the door for the introduction of Slavery into Territories now free, would also have opened the door to litigation and strife among the future inhabitants thereof, to the ruin of their peace and prosperity, was defeated in the House of Representatives, its passage, in hot haste, by a majority, embracing several senators who voted in open violation of the known will of their constituents, should warn the people to see to it, that their representatives be not suffered to betray them. There must be no more Compromises with Slavery; if made they must be repealed.

Resolved, That we demand freedom and established institutions for our brethren in Oregon, now exposed to hardships, peril and massacre by the reckless hostility of the Slave Power to the establishment of Free Government for Free Territories; and not only for them, but for our new brethren in California and New-Mexico.

Resolved, It is due not only to this occasion, but to the whole people of the United States, that we should also declare ourselves on certain other questions of National Policy: therefore,

Resolved, That we demand Cheap Postage for the People; a retrenchment of the expenses and patronage of the Federal Government; the abolition of all unnecessary offices and salaries; and the election by the people of all civil officers in the service of the government, so far as the same may be practicable.

Resolved, That River and Harbor improvements, when demanded by the safety and convenience of commerce with foreign nations, or among the several States, are objects of national concern, and that it is the duty of Congress, in the exercise of its constitutional powers, to provide therefor.

Resolved, That the free grant to actual settlers, in consideration of the expenses they incur in making settlements in the wilderness, which are usually fully equal to their actual cost, and of the public benefits resulting therefrom, of reasonable portions of the public lands, under suitable limitations, is a wise and just measure of public policy, which will promote in various ways the interests of all the States of this Union; and we therefore recommend it to the favorable consideration of the American people.

Resolved, That the obligations of honor and patriotism require the earliest practicable payment of the national debt, and we are therefore in favor of such a tariff of duties as will raise revenue adequate to defray the necessary expenses of the Federal Government, and to pay annual instalments of our debt, and the interest thereon

Resolved, That we inscribe on our own banner, "Free Soil, Free Speech, Free Labor, and Free Men," and under it we will fight on, and fight ever, until a triumphant victory shall reward our exertions.

WHIG NATIONAL CONVENTION, 1852.

This body assembled at Baltimore on the 16th of June, and chose Gen. John G. Chapman, of Md., as presiding officer, and, after an exciting session of six days, nominated Gen. Winfield Scott as President, on the 53d ballot, as follows:

Ballots.	Scott.	Fillmore.	Webster.	Ballots.	Scott.	Fillmore	Webster.
1.	131	133	29	28.	134	128	30
2.	133	131	29	29.	134	128	30
3.	133	131	29	30.	134	128	29
4.	134	130	29	31.	134	128	30
5.	130	133	30	32.	134	128	30
6.	133	131	29	33.	134	128	29
7.	131	133	28	34.	134	126	28
8.	133	131	28	35.	134	128	28
9.	133	133	29	36.	136	127	28
10.	135	130	29	37.	133	128	28
11.	134	131	28	38.	136	127	29
12.	134	130	28	39.	134	128	30
13.	134	130	28	40.	132	129	32
14.	133	130	29	41.	132	129	32
15.	133	130	29	42.	134	128	30
16.	135	129	28	43.	134	128	30
17.	132	131	29	44.	133	129	30
18.	132	131	28	45.	133	127	32
19.	132	131	29	46.	134	127	31
20.	132	131	29	47.	135	129	29
21.	133	131	28	48.	137	124	30
22.	132	130	30	49.	139	122	30
23.	132	130	30	50.	142	122	28
24.	133	129	30	51.	142	120	29
25.	133	128	31	52.	146	119	27
26.	134	128	30	53.	159	112	21
27.	134	128	30	Necessary to choose—147.			

William A. Graham, of North Carolina, was nominated for Vice-President on the second ballot.

The Convention adopted the following

PLATFORM:

The Whigs of the United States, in Convention assembled, adhering to the great conservative principles by which they are controled and governed, and now as ever relying upon the intelligence of the American people, with an abiding confidence in their capacity for self-government, and their devotion to the Constitution and the Union, do proclaim the following as the political sentiments and determination for the establishment and maintenance of which their national organization as a party was effected.

First. The government of the United States is of a limited character, and it is confined to the exercise of powers expressly granted by the Constitution, and such as may be necessary and proper for carrying the granted powers into full execution, and that powers not granted or necessarily implied are reserved to the States respectively and to the people.

Second. The State Governments should be held secure

to their reserved rights, and the General Government sustained on its constitutional powers, and that the Union should be revered and watched over as the palladium of our liberties.

Third. That while struggling freedom everywhere enlists the warmest sympathy of the Whig party, we still adhere to the doctrines of the Father of his Country, as announced in his Farewell Address, of keeping ourselves free from all entangling alliances with foreign countries, and of never quitting our own to stand upon foreign ground; that our mission as a republic is not to propagate our opinions, or impose on other countries our forms of government, by artifice or force; but to teach by example, and show by our success, moderation and justice, the blessings of self-government, and the advantage of free institutions.

Fourth. That, as the people make and control the Government, they should obey its constitution, laws and treaties as they would retain their self-respect, and the respect which they claim and will enforce from foreign powers.

Fifth. Government should be conducted on principles of the strictest economy; and revenue sufficient for the expenses thereof, in time, ought to be derived mainly from a duty on imports, and not from direct taxes; and on laying such duties sound policy requires a just discrimination, and, when practicable, by specific duties, whereby suitable encouragement may be afforded to American industry, equally to all classes and to all portions of the country; an economical administration of the Government, in time of peace, ought to be derived from duties on imports, and not from direct taxation; and in laying such duties, sound policy requires a just discrimination, whereby suitable encouragement may be afforded to American industry, equally to all classes, and to all parts of the country.

Sixth. The Constitution vests in Congress the power to open and repair harbors, and remove obstructions from navigable rivers, whenever such improvements are necessary for the common defense, and for the protection and facility of commerce with foreign nations, or among the States—said improvements being in every instance national and general in their character.

Seventh. The Federal and State Governments are parts of one system, alike necessary for the common prosperity, peace and security, and ought to be regarded alike with a cordial, habitual and immovable attachment. Respect for the authority of each, and acquiescence in the just constitutional measures of each, are duties required by the plainest considerations of National, State and individual welfare.

Eighth. That the series of acts of the 32d Congress, the Act known as the Fugitive Slave law included, are received and acquiesced in by the Whig party of the United States as a settlement in principle and substance of the dangerous and exciting questions which they embrace; and, so far as they are concerned, we will maintain them, and insist upon their strict enforcement, until time and experience shall demonstrate the necessity of further legislation to guard against the evasion of the laws on the one hand and the abuse of their powers on the other—not impairing their present efficiency; and we deprecate all further agitation of the question thus settled, as dangerous to our peace, and will discountenance all efforts to continue or renew such agitation, whenever, wherever, or however the attempt may be made; and we will maintain this system as essential to the nationality of the Whig party, and the integrity of the Union.

The above propositions were unanimously adopted with the exception of the last, which was carried by a vote of 212 to 70: the delegates who voted against it being supporters of Scott as against Fillmore and Webster in the ballotings above given.

The vote by States, on this (Compromise) resolution, was as follows:

YEAS—Maine, 4; New-Hampshire, 5; Vermont, 5; Massachusetts, 3; Rhode Island, 4; Connecticut, 4; New-York, 11; New-Jersey, 7; Pennsylvania, 21; Delaware, 3; Maryland, 8; Virginia, 14; North Carolina, 10; South Carolina, 8; Georgia, 10; Alabama, 9; Mississippi, 7; Louisiana, 6; Ohio, 8; Kentucky, 12; Tennessee, 12; Indiana, 7; Illinois, 6; Missouri, 9; Arkansas, 4; Florida, 3; Iowa, 4; Wisconsin, 4; Texas, 4; —212.

NAYS—Maine, 4; Connecticut, 1; New-York, 22; Pennsylvania, 6; Ohio, 15; Wisconsin, 1; Indiana, 6; Illinois, 5; Michigan, 6; California, 4—70.

GEN. SCOTT'S ACCEPTANCE.

Gen. Scott accepted the nomination and Platform in the following letter.

WASHINGTON, *June 24th*, 1852.

SIR: I have had the honor to receive from your hands the official notice of my unanimous nomination as the Whig candidate for the office of President of the United States, together with a copy of the resolutions passed by the Convention, expressing their opinions upon some of the most prominent questions of national policy.

This great distinction, conferred by a numerous, intelligent and patriotic body, representing millions of my countrymen, sinks deep into my heart; and remembering the very eminent names which were before the Convention in amicable competition with my own, I am made to feel, oppressively, the weight of responsibility belonging to my new position. Not having written a word to procure this distinction, I lost not a moment after it had been conferred in addressing a letter to one of your members, to signify what would be, at the proper time, the substance of my reply to the Convention : and I now have the honor to repeat in a more formal manner, as the occasion justly demands, that I accept the nomination with the resolutions annexed. The political principles and measures laid down in those resolutions are so broad that but little is left for me to add. I therefore barely suggest in this place, that should I, by the partiality of my countrymen, be elevated to the Chief Magistracy of the Union, I shall be ready, in my connection with Congress, to recommend or approve of measures in regard to the management of the public domain, so as to secure an early settlement of the same, favorable to actual settlers, but consistent, nevertheless, with a due regard to the equal rights of the whole American people in that vast national inheritance; and also to recommend or approve of a single alteration in our naturalization laws, suggested by my military experience, viz : Giving to all foreigners the right of citizenship, who shall faithfully serve, in time of war, one year on board of our public ships, or in our land forces, regular or volunteer, on their receiving an honorable discharge from the service. In regard to the general policy of the administration, if elected, I should, of course, look among those who may approve that policy for the agents to carry it into execution; and I should seek to cultivate harmony and fraternal sentiments throughout the Whig party, without attempting to reduce its members, by proscription, to exact uniformity to my own views.

But I should at the same time be rigorous in regard to qualifications for office, retaining and appointing no one either deficient in capacity or integrity, or in devotion to liberty, to the Constitution and the Union. Convinced that harmony or good will between the different quarters of our broad country is essential to the present and the future interests of the Republic, and with a devotion to those interests that can know no South and no North, I should neither countenance nor tolerate any sedition, disorder, faction or resistance to the law or the Union on any pretext, in any part of the land, and I should carry into the civil administration this one principle of military conduct—obedience to the legislative and judicial departments of government, each in its constitutional sphere, saving only in respect to the Legislature, the possible resort to the veto power, always to be most cautiously exercised, and under the strictest restraints and necessities.

Finally, for my strict adherence to the principles of the Whig party, as expressed in the resolutions of the Convention, and herein suggested, with a sincere and earnest purpose to advance the greatness and happiness of the Republic, and thus to cherish and encourage the cause of constitutional liberty throughout the world, avoiding every act and thought that might involve our country in an unjust or unnecessary war, or impair the faith of treaties, and discountenancing all political agitations injurious to the interests of society and dangerous to the Union, I can offer no other pledge or guarantee than the known incidents of a long public life, now undergoing the severest examination Feeling myself highly fortunate in my associate on the ticket, and with a lively sense of my obligations to the Convention, and to your personal courtesies, I have the honor to remain, sir. with great esteem, your most obedient servant,

WINFIELD SCOTT.

To HON. J. G. CHAPMAN, *President of the Whig National Convention.*

DEMOCRATIC CONVENTION—1852.

This Convention assembled at Baltimore on the 1st of June, John W. Davis, of Indiana, presided, and the two-thirds rule was adopted. Gen. Franklin Pierce, of New Hampshire, was nominated for President on the 49th ballot, as follows

Ballots.	Cass.	Buchanan.	Douglas.	Marcy.	Butler.	Houston.	Dodge.	Lane.	Dickinson.	Pierce.
1.	116	93	20	27	2	8	3	13	1	—
2.	118	95	23	27	1	6	3	13	1	—
3.	119	94	21	26	1	7	3	13	1	—
4.	115	89	31	25	1	7	3	13	1	—
5.	114	88	34	26	1	8	3	13	1	—
6.	114	88	34	26	1	8	3	13	1	—
7.	113	88	34	26	1	9	3	13	1	—
8.	113	88	34	26	1	9	3	13	1	—
9.	112	87	39	27	1	8	—	13	1	—
10.	111	86	40	27	1	8	—	14	1	—
11.	101	87	50	27	1	8	—	13	1	—
12.	98	88	51	27	1	9	—	13	1	—
13.	98	88	51	26	1	10	—	13	1	—
14.	99	87	51	26	1	10	—	13	1	—
15.	99	87	51	26	1	10	—	13	1	—
16.	99	87	51	26	1	10	—	13	1	—
17.	99	87	50	26	1	11	—	13	1	—
18.	96	85	56	25	1	11	—	13	1	—
19.	89	85	63	26	1	10	—	13	1	—
20.	81	92	64	26	1	10	—	13	1	—
21.	60	102	64	26	13	9	—	13	1	—
22.	53	104	77	26	15	9	—	13	1	—
23.	37	103	78	26	19	11	—	13	1	—
24.	33	103	80	26	23	9	—	13	1	—
25.	34	101	81	26	24	9	—	13	1	—
26.	33	101	80	26	24	10	—	13	1	—
27.	32	98	85	26	24	9	—	13	1	—
28.	23	96	88	26	25	11	—	13	1	—
29.	27	93	91	26	25	12	—	13	1	—
30.	33	91	92	26	20	12	—	13	1	—
31.	64	79	92	26	16	10	—	—	1	—
32.	98	74	80	26	1	8	—	—	1	—
33.	123	72	60	25	2	6	—	—	1	—
34.	130	49	53	23	1	5	—	—	16	—
35.	131	39	52	44	1	5	—	—	1	15
36.	122	28	43	58	1	5	—	—	1	30
37.	120	28	37	70	1	5	—	—	1	29
38.	107	28	33	84	1	5	—	—	1	29
39.	106	28	33	85	1	5	—	—	1	29
40.	106	27	33	85	1	5	—	—	1	29
41.	107	27	33	85	1	5	—	—	1	29
42.	101	27	33	91	1	5	—	—	1	29
43.	101	27	33	91	1	5	—	—	1	29
44.	101	27	33	91	1	5	—	—	1	29
45.	96	27	32	97	1	5	—	—	1	29
46.	78	28	32	97	1	5	—	—	1	44
47.	75	28	33	95	1	5	—	—	1	49
48.	73	28	33	90	1	6	—	—	1	55
49.	2	—	2	—	2	—	—	—	—	282

The first vote for Vice-President was as follows

Wm. R. King, of Ala...	126	Wm. O. Butler, of Ky...	27
G. J. Pillow, of Tenn...	25	Robt. Strange, of N. C...	23
D. R. Atchison, of Mo..	25	S. U. Downs, of La....	30
T. J. Rusk, of Texas,..	12	J. B. Weller, of Cal....	28
Jeff. Davis, of Miss.....	2	Howell Cobb, of Ga....	2

Wm. R. King, of Alabama, was unanimously nominated on the second ballot.

THE PLATFORM.

The Platform was made up of resolves. Here follow 1, 2, and 3, of that of 1848, with 1, 2, 3, and 4 of that of 1840, (see them heretofore), to which were added the following :

Resolved, That it is the duty of every branch of the Government to enforce and practice the most rigid economy in conducting our public affairs, and that no more revenue ought to be raised than is required to defray the necessary expenses of the Government, and for the gradual but certain extinction of the public debt.

Resolved, That Congress has no power to charter a National Bank ; that we believe such an institution one of deadly hostility to the best interests of the country, dangerous to our republican institutions and the liberties of the people, and calculated to place the business of the country within the control of a concentrated money power, and that above the laws and the will of the people ; and that the results of Democratic legislation, in this and all other financial measures, upon which issues have been made between the two political parties of the country have demonstrated to candid and practical men of all, parties, their soundness, safety, and utility, in all business pursuits.

Resolved, That the separation of the moneys of the Government from Banking Institutions, is indispensable for the safety of the funds of the Government, and the rights of the people.

Resolved, That the liberal principles embodied by Jefferson in the Declaration of Independence, and sanctioned in the Constitution, which makes ours the land of liberty, and the asylum of the oppressed of every nation, have ever been cardinal principles in the Democratic faith ; and every attempt to abridge the privilege of becoming citizens and the owners of soil among us, ought to be resisted with the same spirit which swept the alien and sedition laws from our statute book.

Resolved, That Congress has no power under the Constitution to interfere with, or control the domestic institutions of the several States, and that such States are the sole and proper judges of everything appertaining to their own affairs, and prohibited by the Constitution ; that all efforts of the Abolitionists or others, made to induce Congress to interfere with questions of Slavery, or to take incipient steps in relation thereto, are calculated to lead to the most alarming and dangerous consequences ; and that all such efforts have an inevitable tendency to diminish the happiness of the people, and endanger the stability and permanency of the Union, and ought not to be countenanced by any friend of our political institutions.

Resolved, That the foregoing proposition covers, and is intended to embrace, the whole subject of Slavery agitation in Congress ; and therefore, the Democratic party of the Union, standing on this National Platform, will abide by, and adhere to, a faithful execution of the acts known as the Compromise measures settled by the last Congress —the act for reclaiming fugitives from service or labor included ; which act, being designed to carry out an express provision of the Constitution, cannot with fidelity thereto be repealed, nor so changed as to destroy or impair its efficiency.

Resolved, That the Democratic party will resist all attempts at renewing in Congress, or out of it, the agitation of the Slavery question, under whatever shape or color the attempt may be made.

[Here follow the Resolutions of 1848, against the distribution of the proceeds of the Public Land Sales, and against the abridgment of the veto power of the President.]

Resolved, That the Democratic party will faithfully abide by and uphold the principles laid down in the Kentucky and Virginia Resolutions of 1792 and 1798, and in the report of Mr. Madison to the Virginia Legislature in 1799 ; that it adopts those principles as constituting one of the main foundations of its political creed, and is resolved to carry them out in their obvious meaning and import.

Resolved, That the war with Mexico, upon all the principles of patriotism and the law of nations, was a just and necessary war on our part, in which no American citizen should have shown himself opposed to his country, and neither morally nor physically, by word or deed, given aid and comfort to the enemy.

Resolved, That we rejoice at the restoration of friendly relations with our sister Republic of Mexico, and earnestly desire for her all the blessings and prosperity which we enjoy under Republican Institutions, and we congratulate the American people on the results of that war which have so manifestly justified the policy and conduct of the Democratic party, and insured to the United States indemnity for the past, and security for the future.

Resolved, That, in view of the condition of popular institutions in the old world, a high and sacred duty is devolved with increased responsibility upon the Democracy of this country, as the party of the people, to uphold and maintain the rights of every State, and thereby the Union of States, and to sustain and advance among them constitutional liberty, by continuing to resist all monopolies and exclusive legislation for the benefit of the few at the expense of the many, and by a vigilant and constant adherence to those principles and compromises of the CONSTITUTION, which are broad enough and strong enough to embrace and uphold the Union as it is, and the Union as it should be, in the full expansion of the energies and capacity of this great and progressive people.

FREE DEMOCRATIC CONVENTION—1852.

The Free-Soil Democracy held a National Convention at Pittsburgh, on the 11th August, 1852, Henry Wilson, of Mass., presiding. All the Free States were represented, together with Delaware, Virginia, Kentucky and Maryland. John P. Hale, of N. H., was nominated for President, with Geo. W. Julian, of Indiana, for Vice-President. The Convention adopted the following:

PLATFORM:

Having assembled in National Convention as the Democracy of the United States, united by a common resolve to maintain right against wrong, and Freedom against Slavery: confiding in the intelligence, patriotism, and discriminating justice of the American people, putting our trust in God for the triumph of our cause, and invoking his guidance in our endeavors to advance it, we now submit to the candid judgment of all men the following declaration of principles and measures:

1. That governments, deriving their just powers from the consent of the governed, are instituted among men to secure to all those inalienable rights of life, liberty, and the pursuit of happiness with which they are endowed by their Creator, and of which none can be deprived by valid legislation, except for crime.

2. That the true mission of American Democracy is to maintain the Liberties of the People, the Sovereignty of the States, and the perpetuity of the Union, by the impartial application to public affairs, without sectional discriminations of the fundamental principles of human rights, strict justice and an economical administration.

3. That the Federal Government is one of limited powers, derived solely from the Constitution, and the grants of power therein ought to be strictly construed by all the departments and agents of the Government, and it is inexpedient and dangerous to exercise doubtful constitutional powers.

4. That the Constitution of the United States, ordained to form a more perfect Union, to establish Justice and secure the blessings of Liberty, expressly denies to the General Government all power to deprive any person of life, liberty or property without due process of law; and, therefore, the Government having no more power to make a slave than to make a king, and no more power to establish Slavery than to establish a Monarchy, should at once proceed to relieve itself from all responsibility for the existence of Slavery, wherever it possesses constitutional power to legislate for its extinction.

5. That, to the persevering and importunate demands of the Slave power for more Slave States, new Slave Territories and the nationalization of Slavery, our distinct and final answer is—no more Slave States, no Slave Territory, no nationalized Slavery, and no national Legislation for the extradition of Slaves.

6. That Slavery is a sin against God, and a crime against man, which no human enactment nor usage can make right; and that Christianity, humanity, and patriotism alike demand its abolition.

7. That the Fugitive Slave Act of 1850, is repugnant to the Constitution, to the principles of the common law, to the spirit of Christianity, and to the sentiments of the civilized world. We therefore deny its binding force upon the American people, and demand its immediate and total repeal.

8. That the doctrine that any human law is a finality, and not subject to modification or repeal, is not in accordance with the creed of the founders of our Government, and is dangerous to the liberties of the people.

9. That the Acts of Congress, known as the Compromise Measures of 1850, by making the admission of a sovereign State contingent upon the adoption of other measures demanded by the special interest of Slavery; by their omission to guarantee freedom in the free Territories; by their attempt to impose unconstitutional limitations on the power of Congress and the people—to admit new States; by their provisions for the assumption of five millions of the State debt of Texas, and for the payment of five millions more, and the cession of a large territory to the same State under menace, as an inducement to the relinquishment of a groundless claim, and by their invasion of the sovereignty of the States and the liberties of the people through the enactment of an unjust, oppressive, and unconstitutional Fugitive Slave Law, are proved to be inconsistent with all the principles and maxims of Democracy, and wholly inadequate to the settlement of the questions of which they are claimed to be an adjustment.

10. That no permanent settlement of the Slavery question can be looked for except in the practical recognition of the truth that Slavery is sectional and Freedom national; by the total separation of the General Government from Slavery, and the exercise of its legitimate and constitutional influence on the side of Freedom; and by leaving to the States the whole subject of Slavery and the extradition of fugitives from service.

11. That all men have a natural right to a portion of the soil; and that as the use of the soil is indispensable to life, the right of all men to the soil is as sacred as their right to life itself.

12. That the Public Lands of the United States belong to the People, and should not be sold to individuals nor granted to corporations, but should be held as a sacred trust for the benefit of the people, and should be granted in limited quantities, free of cost, to landless settlers.

13. That a due regard for the Federal Constitution, a sound administrative policy, demand that the funds of the General Government be kept separate from Banking institutions; that inland and ocean postage should be reduced to the lowest possible point; that no more revenue should be raised than is required to defray the strictly necessary expenses of the public service, and to pay off the public Debt; and that the power and patronage of the Government should be diminished, by the abolition of all unnecessary offices, salaries, and privileges, and by the election, by the people, of all civil officers in the service of the United States, so far as may be consistent with the prompt and efficient transaction of the public business.

14. That River and Harbor Improvements, when necessary to the safety and convenience of commerce with foreign nations, or among the several States, are objects of national concern; and it is the duty of Congress, in the exercise of its constitutional powers, to provide for the same.

15. That emigrants and exiles from the old world should find a cordial welcome to homes of comfort and fields of enterprise in the new; and every attempt to abridge their privilege of becoming citizens and owners of the soil among us, ought to be resisted with inflexible determination.

16. That every nation has a clear right to alter or change its own government, and to administer its own concerns in such manner as may best secure the rights and promote the happiness of the people; and foreign interference with that right is a dangerous violation of the law of nations, against which all independent governments should protest, and endeavor by all proper means to prevent; and especially is it the duty of the American Government, representing the Chief Republic of the world, to protest against, and by all proper means to prevent the intervention of kings and emperors against Nations seeking to establish for themselves Republican or constitutional governments.

17. That the Independence of Hayti ought to be recognized by our Government, and our commercial relations with it placed on the footing of the most favored nations.

18. That as by the Constitution, "the citizens of each State shall be entitled to all the privileges and immunities of citizens in the several States," the practice of imprisoning colored seamen of other States, while the vessels to which they belong lie in port, and refusing the exercise of the right to bring such cases before the Supreme Court of the United States, to test the legality of such proceedings, is a flagrant violation of the Constitution, and an invasion of the rights of the citizens of other States utterly inconsistent with the professions made by the slaveholders, that they wish the provisions of the Constitution faithfully observed by every State in the Union.

19. That we recommend the introduction into all treaties hereafter to be negotiated between the United States and foreign nations, of some provision for the amicable settlement of difficulties by a resort to decisive arbitrations.

20. That the Free Democratic Party is not organized to aid either the Whig or Democratic wing of the great Slave Compromise party of the nation, but to defeat them both; and that repudiating and renouncing both, as hopelessly corrupt, and utterly unworthy of confidence, the purpose of the Free Democracy is to take possession of the Federal Government, and administer it for the better protection of the rights and interests of the whole people.

21. That we inscribe on our banner, Free Soil, Free Speech, Free Labor and Free Men, and under it will fight on and fight ever until a triumphant victory shall reward our exertions.

22. That upon this Platform the Convention presents to the American people as a candidate for the office of

President of the United States, JOHN P. HALE, of New-Hampshire, and as a candidate for the office of Vice-President of the United States, GEORGE W. JULIAN, of Indiana, and earnestly commend them to the support of all Freemen and all parties.

The result of this contest was an overwhelming triumph of the regular Democracy : Pierce and King carrying every State except Massachusetts, Vermont, Kentucky, and Tennessee, which cast their votes for Gen. Scott. The Free Democratic vote in several States would have given those States to Scott, had it been cast for him.

REPUBLICAN NATIONAL CONVENTION—1856.

This Convention met at Philadelphia on the 17th of June, and chose Col. Henry S. Lane, of Indiana, as presiding officer. An informal ballot for President resulted as follows :

States.	Fremont.	McLean.	States.	Fremont	McLean
Maine,	13	11	Indiana	18	21
New-Hampshire	15	—	Illinois	14	19
Vermont	15	—	Michigan	18	—
Massachusetts	39	—	Wisconsin	15	—
Rhode Island	12	—	Iowa	12	—
Connecticut	18	—	Minnesota	—	3
New-York	93		Kansas	9	—
New-Jersey	7	14	Nebraska	—	3
Pennsylvania	10	71	Kentucky	5	—
Delaware	—		California	12	—
Maryland	4			—	—
Ohio	30	39		359	196

New-York also gave two votes for Sumner and one for Seward.

Col. John C. Fremont was thereupon unanimously nominated.

William L. Dayton was nominated for Vice-President, receiving, on the informal ballot, 259 votes to 43 for David Wilmot; 110 for Abraham Lincoln; 7 for Thomas Ford; 35 for Charles Sumner; 4 for Cassius M. Clay; 15 for Jacob Collamer; 2 for J. R. Giddings; 2 for W. F. Johnston; 46 for N. P. Banks; 1 for A. C. M. Pennington; 5 for Henry Wilson; 9 for John A. King; 3 for Henry C. Carey; and 8 for Gen. S. C. Pomeroy of Kansas. A formal ballot was then taken, when Mr. Dayton was nominated unanimously.

The Convention adopted the following

PLATFORM :

This Convention of Delegates, assembled in pursuance of a call addressed to the people of the United States, without regard to past political differences or divisions, who are opposed to the repeal of the Missouri Compromise, to the policy of the present Administration, to the extension of Slavery into Free Territory ; in favor of admitting Kansas as a Free State, of restoring the action of the Federal Government to the principles of Washington and Jefferson, and who purpose to unite in presenting candidates for the offices of President and Vice-President, do resolve as follows:

Resolved, That the maintenance of the principles promulgated in the Declaration of Independence and embodied in the Federal Constitution is essential to the preservation of our Republican Institutions, and that the Federal Constitution, the rights of the States, and the Union of the States, shall be preserved.

Resolved, That with our republican fathers we hold it to be a self-evident truth, that all men are endowed with the inalienable rights to life, liberty, and the pursuit of happiness, and that the primary object and ulterior designs of our Federal Government were, to secure these rights to all persons within its exclusive jurisdiction ; that, as our republican fathers, when they had abolished Slavery in all our national territory, ordained that no person should be deprived of life, liberty or property without due process of law, it becomes our duty to maintain this provision of the Constitution against all attempts to violate it for the purpose of establishing Slavery in any territory of the United States, by positive legislation, prohibiting its existence or extension therein. That we deny the authority of Congress, of a territorial legislature, of any individual or association of individuals, to give legal existence to Slavery in any territory of the United States, while the present Constitution shall be maintained.

Resolved, That the Constitution confers upon Congress sovereign power over the territories of the United States for their government, and that in the exercise of this power it is both the right and the duty of Congress to prohibit in the territories those twin relics of barbarism —Polygamy and Slavery.

Resolved, That while the Constitution of the United States was ordained and established by the people in order to form a more perfect Union, establish justice, insure domestic tranquillity, provide for the common defense, and secure the blessings of liberty, and contains ample provisions for the protection of the life, liberty and property of every citizen, the dearest constitutional rights of the people of Kansas have been fraudulently and violently taken from them—their territory has been invaded by an armed force—spurious and pretended legislative, judicial and executive officers have been set over them, by whose usurped authority, sustained by the military power of the Government, tyrannical and unconstitutional laws have been enacted and enforced—the rights of the people to keep and bear arms have been infringed—test oaths of an extraordinary and entangling nature have been imposed. as a condition of exercising the right of suffrage and holding office—the right of an accused person to a speedy and public trial by an impartial jury has been denied—the right of the people to be secure in their persons, houses, papers and effects against unreasonable searches and seizures has been violated—they have been deprived of life, liberty and property without due process of law—that the freedom of speech and of the press has been abridged—the right to choose their representatives has been made of no effect—murders, robberies and arsons have been instigated and encouraged, and the offenders have been allowed to go unpunished—that all these things have been done with the knowledge, sanction and procurement of the present Administration, and that for this high crime against the Constitution, the Union and Humanity, we arraign the Administration, the President, his advisers, agents, supporters, apologists and accessories, either before or after the facts, before the country and before the world, and that it is our fixed purpose to bring the actual perpetrators of these atrocious outrages, and their accomplices, to a sure and condign punishment hereafter.

Resolved, That Kansas should be immediately admitted as a State of the Union, with her present free Constitution, as at once the most effectual way of securing to her citizens the enjoyment of the rights and privileges to which they are entitled ; and of ending the civil strife now raging in her territory.

Resolved, That the highwayman's plea, that "might makes right," embodied in the Ostend Circular, was in every respect unworthy of American diplomacy, and would bring shame and dishonor upon any government or people that gave it their sanction.

Resolved, That a railroad to the Pacific Ocean, by the most central and practicable route, is imperatively demanded by the interests of the whole country, and that the Federal Government ought to render immediate and efficient aid in its construction; and, as an auxiliary thereto, the immediate construction of an emigrant route on the line of the railroad.

Resolved, That appropriations by Congress for the improvement of rivers and harbors, of a national character, required for the accommodation and security of our existing commerce, are authorized by the Constitution, and justified by the obligation of government to protect the lives and property of its citizens.

This contest resulted in the election of the Democratic nominees, Buchanan and Breckinridge, who received the electoral votes of

New-Jersey, 7; Pennsylvania, 27; Delaware, 3; Virginia, 15; North Carolina, 10; South Carolina, 8; Georgia, 10; Alabama, 9; Mississippi, 7; Louisiana, 6; Tennessee, 12; Kentucky, 12; Indiana, 13; Illinois, 11: Missouri, 9; Arkansas, 4; Florida, 3; Texas, 4; California, 4.—174.

For Fremont and Dayton: Maine, 8; New-Hampshire, 5; Vermont, 5; Massachusetts, 13; Rhode Island, 4;

Connecticut, 6; New-York, 85; Ohio, 23; Michigan, 6 Iowa, 4; Wisconsin, 5 – 114.
Fillmore and Donelson, Maryland, 8.

AMERICAN NATIONAL CONVENTION—1856.

The American National Council met in Philadelphia February 19, 1856. All the States except four or five were represented. E. B. Bartlett, of Ky., President of the National Council presided, and, after a rather stormy session of three days, devoted mainly to the discussion of a Party Platform, the following, on the 21st, was adopted:

AMERICAN PLATFORM.

1. An humble acknowledgment to the Supreme Being, for his protecting care vouchsafed to our fathers in their successful Revolutionary struggle, and hitherto manifested to us, their descendants, in the preservation of the liberties, the independence, and the union of these States.

2. The perpetuation of the Federal Union and Constitution, as the palladium of our civil and religious liberties, and the only sure bulwarks of American Independence.

3. *Americans must rule America;* and to this end *native*-born citizens should be selected for all State, Federal and municipal offices of government employment, in preference to all others. *Nevertheless,*

4. Persons born of American parents residing temporarily abroad, should be entitled to all the rights of native-born citizens.

5. No person should be selected for political station (whether of native or foreign birth), who recognizes any allegiance or obligation of any description to any foreign prince, potentate or power, or who refuses to recognize the Federal and State Constitutions (each within its sphere) as paramount to all other laws, as rules of political action.

6. The unqualified recognition and maintenance of the reserved rights of the several States, and the cultivation of harmony and fraternal good will between the citizens of the several States, and to this end, non-interference by Congress with questions appertaining solely to the individual States, and non-intervention by each State with the affairs of any other State.

7. The recognition of the right of native-born and naturalized citizens of the United States, permanently residing in any territory thereof, to frame their constitution and laws, and to regulate their domestic and social affairs in their own mode, subject only to the provisions of the Federal Constitution, with the privilege of admission into the Union whenever they have the requisite population for one Representative in Congress : *Provided, always,* that none but those who are citizens of the United States, under the Constitution and laws thereof, and who have a fixed residence in any such Territory, ought to participate in the formation of the Constitution, or in the enactment of laws for said Territory or State.

8. An enforcement of the principles that no State or Territory ought to admit others than citizens to the right of suffrage, or of holding political offices of the United States.

9. A change in the laws of naturalization, making a continued residence of twenty-one years, of all not heretofore provided for, an indispensable requisite for citizenship hereafter, and excluding all paupers, and persons convicted of crime, from landing upon our shores ; but no interference with the vested rights of foreigners.

10. Opposition to any union between Church and State ; no interference with religious faith or worship, and no test oaths for office.

11. Free and thorough investigation into any and all alleged abuses of public functionaries, and a strict economy in public expenditures.

12. The maintenance and enforcement of all laws constitutionally enacted until said laws shall be repealed, or shall be declared null and void by competent judicial authority.

13. Opposition to the reckless and unwise policy of the present Administration in the general management of our national affairs, and more especially as shown in removing "Americans" (by designation) and Conservatives in principle, from office, and placing foreigners and Ultraists in their places ; as shown in a truckling subserviency to the stronger, and an insolent and cowardly bravado toward the weaker powers ; as shown in reopening sectional agitation, by the repeal of the Missouri Compromise ; as shown in granting to unnaturalized foreigners the right of suffrage in Kansas and Nebraska ; as shown in its vacillating course on the Kansas and Nebraska question ; as shown in the corruptions which pervade some of the Departments of the Government ; as shown in disgracing meritorious naval officers through prejudice or caprice : and as shown in the blundering mismanagement of our foreign relations.

14. Therefore, to remedy existing evils, and prevent the disastrous consequences otherwise resulting therefrom, we would build up the "American Party" upon the principles herein before stated.

15. That each State Council shall have authority to amend their several constitutions, so as to abolish the several degrees and substitute a pledge of honor, instead of other obligations, for fellowship and admission into the party.

16. A free and open discussion of all political principles embraced in our Platform.

On the following day (Feb. 22,) the American National Nominating Convention, composed mostly of the same gentlemen who had deliberated as the National Council, organized at Philadelphia, with 227 delegates in attendance, Maine, Vermont, Georgia, and South Carolina, being the only States not represented. Ephraim Marsh, of New-Jersey, was chosen to preside, and the Convention remained in session till the 25th, and, after disposing of several cases of contested seats, discussed at considerable length, and with great warmth, the question of the power of the National Council to establish a Platform for the Convention, which should be of binding force upon that body. Finally, Mr. Killinger, of Pennsylvania, proposed the following :

Resolved, That the National Council has no authority to prescribe a Platform of principles for this Nominating Convention, and that we will nominate for President and Vice-President no man who is not in favor of interdicting the introduction of Slavery into Territory north 36° 30' by congressional action.

A motion to lay this resolution on the table was adopted, 141 to 59. A motion was then made to proceed to the nomination of a candidate for President, which was carried, 151 to 51, the Anti-Slavery delegates, or North Americans, as they were called, voting in the negative, and desiring to postpone the nomination. But being beaten at all points, they (to the number of about 50) either withdrew or refused to take any further part in the proceedings of the Convention, and many of them subsequently supported Col. Fremont for President.

An informal ballot was then taken for President, which resulted as follows :

M. Fillmore, of N. Y.....	71	John Bell, Tennessee...	5
George Law, N. Y.......	27	Kenneth Raynor, N. C..	2
Garrett Davis, Ky......	13	Erastus Brooks, N. Y....	2
John McLean, Ohio....	7	Lewis D. Campbell, Ohio.	1
R. F. Stockton, N. J.....	8	John M. Clayton, Del....	1
Sam. Houston, Texas...	6		

A formal ballot was then taken, when Mr. Fillmore was nominated as follows :

Fillmore, 179 ; Law, 24 ; Raynor, 14 ; McLean, 18 ; Davis, 10 ; Houston, 3.
Necessary to a choice, 122.

Millard Fillmore was then declared to be the nominee.

A ballot was then taken for Vice-President, and Andrew Jackson Donelson, of Tennessee, was nominated as follows :

A. J. Donelson, Ten., 181 ; Percy Walker, Ala., 8 ; Henry J. Gardner, Mass., 8 ; Kenneth Raynor, N. C., 8.
Mr. Donelson was then declared to be unani-

mously nominated, and the Convention adjourned.

———

DEMOCRATIC NATIONAL CONVENTION—1856.

This Convention met at Cincinnati on the 2d of June, and chose John E. Ward, of Georgia, to preside, and nominated James Buchanan on the 17th ballot, as follows:

Ballots.	Buchanan.	Pierce.	Douglas.	Cass.
1.	135	122	33	5
2.	139	119½	3½	6
3.	139½	119	32	5½
4.	141¼	119	30	5½
5.	140	119½	31	5½
6.	155	117½	28	5½
7.	143½	89	58	5½
8.	147½	87	56	5½
9.	146	87	56	7
10.	150½	80½	59½	5½
11.	147½	80	63	5½
12.	148	79	63½	5½
13.	150	77½	63	5½
14.	152½	75	63	5½
15.	168½	3½	118½	4½
16.	168	—	121	6
17.	296	—	—	—

M Buchanan having been unanimously nominated for President, the Convention proceeded to ballot for a candidate for Vice-President, the first ballot resulting as follows:

J. A. Quitman, Miss.,.. 59	J. C. Breckinridge, Ky.,.. 55
Linn Boyd, Ky.,....... 33	B. Fitzpatrick, Ala.,..... 11
A. V. Brown, Tenn.,.... 29	H. V. Johnson, Ga.,..... 31
J. A. Bayard, Del.,.... 31	Trusten Polk, Mo.,...... 5
T. J. Rusk, Texas,..... 2	J. C. Dobbin, N. C.,..... 13

On the second ballot, the name of Gen. Quitman was withdrawn, as were also those of other leading candidates, and Mr. Breckinridge was unanimously nominated.

The Convention adopted the following

PLATFORM:

Resolved, That the American Democracy place their trust in the intelligence, the patriotism, and the discriminating justice of the American people.

Resolved, That we regard this as a distinctive feature of our political creed, which we are proud to maintain before the world as a great moral element in a form of government springing from and upheld by the popular will; and we contrast it with the creed and practice of Federalism, under whatever name or form, which seeks to palsy the will of the Constituent, and which conceives no imposture too monstrous for the popular credulity.

Resolved, therefore, That entertaining these views, the Democratic party of this Union, through their delegates, assembled in general Convention, coming together in a spirit of concord, of devotion to the doctrines and faith of a free representative government, and appealing to their fellow-citizens for the rectitude of their intentions, renew and reassert before the American people, the declarations of principles avowed by them, when, on former occasions, in general Convention, they have presented their candidates for the popular suffrage.

1. That the Federal Government is one of limited power, derived solely from the Constitution, and the grants of power made therein ought to be strictly construed by all the departments and agents of the Government, and that it is inexpedient and dangerous to exercise doubtful constitutional powers.

2. That the Constitution does not confer upon the General Government the power to commence and carry on a general system of internal improvements.

3. That the Constitution does not confer authority upon the Federal Government, directly or indirectly, to assume the debts of the several States, contracted for local and internal improvements, or other State purposes, nor would such assumption be just or expedient.

4. That justice and sound policy forbid the Federal Government to foster one branch of industry to the detriment of another, or to cherish the interests of one portion of our common country; that every citizen and every section of the country has a right to demand and insist upon an equality of rights and privileges, and a complete and ample protection of persons and property from domestic violence and foreign aggression.

5. That it is the duty of every branch of the Government to enforce and practice the most rigid economy in conducting our public affairs, and that no more revenue ought to be raised than is required to defray the necessary expenses of the government, and gradual but certain extinction of the public debt.

6. That the proceeds of the public lands ought to be sacredly applied to the national objects specified in the Constitution, and that we are opposed to any law for the distribution of such proceeds among the States, as alike inexpedient in policy, and repugnant to the Constitution.

7. That Congress has no power to charter a National Bank; that we believe such an institution one of deadly hostility to the best interests of this country, dangerous to our republican institutions and the liberties of the people, and calculated to place the business of the country within the control of a concentrated money power and above the laws and will of the people; and the results of the Democratic legislation in this and all other financial measures upon which issues have been made between the two political parties of the country, have demonstrated to candid and practical men of all parties their soundness, safety and utility in all business pursuits.

8. That the separation of the moneys of the Government from banking institutions is indispensable to the safety of the funds of the Government and the rights of the people.

9. That we are decidedly opposed to taking from the President the qualified Veto power, by which he is enabled, under restrictions and responsibilities amply sufficient to guard the public interests, to suspend the passage of a bill whose merits cannot secure the approval of two-thirds of the Senate and House of Representatives, until the judgment of the people can be obtained thereon, and which has saved the American people from the corrupt and tyrannical dominion of the Bank of the United States, and from a corrupting system of general internal improvements.

10. That the liberal principles embodied by Jefferson in the Declaration of Independence, and sanctioned in the Constitution, which makes ours the land of liberty and the asylum of the oppressed of every nation, have ever been cardinal principles in the Democratic faith; and every attempt to abridge the privilege of becoming citizens and the owners of soil among us ought to be resisted with the same spirit which swept the alien and sedition laws from our statute books.

And whereas, Since the foregoing declaration was uniformly adopted by our predecessors in National Convention, an adverse political and religious test has been secretly organized by a party claiming to be exclusively American, and it is proper that the American Democracy should clearly define its relations thereto; and declare its determined opposition to all secret political societies, by whatever name they may be called.

Resolved, That the foundation of this Union of States having been laid in, and its prosperity, expansion, and preëminent example of free government, built upon entire freedom in matters of religious concernment, and no respect of persons in regard to rank, or place of birth, no party can justly be deemed national, constitutional, or in accordance with American principles, which bases its exclusive organization upon religious opinions and accidental birth-place. And hence a political crusade in the nineteenth century, and in the United States of America, against Catholics and foreign-born, is neither justified by the past history nor future prospects of the country, nor in unison with the spirit of toleration, and enlightened freedom which peculiarly distinguishes the American system of popular government.

Resolved, That we reiterate with renewed energy of purpose the well considered declarations of former conventions upon the sectional issue of domestic slavery, and concerning the reserved rights of the States:

1. That Congress has no power under the Constitution to interfere with or control the domestic institutions of the several States, and that all such States are the sole and proper judges of everything appertaining to their own affairs not prohibited by the Constitution; that all efforts of the Abolitionists or others made to induce Congress to interfere with questions of Slavery, or to take incipient steps in relation thereto, are calculated to lead to the most alarming and dangerous consequences, and that all such efforts have an inevitable tendency to diminish the happiness of the people and endanger the stability and permanency of the Union, and ought not to be countenanced by any friend of our political institutions.

2. That the foregoing proposition covers and was intended to embrace the whole subject of Slavery agitation in Congress, and therefore the Democratic party of the

Union, standing on this national platform, will abide by and adhere to a faithful execution of the acts known as the Compromise Measures, settled by the Congress of 1850: "the act for reclaiming fugitives from service or labor" included; which act, being designed to carry out an express provision of the Constitution, cannot, with fidelity thereto, be repealed, or so changed as to destroy or impair its efficiency.

3. That the Democratic Party will resist all attempts at renewing, in Congress or out of it, the agitation of the Slavery question, under whatever shape or color the attempt may be made.

4. That the Democratic Party will faithfully abide by and uphold the principles laid down in the Kentucky and Virginia resolutions of 1797 and 1798, and in the report of Mr. Madison to the Virginia Legislature in 1799 —that it adopts these principles as constituting one of the main foundations of its political creed, and is resolved to carry them out in their obvious meaning and import.

And that we may more distinctly meet the issue on which a sectional party, subsisting exclusively on Slavery agitation, now relies to test the fidelity of the people, North and South, to the Constitution and the Union—

1. *Resolved*, That claiming fellowship with and desiring the coöperation of all who regard the preservation of the Union under the Constitution as the paramount issue, and repudiating all sectional parties and platforms concerning domestic Slavery, which seek to embroil the States and incite to treason and armed resistance to law in the Territories, and whose avowed purpose, if consummated, must end in civil war and disunion, the American Democracy recognize and adopt the principles contained in the organic laws establishing the Territories of Nebraska and Kansas, as embodying the only sound and safe solution of the Slavery question, upon which the great national idea of the people of this whole country can repose in its determined conservation of the Union, and non-interference of Congress with Slavery in the Territories or in the District of Columbia.

2. That this was the basis of the compromises of 1850, confirmed by both the Democratic and Whig parties in National Conventions, ratified by the people in the election of 1852, and rightly applied to the organization of the Territories in 1854.

3. That by the uniform application of the Democratic principle to the organization of Territories, and the admission of new States with or without domestic Slavery, as they may elect, the equal rights of all the States will be preserved intact, the original compacts of the Constitution maintained inviolate, and the perpetuity and expansion of the Union insured to its utmost capacity of embracing, in peace and harmony, every future American State that may be constituted or annexed with a republican form of government.

Resolved, That we recognize the right of the people of all the Territories, including Kansas and Nebraska, acting through the legally and fairly expressed will of the majority of the actual residents, and whenever the number of their inhabitants justifies it, to form a Constitution, with or without domestic Slavery, and be admitted into the Union upon terms of perfect equality with the other States.

Resolved, finally, That in view of the condition of popular institutions in the Old World (and the dangerous tendencies of sectional agitation, combined with the attempt to enforce civil and religious disabilities against the rights of acquiring and enjoying citizenship in our own land), a high and sacred duty is involved with increased responsibility upon the Democratic Party of this country, as the party of the Union, to uphold and maintain the rights of every State and thereby the Union of the States—and to sustain and advance among us constitutional liberty, by continuing to resist all monopolies and exclusive legislation for the benefit of the few at the expense of the many, and by a vigilant and constant adherence to those principles and compromises of the Constitution — which are broad enough and strong enough to embrace and uphold the Union as it was, the Union as it is, and the Union as it shall be—in the full expression of the energies and capacity of this great and progressive people.

1. *Resolved*, That there are questions connected with the foreign policy of this country which are inferior to no domestic question whatever. The time has come for the people of the United States to declare themselves in favor of free seas, and progressive free trade throughout the world, and, by solemn manifestations, to place their moral influence at the side of their successful example.

2. *Resolved*, That our geographical and political position with reference to the other states of this continent, no less than the interest of our commerce and the development of our growing power, requires that we should hold sacred the principles involved in the Monroe doctrine. Their bearing and import admit of no misconstruction, and should be applied with unbending rigidity.

3. *Resolved*, That the great highway, which nature as well as the assent of States most immediately interested in its maintenance has marked out for free communication between the Atlantic and the Pacific Oceans, constitutes one of the most important achievements realized by the spirit of modern times, in the unconquerable energy of our people; and that result would be secured by a timely and efficient exertion of the control which we have the right to claim over it; and no power on earth should be suffered to impede or clog its progress by any interference with relations that it may suit our policy to establish between our Government and the government of the States within whose dominions it lies; we can under no circumstance surrender our preponderance in the adjustment of all questions arising out of it.

4. *Resolved*, That, in view of so commanding an interest, the people of the United States cannot but sympathize with the efforts which are being made by the people of Central America to regenerate that portion of the continent which covers the passage across the interoceanic isthmus.

5. *Resolved*, That the Democratic Party will expect of the next Administration that every proper effort be made to insure our ascendency in the Gulf of Mexico, and to maintain permanent protection to the great outlets through which are emptied into its waters the products raised out of the soil and the commodities created by the industry of the people of our western valleys and of the Union at large.

Resolved, That the Administration of Franklin Pierce has been true to Democratic principles, and therefore true to the great interests of the country; in the face of violent opposition, he has maintained the laws at home, and vindicated the rights of American citizens abroad; and therefore we proclaim our unqualified admiration of his measures and policy.

WHIG CONVENTION—1856.

A Whig National Convention met at Baltimore on the 17th of Sept., 1856—Edward Bates, of Missouri, presiding. The nominations of Millard Fillmore for President, and Andrew J. Donelson for Vice-President, were unanimously concurred in. The Convention adopted the following

PLATFORM:

Resolved, That the Whigs of the United States, now here assembled, hereby declare their reverence for the Constitution of the United States, their unalterable attachment to the National Union, and a fixed determination to do all in their power to preserve them for themselves and their posterity. They have no new principles to announce; no new platform to establish; but are content to broadly rest—where their fathers rested—upon the Constitution of the United States, wishing no safer guide, no higher law.

Resolved, That we regard with the deepest interest and anxiety the present disordered condition of our national affairs—a portion of the country ravaged by civil war, large sections of our population embittered by mutual recriminations; and we distinctly trace these calamities to the culpable neglect of duty by the present national administration.

Resolved, That the Government of the United States was formed by the conjunction in political unity of wide spread geographical sections materially differing, not only in climate and products, but in social and domestic institutions; and that any cause that shall permanently array the different sections of the Union in political hostility and organized parties founded only on geographical distinctions must inevitably prove fatal to a continuance of the National Union.

Resolved, That the Whigs of the United States declare, as a fundamental article of political faith, an absolute necessity for avoiding geographical parties. The danger, so clearly discerned by the Father of his Country, has now become fearfully apparent in the agitation now convulsing the nation, and must be arrested at once if we would preserve our Constitution and our Union from dismemberment, and the name of America from being blotted out from the family of civilized nations.

Resolved, That all who revere the Constitution and the Union, must look with alarm at the parties in the field in the present Presidential campaign—one claiming only to represent sixteen Northern States, and the other appealing mainly to the passions and prejudices of the Southern States; that the success of either faction must add fuel to the flame which now threatens to wrap our dearest interests in a common ruin.

Resolved, That the only remedy for an evil so appalling is to support a candidate pledged to neither of the geographical sections now arrayed in political antagonism, but holding both in a just and equal regard. We congratulate the friends of the Union that such a candidate exists in Millard Fillmore.

Resolved, That, without adopting or referring to the peculiar doctrines of the party which has already selected Mr. Fillmore as a candidate, we look to him as a well-tried and faithful friend of the Constitution and the Union, eminent alike for his wisdom and firmness—for his justice and moderation in our foreign relations—for his calm and pacific temperament, so well becoming the head of a great nation—for his devotion to the Constitution in its true spirit—his inflexibility in executing the laws; but, beyond all these attributes, in possessing the one transcendent merit of being a representative of neither of the two sectional parties now struggling for political supremacy.

Resolved, That, in the present exigency of political affairs, we are not called upon to discuss the subordinate questions of administration in the exercising of the Constitutional powers of the Government. It is enough to know that civil war is raging, and that the Union is in peril; and we proclaim the conviction that the restoration of Mr. Fillmore to the Presidency will furnish the best if not the only means of restoring peace.

In the election which ensued, Mr. Fillmore received the vote of Maryland only, while Mr. Buchanan obtained those of the 14 other Slave States, and of New-Jersey, Pennsylvania, Indiana, Illinois and California, making 172 in all. Col. Fremont received the votes of the eleven other Free States, making 114 in all. Pennsylvania and Illinois, had they voted for Col. Fremont, would have given him the election.

REPUBLICAN CONVENTION—1860.

A Republican National Convention assembled at Chicago, Illinois, on Wednesday, May 16th, 1860, delegates being in attendance from all the Free States, as also from Delaware, Maryland, Virginia, Kentucky, Missouri, Texas,* the Territories of Kansas and Nebraska, and the District of Columbia.

Gov. Morgan, of New-York, as Chairman of the National Executive Committee, nominated David Wilmot as temporary Chairman, and he was chosen. The usual Committees on permanent organization, credentials, etc., were appointed, and the Convention was permanently organized by the selection of George Ashmun, of Massachusetts, as President, with a Vice-President and a Secretary from each State and Territory represented. A Committee, of one from each State and Territory, was appointed to draft suitable resolutions, or in other words a Platform, and the Convention adjourned.

On the following day, an interesting debate arose on a proposition to require a vote equal to a majority of full delegations from all the States to nominate candidates for President and Vice-President; which, with the delegates actually in attendance, would have been about equivalent to a two-third rule. This proposition was voted down, and the Convention decided, by a vote of 331 to 130, that only a majority of

those present and voting should be required to nominate candidates. The following Platform was adopted, and, without taking a ballot for President, the Convention again adjourned.

PLATFORM OF 1860.

Resolved, That we, the delegated representatives of the Republican electors of the United States, in Convention assembled, in discharge of the duty we owe to our constituents and our country, unite in the following declarations:

1. That the history of the nation, during the last four years, has fully established the propriety and necessity of the organization and perpetuation of the Republican party, and that the causes which called it into existence are permanent in their nature, and now, more than ever before, demand its peaceful and constitutional triumph.

2. That the maintenance of the principles promulgated in the Declaration of Independence and embodied in the Federal Constitution, "That all men are created equal; that they are endowed by their Creator with certain inalienable rights; that among these are life, liberty and the pursuit of happiness; that, to secure these rights, governments are instituted among men, deriving their just powers from the consent of the governed," is essential to the preservation of our Republican institutions; and that the Federal Constitution, the Rights of the States, and the Union of the States, must and shall be preserved.

3. That to the Union of the States this nation owes its unprecedented increase in population, its surprising development of material resources, its rapid augmentation of wealth, its happiness at home and its honor abroad; and we hold in abhorrence all schemes for Disunion, come from whatever source they may: And we congratulate the country that no Republican member of Congress has uttered or countenanced the threats of Disunion so often made by Democratic members, without rebuke and with applause from their political associates; and we denounce those threats of disunion, in case of a popular overthrow of their ascendency, as denying the vital principles of a free government, and as an avowal of contemplated treason, which it is the imperative duty of an indignant People sternly to rebuke and forever silence.

4. That the maintenance inviolate of the rights of the States, and especially the right of each State to order and control its own domestic institutions according to its own judgment exclusively, is essential to that balance of powers on which the perfection and endurance of our political fabric depends; and we denounce the lawless invasion by armed force of the soil of any State or Territory, no matter under what pretext, as among the gravest of crimes.

5. That the present Democratic Administration has far exceeded our worst apprehensions, in its measureless subserviency to the exactions of a sectional interest, as especially evinced in its desperate exertions to force the infamous Lecompton Constitution upon the protesting people of Kansas; in construing the personal relation between master and servant to involve an unqualified property in persons; in its attempted enforcement, everywhere, on land and sea, through the intervention of Congress and of the Federal Courts of the extreme pretensions of a purely local interest; and in its general and unvarying abuse of the power intrusted to it by a confiding people.

6. That the people justly view with alarm the reckless extravagance which pervades every department of the Federal Government; that a return to rigid economy and accountability is indispensable to arrest the systematic plunder of the public treasury by favored partisans; while the recent startling developments of frauds and corruptions at the Federal metropolis, show that an entire change of administration is imperatively demanded.

7. That the new dogma that the Constitution, of its own force, carries Slavery into any or all of the Territories of the United States, is a dangerous political heresy, at variance with the explicit provisions of that instrument itself, with cotemporaneous exposition, and with legislative and judicial precedent; is revolutionary in its tendency, and subversive of the peace and harmony of the country.

8. That the normal condition of all the territory of the United States is that of freedom: That as our Republican fathers, when they had abolished Slavery in all our national territory, ordained that " no person should be deprived of life, liberty, or property, without due process of law," it becomes our duty, by legislation, whenever such legislation is necessary, to maintain this provision of the Constitution against all attempts to violate it; and we deny the authority of Congress, of a territorial legis-

---

* The delegation from Texas has since been proved fraudulent, having been got up in Michigan to effect a personal end.

lature, or of any individuals, to give legal existence to Slavery in any Territory of the United States.

9. That we brand the recent re-opening of the African slave-trade, under the cover of our national flag, aided by perversions of judicial power, as a crime against humanity and a burning shame to our country and age; and we call upon Congress to take prompt and efficient measures for the total and final suppression of that execrable traffic.

10. That in the recent vetoes, by their Federal Governors, of the acts of the Legislatures of Kansas and Nebraska, prohibiting Slavery in those Territories, we find a practical illustration of the boasted Democratic principle of Non Intervention and Popular Sovereignty embodied in the Kansas-Nebraska bill, and a demonstration of the deception and fraud involved therein.

11. That Kansas should, of right, be immediately admitted as a State under the Constitution recently formed and adopted by her people, and accepted by the House of Representatives.

12. That, while providing revenue for the support of the General Government by duties upon imports, sound policy requires such an adjustment of these imposts as to encourage the development of the industrial interests of the whole country: and we commend that policy of national exchanges which secures to the working men liberal wages, to agriculture remunerating prices, to mechanics and manufacturers an adequate reward for their skill, labor, and enterprise, and to the nation commercial prosperity and independence.

13. That we protest against any sale or alienation to others of the Public Lands held by actual settlers, and against any view of the Homestead policy which regards the settlers as paupers or suppliants for public bounty; and we demand the passage by Congress of the complete and satisfactory Homestead measure which has already passed the House.

14. That the Republican Party is opposed to any change in our Naturalization Laws or any State legislation by which the rights of citizenship hitherto accorded to immigrants from foreign lands shall be abridged or impaired; and in favor of giving a full and efficient protection to the rights of all classes of citizens, whether native or naturalized, both at home and abroad.

15. That appropriations by Congress for River and Harbor improvements of a National character, required for the accommodation and security of an existing commerce, are authorized by the Constitution, and justified by the obligations of Government to protect the lives and property of its citizens.

16. That a Railroad to the Pacific Ocean is imperatively demanded by the interests of the whole country; that the Federal Government ought to render immediate and efficient aid in its construction; and that, as preliminary thereto, a daily Overland Mail should be promptly established.

17. Finally, having thus set forth our distinctive principles and views, we invite the coöperation of all citizens, however differing on other questions, who substantially agree with us in their affirmance and support.

On the following day, Friday, May 18th, the Chair having announced that the naming of candidates for President was in order, Wm. M. Evarts, of New-York, named William H. Seward.

Mr. Judd, of Illinois, named Abraham Lincoln. Mr. Dudley, of New-Jersey, nominated Wm. L. Dayton. Gov. Reeder, of Pennsylvania, nominated Simon Cameron. Mr. Cartter, of Ohio, nominated Salmon P. Chase. Francis P. Blair, of Maryland, nominated Edward Bates, of Missouri.

Indiana seconded the nomination of Abraham Lincoln. Mr. Austin Blair, of Michigan, seconded the nomination of Mr. Seward; so also did Carl Schurz, of Wisconsin, Mr. Worth, of Minnesota, and Mr. Wilder, of Kansas.

Mr. Corwin, of Ohio, nominated Judge McLean.

Mr. Delano, of Ohio, seconded the nomination of Mr. Lincoln, as did also one of the delegates from Iowa.

The balloting then proceeded, with the following result:

FIRST BALLOT.

States.	Seward.	Lincoln.	Wade.	Cameron.	Bates.	McLean.	Read.	Chase.	Dayton.	Sumner.	Fremont.	Collamer.
Maine	10	6	—	—	—	—	—	—	—	—	—	—
New-Hampshire	1	7	—	—	—	—	—	1	—	—	1*	—
Vermont	—	—	—	—	—	—	—	—	—	—	—	10
Massachusetts	21	4	—	—	—	—	—	—	—	—	—	—
Rhode Island	—	—	—	—	1	5	1	1	—	—	—	—
Connecticut	—	2	1	—	7	—	—	2	—	—	—	—
New-York	70	—	—	—	—	—	—	—	—	—	—	—
New-Jersey	—	—	—	—	—	—	—	—	14	—	—	—
Pennsylvania	1½	4	—	47½	—	1	—	—	—	—	—	—
Maryland	3	—	—	—	8	—	—	—	—	—	—	—
Delaware	—	—	—	—	.6	—	—	—	—	—	—	—
Virginia	8	14	—	1	—	—	—	—	—	—	—	—
Kentucky	5	6	2	—	—	1	—	8	—	1	—	—
Ohio	—	8	—	—	—	4	—	34	—	—	—	—
Indiana	—	26	—	—	—	—	—	—	—	—	—	—
Missouri	—	—	—	—	18	—	—	—	—	—	—	—
Michigan	12	—	—	—	—	—	—	—	—	—	—	—
Illinois	—	22	—	—	—	—	—	—	—	—	—	—
Texas	4	—	—	—	2	—	—	—	—	—	—	—
Wisconsin	10	—	—	—	—	—	—	—	—	—	—	—
Iowa	2	2	—	1	1	1	—	1	—	—	—	—
California	8	—	—	—	—	—	—	—	—	—	—	—
Minnesota	8	—	—	—	—	—	—	—	—	—	—	—
Oregon	—	—	—	—	5	—	—	—	—	—	—	—
Territories.												
Kansas	6	—	—	—	—	—	—	—	—	—	—	—
Nebraska	2	1	—	1	—	—	—	2	—	—	—	—
Dis. of Columbia	2	—	—	—	—	—	—	—	—	—	—	—
Total	173½	102	3	50½	48	12	1	49	14	1	1	10

Whole number of votes, 465. Necessary to a choice, 233.

The second ballot was then taken.

Mr. Cameron's name was withdrawn.

SECOND BALLOT.

States.	Seward.	Lincoln.	Bates.	Cameron.	McLean.	Chase.	Dayton.	C. M. Clay.
Maine	10	6	—	—	—	—	—	—
New-Hampshire	1	9	—	—	—	—	—	—
Vermont	—	10	—	—	—	—	—	—
Massachusetts	22	4	—	—	—	—	—	—
Rhode Island	—	3	—	—	2	3	—	—
Connecticut	—	4	4	—	—	2	—	2
New-York	70	—	—	—	—	—	—	—
New-Jersey	4	—	—	—	—	—	10	—
Pennsylvania	2½	48	—	1	2½	—	—	—
Maryland	3	—	8	—	—	—	—	—
Delaware	—	6	—	—	—	—	—	—
Virginia	8	14	—	1	—	—	—	—
Kentucky	7	9	—	—	—	6	—	—
Ohio	—	14	—	—	3	29	—	—
Indiana	—	26	—	—	—	—	—	—
Missouri	—	—	18	—	—	—	—	—
Michigan	12	—	—	—	—	—	—	—
Illinois	—	22	—	—	—	—	—	—
Texas	6	—	—	—	—	—	—	—
Wisconsin	10	—	—	—	—	—	—	—
Iowa	2	5	—	—	½	½	—	—
California	8	—	—	—	—	—	—	—
Minnesota	8	—	—	—	—	—	—	—
Oregon	—	—	5	—	—	—	—	—
Territories.								
Kansas	6	—	—	—	—	—	—	—
Nebraska	3	1	—	—	—	—	—	—
District of Columbia	2	—	—	—	—	—	—	—
Total	184½	181	35	2	8	42½	10	2

The third ballot was taken amid excitement, and cries for "the ballot." Intense feeling existed during the voting, each vote being awaited in breathless silence and expectancy.

The progress of the ballot was watched with most intense interest, especially toward the last, the crowd becoming silent as the contest narrowed down. The States, as called, voted as follows:

* Previously withdrawn.

THIRD BALLOT.

States.	Seward.	Bates.	Chase.	Lincoln.	McLean.	Dayton.	C. M. Cla[y]
Maine.........10	—	—	6	—	—	—
New-Hampshire. 1	—	—	9	—	—	—
Vermont........—	—	—	10	—	—	—
Massachusetts....18	—	—	8	—	—	—
Rhode Island.... 1	—	1	5	1	—	—
Connecticut..... 1	4	2	4	—	—	1
New-York.......70	—	—	—	—	—	—
New-Jersey...... 5	—	—	8	—	1	—
Pennsylvania....—	—	—	52	2	—	—
Maryland....... 2	—	—	9	—	—	—
Delaware... ...—	—	—	6	—	—	—
Virginia........ 8	—	—	14	—	—	—
Kentucky 6	—	4	13	—	—	—
Ohio.............—	—	15	29	2	—	—
Indiana.........—	—	—	26	—	—	—
Missouri........—	18	—	—	—	—	—
Michigan.......12	—	—	—	—	—	—
Illinois..........—	—	—	22	—	—	—
Texas.......... 6	—	—	—	—	—	—
Wisconsin......10	—	—	—	—	—	—
Iowa............ 2	—	½	5½	—	—	—
California....... 8	—	—	—	—	—	—
Minnesota...... 8	—	—	—	—	—	—
Oregon......... 1	—	—	4	—	—	—
Territories.							
Kansas......... 6	—	—	—	—	—	—
Nebraska... ... 3	—	2	1	—	—	—
Dist. of Columbia 2	—	—	—	—	—	—
	180	22	24½	231½	5	1	1

This gave Lincoln 231½ votes, or within 2½ of a nomination.

Before the result was announced, Mr. Cartter, of Ohio, said—I rise, Mr. Chairman, to announce the change of four votes from Ohio, from Mr. Chase to Abraham Lincoln.

This announcement, giving Mr. Lincoln a majority, was greeted by the audience with the most enthusiastic and thundering applause.

Mr. McCrillis, of Maine, making himself heard, said that the young giant of the West is now of age. Maine casts for him her 16 votes.

Mr. Andrew, of Massachusetts, changed the vote of that State, giving 18 to Mr. Lincoln and 8 to Mr. Seward.

Mr. B. Gratz Brown, of Missouri, desired to change the 18 votes of Missouri to the gallant son of the West, Abraham Lincoln. Iowa, Connecticut, Kentucky, and Minnesota also changed their votes. The result of the third ballot was announced:

> Whole number of votes cast 466
> Necessary to a choice............234

Abraham Lincoln had received 354, and was declared duly nominated.

On motion of Wm. M. Evarts, of New-York, seconded by Mr. Andrew, of Massachusetts, the nomination was then made unanimous.

On motion of Mr. Evarts, of New-York, the Convention now took a recess till 5 o'clock, to afford time for consultation as to Vice-President.

At 5 o'clock the Convention rëassembled, listened to nominations, and then proceeded to ballot.

The following is a record of the ballotings for Vice-President:

[NOTE.—Col. Fremont had sent a letter by one of the delegates from California, withdrawing his name from the list of candidates for President. This letter was published before the meeting of the Convention.]

FIRST BALLOT.

States.	C. M. Clay	Banks.	Reeder.	Hickman.	Hamlin.	ead.	. W.Davis	ayton.	ouston.
Maine............—	—	—	—	16	—	—	—	—
New-Hampshire...—	—	—	—	10	—	—	—	—
Vermont..........—	—	—	—	10	—	—	—	—
Massachusetts....—	20	1	1	1	—	—	—	—
Rhode Island.. ..—	—	—	—	8	—	—	—	—
Connecticut....... 2	1	—	2	5	—	—	—	—
New-York......... 9	4	2	11	35	1	—	—	—
New-Jersey........ 1	—	7	—	6	—	—	—	—
Pennsylvania..... 4¼	2½	24	7	11	—	—	3	—
Maryland......... 2	—	—	1	8	—	—	—	—
Delaware......... 3	—	—	1	2	—	—	—	—
Virginia.........23	—	—	—	—	—	—	—	—
Kentucky.........23	—	—	—	—	—	—	—	—
Ohio.............. —	—	—	—	48	—	—	—	—
Indiana.........18	—	—	—	8	—	—	—	—
Missouri..........—	9	—	9	—	—	—	—	—
Michigan......... 4	—	—	—	8	—	—	—	—
Illinois.......... 2	—	16	2	2	—	—	—	—
Texas............—	—	—	—	—	—	—	—	—
Wisconsin........ 5	—	—	—	5	—	—	—	—
Iowa ....—	1	1	—	6	—	—	—	—
California........—	—	—	8	—	—	—	—	—
Minnesota........ 1	—	—	1	6	—	—	—	—
Oregon..........—	1	—	3	1	—	—	—	—
Territories.									
Kansas...........—	—	—	6	—	—	—	—	—
Nebraska......... 1	—	—	5	—	—	—	—	—
Dist. of Columbia.. 2	—	—	—	—	—	—	—	—
Total.......101¼	38½	51	58	194	1	8	3	6

Total 461. Necessary to a choice, 232.

THE SECOND BALLOT.

States.	Hamlin.	Clay.	Hickman.
Maine......................... 16	—	—
New-Hampshire. 10	—	—
Vermont........................ 10	—	—
Massachusetts................. 26	—	—
Rhode Island 8	—	—
Connecticut................ 10	—	—
New-York...................... 70	—	—
New-Jersey.................... 14	—	—
Pennsylvania.................. 54	—	—
Maryland...................... 10	1	—
Delaware...................... 6	—	—
Virginia...................... —	23	—
Kentucky..................... —	28	—
Ohio......................... 46	—	—
Indiana...................... 12	14	—
Missouri...................... 13	5	—
Michigan..................... 8	4	—
Illinois...................... 20	2	—
Texas........................ —	6	—
Wisconsin 5	5	—
Iowa........................ 3	1	—
California...... 7	1	—
Minnesota.... 7	1	—
Oregon....................... 3	—	2
Territories			
Kansas....................... 2	1	3
Nebraska..................... —	—	6
District of Columbia............. 2	—	—
Total.................... 367	86	13

Massachusetts withdrew the name of Mr. Banks, and cast 26 votes for Mr. Hamlin.

Pennsylvania withdrew the name of Gov. Reeder, and cast 54 votes for Mr. Hamlin.

On motion of Mr. Blakey, of Kentucky, the nomination was made unanimous.

Mr. J. R. Giddings, of Ohio, offered and the Convention adopted the following:

Resolved, That we deeply sympathize with those men who have been driven, some from their native States and others from the States of their adoption, and are now exiled from their homes on account of their opinions; and we hold the Democratic party responsible for the gross violations of that clause of the Constitution which declares that citizens of each State shall be entitled to all the privileges and immunities of citizens of the several States.

Mr. Ashmun made a brief speech, and the Convention adjourned *sine die*, with nine hearty cheers for the ticket.

NATIONAL REPUBLICAN COMMITTEE.

The Convention previous to its adjournment made choice of the following gentlemen as the National Committee for the next four years:

Maine—CHARLES J. GILMAN, Brunswick.
New-Hampshire—GEORGE G. FOGG, Concord.
Vermont—LAWRENCE BRAINARD, St. Albans.
Massachusetts—JOHN Z. GOODRICH, Stockbridge.
Rhode Island—THOMAS G. TURNER, Providence.
Connecticut—GIDEON WELLES, Hartford.
New-York—EDWIN D. MORGAN, Albany.
New-Jersey—DENNING DUER, N. Y. City.
Pennsylvania—EDWARD MCPHERSON, Gettysburg
Delaware—NATHANIEL B. SMITHERS, Dover.
Maryland—JAMES F. WAGNER, Baltimore.
Virginia—ALFRED CALDWELL, Wheeling.
Ohio—THOMAS SPOONER, Reading, Hamilton Co.
Indiana—SOLOMON MEREDITH, Centerville.
Illinois—NORMAN B. JUDD, Chicago.
Michigan—AUSTIN BLAIR, Jackson.
Wisconsin—CARL SCHURZ, Milwaukee.
Iowa—ANDREW J. STEVENS, Des Moines.
Minnesota—JOHN MCKUSICK, Stillwater.
Missouri—ASA S. JONES, St. Louis.
Kentucky—CASSIUS M. CLAY, Whitehall.
California—D. W. CHEESMAN, Oroville.
Oregon—W. FRANK JOHNSON, Oregon City.
Kansas—WILLIAM A. PHILLIPS, Lawrence.
Nebraska—O. H. IRISH, Nebraska City.
Dist. of Columbia, JOSEPH GERHARDT, Washington.

At a meeting held in Chicago, May 18th, 1860, the Committee organized by choosing the Hon. E. D. Morgan, of New-York, Chairman, and George G. Fogg, of New-Hampshire, Secretary. Subsequently, the following persons were constituted the Executive Committee:

E. D. MORGAN, of New-York.
GIDEON WELLES, of Connecticut.
N. B. JUDD, of Illinois.
CARL SCHURZ, of Wisconsin.
JOHN Z. GOODRICH, of Massachusetts.
DENNING DUER, of New-Jersey.
GEO. G. FOGG, of New-Hampshire.

CONSTITUTIONAL UNION CONVENTION—1860.

A Convention of Delegates, coming from twenty States, and claiming to represent the "Constitutional Union Party," met at Baltimore on the 9th of May, and nominated for President John Bell, of Tennessee, and for Vice-President Edward Everett, of Massachusetts. The ballotings for President resulted as follows:

	1st.	2d.		1st.	2d.
John Bell,	68¼	138	Edward Everett,	25	9½
Sam. Houston,	57	69	Wm. L. Goggin,	3	—
John M. Botts,	9¼	7	Wm. A. Graham,	22	18
John McLean,	21	1	Wm. L. Sharkey,	7	8½
J. J. Crittenden,	28	1	Wm. C. Rives,	13	—

Necessary to a choice, 1st ballot, 128; second ballot, 127.

The nomination of Mr. Bell was thereupon made unanimous.

Mr. Everett was unanimously nominated for Vice-President.

The Convention adopted the following as their

PLATFORM.

Whereas, Experience has demonstrated that Platforms adopted by the partisan Conventions of the country have had the effect to mislead and deceive the people, and at the same time to widen the political divisions of the country, by the creation and encouragement of geographical and sectional parties ; therefore,

Resolved, That it is both the part of patriotism and of duty *to recognize* no political principle other than THE CONSTITUTION OF THE COUNTRY, THE UNION OF THE STATES AND THE ENFORCEMENT OF THE LAWS, and that, as representatives of the Constitutional Union men of the country in National Convention assembled, we hereby pledge ourselves to maintain, protect and defend, separately and unitedly, these great principles of public liberty and national safety, against all enemies at home and abroad, believing that thereby peace may once more be restored to the country, the rights of the People and of the States reëstablished, and the Government again placed in that condition, of justice, fraternity and equality, which, under the example and Constitution of our fathers, has solemnly bound every citizen of the United States to maintain a more perfect union, establish justice, insure domestic tranquillity, provide for the common defense, promote the general welfare, and secure the blessings of liberty to ourselves and our posterity.

DEMOCRATIC CONVENTION—1860.

A Democratic National Convention assembled at Charleston, S. C., on the 23d of April, 1860, with full delegations present from every State in the Union, and double delegations from Illinois and New-York. One of the New-York delegations was elected by the State Nominating Convention which met at Syracuse the preceding autumn ; while its rival was elected by districts, and led by Fernando Wood, Mayor of the commercial emporium. From Illinois, one of the delegations was favorable to Senator Douglas, and the other opposed to that gentleman. Tickets of admission were given by the National Committee to the former or "Soft" Delegation from New York, thus deciding, so far as their power extended, against the Wood or "Hard" contestants, who were understood to be opposed to the nomination of Douglas.

Francis B. Flournoy, of Arkansas, was chosen temporary chairman, and the Convention opened with an angry and stormy debate on the question of the disputed seats. Mr. Fisher, of Va., presented a protest from Mayor Wood, on behalf of his delegation, against their exclusion from the Hall. The reading of the protest was ruled out of order, and, after a wrangling debate, committees were appointed on Permanent Organization and Credentials, and the communication of Mayor Wood was referred without reading to the latter.

On the following day, the Committee on Organization reported the name of Caleb Cushing, of Mass., for President, with one Vice-President and one Secretary from each State, which report was adopted. They also reported a rule "that in any State in which it has not "been provided or directed by its State Convention how its vote may be given, the "Convention will recognize the right of each "delegate to cast his individual vote." Which was also adopted.

A Committee on Resolutions and Platform was now appointed ; and it was voted that no ballot for President and Vice-President should be taken till after the adoption of a Platform. Adjourned.

On the following day, the only progress made by the Convention was the settlement of the question of contested seats, by confirming the sitting delegates ; that is, the "Softs" from New-York, and the Douglas men from Illinois. On the 26th, no progress was made, though there was much angry debate and many threats of bolting on the part of delegates from the Cotton States, unless their views in regard to Platform should be adopted.   •

On the 27th, the Platform Committee, failing to agree. presented an assortment of Platforms, from which the Convention was expected to make its selection. The majority report, presented by Mr. Avery, of N. C., was as follows:

Resolved, That the Platform adopted at Cincinnati be affirmed, with the following resolution:

That the National Democracy of the United States hold these cardinal principles on the subject of Slavery in the Territories: First, that Congress has no power to abolish Slavery in the Territories; second, that the Territorial Legislature has no power to abolish Slavery in the Territories, nor to prohibit the introduction of slaves therein, nor any power to destroy or impair the right of property in slaves by any legislation whatever.

Resolved, That the enactments of State Legislatures to defeat the faithful execution of the Fugitive Slave Law are hostile in character, subversive of the Constitution, and revolutionary in their effects.

Resolved, That it is the duty of the Federal Government to protect the rights of person and property on the high seas, in the Territories, or wherever else its jurisdiction extends.

Resolved, That it is the duty of the Government of the United States to afford protection to naturalized citizens from foreign countries.

Resolved, That it is the duty of the Government of the United States to acquire Cuba at the earliest practicable moment.

The principal minority report, which was presented by Mr. Henry B. Payne, of Ohio, and signed by the members of the committee from Maine. New-Hampshire, Vermont, Rhode Island, Connecticut, New-Jersey, Ohio, Indiana, Illinois, Michigan, Wisconsin, Iowa, Minnesota, New-York, and Pennsylvania, (all the Free States except California, Oregon, and Massachusetts), reaffirmed the Cincinnati Platform; declared that all rights of property are judicial in their character, and that the Democracy pledge themselves to defer to the decisions of the Supreme Court on the subject; ample protection to citizens, native or naturalized, at home or abroad; aid to "a Pacific Railroad;" the acquisition of Cuba, and that all State resistance to the Fugitive Slave Law is revolutionary and subversive of the Constitution.

Gen. Benj. F. Butler, of Massachusetts, presented another minority report, reaffirming the Cincinnati Platform, and declaring Democratic principles unchangeable in their nature when applied to the same subject matter, and only recommending, in addition to the Cincinnati Platform, a resolution for the protection of all citizens, whether native or naturalized.

Mr. Payne stated that his report, although a minority one, represented one hundred and seventy-two electoral votes, while the majority report represented only one hundred and twenty-seven electoral votes.

Mr. James A. Bayard (U. S. Senator), of Delaware, presented another series of resolutions, as follows:

The first affirmed the Cincinnati Platform.

The second declared that Territorial Governments are provisional and temporary, and that during their existence all citizens of the United States have an equal right to settle in the Territories without their rights of either person or property being destroyed or impaired by Congressional or Territorial 'egislation.

The third. that it is the duty of the Govern-

ment to protect the rights of persons or property on the high seas, in the Territories, or wherever else its constitutional authority extends.

The fourth that, when the settlers in a Territory have adequate population to form a State Constitution, the right of Sovereignty commences, and, being consummated by their admission into the Union, they stand upon an equal footing with the citizens of other States, and that a State thus organized is to be admitted into the Union, Slavery or no Slavery.

The day was spent in fierce debate, without coming to a vote on any of these various propositions.

On the 28th, Senator Wm. Bigler, of Pennsylvania, moved that the majority and minority reports be recommitted to the Convention, with instructions to report in an hour, the following resolutions:

Resolved, That the Platform adopted by the Democratic party at Cincinnati be affirmed, with the following explanatory resolution:

Resolved, That the Government of a Territory, organized by an act of Congress, is provisional and temporary, and, during its existence, all citizens of the United States have an equal right to settle in the Territory, without their rights, either of person or property, being destroyed or impaired by Congressional or Territorial Legislation.

Resolved, That the Democratic party stands pledged to the doctrine that it is the duty of Government to maintain all the constitutional rights of property, of whatever kind, in the Territories, and to enforce all the decisions of the Supreme Court in reference thereto

Resolved, That it is the duty of the United States to afford ample and complete protection to all its citizens, whether at home or abroad, and whether native or foreign

Resolved, That one of the necessities of the age, in a military, commercial and postal point of view, is speedy communication between the Atlantic and Pacific States; and the Democratic Party pledge such Constitutional Government aid as will insure the construction of a railroad to the Pacific coast at the earliest practical period.

Resolved, That the Democratic Party are in favor of the acquisition of the Island of Cuba, on such terms as shall be honorable to ourselves and just to Spain.

Resolved, That the enactments of State Legislatures to defeat the faithful execution of the Fugitive Slave Law, are hostile in character, subversive of the Constitution, and revolutionary in their effect.

Mr. Bigler moved the previous question.

Mr. W. Montgomery (M. C.), of Pennsylvania, moved to lay Mr. Bigler's motion on the table. He did not regard as a compromise a proposition for a Congressional Slave Code and the reopening of the African Slave Trade; but, learning that the adoption of his motion would have the effect of tabling the whole subject, he withdrew it. A division of the question was called for, and the vote was first taken on the motion to recommit, which was carried, 152 to 151; but the proposition to instruct the committee was laid on the table, 242½ to 56½, as follows:

Yeas.—Maine, 8; New-Hampshire, 5; Vermont, 5; Massachusetts, 12½; Rhode Island, 4; Connecticut, 5; New-York, 35; Pennsylvania, 8; Delaware, 3; Maryland, 5½; Virginia, 15; North Carolina, 10; South Ca.olina, 8; Georgia, 10; Florida, 3; Alabama, 9; Louisiana, 6; Mississippi, 7; Texas, 4; Arkansas, 4; Missouri, 4; Kentucky, 5; Ohio, 23; Indiana, 13; Illinois, 11; Michigan, 6; Iowa, 4; Minnesota, 4; California, 3½—242½.

Nays.—Massachusetts, ½; Connecticut, 1; New-Jersey, 7; Pennsylvania, 15; Maryland, 2½; Missouri, 9; Tennessee, 11; Kentucky, 7; Indiana, 6; Wisconsin, 5; California, ½; Oregon, 3—56½.

Subsequently, on the same day. Mr. Avery,

from the majority of the Committee on Platform, reported the following:

Resolved, That the platform adopted by the Democratic party at Cincinnati be affirmed, with the following explanatory Resolutions:

First. That the government of a Territory organized by an act of Congress, is provisional and temporary; and, during its existence, all citizens of the United States have an equal right to settle with their property in the Territory without their rights, either of person or property, being destroyed or impaired by congressional or territorial legislation.

Second. That it is the duty of the Federal Government, in all its departments, to protect, when necessary, the rights of persons and property in the Territories, and wherever else its constitutional authority extends.

Third. That when the settlers in a Territory having an adequate population form a State Constitution, the right of sovereignty commences, and, being consummated by admission into the Union, they stand on an equal footing with the people of other States; and the State thus organized ought to be admitted into the Federal Union, whether its constitution prohibits or recognizes the institution of Slavery.

Fourth. That the Democratic party are in favor of the acquisition of the Island of Cuba, on such terms as shall be honorable to ourselves and just to Spain, at the earliest practicable moment.

Fifth. That the enactments of State legislatures to defeat the faithful execution of the Fugitive Slave Law, are hostile in character, subversive of the Constitution, and revolutionary in their effect.

Sixth. That the Democracy of the United States recognize it as the imperative duty of this Government to protect the naturalized citizen in all his rights, whether at home or in foreign lands, to the same extent as its native-born citizens.

Whereas, one of the greatest necessities of the age, in a political, commercial, postal and military point of view, is a speedy communication between the Pacific and Atlantic coasts: Therefore be it

Resolved, That the Democratic party do hereby pledge themselves to use every means in their power to secure the passage of some bill, to the extent of the constitutional authority of Congress, for the construction of a Pacific Railroad, from the Mississippi River to the Pacific Ocean, at the earliest practicable moment.

Mr. Avery took the floor, and spoke at length in favor of his report, and in the course of his remarks said:

I have stated that we demand at the hands of our Northern brethren upon this floor that the great principle which we cherish should be recognized, and in that view I speak the common sentiments of our constituents at home; and I intend no reflection upon those who entertain a different opinion, when I say that the results and ultimate consequences to the Southern States of this confederacy, if the Popular Sovereignty doctrine be adopted as the doctrine of the Democratic party, would be as dangerous and subversive of their rights as the adoption of the principle of Congressional intervention or prohibition. We say that, in a contest for the occupation of the Territories of the United States, the Southern men encumbered with slaves cannot compete with the Emigrant Aid Society at the North. We say that the Emigrant Aid Society can send a voter to one of the Territories of the United States, to determine a question relating to slavery, for the sum of $200, while it would cost the Southern man the sum of $1500. We say, then, that wherever there is competition between the South and North, that the North can and will, at less expense and difficulty, secure power, control and dominion over the Territories of the Federal Government; and if, then, you establish the doctrine that a Territorial Legislature which may be established by Congress in any Territory has the right, directly or indirectly, to affect the institution of Slavery, then you can see that the Legislature by its action, either directly or indirectly, may finally exclude every man from the slaveholding States as effectually as if you had adopted the Wilmot Proviso out and out. . . . .

But we are told that, in advocating the doctrine we now do, we are violating the principles of the Cincinnati platform. They say that the Cincinnati platform is a Popular Sovereignty platform; that it was intended to present and practically enforce that great principle. Now, we who made this report deny that this is the true construction of the Cincinnati platform. We of the South say that when we voted for the Cincinnati platform we understood, from the fact that the Territories stand in the same position as the District of Columbia, that non-interference and non-intervention in the Territories was that same sort of non-interference and non-intervention forbidden in the Dis-

trict of Columbia. Now, we maintain that Congress has no right to prohibit or abolish Slavery in the District of Columbia. Why? Because it is an existing institution. It becomes the duty of Congress under the Constitution to protect and cherish the right of property in slaves in that District, because the Constitution does not give them the power to prohibit or establish Slavery. Every session of Congress, Northern men, Southern men, men of all parties, are legislating to protect, cherish and uphold the institution of Slavery in the District of Columbia. . . . .

It is said that the Cincinnati platform is ambiguous, and that we must explain it. At the South, we have maintained that it had no ambiguity; that it did not mean Popular Sovereignty; but our Northern friends say that it does mean Popular Sovereignty. Now, if we are going to explain it and to declare its principles, I say let us either declare them openly, boldly, squarely, or let us leave it as it is in the Cincinnati Platform. I want, and we of the South want, no more doubtful platforms upon this or any other question. We desire that this Convention should take a bold, square stand. What do the minority of the committee propose? Their solution is to leave the question to the decision of the Supreme Court, and agree to abide by any decision that may be made by that tribunal between the citizens of a Territory upon the subject. Why, gentlemen of the minority, you cannot help yourselves. That is no concession to us. There is no necessity for putting that in the platform, because I take it for granted that you are all law-abiding citizens. Every gentleman here from a non-slaveholding State is a law-abiding citizen; and if he be so, why we know that when there is a decision of the Supreme Court, even adverse to his views, he will submit to it. . . . . .

You say that this is a judicial question. We say that it is not. But if it be a judicial question, it is immaterial to you how the platform is made, because all you will have to say is, "this is a judicial question; the majority of the Convention were of one opinion; I may entertain my own opinion upon the question; let the Supreme Court settle it." . .

Let us make a platform about which there can be no doubt, so that every man, North and South, may stand side by side on all issues connected with Slavery, and advocate the same principles. That is all we ask. All we demand at your hands is, that there shall be no equivocation and no doubt in the popular mind as to what our principles are.

Mr. H. B. Payne, of Ohio, replied at length, and, in the course of his argument, said:

The question of Slavery had distracted the Courts and the party since 1820, and we hoped by the Compromise measures of 1850, the Kansas law of 1854, and the Platform of 1852 and 1856, that the policy of the Democratic party was a united and settled policy in respect to African slavery. . . . . The Democracy of the North have, throughout, stood by the South in vindication of their constitutional rights. For this they claim no credit. They have simply discharged their constitutional duty; and, though some Southern Senators may rise in their places and stigmatize us as unsound and rotten, we say we have done it in good faith, and we challenge contradiction. We have supposed that this doctrine of Popular Sovereignty was a final settlement of the Slavery difficulty. You so understood it in the South. We are not claiming anything in our Platform but what the Cincinnati Platform was admitted to have established. . . . .

What was the doctrine of 1856? Non-intervention by Congress with the question of Slavery, and the submission of the question of Slavery in the Territories, under the Constitution, to the People.

It is said that one construction has been given to the Platform at the South and another at the North. He could prove from the Congressional debates that from 1850 to 1856 there was not a dissenting opinion expressed in Congress on this subject.

To show that Squatter Sovereignty had been generally accepted as the true Democratic doctrine, Mr. Payne quoted from eminent Southern Democratic Statesmen as follows:

FROM A SPEECH OF HON. HOWELL COBB, OF GEORGIA.

"I stand upon a principle. I hold that the will of the majority of the people of Kansas should decide this question, and I say here to-night, before this people and before this country, that I, for one, shall abide the decision of the people there. I hold to the right of the People to self-government. I am willing for them to decide this question."

FROM THE SAME.

"I would not plant Slavery upon the soil of any portion of God's earth against the will of the people. The

Government of the United States should not force the institution of Slavery upon the people either of the 'Territories,' or of the States against the will of the people, though my voice could bring about that result."

FROM A SPEECH OF VICE-PRESIDENT BRECKINRIDGE.

" But those who hold that the Territorial Legislature cannot pass a law prohibiting Slavery, admit that, unless the Territorial Legislature pass laws for its protection, Slavery will not go there. Therefore, practically, a majority of the people represented in the Territorial Legislature decides the question. Whether they decide it by prohibiting it, according to the one doctrine, or by refusing to pass laws to protect it, as contended for by the other party, is immaterial. The majority of the people, by the action of the Territorial Legislature, will decide the question, and all must abide the decision when made."

FROM THE SAME.

" But if non-intervention by Congress be the principle that underlies the Compromise of 1850, then the prohibition of 1820, being inconsistent with that principle, should be removed, and perfect non-intervention thus be established by law.

" Among many misrepresentations sent to the country by some of the enemies of this bill, perhaps none is more flagrant, than the charge that it proposes to legislate Slavery into Nebraska and Kansas. Sir, if the bill contained such a feature it would not receive my vote. The right to establish involves the correlative right to prohibit, and, denying both, I would vote for neither."

FROM THE SAME.

" Upon the distracting question of domestic Slavery, their position is clear. The whole power of the Democratic organization is pledged to the following propositions: That Congress shall not interpose upon this subject in the States, in the Territories, or in the District of Columbia ; that the people of each Territory shall determine the question for themselves, and be admitted into the Union upon a footing of perfect equality with the original States, without discrimination on account of the allowance or prohibition of Slavery."

FROM A SPEECH BY HON. JAMES L. ORR, OF S. C.

" Now, I admit that there is a difference of opinion amongst Democrats as to whether this feature of Squatter Sovereignty be in the bill or not. But the great point upon which the Democratic party at Cincinnati rested was, that the government of the Territories had been transferred from Congress, and, carrying out the spirit and genius of our institutions, had been given to the people of the Territories."

FROM A SPEECH BY HON. A. H. STEPHENS, OF GEORGIA.

" The whole question of Slavery or No Slavery was to be left to the people of the Territories, whether North or South of 36° 30', or any other line. The question was to be taken out of Congress, where it had been improperly thrust from the beginning, and to be left to the people concerned in the matter to decide for themselves. This, I say, was the position originally held by the South when the Missouri Restriction was at first proposed. The principle upon which that position rests, lies at the very foundation of all our Republican institutions: it is that the citizens of every distinct and separate community or State should have the right to govern themselves in their domestic matters as they please, and that they should be free from intermeddling restriction and arbitrary dictation on such matters, from any other Power or Government, in which they have no voice."

Mr. Payne continued. But for consuming time, he could read for half an hour, to show that every eminent Southern man had held the same opinion on the doctrine of popular sovereignty.

Mr. Payne would read from the Cincinnati Platform to show what it laid down. All should be familiar with it :

" The American Democracy recognize and adopt the principles contained in the organic laws, establishing the Territories of Kansas and Nebraska as embodying the only sound and safe solution of the 'Slavery Question' upon which the great National idea of the People of this whole country can repose in its determined conservatism of the Union—non-interference by Congress with Slavery in State and Territory, or in the District of Columbia."

They nominated Mr. Buchanan on that Platform, agreed on by the representatives of every State in the Union, as the official record would show. There was not one dissenting voice in the whole list of States. In casting the vote of North Carolina, his friend, Mr. Avery,

then acting as Chairman of his Delegation, and now presenting the majority report announced:

" North Carolina gives ten votes for the Platform, and will give ten thousand majority in November."

In his letter of acceptance, Mr. Buchanan, in an emphatic and clear manner, thus expressed his views of this Platform :

" The recent legislation of Congress respecting domestic Slavery, derived, as it has been, from the original and pure fountain of legitimate political power, the will of the majority, promises, ere long, to allay the dangerous excitement. This legislation is founded on principles as ancient as Free government itself, and in accordance with them has simply declared that *the people of a Territory, like those of a State, shall decide for themselves, whether Slavery shall or shall not exist within their limits.*"

Mr. Payne had extracts yet behind of speeches from Stephens, of Georgia, one of the most distinguished Statesmen of the South—from Mr. Benjamin, of Louisiana—Mason, of Virginia—more qualified, he admitted, but still emphatic. The Senator from Delaware, too, Mr. Bayard, had fully indorsed the doctrine of Popular Sovereignty.

So had Mr. Badger, of North Carolina, and Judge Butler of South Carolina. Mr. Hunter of Virginia, certainly one of the wisest and purest statesmen which the Democracy now numbers amongst her leaders in the land—he, also, says that the people shall have the right to decide on all questions relating to their domestic institutions. In his speech, he used these words, almost identical with the Platform of the minority :

" The bill provides that the Legislatures of these Territories shall have power to legislate over all rightful subjects of legislation consistently with the Constitution. And, if they should assume powers which are thought to be inconsistent with the Constitution, the Courts will decide that question whenever it may be raised. There is a difference of opinion among the friends of this measure as to the extent of the limits which the Constitution imposes upon the Territorial Legislatures. This bill proposes to leave these differences to the decision of the Courts. To that tribunal I am willing to leave this decision, as it was once before proposed to be left by the celebrated Compromise of the Senator from Delaware."

He also read an extract of a similar character from a speech by Mr. Toombs, of Georgia, one of the boldest men on the floor of the American Senate, taking ground in favor of non-intervention by Congress.

Need he accumulate these extracts to show that not a single statesman who has figured in Congress, of late years, but has taken this high ground?

Mr. Samuels, of Iowa, presented the following report on behalf of the minority of the Platform Committee :

1. *Resolved*, That we, the Democracy of the Union, in Convention assembled, hereby declare our affirmance of the resolutions unanimously adopted and declared as a platform of principles by the Democratic Convention at Cincinnati, in the year 1856, believing that Democratic principles are unchangeable in their nature, when applied to the same subject matters ; and we recommend as the only further resolutions the following :

Inasmuch as differences of opinion exist in the Democratic Party as to the nature and extent of the powers of a Territorial Legislature, and as to the powers and duties of Congress, under the Constitution of the United States, over the institution of Slavery within the Territories:

2. *Resolved*, That the Democratic Party will abide by the decisions of the Supreme Court of the United States on the questions of Constitutional law.

3. *Resolved*, That it is the duty of the United States to afford ample and complete protection to all its citizens, whether at home or abroad, and whether native or foreign.

4. *Resolved*, That one of the necessities of the age, in a military, commercial, and postal point of view, is speedy communication between the Atlantic and Pacific States ; and the Democratic Party pledge such Constitutional Government aid as will insure the construction of a railroad to the Pacific coast, at the earliest practicable period.

5. *Resolved*, That the Democratic party are in favor of the acquisition of the Island of Cuba, on such terms as shall be honorable to ourselves and just to Spain.

6. *Resolved*, That the enactments of State Legislatures to defeat the faithful execution of the Fugitive Slave Law, are hostile in character, subversive of the Constitution, and revolutionary in their effect.

Gen. Butler, of Massachusetts, again reported

(as a minority) the Cincinnati Platform without alteration.

It was evident, even before the report of the majority was presented, that it would not be sustained by the Convention, though the Free-State majority evinced not only willingness but anxiety to conciliate their Southern brethren at any sacrifice not absolutely ruinous.

The majority of the Convention, confident of their power to reject the majority report, were anxious for a vote; but the minority seemed determined to stave off definite action for that day, and carried their point by a system currently termed "filibustering," which would have done no discredit to the House of Representatives at Washington. The confusion and hubbub which prevailed may be comprehended perhaps, by the following extract from the official report of the proceedings:

Mr. Bigler obtained the floor, and desired to suggest to the Convention that, by common consent, and without any further struggle, they should adjourn. (Cries of " I object !" " I object !")

Mr. Hunter, of Louisiana.—I appeal to my Democratic friends of the South and my Democratic friends from all parts of the Union——(Cries of "order !" "order !" and the greatest disorder prevailing in the Hall.)

The President—The Chair begs leave, once for all, to state—and the Chair entreats the Convention to listen to this declaration—that it is physically impossible for the Chair to go on in a contest with six hundred men as to who shall cry out loudest; and unless the Convention will come to order, and gentlemen take their places and proceed in order, the Chair will feel bound in duty to the Convention as well as to himself, to leave the chair. (Applause.) The Chair will wait to see whether it is possible to have order in the House.

Mr. Samuels, of Iowa, appealed to the Convention to listen to a proposition of Mr. Hunter of Louisiana.

The President.—The Chair will entertain no motion until the Convention is restored to order, and when that is done, the Chair desires to make another suggestion to the Convention. The Chair has already stated that it is physically impossible for him to go on with the business of the Convention, so long as one-half of the members are upon their feet and engaged in clamor of one sort or another. The Chair begs leave to repeat that he knows but one remedy for such disorder, and that is for your residing officer to leave the chair. He, of course, would deeply regret that painful necessity ; but it would be a less evil than that this incessant confusion and disorder, presenting such a spectacle to the people of South Carolina, should continue to prevail in this most honorable body of so many respectable gentlemen of the highest standing in the community, engaged in debate and deliberation upon the dearest interests of the country. (Applause.)

It was finally agreed that the vote should be taken the next day—or rather the following Monday, and the Convention adjourned.

On Monday the 30th, the President stated the question as follows:

The Convention will remember that, in the first place, the gentleman from North Carolina (Mr. Avery) reported the resolutions of the majority of the committee. Thereupon the gentleman from Iowa (Mr. Samuels) moved an amendment to these resolutions, by striking out all after the word "resolved," and to insert the resolutions proposed by him, in behalf of a portion of minority of the committee. After which, the gentleman from Massachusetts (Mr. Butler) moved, in behalf of another portion of the minority committee, to amend the amendment, by striking out all after the word "resolved," and inserting the proposition proposed by him on behalf of that minority. The first question will be, therefore, upon the amendment moved by the gentleman from Massachusetts (Mr. Butler). If that amendment falls, the Convention will then come to a vote upon the amendment moved by the gentleman from Iowa (Mr. Samuels). If, however, the amendment of Mr. Butler prevails, then that amendment will have taken the place of the amendment moved by Mr. Samuels, and the next question will be upon substituting it in the place

of the original resolution proposed by the gentleman from North Carolina.

Mr. Butler's Platform affirms the Cincinnati Platform, and adds a resolution for the protection of citizens abroad.

The vote was then taken by States on Mr. Butler's amendment, with the following result; yeas 105, nays 198:

Yeas—Maine, 3; Massachusetts, 8; Connecticut, 2½; New-Jersey, 5; Pennsylvania, 16½; Delaware, 3; Maryland, 5½; Virginia, 12½; North Carolina, 10; Georgia, 10; Missouri, 4½; Tennessee, 11; Kentucky, 9; Minnesota, 1½; Oregon, 3—105.

Nays—Maine, 5; New-Hampshire, 5; Vermont, 5; Massachusetts, 5; Rhode Island, 4; Connecticut, 3½; New-York, 35; New-Jersey, 2; Pennsylvania, 10½; Maryland, 2½; Virginia, 2½; South Carolina, 8; Florida, 3; Alabama, 9; Louisiana, 6; Mississippi, 7; Texas, 4; Arkansas, 4; Missouri, 4½; Tennessee, 1; Kentucky, 3; Ohio, 23; Indiana, 13; Illinois, 11; Michigan, 6; Wisconsin, 5; Iowa, 4; Minnesota, 2½; California, 4—198.

So the amendment was rejected.

The minority report (that of Mr. Samuels) was then read, and, after ineffectual attempts to table the subject and proceed to a nomination, the vote was taken and the minority report was adopted as an amendment or substitute, as follows:

Yeas—Maine, 8; New-Hampshire, 5; Vermont, 5; Massachusetts, 7; Rhode Island, 4; Connecticut, 6; New-York, 35; New-Jersey, 5; Pennsylvania, 12; Maryland, 3½; Virginia, 1; Missouri, 4; Tennessee, 1; Kentucky, 2½; Ohio, 23; Indiana, 13; Illinois, 11; Michigan, 6; Wisconsin, 5; Iowa, 4; Minnesota, 4—165.

Nays—Massachusetts, 6; New-Jersey, 2; Pennsylvania, 15; Delaware, 3; Maryland, 4½; Virginia, 14; North Carolina, 10; South Carolina, 8; Georgia, 10; Florida, 3; Alabama, 9; Louisiana, 6; Mississippi, 7; Texas, 4; Arkansas, 4; Missouri, 5; Tennessee, 11; Kentucky, 9½; California, 4; Oregon, 3—138.

The question was then taken on the adoption of the report as amended, the vote being taken on each resolution separately, and with the exception of the one pledging the Democratic party to abide by the decisions of the Supreme Court on the subject of Slavery in the Territories—which was rejected—they were adopted by a vote which was nearly unanimous.

The delegation from Alabama, by its Chairman, then presented a written protest, signed by all its members, announcing their purpose to withdraw from the Convention. They were followed by the delegations from Mississippi, Florida, Texas, all the Louisiana delegation except two, all the South Carolina delegation except three, three of the Arkansas delegation, two of the Delaware delegation (including Senator Bayard) and one from North Carolina.

The order of their withdrawal was as follows:

ALABAMA PROTESTS AND WITHDRAWS.

Mr. Walker, of Alabama.—Mr. President, I am instructed by the Alabama delegation to submit to this Convention a communication, and, with your permission, I will read it.

To the Hon. Caleb Cushing,

President of the Democratic National Convention, now in session in the City of Charleston, South Carolina :

The undersigned delegates, representing the State of Alabama in this Convention, respectfully beg leave to lay before your honorable body the following statements of facts:

On the eleventh day of January, 1860, the Democratic party of the State of Alabama met in Convention, in the city of Montgomery, and adopted, with singular unanimity, a series of resolutions herewith submitted:

1. *Resolved by the Democracy of the State of Alabama in Convention assembled,* That holding all issues and principles upon which they have heretofore affiliated and acted with the National Democratic Party to be inferior in dignity and importance to the great question of Slavery, they content themselves

wih a general re-affirmance of the Cincinnati platform as to such issues, and also indorse said platform as to slavery, together with the following resolutions :

2. *Resolved further*, That we re-affirm so much of the first resolution of the platform adopted in the Convention by the Democracy of this State, on the 8th of January, 1856, as relates to the subject of Slavery, to-wit : "The unqualified right of the people of the Slaveholding States to the protection of their property in the States, in the Territories, and in the wilderness, in which Territorial Governments are as yet unorganized."

3. *Resolved further*, That in order to meet and clear away all obstacles to a full enjoyment of this right in the Territories, we re-affirm the principle of the 9th resolution of the Platform adopted in Convention by the Democracy of this State, on the 14th of February, 1848, to wit : "That it is the duty of the General Government, by all proper legislation, to secure an entry into those Territories to all the citizens of the United States, together with their property of every description, and that the same should be protected by the United States while the Territories are under its authority."

4. *Resolved further*, That the Constitution of the United States is a compact between sovereign and co-equal States, united upon the basis of perfect equality of rights and privileges.

5. *Resolved further*, That the Territories of the United States are common property, in which the States have equal rights, and to which the citizens of every State may rightfully emigrate, with their slaves or other property recognized as such in any of the States of the Union, or by the Constitution of the United States.

6. *Resolved further*, That the Congress of the United States has no power to abolish Slavery in the Territories, or to prohibit its introduction into any of them.

7. *Resolved further*, That the Territorial Legislatures, created by the legislation of Congress, have no power to abolish Slavery, or to prohibit the introduction of the same, or to impair by unfriendly legislation the security and full enjoyment of the same within the Territories ; and such constitutional power certainly does not belong to the people of the Territories in any capacity, before, in the exercise of a lawful authority, they form a Constitution preparatory to admission as a State into the Union ; and their action, in the exercise of such lawful authority, certainly cannot operate or take effect before their actual admission as a State into the Union.

8. *Resolved further*, That the principles enunciated by Chief Justice Taney, in his opinion in the *Dred Scott* case, deny to the Territorial Legislature the power to destroy or impair, by any legislation whatever, the right of property in slaves, and maintain it to be the duty of the Federal Government, in *all* of its departments, to protect the rights of the owner of such property in the Territories ; and the principles so declared are hereby asserted to be the rights of the South, and the South should maintain them.

9. *Resolved further*, That we hold all of the foregoing propositions to contain *cardinal principles*—true in themselves—and just and proper, and necessary for the safety of all that is dear to us ; and we do hereby instruct our delegates to the Charleston Convention to present them for the calm consideration and approval of that body—from whose justice and patriotism we anticipate their adoption.

10. *Resolved further*, That our delegates to the Charleston Convention are hereby expressly instructed to insist that said Convention shall adopt a platform of principles, recognizing distinctly the rights of the South, as asserted in the foregoing resolutions ; and if the said National Convention shall refuse to adopt, in substance, the propositions embraced in the preceding resolutions, prior to nominating candidates, our delegates to said Convention are hereby positively instructed to withdraw therefrom.

11. *Resolved further*, That our delegates to the Charleston Convention shall cast the vote of Alabama as a unit, and a majority of our delegates shall determine how the vote of this State shall be given.

12. *Resolved further*, That an Executive Committee, to consist of one from each Congressional District, be appointed, whose duty it shall be, in the event that our delegates withdraw from the Charleston Convention, in obedience to the 10th resolution, to call a Convention of the Democracy of Alabama to meet at an early day to consider what is best to be done.

Under these resolutions, the undersigned received their appointment, and participated in the action of this Convention.

By the resolution of instruction, the tenth in the series, we were directed to insist that the platform adopted by this Convention should embody, "in whole," the propositions embraced in the preceding resolutions, prior to nominating candidates.

Anxious, if possible, to continue our relations with this Convention, and thus to maintain the nationality of the Democratic party, we agreed to accept, as the substance of the Alabama platform, either of the two reports submitted to this Convention by the majority of the Committee on Resolutions—this majority representing not only a majority of the States of the Union, but also the only States at all likely to be carried by the Democratic party in the Presidential election. We beg to make these reports a part of this communication.

[See heretofore the two sets of resolutions reported by Mr. Avery.]

These reports received the indorsement in the Committee on Resolutions of every Southern State, and, had either of them been adopted as the platform of principles of the Democratic party, although possibly in some respects subject to criticism, we should not have felt ourselves in duty bound to withhold our acquiescence.

But it has been the pleasure of this Convention, by an almost exclusive sectional vote, not representing a majority of the Democratic electoral vote, to adopt a platform which does not, in our opinion, nor in the opinion of those who urge it, embody in substance the principles of the Alabama resolutions. That Platform is as follows :

[Here follow Mr. Samuels' resolutions as adopted. See Platform.]

The points of difference between the Northern and Southern Democracy are :

1st. As regards the *status* of Slavery as a political institution in the Territories whilst they remain Territories, and the power of the people of a Territory to exclude it by unfriendly legislation ; and

2d. As regards the duty of the Federal Government to protect the owner of slaves in the enjoyment of his property in the Territories so long as they remain such.

This Convention has refused, by the Platform adopted, to settle either of these propositions in favor of the South. We deny to the people of a Territory any power to legislate against the institution of Slavery ; and we assert that it is the duty of the Federal Government, in all its departments, to protect the owner of slaves in the enjoyment of his property in the Territories. These principles, as we state them, are embodied in the Alabama Platform.

Here, then, is a plain, explicit and direct issue between this Convention and the constituency which we have the honor to represent in this body.

Instructed as we are, not to waive this issue, the contingency, therefore, has arisen, when, in our opinion, it becomes our duty to withdraw from this Convention. We beg, sir, to communicate this fact through you, and to assure the Convention that we do so in no spirit of anger, but under a sense of imperative obligation, properly appreciating its responsibilities and cheerfully submitting to its consequences.

L. P. WALKER, Chairman.	O. O. HARPER,
J. S. LYON,	LEWIS H. CATO,
JOHN A. WINSTON,	JNO. W. PORTIS,
ROBERT G. SCOTT,	F. G. NORMAN,
A. B. MEEK,	W. C. GUILD,
J. R. BREARE,	JULIUS C. B. MITCHELL,
H. D. SMITH,	W. C. SHERROD,
JAS. IRWIN,	G. G. GRIFFIN,
W. L. YANCEY,	J. T. BRADFORD,
D. W. BAINE,	T. J. BURNETT,
N. H. R. DAWSON,	A. G. HENRY,
R. M. PATTON,	WM. M. BROOKS,
W. C. MCIVER,	R. CHAPMAN.

Mr. Walker also presented a resolution to the effect that no other person than the retiring delegates had any authority to represent Alabama in the Convention.

The Alabama delegation then withdrew from the hall.

MISSISSIPPI WITHDRAWS.

Mr. Barry, of Mississippi.—I am instructed by the Mississippi delegation to state that they retire from the Convention with the delegation from Alabama. (Cheers.) They have prepared a protest, which they desire to submit, but by accident it is not now here. I desire also to state that they have adopted unanimously a resolution that they are the only delegates—which is uncontested— and that no one is or shall be authorized to represent them in their absence upon the floor of the Convention. (Cheers.)

Mr. Mouton, of Louisiana.—Mr. President, I have but a short communication to make to the Convention. I do not do it as an individual. I am authorized to say by the delegates representing Louisiana in this Convention, that they will not participate any longer in the proceedings of this Convention. (Cheers.) Heretofore we have been in the habit of saying that the Democracy of the country was harmonious. (Laughter.) Can we say so to-day with any truth? Are we not divided, and divided in such a manner that we can never be reconciled, because we are divided upon principle? Can we agree to the Platform adopted by the majority of the Convention, and then go home to our constituents and put one construction on it, while Northern Democrats put another? No, Mr. President, I think I speak the sentiment of my State when I say that she will never play such a part. (Cheers.) If we are to fight the Black Republicans together, let us do it with a bold front; let us use the same arms; let us sustain the same principles. I was willing, this morning, in order to do away with the necessity of all these votes, and to ascertain if there was a majority here ready to impose upon us such a Platform—I was willing, myself, that the majority of the Convention should retire and prepare such a Platform as suited them, and to take a vote upon it, and if that Platform did not give us those guarantees which we are entitled to under the Constitution, then we would have been ready to do what we are now doing. The Platform which the majority of this Convention has adopted does not give us those guarantees which we are entitled to for the protection of our property in the Territories. We wish to wear no two faces in this contest. We wish to meet the Black Republicans with their abominable doctrines boldly; and if our friends, the Democrats from the Free States, cannot join us and fight with us, we must fight our own battle. We are ready to meet the issue made by the Black Republicans like men, but we shall battle for what we conceive to be the truth, and not for profit. For these reasons, I am authorized by my delegation to announce that they withdraw from the Convention. At the same time, I should state the fact that two of the delegation do not join us in this movement. (Loud cheers.) At the same time, I should state that those who sent us here instructed us to vote as a unit, and we contend, therefore, that we are entitled to give the whole vote of the State, and that no one else is entitled to give it or to divide it.

Mr. Mouton made some additional remarks, but owing to the confusion which prevailed in the hall, the reporter was unable to hear them.

Mr. Glenn, of Mississippi.—Mr. President and gentlemen of this Convention: For the first time, for the only time, for the last time, in the name of the State that I have the honor in part to represent here, I desire to say but a few words to this Convention. I hold in my hand the solemn act of her delegation upon this floor, and I say to you, gentlemen, that it is not a hasty action; that it is not one conceived in passion, or carried out in caprice or disappointment. It is the firm resolve of the great body of the people whom we represent, which was expressed in the Convention that sent us here, and that resolve, that people, and we, their representatives, will maintain at all cost and at all hazards. (Loud cheers.)

We came here not to dictate to the representatives of other sovereign States. Since we have been here, our intercourse has been courteous so far as personalities are concerned. We have all sought, and I believe have all been able, to conduct ourselves as gentlemen. But we did not come here to exercise the courtesies of life alone. We came to settle the principles upon which our party must rest and must stand. We came here, gentlemen of the North, not to ask you to adopt a principle which you could say was opposed to your consciences and to your principles. We did not believe it to be so. We came as equal members of a common confederacy, simply to ask you to acknowledge our equal rights within that confederacy. (Cheers.) Sir, at Cincinnati we adopted a Platform on which we all agreed. Now answer me, ye men of the North, of the East, of the South, and of the West, what was the construction placed upon that Platform in different sections of the Union? You at the West said it meant one thing. we of the South said it meant another. Either we were right or you were right; we were wrong or you were wrong. We came here to ask you which was right and which was wrong. You have maintained your position. You say that you cannot give us an acknowledgment of that right, which I tell you here now, in coming time will be your only safety in your contests with the Black Republicans of Ohio and of the North. (Cheers.)

Why, sir, turn back to the history of your own leading men. There sits a distinguished gentleman, (Hon. Charles E. Stuart, of Michigan,) once a representative of one of the sovereign States of the Union in the Senate, who then voted that Congress had the constitutional power to pass the Wilmot Proviso, and to exclude Slavery from the Territories; and now, when the Supreme Court has said that it has not that power, he comes forward and tells Mississippians that that same Congress is impotent to protect that same species of property. There sits my distinguished friend, the Senator from Ohio, (Mr. Pugh,) who, but a few nights since, told us from that stand that if a Territorial Government totally misused their powers or abused them, Congress could wipe out that Territorial Government altogether. And yet, when we come here and ask him to give us protection in case that Territorial Government robs us of our property and strikes the star which answers to the name of Mississippi from the flag of the Union, so far as the Constitution gives her protection, he tells us, with his hand upon his heart—as Gov. Payne, of Ohio, had before done—that they will part with their

lives before they will acknowledge the principle which we contend for.

Gentlemen, in such a situation of things in the Convention of our great party, it is right that we should part. Go your way, and we will go ours. The South leaves you —not like Hagar, driven into the wilderness, friendless and alone—but I tell Southern men here, and for them, I tell the North, that, in less than sixty days, you will find a united South standing side by side with us. (Prolonged and enthusiastic cheering.)

We stand firm and immovable, and while we respect you, we must respect ourselves. And, gentlemen, let me say to you of the North now, that the time may come when you will need us more than we need you. I speak to those who represent " the green hills of New England ;" I speak to the " imperial center " of the Union. There slumbers in your midst a latent spark—not of political sectionalism, but of social discord—which may yet require the conservative principles of the South to save your region of country from anarchy and confusion. We need not your protection. The power of the Black Republicans is nothing to us. We are safe in our own strength and security, so long as we maintain our rights.

Gentlemen, I have detained you too long. I ask, in conclusion, that the few words which are here written— words of courtesy, but words of truth so far as my glorious State is concerned—may be read in your hearing.

Mr. Mathews, of Mississippi, then read the following document.

To the President of the Democratic Convention :

Sir : As Chairman of the delegation, which has the honor to represent the State of Mississippi upon this floor, I desire to be heard by you and by the Convention.

In common consultation we have met here, the representatives of sister States, to resolve the principles of a great party. While maintaining principles, we profess no spirit save that of harmony, conciliation, the success of our party, and the safety of our organization. But to the former the latter must yield—for no organization is valuable without it, and no success is honorable which does not crown it.

We came here simply asking a recognition of the equal rights of our State under the laws and Constitution of our common Government; that our right to property should be asserted, and the protection of that property, when necessary, should be yielded by the Government which claims our allegiance. We had regarded government and protection as correlative ideas, and that so long as the one was maintained the other still endured.

After a deliberation of many days, it has been announced to us by a controlling majority of Representatives of nearly one-half the States of this Union, and that too, in the most solemn and impressive manner, that our demand cannot be met and our rights cannot be recognized. While it is granted that the capacity of the Federal Government is ample to protect all other property within its jurisdiction, it is claimed to be impotent when called upon to act in favor of a species of property recognized in fifteen sovereign States. Within those States, even Black Republicans admit it to be guaranteed by the Constitution, and to be only assailed by a Higher Law ; without them, they claim the power to prohibit or destroy it. The controling majority of Northern representatives on this floor, while they deny all power to destroy, equally deny all power to protect ; and this, they assure us, is, and must, and shall be the condition of our coöperation in the next Presidential election.

In this state of affairs, our duty is plain and obvious. The State which sent us here, announced to us her principles. In common with seventeen of her sister States, she has asked a recognition of her Constitutional rights. These have been plainly and explicitly denied to her. We have offered to yield everything except an abandonment of her rights—everything except her honor—and it has availed us nothing.

As the Representatives of Mississippi, knowing her wishes—as honorable men, regarding her commands—we withdraw from the Convention, and, as far as our action is concerned, absolve her from all connection with this body, and all responsibility for its action.

To you, sir, as presiding officer of the Convention while it has existed in its integrity, we desire, collectively as a delegation, and individually as men, to tender the highest assurances of our profound respect and consideration.

Signed : D. C. Glen, Chairman of the Mississippi delegation ; George H. Gordon, James Drone, Beverly Mathews, J. T. Simms, Joseph R. Davis, W. S. Wilson, Isaac Enloe, Charles Edward Hooker, W. H. H. Tison, Ethelbert Barksdale, W. S. Barry, J. M. Thomson.

Mr. Mathews then announced that a meeting

of all those who sympathized with them in this movement would be held at 8 o'clock this evening, in St. Andrew's Hall.

The Mississippi delegation then withdrew from the Convention.

SOUTH CAROLINA WITHDRAWS.

The Hon. James Simons, of South Carolina.—Mr. President, I am directed by the delegation from South Carolina respectfully to present the following document.

To the Hon. Caleb Cushing,

President of the Charleston Convention:

We, the undersigned Delegates appointed by the Democratic State Convention of South Carolina, beg leave respectfully to state that, according to the principles enunciated in their Platform at Columbia, the power, either of the Federal Government or of its agent, the Territorial Government, to abolish or legislate against property in slaves, by either direct or indirect legislation, is especially denied; and as the Platform adopted by the Convention palpably and intentionally prevents any expression affirming the incapacity of the Territorial Government so to legislate, that they would not be acting in good faith to their principles, or in accordance with the wishes of their constituents, to longer remain in this Convention, and they hereby respectfully announce their withdrawal therefrom.

James Simons,	Thos. Y. Simons,
S. McGowan,	Jas. Patterson,
B. H. Wilson,	B. H. Brown,
R. B. Boylston,	J. A. Metts,
Jas. H. Witherspoon,	John S. Preston,
E. W. Charles,	Frankland Gaillard.

G. N. Reynolds, Jr.

The reading of this paper was greeted with frequent bursts of most enthusiastic cheering on the floor and in the galleries.

I am further instructed to say, that the communication is signed by all the delegation but three members.

The South Carolina delegation then withdrew from the Convention amidst loud cheering.

FLORIDA RETIRES.

Mr. Milton, of Florida.—Mr. President: Representing the State of Florida, it is with feelings of sadness that I present myself before you to bid adieu to the men of talent and men of high and noble feelings from the North and West, who have met us here upon this occasion. But differences have arisen between us which, as honorable men, we cannot adjust. It has been asked, time and again, why we should invite gentlemen from the Northwest, the North and the East, to come and occupy higher ground than we did when we stood together and triumphed on the Cincinnati Platform? Since that time, gentlemen, according to your own report, a mighty power has arisen in your midst, deriving much of its strength and support from the Democrats of the North. I allude to the Black Republican party—a party which promulgates to the country that they have a higher law, a law known only to themselves—I hope not known to you—but superior to the Constitution. And, gentlemen, let me tell you that we came here expecting to be met hand in hand, and heart in heart, and to have formed a line shoulder to shoulder with you to drive back this swelling tide of fanaticism. But, gentlemen, how have we been met by you? I am proud to say that we have been met with high-toned generosity by Oregon and California. (Cheers.) I am proud to say that supporters of our claim for equal rights have boldly presented themselves from the good old State of Pennsylvania. (Cheers.) While we have entertained great respect for your talent and integrity, yet we bid adieu to you of the Northwest without so much feeling of regret, as you have hardened your hearts and stiffened your necks against the rights of the South. (Cheers and laughter.) But, we say to you, gentlemen from Oregon and California, and Pennsylvania and other States, who have come forward with the hand of fellowship, that we part from you with feelings of heartfelt sorrow.

Mr. Randall, of Pennsylvania.—And New-Jersey.

Mr. Milton.—I did not forget New-Jersey, nor could I forget Massachusetts. My remark was general. Wherever and whenever a gentleman from the North, the East or the West, has had the manliness to rise up and vindicate our rights, our hearts have been at his command. (Cheers.)

We thank you, gentlemen, for the courtesies we have received amongst you, and which we have returned with the kindest feelings of our hearts. We part from you without any unkind feeling. We respect you as gentlemen, but differing, as we do, upon principles vital to our most sacred interests, in the same spirit of wisdom and affection which caused Abraham and Lot to pass on, one in one direction and the other in a different one, we bid you a most respectful adieu. (Loud cheers.) One more remark, and I have done. The delegation from the State of Florida has unanimously passed a resolution that no one is authorized, when we shall retire, to represent Florida in this Convention. I confess, in all frankness, that I deem the resolution wholly unnecessary, because I believe there is too high a sense of honor amongst gentlemen here from the North, and the East, and the West, to permit any man to skulk in here to represent Florida.

Mr. Eppes, of Florida, then read the following protestation :

To the Hon. Caleb Cushing,

President of the Democratic National Convention :

The undersigned, Democratic delegates from the State of Florida, enter this their solemn protest against the action of the Convention in voting down the Platform of the majority.

Florida, with her Southern sisters, is entitled to a clear and unambiguous recognition of her rights in the Territories, and this being refused by the rejection of the majority report, we protest against receiving the Cincinnati Platform with the interpretation that it favors the doctrine of Squatter Sovereignty in the Territories— which doctrine, in the name of the people represented by us, we repudiate.

T. J. Eppes, B. F. Wardlaw, John Milton, J. B. Owens, C. F. Dyke, delegates from Florida.

The delegates from Florida, before retiring, have unanimously adopted the following Resolution :

Resolved, That no person, not a regularly appointed delegate, has a right to cast the vote of the State of Florida in this Convention.

John Milton, Chairman of Delegation.

TEXAS WITHDRAWS.

Mr. Bryan, of Texas, who was received with loud cheers, said : Mr. President and gentlemen of the Convention— Texas, through her delegates on this floor, on the land of Calhoun, where "truth, justice and the Constitution" was proclaimed to the South, says to the South—this day you stand erect. (Loud cheers.) Whilst we deprecate the necessity which calls for our parting with the delegates from the other States of this Confederacy, yet it is an event that we, personally, have long looked to. Educated in a Northern College, I there first learned that there was a North and a South ; there were two literary Societies, one Northern and the other Southern. In the Churches, the Methodist Church, the Baptist Church, the Presbyterian Church, are North and South. Gentlemen of the North and Northwest, God grant that there may be but one Democratic party ! It depends upon your action, when you leave here, whether it shall be so. Give not aid and comfort to the Black Republican hosts ; but say to the South, "You are our equals in this Confederacy, and your lives, your persons and property, equally with those of the Northern States, are protected by the Constitution of the Federal Union." What is it that we, the Southern Democrats, are asking you to acknowledge ? Analyze it and see the meaning ; and it is this—that we will not ask quite as much of you as the Black Republicans, and if you only grant what we ask, we can fight them. We blame you not if you really hold these opinions, but declare them openly, and let us separate, as did Abraham and Lot. I have been requested to read this protest on the part of the delegates from Texas, and to ask the courtesy of the Convention that it be spread upon the minutes of its proceedings.

Hon. Caleb Cushing,

President of the Democratic National Convention :

The undersigned, delegates from the State of Texas, would respectfully protest against the late action of this Convention, in refusing to adopt the report of the majority of the Committee on Resolutions, which operates as the virtual adoption of principles affirming doctrines in opposition to the decision of the Supreme Court in the *Dred Scott* case, and in conflict with the Federal Constitution, and especially opposed to the platform of the Democratic party of Texas, which declares:

1st. That the Democratic party of the State of Texas reaffirm and concur in the principles contained in the platform of the National Democratic Convention, held at Cincinnati in June, 1856, as a true expression of political faith and opinion, and herewith reassert and set forth the principles therein contained, as embracing the only doctrine which can preserve the integrity of the Union and the equal rights of the States, "expressly rejecting any interpretation thereof favoring the doctrine known as Squatter Sovereignty," and that we will continue to adhere to and abide by the principles and doctrines of the Virginia and Kentucky resolutions of 1798 and 1799 and Mr. Madison's report relative thereto.

2d. That it is the right of every citizen to take his property, of any kind, including slaves, into the common territory belonging equally to all the States of the Confederacy, and to have it protected there under the Federal Constitution. Neither Congress nor a Territorial Legislature, nor any human power, has any authority, either directly or indirectly, to impair these sacred rights; and they having been affirmed by the decision of the Supreme Court in the *Dred Scott* case, we declare that it is the duty of the Federal Government, the common agent of all the States, to establish such government, and enact such laws for the Territories, and so change the same, from time to time, as may be necessary to insure the protection and preservation of these rights, and prevent every infringement of the same. The affirmation of this principle of the duty of Congress to simply protect the rights of property, is nowise in conflict with the heretofore established and well-organized principles of the Democratic party, that Congress does not possess the power to legislate Slavery into the Territories, or to exclude it therefrom.

Recognizing these declarations of principles as instructions to us for our government in the National Convention, and believing that a repudiation of them by all the Northern States, except the noble States of Oregon and California, the whole vote of which is more than doubtful in the ensuing Presidential election, demand from us our unqualified disapproval.

The undersigned do not deem this the place or time to discuss the practical illustration that has been given of the irrepressible conflict between the Northern and Southern States, that has prevailed in this Convention for the last week.

It is sufficient to say that, if the principles of the Northern Democracy are properly represented by the opinion and action of the majority of the delegates from that section on this floor, we do not hesitate to declare that their principles are not only not ours, but, if adhered to and enforced by them, will destroy this Union.

In consideration of the foregoing facts, we cannot remain in the Convention. We consequently respectfully withdraw, leaving no one authorized to cast the vote of the State of Texas.

Guy M. Bryan, Chairman; F. R. Lubbock, F. S. Stockdale, E. Greer, H. R. Runnells, Wm. B. Ochiltree, M. W. Covey, Wm. H. Parsons, R. Ward, J. F. Crosby.

ARKANSAS RETIRES.

Mr. Burrow, of Arkansas, read the following protest.

Hon. Caleb Cushing,
President of Charleston Convention:

The undersigned, delegates accredited by the Democracy of Arkansas to represent said Democracy in the Convention of the Democracy of the United States, assembled on the 23d April, 1860, beg leave to submit the following protest, against certain actions of this Convention, and statement of the causes which, in their opinion, require them to retire from this Convention:

1st. The Convention of the Democracy of the State of Arkansas, convened at Little Rock on the 2d day of April, 1860, passed among other things, the following resolutions, viz.:

1st. *Resolved,* We the Democracy of Arkansas, through our representatives in Convention assembled, proclaim our confidence in the virtue and intelligence of the people, and unabated faith in the principles of the Democracy.

2d. We re-affirm the political principles enunciated in the Cincinnati platform by the Democracy of the United States in June, 1856, and assert as illustrative thereof, that neither Congress nor a Territorial Legislature, whether by direct legislation or by legislation of an indirect and unfriendly character, possesses the power to annul or impair the constitutional rights of any citizen of the United States to take his slave property into the common Territories, and there hold and enjoy the same, and that if experience should at any time prove the judiciary and executive power do not possess the means to insure protection to constitutional rights in a Territory—and if the Territorial Government should fail or refuse to provide the necessary remedies for that purpose, it will be the duty of Congress to supply the deficiency.

3d. That the representatives of the Democracy of Arkansas in the Charleston Convention be instructed to insist upon the recognition by said Convention of the purpose hereinbefore declared, prior to balloting for any candidate for the Presidency; and if said Convention refuse to recognize the rights of the South in the Territories of the United States, the repre-

sentatives of the Democracy of Arkansas be instructed to retire from said Convention, and refuse to aid in the selection of any candidate whomsoever by said Convention.

4th. That the unity of the Democratic party and the safety of the South demands the adoption of the two-thirds rule by the Charleston Convention of the Democracy of the United States, and that our delegates to said Convention be required to insist upon and maintain the adoption thereof as an indispensable necessity.

In accordance with the instructions contained in resolution 3d above, one of the undersigned had the honor, on the second day of the session of this Convention, to offer to the consideration of this Convention the following resolution, viz.:

"*Resolved,* That the Convention will not proceed to nominate a candidate for the Presidency until the Platform shall have been made"—

Which said resolution was passed by the Convention with great unanimity. Subsequently, the Committee on Resolutions and Platform, appointed by the Convention, in accordance with the usages and customs of the Democratic party of the United States, agreed upon and reported to this Convention a platform of principles, recognizing the principle contained in the resolutions of the Democracy of Arkansas, above recited, and fully asserting the equal rights of the Southern States in the common Territories of the United States, and the duty of the Federal Government to protect those rights when necessary, according to the usages and customs of the Democracy of the United States, as developed by the practice of said Democracy assembled in Convention on former occasions, and in strict accordance, as is believed by the undersigned, with the compact and agreement made by and between the Democrats of the several States, upon which the Conventions of the Democracy of the United States were agreed first to be founded, and assented to by the several Southern States. The report and determination of the Committee on Platform became and was henceforward the platform of the Democracy of the United States, and this Convention had no duty to perform in relation thereto but to receive, confirm and publish the same, and cause it to be carried into effect wherever in the respective States the Democracy were able to enforce their decrees at the ballot box.

The undersigned are confirmed in this opinion by reference not only to the history of the past, which shows that in all instances the sovereignty of the States, and not the electoral votes of the States, has uniformly been represented in the Committee on Platforms, and that the report of the Committee has invariably been registered as the supreme law of the Democratic party by unanimous consent of the entire Convention, without changing or in any manner altering any part or portion thereof. It is asserted, as a part of our traditional policy, and confidently believed, that the Democracy of the United States, by a peculiar system of checks and balances, formed after the fashion of the Federal Government, were contracted and bound themselves to fully recognize the sovereignty of the States in making the platform, and the population or masses of the States in naming the candidate to be placed on the platform. That many States have been uniformly allowed to vote the full strength of their electoral college in these Conventions when it was well known that said States never heretofore, and probably would never hereafter give a single electoral vote at the polls to the candidate which they had so large a share in nominating, cannot be accounted for on any other principle than that it was intended only as a recognition of the sovereignty and equality of said States.

Would it be right at this time for the numerical majority to deprive all the Black Republican States represented on this floor of their representation, which by custom they have so long enjoyed, simply because it is now evident that they are or will be unable to vote the Democratic ticket in the next Presidential election?

By common consent we say that a reckless numerical majority should not be thus allowed to tread under foot the vested rights of those States and well established usages and customs of the party.

If thus it be wrong for the numerical majority to deprive the Black Republican States of this long vested right, how much more unjust is it for the numerical majority to deprive *all* the States of their vested right to make and declare the platform in the usual and customary manner? and when we call to mind that the numerical majority resides chiefly in the Black Republican States, to whom the South has uniformly accorded so large a privilege, in naming candidates who were alone to be elected by Southern votes, we have much reason to believe that he to whom you gave an inch seems emboldened thereby to demand an ell.

The undersigned beg leave to state that many patriotic States' Right Democrats in the South, have long contended that these Conventions of the Democracy, representing in fact the whole consolidated strength of the Union, acting through party sympathy upon the individual members of society, would ultimate in a despotic, colossal centralism, possessed of power to override and destroy at its will and pleasure the constitutions and reserved rights of any and all the States. The South, however, has heretofore felt safe because of the checks and balances imposed upon the machinery of the Conventions. The South felt that where she retained an equal power to write the creed of faith, she could trust her Northern sisters, with their immense populations, to name the candidate; and all would alike support the creed and the candidate.

The undersigned, well knowing the hostility of the Northern masses toward the "peculiar institutions" of the South, and calling to mind the relative numbers of the Northern and Southern States, assert with confidence that no Southern State in the Union would ever have consented to surrender, so abjectly and hopelessly, all their fortunes to the numerical majority who have just now voted to set aside the Platform, unless upon the full assurance that the States were entitled by agreement to make and establish the creed of faith and prescribe the rule of action. This violation of plighted faith on the part of the numerical majority—this violation of the well established usage and custom of the party—drive us to the conclusion that we cannot longer safely trust the fortunes of Slaveholding States to the chances of the numerical majority in a Convention, where all the Black Republicans of the Union, the immense populations of Massachusetts, New-York, Pennsylvania and Ohio, and other Northern States, are fully represented, on the one side, against the small populations from the slave States on the other. Had these populations adhered strictly to the usages and customs of the party, longer association might have been practicable; but annihilation is staring us in the face, and we are admonished of our duty to stand upon our reserved rights.

We declare, therefore, that we believe our mission to this Convention at an end:

1st. Because the numerical majority have usurped the prerogatives of the States in setting aside the Platform made by the States, and have thus unsettled the basis of this Convention, and thereby permanently disorganized its constitution. Its decrees, therefore, become null and void.

2d. Because we were positively instructed by the Democracy of Arkansas to insist on the recognition of the equal rights of the South in the common Territories, and protection to those rights by the Federal Government, prior to any nomination of a candidate; and as this Convention has refused to recognize the principle required by the State of Arkansas, in her popular Convention first, and twice subsequently re-asserted by Arkansas, together with all her Southern sisters, in the report of a Platform to this Convention; and as we cannot serve two masters, we are determined first to serve the Lord our God. We cannot ballot for any candidate whatsoever.

3d. In retiring, we deny to any person, or persons, any right whatever to cast hereafter, in this Convention, either our vote or the vote of Arkansas on any proposition which may, or can, possibly come up for consideration. The Delegates of Arkansas cannot take any part in placing a sound candidate on an unsound platform, because it would disgrace any sound Southern man who would consent to stand on such a platform; and, as a Squatter Sovereignty Platform has been adopted, we believe good faith and honor requires that the Chief of Squatter Sovereignty should be placed on it. We wish no part or lot in such misfortune, nor do we believe that we can safely linger under the shade of the upas tree, this day planted certainly.

P. JORDAN,
B. BURROW,
VAN H. MANNING.

Mr. Burrow stated, after reading the paper, that the gentlemen who had signed represented both wings of the State—all its public men, its hopes, it character, and its fortunes.

Mr. Johnson, of Arkansas, as Chairman of the Arkansas delegation, desired to say a single word to go along with the paper which had been read. It was his desire that that portion of the Arkansas delegation who had concluded to leave the Convention should have paused until the delegation could have had a consultation. Why did he hesitate? It was because he conceived that the stability of the Union itself was involved in the action taken here by the Southern representatives.

He had been taught from childhood to believe that if the Union was to be preserved at all, it was to be preserved by the Democratic party as a unit. (Cheers.) He wished to consult with other Southern men as to the best course to be pursued—(cheers)—reserving to himself the right to decide the question, which he would do in a few hours. His heart and all the feelings of his nature were with those Southern men who had seen proper to leave the Convention; but, at the same time, he hesitated between his personal feelings and his duty to his own people. If he could get a good sound Southern man for President, he would be willing to take him on this platform. (Cheers.)

The Georgia delegation asked leave to retire for consultation, which was granted.

Messrs. Bayard and Whiteley, two of the six delegates from Delaware, retired from the Convention and joined the seceders.

Mr. Saulsbury, (U. S. Senator,) of Delaware, stated his reason for not retiring with his colleagues, and the Convention adjourned.

On Tuesday, May 1st, the President stated the regular order of business to be the motions to reconsider, and the motions to lay the motions to reconsider on the table, by which the various resolutions constituting the Platform were adopted. Pending the determination of these questions, yesterday evening, the chairman of several of the delegations rose to questions of privilege, under which their delegations retired from the hall. When the Convention adjourned the gentleman from Illinois (Mr. Merrick) was upon the floor.

GEORGIA RETIRES.

Mr. Benning of Georgia.—Mr. President: On yesterday afternoon the delegation from Georgia obtained the leave of the Convention to retire for the purpose of consulting as to the course they would pursue in consequence of the action taken by the Convention in the previous part of the day. They retired, and they have since been engaged in consultation. They have considered the questions involved, with as much maturity and care as they could bestow upon them, and they have come to a conclusion as to the course they ought to pursue. That conclusion is contained in two resolutions which I hold in my hand, and which I will now read to the Convention.

Resolved, That, upon the opening of the Convention this morning, our Chairman be requested to state to the President that the Georgia delegation, after mature deliberation, have felt it be their duty, under existing circumstances, not to participate further in the deliberations of the Convention, and that, therefore, the delegation withdraw.

Resolved, That all who acquiesce in the foregoing resolution sign the same, and request the Convention to enter it on their records.

(Signed,)

JUNIUS WINGFIELD,	HENRY L. BENNING,
HENRY R. JACKSON,	P. TRACY,
J. M. CLARK,	JEFFERSON N. LAMAR,
WM. M. SLAUGHTER,	EDMOND J. McGEBER,
JOHN A. JONES,	GEO. HILLYER,
DAVID C. BARROW,	MARK JOHNSTON,
JAS. J. DIAMAN,	EDWARD R. HARDEN,
A. FRANKLIN HILL,	JOHN H. LUMPKIN,
ED. L. STROHECKER,	G. G. FAIR,
O. C. GIBSON,	JAMES HOGE,
HENRY O. THOMAS,	W. J. JOHNSON.

The undersigned, delegates from Georgia, having voted in the meeting of the delegation against withdrawing from the Convention, yet, believe, under the instructions contained in the resolution of the Georgia Convention, that the vote of the majority should control our motion, and we therefore withdraw with the majority.

J. T. IRVIN,	JULIAN HARTRIDGE,
W. H. HULL,	L. H. DRISCOE.

This paper is signed by twenty-six out of the thirty-three or thirty-four delegates in that Convention from the State of Georgia.

I have now, Mr. President, discharged the duty which has been intrusted to me by my delegation.

The majority of the Georgia delegation then retired from the hall.

Mr. Johnson, of Arkansas.—I do not desire to detain this Convention for a moment. On yesterday evening I stated to the Convention that I should come here this morning and tell them what was my conclusion, and what was the conclusion of the portion of the delegation from the State of Arkansas which then thought proper to remain in the Convention. We are now ready to take that step which our judgment dictates to be right. In accordance with our duty here, we wanted time to pause and consider calmly with our sister Southern States, in relation to the proper course to be pursued. We have calmly and with deliberation considered the matter, and we believe it to be an imperative duty which we owe to the South, and we are ready to take our course.

Now, sir, I desire to appeal to Virginia, the mother of States, and the mother of Democracy, and to ask them whether the principle contained in the majority report of this Convention, signed by seventeen States, is right or is wrong? Did you indorse it, or did you not?

Mr. Smith, of Wisconsin, raised the question of order, that the gentleman had no right to make sectional appeals in this Convention.

Mr. Johnson.—I desire to do no such thing. I do not understand the principles of the majority report to be sectional. I understand them to be national. But, Mr. President, I only desire, in behalf of a portion of the delegates, to say that we came here with a view to stand by the principles of our people and of the Union, and when we have found the Convention acting in violation of those principles, we feel ourselves compelled to retire from the Hall. I will only remark in conclusion, that the Vice-President from my State has been charged with presenting a protest on the part of a portion of our declaration.

Mr. Terry, of Arkansas, then read the following paper to the Convention:

To the Hon. Caleb Cushing, *President:*

The undersigned, Delegates from Arkansas, ask permission to make the following statement: We have, thus far, abstained from taking any active part in the measures which were consummated on yesterday, in this Convention, by the withdrawal, in whole or in part, of several Southern States. We have counseled our Southern friends to patience and forbearance; and, while we were conscious of causes sufficient to induce them to this step, yet we still hoped some more auspicious event would transpire that would avert its necessity. Nothing has occurred to palliate these causes. Hence we cannot hesitate in our course, and therefore ask permission to withdraw and surrender to our State the high trust reposed in us. To you, sir, who have with so much ability presided over our deliberations, and meted out justice with an even hand, we part with sorrow. Hoping that the cloud which now hangs over our beloved country may be dispelled, and her counsels directed by some statesman like yourself—able, honest, just and true.

Francis Terry, Vice-President.
J. P. Johnson, Ch'n of Delegation.
F. W. Hoadley, Secretary.

Charleston, *May 1st*, 1860.

The Tennessee Delegation asked and obtained leave to retire for consultation.

The Delegation from Virginia, and portions of the Delegations from Kentucky, North Carolina and Maryland, had leave to retire for consultation.

Mr. Flournoy, of Arkansas.—May I be indulged in one remark? My voice is "Never give up the ship"—(applause)—though the fearful storm rages around us—though she may have lost some spars and masts—though she may have some cracked ribs. Sir, for myself, I will be one of that gallant crew who, though the storm rages, though the spars and masts are gone, though ribs be broken—I will, until the noble vessel be swallowed up by the devouring waves, continue to unite with them in the reiterated cry of " Live, live the Republic !" (Great applause.)

Mr. President, I am a Southern man. Yes, sir, I have been reared amidst the institution. All I have is the product of slave labor. I believe the institution a patriarchal one, and beneficial alike to master and slave. The bread which supports my own wife and tender babe is the product of slave labor. I trust, then, that, like Cæsar's wife, I am "above suspicion."

LOUISIANA WITHDRAWS.

To the Hon. Caleb Cushing,
President of the Democratic Convention:

Sir: The undersigned delegates from the State of Louisiana, in withdrawing from the Convention, beg leave to make the following statement of facts:

On the 5th day of March, 1860, the Democracy of Louisiana assembled in State Convention at Baton Rouge, and unanimously adopted the following declaration of their principles:

Resolved, That the Territories of the United States belong to the several States as their common property, and not to individual citizens thereof, that the Federal Constitution recognizes property in slaves; and as such, the owner thereof is entitled to carry his slaves into any Territory in the United States; to hold them there as property; and in case the people of the Terri-

tories, by inaction, unfriendly legislation or otherwise, should endanger the tenure of such property, or discriminate against it by withholding that protection given to other species of property in the Territories, it is the duty of the General Government to interpose, by the active exertion of its constitutional power, to secure the rights of the slaveholder.

The principles enunciated in the foregoing resolution are guaranteed to us by the Constitution of the United States, and their unequivocal recognition by the Democracy of the Union we regard as essential, not only to the integrity of the party, but to the safety of the States whose interests are directly involved. They have been embodied in both of the series of resolutions presented to the Convention by a majority of the States of the Union, and have been rejected by a numerical vote of the delegates.

The Convention has, by this vote, refused to recognize the fundamental principles of the Democracy of the State we have the honor to represent, and we feel constrained, in obedience to a high sense of duty, to withdraw from its deliberations, and unanimously to enter our solemn protest against its action.

We ask that the communication may be spread upon the minutes of the Convention, and beg leave to express our appreciation of ,the justice and dignity which have characterized your action as its presiding officer.

[Signed,]

<table>
<tr><td>A. Mouton,</td><td>E. Lawrence,</td></tr>
<tr><td>John Tarleton,</td><td>A. Talbot,</td></tr>
<tr><td>Richard Taylor,</td><td>B. W. Pearce,</td></tr>
<tr><td>Emile Laskre,</td><td>R. A. Hunter,</td></tr>
<tr><td>F. H. Hatch,</td><td>D. D. Withers.</td></tr>
</table>

The undersigned, in explanation of their position, beg leave to annex the following statement, viz. :.

Whilst we took the same view with our colleagues, that the platform of principles, as adopted by this Convention, was not what was expected by Louisiana, and desired by ourselves, as sufficient to guard the rights of that State, and of the whole South, under the Constitution, are now unwilling precipitately to retire from the Convention, until all hope of accommodation shall have been exhausted, and until the last moment had arrived, at which, in justice to our own honor, and the interest and dignity of our own State, we would be forced to retire. We, therefore, were opposed to the retirement of the delegation at the time it was made; but believing that the other members of the delegation were actuated by the same high motives which governed our own opinions, and desiring our State to present a firm, undivided front, we being in the minority of the delegation, were willing to yield, and did yield, our opinions to the judgment of the majority.

J. A. McHatton,
Charles Jones,

Charleston, S. C,, *May* 1, 1860.

A VOICE FROM GEORGIA.

Mr. Gaulden, of Georgia, addressed the Convention, giving his reasons for not retiring with his colleagues, as follows:

Mr. President, and Fellow Democrats: As I stated to you a few moments ago, I have been confined to my room by severe indisposition, but, learning of the commotion and the intense excitement which were existing upon the questions before this body, I felt it to be my duty, feeble as I was, to drag myself out to the meeting of my delegation, and when there I was surprised to find a large majority of that delegation voting to secede at once from this body. I disagree with those gentlemen. I regret to disagree with my brethren from the South upon any of the great questions which interest our common country. I am a Southern States' Rights man; I am an African Slave-trader. I am one of those Southern men who believe that Slavery is right, morally, religiously, socially, and politically. (Applause.) I believe that the institution of Slavery has done more for this country, more for civilization, than all other interests put together. I believe if it were in the power of this country to strike down the institution of Slavery, it would put civilization back 200 years. Holding, then, this position, that Slavery is right in the point of view I have stated, I would demand of the General Government our whole rights in this regard. I believe that the General Government by the Constitution never had any right to legislate upon this subject. I believe that our Government was a confederation of States for certain specified objects with limited powers; that the domestic relations of each State are to be and should be left to themselves; that this eternal Slavery question has been the bone of contention between the North and South, which if kept in the halls of Congress must break up this Government. I am one of those who believe in non-intervention, either in the States or the Territories.

(Applause.) I am not in favor of breaking up this Government upon an impracticable issue, upon a mere theory I believe that this doctrine of protection to slavery in the Territories is a mere theory, a mere abst action. (Applause.) Practically, it can be of no consequence to the South, for the reason that the infant has been strangled before it was born. (Laughter.) You have cut off the supply of Slaves; you have crippled the institution of Slavery in the States by your unjust laws, and it is mere folly and madness now to ask for protection for a nonentity, for a thing which is not there. We have no slaves to carry to these Territories. We can never make another Slave State with our present supply of slaves. But if we could, it would not be wise, for the reason, that if you make another Slave State from our new Territories with the present supply of slaves, you will be obliged to give up another State, either Maryland, Delaware, or Virginia, to Free Soil upon the North. Now, I would deal with this question, fellow-Democrats, as a practical one. When I can see no possible practical good to result to the country from demanding legislation upon this theory, I am not prepared to disintegrate and dismember the great Democratic party of this Union. I believe that the hopes of this country depend upon the maintenance of the great Democratic party North. It is no trouble for a man to be a saint in Heaven.

> " When the devil was sick,
> The devil a monk would be :
> The devil got well,
> But devil a monk was he."   (Great laughter.)

We, the Democracy of the South, are mere carpet-knights. It is no trouble for us to be Democrats. (Applause and laughter.) When I look to the Northern Democrats, I see them standing up there and breasting the tide of fanaticism, oppression, wrong, and slander, with which they have to contend. I view in these men types of the old ancient Romans ; I view in them all that is patriotic and noble ; and, for one, I am not willing to cut loose from them. (Great cheering.) I say, then, that I will hold on to my Democratic friends of the North to the last day of the week—late in the evening. (Great laughter.) I am not willing to present to them a half issue of this sort. I am not willing to disintegrate, dismember, and turn them over to the ruthless hands of the thieving Black Republicans of the North. I would ask my friends of the South to come up in a proper spirit, ask our Northern friends to give us all our rights, and take off the ruthless restrictions which cut off the supply of slaves from foreign lands. As a matter of right and justice to the South, I would ask the Democracy of the North to grant us this thing, and I believe they have the patriotism and honesty to do it, because it is right in itself. I tell you, fellow-Democrats, that the African Slave-trader is the true Union man. (Cheers and laughter.) I tell you that the Slave-trading of Virginia is more immoral, more unchristian in every possible point of view, than that African Slave-trade which goes to Africa and brings a heathen and worthless man here, makes him a useful man, Christianizes him, and sends him and his posterity down the stream of time to join in the blessings of civilization. (Cheers and laughter.) Now, fellow-Democrats, so far as any public expression of the State of Virginia—the great Slave-trading State of Virginia—has been given, they are all opposed to the Af ican Slavet-rade.

Dr. Reed of Indiana.—I am from Indiana, and I am in favor of it.

Mr. Gaulden—Now, gentlemen, we are told, upon high authority, that there is a certain class of men who strain at a gnat and swallow a camel. Now, Virginia, which authorizes the buying of Christian men, separating them from their wives and children, from all the relations and associations amid whom they have lived for years, rolls up her eyes in holy horror when I would go to Africa, buy a savage, and introduce him to the blessings of civilization and Christianity. (Cheers and laughter.)

Mr. Rynders of N. Y.—You can get one or two recruits from New-York to join with you.

The President.—The time of the gentleman has expired. (Cries of " Go on ! Go on !")

The President—stated that if it was the unanimous wish of the Convention, the gentleman could proceed.

Mr. Gaulden.—Now, Fellow-Democrats, the slave-trade in Virginia forms a mighty and powerful reason for its opposition to the African slave-trade, and in this remark I do not intend any disrespect to my friends from Virginia. Virginia, the Mother of States and of statesmen, the Mother of Presidents, I apprehend may err as well as other mortals. I am afraid that her error in this regard lies in the promptings of the almighty dollar. It has been my fortune to go into that noble old State to buy a few darkies, and I have had to pay from $1,000 to $2,000 a head, when I could go to Africa and buy better negroes for $50 apiece. (Great laughter.) Now, unquestionably, it is to the interest of Virginia to break down the African slave-trade when she can sell her negroes at $2,000. She knows that the African slave-trade would break up her monopoly, and hence her objection to it. If any of you Northern Democrats—for I have more faith in you than I have in the Carpet-Knight Democracy of the South—will go home with me to my plantation in Georgia, but a little way from here, I will show you some darkies that I bought in Maryland, some that I bought in Virginia, some in Delaware, some in Florida, some in North Carolina, and I will also show you the pure African, the noblest Roman of them all. (Great laughter.) Now, Fellow-Democrats, my feeble health and failing voice, admonish me to bring the few remarks I have to make to a close. (Cries of " Go on, go on.") I am only sorry that I am not in a better condition than I am to vindicate before you to-day the words of truth, of honesty, and of right, and to show you the gross inconsistencies of the South in this rega. d. I came from the First Congressional District of the State of Georgia. I represent the African Slave-trade interests of that section. (Applause.) I am proud of the position I occupy in that respect. I believe that the African slave-trader is a true missionary, and a true Christian (applause), and I have pleaded with my delegation from Georgia to put this issue squarely to the Northern Democracy, and say to them, Are you prepared to go back to first principles, and take off your unconstitutional restrictions. and leave this question to be settled by each State? Now do this, fellow-citizens, and you will have peace in the country. But so long as your Federal Legislature takes jurisdiction of this question, so long will there be war, so long will there be ill-blood, so long will there be strife, until this glorious Union of ours shall be disrupted and go out in blood and night forever. I advocate the repeal of the laws prohibiting the African Slave-trade, because I believe it to be the true Union movement. I do not believe that sections whose interests are so different as the Southern and Northern States can ever stand the shocks of fanaticism, unless they be equally balanced. I believe by reopening this trade, and giving us negroes to populate the Territories, that the equilibrium of the two sections will be maintained. But if the South lies supinely by, and allows the people of the North to people all the Territories, until we come to be a hopeless fraction in the Government, then that gallant band of Democrats North may in vain attempt to stay the torrent that will roll down upon us. It will not be in your power to do it. It should be the object of the South now to say to the North : Let us have all our rights in this matter ; let us take off these restrictions against the African Slave-trade, and leave it to each State to settle for itself. Then we would want no protection, and then I would be willing to let you have as much Squatter Sovereignty as you wish. Give us an equal chance, and I tell you the institution of Slavery will take care of itself. We will give you all the Squatter Sovereignty that the North can desire, Mr. Douglas, or anybody else, if you will take off the unconstitutional restrictions on the Slave-trade and let the negroes come. Then, gentlemen, we should proceed harmoniously, go on to prosper and prospering, until the last trump of God should sound ; until time was merged in the ocean of eternity. (Applause.) I say, Fellow-Democrats, that I remained here because I have great faith in the Northern Democracy. If I am forced to part with you, it will be with a bleeding heart. I know not exactly what position I occupy here (laughter), for the majority of my delegation have voted to secede. We came here instructed to vote as a unit. Whether the minority are bound to go out with the majority is a question which I have not yet fully determined in my own mind, but at any rate, I told them this morning, and I tell them now, I will not go out yet ; I intend to stay here ; I intend to hold on to the great Democratic Party of the Union so long as I can consistently with honor and propriety, for I believe that if we break up in a row here, and the Democratic Party of the country is destroyed, this Union falls as certainly as the sun rises and sets. I warn you, seceders, if your action here to-day should have the effect of dismembering and destroying the great Democratic Party of the North, that you destroy this Government beyond all question (applause) ; and the Union falls, and falls forever ! Now, I am not a disunionist. I love this Union for the memories of the past and for the hopes of the future. (Applause.) The blood of my ancestors was poured out around this city and throughout the South to rear aloft the proud banner of our glorious Union. I, as an humble descendant of theirs, feel bound to maintain this Union and the Constitution so long, and no longer than I can do it honorably and justly to myself and my country. But I do not yet despair of the Republic. Entertaining, as I do, such profound respect, nay, almost veneration for the justice of the Democracy of the North, I will yet stand by you for a time. I will do all that in me lies to heal these differences. I trust that the result of our deliberations will be the nomination of such a man as will give peace to the country and success to the great Democratic National Party of the Union. (Great applause.)

The Convention having decided to proceed to ballot for President, at 4 P.M., Wm. Howard, of Tennessee, moved that two-thirds (202) of a full Convention (303) be required to nominate. which, after much discussion and confusion, was adopted—141 to 112—as follows:

YEAS:—Maine, 3; Massachusetts, 8½; Connecticut, 2½; New-York, 35; New-Jersey, 5½; Pennsylvania, 17½; Delaware, 2; Maryland, 6; Virginia, 15; North Carolina. 10; South Carolina, 1; Missouri, 4½; Tennessee, 11; Kentucky, 11; Minnesota, 1½; California, 4; Oregon, 3—141.

NAYS:—Maine, 5; New-Hampshire, 5; Vermont, 5; Massachusetts, 4½; Rhode Island, 4; Connecticut, 3½; New-Jersey, 1½; Pennsylvania, 9½; Maryland, 2; Arkansas, 1; Missouri, 4½; Tennessee, 1; Kentucky, 1; Ohio, 23; Indiana, 13; Illinois, 11; Michigan, 6; Wisconsin, 5; Iowa, 4; Minnesota, 2½—112.

Candidates were put in nomination, and the Convention proceeded to ballot, as follows:

	Douglas.	Guthrie.	Hunter.	Dickinson.	A. Johnson	Lane.	Jeff. Davis	Toucey.	F. Pierce.
1st Ballot	145½	35	42	7	12	6	1½	2½	1
2	147	36½	41½	6½	12	6	1	2½	—
3	148½	42	36	6½	12	6	1	1	—
4	149	37½	41½	5	12	6	1	—	—
5	149½	37½	41	5	12	6	1	—	—
6	149½	39½	41	3	12	7	—	—	—
7	150½	38½	41	4	11	6	1	—	—
8	150½	38½	40½	4½	11	6	1½	—	—
9	150½	41	39½	1	—	6	1½	—	—
10	150½	39½	39	4	12	5½	1½	—	—
11	150½	39½	38	4	12	6½	1½	—	—
12	150½	39½	38	4	12	6	1½	—	—
13	149½	39½	28½	1	12	20	1	—	—
14	150	41	27	½	12	20½	1	—	—
15	150	41½	26½	½	12	20½	1	—	—
16	150	42	26	½	12	20½	1	—	—
17	150	42	26	½	12	20½	1	—	—
18	150	41½	26	1	12	20½	1	—	—
19	150	41½	26	1	12	20½	1	—	—
20	150	42	26	½	12	20½	1	—	—
21	150½	41½	26	½	12	20½	1	—	—
22	150½	41½	26	½	12	20½	1	—	—
23	152½	41½	25	½	12	19½	1	—	—
24	151½	41½	25	1½	12	19½	1	—	—
25	151½	41½	25	1½	12	19½	1	—	—
26	151½	41½	25	12	12	9	1	—	—
27	151½	42½	25	12	12	8	1	—	—
28	151½	42	25	12½	12	8	1	—	—
29	151½	42	25	13	12	7½	1	—	—
30	151½	45	25	13	11	5½	1	—	—
31	151½	47½	32½	3	11	5½	1	—	—
32	151½	47½	22½	3	11	5½	1	—	—
33	152½	47½	22½	3	11	14½	1	—	—
34	152½	47½	22½	5	11	12½	1	—	—
35	152	47½	22	4½	12	13	1	—	—
36	151½	48	22	4½	12	13	1	—	—
37	151½	64½	16	5½	½	12½	1½	—	—
38	151½	66	16	5½	—	13	—	—	—
39	151½	66½	16	5½	—	12½	—	—	—
40	151½	66½	16	5½	—	12½	—	—	—
41	151½	66½	16	5½	—	12½	—	—	—
42	151½	66½	16	5	—	13	—	—	—
43	151½	65½	16	5	—	13	1	—	—
44	151½	65½	16	5	—	13	1	—	—
45	151½	65½	16	5	—	13	1	—	—
46	151½	65½	16	5	—	13	1	—	—
47	151½	65½	16	5	—	13	1	—	—
48	151½	65½	16	5	—	13	1	—	—
49	151½	65½	16	4	—	14	1	—	—
50	151½	65½	16	4	—	14	1	—	—
51	151½	65½	16	4	—	14	1	—	—
52	151½	65½	16	4	—	14	1	—	—
53	151½	65½	16	4	—	14	1	—	—
54	151½	61	20½	2	—	16	1	—	—
55	151½	65½	16	4	—	14	1	—	—
56	151½	65½	16	4	—	14	1	—	—
57	151½	65½	16	4	—	14	1	—	—

On the 3d of May, and the 10th day of the session, Mr. Russell, of Virginia, offered the following:

Resolved. That when this Convention adjourns to-day, it adjourn to re-assemble at Baltimore, Md., on Monday, the 18th day of June, and that it be respectfully recommended to the Democratic party of the several States to make provision for supplying all vacancies in their respective delegations to this Convention when it shall re-assemble. (Applause.)

After the failure of attempts to change the place of meeting to New-York, Philadelphia, etc., and also to change the time to a later period, the resolve was adopted—195 to 55—as follows:

YEAS:—Maine, 5; New-Hampshire, 5; Vermont, 5; Massachusetts, 10; Rhode Island, 4; Connecticut, 6; New-York, 35; New-Jersey, 2; Pennsylvania, 23½; Maryland, 5; Virginia, 14½; Arkansas, 1; Missouri, 6; Tennessee, 7; Ohio, 23; Indiana, 13; Illinois, 11; Michigan, 6; Wisconsin, 5; Iowa 4, Minnesota, 4; California 3—195.

NAYS:—Maine, 3; Connecticut, 3; New-Jersey, 5; Pennsylvania, 3; Maryland, 3; Virginia, ½; North-Carolina, 14, Missouri, 3; Tennessee, 5; Kentucky, 2—55.

Gen. Cushing. the President, made a brief speech, and the Convention adjourned to meet again in Baltimore, on the 18th of June succeeding.

SECEDERS.

The retiring delegates met at St. Andrew's Hall, and were waited on with manifestations of sympathy by a portion of the Wood Delegation, from New-York, who, however, were not invited or admitted to seats. The seceders organized by the appointment of Senator James A. Bayard, of Delaware, as Chairman, and, after much animated discussion, adopted the following Platform:

Resolved, That the Platform adopted by the Democratic party at Cincinnati be affirmed, with the following explanatory Resolutions:

First, That the Government of a Territory organized by an act of Congress, is provisional and temporary; and, during its existence, all citizens of the United States have an equal right to settle with their property in the Territory without their rights, either of person or property, being destroyed or impaired by Congressional or Territorial Legislation.

Second, That it is the duty of the Federal Government, in all its departments, to protect when necessary the rights of persons and property in the Territories, and wherever else its Constitutional authority extends.

Third, That when the settlers in a Territory having an adequate population form a State Constitution in pursuance of law, the right of sovereignty commences, and, being consummated by admission into the Union, they stand on an equal footing with the people of other States ; and the State thus organized ought to be admitted into the Federal Union, whether its Constitution prohibits or recognizes the institution of Slavery.

Fourth, That the Democratic party are in favor of the acquisition of the Island of Cuba, on such terms as shall be honorable to ourselves and just to Spain, at the earliest practicable moment.

Fifth, That the enactments of State Legislatures to defeat the faithful execution of the Fugitive Slave Law, are hostile in character, subversive of the Constitution, and revolutionary in their effect.

Sixth, That the Democracy of the United States recognize it as the imperative duty of this Government to protect the naturalized citizen in all his rights, whether at home or in foreign lands, to the same extent as its native-born citizens.

Whereas, one of the greatest necessities of the age, in a Political, Commercial, Postal and Military point of view, is a speedy communication between the Pacific and Atlantic coasts. Therefore, be it

Resolved, That the Democratic party do hereby pledge themselves to use every means in their power to secure the passage of some bill to the extent of the Constitutional authority of Congress for the construction of a Pacific Railroad from the Mississippi River to the Pacific Ocean, at the earliest practicable moment.

After talking for four days, the Seceders' Convention adjourned to meet in Richmond, Virginia, on the second Monday in June. Delegates were present from the following States: Alabama, Texas, Arkansas, Missouri, Louisiana, Mississippi, Florida, Georgia, South Carolina, Virginia, Dela are

THE SECEDERS AT RICHMOND.

According to adjournment, the Seceding delegates met at Richmond, Va., on the 11th June. Delegates were present from Alabama, Arkansas, Texas, Louisiana, Mississippi, Georgia, South Carolina, Florida, 2d Congressional District of Tennessee, and the 7th Electoral District of Virginia. The Hon. John Erwin, of Alabama, was chosen President, with several Vice-Presidents and Secretaries. The Convention adopted the following resolutions, and on the 12th, at 12 o'clock, adjourned:

Resolved, That as the delegation from States represented in this Convention are assembled upon the basis of the platform recommended by a majority of the States at Charleston, which we indorse, we deem it unnecessary to take any further action on the subject at the present time.

Resolved, That. when this Convention adjourn it adjourn to meet in this city on Thursday, the 21st inst.; provided that the President of this Convention may call it together at an earlier or a later day, if it be deemed necessary.

The Convention reassembled on the 21st; but, without doing any business, adjourned to the following day, and so continued to meet and adjourn, awaiting the action of the Convention at Baltimore, till after the nomination of Breckinridge and Lane; when such of the Delegates as had not joined the Seceders in Baltimore, adopted the candidates and platform of the Breckinridge party, and adjourned *sine die*.

THE NATIONAL DEMOCRATIC CONVENTION AT BALTIMORE.

In accordance with the adjournment at Charleston, the National Democratic Convention reassembled at Baltimore, on Monday, the 18th June, and held their sessions in the Front street theatre.

At eleven o'clock, President Cushing, who appeared on the platform but did not take the chair, directed the Secretary to call the roll of States in order to ascertain if the delegates were present.

On the calling of the roll, the following States were found to be fully represented: Maine, New-Hampshire, Vermont, Massachusetts, Rhode Island, New-York, New-Jersey, Maryland, Virginia, North Carolina, Missouri, Ohio, Indiana, Illinois, Michigan, Wisconsin, Iowa, Minnesota, California, Oregon.

Connecticut was represented in part, there being some misunderstanding as to the hour of meeting, which had been fixed at 10 o'clock.

Two delegates were present from Delaware.

When the State of South Carolina was called, the Chair directed that only those States be called which were present at the adjournment of the Convention at Charleston, consequently South Carolina, Georgia, Florida, Alabama, Louisiana, Mississippi, Arkansas and Texas, were not called.

In consequence of a misapprehension as to the time, the President delayed calling the Convention to order till 12 o'clock, when he took the Chair and said:

GENTLEMEN OF THE CONVENTION: Permit me, in the first place, to congratulate you upon your being reassembled here for the discharge of your important duties in the interests of the Democratic party of the United States; and I beg leave, in the second place, to communicate to the Convention the state of the various branches of its business, as they now come up for consideration before you.

Prior to the adjournment of the Convention, two principal subjects of action were before it. One, the adoption of the doctrinal resolutions constituting the platform of the Convention; the other, voting upon the question of the nomination of a candidate for the Presidency.

In the course of the discussion on the adoption of a platform, the Convention adopted a vote, the effect of which was to amend the report of the majority of the Committee on Platform by substituting the report of the minority of that Committee; and after the adoption of that motion, and the substitution of the minority for the majority report, a division was called for upon the several resolutions constituting that platform, being five in number. The 1st, 3d, 4th and 5th of those resolutions were adopted by the Convention, and the 2d was rejected. After the vote on the adoption of the 1st, 3d, 4th and 5th of those resolutions, a motion was made in each case to reconsider the vote, and to lay that motion of reconsideration upon the table. But neither of those motions to reconsider or to lay on the table was put, the putting of those motions having been prevented by the intervention of questions of privilege, and the ultimate vote competent in such case, to wit, on the adoption of the report of the majority as amended by the report of the minority, had not been acted upon by the Convention. So that at the time when the Convention adjourned there remained pending before it these motions, to wit; To reconsider—the resolutions constituting the platform, and the ulterior question of adopting the majority as amended by the substitution of the minority report. Those questions, and those only, as the Chair understood the motions before the Convention, were not acted upon prior to the adjournment.

After the disposition of the intervening questions of privilege, a motion was made by Mr. McCook, of Ohio, to proceed to vote for candidates for President and Vice-President. Upon that motion, the Convention instructed the Chair (not, as has been erroneously supposed, in the recess of the Convention, the Chair determining for the Convention, but the Convention instructing the Chair) to make no declaration of a nomination except upon a vote equivalent to two-thirds in the Electoral College of the United States, and upon that balloting, no such vote being given, that order was, upon the motion of the gentleman from Virginia (Mr. Russell), laid on the table, for the purpose of enabling him to propose a motion, which he subsequently did, that the Convention adjourn from the city of Charleston to the city of Baltimore, and with a provision concerning the filling of vacancies embraced in the same resolution, which resolution the Secretary will please read.

The Secretary read the resolution as follows:

" *Resolved*, That when this Convention adjourns to-day, it adjourn to reassemble at Baltimore, Md., on Monday, the 18th day of June, and that it be respectfully recommended to the Democratic party of the several States, to make provision for supplying all vacancies in their respective delegates to this Convention when it shall reassemble."

The President.—The Convention will thus perceive that the order adopted by it provided, among other things, that it is respectfully recommended to the Democratic party of the several States to make provisions for supplying all vacancies in their respectives delegation to this Convention when it shall reassemble. What is the construction of that resolution?—what is the scope of its application?—is a question not for the Chair to determine or to suggest to the Convention, but for the Convention itself to determine.

However that may be, in the preparatory arrangements for the present assembling of this Convention, there were addressed to the Chair the credentials of members elected, or purporting to be elected, affirmed and confirmed by the original Conventions and accredited to this Convention. In three of those cases, or perhaps four, the credentials were authentic and complete, presenting no question of controverting delegates. In four others, to wit—the States of Georgia, Alabama, Louisiana and Deleware—there were contesting applications. Upon those applications the Chair was called to determine whether it possessed any power to determine *prima facie* membership of this Convention. That question was presented 'n its most absolute and complete form in the case of Mississippi, where there was no contest either through irregularity of form or of competing delegations, and so also in the cases of Florida, Texas and Arkansas. In those four States, there being an apparent authenticity of commission, the Chair was called upon to determine the naked, abstract question whether he had power, peremptorily and preliminarily, to determine the *prima facie* membership of alleged members of this Convention. The Chair would gladly have satisfied himself that he had this power, but upon examining the source of his power, to wit—the rules of the House of Representatives—he was unable to discern that he had any authority, even *prima facie*, to scrutinize and canvass credentials, although they were such as, upon their face, were free from contest or controversy either of form or of substance, and therefore he deemed it his duty to reserve the determination of that question to be submitted to the Convention. And in due time the Chair will present that question as one of privilege to this body.

Gentlemen, the Convention is now in order for the transaction of business.

The Address of the President was delivered in a clear, loud voice, with much emphasis, and was listened to with close attention. The statement of the position in which the business was left at the time of the adjournment at Charleston, created an evident sensation, inasmuch as it indicated that, according to the opinion of the Chair, the platform question, as well as the resolution declaring that a vote equal to two-thirds of the full electoral college to be necessary to the nomination of a candidate for the Presidency, were each in a position to be again brought up for the action of the Convention.

ADMISSION OF DELEGATES.

Mr. Howard, of Tennessee, offered the following resolution:

Resolved, that the President of this Convention direct the Sergeant-at-Arms to issue tickets of admission to the delegates of the Convention as originally constituted and organized at Charleston.

Mr. Cavanaugh, of Minnesota, moved to lay the resolution on the table, and upon that motion called for a vote by States; but by request withdrew his motion to permit Mr. Sanford E. Church, of N. Y., to offer the following, which was read for the information of the Convention and created much excitement:

Resolved, That the credentials of all persons claiming seats in this Convention made vacant by the secession of delegates at Charleston be referred to the Committee on Credentials, and said Committee is hereby instructed, as soon as practicable, to examine the same and report the names of persons entitled to such seats, with the district—understanding, however, that every person accepting a seat in this Convention is bound in honor and good faith to abide by the action of this Convention and support its nominations.

After a running debate on questions of order, in which Messrs. Cochrane, of N. Y., Saulsbury, of Del., Clark, of Mo., Montgomery, of Pa., Cavanaugh, of Min., and the Chair participated.

Mr. Church moved his resolution as an amendment to that offered by Mr. Howard, and upon that he called for the previous question.

Messrs. Gilmor and Randall rose to debate the question, but the Chair ruled debate not in order.

Mr. Avery, of North Carolina.—I call for a division of the question, so that the first question shall be upon referring those credentials to the Committee, and the second question upon the proposition to initiate test-oaths in the Democratic Convention. [Applause.]

The Chair could not entertain such a proposition at that time, as the previous question had been demanded. The question was—Would the Convention second the demand for the previous question?

Mr. Russell, of Va.—I ask that this Convention will allow me to make a friendly, candid and sincere appeal to the gentleman who made the call for the previous question (Mr. Church, of New-York) to withdraw his call.

The President.—The Chair has no authority over that question.

Mr. Russell.—I ask the Chair to appeal to the gentleman to allow fair play in this Convention.

Mr. Stuart, of Mich.—I insist that the Chair preserve order.

The President.—The gentleman from Virginia (Mr. Russell) is not in order.

Mr. Russell.—If we are to be constrained to silence, I beg gentlemen to consider the silence of Virginia as somewhat ominous. (Applause and hisses.)

The question was stated to be upon seconding the demand for the previous question. Being taken *viva voce*,

The President stated that the noes appeared to have it

Mr. Richardson, of Ill., doubted the announcement, and asked that the vote be taken by States, which was ordered.

Mr. Brodhead, of Pa., stated that Mr. Church was willing to withdraw his call for the previous question.

The Chair decided that it was too late.

Mr. Saulsbury, of Delaware, moved a recess to 4 P.M. Lost: 73½ to 178½.

Mr. Howard, of Tennessee.—I hold in my hand a respectful communication from one of the States of this Union, Mississippi, not now represented upon this floor, addressed to the President of this Convention. I desire that it be read for the information of the Convention.

The President.—It can only be done by common consent, as the seconding the demand for the previous question is now pending.

Cries of "object," "object," from various quarters.

The President—Objection being made to reading this communication, the Secretary will proceed to call the roll of States upon the seconding the demand for the previous question.

The question being then taken by States upon seconding the demand for the previous question, it was not agreed to.

YEAS.—Maine, 6; New-Hampshire, 5; Vermont, 4½; Massachusetts, 4; Connecticut, 3½; New-Jersey, 2¼; Pennsylvania, 9½; Maryland, 2; Missouri, 2½; Tennessee, 3; Kentucky, 1½; Ohio, 23; Indiana, 13; Illinois, 11; Michigan, 6; Wisconsin, 5; Iowa, 4; Minnesota, 2¼—108¼.

NAYS.—Maine, 2; Vermont, ½; Massachusetts, 8½; Rhode Island, 4; Connecticut, 2—one absent; New-York, 35; New-Jersey, 4½; Pennsylvania, 16½; Delaware, 2; Maryland, 6; Virginia, 15; North Carolina, 10; Arkansas, 1; Missouri, 6½; Tennessee, 8; Kentucky, 10½; Minnesota, 1½; California, 4; Oregon, 3—140½.

On calling the roll, the New-York delegation asked permission to retire for consultation, and during the interim there was an entire cessation of business. The vote of the State as a unit was finally rendered against the call for the previous question.

The question was then stated to be upon the amendment to the amendment.

Mr. Gilmor, of Pennsylvania, offered the following amendment to Mr. Church's resolution:

Resolved, That the President of the Convention be directed to issue tickets of admission to seats in the Convention, to the delegates from the States of Texas, Florida, Mississippi, and Arkansas, in which States there are no contesting delegations.

Without taking a vote on Mr. Gilmor's resolution, the Convention, on motion of Mr. Randall, of Pa., took a recess till 5 P.M.

When the Convention reassembled, the President said: Mr. Randall, of Pennsylvania, has the floor upon an amendment moved by Mr. Gilmor, of Pennsylvania.

Before proceeding in the debate, the Chair begs leave to state to the Convention that he has had placed in his hands the credentials of gentlemen claiming seats in the Convention, from the States of Delaware, Georgia, Alabama, Florida, Mississippi, Louisiana, Texas, and Arkansas, including in that enumeration the letter presented to the Convention, in his place, by Mr. Howard, of Tennessee, in behalf of the gentlemen claiming seats from the State of Mississippi, and in addition to that, there has been addressed to the Chair, a communication from Mr. Chaffee, claiming a seat from the State of Massachusetts. The Chair deems it his duty to communicate the fact to the Convention that those several documents have been placed in his hands, to be presented at the proper time to the consideration of the Convention.

Mr. Gilmor, of Pennsylvania.—I have made a small addition to the amendment I offered this morning to the amendment of the gentleman from New-York (Mr. Church), for the purpose of covering the cases mentioned by the Chair just now.

The amendment, as modified, was read as follows:

Resolved, That the President of the Convention be authorized to issue tickets of admission to seats in this Convention, to the delegates from the States of Arkansas, Texas, Florida, and Mississippi, in which States there are no contesting delegations, and that in those States, to wit: Delaware, Georgia, Alabama, and Louisiana, where there are contesting delegations, a Committee on Credentials shall be appointed, by the several delegations, to report upon said States.

After discussing points of order, Mr. Clark, of Missouri, offered a substitute for Mr. Gilmor's amendment, which was read for the information of the Convention, as follows:

Strike out the proviso in the amendment of Mr. Church, of New-York, and add the following:

Resolved, That the citizens of the several States of the Union have an equal right to settle and remain in the Territories of the United States, and to hold therein, unmolested by any legislation whatever, their slave and other property; and that this Convention recognizes the opinion of the Supreme Court of the United States in the Dred Scott case, as a true exposition of the Constitution in regard to the rights of the citizens of the several States and Territories of the United States, upon all subjects concerning which it treats; and that the members of this Convention pledge themselves, and require all others who may be authorized as delegates to make the same pledge, to support the Democratic candidates, fairly and in good faith, nominated by this Convention according to the usages of the National Democratic Party.

Mr. Randall then took the floor and opposed the amendment of Mr. Church, and favored that of Mr. Gilmor.

The amendment of the gentleman from New York imposes a condition upon the returning members of the several States that seceded at Charleston. I deny the power of the Convention to impose any such condition. The right of their constituents is unqualified and beyond the power of this Convention, to send their representatives to this body without condition and without limitation. (Applause and hisses). It is an interference with the right of the constituents of seven seceding States to impose any qualification upon their representatives in this body. I deny its equity or its justice. We who sit here—the honorable gentleman who moved the amendment, the President, the Vice-Presidents of this body—all who sit here, are unfettered by any such limitation or condition. (Applause.) What justice in imposing upon others the condition that they shall come in here as slaves, with the bands and the iron fetters about them, with no right to exercise their judgment or their patriotism, except as the majority of this body may choose to indicate? I deny the power or the right. The proposition has been put in the least offensive shape.

It is said in the amendment that it is " understood." Understood! an apology for the broad declaration of a naked invasion of the rights of freemen. Not that the members of this body thus admitted have denied the right, but it is understood that they are pledged to do what other members are not pledged to do—to conform to the decision of the majority. Mr. President and gentlemen, I invoke you to look at the injustice of every such qualification—a qualification which no honorable man, except under very peculiar circumstances, could ever submit to; a qualification which it is known that the representatives of these seven seceding States will never submit to. (Applause and hisses.) But, Mr. President and brethren of the great Democratic family, who are now contending for the success of the Democratic cause, I ask you to halt, not simply upon the ground of right and justice, but of policy. Not a member of this body but knows that the representatives of those States will not give any such pledge (applause and hisses); that it is tantamount to a declaration of secession from the body. (Applause and hisses.)

The debate was continued by Messrs. Richardson, of Ill., Cochrane, of N. Y., Montgomery, of Pa., Merrick, of Ill., King, of Mo., and West of Ct., against Mr. Gilmor's amendment, and by Messrs. Russell, of Va., Ewing, of Tenn., Loring, of Mass., Hunter, of Mo., Avery, of N. C., and Atkins, of Tenn., in favor. At last, Mr. Atkins moved the previous question, which was sustained, 233 to 18¾, and the Convention adjourned till Tuesday morning.

On the reassembling of the Convention, Mr. Church asked and obtained unanimous consent to make a proposition which he thought would produce harmony. He said:

Upon consultation with the gentleman (Mr. Gilmor , who moved that amendment to my amendment, we have agreed, if it meets the approbation of this Convention, for the purpose of harmonizing the action of this Convention, to an arrangement alike honorable to both sides, and which, if carried out, will terminate the controversy as to pending questions. The proposition which has been made and accepted is simply this: The gentleman from Pennsylvania (Mr. Gilmor) is to withdraw his amendment to my amendment, and then I am to withdraw the latter part of my resolutions, leaving only a simple resolution of reference to the Committee on Credentials. (Applause).

This proposition was accepted, and the resolution, as thus amended, was adopted without a division. Vacancies in the Committee on Credentials were filled, and the committee, as now constituted, consisted of the following gentlemen:

C. D. Jameson, Me.; A. P. Hughes, N. H.; Stephen Thomas, Vt.; Oliver Stevens, Mass.; George H. Brown, R. I.; James Gallagher, Conn.; Delos De Wolfe, N. Y.; A. R. Spear, N. J.; H. M. Forth, Pa.; W. S. Gittings, Md.; E. W. Hubbard, Va.; R. R. Bridges, N. C.; B. F. Perry, S. C.; James B. Steadman, Ohio; W. H. Carrol, Tenn.; S. A. Hall, Ind.; W. J. Allen, Ill.; John M. Krum, Mo.; Benj. Follet, Mich.; D. O. Finch, Iowa; P. H. Smith, Wis.; H. H. Sibley, Minn.; J. H. Beverly, Del.; Isaac J. Stevens, Oregon; G. H. Morrow, Kentucky; D. S. Gregory, Cal.

A paper was presented from Mr. O'Fallon, of Missouri, who had acted at Charleston in the place of one of the regularly appointed delegates from that State, but had been refused a ticket in Baltimore, asking admission.—His case was referred to the Committee on Credentials.

The memorial of the contesting delegates from Arkansas was also presented, and was handed to the Committee on Credentials. And the Committee took a recess till 5 P.M., at which time it reassembled, but, the Committee on Credentials not being ready to report, the Convention, without transacting any business, adjourned to 10 o'clock the following day, 20th.

The Convention met at the usual hour, on Wednesday, the 20th, but, in consequence of the delay of the Committee on Credentials in reporting, no business was transacted.

REPORT OF THE COMMITTEE ON CREDENTIALS.

On Thursday, the 21st, the Committee on Credentials presented their report, or rather reports, for there were three ; the majority report being presented by Mr. Krum, of Missouri, as follows :

1st. *Resolved*, That George H. Gordon, E. Barksdale, W. F. Barry, H. C. Chambers, Jos. R. Davis, Beverly Matthew, Charles Clarke, W. L. Featherston, P. F. Slidell, C. G. Armistead, W. F. Avaunt, and T. J. Hucston, are entitled to seats in this Convention as delegates from the State of Mississippi.

2d. *Resolved*, That Pierre Soulé, F. Cotterman, R. C. Wickliffe, Michael Ryan, Maunsell White, Charles Bienvenala, Gustav Lenroy, J. C. Morse, A. S. Heron, N. D. Colburn, J. N. T. Richardson and J. L. Walker are entitled to seats in this Convention as delegates from the State of Louisiana.

3d. *Resolved*, That R. W. Johnson, T. C. Hindman, J. P. Johnson, Henry Carroll, J. Gould, and John A. Jordan, be entitled to seats as Delegates from the State of Arkansas, with power to cast *two* votes, and that Thomas H. Bradley, M. Hooper, and D. C. Cross be also admitted to seats as delegates from the same State, with power to cast *one* vote; and, in case either portion of said delegates shall refuse or neglect to take their said seats and to cast their said votes, the other portion of said delegates taking seats in this Convention shall be entitled to cast the entire three votes of said State.

4th. *Resolved*, That J. M. Bryan, F. R. Lubbock, F. S. Stockdale, E. Green, H. R. Runnels, Wm. B. Ochiltree, M. W. Carey, Wm. H. Parrows, R. Ward, J. F. Crosby, B. Burrows, and V. H. Manning are entitled to seats from Texas.

5th. *Resolved*, That James A. Bayard and William G. Whiteley are entitled to seats from the county of New-Castle, Del.

6th. *Resolved*, That K. S. Chaffee, who was duly admitted at Charleston as a delegate from the fifth congressional district of Massachusetts, is still entitled to said seat in this Convention, and that B. F. Hallett, who has assumed said seat, is not entitled thereto.

7th. *Resolved*, That John O'Fallon, who was duly admitted at Charleston as a delegate from the eighth electoral district of Missouri, is still entitled to said seat in this Convention, and that Johnson B. Gardy, who has assumed said seat, is not entitled thereto.

8th. *Resolved*, That R. A. Baker, D. C. Humphrey, John Forsyth, Wm. Jewett, I. I. Seibles, S. C. Posey, L. E. Parsons, Joseph C. Bradley, Thomas B. Cooper, James Williams, C. H. Brynan, Daniel W. Weakley, L. M. B. Martyr, John W. Howard, W. R. R. Wyatt, B. Hanson, Thos. M. Matthews, and Norbert M. Lord are entitled to seats in the Convention as delegates from the State of Alabama.

9th, *Resolved*, That the delegation from the State of Georgia, of which H. L. Benning is chairman, be admitted to seats in the Convention, with power to cast one-half of the vote of said State, and that the delegation from said State, of which Col. Gardner is chairman, be also admitted to the Convention, with power to cast one-half of the vote of said State ; and if either of said delegations refuse or neglect to cast the vote as above indicated, that in said case the delegates present in the Convention be authorized to cast the full vote of said State.

Mr. Stevens, of Oregon.—I rise, Mr. President, to present the report of a minority of the Committee on credentials, and will proceed to read

MINORITY REPORT.

To the President of the Democratic National Convention:

Sir: We, the undersigned, members of the Committee on Credentials, feel constrained to dissent from many of the views and a large portion of the action of the majority of the Committee in respect to the rights of delegates to seats referred to them by the Convention, and to respectfully recommend the adoption of the following resolutions:

1. *Resolved,* That B. F. Hallett is entitled to a seat in this Convention, as a delegate from the 5th Congressional district of the State of Massachusetts.

2. *Resolved,* That Johnson B. Gardy is entitled to a seat in this Convention as a delegate from the 8th Congressional district of the State of Missouri.

3. *Resolved,* That James A. Bayard and William G. Whiteley are entitled to seats in this Convention as delegates from the State of Delaware.

4. *Resolved,* That the delegation headed by R. W. Johnson are entitled to seats in this Convention as delegates from the State of Arkansas.

5. *Resolved,* That the delegation of which George W. Bryan is chairman are entitled to seats in this Convention from the State of Texas.

6. *Resolved,* That the delegation of which John Tarleton is chairman are entitled to seats in this convention as delegates from the State of Louisiana.

7. *Resolved,* That the delegation of which L. P. Walker is chairman are entitled to seats in this Convention as delegates from the State of Alabama.

8. That the delegation of which Henry L. Benning is chairman are entitled to seats in this Convention as delegates from the State of Georgia.

9. *Resolved,* That the delegation from the State of Florida accredited to the Charleston Convention are invited to take seats in this Convention and cast the vote of the State of Florida.

The Committee presented an elaborately argued report to sustain their resolutions, which was signed by

I. I. STEVENS, Oregon,   E. W. HUBBARD, Va.,
A. R. SPEER, N. J.,   R. R. BRIDGERS, N. C.,
H. M. NORTH, Penn.,   W. H. CARROLL, Tenn.,
JOHN H. BEWLEY, Del.,   GEO. H. MORROW, Ky.,
D. S. GREGORY, Cal.

In the points of difference between the majority and minority reports of the Committee on Credentials, I concur in the conclusions of the minority report in the cases of Georgia, Alabama, Missouri and Massachusetts.

AARON V. HUGHES, New-Hampshire.

Mr. Gittings, of Maryland, presented still another report, concluding with the following resolutions:

Resolved, That so much of the majority report of the Committee on Credentials as relates to Massachusetts, Missouri, Delaware, Arkansas, Georgia, Louisiana and Texas, be adopted.

Resolved, That the delegation of which L. P. Walker is chairman, be, and they are hereby, declared the only regularly authorized representatives of the State of Alabama, and as such are entitled to seats in the National Democratic Convention.

Mr. Stevens demanded the previous question, which was sustained by the Convention, and the main question was ordered, but, without taking the vote, the Convention adjourned.

When the Convention assembled on the 22d, Mr. Gittings.withdrew his report, which brought the minority report proper—that of Mr. Stevens, of Oregon—first in order, and the question being put on the substitution of the whole minority report for the report of the majority, the motion was lost, 100½ to 150, as follows:

YEAS—Maine, 2½; New-Hampshire, ½; Vermont, 1½; Massachusetts, 8; Connecticut, 2¼; New-Jersey, 4; Penn-

sylvania, 17; Delaware, 2; Maryland, 5¼; Virginia, 14; North Carolina, 9; Arkansas, ½; Missouri, 5; Tennessee, 10; Kentucky, 10; Minnesota, 1½; California, 4; Oregon, 3—100¼.

NAYS—Maine, 5½; New-Hampshire, 4½; Vermont, 3½; Massachusetts, 5; Rhode Island, 4; Connecticut, 3½; New-York, 35; New-Jersey, 3; Pennsylvania, 10; Maryland, 2; Virginia, 1; North Carolina, 1; Arkansas, ½; Missouri, 4; Tennessee, 1; Kentucky, 2; Ohio, 23; Indiana, 13; Illinois, 11; Michigan, 6; Wisconsin, 5; Iowa, 4; Minnesota, 2½—150.

Maryland, ½ vote not voted; Tennessee, 1 vote not cast.

The question then recurred on adopting the majority report. A division being called for, the vote was taken on the first resolution, admitting the original delegates from Mississippi, which was adopted almost unanimously, 250 to 2¼.

The vote was then taken on the second resolution, admitting the Soulé (Douglas) Delegates from Louisiana, which resulted—Ays, 153; Nays, 98— as follows:

YEAS—Maine, 5¼; New-Hampshire, 4¼; Vermont, 4½; Massachusetts, 5; Rhode Island, 4; Connecticut, 3½; New-York, 35; New-Jersey, 2½; Pennsylvania, 10; Maryland, 2½; Virginia, 1; North Carolina, 2; Arkansas, ½; Missouri, 4; Tennessee, 2; Kentucky, 2; Ohio, 23; Indiana, 13; Illinois, 11; Michigan, 6; Wisconsin, 5; Iowa, 4; Minnesota, 2½—153.

NAYS—Maine, 2½; New-Hampshire, ½; Vermont, ½; Massachusetts, 8; Connecticut, 2¼; New-Jersey, 4½; Pennsylvania, 17; Delaware, 2; Maryland, 5¼; Virginia, 13; North Carolina, 8; Arkansas, ½; Missouri, 5; Tennessee, 10; Kentucky, 10; Minnesota, 1¼; California, 4; Oregon, 3—98.

So the second resolution was adopted.

The question was then taken on the third resolution, admitting Col. Hindman and his colleagues (the original delegates) with power to cast two votes, and Mr. Hooper and his colleagues (the contestants) with power to cast one vote; and providing that, if either set of delegates refuse to take seats, the other shall be entitled to cast the whole vote of the State, (Arkansas).

A division of the question being called for, the President decided that the resolution was divisible.

The question was taken on the three several propositions, viz.:—1st. The admission of the Hindman delegates, which was adopted, 182 to 69. 2d. The admission of the Hooper delegates, which was adopted, 150 to 100¼. 3d. On the giving power to one set to cast the whole vote if the other set withdrew, which was adopted without a division.

A vote was then taken on the fourth resolution of the majority report, admitting the original delegation from the State of Texas, which was adopted almost unanimously.

A vote was next taken on the fifth resolution, admitting Bayard and Whiteley from Delaware. Adopted without division.

The sixth resolution, giving R. L. Chaffee the seat in the Massachusetts delegation contested by Mr. Hallett, was then adopted—yeas, 138, nays, 111¼.

Mr. Stuart, of Michigan, at this point, made motions to reconsider each vote taken, and to lay the same on the table, it being understood that the motions were not to be put till votes on all the propositions had been taken.

The seventh resolution, declaring J. O'Fallon entitled to the seat in the Missouri delegation claimed by John B. Gardy, was then adopted—yeas, 138½, nays, 112.

The eighth resolution, admitting the contesting delegates from Alabama, was next adopted. Yeas, 148½; Nays, 101¼.

The question then being on the ninth and last resolution of the majority report, admitting both delegations from Georgia, and dividing the vote of the State between them, with the provision that, if either refused to take seats, the remaining delegates cast the vote of the State.

Before the vote was taken, Mr. Seward, of Georgia, presented a communication from Col. Gardner, Chairman of the contesting delegates from Georgia, withdrawing from the contest, and the resolution was lost—106¼ to 145. The original (seceding) delegation from Georgia, headed by H. L. Benning, was subsequently admitted.

The President stated the next question to be upon laying upon the table the motion to reconsider the vote by which the Convention refused to substitute the resolutions reported by the minority of the Committee on Credentials for those reported by the majority of said Committee.

The question being then taken by States, the motion to lay on the table was not agreed to—yeas, 113¼; Nays, 128¼ —as follows:

YEAS—Maine, 5¼; New-Hampshire, 8; Vermont, 4¼; Massachusetts, 5; Rhode Island, 4; Connecticut, 3¼; New-

Jersey, 3½; Pennsylvania, 10; Maryland, 2; North Carolina, 1; Arkansas, ½; Missouri, 4½; Kentucky, 2; Ohio, 23; Indiana, 13; Illinois, 11; Michigan, 6; Wisconsin, 5; Iowa, 4; Minnesota, 2½—113½.

NAYS—Maine, 2¼; New-Hampshire, 2; Vermont, ½; Massachusetts, 8; Connecticut, 2½; New-York, 35; New-Jersey, 3½; Pennsylvania, 17; Delaware, 2; Maryland, 6; Virginia, 15; North Carolina, 9; Arkansas, ½; Missouri, 4½; Tennessee, 12; Kentucky, 10; Minnesota, 1½; California, 4; Oregon, 3—138½.

When New-York was called, her delegates asked time to consult, but finally gave her thirty-five votes against the motion to lay upon the table, which, had it prevailed, would have precluded all further reconsideration of the subject.

The question recurred upon the motion to reconsider the vote rejecting the minority resolutions.

Mr. Cessna, of Pa., moved the previous question, which was sustained, and the question being taken by States, the motion to reconsider was rejected—103 to 149—as follows:

YEAS—Maine, 2¼; New-Hampshire, 2; Vermont, 1; Massachusetts, 8; Connecticut, 2½; New-Jersey, 4½; Pennsylvania, 17; Delaware, 2; Maryland, 6; Virginia, 15; North Carolina, 9; Arkansas, ½; Missouri, 4½; Tennessee, 10; Kentucky, 10; Minnesota, 1½; California, 4; Oregon, 3—103.

NAYS—Maine, 5½; New-Hampshire, 3; Vermont, 4; Massachusetts, 5; Rhode Island, 4; Connecticut, 3½; New-York, 35; New-Jersey, 2½; Pennsylvania, 10; Maryland, 2; North Carolina, 1; Arkansas, ½; Missouri, 4½; Tennessee, 2; Kentucky, 2; Ohio, 23; Indiana, 13; Illinois, 11; Michigan, 6; Wisconsin, 5; Iowa, 4; Minnesota, 2½—149.

The several motions to lay on the table the question of reconsidering the votes by which each of the resolutions of the majority had been adopted. were then put and carried in the affirmative, and the several delegates who had been voted in were then admitted to seats.

VIRGINIA WITHDRAWS.

Mr. Russell, of Virginia.—If it be the pleasure of yourself, Mr. President and the Convention, I will now make the brief announcement of which I made mention this morning.

I will detain the Convention but a very brief time. I understand that the action of this Convention upon the various questions arising out of the reports from the Committee on Credentials has become final, complete and irrevocable. And it has become my duty now, by direction of a large majority of the delegation from Virginia, respectfully to inform this body that it is inconsistent with their convictions of duty to participate longer in its deliberations. (Loud applause in the Convention and in the galleries, with loud cries from the galleries.)

The disorder continued for some minutes, after which

Mr. Russell resumed—The delegates from Virginia, who participate in this movement, have come to the conclusion which I have announced, after long, mature and anxious deliberation, and after, in their judgment, having exhausted all honorable efforts to obviate this necessity. In addition to the facts which appear upon your record, I desire the attention of this body long enough only to state that it is ascertained that the delegations to which you, sir, under the order of this Convention, have just directed tickets to be issued—some of them at least and all of them whom we regard as the representatives of the Democracy of their States—will decline to join here in the deliberations of this body. For the rest, the reasons which impel us to take this important step will be rendered to those to whom only we are responsible, the Democracy of the Old Dominion. To you, sir, and to the body over which you preside, I have only to say in addition that we bid you a respectful adieu.

The portion of the delegation from Virginia which retired then left their seats and proceeded out of the Hall, shaking hands with members of various delegations as they passed along.

Mr. Moffatt, of Virginia—made a speech in defense of his course, and that of his colleagues who remained in the Convention.

WITHDRAWAL OF NORTH CAROLINA.

Mr. Lander, of North Carolina.—Mr. President, painful as the duty is, it is, nevertheless, my duty to announce here, as a representative of the delegates from North Carolina, that a very large majority of them are compelled to retire permanently from this Convention on account of the unjust action, as we conceive, that has this day been perpetrated upon some of our sovereign States and fellow citizens of the South. We of the South have heretofore maintained and supported the Northern Democracy for the reason that they are willing to attribute to us in the South equality in the Union. The vote to-day has satisfied the majority of the North Carolina delegates that, that being refused by our brethren of the Northern Democracy, North Carolina—Rip Van Winkle, as you may call her—can no longer remain in this Convention. The rights of sovereign States and of gentlemen of the South have been denied by a majority of this body. We cannot act, as we conceive, in view of this wrong. I use the word "wrong" with no intention to reflect upon those gentlemen of the North Carolina delegation who differ with me or with the majority of the delegation. For these reasons, without assigning any more, as I have no idea of inflicting a speech upon this Convention, who are in no state of preparation to receive it, I announce that eight out of ten of the votes of North Carolina ask to retire.

WITHDRAWAL OF TENNESSEE.

Mr. Ewing, of Tennessee.—Mr. President, in behalf of the delegation from Tennessee, I beg leave to address this Convention upon this occasion, so important, and, to us, so solemn in its consequences. The delegation from Tennessee have exhibited, so far as they knew how, every disposition to harmonize this Convention, and to bring its labors to a happy result. They were the first, when the majority platform was not adopted, to seek for some proposition for compromise—something that would enable us to harmonize. They have a candidate who was dear to them. They cast away his prospect for the sake of harmony. They have yielded all that they can. They have endeavored, with all their power, to accomplish the result they came here for; but they fear that the result is not to be accomplished in a manner that can render a just and proper account to their constituents. We have consulted together, and, after anxious and long deliberation, without knowing exactly what phase this matter might finally present, we have not adopted any decisive rule for our action; but a large majority of our delegates—some twenty to four—have decided that, upon the result now obtained, we shall ask leave of this Convention to retire, that we may consult and announce our final action. We shall take no further part in the deliberations of this Convention, unless our minds should change; and of that I can offer you no reasonable hope.

A PORTION OF MARYLAND WITHDRAWS.

Mr. Johnson, of Maryland.—Mr. President, I am authorized by my colleagues to report the state of facts in regard to a portion of the Maryland delegation. Representing, in part, a district in Maryland upon which the first blood of the irrepressible conflict was shed, a district which sent fifteen men in midwinter to the rescue of Philadelphia and New-Jersey, we are obliged now to take a step which dissolves our connection with you, and to bid you a final adieu. We have made all sacrifices for the grand old Democratic party, whose mission it has been to preserve the Constitution and to care for the Republic for more than sixty years, until it now seems as if you were going to substitute a man in the place of principle. (Calls to order.) I desire to be respectful. I desire to say that the action of the majority of the late Convention—a majority created by the operation of a technical unit rule imposed upon the Convention contrary to Democratic precedent and usage—States have been disfranchised, and districts deprived of their rights, until, in our opinion, it is no longer consistent with our honor or our rights, or the rights of our constituents, to remain here. Cherishing deeply and warmly the remembrance of the many galiant deeds you have done for us in times past, hoping that hereafter no occasion may ever occur to weaken this feeling, I now, on behalf of the representatives of Maryland, tell you that in all future time, and in all future contests, our lot is cast with the people of the South. Their God shall be our God, and their country our country. (Applause.)

Mr. Glass, of Virginia, declined any further participation in the proceedings of the Convention, but did not indorse the action of his colleagues in withdrawing.

Mr. Watterson, of Tennessee, declined to withdraw.

CALIFORNIA WITHDRAWS—AN EXCITEMENT.

Mr. Smith, of California, said: While I cannot say with the gentleman from Tennessee (Mr. Jones) that my Democracy dates back to that time of which I have no recollection, yet I can say that it is unspotted as the vault of heaven. California is here with melancholy face— California is here with a lacerated heart, bleeding and weeping over the downfall and the destruction of the Democratic party. (Applause and laughter.) Yes, sir, the destruction of the Democratic party, consummated by assassins now grinning upon this floor. (Loud cries of "order," "order," "put him out," and great confusion.)

DELAWARE WITHDRAWS.

Mr. Saulsbury did not desire to occupy the attention of the Convention but for a moment. The delegates from his State had done all in their power to promote the harmony and unity of this Convention, and it was their purpose to continue to do so. I am, however, instructed by the delegation to announce that they desire to be excused from voting on any further ballots or votes, unless circumstances should alter this determination. It is our desire to be left free to act or not act, their desire being to leave the question open for the consideration of their constituents after their return home.

Mr. Steele, of North Carolina, briefly addressed the Convention, stating that he, for the present, at least, should not retire.

After explanations and debate, the motion "Shall the main question be now put." (to go into nomination of candidates for President and Vice-President) was carried, and the Convention adjourned.

KENTUCKY WITHDRAWS IN PART.

On Saturday (23d), Mr. Caldwell, of Kentucky, in behalf of the delegation from that State, said:

The circumstances in which we (the Kentucky Delegation) are placed are exceedingly embarrassing, and we have not therefore been enabled to come to an entirely harmonious conclusion. The result is, however, that nine of the delegates of Kentucky remain in the Convention. (applause.) There are ten delegates who withdraw from the Convention.

The exact character of their withdrawal is set forth in a single paragraph, with their names appended, which I desire the Secretary to read before I sit down. There are five others—completing the delegation—who desire for the present to suspend their connection with the action of this Convention. I will add here, that there may be no misunderstanding, that I myself am one of those five, and we have also signed a short paper, which I shall also ask the Secretary to read to the Convention.

I am requested by those who withdraw from the Convention, and by those who suspend their action for the present with the Convention, to say that it is their wish that their seats in this Convention shall not be filled or occupied by any others; and that no one shall claim the right to cast their votes. The right of those remaining in the Convention to cast their individual vote, is not by us questioned in any degree. But we enter our protest against any one casting our vote.

I will ask the Secretary to read the papers I have indicated, and also one which a gentleman of our delegation has handed me, which he desires to be read. I ask that the three papers be read.

The first paper read was signed James G. Leach, the writer of which animadverted in rather strong terms upon the action of the Convention, in the matter of the admission and rejection of delegates from certain States. The communication was regarded as disrespectful to the Convention, and, on motion of Mr. Payne, of Ohio, it was returned to the writer. The Secretary then read the other two communications from the Kentucky delegation as follows :

To the Hon. Caleb Cushing, President of the National Democratic Convention, assembled in the city of Baltimore:

The Democratic Convention for the State of Kentucky, held in the city of Frankfort, on the 9th day of January, 1860, among others, adopted the following resolution:

Resolved, That we pledge the Democracy of Kentucky to an honest and industrious support of the nominee of the Charleston Convention.

Since the adoption of this resolution, and the assembling of this Convention, events have transpired not then contemplated, notwithstanding which we have labored diligently to preserve the harmony and unity of said Convention; but discord and disintegration have prevailed to such an extent that we feel that our efforts cannot accomplish this end.

Therefore, without intending to vacate our seats, or to join or participate in any other Convention or organization in this city, and with the intention of again co-operating with this Convention, should its unity and harmony be restored by any future event, we now de-clare that we will not participate in the meantime in the deliberations of this Convention, nor hold ourselves or constituents bound by its action, but leave both at full liberty to act as future circumstances may dictate.

N. W. WILLIAMSON,	W. BRADLEY,
G. A. CALDWELL,	SAMUEL B. FIELD,
THOS. J. YOUNG.	

Resolved, That the Chairman of our delegation be instructed to inform the Convention in our behalf that, in the present condition of that body, we deem it inconsistent with our duty to ourselves and our constituents to participate further in its deliberations. Our reasons for so doing will be given to the Democracy of Kentucky.

JNO. DISHMAN,	L. GREEN,
J. S. KENDALL,	R. M JOHNSON,
JOS. B. BECK,	CAL. BUTLER,
D. W. QUARLES,	R. NICKEE,
COLBERT CECIL,	JAMES G. LEACH.

Mr. Reed, of Ky., spoke briefly in defense of the course of the nine delegates from that State, who remained with the Convention.

MISSOURI DEFINES HER POSITION.

Mr. Clark, of Missouri, announced as the result of a consultation of a portion of the Missouri delegation, that two of that delegation had decided to withdraw from the Convention.

Mr. Hill, of N. C., who had refused to retire with his colleagues on the previous day, now announced his intention of withdrawing.

Mr. Cessna, of Pennsylvania, called for the vote upon his resolution to proceed to nominate candidates for President and Vice-President.

MR. CUSHING RESIGNS THE CHAIR.

Mr. Cushing resigned his post as presiding officer, in a brief speech, and left the chair.

Gov. Tod, of Ohio, immediately assumed the chair, and was greeted with enthusiastic and hearty cheers. After order was restored, he said :

As the present presiding officer of this Convention by common consent of my brother Vice-Presidents, with great diffidence I assume the chair. When I announce to you that for thirty-four years I have stood up in that district so long misrepresented by Joshua R. Giddings, with the Democratic banner in my hand (applause), I know that I shall receive the good wishes of this Convention, at least, for the discharge of the duties of the chair. If there are no privileged questions intervening, the Secretary will proceed with the call of the States.

MASSACHUSETTS DESIRES A HEARING.

Mr. Butler, of Mass., addressed the chair, and desired to present a protest. Objection was made by Mr. Cavanaugh, of Minnesota, and the States were called on the question of proceeding to a vote for President. When Massachusetts was called, Mr. Butler said: Mr. President, I have the instruction of a majority of the delegation from Massachusetts to present a written protest. I will send it to the Chair to have it read. (Calls to order.) And further, with your leave, I desire to say what I think will be pleasant to this Convention. First, that, while a majority of the delegation from Massachusetts do not purpose further to participate in the doings of this Convention, we desire to part, if we may, to meet you as friends and Democrats again. We desire to part in the same spirit of manly courtesy with which we came together. Therefore, if you will allow me, instead of reading to you a long document, I will state, within parliamentary usage, exactly the reasons why we take the step we do.

Thanking the Convention for their courtesy, allow me to say that though we have protested against the action of this body excluding the delegates, although we are not satisfied with that action—

We have not discussed the question, Mr. President, whether the action of the Convention, in excluding certain delegates, could be any reason for withdrawal. We now put our withdrawal before you, upon the simple ground, among others, that there has been a withdrawal in part of a majority of the States, and further (and that, perhaps, more personal to myself), upon the ground that I will not sit in a Convention where the African slave-trade—which is piracy by the laws of my country—is approvingly advocated. (Great sensation.)

A portion of the Massachusetts delegation here retired.

Mr. Stevens, of Massachusetts, said—I am not ready at this moment to cast the vote of Massachusetts, the delegation being in consultation as to their rights.

The call proceeded, the chairman of each Convention making a speech on delivering the vote of his State; and Mr. Stevens finally stated that, although a portion of the Massachusetts delegation had withdrawn, he was instructed by his remaining colleagues to cast the entire vote of the State.

Mr. Russell, of New-York, withdrew the name of Horatio Seymour as a candidate. The following is the result of the ballotings for President:

STATES.	FIRST BALLOT.			SECOND BALLOT.		
	Douglas.	Breckinridge.	Guthrie.	Douglas.	Breckinridge.	Guthrie.
Maine	5½	—	—	7	—	—
New-Hampshire	5	—	—	5	—	—
Vermont	5	—	—	5	—	—
Massachusetts	10	—	—	10	—	—
Rhode Island	4	—	—	4	—	—
Connecticut	3⅞	1	—	3⅞	⅛	—
New-York	35	—	—	35	—	—
New-Jersey	2¼	—	—	2¼	—	—
Pennsylvania	10	3	3	10	7	2¼
Maryland	2½	—	—	2½	—	—
Virginia	1½	—	—	3	—	—
North Carolina	1	—	—	1	—	—
Alabama	9	—	—	9	—	—
Louisiana	6	—	—	6	—	—
Arkansas	1	½	—	1¼	—	—
Missouri	4¼	—	1½	4¼	—	1½
Tennessee	3	—	—	3	—	—
Kentucky	—	—	4½	3	—	1½
Ohio	23	—	—	23	—	—
Indiana	13	—	—	13	—	—
Illinois	11	—	—	11	—	—
Michigan	6	—	—	6	—	—
Wisconsin	5	—	—	5	—	—
Iowa	4	—	—	4	—	—
Minnesota	2½	½	1	4	—	—
Total	173½	5	10	181½	7¼	5¼

On the first ballot, Henry A. Wise, of Virginia, received ½ a vote from Maryland; Bocock, of Va., received 1 vote from Virginia; Daniel S. Dickinson, ½ vote from Virginia; and Horatio Seymour 1 vote from Pennsylvania.

On the announcement of the first ballot, Mr. Church, of New-York, offered the following:

Resolved unanimously, That Stephen A. Douglas, of the State of Illinois, having now received two-thirds of all the votes given in this Convention, is hereby declared, in accordance with the rules governing this body, and in accordance with the uniform customs and rules of former Democratic National Conventions, the regular nominee of the Democratic party of the United States, for the office of President of the United States.

Mr. Jones, of Pennsylvania, raised the point of order, that the resolution proposed practically to rescind a rule of the Convention (requiring two-thirds of a full Convention, 202 votes, to nominate), and could not, under the rules, be adopted without one day's notice.

The Chair ruled that the resolution was in order, and after a lengthy and animated debate it was withdrawn till after another ballot should be taken. When the result of the second ballot had been announced, Mr. Church's resolution was called up again and passed.

Benj. Fitzpatrick, of Alabama, was nominated for Vice-President, receiving 198½ votes, and Mr. William C. Alexander, of N. J., 1. [Mr. Fitzpatrick declined the nomination two days afterward, and the National Committee supplied the vacancy, by the nomination of Herschel V. Johnson, of Georgia].

Gov. Wickliffe, of Louisiana, offered the following resolution as an addition to the Platform adopted at Charleston:

Resolved, That in its accordance with the interpretation of the Cincinnati Platform, that, during the existence of the Territorial Governments, the measure of restriction, whatever it may be, imposed by the Federal Constitution on the power of the Territorial Legislature over the subject of the domestic relations, as the same has been, or shall hereafter be, finally determined by the Supreme Court of the United States, should be respected by all good citizens, and enforced with promptness and fidelity by every branch of the General Government.

Mr. Payne, of Ohio, moved the previous question, and this resolution was adopted, with only two dissenting votes.

THE SECEDERS' CONVENTION.

The delegates who had withdrawn from the Convention at the Front-Street Theater, together with the delegations from Louisiana and Alabama, who were refused admission to that Convention, met at the Maryland Institute on Saturday the 28th of June. Twenty-one States were represented either by full or partial delegations. The States not represented at all were Connecticut, Illinois, Indiana, Iowa, Maine, Michigan, New-Hampshire, New-Jersey, Ohio, Rhode Island, South Carolina, and Wisconsin.

The Hon. Caleb Cushing, of Massachusetts, was chosen to preside, assisted by vice-presidents and secretaries.

The Convention adopted a rule requiring a vote of two-thirds of all the delegates present to nominate candidates for President and Vice-President; also that each delegate cast the vote to which he is entitled, and that each State cast only the number of votes to which it is entitled by its actual representation in the Convention.

The delegates from South Carolina and Florida accredited to the Richmond Convention, were invited to take seats in this.

A committee of five, of which Mr. Caleb Cushing was chairman, was appointed to address the Democracy of the Union upon the principles which have governed the Convention in making the nominations, and in vindication of the principles of the party. The Convention also decided that the next Democratic National Convention be held at Philadelphia.

Mr. Avery, of N. C., chairman of Committee on Resolutions, reported, with the unanimous sanction of the Committee, the Platform reported by the majority of the Platform Committee at Charleston, and rejected by the Convention, (see page 30) which was unanimously adopted.

The Convention adopted a resolution instructing the National Committee not to issue tickets of admission to their next National Convention in any case where there is a *bona fide* contestant.

The Convention then proceeded to ballot for a candidate for President; and John C. Breckinridge, of Ky., received the unanimous vote of the delegates present as follows:

Vermont	½	Florida	3	Tennessee	9½
Massachusetts	8	Alabama	9	Kentucky	4½
New-York	2	Louisiana	6	Minnesota	1
Pennsylvania	4	Mississippi	7	California	4
Maryland	4¼	Texas	4	Oregon	3
Virginia	11½	Arkansas	4		
North Carolina	8¼	Missouri	1		105
Georgia	10				

For Vice-President Gen. Joseph Lane, of Oregon, received the unanimous vote of the Convention (105), on the first ballot. And then, after listening to a speech from Mr. Yancy, the Convention adjourned *sine die*.

HISTORY OF THE STRUGGLE

FOR

SLAVERY EXTENSION OR RESTRICTION.

MAINLY BY DOCUMENTS.

SLAVERY IN THE COLONIES.

LUST of gold and power was the main impulse of Spanish migration to the regions beyond the Atlantic. And the soft and timid Aborigines of tropical America, especially of its islands, were first compelled to surrender whatever they possessed of the precious metals to the imperious and grasping strangers; next forced to disclose to those strangers the sources whence they were most readily obtained; and finally driven to toil and delve for more, wherever power and greed supposed they might most readily be obtained. From this point, the transition to general enslavement was ready and rapid. The gentle and indolent natives, unaccustomed to rugged, persistent toil, and revolting at the harsh and brutal severity of their Christian masters, had but one unfailing resource—death. Through privation, hardship, exposure, fatigue and despair, they drooped and died, until millions were reduced to a few miserable thousands within the first century of Spanish rule in America.

A humane and observant priest (Las Casas,) witnessing these cruelties and sufferings, was moved by pity to devise a plan for their termination. He suggested and urged the policy of substituting for these feeble and perishing "Indians" the hardier natives of Western Africa, whom their eternal wars and marauding invasions were constantly exposing to captivity and sale as prisoners of war, and who, as a race, might be said to be inured to the hardships and degradations of Slavery by an immemorial experience. The suggestion was unhappily approved, and the woes and miseries of the few remaining Aborigines of the islands known to us as "West Indies," were inconsiderably prolonged by exposing the whole continent for unnumbered generations to the evils and horrors of African Slavery. The author lived to perceive and deplore the consequences of his expedient.

The sanction of the Pope having been obtained for the African Slave-trade by representations which invested it with a look of philanthropy, Spanish and Portuguese mercantile avarice was readily enlisted in its prosecution, and the whole continent, North and South of the tropics, became a Slave-mart before the close of the sixteenth century.

Holland, a comparatively new and Protestant State, unable to shelter itself from the reproaches of conscience and humanity behind a Papal bull, entered upon the new traffic more tardily; but its profits soon overbore all scruples, and British merchants were not proof against the glittering evidences of their success. But the first slave ship that ever entered a North American port for the sale of its human merchandise, was a Dutch trading-vessel which landed twenty negro bondmen at Jamestown, the nucleus of Virginia, almost simultaneously with the landing of the Pilgrims of the May-flower on Plymouth Rock, December 22d, 1620.

The Dutch slaver had chosen his market with sagacity. Virginia was settled by CAVALIERS—gentlemen-adventurers aspiring to live by their own wits and other men's labor—with the necessary complement of followers and servitors. Few of her pioneers cherished any earnest liking for downright, persistent, muscular exertion; yet some exertion was urgently required to clear away the heavy forest which all but covered the soil of the infant colony, and grow the tobacco which early became its staple export, by means of which nearly everything required by its people but food was to be paid for in England. The slaves, therefore, found ready purchasers at satisfactory prices, and the success of the first venture induced others; until not only Virginia but every part of British America was supplied with African slaves.

This traffic, with the bondage it involved, had no justification in British nor in the early colonial laws; but it proceeded, nevertheless, much as an importation of dromedaries to replace with presumed economy our horses and oxen might now do. Georgia was the first among the colonies to resist and condemn it in her original charter under the lead of her noble founder-governor, General Oglethorpe; but the evil was too formidable and inveterate for local extirpation, and a few years saw it established, even in Georgia; first evading or defying, and at length molding and transforming the law.

It is very common at this day to speak of our revolutionary struggle as commenced and hurried forward by a union of Free and Slave colonies; but such is not the fact. However slender and dubious its legal basis, Slavery existed in each and all of the colonies that united to declare and maintain their independence. Slaves were proportionately more numerous in certain portions of the South; but they were held with impunity throughout the North, advertised like dogs or horses, and sold at auction, or otherwise, as chattels. Vermont, then a territory in dispute between New-Hampshire and New-York, and with very few civilized inhabitants, mainly on its Southern and Eastern borders, is probably the only portion of the revolutionary confederation never polluted by the tread of a slave.

The spirit of liberty, aroused or intensified by the protracted struggle of the colonists against usurped and abused power in the mother country, soon found itself engaged in natural antagonism against the current form of domestic despotism. "How shall we complain of arbitrary or unlimited power exerted over us, while we exert a still more despotic and inexcusable power over a dependent and benighted race?" was very fairly asked. Several suits were brought in Massachusetts—where the fires of liberty burnt earliest and brightest—to test the legal right of slave-holding; and the leading Whigs gave their money and their legal services to support these actions, which were generally, on one ground or another, successful. Efforts for an express law of emancipation, however, failed even in Massachusetts; the Legislature, doubtless, apprehending that such a measure, by alienating the slave-holders, would increase the number and power of the Tories; but in 1777, a privateer having brought a lot of captured slaves into Jamaica, and advertised them for sale, the General Court, as the Legislative Assembly was called, interfered and had them set at liberty. The first Continental Congress which resolved to resist the usurpations and oppressions of Great Britain by force, had already declared that our struggle would be "for the rights of human nature," which the Congress of 1776, under the lead of Thomas Jefferson, expanded into the noble affirmation of the right of "all men to life, liberty, and the pursuit of happiness," contained in the immortal preamble to the Declaration of Independence. A like averment that "all men are born free and equal," was in 1780 inserted in the Massachusetts Bill of Rights; and the Supreme Court of that State, in 1783, on an indictment of a master for assault and battery, held this declaration a bar to slave-holding henceforth in the State.

A similar clause in the second Constitution of New-Hampshire was held by the courts of that State to secure Freedom to every child, born therein after its adoption. Pennsylvania, in 1780, passed an act prohibiting the further introduction of slaves, and securing Freedom to all persons born in that State thereafter. Connecticut and Rhode-Island passed similar acts in 1784. Virginia, in 1778, on motion of Mr. Jefferson, prohibited the further importation of slaves; and in 1782, removed all legal restrictions on emancipation: Maryland adopted both of these in 1783. North-Carolina, in 1786, declared the introduction of slaves into that State "of evil consequence, and highly impolitic," and imposed a duty of £5 per head thereon. New-York and New-Jersey followed the example of Virginia and Maryland, including the domestic in the same interdict with the foreign slave-trade. Neither of these States, however, declared a general emancipation until many years thereafter, and Slavery did not wholly cease in New-York until about 1830, nor in New-Jersey till a much later date. The distinction of Free and Slave States, with the kindred assumption of a natural antagonism between the North and South, was utterly unknown to the men of the Revolution.

Before the Declaration of Independence, but during the intense ferment which preceded it, and distracted public attention from everything else, Lord Mansfield had rendered his judgment from the King's Bench, which expelled Slavery from England, and ought to have destroyed it in the colonies as well. The plaintiff in this famous case was James Somerset, a native of Africa, carried to Virginia as a slave, taken thence by his master to England, and there incited to resist the claim of his master to his services, and assert his right to liberty. In the first recorded case, involving the legality of modern Slavery in England, it was held (1677) that negroes, "being usually bought and sold among merchants as merchandise, and *also being infidels*, there might be a property in them sufficient to maintain trover." But this was overruled by Chief Justice Holt from the King's Bench (1697,) ruling that "so soon as a negro lands in England, he is free;" and again, (1702) that "there is no such thing as a slave by the law of England." This judgment proving exceedingly troublesome to planters and merchants from slave-holding colonies visiting the mother country with their servants, the merchants concerned in the American trade, in 1729, procured from Yorke and Talbot, the Attorney General and Solicitor General of the Crown, a written opinion that negroes, legally enslaved elsewhere, might be held as slaves in England, and that even baptism was no bar to the master's claim. This opinion was, in 1749, held to be sound law by Yorke (now Lord Hardwicke,) sitting as judge, on the ground that, if the contrary ruling of Lord Holt were upheld, it would abolish Slavery in Jamaica or Virginia as well as in England; British law being paramount in each. Thus the law stood until Lord Mansfield, in Somerset's case, reversed it with evident reluctance, and after having vainly endeavored to bring about an accommodation between the parties. When delay would serve no longer, and a judgment must be rendered, Mansfield declared it in these memorable words:

"We cannot direct the law: the law must direct us. . . . . The state of Slavery is of such a nature that it is incapable of being introduced on any reasons, moral or political, but only by positive law, which preserves its force long after the reasons, occasion, and time itself whence it was created, is erased from the memory. It is so odious that nothing can be sufficient to support it but positive law. Whatever inconveniences, therefore, may follow from the decision, I cannot say that this case is allowed or approved by the law of England, and therefore the black must be discharged."

The natural, if not necessary, effect of this decision on Slavery in these colonies had their connection with the mother country been continued, is sufficiently obvious.

SLAVERY UNDER THE CONFEDERATION.

The disposition or management of unpeopled territories, pertaining to the thirteen recent colonies now confederated as independent States, early became a subject of solicitude and of bickering among those States, and in Congress. By the terms of their charters, some of the colonies had an indefinite extension westwardly, and were only limited by the power of the grantor. Many of these charters conflicted with each other—the same territory being included within the limits of two or more totally distinct colonies. As the expenses of the Revolutionary struggle began to bear heavily on the resources of the States, it was keenly felt by some that their share in the advantages of the expected triumph would be less than that of others. Massachusetts, Connecticut, New-York, Virginia, North Carolina, and Georgia, laid claim to spacious dominions outside of their proper boundaries; while New-Hampshire (save in Vermont), Rhode Island, New-Jersey, Maryland, Delaware, and South Carolina, possessed no such boasted resources to meet the war-debts constantly augmenting. They urged, therefore, with obvious justice, that these unequal advantages ought to be surrendered, and all the lands included within the territorial limits of the Union, but outside of the proper and natural boundaries of the several States, respectively, should be ceded to, and held by, Congress, in trust for the common benefit of all the States, and their proceeds employed in satisfaction of the debts and liabilities of the Confederation. This reasonable requisition was ultimately, but with some reservations, responded to.

The IXth Continental Congress, under the Articles of Confederation, assembled at Philadelphia, Nov. 3, 1783, but adjourned next day to Annapolis, Md. The House was soon left without a quorum, and so continued most of the time — of course, doing no business—till the 1st of March, 1784, when the delegates from Virginia, in pursuance of instructions from the Legislature of that State, signed the conditional deed of cession to the Confederation of her claims to territory northwest of the Ohio River. New-York, Connecticut, and Massachusetts had already made similar concessions to the Confederation of their respective claims to territory westward of their present limits. Congress hereupon appointed Messrs. Jefferson of Virginia, Chase of Maryland, and Howell of Rhode Island, a Select Committee to report a Plan of Government for the Western Territory. This plan, drawn up by Thomas Jefferson, provided for the government of *all* the Western territory, including that portion which had not yet been, but which, it was reasonably expected, would be, surrendered to the Confederation by the States of North Carolina and Georgia (and which now forms the States of Tennessee, Alabama and Mississippi), as well as that which had already been conceded by the more northern States.

The report of the committee was in the following words:

THE JEFFERSONIAN ORDINANCE, 1784.

Resolved, That *the territory ceded, or to be ceded by individual States* to the United States, whensoever the same shall have been purchased of the Indian inhabitants and offered for sale by the United States, shall be formed into additional States, bounded in the following manner, as nearly as such cessions will admit: that is to say, northwardly and southwardly by parallels of latitude, so that each State shall comprehend from south to north, two degrees of latitude, beginning to count from the completion of thirty-one degrees north of the equator; [the then southern boundary of the U. S.] but any territory northwardly of the forty-seventh degree shall make part of the State next below. And eastwardly and westwardly they shall be bounded, those on the Mississippi, by that river on one side, and the meridian of the lowest point of the rapids of the Ohio on the other; and those adjoining on the east, by the same meridian on their western side, and on their eastern by the meridian of the western cape of the mouth of the Great Kanawha. And the territory eastward of this last meridian, between the Ohio, Lake Erie, and Pennsylvania, shall be one State.

That the settlers within the territory so to be purchased and offered for sale shall, either on their own petition or on the order of Congress, receive authority from them, with appointments of time and place, for their free males of full age to meet together for the purpose of establishing a temporary government, to adopt the constitution and laws of any one of these States, so that such laws nevertheless shall be subject to alteration by their ordinary Legislature, and to erect, subject to a like alteration, counties or townships for the election of members for their Legislature.

That such temporary government shall only continue in force in any State until it shall have acquired twenty thousand free inhabitants, when, giving due proof thereof to Congress, they shall receive from them authority, with appointments of time and place, to call a convention of representatives to establish a permanent constitution and government for themselves: *Provided, That both the temporary and permanent governments be established on these principles as their basis:*

1. That they shall forever remain a part of the United States of America.

2. That in their persons, property, and territory, they shall be subject to the Government of the United States in Congress assembled, and to the Articles of Confederation in all those cases in which the original States shall be so subject.

3. That they shall be subject to pay a part of the Federal debts, contracted or to be contracted, to be apportioned on them by Congress, according to the same common rule and measure by which apportionments thereof shall be made on the other States.

4. That their respective governments shall be in republican forms, and shall admit no person to be a citizen who holds a hereditary title.

5. *That after the year* 1800 *of the Christian era, there shall be neither slavery nor involuntary servitude in any of the said States*, otherwise than in punishment of crimes, whereof the party shall have been duly convicted to have been personally guilty.

That whenever any of the said States shall have, of free inhabitants, as many as shall then be in any one of the least numerous of the thirteen original States, such State shall be admitted, by its Delegates, into the Congress of the United States, on an equal footing with the said original States; after which the assent of two-thirds of the United States, in Congress assembled, shall be requisite in all those cases wherein, by the Confederation, the assent of nine States is now required, provided the consent of nine States to such admission may be obtained according to the eleventh of the Articles of Confederation. Until such admission by their Delegates into Congress, any of the said States, after the establishment of their temporary government, shall have authority to keep a sitting member in Congress, with a right of debating, but not of voting.

That the territory northward of the forty-fifth degree, that is to say, of the completion of forty-five degrees from the equator, and extending to the Lake of the Woods, shall be called *Sylvania;* that of the territory under the forty-fifth and forty-fourth degress, that which lies westward of Lake Michigan, shall be called *Michigania;* and that which is eastward thereof, within the peninsula formed by the lakes and waters of Michigan, Huron, St. Clair, and Erie, shall be called *Chersonesus,* and shall include any part of the peninsula which may extend above the forty-fifth degree. Of the territory under the forty-third and forty-second degrees, that to the westward, through which the Assenisipi or Rock River runs, shall be called *Assenisipia;* and that to the eastward, in which are the fountains of the Muskingum, the two Miamies of the Ohio, the Wabash, the Illinois, the Miami of the Lake, and the Sandusky rivers, shall be called *Metropotamia.* Of the territory which lies under the forty-first and fortieth degrees, through which the river Illinois runs, shall be called *Illinoia;* that next adjoining to the eastward, *Saratoga;* and that between this last and Pennsylvania, and extending from the Ohio to Lake Erie, shall be called *Washington.* Of the territory which lies under the thirty-ninth and thirty-eighth degrees, to which shall be added so much of the point of land within the fork of the Ohio and Mississippi as lies under the thirty-seventh degree; that to the westward, within and adjacent to which are the confluences of the rivers Wabash, Shawanee, Tanisee, Ohio, Illinois, Mississippi, and Missouri, shall be called *Polypotamia;* and that to the eastward, further up the Ohio, otherwise called the Pelisipi, shall be called *Pelisipia.*

That all the preceding articles sha'l be formed into a charter of compact, shall be duly executed by the President of the United States, in Congress assembled, under his hand and the seal of the United States, shall be promulgated, and *shall stand as fundamental conditions* between the thirteen original States and those newly described, *unalterable* but by the joint consent of the United States, in Congress assembled, and of the particular State within which such alteration is proposed to be made.

April 19, this reported plan came up for consideration in Congress. Mr. Spaight of N. C. moved that the 5th proposition (prohibiting Slavery after the year 1800) be stricken out of the plan of ordinance, and Mr. Read of S. C. seconded the motion. The question was put in this form: "Shall the words moved to be stricken out stand?" and on this question the Ayes and Noes were taken, and resulted as follows:

N. Hampshire	Mr. Foster,	ay	*Ay.*
	Mr. Blanchard,	ay	
Massachusetts	Mr. Gerry,	ay	*Ay.*
	Mr. Partridge,	ay	
Rhode Island	Mr. Ellery,	ay	*Ay.*
	Mr. Howell,	ay	
Connecticut	Mr. Sherman,	ay	*Ay.*
	Mr. Wadsworth,	ay	
New-York	Mr. De Witt,	ay	*Ay.*
	Mr. Paine,	ay	
New-Jersey	Mr. Dick,	ay	*
Pennsylvania	Mr. Mifflin,	ay	*Ay.*
	Mr. Montgomery,	ay	
	Mr. Hand,	ay	
Maryland	Mr. McHenry,	no	*No.*
	Mr. Stone,	no	
Virginia	Mr. Jefferson,	ay	*No.*
	Mr. Hardy,	no	
	Mr. Mercer,	no	
N. Carolina	Mr. Williamson,	ay	*Divided*
	Mr. Spaight,	no	
S. Carolina	Mr. Read,	no	*No.*
	Mr. Beresford,	no	

Here we find the votes *sixteen* in favor of Mr. Jefferson's restriction to barely *seven* against it, and the States divided *six* in favor to *three* against it. But the Articles of Confederation (Art. IX.) required an affirmative vote of a majority of all the States—that is, a vote of seven States—to carry a proposition; so this clause was defeated through the absence of one delegate from New-Jersey, in spite of a vote of more than two to one in its favor. Had the New-Jersey delegation been full, it must, to a moral certainty, have prevailed; had Delaware then been represented, it would probably have been carried, even without New-Jersey. Yet, it is this vote, so given and recorded, that Mr. Douglas in his "Harper" essay claims as sus-

---

taining his views of "non-intervention by Congress."

The Ordinance, thus depleted, after undergoing some further amendments, was finally approved April 23d—all the delegates, but those from South Carolina, voting in the affirmative.

In 1787, the last Continental Congress, sitting in New-York simultaneously with the Convention at Philadelphia which framed our Federal Constitution, took up the subject of the government of the Western Territory, raising a Committee thereon, of which Nathan Dane, of Massachusetts, was Chairman. That Committee reported (July 11th), "An Ordinance for the government of the Territories of the United States, *Northwest of the Ohio*"—the larger area contemplated by Mr. Jefferson's bill not having been ceded by the Southern States claiming dominion over it. This bill embodied many of the provisions originally drafted and reported by Mr. Jefferson, but with some modifications, and concludes with six unalterable articles of perpetual compact, the last of them as follows:

"There shall be neither Slavery nor involuntary servitude, in the said Territory, otherwise than in punishment of crimes, whereof the parties shall be duly convicted."

To this was added, prior to its passage, the stipulation for the delivery of fugitives from labor or service, soon after embodied in the Federal Constitution; and in this shape, the entire ordinance was adopted (July 13th) by a unanimous vote, Georgia and the Carolinas concurring.

UNDER THE CONSTITUTION.

The old Articles of Confederation having proved inadequate to the creation and maintenance of a capable and efficient national or central authority, a Convention of Delegates from the several States, was legally assembled in Philadelphia, in 1787—George Washington, President; and the result of its labors was our present Federal Constitution, though some amendments mainly of the nature of restrictions on Federal power, were proposed by the several State Conventions assembled to pass upon that Constitution, and adopted. The following are all the provisions of that instrument, which are presumed to bear upon the subject of Slavery:

(Preamble): We, the people of the United States, in order to form a more perfect Union, establish justice, insure domestic tranquillity, provide for the common defense, promote the general welfare, and secure the blessings of liberty to ourselves and our posterity, do ordain and establish this Constitution for the United States of America.

Art. I. § 1. All legislative powers herein granted, shall be vested in a Congress of the United States, which shall consist of a Senate and House of Representatives.

§ 2. . . . . Representatives and direct taxes shall be apportioned among the several States which may be included within this Union, according to their respective numbers, which shall be determined, by adding to the whole number of free persons, including those bound to servitude for a term of years, and excluding Indians not taxed, three-fifths of all other persons.

§ 9. The migration or importation of such persons as any of the States now existing shall think proper to admit, shall not be prohibited by the Congress prior to the year 1808; but a tax or duty may be imposed, not exceeding ten dollars on each person.

The privilege of the writ of *habeas corpus* shall not be suspended, unless when, in cases of rebellion or invasion, the public safety may require it.

No bill of attainder or *ex post facto* laws shall be passed.

Art. III. § 3. Treason against the United States

shall consist only in levying war against them, or in adhering to their enemies, giving them aid and comfort.

Art. IV. § 2. The citizens of each State shall be entitled to all the privileges of citizens, in the several States.

No person held to service or labor in one State, under the laws thereof, escaping into another, shall, in consequence of any law or regulation therein, be discharged from such service or labor, but shall be delivered up on claim of the party to whom such service or labor may be due.

The Congress shall have power to dispose of and make all needful rules and regulations respecting the territory or other property belonging to the United States : and nothing in this Constitution shall be so construed as to prejudice any claims of the United States, or of any particular State.

§ 4. The United States shall guarantee to every State in this Union a republican form of government, and shall protect each of them against invasion ; and on application of the legislature, or of the executive when the legislature cannot be convened, against domestic violence.

Art. VI. This Constitution, and the laws of the United States, which shall be made in pursuance thereof, and all the treaties made, or which shall be made, under the authority of the United States, shall be the supreme law of the land ; and the judges in every State shall be bound thereby, anything in the Constitution or laws of any State to the contrary notwithstanding.

The above are all—and perhaps more than all—the clauses of the Constitution, that have been quoted on one side or the other as bearing upon the subject of Slavery.

It will be noted that the word "slave" or "slavery" does not appear therein. Mr. Madison, who was a leading and observant member of the Convention, and who took notes of its daily proceedings, affirms that this silence was designed—the Convention being unwilling that the Constitution of the United States should recognize property in human beings. In passages where slaves are presumed to be contemplated, they are uniformly designated as "persons," never as property. Contemporary history proves that it was the belief of at least a large portion of the delegates that Slavery could not long survive the final stoppage of the slave-trade, which was expected to (and did) occur in 1808. And, were Slavery this day banished forever from the country, there might, indeed, be some superfluous stipulations in the Federal compact or charter ; but there are none which need be repealed, or essentially modified.

A direct provision for the restoration of fugitive slaves to their masters was, at least once, voted down by the Convention. Finally, the clause respecting persons "held to service or labor," was proposed by Mr. Butler, of South Carolina, and adopted with little or no opposition.

The following, among the amendments to the Constitution, proposed by the ratifying conventions of one or more States, and adopted, are supposed by some to bear on the questions now agitated relative to Slavery :

Art. I. Congress shall make no law respecting an establishment of religion, or prohibiting the free exercise thereof ; or abridging the freedom of speech, or of the Press, or of the rights of the people peacefully to assemble, and to petition the Government for a redress of grievances.

Art. II. A well-regulated militia being necessary to the security of a free State, the right of the people to keep and bear arms shall not be infringed.

Art. V. No persons shall be . . . . deprived of life, liberty, or property, without due process of law ; nor shall private property be taken for public use without just compensation.

CESSIONS OF SOUTHERN TERRITORY.

The State of Kentucky was set off from the State of Virginia in 1790, by mutual agreement, and admitted into the Union by act of Congress, passed February 4th, 1791 ; to take effect June 1st, 1792. It was never a territory of the United States, nor under Federal jurisdiction, except as a State, and inherited Slavery from the "Old Dominion."

The State of North Carolina, like several others, claimed, during and after the Revolution, that her territory extended westward to the Mississippi.

On the 22d of December, 1799—one month after the ratification of the Federal Constitution—North Carolina passed an act, ceding, on certain conditions, all her territory west of her present limits to the United States. Among the conditions exacted by her, and agreed to by Congress (Act approved April 2nd, 1790) is the following :

Provided always, that no regulations made, or to be made, by Congress shall tend to emancipate slaves.

Were it not then conceded that Congress had the power to make regulations for the territories which would "tend to emancipate slaves," this proviso would be utterly meaningless.

Georgia, in like manner, ceded (April 2nd, 1802) the territories lying west of her present limits, now forming the States of Alabama and Mississippi. Among the conditions exacted by her, and accepted by the United States, is the following :

Fifthly. That the territory thus ceded shall become a State, and be admitted into the Union as soon as it shall contain sixty thousand free inhabitants, or, at an earlier period, if Congress shall think it expedient, on the same conditions and restrictions, with the same privileges, and in the same manner, as is provided in the ordinance of Congress of the 13th day of July, 1787, for the government of the Western territory of the United States ; which ordinance shall, in all its parts, extend to the territory contained in the present act of cession, the article only excepted which forbids slavery.

EARLY ATTEMPTS TO OVERRIDE THE ORDINANCE.

When Ohio (1802-3) was made a State, the residue of the vast regions originally conveyed by the ordinance of '87 was continued under Federal pupilage, by the name of "Indiana Territory," whereof Wm. Henry Harrison (since President) was appointed Governor. It was quite commonly argued that, though Slavery was injurious in the long run, yet, as an expedient while clearing away the heavy forests, opening settlements in the wilderness, and surmounting the inevitable hardships and privations of border life, it might be tolerated, and even regarded with favor. Accordingly, the new Territory of Indiana made repeated efforts to procure a relaxation in her favor of the restrictive clause of the Ordinance of '87, one of them through the instrumentality of a Convention assembled in 1802-3, and presided over by the Territorial Governor ; so he, with the great body of his fellow-delegates, memorialized Congress, among other things, to suspend temporarily the operation of the sixth article of the Ordinance aforesaid This memorial was referred in the House to a select committee of three, two of them from Slave States, with the since celebrated John Randolph as chairman.

On the 2nd of March, 1803, Mr. Randolph made what appears to have been a unanimous report from this Committee, of which we give so much as relates to Slavery—as follows:

The rapid population of the State of Ohio sufficiently evinces, in the opinion of your Committee, that the labor of slaves is not necessary to promote the growth and settlement of colonies in that region; that this labor—demonstrably the dearest of any—can only be employed in the cultivation of products more valuable than any known to that quarter of the United States; that the Committee deem it highly dangerous and inexpedient to impair a provision wisely calculated to promote the happiness and prosperity of the northwestern country, and to give strength and security to that extensive frontier. In the salutary operation of this sagacious and benevolent restraint, it is believed that the inhabitants of Indiana will, at no very distant day, find ample remuneration for a temporary privation of labor, and of emigration.

The Committee proceed to discuss other subjects set forth in the prayer of the memorial, and conclude with eight resolves, whereof the only one relating to Slavery is as follows:

Resolved, That it is inexpedient to suspend, for a limited time, the operation of the sixth article of the compact between the original States and the people and States west of the river Ohio.

This Report having been made at the close of the Session, was referred at the next to a new Committee, whereof Cæsar Rodney, a new Representative from Delaware, was Chairman. Mr. Rodney, from this Committee, reported (February 17th, 1804),

That, taking into their consideration the facts stated in the said memorial and petition, they are induced to believe that a qualified suspension, for a limited time, of the sixth article of compact between the original States and the people and States west of the river Ohio, might be productive of benefit and advantage to said Territory.

The Report goes on to discuss the other topics embraced in the Indiana memorial, and concludes with eight resolves, of which the first (and only one relative to Slavery) is as follows:

R*solved, That the sixth article of the Ordinance of 1787, which prohibited Slavery within the said Territory, be suspended in a qualified manner, for ten years, so as to permit the introduction of slaves, born within the United States, from any of the individual States; provided, that such individual State does not permit the importation of slaves from foreign countries: and provided, further, that the descendants of all such slaves shall, if males, be free at the age of twenty-five years, and, if females, at the age of twenty-one years.

The House took no action on this Report.

The original memorial from Indiana, with several additional memorials of like purport, was again, in 1805-6, referred by the House to a select committee, whereof Mr. Garnett of Virginia was chairman, who, on the 14th of February, 1806, made a report in favor of the prayer of the petitioners—as follows:

That, having attentively considered the facts stated in the said petitions and memorials, they are of opinion that a qualified suspension, for a limited time, of the sixth article of the compact between the original States, and the people and States west of the river Ohio, would be beneficial to the people of the Indiana Territory. The suspension of this article is an object almost universally desired in that Territory.

After discussing other subjects embodied in the Indiana memorial, the Committee close with a series of Resolves, which they commend to the adoption of the House. The first and only one germane to our subject is as follows:

Resolved, That the sixth article of the Ordinance of 1787, which prohibits Slavery within the Indiana Territory, be suspended for ten years, so as to permit the introduc-

tion of slaves, born within the United States, from any of the individual States.

This report and resolve were committed and made a special order on the Monday following, but were never taken into consideration.

At the next session, a fresh letter from Gov. William Henry Harrison, inclosing resolves of the Legislative Council and House of Representatives in favor of suspending, for a limited period, the sixth article of compact aforesaid, was received (Jan. 21st, 1807) and referred to a Select Committee, whereof Mr. B. Parke, delegate from said Territory, was made Chairman. The entire Committee (Mr. Nathaniel Macon, of N. C., being now Speaker,) consisted of

MESSRS. ALSTON, of N. C.   RHEA, of Tenn.
MASTERS, of N. Y.   SANDFORD, of Ky.
MORROW, of Ohio.   TRIGG, of Va.
PARKE, of Ind.

Mr. Parke, from this Committee, made (Feb. 12th,) a third Report to the House in favor of granting the prayer of the memorialists.

This report, with its predecessors, was committed, and made a special order, but never taken into consideration.

The same letter of Gen. Harrison, and resolves of the Indiana Legislature, were submitted to the Senate, Jan. 21st, 1807. They were laid on the table " for consideration," and do not appear to have even been referred at that session; but at the next, or first session of the fourth Congress, which convened Oct. 26th, 1807, the President (Nov. 7th) submitted a letter from Gen. Harrison and his Legislature—whether a new or old one does not appear—and it was now referred to a Select Committee, consisting of Messrs. J. Franklin, of N. C., Kitchel, of N. J., and Tiffin, of Ohio.

Nov. 13th, Mr. Franklin, from said committee, reported as follows:

The Legislative Council and House of Representatives, in their resolutions, express their sense of the propriety of introducing Slavery into their Territory, and solicit the Congress of the United States to suspend, for a given number of years, the sixth article of compact, in the ordinance for the government of the Territory northwest of the Ohio, passed on the 13th day of July, 1787. That article declares: " There shall be neither Slavery nor involuntary servitude within the said Territory."
The citizens of Clark County, in their remonstrance, express their sense of the impropriety of the measure, and solicit the Congress of the United States not to act on the subject, so as to permit the introduction of slaves into the Territory; at least, until their population shall entitle them to form a Constitution and State Government.
Your Committee, after duly considering the matter, respectfully submit the following resolution:
Resolved, That it is not expedient at this time to suspend the sixth article of compact for the government of the Territory of the United States northwest of the river Ohio.

And here ended, so far as we have been able to discover, the effort, so long and earnestly persisted in, to procure a suspension of the restriction in the Ordinance of 1787, so as to admit Slavery, for a limited term, into the Territory lying between the Ohio and Mississippi rivers, now forming the States of Ohio, Indiana, Illinois, Michigan, and Wisconsin.

THE FIRST MISSOURI STRUGGLE.

The vast and indefinite Territory known as Louisiana, was ceded by France to the United States in the year 1803, for the sum of $15,000,-000, of which $3,750,000 was devoted to the payment of American claims on France. This territory had just before been ceded by Spain to France without pecuniary consideration. Slave-holding had long been allowed therein, alike under Spanish and French rule, and the Treaty of Cession contained the following stipulation:

Art. III. The inhabitants of the ceded Territory shall be incorporated into the Union of the United States, and admitted as soon as possible, according to the principles of the Federal Constitution, to the enjoyment of all the rights, advantages and immunities of citizens of the United States; and in the meantime they shall be maintained and protected in the free enjoyment of their liberty, property, and the religion which they profess.

The State of Louisiana, embodying the southern portion of this acquired territory, was recognized by Congress in 1811, and fully admitted in 1812, with a State Constitution. Those who chose to dwell among the inhabitants of the residue of the Louisiana purchase, henceforth called Missouri Territory, continued to hold slaves in its sparse and small but increasing settlements, mainly in its southeastern quarter, and a pro-Slavery Court—perhaps any Court—would undoubtedly have pronounced Slavery legal anywhere on its vast expanse, from the Mississippi to the crests of the Rocky Mountains, if not beyond them, and from the Red River of Louisiana to the Lake of the Woods.

The XVth Congress assembled at Washington, on Monday, Dec. 1st, 1817. Henry Clay was chosen Speaker of the House. Mr. John Scott appeared on the 8th, as delegate from Missouri Territory, and was admitted to a seat as such. On the 16th of March following, he presented petitions of sundry inhabitants of Missouri, in addition to similar petitions already presented by him, praying for the admission of Missouri into the Union as a State, which were, on motion, referred to a Select Committee, consisting of

Messrs. Scott, of Mo.; Poindexter, of Miss.; Robertson, of Ky.; Hendricks, of Ind.; Livermore, of N. H.; Mills, of Mass.; Baldwin, of Pa.

April 3d, Mr. Scott, from this Committee, reported a bill to authorize the people of Missouri Territory to form a Constitution and State Government, and for the admission of such State into the Union on an equal footing with the original States; which bill was read the first and second time, and sent to the Committee of the Whole, where it slept for the remainder of the session.

That Congress convened at Washington for its second session, on the 16th of November, 1818. Feb. 13th, the House went into Committee of the Whole—Gen. Smith, of Md., in the Chair—and took up the Missouri bill aforesaid, which was considered through that sitting, as also that of the 15th, when several amendments were adopted, the most important of which was the following, moved in Committee by Gen. James Tallmadge, of Duchess county, New-York, (lately deceased):

And provided also, That the further introduction of Slavery or involuntary servitude be prohibited, except for the punishment of crimes, whereof the party shall be duly convicted: and that all children of slaves, born within the said State, after the admission thereof into the Union, shall be free, but may be held to service until the age of twenty-five years.

On coming out of Committee, the Yeas and Nays were called on the question of agreeing to this amendment, which was sustained by the following vote: [taken first on agreeing to so much of it as precedes and includes the word "convicted."]

Yeas—For the Restriction:

New-Hampshire	4	New-York	23
Massachusetts	15	New-Jersey	5
Rhode Island	1	Pennsylvania	20
Connecticut	7	Ohio	5
Vermont	5	Indiana	1
Delaware	1		

Total Yeas 87—only one (Delaware) from a Slave State.

Nays—Against the Restriction:

Massachusetts	3	Virginia	18
New-York	3	North Carolina	13
New-Jersey	1	South Carolina	6
New-Hampshire	1	Georgia	4
Ohio	1	Kentucky	9
Illinois	1	Tennessee	4
Delaware	1	Mississippi	1
Maryland	9	Louisiana	1

Total Nays, 76—10 from Free States, 66 from Slave States.

The House now proceeded to vote on the residue of the reported amendment (from the word "convicted" above), which was likewise sustained.—Yeas, 82; Nays, 78.

So the whole amendment—as moved by Gen. Tallmadge in Committee of the Whole, and there carried—was sustained when reported to the House.

Mr. Storrs, of New York (opposed to the Restriction), now moved the striking out of so much of the bill as provides that the new State shall be admitted into the Union " on an equal footing with the original States "—which, he contended, was nullified by the votes just taken. The House negatived the motion.

Messrs. Desha, of Ky., Cobb, of Ga., and Rhea, of Tenn., declared against the bill as amended.

Messrs. Scott, of Mo., and Anderson, of Ky., preferred the bill as amended, to none.

The House ordered the bill, as amended, to a third reading; Yeas, 98; Nays, 56. The bill thus passed the House next day, and was sent to the Senate.

The following sketch of the debate on this question (Feb. 15th) is condensed from that in the Appendix to *Niles's Register*, vol. xvi.

HOUSE OF REPRESENTATIVES, FEB. 15, 1819.

Mr. Tallmadge, of New York, having moved the following amendment on the Saturday preceding—

" *And provided that the introduction of Slavery, or involuntary servitude, be prohibited, except for the punishment of crimes, whereof the party has been duly convicted; and that all children born within the said State, after the admission thereof into the Union, shall be declared free at the age of 25 years,*"

Mr. Fuller, of Massachusetts, argued that, to effect a concert of interests, it was proper to make concessions. The States where Slavery existed not only claimed the right to continue it, but it was manifest that a general emancipation of slaves could not be asked of them. Their political existence would have been in jeopardy; both masters and slaves must have been involved in the most fatal consequences.

To guard against such intolerable evils, it is provided in the Constitution, " that the migration or importation of such persons, as any of the *existing* States think proper to admit, shall not be prohibited till 1808.—Art. 1, sec. 9. And it is provided elsewhere, that persons held to service by the laws of any State, shall be given up by other States, to which they may have escaped, etc.—Art. 4, sec. 2. These provisions effectually recognized the right in the

States, which, at the time of framing the Constitution, held the blacks in Slavery, to *continue* so to hold them until they should think proper to meliorate their condition. The Constitution is a compact among all the States then existing, by which certain principles of government are established for the whole, and for each individual State. The *predominant* principle in both respects is, that ALL MEN ARE FREE, and have an EQUAL RIGHT TO LIBERTY, and all other privileges; or, in other words, the predominant principle is REPUBLICANISM, in its largest sense. But, then, the same compact contains certain exceptions. The States then holding slaves are *permitted*, from the necessity of the case, and for the sake of union, to exclude the republican principle so far, and *only* so far, as to retain their slaves in servitude, and also their progeny, as had been the usage, until they should think it proper or safe to conform to the pure principle, by abolishing Slavery. The compact contains on its face the *general* principle and the *exceptions*. But the attempt to extend Slavery to the *new States*, is in direct violation of the clause which guarantees a republican form of government to all the States. This clause, indeed, must be construed in connection with the exceptions before mentioned; but it cannot, without violence, be applied to any other States than those in which Slavery was allowed at the formation of the Constitution.

The Speaker (Clay) cites the first clause in the 2d section of the 4th article—"The citizens of each State shall be entitled to all the privileges and immunities of citizens of the several States," which he thinks would be violated by the condition proposed in the Constitution of Missouri. To keep slaves—to make one portion of the population the property of another—hardly deserves to be called a *privilege*, since what is gained by the masters must be lost by the slaves. But, independently of this consideration, I think the observations already offered to the committee, showing that holding the black population in servitude is an exception to the general principles of the Constitution, and cannot be allowed to extend beyond the fair import of the terms by which that exception is provided, are a sufficient answer to the objection. The gentleman proceeds in the same train of reasoning, and asks, if Congress can require one condition, how many more can be required, and where these conditions will end? With regard to a republican constitution, Congress are *obliged* to require that condition, and that is enough for the present question; but I contend, further, that Congress has a right, at their discretion, to require any other reasonable condition. Several others were required of Ohio, Indiana, Illinois and Mississippi. The State of Louisiana, which was a part of the territory ceded to us at the same time with Missouri, was required to provide in her Constitution for trials by jury, the writ of habeas corpus, the principles of civil and religious liberty, with several others, peculiar to that State. These, certainly, are none of them more indispensable ingredients in a republican form of government than the equality of privileges of all the population; yet these have not been denied to be reasonable, and warranted by the National Constitution in the admission of new States. . . . .

One gentleman, however, has contended against the amendment, because it abridges the rights of the slave-holding States to transport their slaves to the new States, for sale or otherwise. This argument is attempted to be enforced in various ways, and particularly by the clause in the Constitution last cited. It admits, however, of a very clear answer, by recurring to the 9th section of article 1st, which provides that " the *migration* or importation of such persons as any of the States then existing shall admit, shall not be prohibited by Congress till 1808." This clearly implies that the *migration* and importation *may* be prohibited *after* that year. The importation has been prohibited, but the migration has not hitherto been restrained; Congress, however, may restrain it, when it may be judged expedient.

The expediency of this measure is very apparent. The opening of an extensive slave market will tempt the cupidity of those who, otherwise, perhaps, might gradually emancipate their slaves. We have heard much, Mr. Chairman, of the Colonization Society; an institution which is the favorite of the humane gentlemen in the slave-holding States. They have long been lamenting the miseries of Slavery, and earnestly seeking for a remedy compatible with their own safety, and the happiness of their slaves. At last, the great desideratum is found—a colony in Africa for the emancipated blacks. How will the generous intentions of these humane persons be frustrated, if the price of slaves is to be doubled by a new and boundless market! Instead of emancipation of the slaves, it is much to be feared that unprincipled wretches will be found kidnapping those who are already free, and transporting and selling the hapless victims into hopeless bondage. Sir I really hope that

Congress will not contribute to discountenance and render abortive the generous and philanthropic views of this most worthy and laudable society.

Mr. Tallmadge, of New York, followed—

Sir, said he, it has been my desire and my intention to avoid any debate on the present painful and unpleasant subject. When I had the honor to submit to this House the amendment now under consideration, I accompanied it with a declaration that it was intended to confine its operation to the newly acquired Territory across the Mississippi; and I then expressly declared that I would in no manner intermeddle with the slave-holding States, nor attempt manumission in any one of the original States in the Union. Sir, I even went further, and stated that I was aware of the delicacy of the subject—and, that I had learned from Southern gentlemen the difficulties and the dangers of having free blacks intermingling with slaves; and, on that account, and with a view to the safety of the white population of the adjoining States, I would not even advocate the prohibition of Slavery in the Alabama Territory; because, surrounded as it was by slave-holding States, and with only imaginary lines of division, the intercourse between slaves and free blacks could not be prevented, and a servile war might be the result. While we deprecate and mourn over the evil of Slavery, humanity and good morals require us to wish its abolition, under circumstances consistent with the safety of the white population. Willingly, therefore, will I submit to an evil which we cannot safely remedy. I admitted all that had been said of the danger of having free blacks visible to slaves, and, therefore, did not hesitate to pledge myself that I would neither advise nor attempt coercive manumission. But, sir, all these reasons cease when we cross the banks of the Mississippi, into a Territory separated by a natural boundary—a newly acquired Territory, never contemplated in the formation of our government, not included within the Compromise or mutual pledge in the adoption of our Constitution—a new Territory acquired by our common fund, and which ought justly to be subject to our common legislation.

Sir, when I submitted the amendment now under consideration, accompanied with these explanations, and with these avowals of my intentions and of my motives I did expect that gentlemen who might differ from me in opinion would appreciate the liberality of my views, and would meet me with moderation, as upon a fair subject for general legislation. I did expect, at least, that the frank declaration of my views would protect me from harsh expressions, and from the unfriendly imputations which have been cast out on this occasion. But, sir, such has been the character and the violence of this debate, and expressions of so much intemperance, and of an aspect so threatening have been used, that continued silence on my part would ill become me, who had submitted to this House the original proposition.

Sir, has it already come to this: that in the Congress of the United States—that, in the Legislative councils of Republican America, the subject of Slavery has become a subject of so much feeling—of such delicacy—of such danger, that it cannot safely be discussed? Are members who venture to express their sentiments on this subject, to be accused of talking to the galleries, with intention to excite a servile war; and of meriting the fate of Arbuthnot and Ambrister? Are we to be told of the dissolution of the Union, of civil war and of seas of blood? And yet, with such awful threatenings before us, do gentlemen, in the same breath, insist upon the encouragement of this evil; upon the extension of this monstrous scourge of the human race? An evil so fraught with such dire calamities to us as individuals, and to our nation, and threatening, in its progress, to overwhelm the civil and religious institutions of the country, with the liberties of the nation, ought at once to be met, and to be controlled. If its power, its influence, and its impending dangers, have already arrived at such a point, that it is not safe to discuss it on this floor, and it cannot now pass under consideration as a proper subject for general legislation, what will be the result when it is spread through your widely-extended domain? Its present threatening aspect, and the violence of its supporters, so far from inducing me to yield to its progress, prompt me to resist its march. Now is the time. It must now be met, and the extension of the evil must now be prevented, or the occasion is irrecoverably lost, and the evil can never be controlled.

Sir, extend your view across the Mississippi, over your newly-acquired Territory—a Territory so far surpassing, in extent, the limits of your present country, that country which gave birth to your nation—which achieved your Revolution—consolidated your Union—formed your Constitution, and has subsequently acquired so much glory, hangs but as an appendage to the extended empire over which your Republican Government is now called to bear sway. Look down the long vista of futurity ; see your empire, in extent unequaled, in advantageous situation without a parallel, and occupying all the valuable part of one continent. Behold this extended empire, inhabited by the hardy sons of American freemen, knowing their rights, and inheriting the will to protect them—owners of the soil on which they live, and interested in the institutions which they labor to defend ; with two oceans laving your shores, and tributary to your purposes, bearing on their bosoms the commerce of our people ; compared to yours, the governments of Europe dwindle into insignificance, and the whole world is without a parallel. But, sir, reverse this scene ; people this fair domain with the slaves of your planters ; extend *Slavery*, this bane of man, this abomination of heaven, over your extended empire, and you prepare its dissolution ; you turn its accumulated strength into positive weakness ; you cherish a canker in your breast ; you put poison in your bosom ; you place a vulture preying on your heart—nay, you whet the dagger and place it in the hands of a portion of your population, stimulated to use it, by every tie, human and divine. The envious contrast between your happiness and their misery, between your liberty and their slavery, must constantly prompt them to accomplish your destruction. Your enemies will learn the source and the cause of your weakness. As often as external dangers shall threaten, or internal commotions await you, you will then realize that, by your own procurement, you have placed amidst your families, and in the bosom of your country, a population producing at once the greatest cause of individual danger, and of national weakness. With this defect, your government must crumble to pieces, and your people become the scoff of the world.

Sir, we have been told, with apparent confidence, that we have no right to annex conditions to a State, on its admission into the Union ; and it has been urged that the proposed amendment, prohibiting the further introduction of Slavery, is unconstitutional. This position, asserted with so much confidence, remains unsupported by any argument, or by any authority derived from the Constitution itself. The Constitution strongly indicates an opposite conclusion, and seems to contemplate a difference between the old and the new States. The practice of the government has sanctioned this difference in many respects.

Sir, we have been told that this is a new principle for which we contend, never before adopted, or thought of. So far from this being correct, it is due to the memory of our ancestors to say, it is an old principle, adopted by them, as the policy of our country. Whenever the United States have had the right and the power, they have heretofore prevented the extension of Slavery. The States of Kentucky and Tennessee were taken off from other States, and were admitted into the Union without condition, because their lands were never owned by the United States. The Territory northwest of the Ohio is all the land which ever belonged to them. Shortly after the cession of those lands to the Union, Congress passed, in 1787, a compact, which was declared to be unalterable, the sixth article of which provides that, "*there shall be neither Slavery nor involuntary servitude in the said Territory, otherwise than in the punishment for crimes, whereof the parties shall have been duly convicted.*" In pursuance of this compact, all the States formed from that Territory have been admitted into the Union upon various conditions, and, amongst which, the sixth article of this compact is included as one.

Let gentlemen also advert to the law for the admission of the State of Louisiana into the Union ; they will find it filled with conditions. It was required not only to form a Constitution upon the principles of a republican government, but it was required to contain the "fundamental principles of civil and religious liberty." It was even required, as a condition of its admission, to keep its records, and its judicial and its legislative proceedings, in the English language ; and also to secure the trial by jury, and to surrender all claim to unappropriated lands in the Territory, with the prohibition to tax any of the United States' lands.

After this long practice and constant usage to annex conditions to the admission of a State into the Union, will gentlemen yet tell us it is unconstitutional, and talk of our principles being novel and extraordinary ?

Mr. Scott, of Missouri, said :

He trusted that his conduct, during the whole of the time in which he had had the honor of a seat in the House, had convinced gentlemen of his disposition not to obtrude his sentiments on any other subjects than those on which the interest of his constituents, and of the Territory he re-

presented, were immediately concerned. But when a question such as the amendments proposed by the gentlemen from New York (Messrs. Tallmadge and Taylor), was presented for consideration, involving constitutional principles to a vast amount, pregnant with the future fate of the Territory, portending destruction to the liberties of that people, directly bearing on their rights of property, their state rights, their all, he should consider it as a dereliction of his duty, as retreating from his post, nay, double criminality, did he not raise his voice against their adoption.

Mr. Scott entertained the opinion, that, under the Constitution, Congress had not the power to impose this, or any other restriction, or to require of the people of Missouri their assent to this condition, as a pre-requisite to their admission into the Union. He contended this from the language of the Constitution itself, from the practice in the admission of new States under that instrument, and from the express terms of the treaty of cession. The short view he intended to take of those points would, he trusted, be satisfactory to all those who were not so anxious to usurp power as to sacrifice to its attainment the principles of our government, or who were not desirous of prostrating the rights and independence of a State to chimerical views of policy or expediency. The authority to admit new States into the Union was granted in the third section of the fourth article of the Constitution, which declared that "new States may be admitted by the Congress into the Union." The only power given to the Congress by this section appeared to him to be, that of passing a law for the admission of the new State, leaving it in possession of all the rights, privileges, and immunities, enjoyed by the other States ; the most valuable and prominent of which was that of forming and modifying their own State Constitution, and over which Congress had no superintending control, other than that expressly given in the fourth section of the same article, which read, "The United States shall guarantee to every State in this Union a republican form of government." This end accomplished, the guardianship of the United States over the Constitutions of the several States was fulfilled ; and all restrictions, limitations and conditions beyond this, was so much power unwarrantably assumed. In illustration of this position, he would read an extract from one of the essays written by the late President Madison, contemporaneously with the Constitution of the United States, and from a very celebrated work : "In a confederacy founded on republican principles, and composed of republican members, the superintending government ought clearly to possess authority to defend the system against aristocratic or monarchical innovations. The more intimate the nature of such an union may be, the greater interest have the members in the political institutions of each other, and the greater right to insist that the forms of government under which the compact was entered into, should be substantially maintained. But this authority extends no further than to a *guarantee of a republican form of* government, which supposes a preëxisting government of the form which is to be guaranteed. As long, therefore, as the existing republican forms are continued by the States, they are guaranteed by the Federal Constitution. Whenever the States may choose to substitute other republican forms, they have a right to do so, and to claim the Federal guarantee for the latter. The *only restriction* imposed on them is, that they shall not exchange republican for anti-republican Constitutions ; a restriction which, it is presumed, will hardly be considered as a grievance."

Mr. Scott believed it to be a just rule of interpretation, that the enumeration of powers delegated to Congress weakened their authority in all cases not enumerated ; and that beyond those powers enumerated they had none, except they were essentially necessary to carry into effect those that were given. The second section of the fourth article of the Constitution, which declared that "the citizens of each State shall be entitled to all the privileges and immunities of citizens in the several States," was satisfactory, to his judgment, that it was intended the citizens of each State, forming a part of one harmonious whole, should have, in all things, *equal privileges ;* the necessary consequence of which was, that every man, in his own State, should have the same rights, privileges, and powers, that any other citizen of the United States had in his own State ; otherwise, discontent and murmurings would prevail against the general government who had deprived him of this equality.

For example, if the citizens of Pennsylvania, or Virginia, enjoyed the right, in their own State, to decide the question whether they would have Slavery or not, the citizens of Missouri, to give them the same privileges, must have the same right to decide whether they would or would not tolerate Slavery in their State ; if it were otherwise, then the citizens of Pennsylvania and Virginia would have more rights, privileges and powers in their respective States, than the . tizens of Missouri would have in theirs. Mr. S. said he would make another quotation from the same work he had before been indebted to, which he believed had considerable bearing on this subject. "The powers delegated by the proposed Constitution, to the Federal Government, are few and defined; those which are to remain in the State Governments, are numerous and indefinite; the former will be exercised principally on external objects, as war, peace, negotiation, and foreign commerce, with which last the powers of taxation will, for the most part, be connected. The powers reserved to the several States will extend to all the objects, which in the ordinary course of affairs concern the lives, liberties, and properties of the people, and the internal order, improvement, and prosperity of the State." The applicability of this doctrine to the question under consideration was so obvious, that he would not detain the House to give examples, but leave it for gentlemen to make the application. . . . .

Mr. Scott believed, that the practice under the Constitution had been different from that now contended for by gentlemen; he was unapprised of any similar provision having ever been made, or attempted to be made, in relation to any other new State heretofore admitted. The argument drawn from the States formed out of the Territory northwest of the river Ohio, he did not consider as analogous; that restriction, if any, was imposed in pursuance of a compact, and only, so far as Congress could do, carried into effect the disposition of Virginia in reference to a part of her own original Territory, and was, in every respect, more just, because that provision was made and published to the world at a time when but few, if any, settlements were formed within that tract of country; and the children of those people of color belonging to the inhabitants then there, have been, and still were, held in bondage, and were not free at a given age, as was contemplated by the amendment under consideration; nor did he doubt but that it was competent for any of those States admitted in pursuance of the Ordinance of '87, to call a Convention, and so to alter their Constitution as to allow the introduction of slaves, if they thought proper to do so. To those gentlemen who had in their argument, in support of the amendments, adverted to the instance where Congress had, by the law authorizing the people of Louisiana to form a Constitution and State Government, exercised the power of imposing the terms and conditions on which they should be permitted to do so, he would recommend a careful examination and comparison of those terms with the Constitution of the United States, when, he doubted not, they would be convinced that these restrictions were only such as were in express and positive language defined in the latter instrument, and would have been equally binding on the people of Louisiana had they not been enumerated in the law giving them authority to form a Constitution for themselves.

Mr. S. said, he considered the contemplated conditions and restrictions, contained in the proposed amendments, to be unconstitutional and unwarrantable, from the provisions of the Treaty of Cession, by the third article of which it was stipulated, that "the inhabitants of the ceded Territory shall be incorporated in the Union of the United States, and admitted, as soon as possible, according to the principles of the Federal Constitution, to the enjoyment of all the rights, advantages, and immunities of citizens of the United States, and, in the mean time, they shall be maintained and protected in the free enjoyment of their liberty, property, and the religion which they profess."

The people were not left to the wayward discretion of this or any other government, by saying that they *may be incorporated* in the Union. The language was different and imperative: "*they shall be incorporated.*" Mr. Scott understood by the term *incorporated*, that they were to form a constituent part of this republic; that they were to become joint partners in the character and councils of the country, and in the national losses and national gains; as a Territory they were not an essential part of the Government; they were a mere province, subject to the acts and regulations of the General Government in all cases whatsoever. As a Territory, they had not all the *rights, advantages and immunities*, of citizens of the United States. Mr. S himself furnished an example, that, in their present condition, they had not all the rights of the other citizens of the Union. Had he a vote in this House? and yet these people were, during the war, subject to certain taxes imposed by Congress. Had those people any voice to give in the imposition of taxes to which they were subject, or in the disposition of the funds of the nation, and particularly those arising from the sales of the public lands, to which they already had, and still would largely contribute? Had they a voice to give in selecting the officers of this Government, or many

of their own? In short, in what had they equal *rights, advantages and immunities*, with the other citizens of the United States, but in the privilege to submit to a procrastination of their rights, and in the advantage to subscribe to your laws, your rules, your taxes, and your powers, even without a hearing? Those people were also "to be admitted into the Union as soon as possible." Mr. Scott would infer from this expression, that it was the understanding of the parties, that so soon as any portion of the Territory, of sufficient extent to form a State, should contain the number of inhabitants required by law to entitle them to a representative on the floor of this House, that they then had the right to make the call for admission, and this admission, when made, was to be, not on conditions that gentlemen might deem expedient, not on conditions referable to future political views, not on conditions that the Constitution the people should form should contain a clause that would particularly open the door for emigration from the North or from the South, not on condition that the future population of the State should come from a Slaveholding or Non-Slaveholding State, "*but according to the principles of the Federal Constitution,*" and none other.

Mr. Scott had trusted that gentlemen who professed to be actuated by motives of humanity and principle would not encourage a course of dissimulation, or, by any vote of theirs, render it necessary for the citizens of Missouri to act equivocally to obtain their rights. He was unwilling to believe, that political views alone led gentlemen on this or any other occasion; but, from the language of the member from New-York (Mr. Taylor), he was compelled to suspect that they had their influence upon him. That gentleman has told us, that if ever he left his present residence, it would be for Illinois or Missouri; at all events, he wished to send out his brothers and his sons. Mr. Scott begged that gentleman to relieve him from the awful apprehension excited by the prospect of this accession of population. He hoped the House would excuse him while he stated, that he did not desire that gentleman, his sons, or his brothers, in that land of brave, noble, and independent freemen. The member says that the latitude is too far North to admit of Slavery there. Would the gentleman cast his eye on the map before him, he would there see, that a part of Kentucky, Virginia, and Maryland, were as far North as the Northern boundary of the proposed State of Missouri. Mr. Scott would thank the gentleman if he would condescend to tell him what precise line of latitude suited his conscience, his humanity, or his political views, on this subject. Could that member be serious, when he made the parallel of latitude the measure of his good-will to those unfortunate blacks? Or was he trying how far he could go in fallacious argument and absurdity, without creating one blush even on his own cheek, for inconsistency? What, starve the negroes out, pen them up in the swamps and morasses, confine them to Southern latitudes, to long, scorching days of labor and fatigue, until the race becomes extinct, that the fair land of Missouri may be tenanted by that gentleman, his brothers, and sons? He expected from the majority of the House a more liberal policy, and better evidence that they really were actuated by humane motives.

The House bill, thus passed, reached the Senate, February 17th, when it was read twice and sent to a Select Committee already raised on a like application from Alabama, consisting of

Messrs. Tait, of Georgia; Morrow, of Ohio; Williams, of Mississippi; Edwards, of Illinois; Williams, of Tennessee.

On the 22nd, Mr. Tait, from this Committee, reported the bill with amendments, striking out the Anti-Slavery restrictions inserted by the House. This bill was taken up in Committee of the Whole, on the 27th, when Mr. Wilson of New-Jersey moved its postponement to the 5th of March—that is, to the end of the session—negatived: Yeas 14; Nays 23.

The Senate then proceeded to vote on agreeing to the amendments reported by the Select Committee, viz.: 1, to strike out of the House bill the following:

And that all children of slaves born within the said State, after the admission thereof into the Union, shall be Free, but may be held to service until the age of twenty-one years.

Which was stricken out by the following vote:

Yeas—Against the Restriction —27. Nays—For the Restriction —7.

The Senate then proceeded to vote on the residue of the House Restriction, as follows:

And provided also, That the further introduction of Slavery or involuntary servitude be prohibited, except for the punishment of crimes, whereof the party shall have been duly convicted.

The vote on this clause was as follows:

Yeas—For striking out the Restriction —22. Nays —Against striking out —16.

The bill thus amended was ordered to be engrossed, and was (March 2nd—last day but one of the Session) read a third time, and passed without a division. The bill was on that day returned to the House, and the amendments of the Senate read: whereupon, Mr. Tallmadge, of New-York, moved that the bill be postponed indefinitely. Yeas 69; Nays 74.

[The record shows hardly a vote changed from Yea, on the original passage of the Restriction, to Nay now, but many members who voted then were now absent or silent.]

The vote was then taken on concurring in the Senate's amendments, as aforesaid, and the House refused to concur; Yeas 76; Nays 78.

[Hardly a vote changed; but more members voting than on the previous division, and less than when the Restriction was carried.]

The bill was now returned to the Senate, with a message of non-concurrence; when Mr. Tait moved that the Senate adhere to its amendment, which was carried without a division. The bill being thus remanded to the House, Mr. Taylor, of New-York, moved that the House adhere to its disagreement, which prevailed. Yeas 78; Nays 66. So the bill fell between the two Houses, and was lost.

The Southern portion of the then Territory of Missouri (organized by separation from Louisiana in 1812) was excluded from the proposed State of Missouri, and organized as a separate Territory, entitled Arkansas.

The bill being under consideration, Mr. Taylor, of New-York, moved that the foregoing restriction be applied to it also; and the clause, proposing that slaves born therein after the passage of this act be free at twenty-five years of age, was carried (February 17th) by 75 Yeas to 73 Nays; but that providing against the further introduction of Slaves was lost; Yeas 70; Nays 71. The next day, the clause just adopted was stricken out, and the bill ultimately passed without any allusion to Slavery. Arkansas of course became a Slave Territory, and ultimately (1836) a Slave State.

THE SECOND MISSOURI STRUGGLE.

A new Congress assembled on the 6th of December, 1819. Mr. Clay was again chosen Speaker. On the 8th, Mr. Scott, delegate from Missouri, moved that the memorial of her Territorial Legislature, as also of several citizens, praying her admission into the Union as a State, be referred to a Select Committee; carried, and Messrs. Scott, of Missouri, Robertson, of Kentucky, Terrell, of Georgia, Strother, of Virginia, and De Witt, of New-York, (all but the last from the Slave region,) were appointed said committee.

Mr. Strong, of New-York, that day gave notice of a bill "To prohibit the further extension of Slavery in the United States."

On the 14th, Mr. Taylor, of New-York, moved a Select Committee on this subject, which was granted; and the mover, with Messrs. Livermore, of New-Hampshire, Barbour, (P. P.) of Virginia, Lowndes, of South-Carolina, Fuller, of Massachusetts, Hardin, of Kentucky, and Cuthbert, of Georgia, were appointed such committee, A majority of this Committee being Pro-Slavery, Mr. Taylor could do nothing; and on the 28th the Committee was, on motion, discharged from the further consideration of the subject.

On the same day, Mr. Taylor moved:

That a Committee be appointed with instructions to report a bill prohibiting the further admission of slaves into the Territories of the United States West of the river Mississippi.

On motion of Mr. Smith, of Maryland, this resolve was sent to the Committee of the Whole, and made a special order for January 10th; but it was not taken up, and appears to have slept the sleep of death.

In the Senate, the memorial of the Missouri Territorial Legislature, asking admission as a State, was presented by Mr. Smith, of South-Carolina, December 29th, and referred to the Judiciary Committee, which consisted of

Messrs. Smith, of South Carolina; Leake, of Mississippi; Burrill, of Rhode Island; Logan, of Kentucky; Otis of Massachusetts.

DANIEL WEBSTER ON SLAVERY EXTENSION.

The following is extracted from the "Memorial to the Congress of the United States, on the subject of restraining the increase of Slavery in New *States* to be admitted into the Union," in pursuance of a vote of the inhabitants of Boston and its vicinity, assembled at the State House on the 3d of December, 1819, which was drawn up by Daniel Webster, and signed by himself, George Blake, Josiah Quincy, James T. Austin, etc. It is inserted here instead of the resolves of the various New England Legislatures, as a fuller and clearer statement of the views of the great body of the people of that section during the pendency of the Missouri question:

"MEMORIAL

To the Senate and House of Representatives of the United States, in Congress assembled :

The undersigned, inhabitants of Boston and its vicinity, beg leave most respectfully and humbly to represent: That the question of the introduction of Slavery into the new States to be formed on the west side of the Mississippi River, appears to them to be a question of the last importance to the future welfare of the United States. If the progress of this great evil is ever to be arrested, it seems to the undersigned that this is the time to arrest it. A false step taken now, cannot be retraced; and it appears to us that the happiness of unborn millions rests on the measure which Congress on this occasion may adopt. Considering this as no local question, nor a question to be decided by a temporary expediency, but as involving great interests of the whole United States, and affecting deeply and essentially those objects of common defense, general welfare, and the perpetuation of the blessings of liberty, for which the Constitution itself was formed, we have presumed, in this way, to offer our sentiments and express our wishes to the National Legislature. And, as various reasons have been suggested against prohibiting Slavery in the new States, it may perhaps be permitted to us to state our reasons, both for believing that Congress possesses the Constitutional power to make such prohibition a condition, on the admission of a new State into the Union, and that it is just and proper that they should exercise that power.

"And in the first place, as to the Constitutional authority of Congress. The Constitution of the United

States has declared that " Congress shall have power to dispose of and make all needful rules and regulations respecting the Territory or other property belonging to the United States : and nothing in this Constitution shall be so construed as to prejudice the claims of the United States or of any particular State." It is very well known, that the saving in this clause of the claims of any particular State, was designed to apply to claims by the then existing States, of territory which was also claimed by the United States as their own property. It has, therefore, no bearing on the present question. The power, then, of Congress over its own Territories, is, by the very terms of the Constitution, unlimited. It may make all " needful rules and regulations," which of course include all such regulations as its own views of policy or expediency shall, from time to time, dictate. If, therefore, in its judgment it be needful for the benefit of a Territory to enact a prohibition of Slavery, it would seem to be as much within its power of Legislation as any other act of local policy. Its sovereignty being complete and universal as to the Territory, it may exercise over it the most ample jurisdiction in every respect. It possesses, in this view, all the authority which any State Legislature possesses over its own Territory ; and if any State Legislature may, in its discretion, abolish or prohibit Slavery within its own limits, in virtue of its general Legislative authority, for the same reason Congress also may exercise the like authority over its own Territories. And that a State Legislature, unless restrained by some Constitutional provision, may so do, is unquestionable, and has been established by general practice. . . . .

If the constitutional power of Congress to make the proposed prohibition be satisfactorily shown, the justice and policy of such prohibition seem to the undersigned to be supported by plain and strong reasons. The permission of Slavery in a new State, necessarily draws after it an extension of that inequality of representation, which already exists in regard to the original States. It cannot be expected that those of the original States, which do not hold slaves, can look on such an extension as being politically just. As between the original States the representation rests on compact and plighted faith ; and your memorialists have no wish that that compact should be disturbed, or that plighted faith in the slightest degree violated. But the subject assumes an entirely different character, when a new State proposes to be admitted. With her there is no compact, and no faith plighted ; and where is the reason that she could come into the Union with more than an equal share of political importance and political power? Already the ratio of representation, established by the Constitution, has given to the States holding slaves twenty members of the House of Representatives more than they would have been entitled to, except under the particular provision of the Constitution. In all probability, this number will be doubled in thirty years. Under these circumstances, we deem it not an unreasonable expectation that the inhabitants of Missouri should propose to come into the Union, renouncing the right in question, and establishing a Constitution prohibiting it forever. Without dwelling on this topic, we have still thought it our duty to present it to the consideration of Congress. We present it with a deep and earnest feeling of its importance, and we respectfully solicit for it the full consideration of the National Legislature.

Your memorialists were not without the hope that the time had at length arrived when the inconvenience and the danger of this description of population had become apparent in all parts of this country and in all parts of the civilized world. It might have been hoped that the new States themselves would have had such a view of their own permanent interests and prosperity as would have led them to prohibit its extension and increase. The wonderful increase and prosperity of the States north of the Ohio is unquestionably to be ascribed, in a great measure, to the consequences of the ordinance of 787 and few ndeed, are the occasions, in the history of nations, which so much can be done, by a single act, for the benefit of future generations, as was done by that ordinance, and as may now be done by the Congress of the United States. We appeal to the justice and to the wisdom of the National Councils to prevent the further progress of a great and serious evil. We appeal to those who look forward to the remote consequences of their measures, and who cannot balance a temporary or trifling inconvenience, if there were such, against a permanent, growing, and desolating evil. We cannot forbear to remind the two Houses of Congress that the early and decisive measures adopted by the American Government for the abolition of the slave-trade, are among the proudest memorials of our nation's glory. That Slavery was ever tolerated in the Republic is, as yet, to be attributed to the policy of another Government. No imputation, thus far, rests on

any portion of the American Confederacy. The Missouri Territory is a new country. If its extensive and fertile field shall be opened as a market for slaves, the Government will seem to become a party to a traffic which, in so many acts, through so many years, it has denounced as impolitic, unchristian, inhuman. To enact laws to punish the traffic, and, at the same time, to tempt cupidity and avarice by the allurements of an insatiable market, is inconsistent and irreconcilable. Government, by such a course, would only defeat its own purposes, and render nugatory its own measures. Nor can the laws derive support from the manners of the people, if the power of moral sentiment be weakened by enjoying, under the permission of Government, great facilities to commit offenses. The laws of the United States have denounced heavy penalties against the traffic in slaves, because such traffic is deemed unjust and inhuman. We appeal to the spirit of these laws. We appeal to this justice and humanity. We ask her whether they ought not to operate, on the present occasion, with all their force? We have a strong feeling of the injustice of any toleration of Slavery. Circumstances have entailed it on a portion of our community, which cannot be immediately relieved from it without consequences more injurious than the suffering of the evil. But to permit it in a new country, where yet no habits are formed which render it indispensable, what is it, but to encourage that rapacity, and fraud and violence, against which we have so long pointed the denunciations of our penal code? What is it, but to tarnish the proud fame of the country? What is it, but to throw suspicion on its good faith, and to render questionable all its professions of regard for the rights of humanity and the liberties of mankind?

As inhabitants of a free country—as citizens of a great and rising Republic—as members of a Christian community—as living in a liberal and enlightened age, and as feeling ourselves called upon by the dictates of religion and humanity, we have presumed to offer our sentiments to Congress on this question, with a solicitude for the event far beyond what a common occasion could inspire."

Instead of reprinting the Speeches elicited by this fruitful theme, which must necessarily, to a great extent, be a mere reproduction of ideas expressed in the debate of the last session, already given, we here insert the Resolves of the Legislatures of New-York, New-Jersey, Pennsylvania, Delaware and Kentucky—the first three being unanimous expressions in favor of Slavery Restriction ; the fourth, from a Slave State, also in favor of such Restriction, though probably not unanimously agreed to by the Legislature ; the last against Restriction, and also (we presume) unanimous. The Legislatures of the Free States were generally unanimous for Restriction ; those of the Slave States (Delaware excepted) against it. It is not deemed necessary to print more than the following :

NEW-YORK.

State of New-York, in Assembly, Jan. 17, 1820 :

Whereas, The inhibiting the further extension of Slavery in these United States is a subject of deep concern among the people of this State ; and whereas we consider Slavery as an evil much to be deplored ; and that every constitutional barrier should be interposed to prevent its further extension ; and that the Constitution of the United States clearly gives Congress the right to require of new States, not comprised within the original boundaries of these United States, the prohibition of Slavery, as a condition of its admission into the Union : Therefore,

Resolved (if the honorable the Senate concur herein), That our Senators be instructed, and our Representatives in Congress be requested, to oppose the admission as a State into the Union, any territory not comprised as aforesaid, without making the prohibition of Slavery therein an indispensable condition of admission ; therefore,

Resolved, That measures be taken by the clerks of the Senate and Assembly of this State, to transmit copies of the preceding resolutions to each of our Senators and Representatives in Congress.

(Unanimously concurred in by the Senate.)

NEW-JERSEY.

HOUSE OF REPRESENTATIVES, }
January 24th, 1820. }

Mr. Wilson, of N. J., communicated the following Resolutions of the Legislature of the State of New-Jersey, which were read:

Whereas, A Bill is now depending in the Congress of the United States, on the application of the people in the Territory of Missouri for the admission of that Territory as a State into the Union, not containing provisions against Slavery in such proposed State, and a question is made upon the right and expediency of such provision,

The representatives of the people of New-Jersey, in Legislative Council and General Assembly of the said State, now in session, deem it a duty they owe to themselves, to their constituents, and posterity, to declare and make known the opinions they hold upon this momentous subject; and,

1. *They do resolve and declare,* That the further admission of Territories into the Union, without restriction of Slavery, would, in their opinion, essentially impair the right of this and other existing States to equal representation in Congress (a right at the foundation of the political compact), inasmuch as such newly-admitted slaveholding States would be represented on the basis of their slave population; a concession made at the formation of the Constitution in favor of the then existing States, but never stipulated for new States, nor to be inferred from any article or clause in that instrument.

2. *Resolved,* That to admit the Territory of Missouri as a State into the Union, without prohibiting Slavery there, would, in the opinion of the representatives of the people of New-Jersey aforesaid, be no less than to sanction this great political and moral evil, furnish the ready means of peopling a vast Territory with slaves, and perpetuate all the dangers, crimes, and pernicious effects of domestic bondage.

3. *Resolved,* As the opinion of the Representatives aforesaid, That inasmuch as no Territory has a right to be admitted into the Union, but on the principles of the Federal Constitution, and only by a law of Congress, consenting thereto on the part of the existing States, Congress may rightfully, and ought to refuse such law, unless upon the reasonable and just conditions, assented to on the part of the people applying to become one of the States.

4. *Resolved,* In the opinion of the Representatives aforesaid, That the article of the Constitution which restrains Congress from prohibiting the migration or importation of slaves, until after the year 1808, does, by necessary implication, admit the general power of Congress over the subject of Slavery, and concedes to them the right to regulate and restrain such migration and importation after that time, into the ex sting, or any newly-to-be-created State.

5. *Resolved,* As the opinion of the Representatives of the people of New-Jersey aforesaid, That inasmuch as Congress have a clear right to refuse the admission of a Territory into the Union, by the terms of the Constitution, they ought, in the present case, to exercise that absolute discretion in order to preserve the political rights of the several existing States, and prevent the great national disgrace and multiplied mischiefs, which must ensue from conceding it, as a matter of right, in the immense Territories yet to claim admission into the Union beyond the Mississippi, that they may tolerate Slavery.

6. *Resolved,* (with the concurrence of Council,) That the Governor of this State be requested to transmit a copy of the foregoing resolutions to each of the Senators and Representatives of this State in the Congress of the United States.

PENNSYLVANIA.

HOUSE OF REPRESENTATIVES, }
December 11th, 1819. }

A motion was made by Mr. Duane and Mr. Thackara, and read as follows:

The Senate and House of Representatives of the Commonwealth of Pennsylvania, while they cherish the right of the individual States to express their opinion upon all public measures proposed in the Congress of the Union, are aware that its usefulness must in a great degree depend upon the discretion with which it is exercised; they believe that the right ought not to be resorted to upon trivial subjects or unimportant occasions; but they are also persuaded that there are moments when the neglect to exercise it would be a dereliction of public duty.

Such an occasion, as in their judgment demands the frank expression of the sentiments of Pennsylvania, is now presented. A measure was ardently supported in the last Congress of the United States, and will probably be as earnestly urged during the existing session of that body, which has a palpable tendency to impair the political relations of the several States; which is calculated to mar the social happiness of the present and future generations; which, if adopted, would impede the march of humanity and Freedom through the world; and would transfer from a misguided ancestry an odious stain and fix it indelibly upon the present race—a measure, in brief, which proposes to spread the crimes and cruelties of Slavery from the banks of the Mississippi to the shores of the Pacific. When a measure of this character is seriously advocated in the republican Congress of America, in the nineteenth century, the several States are invoked by the duty which they owe to the Deity, by the veneration which they entertain for the memory of the founders of the Republic, and by a tender regard for posterity, to protest against its adoption, to refuse to covenant with crime, and to limit the range of an evil that already hangs in awful boding over so large a portion of the Union.

Nor can such a protest be entered by any State with greater propriety than by Pennsylvania. This Commonwealth has as sacredly respected the rights of other States as it has been careful of its own; it has been the invariable aim of the people of Pennsylvania to extend to the universe, by their example, the unadulterated blessings of civil and religious freedom; and it is their pride that they have been at all times the practical advocates of those improvements and charities among men which are so well calculated to enable them to answer the purposes of their Creator; and above all, they may boast that they were foremost in removing the pollution of Slavery from among them.

If, indeed, the measure, against which Pennsylvania considers it her duty to raise her voice, were calculated to abridge any of the rights guaranteed to the several States; if, odious as Slavery is, it was proposed to hasten its extinction by means injurious to the States upon which it was unhappily entailed, Pennsylvania would be among the first to insist upon a sacred observance of the Constitutional compact. But it cannot be pretended that the rights of any of the States are at all to be affected by refusing to extend the mischiefs of human bondage over the boundless regions of the West, a Territory which formed no part of the Union at the adoption of the Constitution; which has been but lately purchased from a European Power by the people of the Union at large; which may or may not be admitted as a State into the Union at the discretion of Congress; which must establish a Republican form of Government, and no other; and whose climate affords none of the pretexts urged for resorting to the labor of natives of the torrid zone; such a Territory has no right, inherent or acquired, such as those States possessed which established the existing Constitution. When that Constitution was framed in September, 1787, the concession that three-fifths of the slaves in the States then existing should be represented in Congress, could not have been intended to embrace regions at that time held by a foreign power. On the contrary, so anxious were the Congress of that day to confine human bondage within its ancient home, that on the 13th of July, 1787, that body unanimously declared that Slavery or involuntary servitude should not exist in the extensive Territories bounded by the Ohio, the Mississippi, Canada and the Lakes; and in the ninth article of the Constitution itself, the power of Congress to prohibit the emigration of servile persons after 1808, is expressly recognized; nor is there to be found in the statute-book a single instance of the admission of a Territory to the rank of a State, in which Congress have not adhered to the right, vested in them by the Constitution, to stipulate with the Territory upon the conditions of the boon.

The Senate and House of Representatives of Pennsylvania, therefore, cannot but deprecate any departure from the humane and enlightened policy pursued not only by the illustrious Congress which framed the Constitution, but by their successors without exception. They are persuaded that, to open the fertile regions of the West to a servile race, would tend to increase their numbers beyond all past example, would open a new and steady market for the lawless venders of human flesh, and would render all schemes for obliterating this most foul blot upon the American character, useless and unavailing.

Under these convictions, and in the full persuasion that upon this topic there is but one opinion in Pennsylvania—

"*Resolved by the Senate and House of Representatives of the Commonwealth of Pennsylvania,* That the Senators of this State in the Congress of the United States be, and they are hereby instructed, and that the Representatives of this State in the Congress of the United States be, and they are hereby requested, to vote against the admission of any Territory as a State into the Union, unless said Territory shall stipulate and agree that " the further introduction of **Slavery** or involuntary servitude, except for the punishment of crimes whereof the party shall have been duly convicted, shall be prohibited ; and that all children born within the said Territory, after its admission into the Union as a State, shall be free, but may be held to service until the age of twenty-five years "

Resolved, That the Governor be, and he is hereby, requested to cause a copy of the foregoing preamble and resolution to be transmitted to each of the Senators and Representatives of this State in the Congress of the United States.

Laid on the table.

THURSDAY, December 16, 1819.

Agreeably to the order of the day, the House resumed the consideration of the resolutions postponed on the 14th inst., relative to preventing the introduction of Slavery into States hereafter to be admitted into the Union. And on the question, " Will the House agree to the resolution?" the Yeas and Nays were required by Mr. Randall and Mr. Souder, and stood—Yeas 74—(54 Democrats, 20 Federalists) ; Nays *none.* Among the Yeas were David R Porter, late Governor. Josiah Randall of Philadelphia, late Whig, now a leading Democrat, William Wilkins, late minister to Russia, since in the State Senate, Dr. Daniel Sturgeon, late U. S. Senator, etc., etc. William Duane, editor of *The Aurora,* then the Democratic organ, also voted for the resolutions, as he had prominently advocated the principle they asserted.

The Senate unanimously concurred, and the Resolves were signed by Gov. William Findlay.

DELAWARE.

In Senate of the United States, early in 1820, Mr. Van Dyke communicated the following Resolutions of the Legislature of the State of Delaware, which were read :

Resolved, by the Senate and House of Representatives of the State of Delaware, in General Assembly met: That it is, in the opinion of this General Assembly, the constitutional right of the United States, in Congress assembled, to enact and establish, as one of the conditions for the admission of a new State into the Union, a provision which shall effectually prevent the further introduction of Slavery into such State ; and that a due regard to the true interests of such State, as well as of the other States, require that the same should be done.

Resolved, That a copy of the above and foregoing resolution be transmitted, by the Speaker of the Senate, to each of the Senators and Representatives from this State in the Congress of the United States.

KENTUCKY.

In Senate, January 24th, 1820, Mr. Logan communicated the following preamble and Resolutions of the Legislature of the State of Kentucky, which were read :

Whereas, The Constitution of the United States provides for the admission of new States into the Union, and it is just and proper that all such States should be established upon the footing of original States, with a view to the preservation of State Sovereignty, the prosperity of such new State, and the good of their citizens ; *and whereas,* successful attempts have been heretofore made, and are now making, to prevent the People of the Territory of Missouri from being admitted into the Union as a State, unless trammeled by rules and regulations which do not exist in the original States, particularly in relation to the toleration of Slavery.

Whereas, also, if Congress can thus trammel or control the powers of a Territory in the formation of a State government, that body may, on the same principle, reduce its powers to little more than those possessed by the people of the District of Columbia, and whilst professing to make it a Sovereign State, may bind it in perpetual vassalage, and reduce it to the condition of a province ; such State must necessarily become the dependent of Congress, asking such powers, and not the independent State, demanding rights. *And whereas,* it is necessary, in preserving the State Sovereignties in their present rights, that no new State should be subjected to this restriction, any more than an old one, and that there can be no reason or justice why it should not be entitled to the same privileges, when it is bound to bear all the burdens and taxes laid upon it by Congress.

In passing the following resolution, the General Assembly refrains from expressing any opinion either in favor or against the principles of Slavery ; but to support and maintain State rights, which it conceives necessary to be supported and maintained, to preserve the liberties of the free people of these United States, it avows its solemn conviction, that the States already confederated under one common Constitution, have not a right to deprive new States of equal privileges with themselves. Therefore,

Resolved, by the General Assembly of the Commonwealth of Kentucky, That the Senators in Congress from this State be instructed, and the Representatives be requested, to use their efforts to procure the passage of a law to admit the people of Missouri into the Union, as a State, whether those people will sanction Slavery by their Constitution or not.

Resolved, That the Executive of this Commonwealth be requested to transmit this Resolution to the Senators and Representatives of this State in Congress, that it may be laid before that body for its consideration.

The bill authorizing Missouri to form a constitution, etc., came up in the House as a special order, Jan. 24th. Mr. Taylor, of N. Y., moved that it be postponed for one week : Lost : Yeas 87 ; Nays 88. Whereupon the House adjourned. It was considered in committee the next day, as also on the 28th and 30th, and thence debated daily until the 19th of February, when a bill came down from the Senate " to admit the State of *Maine* into the Union," but with a rider authorizing the people of Missouri to form a State Constitution, etc., without restriction on the subject of Slavery.

The House, very early in the session, passed a bill providing for the admission of Maine as a State. This bill came to the Senate, and was sent to its Judiciary Committee aforesaid, which amended it by adding a provision for Missouri as above. After several days' debate in Senate, Mr. Roberts, of Pa., moved to recommit, so as to strike out all but the admission of Maine ; which was defeated (Jan. 14th, 1820)—Yeas 18 ; Nays 25. Hereupon Mr. Thomas, of Ill., (who voted with the majority, as uniformly against any restriction on Missouri) gave notice that he should

" ask leave to bring a bill to prohibit the introduction of Slavery into *the Territories of the United States North and West of the* contemplated *State of Missouri ;*"

—which he accordingly did on the 19th ; when it was read and ordered to a third reading.

[NOTE.—Great confusion and misconception exists in the public mind with regard to the " Missouri Restriction," two totally different propositions being called by that name. The *original* Restriction, which Mr. Clay vehemently opposed, and Mr. Jefferson in a letter characterized as a " fire-bell in the night," contemplated the limitation of Slavery in its exclusion from the *State of Missouri.* This was ultimately defeated, as we shall see. The *second* proposed Restriction was that of Mr. Thomas, just cited, which proposed the exclusion of Slavery, not from the State of Missouri, but *from the Territories of the United States North and West of that State.* This proposition did not emanate from the original Missouri Restrictionists, but from their adversaries, and was but reluctantly and partially accepted by the former.]

The Maine admission bill, with the proposed amendments, was discussed through several days, until, Feb. 16th, the question was taken on the Judiciary Committee's amendments (authorizing Missouri to form a State Constitution, and saying nothing of Slavery), which were adopted by the following vote:

Yeas—Against the Restriction on Missouri, 23.

[20 from Slave States ; 3 from Free States.]

Nays—For Restriction, 21.

[19 from Free States ; 2 from Delaware.]

Mr. Thomas, of Ill., then proposed his amendment, which, on the following day, he withdrew and substituted the following:

And be it further enacted, That in all that Territory ceded by France to the United States under the name of Louisiana which lies north of thirty-six degrees thirty minutes north latitude, excepting only such part thereof as is included within the limits of the State contemplated by this act, Slavery and involuntary servitude, otherwise than in the punishment of crime whereof the party shall have been duly convicted, shall be and is hereby forever prohibited. *Provided always*, that any person escaping into the same, from where labor or service is lawfully claimed in any State or Territory of the United States, such fugitive may be lawfully reclaimed and conveyed to the person claiming his or her labor or service as aforesaid.

Mr. Trimble, of Ohio, moved a substitute for this, somewhat altering the boundaries of the regions shielded from Slavery, which was rejected: Yeas 20 (Northern); Nays 24 (Southern).

The question then recurred on Mr. Thomas's amendment, which was adopted, as follows:

Yeas—For excluding Slavery from all the Territory North and West of Missouri:

Messrs. Brown of La.,	Mellen of Mass.,
Burrill of R. I.,	Morrill of N. H.,
Dana of Conn.,	Otis of Mass.,
Dickerson of N. J.,	Palmer of Vt.,
Eaton of Tenn.,	Parrott of N. H.,
Edwards of Ill.,	Pinkney of Md.,
Horsey of Del.,	Roberts of Pa.,
Hunter of R. I.,	Ruggles of Ohio,
Johnson of Ky.,	Sanford of N. Y.,
Johnson of La..	Stokes of N. C.,
King (Wm. R.) of Ala.,	Thomas of Ill.,
King (Rufus) of N. Y.,	Tichenor of Vt.,
Lanman of Conn.,	Trimble of Ohio,
Leake of Miss.,	Van Dyke of Del.,
Lowrie of Pa.,	Walker of Ala.,
Lloyd of Md.,	Williams of Tenn.,
Logan of Ky.,	Wilson of N. J.—34.

Nays—Against such Restriction:

Messrs. Barbour of Va.,	Pleasants of Va..
Elliott of Ga.,	Smith (Wm.) of S. C..
Gaillard of S. C.,	Taylor of Ind.,
Macon of N. C.,	Walker of Ga.,
Noble of Ind.,	Williams of Miss.—10.

[It will here be seen that the Restriction ultimately adopted—that excluding Slavery from all territory then owned by the United States North and West of the Southwest border of the State of Missouri—was proposed by an early and steadfast opponent of the Restriction originally proposed, relative to Slavery in the contemplated State of Missouri, and was sustained by the votes of fourteen Senators from Slave States, including the Senators from Delaware, Maryland, Kentucky, Tennessee, Alabama, and Louisiana, with one vote each from North Carolina and Mississippi.

The current assumption that this Restriction was proposed by Rufus King, of New-York, and mainly sustained by the antagonists of Slavery Extension, is wholly mistaken. The truth, doubtless, is, that it was suggested by the more moderate opponents of the proposed Restriction on Missouri—and supported also by Senators from Slave States—as a means of overcoming the resistance of the House to Slavery in Missouri. It was, in effect, an offer from the milder opponents of Slavery Restriction to the more moderate and flexible advocates of that Restriction—" Let us have Slavery in Missouri, and we will unite with you in excluding it from all the uninhabited territories North and West of that State." It was in substance an agreement between the North and the South to that

effect, though the more determined champions, whether of Slavery Extension or Slavery Restriction, did not unite in it.]

The bill, thus amended, was ordered to be engrossed for a third reading by the following vote:

Yeas—For the Missouri Bill:

Messrs. Barbour of Va.,	Lloyd of Md.,
Brown of La.,	Logan of Ky.,
Eaton of Tenn.,	Parrott of N. H.,
Edwards of Ill.,	Pinkney of Md.,
Elliott of Ga.,	Pleasants of Va.,
Gaillard of S. C.,	Stokes of N. C..
Horsey of Del.,	Thomas of Ill.,
Hunter of R. I.,	Van Dyke of Del.,
Johnson of Ky.,	Walker of Ala.,
Johnson of La.,	Walker of Ga.,
King of Ala.,	Williams of Miss.,
Leake of Miss.,	Williams of Tenn—24.

Nays—Against the Bill:

Messrs. Burrill of R. I.,	Otis of Mass.,
Dana of Conn.,	Palmer of Vt.,
Dickerson of N. J.,	Roberts of Pa.,
King of N. Y.,	Ruggles of Ohio,
Lanman of Conn.,	Sanford of N. Y.,
Lowrie of Pa.,	Smith of S. C.,
Macon of N. C.,	Taylor of Ind.,
Mellen of Mass.,	Tichenor of Vt.,
Morrill of N. H.,	Trimble of Ohio.,
Noble of Ind.,	Wilson of N. J.—20.

The bill was thus passed (Feb. 18th) without further division, and sent to the House for concurrence. In the House, Mr. Thomas's amendment (as above) was at first rejected by both parties, and defeated by the strong vote of 159 to 18. The Yeas (to adopt) were,

Messrs. Baldwin of Pa.,	Meech, of Vt.,
Bayly of Md.,	Mercer of Va.,
Bloomfield of N. J.,	Quarles of Ky.,
Cocke of Tenn.,	Ringgold of Md.
Crafts of Vt.,	Shaw of Mass.,
Culpepper of N. C.,	Sloan of Ohio ,
Kinsey of N. J.,	Smith of N. J.,
Lathrop of Mass.,	Smith of Md.,
Little of Md.,	Tarr of Pa-—18.

Prior to this vote, the House disagreed to the log-rolling of Maine and Missouri, into one bill by the strong vote of 93 to 72. [We do not give the Yeas and Nays on this decision; but the majority was composed of the representatives of the Free States with only four exceptions; and Mr. Louis McLane of Delaware, who was constrained by instructions from his legislature. His colleague, Mr. Willard Hall, did not vote.]

The members from Free States who voted with the South to keep Maine and Missouri united in one bill were,

Messrs. H. Baldwin of Pa.,	Henry Meigs of N. Y.,
Bloomfield of N. J.,	Henry Shaw of Mass.,

The House also disagreed to the remaining amendments of the Senate (striking out the restriction on Slavery in Missouri) by the strong vote of 102 Yeas to 68 Nays.

[Nearly or quite every Representative of a Free State voted in the majority on this division, with the following from Slave States:

Louis McLane, Del.,	Nelson, Md.,
Alney McLean, Ky.	Trimble, Ky.]

So the House rejected all the Senate's amendments, and returned the bill with a corresponding message.

The Senate took up the bill on the 24th, and debated it till the 28th; when, on a direct vote, it was decided *not* to recede from the attachment of Missouri to the Maine bill: Yeas 21; (19 from Free States and two from Delaware;)

Nays, 23; (20 from Slave States with Messrs. Taylor of Ind., Edwards and Thomas of Ill.)

The Senate also voted not to recede from its amendment prohibiting Slavery west of Missouri, and north of 36° 30', north latitude. (For receding, 9 from Slave States, with Messrs. Noble and Taylor of Ind. : against it, 33—(22 from Slave States, 11 from Free States.) The remaining amendments of the Senate were then insisted on without division, and the House notified accordingly.

The bill was now returned to the House, which, on motion of Mr. John W. Taylor of N. Y., voted to insist on its disagreement to all but Sec. 9 of the Senate's amendments, by Yeas 97 to Nays 76: (all but a purely sectional vote: Hugh Nelson of Va. voting with the North; Baldwin of Pa., Bloomfield of N. J., and Shaw of Mass., voting with the South).

Sec. 9, (the Senate's exclusion of Slavery from the Territory north and west of Missouri) was also rejected—Yeas 160 ; Nays, 14, (much as before). The Senate thereupon (March 2nd) passed the House's Missouri bill, striking out the restriction of Slavery by Yeas 27 to Nays 15, and adding without a division the exclusion of Slavery from the territory west and north of said State. Mr. Trimble again moved the exclusion of Slavery from Arkansas also, but was again voted down, Yeas, 12 ; Nays, 30.

The Senate now asked a conference, which the House granted without a division. The Committee of Conference was composed of Messrs. Thomas of Illinois, Pinkney of Maryland, and Barbour of Va. (all anti-restrictionists), on the part of the Senate, and Messrs. Holmes of Mass., Taylor of N. Y., Lowndes of S. C., Parker of Mass., and Kinsey of N. J., on the part of the House. (Such constitution of the Committee of Conference was in effect a surrender of the Restriction on the part of the House.) John Holmes of Mass., from this Committee, in due time (March 2nd), reported that,

1. The Senate should give up the combination of Missouri in the same bill with Maine.

2. The House should abandon the attempt to restrict Slavery in Missouri.

3. Both Houses should agree to pass the Senate's separate Missouri bill, with Mr. Thomas's restriction or compromising proviso, excluding Slavery from all Territory north and west of Missouri.

The report having been read, the first and most importan questi as put, viz

Will the House concur with the Senate in so much of the said amendments as proposes to strike from the fourth section of the (Missouri) bill the provision prohibiting Slavery or involuntary servitude, in the contemplated State, otherwise than in the punishment of crimes ?

On which question the Yeas and Nays were demanded, and were as follows :

YEAS—*For giving up Restrictions on Missouri :*

MASSACHUSETTS.—Mark Langdon Hill, John Holmes, Jonathan Mason, Henry Shaw—4.
RHODE ISLAND.—Samuel Eddy—1.
CONNECTICUT.—Samuel A. Foot, James Stephens—2.
NEW-YORK.—Henry Meigs, Henry R. Storrs—2.
NEW-JERSEY—Joseph Bloomfield, Charles Kinsey, Bernard Smith—3.
PENNSYLVANIA.—Henry Baldwin, David Fullerton—2.
Total from Free-States 14.

DELAWARE.—Louis McLane—1.
MARYLAND.—Stephenson Archer, Thomas Bayly, Thomas Culbreth, Joseph Kent, Peter Little, Raphael Neale, Samuel Ringgold, Samuel Smith, Henry R. Warfield—9.
VIRGINIA.—Mark Alexander, William S. Archer, Philip P. Barbour, William A. Burwell, John Floyd, Robert S. Garnett, James Johnson, James Jones, William McCoy, Charles F. Mercer, Hugh Nelson, Thomas Nelson, Severn E. Parker, Jas. Pindall, John Randolph, Ballard Smith, Alexander Smyth, George F. Strother, Thomas Van Swearingen, George Tucker, John Tyler, Jared Williams—22.
NORTH CAROLINA.—Hutchins G. Burton, John Culpepper, William Davidson, Weldon N. Edwards, Charles Fisher, Thomas H. Hall, Charles Hooks, Thomas Settle, Jesse Slocumb, James S. Smith, Felix Walker, Lewis Williams—12.
SOUTH CAROLINA.—Josiah Brevard, Elias Earle, James Erwin, William Lowndes, James McCreary, James Overstreet, Charles Pinckney, Eldred Simkins, Sterling Tucker—9.
GEORGIA.—Joel A. Abbot, Thomas W. Cobb. Joel Crawford, John A. Cuthbert, Robert R. Reid, William Terrill—6.
ALABAMA.—John Crowell—1.
MISSISSIPPI.—John Rankin—1.
LOUISIANA.—Thomas Butler—1.
KENTUCKY—Richard C. Anderson, jr., William Brown, Benjamin Hardin, Alney McLean, Thomas Metcalf, Tunstall Quarles, Geo. Robertson, David Trimble—8.
TENNESSEE.—Robert Allen, Henry H. Bryan, Newton Cannon, John Cocke, Francis Jones, John Rhea—5.

Total Yeas from Slave States, 76 ; in all 90.

NAYS—*Against giving up the Restriction on Slavery in Missouri :*

NEW-HAMPSHIRE.—Joseph Buffum, jr., Josiah Butler, Clifton Clagett, Arthur Livermore, William Plumer, jr., Nathaniel Upham—6.
MASSACHUSETTS (including Maine).—Benjamin Adams, Samuel C. Allen, Joshua Cushman, Edward Dowse, Walter Folger, jr., Timothy Fuller, Jonas Kendall, Martin Kinsley, Samuel Lathrop, Enoch Lincoln, Marcus Morton, Jeremiah Nelson, James Parker, Zabdiel Sampson, Nathaniel Silsbee, Ezekiel Whitman—16.
RHODE ISLAND.—Nathaniel Hazard—1.
CONNECTICUT.—Jonathan O. Moseley, Elisha Phelps, John Russ. Gideon Tomlinson—4.
VERMONT.—Samuel C. Crafts, Rollin C. Mallary, Ezra Meech, Charles Rich, Mark Richards, William Strong—6.
NEW-YORK.—Nathaniel Allen, Caleb Baker, Robert Clark, Jacob H. De Witt, John D. Dickinson, John Fay, William D. Ford, Ezra C. Gross, James Guyon, jr., Aaron Hackley, jr., George Hall, Joseph S. Lyman, Robert Monell, Nathaniel Pitcher, Jonathan Richmond, Randall S. Street, James Strong, John W. Taylor, Albert H. Tracy, Solomon Van Rensselear, Peter H. Wendover, Silas Wood—22.
NEW-JERSEY.—Ephraim Bateman, John Linn, Henry Southard—3.
PENNSYLVANIA.—Andrew Boden, William Darlington, George Dennison, Samuel Edwards, Thomas Forrest, Samuel Gross, Joseph Hemphill, Jacob Hibschman, Joseph Heister, Jacob Hostetter, William P. Maclay, David Marchand, Robert Moore, Samuel Moore, John Murray, Thomas Patterson, Robert Philson, Thomas J. Rogers, John Sergeant, Christian Tarr, James M. Wallace—21.
OHIO.—Philemon Beecher, Henry Brush, John W. Campbell, Samuel Herrick, Thomas R. Ross, John Sloane—6.
INDIANA.—William Hendricks—1.
ILLINOIS.—Daniel P. Cook—1.

Total, Nays, 87—all from Free States.

(The members apparently absent on this important division, were Henry W. Edwards of Conn., Walter Case and Honorius Peck of N. Y. and John Condit of N. J., from the Free States; with Lemuel Sawyer of N. C., and David Walker of Ky., from the Slave States. Mr. Clay of Ky., being Speaker, did not vote.)

This defeat broke the back of the Northern resistance to receiving Missouri as a Slave State.

Mr. Taylor, of N. Y., now moved an amendment, intended to include Arkansas Territory ender the proposed Inhibition of Slavery west of Missouri ; but this motion was cut off by the Previous Question, (which then cut off amendments more rigorously, according to the rules of the House, than it now does), and the House proceeded to concur with the Senate in inserting the exclusion of Slavery from the territory west and north of Missouri, instead of that just stricken out by, 134 Yeas to 42 Nays, (the Nays being from the South).   So the bill was *passed* in the form indicated above ; and the bill admitting Maine as a State, (relieved, by a conference, from the Missouri rider,) passed both Houses without a divison, on the following day.

Such was the virtual termination of the struggle for the restriction of Slavery in Missouri, which was beaten by the plan of proffering instead an exclusion of Slavery from all the then federal territory west and north of that State. It is unquestionable that, without this compromise or equivalent, the Northern votes, which passed the bill, could not have been obtained for it.

THE THIRD MISSOURI STRUGGLE.

Though the acceptance of Missouri as a State, with a Slave Constitution, was forever settled by the votes just recorded, a new excitement sprang up on her presenting herself to Congress (Nov. 16, 1820),) with a State Constitution, framed on the 19th of July, containing the following resolutions :

The General Assembly shall have no power to pass laws, First, for the emancipation of slaves without the consent of their owners, or without paying them, before such emancipation, a full equivalent for such slaves so emancipated ; and, Second, to prevent *bona fide* emigrants to this State, or actual settlers therein, from bringing from any of the United States, or from any of their Territories, such persons as may there be deemed to be slaves, so long as any persons of the same description are allowed to be held as slaves by the laws of this State. . . . It shall be their duty, as soon as may be, to pass such laws as may be necessary,

First, to prevent free negroes and mulattoes from coming to, and settling in, this State, under any pretext whatever.

The North, still smarting under a sense of its defeat on the question of excluding Slavery from Missouri, regarded this as needlessly defiant, insulting, and inhuman, and the section last quoted as palpably in violation of that clause of the Federal Constitution which gives to the citizens of each State (which blacks are, in several Free States), the rights of citizens in every State.   A determined resistance to any such exclusion was manifested, and a portion of the Northern Members evinced a disposition to renew the struggle against the further introduction of slaves into Missouri.   At the first effort to carry her admission, the House voted it down—Yeas, 79 ; Nays, 93.   A second attempt to admit her, on condition that she would expunge the obnoxious clause (last quoted) of her Constitution, was voted down still more decisively—Yeas, 6 ; Nays 146.

The House now rested, until a joint resolve, admitting her with but a vague and ineffective qualification, came down from the Senate, where it was passed by a vote of 26 to 18—six Senators from Free States in the affirmative.   Mr. Clay, who had resigned in the recess, and been succeeded, as Speaker, by John W. Taylor, of New-York, now appeared as the leader of the Missouri admissionists, and proposed terms of

compromise, which were twice voted down by the Northern members, aided by John Randolph and three others from the South, who would have Missouri admitted without condition or qualification.   At last, Mr. Clay proposed a Joint Committee on this subject, to be chosen by ballot—which the House agreed to by 101 to 55 ; and Mr. Clay became its Chairman.   By this Committee, it was agreed that a solemn pledge should be required of the Legislature of Missouri that the Constitution of that State should not be construed to authorize the passage of any Act, and that no Act should be passed, " by which any of the citizens of either of the States should be excluded from the enjoyment of the privileges and immunities to which they are entitled under the Constitution of the United States."   The Joint Resolution, amended by the addition of this proviso, passed the House by 86 Yeas to 82 Nays ; the Senate concurred (Feb. 27th, 1821,) by 26 Yeas to 15 Nays—(all Northern but Macon, of N. C.) ;   Missouri complied with the condition, and became an accepted member of the Union.   Thus closed the last stage of the fierce Missouri Controversy, which for a time seemed to threaten—as so many other controversies have harmlessly threatened —the existence of the Union.

EXTENSION OF MISSOURI.

The State of Missouri, as originally organized, was bounded on the west by a line already specified, which excluded a triangle west of said line, and between it and the Missouri, which was found, in time, to be exceedingly fertile and desirable.   It was free soil by the terms of the Missouri compact, and was also covered by Indian reservations, not to be removed without a concurrence of two-thirds of the Senate.   Messrs. Benton and Linn, Senators from Missouri, undertook the difficult task of engineering through Congress a bill including this triangle (large enough to form seven Counties) within the State of Missouri ; which they effected, at the long session of 1835-6, so quietly as hardly to attract attention.   The bill was first sent to the Senate's Committee on the Judiciary, where a favorable report was procured from Mr. John M. Clayton, of Delaware, its Chairman ; and then it was floated through both Houses without encountering the perils of a division.   The requisite Indian treaties were likewise carried through the Senate ; so Missouri became possessed of a large and desirable accession of territory, which has since become one of her most populous and wealthy sections, devoted to the growing of hemp, tobacco, etc., and cultivated by slaves.   This is the most pro-Slavery section of the State, in which was originated, and was principally sustained, that series of inroads into Kansas, corruptions of her ballot-boxes, and outrages upon her people, which earned for their authors the appellation of *Border Ruffians.*

THE ANNEXATION OF TEXAS.

The name of *Texas* was originally applied to a Spanish possession or province, lying between the Mississippi and the Rio Grande del Norte, but not extending to either of these great rivers. It was an appendage of the Viceroyalty of

Mexico, but had very few civilized inhabitants down to the time of the separation of Mexico from Spain. On two or three occasions, bands of French adventurers had landed on its coast, or entered it from the adjoining French colony of Louisiana; but they had uniformly been treated as intruders, and either destroyed or made prisoners by the Spanish military authorities. No line had ever been drawn between the two colonies; but the traditional line between them, south of the Red River, ran somewhat within the limits of the present State of Louisiana.

When Louisiana was transferred by France to the United States, without specification of boundaries, collisions of claims on this frontier was apprehended. General Wilkinson, commanding the United States troops, moved gradually to the west; the Spanish commandant in Texas likewise drew toward the frontier, until they stood opposite each other across what was then tacitly settled as the boundary between the the two countries. This was never afterward disregarded.

In 1819, Spain and the United States seemed on the verge of war. General Jackson had twice invaded Florida, on the assumption of complicity on the part of her rulers and people—first with our British, then with our savage enemies—and had finally overrun, and, in effect, annexed it to the Union. Spain, on the other hand, had preyed upon our commerce during the long wars in Europe, and honestly owed our merchants large sums for unjustifiable seizures and spoliations. A negotiation for the settlement of these differences was carried on at Washington, between John Quincy Adams, Mr. Monroe's Secretary of State, and Don Onis, the Spanish embassador, in the course of which Mr. Adams set up a claim, on the part of this country, to Texas as a natural geographical appendage not of Mexico, but of Louisiana. This claim, however, he eventually waived and relinquished, in consideration of a cession of Florida by Spain to this country—our government agreeing, on its part, to pay the claims of our merchants for spoliations. Texas remained, therefore, what it always had been—a department or province of Mexico, with a formal quit-claim thereto on the part of the United States.

The natural advantages of this region in time attracted the attention of American adventurers, and a small colony of Yankees was settled thereon, about 1819–20, by Moses Austin, of Connecticut. Other settlements followed. Originally, grants of land in Texas were prayed for, and obtained of the Mexican Government, on the assumption that the petitioners were Roman Catholics, persecuted in the United States because of their religion, and anxious to find a refuge in some Catholic country. Thus all the early emigrants to Texas went professedly as Catholics, no other religion being tolerated.

Slavery was abolished by Mexico soon after the consummation of her independence, when very few slaves were, or ever had been, in Texas. But, about 1834, some years after this event, a quiet, but very general, and evidently concerted, emigration, mainly from Tennessee and other southwestern States, began to concentrate itself in Texas. The emigrants carried rifles; many of them were accompanied by slaves; and it was well understood that they did not intend to become Mexicans, much less to relinquish their slaves. When Gen. Sam. Houston left Arkansas for Texas, in 1834–5, the Little Rock *Journal*, which announced his exodus and destination, significantly added: "*We shall, doubtless, hear of his raising his flag there shortly.*" That was a foregone conclusion.

Of course, the new settlers in Texas did not lack pretexts or provocations for such a step. Mexico was then much as she is now, misgoverned, turbulent, anarchical, and despotic. The overthrow of her Federal Constitution by Santa Anna was one reason assigned for the rebellion against her authority which broke out in Texas. In 1835, her independence was declared; in 1836, at the decisive battle of San Jacinto, it was, by the rout and capture of the Mexican dictator, secured. This triumph was won by emigrants from this country almost exclusively; scarcely half a dozen of the old Mexican inhabitants participating in the revolution. Santa Anna, while a prisoner, under restraint and apprehension, agreed to a peace on the basis of the independence of Texas—a covenant which he had no power, and probably no desire, to give effect to when restored to liberty. The Texans, pursuing their advantage, twice or thrice penetrated other Mexican provinces—Tamaulipas, Coahuila, etc.,—and waved their Lone-Star flag in defiance on the banks of the Rio Grande del Norte; which position, however, they were always compelled soon to abandon—once with severe loss. Their government, nevertheless, in reiterating their declaration of independence, claimed the Rio Grande as their western boundary, from its source to its mouth, including a large share of Tamaulipas, Coahuila, Durango, and by far the more important and populous portion of New Mexico. And it was with this claim, expressly set forth in the treaty, that President Tyler and his responsible advisers negotiated the first official project of annexation, which was submitted to the Senate, during the session of 1843–4, and rejected by a very decisive vote: only fifteen (mainly Southern) senators voting to confirm it. Col. Benton, and others, urged this aggressive claim of boundary, as affording abundant reason for the rejection of this treaty; but it is not known that the Slavery aspect of the case attracted especial attention in the Senate. The measure, however, had already been publicly eulogized by Gen. James Hamilton, of S. C., as calculated to "give a Gibraltar to the South," and had, on that ground, secured a very general and ardent popularity throughout the South-West. And, more than a year previously, several northern members of Congress had united in the following :

TO THE PEOPLE OF THE FREE STATES OF THE UNION,

We, the undersigned, in closing our duties to our constituents and our country as members of the 27th Congress, feel bound to call your attention, very briefly, to the project, long entertained by a portion of the people of these United States, still pertinaciously adhered to, and intended soon to be consummated: THE ANNEXATION OF TEXAS TO THIS UNION. In the press of business incident to the last days of a session of Congress, we have not time, did we deem it necessary, to enter upon a detailed statement of the reasons which force upon our minds the conviction that this project is *by no means abandoned :* that a large portion of the country, interested in the continuance of Domestic Slavery and the Slave-trade in these United States, have solemnly and unalterably determined *that it shall be speedily carried into execution;* and that, by this admission of new Slave Territory and Slave States, *the undue ascendency of the Slave-holding power in the Government shall be secured and riveted beyond all redemption ! !*

That it was with these views and intentions that settlements were effected in the province, by citizens of the United States, difficulties fomented with the Mexican Government, a revolt brought about, and an Independent Government declared, *cannot now admit of a doubt ;* and that, hitherto, all attempts of Mexico to reduce her revolted province to obedience have proved unsuccessful, is to be attributed to the unlawful aid and assistance of designing and interested individuals in the United States, and the direct and indirect coöperation of our own Government, *with similar views*, is not the less certain and demonstrable.

The open and repeated enlistment of troops in several States of this Union, in aid of the Texan Revolution ; the intrusion of an American Army, by order of the President, far into the territory of the Mexican Government, at a moment critical for the fate of the insurgents, under pretense of preventing Mexican soldiers from fomenting Indian disturbances, but in reality in aid of, and acting in singular concert and coincidence with, the army of the Revolutionists ; the entire neglect of our Government to adopt any efficient measures to prevent the most unwarrantable aggressions of bodies of our own citizens, enlisted, organized and officered within our own borders, and marched in arms and battle array upon the territory, and against the inhabitants of a friendly government, in aid of freebooters and insurgents, and the premature recognition of the Independence of Texas, by a snap vote, at the heel of a session of Congress, and that, too, at the very session when President Jackson had, by special Message, insisted that "the measure would be contrary to the policy invariably observed by the United States in all similar cases;" would be marked with great injustice to Mexico, and peculiarly liable to the darkest suspicions, *inasmuch as the Texans were almost all emigrants from the United States,* AND SOUGHT THE RECOGNITION OF THEIR INDEPENDENCE WITH THE AVOWED PURPOSE OF OBTAINING THEIR ANNEXATION TO THE UNITED STATES. These occurrences are too well known and too fresh in the memory of all, to need more than a passing notice. These have become matters of history. For further evidence upon all these and other important points, we refer to the memorable speech of John Quincy Adams, delivered in the House of Representatives during the morning hour in June and July, 1838, and to his address to his constituents, delivered at Braintree, 17th September, 1842.

The open avowal of the Texans themselves—the frequent and anxious negotiations of our own Government—the resolutions of various States of the Union—the numerous declarations of members of Congress—the tone of the Southern press—as well as the direct application of the Texan Government, *make it impossible for any man to doubt,* that ANNEXATION, and the formation of several new Slaveholding States, were *originally* the policy and design of the Slaveholding States and the Executive of the Nation.

The same reference will show, very conclusively, that the *particular objects* of this new acquisition of Slave Territory were THE PERPETUATION OF SLAVERY AND THE CONTINUED ASCENDENCY OF THE SLAVE POWER.

The following extracts from a Report on that subject, adopted by the Legislature of Mississippi, from a mass of similar evidence which might be adduced, will show *with what views* the annexation was *then* urged :

"But we hasten to suggest the importance of the annexation of Texas to this Republic upon grounds somewhat local in their complexion, but of an import infinitely grave and interesting to the people who inhabit the Southern portion of this Confederacy, where it is known that a species of domestic Slavery is tolerated and protected by law, whose existence is prohibited by the legal regulations of other States of this Confederacy ; which system of Slavery is held by all, who are familiarly acquainted with its practical effects, *to be of highly beneficial influence to the country within whose limits it is permitted to exist.*

"The Committee feel authorized to say that this system is cherished by our constituents as *the very palladium of their prosperity and happiness,* and whatever ignorant fanatics may elsewhere conjecture, the Committee are fully assured, upon the most diligent observation and reflection on the subject, that *the South does not possess within her limits a blessing with which the affections of her people are so closely entwined and so completely enfibred,* and whose value is more highly appreciated, than that which we are now considering.

* * * * * * *

"It may not be improper here to remark that, during the last session of Congress, when a Senator from Mississippi proposed the acknowledgment of Texan independence, it was found, with a few exceptions, *the members of that body were ready to take ground upon it, as upon the subject of Slavery itself.*

"With all these facts before us, we do not hesitate in believing that these feelings influenced the New England Senators, but one voting in favor of the measure ; and, indeed, Mr. Webster had been bold enough, in a public speech recently delivered in New-York, to many thousand citizens, to declare that the reason that influenced his opposition was his abhorrence of Slavery in the South, and that it might, in the event of its recognition, become a slaveholding State. He also spoke of the efforts making in favor of Abolition ; and that, being predicated upon and aided by the powerful influence of religious feeling, it would become irresistible and overwhelming.

"This language, coming from so distinguished an individual as Mr. Webster, so familiar with the feelings of the North and entertaining so high a respect for public sentiment in New England, speaks so plainly the voice of the North as not to be misunderstood.

"We sincerely hope there is enough good sense and genuine love of country among our fellow-countrymen of the Northern States, *to secure us final justice on this subject ;* yet we cannot consider it safe or expedient for the people of the South to entirely disregard the efforts of the fanatics, and the opinions of such men as Webster, and others who countenance such dangerous doctrines.

"*The Northern States have no interests of their own* which require any *special* safeguards for their defense, save only their domestic manufactures ; and God knows they have already received protection from Government on a most liberal scale ; under which encouragement they have improved and flourished beyond example. *The South has very peculiar interests to preserve ;* interests already violently assailed and boldly threatened.

"*Your Committee are fully persuaded that this protection to her best interests will be afforded by the annexation of Texas ; an equipoise of influence in the halls of Congress will be secured, which will furnish us a permanent guaranty of protection.*"

The speech of Mr. Adams, exposing the whole system of duplicity and perfidy toward Mexico, had marked the conduct of our Government; and the emphatic expressions of opposition which began to come up from all parties in the Free States, however, for a time, nearly silenced the clamors of the South for annexation, and the people of the North have been lulled into the belief that the project is nearly, if not wholly abandoned, and that, at least, there is now no serious danger of its consummation.

Believing this to be a *false and dangerous security ;* that the project has never been abandoned a moment, by its originators and abettors, but that it has been deferred for a more favorable moment for its accomplishment, we refer to a few evidences of more recent development upon which this opinion is founded.

The last Election of President of the Republic of Texas, is understood to have turned, *mainly,* upon the question of *annexation* or *no annexation,* and the candidate favorable to that measure was successful by an overwhelming majority. The sovereign States of Alabama, Tennessee, and Mississippi, have *recently* adopted Resolutions, some, if not all of them, *unanimously,* in favor of annexation, and forwarded them to Congress.

The Hon. Henry A. Wise, a member of Congress from the District in which our present Chief Magistrate resided when elected Vice-President, and who is understood to be more intimately acquainted with the views and designs of the present administration than any other member of Congress, most distinctly avowed his desire for, and expectation of annexation, at the last session of Congress. Among other things, he said, in a speech delivered January 26, 1842 :

"True, if Iowa be added on the one side, Florida will be added on the other. But there the equation must stop. Let one more Northern State be admitted, and the equilibrium is gone—gone forever. The *balance of interests* is gone—the *safeguard* of American property—of the American Constitution—of the American Union, vanished into thin air. *This must be the inevitable result, unless by a treaty with Mexico,* THE SOUTH CAN ADD MORE WEIGHT TO HER END OF THE LEVER ? *Let the South stop at the Sabine,* (the eastern boundary of Texas,) while the North may spread unchecked beyond the Rocky Mountains AND THE SOUTHERN SCALE MUST KICK THE BEAM."

Finding difficulties, perhaps, in the way of a cession by Treaty, in another speech delivered in April, 1842, on a motion made by Mr. Linn, of New-York, to strike out the salary of the Minister to Mexico, on the ground that the design of the EXECUTIVE, in making the appointment, was to accomplish the annexation of Texas, Mr. Wise said, " he earnestly hoped and trusted that the President was as desirous (of annexation) as he was represented to be. We may well suppose the President to be in favor of it, as every wise statesman must be who is not governed by fanaticism, or local sectional prejudices."

He said of Texas, that---

" While she was, as a State, weak and almost powerless in resisting invasion, she was herself irresistible as an invading and a conquering power. She had but a sparse population, and neither men nor money of her own, to raise and equip an army for her own defense ; but let her once raise the flag of foreign conquest—let her once proclaim a crusade against the rich States to the south of her—and in a moment volunteers would flock to her standard in crowds, *from all the States in the great valley of the Mississippi*—men of enterprise and valor, before whom no Mexican troops could stand for an hour. They would leave their own towns, arm themselves, and travel on their own cost, and would come up in thousands, to plant the lone star of the Texan banner on the Mexican capitol. They would drive Santa Anna to the South, and in boundless wealth of captured towns, and rifled churches, and a lazy, vicious, and luxurious priesthood, would soon enable Texas, to pay her soldiery, and redeem her State debt, and push her victorious arms to the very shores of the Pacific. And would not all this extend the bounds of Slavery? Yes, the result would be, that, before another quarter of a century, the extension of Slavery would not stop short of the Western Ocean. *We had but two alternatives before us ; either to receive Texas into our fraternity of States, and thus make her our own, or to leave her to conquer Mexico, and become our most dangerous and formidable rival.*

" To talk of restraining the people of the great Valley from emigrating to join her armies, was all in vain ; and it was equally vain to calculate on their defeat by any Mexican forces, aided by England or not. *They had gone once already ; it was they that conquered Santa Anna at San Jacinto ; and three-fourths of them*, after winning that glorious field, had peaceably returned to their homes. But once set before them the conquest of the rich Mexican provinces, and you might as well attempt to stop the wind. This Government might send its troops to the frontier, to turn them back, and they would run over them like a herd of buffalo.

" Nothing could keep these booted loafers from rushing on, till they kicked the Spanish priests out of the temples they profaned."

Mr. Wise proceeded to insist that a majority of the people of the United States were in favor of the annexation ; at all events, he would risk it with the Democracy of the North.

" Sir," said Mr. Wise, " it is not only the duty of the Government to demand the liquidation of our claims, and the liberation of our citizens, but to go further, and demand the non-invasion of Texas. Shall we sit still while the standard of insurrection is raised on our borders, and let a *horde of slaves, and Indians and Mexicans roll up to the boundary line of Arkansas and Louisiana ?* No. It is our duty at once to say to Mexico, ' *If you strike Texas, you strike us ;*' and if England, standing by, should dare to intermeddle, and ask, ' *Do you take part with Texas ?*' his prompt answer should be, ' *Yes, and against you.*'

" *Such, he would let gentlemen know, was the spirit of the whole people of the great valley of the West.*"

Several other members of Congress, in the same debate, expressed similar views and desires, and they are still more frequently expressed in conversation.

The Hon. Thomas W. Gilmer, a member of Congress from Virginia, and formerly a Governor of that State, numbered as one of the " Guard," and of course understood to be in the counsels of the Cabinet, in a letter bearing date the 10th day of January last, originally designed as a private and confidential letter to a friend, gives it as his deliberate opinion, after much examination and reflection, that TEXAS WILL BE ANNEXED TO THE UNION ; and he enters into a specious argument, and presents a variety of reasons in favor of the measure. He says, among other things :

" Having acquired Louisiana and Florida, we have an interest and a frontier on the Gulf of Mexico, and along our interior to the Pacific, which will not permit us to close our eyes, or fold our arms, with indifference to the events which a few years may disclose in that quarter. We have already had one question of boundary with Texas ; other questions must soon arise, under our revenue laws, and on other points of necessary intercourse, which it will be difficult to adjust. *The institutions of Texas, and her relations with other governments, are yet in that condition which inclines her people (who are our own countrymen,) to unite their destinies with ours.* THIS MUST BE DONE SOON, OR NOT AT ALL. *There are numerous tribes of Indians along both frontiers, which can easily become the cause or the instrument of border wars.*"

None can be so blind *now*, as not to know that the real design and object of the South is, to " ADD NEW WEIGHT TO HER END OF THE LEVER." It was upon that ground that Mr. Webster placed his opposition, in his speech on that subject in New-York, in March, 1837. In that speech, after stating that he saw insurmountable objections to the annexation of Texas, that the purchase of Louisiana and Florida furnished no precedent for it, that the cases were not parallel, and that no such policy or necessity as led to that, required the annexation of Texas, he said :

" Gentlemen, we all see, that by whomsoever possessed, Texas is likely to be a slaveholding country ; and I frankly avow my entire unwillingness to do anything which shall extend the Slavery of the African race on this continent, or add other slaveholding States to the Union. When I say that I regard Slavery as in itself a great moral, social, and political evil, I only use language which has been adopted by distinguished men, themselves citizens of Slaveholding States. I shall do nothing, therefore, to favor or encourage its further extension."

In conclusion he said :

" I see, therefore, no political necessity for the annexation of Texas to the Union ; no advantages to be derived from it , and objections to it of a strong, and, in my judgment, decisive character.

" I believe it to be for the interest and happiness of the whole Union, to remain as it is, without diminution and without addition."

To prevent the success of this nefarious project--to preserve from such gross violation the Constitution of our country, adopted expressly " *to secure the blessings of liberty*," and not the perpetuation of Slavery—and to prevent the speedy and violent dissolution of the Union —we invite you to unite, without distinction of party, in an immediate expression of your views on this subject, in such manner as you may deem best calculated to answer the end proposed.

JOHN QUINCY ADAMS,	NATHANIEL B. BORDEN,
SETH M. GATES,	THOMAS C. CHITTENDEN,
WILLIAM SLADE,	JOHN MATTOCKS,
WILLIAM B. CALHOUN,	CHRISTOPHER MORGAN,
JOSHUA R. GIDDINGS,	JOSHUA M. HOWARD,
SHERLOCK J. ANDREWS,	VICTORY BIRDSEYE,

HILAND HALL.

WASHINGTON, *March 3rd*, 1843.

[NOTE.—The above address was drawn up by Hon. Seth M. Gates, of New-York, at the suggestion of John Quincy Adams, and sent to members of Congress at their residences, after the close of the session, for their signatures. Many more than the above approved heartily of its positions and objects, and would have signed it, but for its premature publication, through mistake. Mr. Winthrop, of Mass., was one of these, with Gov. Briggs, of course ; Mr. Fillmore declined signing it.]

The letters of Messrs. Clay and Van Buren, taking ground against annexation, without the consent of Mexico, as an act of bad faith and aggression, which would necessarily result in war, which appeared in the spring of 1844, make slight allusions, if any, to the Slavery aspect of the case. In a later letter, Mr. Clay declared that he did not oppose annexation on account of Slavery, which he regarded as a temporary institution, which, therefore, ought not to stand in the way of a permanent acquisition. And, though Mr. Clay's last letter on the subject, prior to the election of 1844, reiterated and emphasized all his objections to annexation under the existing circumstances, he did not include the existence of Slavery.

The defeat of Mr. Van Buren, at the Baltimore Nominating Convention—Mr. Polk being selected in his stead, by a body which had been supposed pledged to renominate the ex-President--excited considerable feeling, especially among the Democrats of New-York. A number of their leaders united in a letter, termed the " Secret Circular," advising their brethren, while they supported Polk and Dallas, to be careful to vote for candidates for Congress who would set their faces as a flint against annexation, which was signed by

GEORGE P. BARKER,	DAVID DUDLEY FIELD,
WILLIAM C. BRYANT,	THEODORE SEDGWICK,
J. W. EDMONDS,	THOMAS W. TUCKER,

ISAAC TOWNSEND.

Silas Wright, then a Senator of the United States, and who, as such, had opposed the Tyler Treaty of Annexation, was now run for Governor, as the only man who could carry the State of New-York for Polk and Dallas. In a democratic speech at Skaneateles, N. Y., Mr. Wright had recently declared that he could never consent to Annexation on any terms which would give Slavery an advantage over Freedom. This sentiment was reiterated and amplified in a great Convention of the Democracy, which met at Herkimer, in the autumn of this year.

The contest proceeded with great earnestness throughout the Free States, the supporters of Polk and of Birney (the Abolition candidate for President), fully agreeing in the assertion that Mr. Clay's position was equally favorable to Annexation with Mr. Polk's. Mr. Birney in a letter published on the eve of the Election, declared that he regarded Mr. Clay's election as *more* favorable to Annexation than Mr. Polk's, because, while equally inclined to fortify and extend Slavery, he possessed more ability to influence Congress in its favor.

Before this time, but as yet withheld from, and unknown to, the public, Mr. Calhoun, now President Tyler's Secretary of State, and an early and powerful advocate of Annexation, had addressed to Hon. Wm. R. King, our Embassador at Paris, an official dispatch from which we make the following extracts:

MR. CALHOUN TO MR. KING.

DEPARTMENT OF STATE,
Washington, August 12, 1844.

SIR—I have laid your dispatch, No. 1, before the President, who instructs me to make known to you that he has read it with much pleasure, especially the portion which relates to your cordial reception by the King, and his assurance of friendly feelings toward the United States. The President, in particular, highly appreciates the declaration of the King, that in no event, would any steps be taken by his government in the slightest degree hostile, or which would give to the United States just cause of complaint. It was the more gratifying from the fact, that our previous information was calculated to make the impression that the government of France was prepared to unite with Great Britain in a joint protest against the annexation of Texas, and a joint effort to induce her Government to withdraw the proposition to annex, on condition that Mexico should be made to acknowledge her independence. He is happy to infer from your dispatch that the information, so far as it relates to France, is in all probability without foundation. You did not go further than you ought, in assuring the King that the object of Annexation would be pursued with unabated vigor, and in giving your opinion that a decided majority of the American people were in its favor, and that it would certainly be annexed at no distant day. I feel confident that your anticipation will be fully realized at no distant period.

Every day will tend to weaken that combination of political causes which led to the opposition of the measure, and to strengthen the conviction that it was not only expedient, but just and necessary.

But to descend to particulars: it is certain that while England, like France, desires the independence of Texas, with the view to commercial connections, it is not less so that one of the leading motives of England for desiring it, is the hope that, through her diplomacy and influence, Negro Slavery may be abolished there, and ultimately, by consequence, in the United States and throughout the whole of this continent. That its ultimate abolition throughout the entire continent is an object ardently desired by her, we have decisive proofs in the declaration of the Earl of Aberdeen, delivered to this Department, and of which you will find a copy among the documents transmitted to Congress with the Texan treaty. That she desires its abolition in Texas, and has used her influence and diplomacy to effect it there, the same document, with the correspondence of this Department with Mr. Packenham, also to be found among the documents, furnishes proof not less conclusive. That one of the objects of abolishing it there is to facilitate its abolition in the United States, and throughout the continent, is manifest from the declaration of the Abolition party and societies both in this country and in England. In fact, there is good reason to believe that the scheme of abolishing it in Texas, with a view to its abolition in the United States, and over the continent, originated with the prominent members of the party in the United States ; and was first broached by them in the (so called) World's Convention, held in London in the year 1840, and through its agency brought to the notice of the British Government.

Now, I hold, not only that France can have no interest in the consummation of this grand scheme, which England hopes to accomplish through Texas, if she can defeat the Annexation, but that her interests, and those of all the Continental powers of Europe are directly and deeply opposed to it.

———

The election of James K. Polk as President, and George M. Dallas as Vice-President, (Nov. 1844) having virtually settled, affirmatively, the question of annexing Texas, the XXVIIIth Congress commenced its second session at Washington, on the 2d of December, 1844—Mr. John Tyler being still acting President up to the end of the Congress, March 4th following.

Dec. 19.—Mr. John B. Weller, (then member from Ohio) by leave, introduced a joint resolution, No. 51, providing for the annexation of Texas to the United States, which he moved to the Committee of the Whole.

Mr. E. S. Hamlin, of Ohio, moved a reference of said resolve to a Committee of one from each State, with instructions to report

Whether the annexation of Texas would not extend and perpetuate Slavery in the Slave States, and also, the internal Slave-trade ; and whether the United States Government has any Constitutional power over Slavery *in the States,* either to perpetuate it there, *or to do it away.*

The question on commitment was insisted upon, and first taken—Yeas, 109 (Democrats) ; Nays, 61 (Whigs) ; whereupon it was held that Mr. Hamlin's amendment was defeated, and the original proposition alone committed.

January 10*th*, 1845.—Mr. John P. Hale, of New-Hampshire, (then a Democratic Representative, now a Republican Senator) proposed the following as an amendment to any act or resolve contemplating the annexation of Texas to this Union :

Provided, That immediately after the question of boundary between the United States of America and Mexico shall have been definitively settled by the two Governments, and before any State formed out of the Territory of Texas shall be admitted into the Union, the said Territory of Texas shall be divided as follows, to wit : beginning at a point on the Gulf of Mexico, midway between the Northern and Southern boundaries thereof on the coast ; and thence by a line running in a North-westerly direction to the extreme boundary thereof, so as to divide the same as nearly as possible into two equal parts, and in that portion of said Territory lying South and West of the line to be run as aforesaid, there shall be neither Slavery nor involuntary servitude, otherwise than in the punishment of crimes, whereof the party shall have been duly convicted.

And provided further, That this provision shall be considered as a compact between the people of the United States and the people of the said Territory, and forever remain unalterable, unless by the consent of three-fourths of the States of the Union.

Mr. Hale asked a suspension of the rules, to enable him to offer it now, and have it printed and committed. Refused—Yeas, 92 (not two thirds) ; Nays, 81.

Yeas—All the Whigs* and most of the Democrats from the Free States. with Messrs. Duncan L. Clinch and Alexander H. Stephens, of Georgia, and George W. Summers, of Virginia.

Nays—All the members from Slave States, except the above, with the following from Free States :

MAINE.—Sheppard Cary—1.
NEW-HAMPSHIRE.—Edmund Burke, Moses Norris, jr.—2.
NEW-YORK.—James G. Clinton, Selah B. Strong—2.
PENNSYLVANIA.—James Black, Richard Brodhead, H. D. Foster, *Joseph R. Ingersoll, Michael H. Jenks*—5.
OHIO.—Joseph J. McDowell—1.
INDIANA.—Wm. J. Brown, J. W. Davis, John Pettit—3.

* Except the two here given in *Italics.*

ILLINOIS.—Orlando B. Ficklin, Joseph P. Hoge, Robert Smith—3.

Total Democrats from Free States, 17.

December 12th.—Mr. C. J. Ingersoll, of Pennsylvania, from the Committee on Foreign Affairs, reported a Joint Resolution for annexing Texas to the Union, which was committed and discussed in Committee of the Whole from time to time, through the next month.

January 7th.—Mr. J. P. Hale presented resolves of the Legislature of New-Hampshire, thoroughly in favor of Annexation, and silent on the subject of Slavery, except as follows:

Resolved, That we agree with Mr. Clay, that the re-annexation of Texas will add more Free than Slave States to the Union; and that it would be unwise to refuse a permanent acquisition, which will exist as long as the globe remains, on account of a temporary institution.

January 13th.—Mr. Cave Johnson, of Tennessee, moved that all further debate on this subject be closed at 2 P.M. on Thursday next. Carried—Yeas, 136; Nays, 57; (nearly all the Nays from Slave States.)

January 25th.—The debate, after an extension of time, was at length brought to a close, and the Joint Resolution taken out of Committee, and reported to the House in the following form; (that portion relating to Slavery, having been added in Committee, on motion of Mr. Milton Brown, (Whig) of Tennessee:

Resolved, by the Senate and House of Representatives in Congress assembled, That Congress doth consent that the Territory properly included within, and rightfully belonging to, the Republic of Texas, may be erected into a new State, to be called the State of Texas, with a republican form of Government, to be adopted by the people of said Republic, by deputies in Convention assembled, with the consent of the existing Government, in o.der that the same may be admitted as one of the States of this Union.

2. *And be it further resolved*, That the foregoing consent of Congress is given upon the following conditions, and with the following guaranties, to wit:

First. Said State to be formed, subject to the adjustment by this Government of all questions of boundary that may arise with other governments; and the Constitution thereof, with the proper evidence of its adoption by the people of said Republic of Texas, shall be transmitted to the President of the United States, to be laid before Congress for its final action, on or before the 1st day of January, 1846.

Second. Said State, when admitted into the Union, after ceding to the United States all public edifices,fortifications, barracks, ports and harbors. navy and navy-yards, docks, magazines, arms, armaments, and all other property and means pertaining to the public defense, belonging to the said Republic of Texas, shall retain all the public funds, debts, taxes, and dues of every kind which may belong to, or be due or owing said Republic; and shall also retain all the vacant and unappropriated lands lying within its limits, to be applied to the payment of debts and liabilities of said Republic of Texas; and the residue of said lands, after discharging said debts and liabilities, to be disposed of as said State may direct: but in no event are said debts and liabilities to become a charge upon the United States.

Third. New States of convenient size, not exceeding four in number, in addition to said State of Texas, and having sufficient population,may hereafter,by the consent of said State, be formed out of the Territory thereof, which shall be entitled to admission under the provisions of the Federal Constitution. And such States as may be formed out of that portion of said Territory, lying south of thirty-six degrees thirty minutes north latitude, commonly known as the Missouri Compromise line, shall be admitted into the Union, with, or without Slavery, as the people of each State asking admission may desire; and in such State or States as shall be formed out of said Territory, north of said Missouri Compromise line, Slavery or involuntary servitude (except for crime) shall be prohibited.

Mr. Cave Johnson, of Tennessee, moved the previous question, which the House seconded—Yeas, 113; Nays, 106—and then the amendment aforesaid was agreed to—Yeas, 118; Nays, 101.

Yeas—114 Democrats, and Messrs. Milton Brown, of Tennessee; James Dellet, of Alabama; and Duncan L. Clinch, and Alexander H. Stephens, of Georgia, (4) Southern Whigs.

Nays—all the Whigs present from Free States with all from Slave States, but the four just named; with the following Democrats from Free States:

MAINE.—Robert P. Dunlap, Hannibal Hamlin—2.
VERMONT.—Paul Dillingham, jr.—1.
NEW-HAMPSHIRE.—John P. Hale—1.
CONNECTICUT.—George S. Catlin—1.
NEW-YORK.—Joseph H. Anderson, Charles S. Benton, Jeremiah E. Carey, Amasa Dana, Richard D. Davis, Byram Green, Preston King, Smith M. Purdy, George Rathbun, Orville Robinson, David L. Seymour, Lemuel Stetson—12.
OHIO.—Jacob Brinckerhoff, William C. McCauslen, Joseph Morris, Henry St. John—4.
MICHIGAN.—James B. Hunt, Robert McClelland—2.
Total Democrats from Free States,........23.
Total Whigs from Free and Slave States,....78.

The House then ordered the whole proposition to a third reading forthwith—Yeas, 120; Nays, 97—and passed it, Yeas, 120; Nays, 98.

Yeas—all the Democrats from Slave States, and all the Democrats from Free States, except as above; with Messrs. Duncan L. Clinch, Milton Brown, James Dellet, Willoughby Newton, of Virginia, (who therefrom turned Democrat), and Alexander H. Stephens of Georgia, (now Democrat), from Slave States.

Nays—all the Whigs from Free States; all those from Slave States except as above; with 23 Democrats from Free States.

So the resolve passed the House, and was sent to the Senate for concurrence.

In Senate, several attempts to originate action in favor of Annexation were made at this session, but nothing came of them.

February 24th.—The joint resolution aforesaid from the House was taken up for consideration by 30 Yeas to 11 Nays (all Northern Whigs). On the 27th, Mr. Walker, of Wisconsin, moved to add an alternative proposition, contemplating negotiation as the means of effecting the meditated end.

Mr. Foster, (Whig) of Tennessee, proposed

That the State of Texas, and such other States as may be formed out of that portion of the present Territory of Texas, lying south of thirty-six degrees thirty minutes north latitude, commonly known as the Missouri Compromise line, shall be admitted into the Union with or without Slavery, as the people of each State, so hereafter asking admission, may desire.

On which the question was taken. Yeas, (all Whigs but 3) 18; Nays, 34.

Various amendments were proposed and voted down. Among them, Mr. Foster, of Tenn., moved an express stipulation that Slavery should be tolerated in all States formed out of the Territory of Texas, south of the Missouri line of 36° 30'. Rejected—Yeas, 16 (Southern Whigs, and Sevier, of Arkansas); Nays, 33.

Mr. Miller, of N. J., moved that the existence of Slavery be forever prohibited in the northern and northwestern part of said Territory, west of the 100th degree of latitude west from Greenwich, so as to divide, as equally as may be. the whole of the annexed country between Slaveholding and Non-Slaveholding States.

Yeas, 11; all Northern Whigs, except Mr. Crittenden, Ky. Nays, 33.

The vote in the Senate on the joint resolution for Annexation stood, Yeas, 26, all Democrats but 3; Nays, 25, (all Whigs). In the House, Yeas 134, all Democrats but 1 : Nays, 77, (all Whigs).

THE WILMOT PROVISO.

Texas having been annexed during the summer of 1845, in pursuance of the joint resolution of the two Houses of Congress, a portion of the United States Army, under Gen. Taylor, was, early in the spring of 1846, moved down to the east bank of the Rio Grande del Norte, claimed by Texas as her western boundary, but not so regarded by Mexico. A hostile collision ensued, resulting in war between the United States and Mexico.

It was early thereafter deemed advisable that a considerable sum should be placed by Congress at the President's disposal to negotiate an advantageous Treaty of Peace and Limits with the Mexican Government. A message to this effect was submitted by President Polk to Congress, August 8th, 1846, and a bill in accordance with its suggestions laid before the House, which proceded to consider the subject in Committee of the Whole. The bill appropriating $30,000 for immediate use in negotiations with Mexico, and placing $2,000,000 more at the disposal of the President, to be employed in making peace, Mr. David Wilmot, of Pa., after consultation with other Northern Democrats, offered the following Proviso, in addition to the first section of the bill :

Provided, That as an express and fundamental condition to the acquisition of any territory from the Republic of Mexico by the United States, by virtue of any treaty which may be negotiated between them, and to the use by the Executive of the moneys herein appropriated, neither Slavery nor involuntary servitude shall ever exist in any part of said Territory, except for crime, whereof the party shall be first duly convicted.

This proviso was carried in Committee, by the strong vote of eighty-three to sixty-four—only three Members (Democrats) from the Free-States, it was said, opposing it. (No record is made of individual votes in Committee of the Whole.) The bill was then reported to the House, and Mr. Rathbun, of N. Y., moved the previous question on its engrossment.

Mr. Tibbatts, of Ky., moved that it do lie on the table. Defeated—Yeas, 79 ; (Stephen A. Douglas, John A. McClernand, John Pettit, and Robert C. Schenck, voting with the South to lay on the table ;) Nays 93 ; (Henry Grider and William P. Thomasson, of Ky. (Whigs) voting with the North against it.

The bill was then engrossed for its third reading by Yeas 85, Nays, 80 ; and thus passed without further division. A motion to reconsider was laid on the table—Yeas, 71 ; Nays, 83. So the bill was passed and sent to the Senate, where Mr. Dixon H. Lewis, of Alabama, moved that the Proviso above cited be stricken out; on which debate arose, and Mr. John Davis of Mass., was speaking when, at noon of August 10th, the time fixed for adjournment having arrived, both Houses adjourned without day.

The XXXth Congress assembled Dec. 6, 1847. *Feb.* 28th 1848, Mr. Putnam of New-York moved the following :

Whereas, In the settlement of the difficulties pending between this country and Mexico, territory may be acquired in which Slavery does not now exist.

And whereas, Congress, in the organization of a territorial government, at an early period of our political history, established a principle worthy of imitation in all future time, forbidding the existence of Slavery in free territory ; Therefore,

Resolved, That in any Territory, that may be acquired from Mexico, over which shall be established territorial governments, Slavery, or involuntary servitude, except as a punishment for crime, whereof the party shall have been duly convicted, shall be forever prohibited ; and that in any act or resolution establishing such governments, a fundamental provision ought to be inserted to that effect.

Mr. R. Brodhead, of Penn., moved that this resolution lie on the table. Carried: Yeas, 105 ; Nays, 93.

Yeas—all the members from Slave States, but John W. Houston (Whig), of Delaware, with the following from Free States (all Democrats but Levin) :

MAINE.—Asa W. H. Clapp, Franklin Clark, Jas. S. Wiley, Hezekiah Williams—4.

NEW-YORK.— Ausburn Birdsall, David S. Jackson, Frederick W. Lord, William B. Maclay—4.

PENNSYLVANIA.—Richard Brodhead, Charles Brown, *Lewis C. Levin*, Job Man—4.

OHIO.—William Kennon, jr., John K. Miller, Thomas Richey, William Sawyer—4.

INDIANA.—Charles W. Cathcart, Thomas J. Henley, John Pettit, John L. Robinson, William W. Wick—5.

ILLINOIS.—Orlando B. Ficklin, John A. McClernand, William A. Richardson, Robert Smith, Thomas J. Turner—5.

Nays—all the Whigs and a large majority of the Democrats from Free States, with John W. Houston aforesaid.

This vote terminated all direct action in favor of the Wilmot Proviso for that Session.

July 18th.—In Senate, Mr. Clayton, of Del., from the Select Committee to which was referred, on the 12th inst., the bill providing a territorial government for Oregon, reported a bill to establish Territorial governments for Oregon, New Mexico, and California, which was read. (It proposed to submit all questions as to the rightful existence or extent of Slavery in the Territories to the decision of the Supreme Court of the United States.)

July, 24th.—Second reading. Mr. Baldwin, of Conn., moved to strike out so much of said bill as relates to California and New Mexico. Rejected : Yeas, 17 (Northern Free Soil men of both parties) ; Nays, 37.

The bill was discussed through several succeeding days. On the 26th, Mr. Clarke, of R. I., moved to add to the 6th section :

Provided, however, That no law, regulation, or act of the provisional government of said Territory permitting Slavery or involuntary servitude therein shall be valid, until the same shall be approved by Congress."

Rejected : Yeas, 19 [Col. Benton, and 18 Northern Freesoilers of both parties] ; Nays, 33.

Mr. Reverdy Johnson, of Md., moved to amend the bill by inserting :

Except only, that in all cases of title to slaves, the said writs of error or appeals shall be allowed and decided by the said Supreme Court without regard to the value of the matter, property, or title in controversy ; and except, also, that a writ of error or appeal shall also be allowed to the Supreme Court of the United States from the decision of the said Supreme Court created by this act, or of any judge thereof, or of the district Courts created by this act, or of any judge upon any writ of habeas corpus involving the question of personal freedom.

Carried ; Yeas, 31 (all sorts) ; Nays, 19 (all Southern, but Bright, Dickinson, and Hannegan).

Mr. Baldwin, of Connecticut, moved an additional section, as follows :

Sec. 37. *And be it further enacted*, That it shall be the duty of the attorneys for said Territories, respectively, on the complaint of any person held in involuntary servitude therein, to make application in his behalf in due form of law to the court next thereafter to be holden in said Territory for writ of habeas corpus, to be directed to the person so holding such applicant in service as aforesaid, and to pursue all needful measures in his behalf; and if the decision of such court shall be adverse to the application, or if, on the return of the writ, relief shall be denied to the applicant, on the ground that he is a slave held in servitude in said Territory, said attorney shall cause an appeal to be taken therefrom, and the record of all the proceedings in the case to be transmitted to the Supreme Court of the United States as speedily as may be, and to give notice thereof to the Attorney General of the United States, who shall prosecute the same before said Court, who shall proceed to hear and determine the same at the first term thereof.

Yeas, 15 (all Northern, except Benton); Nays, 31.

Mr. Davis, of Mass., moved to strike out section 12, and insert as follows:

Sec. 12. *And be it further enacted*, That so much of the sixth section of the ordinance of the 13th July, 1787, as is contained in the following words; viz. 'There shall be neither Slavery nor involuntary servitude in the said Territory, otherwise than in the punishment of crimes, whereof the party shall have been duly convicted,' shall be and remain in force in the Territory of Oregon.

This was defeated; Yeas, 21; Nays, 33.

The bill was then engrossed for a third reading; Yeas, 33; Nays, 22; as follows:

Yeas—For Clayton's Compromise:

Messrs. Atchison,	Houston,
Atherton,	Hunter,
Benton,	Johnson, Md.
Berrien,	Johnson, La.
Borland,	Johnson, Ga.
Breese,	King,
Bright,	Lewis,
Butler,	Mangum,
Calhoun,	Mason,
Clayton,	Phelps,
Davis, Miss.	Rusk,
Dickinson,	Sebastian,
Douglas,	Spruance,
Downs,	Sturgeon,
Foote,	Turney,
Hannegan,	Westcott,
	Yulee—33.

Nays—Against Clayton's bill:

Messrs. Allen,	Felch,
Badger,	Fitzgerald,
Baldwin,	Greene,
Bell,	Hale,
Bradbury,	Hamlin,
Clarke,	Metcalf.
Corwin,	Miller,
Davis, Mass.	Niles,
Dayton,	Underwood,
Dix,	Upham,
Dodge,	Walker—22.

So the bill was engrossed, and immediately passed without a division.

July 28th.—This bill reached the House, and was taken up and read twice.

Mr. A. H. Stephens, of Ga., moved that the bill *do lie on the table.* Yeas and Nays orderd, and the motion prevailed: Yeas, 112; Nays, 97.

Yeas, all the Free State Whigs, with 8 Whigs from Slave States; 20 Democrats from Free States.

Nays—21 Democrats from Free States, with 76 Democrats and Whigs from Slave States.

Mr. Pollock, of Pa., moved that this vote be reconsidered, and that the motion to reconsider do lie on the table; which prevailed: Yeas, 113; Nays, 96.

So Mr. Clayton's project of Compromise was defeated.

The next session of the same Congress opened under very different auspices. The Mexican War had been terminated, so that none could longer be deterred from voting for Slavery Exclusion by a fear that the prosecution of hostilities would thereby be embarrassed. General Taylor had been elected President, receiving the votes of Delaware, Maryland, North Carolina, Georgia, Kentucky, Tennessee, Louisiana, and Florida—a moiety of the Slave States—over Gen. Cass, now the avowed opponent of Slavery Restriction. Many of the Northern Democrats considered themselves absolved by this vote from all extra-constitutional obligations to the South, and voted accordingly.

Dec. 13.—Mr. J. M. Root, of Ohio, offered the following:

Resolved, That the Committee on Territories be instructed to report to this House, with as little delay as practicable, a bill or bills providing a Territorial Government for each of the Territories of New Mexico and California, and excluding Slavery therefrom.

A call of the House was had, and the previous question ordered.

Mr. W. P. Hall, of Mo., moved that the same do lie on the table. Lost: Yeas, 80; Nays, 106.

The resolve then passed: Yeas, 108; Nays, 80, viz. :

Yeas—All the Whigs from Free States, and all the Democrats, but those noted as Nays below, including the following, who had voted against the same principle at the former session :

MAINE.—Asa W. H. Clapp, James S. Wiley—2.

NEW-YORK.—Frederick W. Lord—1.

OHIO.—Thomas Richey—1.

INDIANA.—Charles W. Cathcart, Thomas J. Henley, John L. Robinson, William W. Wick—4.

ILLINOIS.—Robert Smith—1.

Messrs. Clark and H. Williams, of Maine, Birdsall and Maclay, of New-York, Brodhead and Mann, of Pa., Pettit, of Ind., Ficklin and McClelland, of Ill., who voted with the South at the former session—now failed to vote.

Mr. Jackson, of N. Y, who then voted with the South, had been succeeded by Mr. H. Greeley, who voted with the North.

Nays—All the Members voting from the Slave States, with the following from the Free States :

NEW-YORK.—Henry C. Murphy—1.

PENNSYLVANIA.—Charles Brown, Charles J. Ingersoll—2.

OHIO.—William Kennon, jun., John K. Miller, William Sawyer—3.

ILLINOIS.—William A. Richardson—1.

IOWA.—Shepherd Leffler—1.

Total Nays from Free States—8.

Mr. Robinson, of Ind, moved a reconsideration of this vote, which motion (Dec. 18), on motion of Mr. Wentworth, of Ill., was laid on the table: Yeas, 105; Nays, 83.

The Civil and Diplomatic Appropriation bill having passed the House in the usual form, came up to the Senate, where it was debated several days.

Feb. 21st.—Mr. Walker, of Wisc., moved an amendment, extending all the laws of the United States, so far as applicable, to the Territories acquired from Mexico.

Mr. Bell, of Tenn., moved to add further sections organizing the State of California, to be admitted into the Union on the 1st of October next. This was rejected: Yeas, 4 (Bell, Dodge of Iowa, Douglas, Davis): Nays, 39.

Feb. 26th.—Mr. Dayton, of N. J., moved that the President be vested with power to provide a suitable temporary government for the Territories. Rejected: Yeas, 8; Nays, 47.

The question recurred on Mr. Walker's amendment, which was carried: Yeas, 29; Nays, 27.

The bill being returned to the House, thus amended, this amendment was (March 2d) voted down: Yeas, 101; Nays, 115—as follows:

Yeas—all the members from the Slave States, with the following from the Free States, viz. :

MAINE—Hezekiah Williams—1.
NEW-YORK—Ausburn Birdsall—1.
PENNSYLVANIA—Samuel A. Bridges, Richard Brodhead, Charles Brown, Charles J. Ingersoll, *Lewis C. Levin*—5.
OHIO—William Kennon, jr., William Sawyer—2.
ILLINOIS—Orlando B. Ficklin, John A. McClernand, William A. Richardson—3.
IOWA—Shepherd Leffler—1.

Total, thirteen from Free States; eighty-eight from Slave States. (Only two from Slave States absent or silent.)

Nays—all the Whigs from Free States, and all the Democrats from Free States, except those named above.

So the House refused to concur in this amendment, and the bill was returned to the Senate accordingly.

The Senate resolved to insist on its amendment, and ask a conference, which was granted, but resulted in nothing. Messrs. Atherton, of N. H., Dickinson, of N. Y., and Berrien, of Ga., were managers on the part of the Senate, and insisted on its amendment, organizing the Territories without restriction as to Slavery. Messrs. Vinton, of Ohio, Nicoll, of N. Y., and Morehead, of Ky., were appointed on the part of the House. These, after a long sitting, reported their inability to agree, and were discharged.

The bill being now returned to the House, Mr. McClernand, of Ill., moved that the House do *recede* from its disagreement. Carried: Yeas, 111; Nays, 106.

Mr. R. W. Thompson, of Ind., moved that the House concur with the Senate, with an amendment, which was a substitute, extending the laws of the United States over said Territories, but leaving them unorganized,—

And that, until the fourth day of July, eighteen hundred and fifty, unless Congress shall sooner provide for the government of said Territories, *the existing laws thereof shall be retained and observed.*

The question being reached on amending the Senate's proposition as proposed by Mr. Thompson, it was carried: Yeas, 111; Nays, 105.

(All the Southern members in the negative, with Levin and a few of the Northern Democrats; the residue, with all the Northern Whigs, in the affirmative.)

The House now proceeded to agree to the Senate's amendment, *as amended* : Yeas, 110; Nays, 103, (the same as before; the friends of the Senate's proposition voting against it, as amended, and *vice versa*, on the understanding that Mr. Thompson's amendment would exclude Slavery.)

The bill as thus amended being returned to the Senate, it refused to agree to the House's amendment, and receded from its own proposition; so the bill was passed and the session closed, with no provision for the government of the newly-acquired Territories.

OREGON.

Aug. 6, 1846.—Mr. Douglas, from the Committee on Territories, reported to the House a bill organizing the Territory of Oregon.

Said bill was discussed in Committee of the Whole. and the following amendment agreed to:

And neither Slavery, nor involuntary servitude shall ever exist in said Territory, except for crime whereof the party shall have been duly convicted.

On coming out of Committee, this amendment was agreed to—Yeas, 108; Nays, 44. (The Nays are all Southern, but Charles J. Ingersoll, Orlando B. Ficklin, and possibly one or two others; and all Democrats, but some half a dozen from the South, of whom Robert Toombs has since turned Democrat.) Stephen A. Douglas did not vote. The bill passed the House without further opposition, was read twice in the Senate, and referred; and Mr. Westcott, of Florida, made a report thereon from the Committee on Territories; but the session closed without further action on the bill.

This Congress reassembled, Dec. 7th, 1846. On the 23d, Mr. Douglas again reported his bill to provide a Territorial government for Oregon, which was read twice and committed: Jan. 11th, 1847, was discussed in Committee, as also on the 12th and 14th, when it was resolved, to close the debate. On the 15th, it was taken out of Committee, when Gen. Burt, of S. C., moved the following addition (already moved, debated, and voted down in Committee) to the clause forbidding Slavery in said Territory :

Inasmuch as the whole of said Territory lies north of thirty-six degrees thirty minutes north latitude, known as the line of the Missouri Compromise.

The purpose of this is clear enough. It was intended to recognize the Missouri line, not as limited to the Territories possessed by the United States at the time said line was established, but as extending to all that has since been, or hereafter should be, acquired, so as to legalize Slavery in any Territory henceforth to be acquired by us south of 36° 30'.

Mr. Burt's amendment was negatived: Yeas, 82; Nays, 114.

The vote was very nearly sectional; but the following members from Free States voted in the minority :

PENNSYLVANIA—Charles J. Ingersoll—1.
ILLINOIS—Stephen A. Douglas, Robt. Smith—2.
IOWA—C. S. Hastings—1. In all, 5.

No member from a Slave State voted in the majority. The bill then passed: Yeas, 134; Nays, 35, (all Southern).

Jan. 15.—The bill reached the Senate, and was sent to the Judiciary Committee, consisting of

Messrs. Ashley, Ark.   Berrien, Ga.   Westcott, Fla.
        Breese, Ill.   Dayton, N. J.

Jan. 25.—Mr. Ashley reported the Oregon bill with amendments, which were ordered to be printed.

29.—Said bill, on motion of Mr. Westcott, was recommitted to the Judiciary Committee.

Feb 10.—Mr. Ashley again reported it with amendments.

March 3.—It was taken up as in Committee of the Whole, when Mr. Evans, of Maine, moved that it be laid on the table. Defeated: Yeas,

19, (all Whigs but Calhoun, of S. C., and Yulee of Florida); Nays, 26, (24 Dem., with Corwin of Ohio, and Johnson of Louisiana.)

Mr. Westcott, of Fla., immediately moved that the bill do lie on the table, which prevailed: Yeas, 26; Nays, 18 (a mixed vote, evidently governed by various motives); but the negatives were all Democrats, but Corwin and Johnson aforesaid. This being the last day of the session, it was evident that the bill, if opposed, as it was certain to be, could not get through, and it was, doubtless, in behalf of other pressing business that many Senators voted to lay this aside. It was, of course, dead for the session.

Dec. 6, 1847.—The XXXth Congress assembled; Robert C. Winthrop (Whig) of Mass. was chosen Speaker of the House. President Polk, in his Annual Message, regretted that Oregon had not already been organized, and urged the necessity of action on the subject.

Feb. 9.—Mr. Caleb B. Smith, of Indiana, reported to the House a bill to establish the territorial government of Oregon; which, by a vote of two-thirds, was made a special order for March 14th. It was postponed, however, to the 28th; when it was taken up and discussed, as on one or two subsequent days. *May* 29th, it was again made a special order next after the Appropriation bills. The President that day sent a special message, urging action on this subject. *July* 25th, it was taken up in earnest; Mr. Wentworth, of Illinois, moving that debate on it in Committee cease at two o'clock this day.

Mr. Geo. S. Houston, of Ala., endeavored to put this motion on the table. Defeated: Yeas 85; Nays 89, (nearly, but not fully, a sectional division). Mr. Geo. W. Jones, of Tenn., moved a reconsideration, which was carried: Yeas, 100; Nays, 88; and the resolution laid on the table: Yeas, 96; Nays, 90.

The bill continued to be discussed, and finally (Aug. 1) was got out of Committee; when Mr. C. B. Smith moved the Previous Question thereon, which was ordered.

Aug. 2.—The House came to a vote on an amendment made in Committee, whereby the following provision of the original bill was stricken out:

That the inhabitants of said Territory shall be entitled to enjoy all and singular, the rights, privileges, and advantages granted and secured to the people of the Territory of the United States northwest of the river Ohio, by the articles of compact contained in the ordinance for the government of said Territory, passed the 13th day of July, seventeen hundred and eighty-seven; and shall be subject to all the conditions, and restrictions, and prohibitions in said articles of compact imposed upon the people of said territory, and—

The House refused to agree to this amendment: Yeas, 88; Nays, 114.

The Members from the Free States who voted with the South to strike out, were—

New York.—Ausburn Birdsall—1.
Ohio.—William Kennon, jun., John K. Miller—2.
Illinois.—Orlando B. Ficklin, John A. McClernand, William A. Richardson—3.
Indiana.—John L. Robinson, William W. Wick—2.
Mr. John W. Houston of Delaware voted in the majority.

The bill was then passed: Yeas, 128; Nays, 71.

[This vote was almost completely sectional.

Mr. Houston, of Delaware, voting in the majority as before: otherwise, members from the Free States in the affirmative; those from the Slave States in the negative.]

Aug. 3.—This bill reached the Senate, when Mr. Badger, of N. C., moved its indefinite postponement: negatived, 47 to 1, (Yulee). It was then sent to the Committee on Territories.

The Senate had had under consideration, from time to time through the Session, a bill of its own, reported by Mr. Douglas, which was finally referred to a select Committee—Mr. Clayton, of Delaware, Chairman—and by said committee reported some days before the reception of the House bill. It was then dropped.

Aug. 5.—Mr. Douglas reported the House bill, with amendments, which were printed.

Aug. 10. — After some days' debate, the Senate proceeded to vote. Mr. Foote, of Miss., moved that the bill do lie on the table. Defeated: Yeas, 15 (Southern); Nays, 36.

On the question of agreeing to this amendment:

Inasmuch as the said Territory is north of thirty-six deg. thirty min., usually known as the [line of the] Missouri Compromise.

It was rejected: Yeas, 2 (Bright and Douglas); Nays, 52.

Mr. Douglas moved to amend the bill, by inserting after the word "enacted:"

That the line of thirty-six degrees and thirty minutes of north latitude, known as the Missouri Compromise line, as defined in the eighth section of an act entitled, "An Act to authorize the people of the Missouri Territory to form a Constitutional and State Government, and for the admission of such State into the Union on an equal footing with the original States, and to prohibit Slavery in certain Territories, approved March 6th, 1820," be, and the same is hereby, declared to extend to the Pacific Ocean; and the said eighth section, together with the compromise therein effected, is hereby revived, and declared to be in full force and binding, for the future organization of the Territories of the United States in the same sense, and with the same understanding with which it was originally adopted; and—

Which was carried: Yeas, 33; Nays, 21; as fol lows:

Yeas—For recognizing the Missouri line as rightfully extending to the Pacific:

Messrs. Atchison,
　　Badger,
　　Bell,
　　Benton,
　　Berrien,
　　Borland,
　　Bright,
　　Butler,
　　Calhoun,
　　Cameron,
　　Davis of Miss.,
　　Dickinson,
　　Douglas,
　　Downs,
　　Fitzgerald,
　　Foote of Miss.,
Hannegan,
Houston,
Hunter,
Johnson of Md.,
Johnson of La.,
Johnson of Ga.,
King,
Lewis,
Mangum,
Mason,
Metcalf,
Pearce,
Sebastian,
Spruance,
Sturgeon,
Turney,
　　　　Underwood—33.

Nays—Against recognizing said line:

Messrs. Allen,
　　Atherton,
　　Baldwin,
　　Bradbury,
　　Breese,
　　Clarke,
　　Corwin,
　　Davis of Mass.,
　　Dayton,
　　Dix,
Dodge,
Felch,
Greene,
Hale,
Hamlin,
Miller,
Niles,
Phelps,
Upham,
Walker,
　　　　Webster—21.

The bill was then engrossed for a third reading: Yeas, 33; Nays, 22; (nearly the same as before—Westcott of Florida added to the Nays—and thus passed).

Aug. 11.—The bill, thus amended, having been returned to the House, the amendment of Mr. Douglas, just recited, was rejected: Yeas, 82; Nays, 121.

Yeas from Free States:

NEW YORK.—Ausburn Birdsall—1.
PENNSYLVANIA.—Charles Brown, Charles J. Ingersoll—2.
Total—3.

Otherwise, from Slave States, all Yeas: from Free States, all Nays.

Aug. 12.—The Senate, after voting down various propositions to lay on the table, etc., finally decided to *recede* from its amendments to the Oregon bill, and pass it as it came from the House: Yeas, 29; Nays, 25 (all from Slave States).

So the bill became a law, and Oregon a Territory, under the original Jefferson or Dane Proviso against Slavery.

THE COMPROMISE OF 1850.

The XXXIst Congress commenced its first Session at Washington, Dec. 3, 1849; but the House was unable to organize—no person receiving a majority of all the votes for Speaker—until the 22nd, when, the Plurality rule having been adopted by a vote of 113 to 106, Mr. Howell Cobb, of Ga., was elected, having 102 votes to 100 for Robert C. Winthrop of Mass., and 20 scattering. It was thereupon resolved—Yeas, 149; Nays, 35—" That Howell Cobb be declared duly elected Speaker;" and on the 24th President Zachary Taylor transmitted to both Houses his first Annual Message, in the course of which he says:

No civil government having been provided by Congress for California, the people of that Territory, impelled by the necessities of their political condition, recently met in Convention, for the purpose of forming a Constitution and State Government; which, the latest advices give me reason to suppose, has been accomplished; and it is believed they will shortly apply for the admission of California into the Union, as a Sovereign State. Should such be the case, and should their constitution be conformable to the requisitions of the Constitution of the United States, I recommend their application to the favorable consideration of Congress.

The people of New-Mexico will also, it is believed, at no very distant period, present themselves for admission into the Union. Preparatory to the admission of California and New-Mexico, the people of each will have instituted for themselves a republican form of government, laying its foundation in such principles, and organizing its power in such form, as to them shall seem most likely to effect their safety and happiness.

By awaiting their action, all uneasiness may be avoided and confidence and kind feeling preserved. With a view of maintaining the harmony and tranquillity so dear to all, we should abstain from the introduction of those exciting topics of a sectional character which have hitherto produced painful apprehensions in the public mind; and I repeat the solemn warning of the first and most illustrious of my predecessors, against furnishing any ground for characterizing parties by geographical discriminations.

Jan. 4.—Gen. Sam. Houston, of Texas, submitted to the Senate the following proposition:

Whereas, The Congress of the United States, possessing only a delegated authority, have no power over the subject of Negro Slavery within the limits of the United States, either to prohibit or interfere with it, in the States, Territories, or District, where, by municipal law, it now exists, or to establish it in any State or Territory where it does not exist; but, as an assurance and guaranty to promote harmony, quiet apprehension and remove sectional prejudice, which by possibility might impair or weaken love and devotion to the Union in any part of the country, it is hereby

Resolved, That, as the people in Territories have the same inherent rights of self-government as the people in the States, if in the exercise of such inherent rights the people in the newly-acquired Territories, by the Annexation of Texas and the acquisition of California and New-Mexico, south of the parallel of 36 degrees and 30 minutes of north latitude, extending to the Pacific Ocean, shall establish Negro Slavery in the formation of their state governments, it shall be deemed no objection to their admission as a State or States into the Union, in accordance with the Constitution of the United States.

Jan. 21.—Gen. Taylor, in answer to a resolution of inquiry, sent a message to the House, stating that he had urged the formation of State Governments in California and New-Mexico.

Feb. 13, 1850.—Gen. Taylor communicated to Congress the Constitution (free) of the State of California.

Jan. 29, 1850.—Mr. Henry Clay, of Kentucky, submitted to the Senate the following propositions, with others, which were made a special order and printed:

1. *Resolved,* That California, with suitable boundaries, ought, upon her application, to be admitted as one of the States of this Union, without the imposition by Congress of any restriction in respect to the exclusion or introduction of Slavery within those boundaries.

2. *Resolved,* That as Slavery does not exist by law, and is not likely to be introduced into any of the territory acquired by the United States from the Republic of Mexico, it is inexpedient for Congress to provide by law either for its introduction into, or exclusion from, any part of the said Territory; and that appropriate territorial governments ought to be established by Congress, in all the said Territory, not assigned as within the boundaries of the proposed State of California, without the adoption of any restriction or condition on the subject of Slavery.

5. *Resolved,* That it is inexpedient to abolish Slavery in the District of Columbia, whilst that institution continues to exist in the State of Maryland, without the consent of that State, without the consent of the people of the District, and without just compensation to the owners of slaves within the District.

6. *But Resolved,* That it *is* expedient to prohibit, within the District, the slave-trade in slaves brought into it from States or places beyond the limits of the District, either to be sold therein as merchandise, or to be transported to other markets without the District of Columbia.

7. *Resolved,* That more effectual provision ought to be made by law, according to the requirement of the Constitution, for the restitution and delivery of persons bound to service or labor in any State, who may escape into any other State or Territory in the Union. And,

8. *Resolved,* That Congress has no power to prohibit or obstruct the trade in slaves between the slaveholding States, but that the admission or exclusion of slaves brought from one into another of them, depends exclusively upon their own particular laws.

Feb. 28.—Mr. John Bell, of Tennessee, submitted to the Senate the following propositions:

Whereas, Considerations of the highest interest to the whole country demand that the existing and increasing dissensions between the North and the South, on the subject of Slavery, should be speedily arrested, and that the questions in controversy be adjusted upon some basis which shall tend to give present quiet, repress sectional animosities, remove, as far as possible, the causes of future discord, and secure the uninterrupted enjoyment of those benefits and advantages which the Union was intended to confer in equal measure upon all its members;

And, whereas, It is manifest, under present circumstances, that no adjustment can be effected of the points of difference unhappily existing between the Northern and Southern sections of the Union, connected with the subject of Slavery, which shall secure to either section all that is contended for, and that mutual concessions upon questions of mere policy, not involving the violation of any constitutional right or principle, must be the basis of every project affording any assurance of a favorable acceptance;

And, whereas, The joint resolution for annexing

Texas to the United States, approved March 1, 1845, contains the following condition and guaranty—that is to say: "New States of convenient size, not exceeding four in number, in addition to said State of Texas, and having sufficient population, may hereafter, by the consent of said State, be formed out of the territory thereof, which shall be entitled to admission under the provisions of the Federal Constitution; and such States as may be formed out of that portion of said Territory lying south of thirty-six degrees thirty minutes north latitude, commonly known as the Missouri Compromise line, shall be admitted into the Union with or without Slavery, as the people of each State, asking admission may desire; and in such State or States as shall be formed out of said territory north of said Missouri Compromise line, Slavery, or involuntary servitude (except for crime), shall be prohibited:" Therefore,

1. *Resolved*, That the obligation to comply with the condition and guaranty above recited in good faith be distinctly recognized, and that, in part compliance with the same, as soon as the people of Texas shall, by an act of their legislature, signify their assent by restricting the limits thereof, within the Territory lying east of the Trinity and south of the Red River, and when the people of the residue of the territory claimed by Texas adopt a constitution, republican in form, they be admitted into Union upon an equal footing in all respects with the original States.

2. *Resolved*, That if Texas shall agree to cede, the United States will accept, a cession of all the unappropriated domain in all the Territory claimed by Texas, lying west of the Colorado and extending north to the forty-second parallel of north latitude, together with the jurisdiction and sovereignty of all the territory claimed by Texas, north of the thirty-fourth parallel of north latitude, and to pay therefor a sum not exceeding —— millions of dollars, to be applied in the first place to the extinguishment of any portion of the existing public debt of Texas, for the discharge of which the United States are under any obligation, implied or otherwise, and the remainder as Texas shall require.

3. *Resolved*, That when the population of that portion of the Territory claimed by Texas, lying south of the thirty-fourth parallel of north latitude and west of the Colorado, shall be equal to the ratio of representation in Congress, under the last preceding apportionment, according to the provisions of the Constitution, and the people of such Territory shall, with the assent of the new State contemplated in the preceding resolution, have adopted a State Constitution, republican in form, they be admitted into the Union as a State, upon an equal footing with the original States.

Resolved, That all the Territory now claimed by Texas, lying north of the thirty-fourth parallel of north latitude, and which may be ceded to the United States by Texas, be incorporated with the Territory of New-Mexico, except such part thereof as lies east of the Rio Grande and south of the thirty-fourth degree of north latitude, and that the Territory so composed form a State, to be admitted into the Union when the inhabitants thereof shall adopt a State Constitution, republican in form, with the consent of Congress; but in the mean time, and until Congress shall give such consent, provision be made for the government of the inhabitants of said Territory suitable to their condition, but without any restriction as to Slavery.

5. *Resolved*, That all the Territory ceded to the United States, by the Treaty of Guadaloupe Hidalgo, lying west of said Territory of New Mexico, and east of the contemplated new State of California, for the present, constitute one Territory, and for which some form of government suitable to the condition of the inhabitants be provided, without any restriction as to Slavery.

6. *Resolved*, That the Constitution recently formed by the people of the western portion of California, and presented to Congress by the President, on the 13th day of February, 1850, be accepted, and that they be admitted into the Union as a State, upon an equal footing in all respects with the original States.

Resolved, That, in future, the formation of State Constitutions, by the inhabitants of the Territories of the United States, be regulated by law; and that no such Constitution be hereafter formed or adopted by the inhabitants of any Territory belonging to the United States, without the consent and authority of Congress.

8. *Resolved*, That the inhabitants of any Territory of the United States, when they shall be authorized by Congress to form a State Constitution, shall have the sole and exclusive power to regulate and adjust all questions of internal State policy, of whatever nature they may be, controlled only by the restrictions expressly imposed by the Constitution of the United States.

9. *Resolved*, That the Committee on Territories be instructed to report a bill in conformity with the spirit and principles of the foregoing resolutions.

A debate of unusual duration, earnestness, and ability ensued, mainly on Mr. Clay's Resolutions. They were regarded by uncompromising champions, whether of Northern or of Southern views, but especially of the latter, as conceding substantially the matter in dispute to the other side. Thus,

January 29th.—Mr. Clay having read and briefly commented on his propositions, *seriatim*, he desired that they should be held over without debate, to give time for consideration, and made a special order for Monday or Tuesday following. But this was not assented to.

Mr. Foote, of Mississippi, spoke against them generally, saying:

If I understand the resolutions properly, they are objectionable, as it seems to me,

1. Because they only assert that it is not *expedient* that Congress should abolish Slavery in the District of Columbia; thus allowing the implication to arise that Congress has power to legislate on the subject of Slavery in the District, which may hereafter be exercised, if it should become expedient to do so; whereas, I hold that Congress has, under the Constitution, no such power at all, and that any attempt thus to legislate would be a gross fraud upon all the States of the Union.

2. The Resolutions of the honorable Senator assert that Slavery does not now exist by law in the Territories recently acquired from Mexico; whereas, I am of opinion that the treaty with the Mexican republic carried the Constitution, *with all its guaranties*, to all the Territory obtained by treaty, and secured the privilege to every Southern slaveholder to enter any part of it, attended by his slave-property, and to enjoy the same therein, free from all molestation or hindrance whatsoever.

3. Whether Slavery is or is not likely to be introduced into these Territories, or into any of them, is a proposition too uncertain, in my judgment, to be at present positively affirmed; and I am unwilling to make a solemn legislative declaration on the point. *Let the future provide the appropriate solution of this interesting question.*

4. Considering, as I have several times heretofore formally declared, the title of Texas to all the Territory embraced in her boundaries, as laid down in her law of 1836, full, complete, and undeniable, I am unwilling to say anything, by resolution or otherwise, which may in the least degree draw that title into question, as I think is done in one of the resolutions of the honorable Senator from Kentucky. . . . .

6. As to the abolition of the *slave-trade* in the District of Columbia, I see no particular objection to it, provided it is done in a delicate and judicious manner, and is not a concession to the menaces and demands of factionists and fanatics. If other questions can be adjusted, this one will, perhaps, occasion but little difficulty.

7. The resolutions which provide for the restoration of fugitives from labor or service, and for the establishment of territorial governments, free from all restriction on the subject of Slavery, have my hearty approval. The last resolution—which asserts that Congress has no power to prohibit the trade in slaves from State to State—I equally approve.

8. If all other questions connected with the subject of Slavery can be satisfactorily adjusted, I see no objection to admitting all California, above the line of 36 degrees 30 minutes, into the Union; *provided another new Slave State can be laid off within the present limits of Texas*, so as to keep the present *equiponderance* between the Slave and Free States of the Union: and provided further, all this is done by way of *compromise, and in order to save the Union,* (as dear to me as to any man living.)

Mr. Mason, of Virginia, after expressing his deep anxiety to "go with him who went furthest, but within the limits of strict duty, in adjusting these unhappy differences," added:

Sir, so far as I have read these resolutions, there is but one proposition to which I can give a hearty assent, and that is the resolution which proposes to organize Territorial governments at once in these Territories, without a declaration one way or the other as to their domestic institutions. But there is another which I deeply regret to see introduced into this Senate, by a Senator from a slaveholding State; it is that which assumes that Slavery does not now exist by law in those countries. I understand one of these propositions to declare that, by law, Slavery is now abolished in New-Mexico and California. That was the very proposition advanced by the non-slaveholding States at the last session; combated and disproved, as I thought, by gentlemen from the slaveholding States and which the Compromise bill was framed to test. So far, I regarded the question of law as disposed of, and it was very clearly and satisfactorily shown to be against the spirit of the resolution of the Senator from Kentucky. If the contrary is true, I presume the Senator from Kentucky would declare that if a law is now valid in the Territories abolishing Slavery, that it could not be introduced there, even if a law was passed creating the institution, or repealing the statutes already existing; a doctrine never assented to, so far as I know, until now, by any Senator representing one of the slaveholding States. Sir, I hold the very opposite, and with such confidence, that at the last session I was willing and did vote for a bill to test this question in the Supreme Court. Yet this resolution assumes the other doctrine to be true, and our assent is challenged to it as a proposition of law.

Mr. Jefferson Davis, of Mississippi, objected specially to so much of Mr. Clay's propositions as relates to the boundary of Texas, to the slave-trade in the Federal district, and to Mr. Clay's avowal in his speech that he did not believe Slavery ever would or could be established in any part of the Territories acquired from Mexico. He continued:

But, sir, we are called upon to receive this as a measure of compromise! As a measure in which we of the minority are to receive nothing. A measure of compromise! I look upon it as but a modest mode of taking that, the claim to which has been more boldly asserted by others; and, that I may be understood upon this question, and that my position may go forth to the country in the same columns that convey the sentiments of the Senator from Kentucky, I here assert, that never will I take less than the Missouri Compromise line extended to the Pacific Ocean, with the specific recognition of the right to hold slaves in the Territory below that line; and that, before such Territories are admitted into the Union as States, slaves may be taken there from any of the United States at the option of the owners. I can never consent to give additional power to a majority to commit further aggressions upon the minority in this Union; and will never consent to any proposition which will have such a tendency, without a full guaranty or counteracting measure is connected with it.

Mr. Clay, in reply, said:

I am extremely sorry to hear the Senator from Mississippi say that he requires, first, the extension of the Missouri Compromise line to the Pacific; and also that he is not satisfied with that, but requires, if I understood him correctly, a positive provision for the admission of Slavery south of that line. And now, sir, coming from a Slave State, as I do, I owe it to myself, I owe it to truth, I owe it to the subject, to state that no earthly power could induce me to vote for a specific measure for the introduction of Slavery where it had not before existed, either south or north of that line. Coming as I do from a Slave State, it is my solemn, deliberate, and well-matured determination that no power—no earthly power—shall compel me to vote for the positive introduction of Slavery either south or north of that line. Sir, while you reproach, and justly, too, our British ancestors for the introduction of this institution upon the Continent of America, I am, for one, unwilling that the posterity of the present inhabitants of California and New-Mexico shall reproach us for doing just what we reproach Great Britain for doing to us. If the citizens of those Territories choose to establish Slavery, I am for admitting them with such provisions in their Constitutions; but then, it will be their own work, and not ours, and their posterity will have to reproach them, and not us, for forming Constitutions allowing the institution of Slavery to exist among them. These are my views, sir, and I choose to express them; and I care not how extensively and universally they are known. The honorable Senator from Virginia has expressed his opinion that Slavery exists in these Territories, and I have no doubt that opinion is sincerely and honestly entertained by him; and I would say with equal sincerity and honesty, that I believe that Slavery nowhere exists within any portion of the Territory acquired by us from Mexico. He holds a directly contrary opinion to mine, as he has a perfect right to do; and we will not quarrel about that difference of opinion.

Mr. William R. King, of Alabama, was inclined to look with favor on Mr. Clay's propositions, and assented to some of them; but he objected to the mode in which California had formed what is called a State Constitution. He preferred the good old way of first organizing Territories, and so training up their people "for the exercise and enjoyment of our institutions." Besides, he thought "there was not that kind of population there that justified the formation of a State Government." On the question of Slavery in the new Territories, he said:

We ask no act of Congress—as has been properly intimated by the Senator from Mississippi—to carry Slavery anywhere. Sir, I believe we have as much Constitutional power to prohibit Slavery from going into the Territories of the United States, as we have to pass an act carrying Slavery there. We have no right to do either the one or the other. I would as soon vote for the Wilmot Proviso as I would vote for any law which required that Slavery should go into any of the Territories.

Mr. Downs, of Louisiana, said:

I must confess that, in the whole course of my life, my astonishment has never been greater than it was when I saw this (Mr. Clay's) proposition brought forward as a compromise; and I rise now, sir, not for the purpose of discussing it at all, but to protest most solemnly against it. I consider this compromise as no compromise at all. What, sir, does it grant to the South? I can see nothing at all.

Mr. Butler, of South Carolina, said:

As I understand it, the Senator from Kentucky's whole proposition of compromise is nothing more than this: That California is already disposed of, having formed a State Constitution, and that Territorial Governments shall be organized for Deseret and New-Mexico, under which, by the operation of laws already existing, a slaveholding population could not carry with them, or own slaves there. What is there in the nature of a compromise here, coupled, as it is, with the proposition that, by the existing laws in the Territories, it is almost certain that slaveholders cannot, and have no right to, go there with their property? What is there in the nature of a compromise here? I am willing, however, to run the risks, and am ready to give to the Territories the governments they require. I shall always think that, under a Constitution giving equal rights to all parties, the slaveholding people, as such, can go to these Territories, and retain their property there. But, if we adopt this proposition of the Senator from Kentucky, it is clearly on the basis that Slavery shall not go there.

The debate having engrossed the attention of the Senate for nearly two months—

March 25.—Mr. Douglas, from the Committee on Territories, reported the following bills:

Senate, 169.—A bill for the admission of California into the Union.
Senate, 170.—A bill to establish the Territorial Governments of Utah and New-Mexico, and for other purposes.

These bills were read, and passed to a second reading.

April 11.—Mr. Douglas moved that Mr. Bell's resolves do lie on the table. Lost: Yeas, 26; Nays, 28.

April 15.—The discussion of Mr. Clay's resolutions still proceeding, Colonel Benton moved that the previous orders be postponed, and that the Senate now proceed to consider the bill (S. 169) for the admission of the State of California.

Mr. Clay moved that this proposition do lie on the table. Carried: Yeas, 27 (for a Compromise); Nays, 24 (for a settlement without compromise).

The Senate now took up Mr. Bell's resolves,

aforesaid, when Mr. Benton moved that they lie on the table. Lost: Yeas, 24; Nays, 28.

Mr. Benton next moved that they be so amended as not to connect or mix up the admission of California with any other question. Lost: Yeas, 23; Nays, 28.

Various modifications of the generic idea were severally voted down, generally by large majorities. ·

On motion of Mr. Foote, of Miss., it was now

Ordered, That the resolutions submitted by Mr. Bell on the 28th February, together with the resolutions submitted on the 29th of January, by Mr. Clay, be referred to a select Committee of thirteen; *Provided*, that the Senate does not deem it necessary, and therefore declines, to express in advance any opinion, or to give any instruction, either general or specific, for the guidance of the said Committee.

April 19.—The Senate proceeded to elect by ballot such Select Committee, which was composed as follows:

Mr. Henry Clay, of Ky., *Chairman.*

Messrs.	
Dickinson, of N. Y.	Cooper, of Pa.
Phelps, of Vt.	Downs, of La.
Bell, of Tenn.	King, of Ala.
Cass, of Mich.	Mangum, of N. C.
Webster, of Mass.	Mason, of Va.
Berrien, of Ga.	Bright, of Ind.

May 8.—Mr. Clay, from said Committee, reported at length, the views and recommendations of the report being substantially as follows:

1. The admission of any new State or States formed out of Texas to be postponed until they shall hereafter present themselves to be received into the Union, when it will be the duty of Congress fairly and faithfully to execute the compact with Texas, by admitting such new State or States.

2. The admission forthwith of California into the Union, with the boundaries which she has proposed.

3. The establishment of Territorial Governments, without the Wilmot Proviso, for New-Mexico and Utah, embracing all the territory recently acquired by the United States from Mexico, not contained in the boundaries of California.

4. The combination of these two last mentioned measures in the same bill;

5. The establishment of the western and northern boundaries of Texas, and the exclusion from her jurisdiction of all New-Mexico, with the grant to Texas of a pecuniary equivalent; and the section for that purpose to be incorporated in the bill admitting California and establishing Territorial Governments for Utah and New-Mexico.

6. More effectual enactments of law to secure the prompt delivery of persons bound to service or labor in one State, under the laws thereof, who escape into another State; and,

7. Abstaining from abolishing Slavery; but, under a heavy penalty, prohibiting the slave-trade in the District of Columbia.

The Senate proceeded to debate from day to day the provisions of the principal bill thus reported, commonly termed "the Omnibus."

June 28.—Mr. Soulé, of Louisiana, moved that all south of 36° 30' be cut off from California, and formed into a Territory entitled South California, and that said Territory

"shall, when ready, able, and willing to become a State, and deserving to be such, be admitted with or without Slavery, as the people thereof shall desire, and make known through their Constitution."

This was rejected: Yeas, 19 (all Southern); Nays, 36.

July 10 —The discussion was interrupted by the death of President Taylor. Millard Fillmore succeeded to the Presidency, and William R. King, of Alabama, was chosen President of the Senate, *pro tempore.*

July 15.—The bill was reported to the Senate and amended so as to substitute " that Congress

shall make no law establishing or prohibiting " Slavery in the new Territories, instead of " in respect to " it. Yeas, 27; Nays, 25.

Mr. Seward moved to add at the end of the 37th section:

But neither Slavery nor involuntary servitude shall be allowed in either of the Territories of New-Mexico or Utah, except on legal conviction for crime.

Which was negatived; Yeas and Nays not taken.

July 17.—The Senate resumed the consideration of the " Omnibus bill."

Mr. Benton moved a change in the proposed boundary between Texas and New-Mexico. Rejected: Yeas, 18; Nays, 36.

Mr. Foote moved that the 34th parallel of north latitude be the northern boundary of Texas throughout. Lost: Yeas, 20; Nays, 34.

July 19.—Mr. King moved that the parallel of 35° 30' be the southern boundary of the State of California. Rejected: Yeas, 20; Nays, 37.

Mr. Davis, of Mississippi, moved 36° 30'. Rejected: Yeas, 23; Nays, 32.

July 23d.—Mr. Turney, of Tenn., moved that the people of California be enabled to form a new State Constitution. Lost: Yeas, 19; Nays, 33.

Mr. Jeff. Davis, of Mississippi, moved to add:

And that all laws and usages existing in said Territory, at the date of its acquisition by the United States, which deny or obstruct the right of any citizen of the United States to remove to, and reside in, said Territory, with any species of property legally held in any of the States of this Union, be, and are hereby declared to be, null and void.

This was rejected: Yeas, 22; Nays, 33.

Yeas—For Davis's amendment:

Messrs.	
Atchison, Mo.	King, Ala.
Barnwell, S. C.	Mangum. N. C.
Bell, Tenn.	Mason, Va.
Berrien, Ga.	Morton, Fla.
Butler, S. C.	Pratt, Md.
Clemens, Ala.	Rusk, Texas.
Davis, Miss.	Sebastian, Ark.
Dawson, Ga.	Soulé, La.
Downs, La.	Turney, Tenn.
Houston, Texas.	Underwood, Ky.
Hunter, Va.	Yulee, Fla.—22.

Nays—Against Davis's amendment:

Messrs.	
Badger, N. C.	Foote, Miss.
Baldwin, Conn.	Greene, R. I.
Benton, Mo.	Hale, N. H.
Bradbury, Me.	Hamlin, Me.
Bright, Ind.	Jones, Iowa.
Cass, Mich.	Miller, N. J.
Chase, Ohio.	Norris, N. H.
Clarke, R. I.	Pearce, Md.
Clay, Ky.	Seward, N. Y.
Cooper, Pa.	Shields, Ill.
Davis, Mass.	Smith, Conn.
Dayton, N. J.	Spruance, Del.
Dickinson, N. Y.	Sturgeon, Pa.
Dodge, Wisc.	Upham, Vt.
Dodge, Iowa.	Wales, Del.
•Felch, Mich.	Walker, Wisc.
Whitcomb, Ind.—33.	

Aug. 10.—The California bill was now taken up. Mr. Yulee, of Fla., moved a substitute, remanding California to a territorial condition, and limiting her southern boundary. Rejected: Yeas, 12 (all Southern); Nays, 35.

Mr. Foote moved a like project, cutting off so much of California as lies south of 36 deg. 30 min., and erecting it into the Territory of Colorado. Rejected: Yeas, 13 (ultra Southern); Nays, 29.

Aug. 12.—Still another proposition to limit

California southwardly, by the line of 36 deg. 30 min., was made by Mr. Turney, and rejected: Yeas, 20 (all Southern); Nays, 30. After defeating Southern motions to adjourn, postpone, and lay on the table, the bill was engrossed for a third reading: Yeas, 33 (all the Senators from Free States, with Bell, Benton, Houston, Spruance, Wales and Underwood); Nays, 19 (all from Slave States). Mr. Clay still absent, endeavoring to restore his failing health.

Aug. 13.—The California bill passed its third reading: Yeas, 34; Nays, 18 (all Southern).

Aug. 14.—The Senate now took up the bill organizing the Territories of New Mexico and Utah (as it was originally reported, prior to its inclusion in Mr. Clay's "Omnibus").

Mr. Chase, of Ohio, moved to amend the bill by inserting:

Nor shall there be in said Territory either Slavery or involuntary servitude, otherwise than in the punishment of crimes whereof the party shall have been duly convicted to have been personally guilty.

Which was rejected: Yeas, 20; Nays, 25.

The bill was then reported complete, and passed to be engrossed.

Aug. 15.—Said bill had its third reading, and was finally passed: Yeas, 27; Nays, 10.

[The Senate proceeded to take up, consider, mature, and pass the Fugitive Slave bill, and the bill excluding the Slave-Trade from the District of Columbia; but the history of these is but remotely connected with our theme]. We return to the House.

Aug. 28.—The California bill was taken up, read twice, and committed.

The Texas bill coming up, Mr. Inge, of Ala. objected to it, and a vote was taken on its rejection: Yeas, 34; Nays, 168; so it was not rejected.

Mr. Boyd, of Ky., moved to amend it so as to create and define thereby the Territories of New-Mexico and Utah, to be slaveholding or not as their people shall determine when they shall come to form State governments. [In other words, to append the bill organizing the Territory of New Mexico to the Texas bill.]

Sept. 7.—The California bill now came up. Mr. Boyd moved his amendment already moved to the Texas bill. Mr. Vinton, of Ohio, declared it out of order. The Speaker again ruled it in order. Mr. Vinton appealed, and the House overruled the Speaker: Yeas (to sustain), 87; Nays, 115.

Mr. Jacob Thompson, of Miss., moved to cut off from California all below 36° 30'. Rejected: Yeas, 76; Nays, 131.

The bill was now ordered to a third reading: Yeas, 151; Nays, 57, and then passed: Yeas, 150; Nays, 56 (all Southern).

The Senate bill organizing the Territory of Utah (without restriction as to Slavery) was then taken up, and rushed through the same day: Yeas, 97; Nays, 85. [The Nays were mainly Northern Free Soil men; but some Southern men, for a different reason, voted with them].

Sept. 9.—The House having returned the Texas Boundary bill, with an amendment (Linn Boyd's), including the bill organizing the Territory of New Mexico therein, the Senate proceeded to consider and agree to the same: Yeas, 31; Nays, 10, namely:

Messrs. Baldwin, Conn.,   Ewing, Ohio,
Benton, Mo.,   Hamlin. Me.,
Chase, Ohio,   Seward, N. Y.,
Davis, Mass.,   Upham, Vt.,
Dodge, Wis.,   Winthrop, Mass.

So all the bills originally included in Mr. Clay's "Omnibus" were passed—two of them in the same bill—after the Senate had once voted to sever them.

THE KANSAS-NEBRASKA STRUGGLE.

Out of the Louisiana Territory, since the admission first of Louisiana and then of Missouri as Slave States, there had been formed the Territories of Arkansas, Iowa, and Minnesota; the first without, and the two others with, Congressional inhibition of Slavery. Arkansas, in due course, became a Slave, Iowa and Minnesota Free States. The destiny of one tier of States, fronting upon, and westward of, the Mississippi, was thus settled. What should be the fate of the next tier?

The region lying immediately westward of Missouri, with much Territory north, as well as a more clearly defined district south of it, was long since dedicated to the uses of the Aborigines —not merely those who had originally inhabited it, but the tribes from time to time removed from the States eastward of the Mississippi. Very little, if any, of it was legally open to settlement by Whites; and, with the exception of the few and small military and trading posts thinly scattered over its surface, it is probable that scarcely two hundred white families were located in the spacious wilderness bounded by Missouri, Iowa, and Minnesota on the east, the British possessions on the north, the crest of the Rocky Mountains on the west, and the settled portion of New-Mexico and the line of 36° 30' on the south, at the time when Mr. Douglas first, at the session of 1852–3, submitted a bill organizing the Territory of Nebraska, by which title the region above bounded had come to be vaguely indicated.

This region was indisputably included within the scope of the exclusion of Slavery from all Federal Territory north of 36° 30', to which the South had assented by the terms of the Missouri compact, in order thereby to secure the admission of Missouri as a Slave State. Nor was it once intimated, during the long, earnest, and searching debate in the Senate on the Compromise Measures of 1850, that the adoption of those measures, whether together or separately, would involve or imply a repeal of the Missouri Restriction. We have seen on a former page how Mr. Clay's original suggestion of a Compromise, which was substantially that ultimately adopted, was received by the Southern Senators who spoke on its introduction, with hardly a qualification, as a virtual surrender of all that the South had ever claimed with respect to the new Territories. And, from the beginning to the close of the long and able discussion which followed, neither friend nor foe of the Compromises, nor of any of them, hinted that one effect of their adoption would be the lifting of the Missouri restriction from the Territory now covered by it. When the Compromises of 1850 were accepted in 1852 by the National Conventions of the two great parties, as a settlement of the distracting controversy therein contemplated, no hint was added that the Nebraska region was opened thereby to Slavery.

Several petitions for the organization of a Territory westward of Missouri and Iowa were presented at the session of 1851–2, but no decisive action taken thereon, until the next session, when,

Dec. 13th.—Mr. W. P. Hall, of Mo., pursuant to notice, submitted to the House a bill to organize the Territory of Platte, which was read twice, and sent to the Committee on Territories. From that Committee,

Feb. 2d, 1853.—Mr. W. A. Richardson, of Ill., reported a bill to organize the Territory of Nebraska, which was read twice and committed.

Feb. 9th.—The bill was ordered to be taken out of Committee, on motion of W. P. Hall.

Feb. 10th.—The bill was reported from the Committee of the Whole to the House, with a recommendation that it do *not* pass.

Mr. Richardson moved the previous question, which prevailed.

Mr. Letcher, of Va., moved that the bill do lie on the table. Lost: Yeas, 49 (mainly Southern); Nays, 107.

The bill was then engrossed, read a third time, and passed. Yeas, 98; Nays, 43, (as before.)

Feb. 11th.—The bill reached the Senate and was referred to the Committee on Territories.

Feb. 17th.—Mr. Douglas reported it without amendment.

March 2d.—(Last day but one of the session), Mr. Douglas moved that the bill be taken up: Lost: Yeas, 20; (all Northern but Atchison and Geyer, of Mo.;) Nays, 25; (21 Southern, 4 Northern.)

March 3rd.—Mr. Douglas again moved that the bill be taken up.

Mr. Borland, of Ark., moved that it do lie on the table. Carried: Yeas, 23; (all Southern but 4;) Nays, 17; (all Northern but Atchison and Geyer.) So the bill was put to sleep for the session.

On the motion to take up—Mr. Rusk of Texas objecting—Mr. Atchison said:

I must ask the indulgence of the Senate to say one word in relation to this matter. Perhaps there is not a State in the Union more deeply interested in this question than the State of Missouri. If not the largest, I will say the best, portion of that Territory, perhaps the only portion of it that in half a century will become a State, lies immediately west of the State of Missouri. It is only a question of time, whether we will organize the Territory at this session of Congress, or whether we will do it at the next session; and, for my own part, I acknowledge now that, as the Senator from Illinois well knows, when I came to this city, at the beginning of the last session, I was perhaps as much opposed to the proposition, as the Senator from Texas now is. The Senator from Iowa knows it; and *it was for reasons which I will not now mention or suggest.* But, sir, I have from reflection and investigation in my own mind, and from the opinions of others—my constituents, whose opinions I am bound to respect—come to the conclusion that now is the time for the organization of this Territory. It is the most propitious time. The treaties with the various Indian tribes, the titles to whose possessions must be extinguished, can better be made now than at any future time; for, as the question is agitated, and as it is understood, white men, speculators, will interpose, and interfere, and the longer it is postponed the more we will have to fear from them, and the more difficult it will be to extinguish the Indian title in that country, and the harder the terms to be imposed. Therefore, Mr. President, for this reason, without going into detail,

I am willing now that the question shall be taken, whether we will proceed to the consideration of the bill or not.

The meaning is here diplomatically veiled, yet is perfectly plain. Gen. Atchison had been averse to organizing this Territory until he could procure a relaxation of the Missouri Restriction as to Slavery; but, seeing no present hope of this, he was willing to waive the point, and assent to an organization under a bill silent with respect to Slavery, and of course leaving the Missouri Restriction unimpaired.

Gen. Pierce was inaugurated President on the 4th March, 1853.

The XXXIIId Congress assembled at Washington, Dec. 5th, 1853, with a large Administration majority in either House. Linn Boyd of Ky., was chosen Speaker of the House. The President's Annual Message contained the following allusion to the subject of Slavery:

It is no part of my purpose to give prominence to any subject which may properly be regarded as set at rest by the deliberate judgment of the people. But, while the present is bright with promise, and the future full of demand and inducements for the exercise of active intelligence, the past can never be without useful lessons of admonition and instruction. If its dangers serve not as beacons, they will evidently fail to fulfill the object of a wise design. When the grave shall have closed over all, who are now endeavoring to meet the obligations of duty, the year 1850 will be recurred to as a period filled with anxious apprehension. A successful war had just terminated. Peace brought with it a vast augmentation of territory. Disturbing questions arose, bearing upon the domestic institutions of one portion of the confederacy, and involving the constitutional rights of the States. But, notwithstanding differences of opinion and sentiment which then existed in relation to details, and specific provisions, the acquiescence of distinguished citizens, whose devotion to the Union can never be doubted, has given renewed vigor to our institutions, and restored a sense of repose and security to the public mind throughout the confederacy. That this repose is to suffer no shock during my official term, if I have power to avert it, those who placed me here may be assured.

Dec. 15.—Mr. A. C. Dodge of Iowa submitted to the Senate a bill (No. 22) "To organize the Territory of Nebraska," which was read twice, and referred to the Committee on Territories.

Jan. 4.—Mr. Douglas, from said Committee, reported said bill with amendments, which were printed. He said in his Report:

The principal amendments which your committee deem it their duty to commend to the favorable action of the Senate, in a special report, are those in which the principles established by the Compromise Measures of 1850, so far as they are applicable to territorial organizations, are proposed to be affirmed, and carried into practical operation within the limits of the new Territory. . . .

With a view of conforming their action to what they regard as the settled policy of the Government, sanctioned by the approving voice of the American People, your Committee have deemed it their duty to incorporate and perpetuate, in their territorial bill, the principles and spirit of those measures. If any other consideration were necessary to render the propriety of this course imperative upon the Committee, they may be found in the fact that the Nebraska country occupies the same relative position to the Slavery question, as did New Mexico and Utah, when those Territories were organized.

It was a disputed point, whether Slavery was prohibited by law in the country acquired from Mexico. On the one hand, it was contended, as a legal proposition, that Slavery having been prohibited by the enactments of Mexico, according to the laws of nations, we received the country with all its local laws and domestic institutions attached to the soil, so far as they did not conflict with the Constitution of the United States; and that a law either protecting or prohibiting Slavery, was not repugnant to that instrument, as was evidenced by the fact that one-half of the States of the Union tolerated, while the other half prohibited, the institution of Slavery. On the other hand, it was insisted that, by virtue of the Constitution of the United States, every citizen had a right to remove to any Territory of the Union, and carry his property with him under the protection of law, whether that property consisted of persons or things. The difficulties arising from this diversity of opinion were greatly aggravated by the fact that there were many persons on both sides of the legal controversy, who were unwilling to abide the decision of the courts on the legal matters in dispute ; thus, among those who claimed that the Mexican laws were still in force, and, consequently, that Slavery was already prohibited in those Territories by valid enactments, there were many who insisted upon Congress making the matter certain, by enacting another prohibition. In like manner, some of those who argued that Mexican law had ceased to have any binding force, and that the Constitution tolerated and protected Slave property in those Territories, were unwilling to trust the decision of the courts upon the point, and insisted that Congress should, by direct enactment, remove all legal obstacles to the introduction of Slaves into those Territories. . . .

Your Committee deem it fortunate for the peace of the country, and the security of the Union, that the controversy then resulted in the adoption of the Compromise Measures, which the two great political parties, with singular unanimity, have affirmed as a cardinal article of their faith, and proclaimed to the world as a final settlement of the controversy and an end of the agitation. A due respect, therefore, for the avowed opinions of Senators, as well as a proper sense of patriotic duty, enjoins upon your Committee the propriety and necessity of a strict adherence to the principles, and even a literal adoption of the enactments of that adjustment, in all their territorial bills, so far as the same are not locally inapplicable. These enactments embrace, among other things, less material to the matters under consideration, the following provisions :

When admitted as a State, the said Territory, or any portion of the same, shall be received into the Union, with or without Slavery, as their constitution may prescribe at the time of their admission ;

That the legislative power and authority of said Territory shall be vested in the Governor and a Legislative Assembly.

That the Legislative power of said Territory shall extend to all rightful subjects of legislation, consistent with the Constitution of the United States, and the provisions of this act ; but no law shall be passed interfering with the primary disposal of the soil ; no tax shall be imposed upon the property of the United States; nor shall the lands or other property of non-residents be taxed higher than the lands or other property of residents.

Jan. 24.—The bill thus reported was considered in Committee of the Whole and postponed to Monday next, when it was made the order of the day.

The bill was further considered Jan. 31st, Feb. 3d, Feb. 5th, and Feb. 6th, when an amendment reported by Mr. Douglas, declaring the Missouri Restriction on Slavery " inoperative and void," being under consideration, Mr. Chase, of Ohio, moved to strike out the assertion that said Restriction

" was superseded by the principles of the legislation of 1850, commonly called the Compromise Measures."

This motion was defeated by Yeas, 13 ; Nays, 30.

Feb. 15.—The bill having been discussed daily until now, Mr. Douglas moved to strike out of his amendment the words above quoted (which the Senate had refused to strike out on Mr. Chase's motion,) and insert instead the following :

Which being inconsistent with the principle of Non-Intervention by Congress with Slavery in the States and Territories, as recognized by the legislation of 1850, (commonly called the Compromise Measures,) is hereby declared inoperative and void ; it being the true intent and meaning of this act not to legislate Slavery into any Territory or State, nor to exclude it therefrom, but to leave the people thereof perfectly free to form and regulate their domestic institutions in their own way, subject only to the Constitution of the United States—

which prevailed—Yeas, 25 ; Nays, 10—as follows :

Yeas—For Douglas's new amendment :

Messrs. Adams,
Atchison,
Bayard,
Bell,
Benjamin,
Brodhead,
Brown,
Butler,
Cass,
Clayton,
Dawson,
Dixon,
Dodge, of Iowa,
Douglas,
Evans,
Fitzpatrick,
Geyer,
Gwin,
Hunter,
Johnson,
Jones, of Iowa,
Jones, of Tenn.,
Mason,
Morton,
Norris,
Pearce,
Pettit,
Pratt,
Sebastian,
Slidell,
Stuart,
Thompson, of Ky.,
Toombs,
Weller,
Williams—35.

Nays—Against said amendment ;

Messrs. Allen,
Chase,
Dodge, of Wisc.,
Everett,
Fish,
Foot,
Houston,
Seward,
Sumner,
Wade—10.

[NOTE.—Prior to this move of Mr. Douglas, Mr. Dixon, (Whig) of Kentucky, had moved to insert a clause directly and plainly *repealing* the Missouri Restriction. Mr. Dixon thought if that was the object, (and he was in favor of it,) it should be approached in a direct and manly way. He was assailed for this in *The Union* newspaper next morning ; but his suggestion was substantially adopted by Douglas, after a brief hesitation. Mr. Dixon's proposition, having been made in Committee, does not appear in the journal of the Senate, or it would here be given in terms.]

The bill was further discussed daily until March 2nd, when the vote was taken on Mr. Chase's amendment, to add to Sec. 14 the following words :

Under which the people of the Territory, through their appropriate representatives, may, if they see fit, prohibit the existence of Slavery therein—

which was rejected : Yeas, 10 ; Nays, 36, as follows :

Yeas—For Mr. Chase's amendment :

Messrs. Chase,
Dodge, of Wisc.,
Fessenden,
Fish,
Foot,
Hamlin,
Seward,
Smith,
Sumner,
Wade—10.

Nays—Against Chase's amendment :

Messrs. Adams,
Atchison,
Badger,
Bell,
Benjamin,
Brodhead,
Brown,
Butler,
Clay, (C. C.),
Clayton,
Dawson,
Dixon,
Dodge, of Iowa,
Douglas,
Evans,
Fitzpatrick,
Gwin,
Houston,
Hunter,
Johnson,
Jones, of Iowa,
Jones, of Tenn.,
Mason,
Morton,
Norris,
Pettit,
Pratt,
Rusk,
Sebastian,
Shields,
Slidell,
Stuart,
Toucey,
Walker,
Weller,
Williams—36.

Mr. Badger, of N. C., moved to add to the aforesaid section :

Provided, That nothing herein contained shall b construed to revive or put in force any law or regulation which may have existed prior to the act of 6th of March, 1820, either protecting, establishing, prohibiting, or abolishing Slavery.

Carried : Yeas, 35 ; Nays, 6.

Mr. Clayton now moved to strike out so much of said Douglas amendment as permits emigrants from Europe, who shall have declared their intention to become citizens, to vote. Carried: Yeas, 23 ; Nays, 21—as follows :

Yeas—For Clayton's amendment :

Messrs. Adams,
Atchison,
Badger,
Bell,
Benjamin,
Brodhead,
Brown,
Butler,
Clay,
Clayton,
Dawson,
Dixon,
Evans,
Fitzpatrick,
Houston,
Hunter,
Johnson,
Jones, of Tenn.,
Mason,
Morton,
Pratt,
Sebastian,
Slidell—23.

Nays—Against Clayton's amendment :

Messrs. Chase,
Dodge, of Wisc.,
Dodge, of Iowa,
Douglas,
Fessenden,
Fish,
Foot,
Gwin,
Hamlin,
Jones, of Iowa,
Norris,
Pettit,
Seward,
Shields,
Smith,
Stuart,
Sumner,
Toucey,
Wade,
Walker,
Williams—21.

Mr. Chase moved to amend, by providing for the appointment of three Commissioners residing in the Territory to organize the Territory, divide it into election districts, notify an election on the first Monday in September then ensuing, etc., at which election the people should choose their own Governor, as well as a Territorial Legislature—the Governor to serve for two years, and the Legislature to meet not later than May, 1855.

This extension of the principle of "Squatter Sovereignty" was defeated—Yeas, 10; Nays, 30.

Mr. Douglas's amendment was then agreed to, and the bill reported from the Committee of the Whole to the Senate.

The question on the engrossment of the bill was now reached, and it was carried: Yeas, 29 ; Nays, 12.

March 3.—The rule assigning Fridays for the consideration of private bills having been suspended, on motion of Mr. Badger, the Senate proceeded to put the Nebraska-Kansas bill on its final passage, when a long and earnest debate ensued. At a late hour of the night Mr. Seward, of New York, addressed the Senate, in opposition to the bill, as follows :

Mr. President : I rise with no purpose of further resisting or even delaying the passage of this bill. Let its advocates have only a little patience, and they will soon reach the object for which they have struggled so earnestly and so long. The sun has set for the last time upon the guaranteed and certain liberties of all the unsettled and unorganized portions of the American continent that lie within the jurisdiction of the United States. To-morrow's sun will rise in dim eclipse over them. How long that obscuration shall last, is known only to the Power that directs and controls all human events. For myself, I know only this—that now no human power will prevent its coming on, and that its passing off will be hastened and secured by others than those now here, and perhaps by only those belonging to future generations.

Sir, it would be almost factious to offer further resistance to this measure here. Indeed, successful resistance was never expected to be made in this Hall. The Senate-floor is an old battle-ground, on which have been fought many contests, and always, at least since 1820, with fortune adverse to the cause of equal and universal freedom. We were only a few here who engaged in that cause in the beginning of this contest. All that we could hope to do —all that we did hope to do—was to organize and prepare the issue for the House of Representatives, to which the country would look for its decision as authoritative, and to awaken the country that it might be ready for the appeal which would be made, whatever the decision of Congress might be. We are no stronger now. Only four-

teen at the first, it will be fortunate if, among the ills and accidents which surround us, we shall maintain that number to the end.

We are on the eve of the consummation of a great national transaction—a transaction which will close a cycle in the history of our country—and it is impossible not to desire to pause a moment and survey the scene around us, and the prospect before us. However obscure we may individually be, our connection with this great transaction will perpetuate our names for the praise or for the censure of future ages, and perhaps in regions far remote. If, then, we had no other motive for our actions than but that of the honest desire for a just fame, we could not be indifferent to that scene and that prospect. But individual interests and ambition sink into insignificance in view of the interests of our country and of mankind. These interests awaken, at least in me, an intense solicitude.

It was said by some in the beginning, and it has been said by others later in this debate, that it was doubtful whether it would be the cause of Slavery or the cause of Freedom that would gain advantages from the passage of this bill. I do not find it necessary to be censorious, nor even unjust to others, in order that my own course may be approved. I am sure that the honorable Senator from Illinois [Mr. Douglas] did not mean that the Slave States should gain an advantage over the Free States ; for he disclaimed it when he introduced the bill. I believe in all candor, that the honorable Senator from Georgia, [Mr. Toombs,] who comes out at the close of the battle as one of the chiefest leaders of the victorious party, is sincere in declaring his own opinion that the Slave States will gain no unjust advantage over the Free States, because he disclaims it as a triumph in their behalf. Notwithstanding all this, however, what has occurred here and in the country, during this contest, has compelled a conviction that Slavery will gain something, and Freedom will endure a severe, though I hope not an irretrievable, loss. The slaveholding States are passive, quiet, and content, and satisfied with the prospective boon ; and the Free States are excited and alarmed with fearful forebodings and apprehensions. The impatience for the speedy passage of the bill, manifested by its friends, betrays a knowledge that this is the condition of public sentiment in the Free States. They thought in the beginning that it was necessary to guard the measure by inserting the Clayton amendment, which would exclude unnaturalized foreign inhabitants of the Territories from the right of suffrage. And now they seem willing, with almost perfect unanimity, to relinquish that safeguard, rather than to delay the adoption of the principal measure for at most a year, perhaps for only a week or a day. Suppose that the Senate should adhere to that condition, which so lately was thought so wise and so important—what then ? The bill could only go back to the House of Representatives, which must either yield or insist ! In the one case or in the other, a decision in favor of the bill would be secured ; for even if the House should disagree, the Senate would have time to recede. But the majority will hazard nothing, even on a prospect so certain as this. They will recede at once, without a moment's further struggle, from the condition, and thus secure the passage of this bill now, to-night. Why such haste ? Even if the question were to go to the country before a final decision here, what would there be wrong in that ? There is no man living who will say that the country anticipated, or that *he* anticipated, the agitation of this measure in Congress, when this Congress was elected, or even when it assembled in December last.

Under such circumstances, and in the midst of agitation, and excitement, and debates, it is only fair to say, that certainly the country has not decided in favor of the bill. The refusal, then, to let the question go to the country, is a conclusive proof that the Slave States, as represented here, expect from the passage of this bill what the Free States insist that they will lose by it—an advantage, a material advantage, and not a mere abstraction. There are men in the Slave States, as in the Free States, who insist always too pertinaciously upon mere abstractions. But that is not the policy of the Slave States to-day. They are in earnest in seeking for, and securing, an object, and an important one. I believe they are going to have it. I do not know how long the advantage gained will last, nor how great or comprehensive it will be. Every Senator who agrees with me in opinion must feel as I do—that under such circumstances he can forego nothing that can be done decently, with due respect to difference of opinion, and consistently with the constitutional and settled rules of legislation, to place the true merits of the question before the country. Questions sometimes occur which seem to have two right sides. Such were the questions that divided the English nation between Pitt and Fox—such the contest between the assailant and the defender of Quebec. The judgment of the world was suspended by its sympathies, and seemed ready to descend in favor of him who should be most gallant in conduct. And so, when both fell with equal chivalry on the same field, the survivors united in raising a common monument to the glorious but rival memories of Wolfe and Montcalm. But this contest involves a moral question. The Slave States so present it. They maintain that African Slavery is not erroneous, not unjust, not inconsistent with the advancing cause of human nature. Since they so regard it, I do not expect to see statesmen representing those States indifferent about a vindication of this system by the Congress of the United States. On the other hand, we of the Free States regard Slavery as erroneous, unjust, oppressive, and therefore absolutely inconsistent with the principles of the American Constitution and Government. Who will expect us to be indifferent to the decisions of the American people and of mankind on such an issue? . . . .

Sir, I am surprised at the pertinacity with which the honorable Senator from Delaware, mine ancient and honorable friend, [Mr. Clayton,] perseveres in opposing the granting of the right of suffrage to the unnaturalized foreigner in the Territories. Congress cannot deny him that right. Here is the third article of that convention by which Louisiana, including Kansas and Nebraska, was ceded to the United States:

"The inhabitants of the ceded territory shall be incorporated in the Union of the United States, and admitted as soon as possible, according to the principles of the Federal Constitution, to the enjoyment of the rights, privileges, and immunities of the citizens of the United States; and in the meantime they shall be maintained and protected in the free enjoyment of their liberty, property, and the religion they profess."

The inhabitants of Kansas and Nebraska are citizens already, and by force of this treaty must continue to be, and as such to enjoy the right of suffrage, whatever laws you make to the contrary. My opinions are well known, to wit: That Slavery is not only an evil, but a local one, injurious and ultimately pernicious to society, wherever it exists, and in conflict with the constitutional principles of society in this country. I am not willing to extend nor to permit the extension of that local evil into regions now free within our empire. I know that there are some who differ from me, and who regard the Constitution of the United States as an instrument which sanctions Slavery as well as Freedom. But if I could admit a proposition so incongruous with the letter and spirit of the Federal Constitution, and the known sentiments of its illustrious founders, and so should conclude that Slavery was national, I must still cherish the opinion that it is an evil; and because it is a national one, I am the more firmly held and bound to prevent an increase of it, tending, as I think it manifestly does, to the weakening and ultimate overthrow of the Constitution itself, and therefore to the injury of all mankind. I know there have been States which have endured long, and achieved much, which tolerated Slavery; but that was not the slavery of caste, like African Slavery. Such Slavery tends to demoralize equally the subjected race and the superior one. It has been the absence of such Slavery from Europe that has given her nations their superiority over other countries in that hemisphere. Slavery, wherever it exists, begets fear, and fear is the parent of weakness. What is the secret of that eternal, sleepless anxiety in the legislative halls, and even at the firesides of the Slave States, always asking new stipulations, new compromises and abrogation of compromises, new assumptions of power and abnegations of power, but fear? It is the apprehension, that, even if safe now, they will not always or long be secure against some invasion or some aggression from the Free States. What is the secret of the humiliating part which proud old Spain is acting at this day, trembling between alarms of American intrusion into Cuba on one side, and British dictation on the other, but the fact that she has cherished Slavery so long and still cherishes it, in the last of her American colonial possessions? Thus far Kansas and Nebraska are safe, under the laws of 1820, against the introduction of this element of national debility and decline. The bill before us, as we are assured, contains a great principle, a glorious principle; and yet that principle, when fully ascertained, proves to be nothing less than the subversion of that security not only within the Territories of Kansas and Nebraska, but within all the other present and future Territories of the United States. Thus it is quite clear that it is not a principle alone that is involved, but that those who crowd this measure with so much zeal and earnestness must expect that either Freedom or Slavery shall gain something by it in those regions. The case, then, stands thus in Kansas and Nebraska: Freedom may lose, but certainly can gain nothing; while Slavery may gain, but as certainly can lose nothing.

So far as I am concerned, the time for looking on the dark side has passed. I feel quite sure that Slavery at most can get nothing more than Kansas; while Nebraska—the wider northern region—will, under existing circumstances, escape, for the reason that its soil and climate are uncongenial with the staples of slave culture—rice, sugar, cotton, and tobacco. Moreover, since the public attention has been so well and so effectually directed toward the subject, I cherish a hope that Slavery may be prevented even from gaining a foothold in Kansas. Congress only gives consent, but it does not and cannot introduce Slavery there. Slavery will be embarrassed by its own overgrasping spirit. No one, I am sure, anticipates the possible reëstablishment of the African Slave-trade. The tide of emigration to Kansas is therefore to be supplied there solely by the domestic fountain of slave production. But Slavery has also other regions besides Kansas to be filled from that fountain. There are all of New Mexico and all of Utah already within the United States; and then there is Cuba, that consumes slave labor and life as fast as any one of the slaveholding States can supply it; and besides these regions, there remains all of Mexico down to the Isthmus. The stream of slave labor flowing from so small a fountain, and broken into several divergent channels will not cover so great a field; and it is reasonably to be hoped that the part of it nearest to the North Pole will be the last to be inundated. But African slave emigration is to compete with free emigration of white men, and the source of this latter tide is as ample as the civilization of the two entire continents. The honorable Senator from Delaware mentioned, as if it were a startling fact, that twenty thousand European immigrants arrived in New-York in one month. Sir, he has stated the fact with too much moderation. On my return to the capital a day or two ago, I met twelve thousand of these emigrants who had arrived in New-York on one morning, and who had thronged the churches on the following Sabbath, to return thanks for deliverance from the perils of the sea, and for their arrival in the land, not of Slavery but of Liberty. I also thank God for their escape, and for their coming. They are now on their way westward, and the news of the passage of this bill, preceding them, will speed many of them toward Kansas and Nebraska. Such arrivals are not extraordinary—they occur almost every week; and the immigration from Germany, from Great Britain, and from Norway, and from Sweden, during the European war, will rise to six or seven hundred thousand souls in a year. And with this tide is to be mingled one rapidly swelling from Asia and from the islands of the South Seas. All the immigrants under this bill, as the House of Representatives overruling you have ordered, will be good, loyal, Liberty-loving, Slavery-fearing citizens. Come on, then, gentlemen of the Slave States. Since there is no escaping your challenge, I accept it in behalf of the cause of Freedom. We will engage in competition for the virgin soil of Kansas, and God give the victory to the side which is stronger in numbers as it is in right.

There are, however, earnest advocates of this bill, who do not expect, and who, I suppose, do not desire, that Slavery shall gain possession of Nebraska. What do they expect to gain? The honorable Senator from Indiana (Mr. Pettit) says that by thus obliterating the Missouri Compromise restriction, they will gain a *tabula rasa*, on which the inhabitants of Kansas and Nebraska may write whatever they will. This is the great principle of the bill, as he understands it. Well, what gain is there in that? You obliterate a Constitution of Freedom. If they write a new constitution of freedom, can the new be better than the old? If they write a Constitution of Slavery, will it not be a worse one? I ask the honorable Senator that. But the honorable Senator says that the people of Nebraska will have the privilege of establishing institutions for themselves. They have now the privilege of establishing free institutions. Is it a privilege, then, to establish Slavery? If so, what a mockery are all our Constitutions, which prevent the inhabitants from capriciously subverting free institutions and establishing institutions of Slavery! Sir, it is a sophism, a subtlety, to talk of conferring upon a country, already secure in the blessings of Freedom, the power of self-destruction.

What mankind everywhere want, is not the removal of the Constitutions of Freedom which they have, that they may make at their pleasure Constitutions of Slavery or of Freedom, but the privilege of retaining Constitutions of Freedom when they already have them, and the removal of Constitutions of Slavery when they have them, that they may establish Constitutions of Freedom in their place. We hold on tenaciously to all existing Constitutions of Freedom. Who denounces any man for diligently adhering to such Constitutions? Who would dare to denounce any one for disloyalty to our existing Constitutions, if they were Constitutions of Despotism and

Slavery? But it is supposed by some that this principle is less important in regard to Kansas and Nebraska than as a general one—a general principle applicable to all other present and future Territories of the United States. Do honorable Senators then indeed suppose they are establishing a principle at all? If so, I think they egregiously err, whether the principle is either good or bad, right or wrong. They are not establishing it, and cannot establish it in this way. You subvert one law capriciously, by making another law in its place. That is all. Will your law have any more weight, authority, solemnity, or binding force on future Congresses, than the first had? You abrogate the law of your predecessors—others will have equal power and equal liberty to abrogate yours. You allow no barriers around the old law, to protect it from abrogation. You erect none around your new law, to stay the hand of future innovators. . . . .

Sir, in saying that your new principle will not be established by this bill, I reason from obvious, clear, well settled principles of human nature. Slavery and Freedom are antagonistical elements in this country. The founders of the Constitution framed it with a knowledge of that antagonism, and suffered it to continue, that it might work out its own ends. There is a commercial antagonism, an irreconcilable one, between the systems of free labor and slave labor. They have been at war with each other ever since the Government was established, and that war is to continue forever. The contest, when it ripens between these two antagonistic elements, is to be settled somewhere; it is to be settled in the seat of central power, in the Federal Legislature. The Constitution makes it the duty of the central Government to determine questions, as often as they shall arise, in favor of one or the other party, and refers the decision of them to the majority of the votes in the two Houses of Congress. It will come back here, then, in spite of all the efforts to escape from it.

This antagonism must end either in a separation of the antagonistic parties—the Slaveholding States and the Free States—or, secondly, in the complete establishment of the influence of the Slave power over the Free—or else, on the other hand, in the establishment of the superior influence of Freedom over the interests of Slavery. It will not be terminated by a voluntary secession of either party. Commercial interests bind the Slave States and the Free States together in links of gold that are riveted with iron, and they cannot be broken by passion or by ambition. Either party will submit to the ascendency of the other, rather than yield the commercial advantages of this Union. Political ties bind the Union together—a common necessity, and not merely a common necessity, but the common interests of empire—of such empire as the world has never before seen. The control of the national power is the control of the great Western Continent; and the control of this continent is to be, in a very few years, the controlling influence in the world. Who is there, North, that hates Slavery so much, or who, South, that hates emancipation so intensely, that he can attempt, with any hope of success, to break a Union thus forged and welded together? I have always heard, with equal pity and disgust, threats of disunion in the Free States, and similar threats in the Slaveholding States. I know that men may rave in the heat of passion, and under great political excitement; but I know that when it comes to a question whether this Union shall stand, either with Freedom or with Slavery, the masses will uphold it, and it will stand until some inherent vice in its Constitution, not yet disclosed, shall cause its dissolution. Now, entertaining these opinions, there are for me only two alternatives, viz.: either to let Slavery gain unlimited sway, or so to exert what little power and influence I may have, as to secure, if I can, the ultimate predominance of Freedom. . . . .

Sir, I have always said that I should not despond, even if this fearful measure should be effected: nor do I now despond. Although, reasoning from my present convictions, I should not have voted for the compromise of 1820, I have labored, in the very spirit of those who established it, to save the landmark of Freedom which it assigned. I have not spoken irreverently even of the compromise of 1850, which, as all men know, I opposed earnestly and with diligence. Nevertheless, I have always preferred the compromises of the Constitution, and have wanted no others. I feared all others. This was a leading principle of the great statesman of the South, (Mr. Calhoun). Said he:

"I see my way in the Constitution; I cannot in a compromise. A compromise is but an act of Congress. It may be overruled at any time. It gives us no security. But the Constitution is stable. It is a rock on which we can stand, and on which we can meet our friends from the non-slaveholding States. It is a firm and stable ground, on which we can better stand in opposition to fanaticism than on the shifting sands of compromise. Let us be done with compromises. Let us go back and stand upon the Constitution."

I stood upon this ground in 1850, defending Freedom upon it as Mr. Calhoun did in defending Slavery. I was overruled then, and I have waited since without proposing to abrogate any compromises.

It has been no proposition of mine to abrogate them now; but the proposition has come from another quarter—from an adverse one. It is about to prevail. The shifting sands of compromise are passing from under my feet, and they are now, without agency of my own, taking hold again on the rock of the Constitution. It shall be no fault of mine if they do not remain firm. This seems to me auspicious of better days and wiser legislation. Through all the darkness and gloom of the present hour, bright stars are breaking, that inspire me with hope, and excite me to perseverance. They show that the day of compromises has past forever, and that henceforward all great questions between Freedom and Slavery legitimately coming here—and none other can come—shall be decided, as they ought to be, upon their merits, by a fair exercise of legislative power, and not by bargains of equivocal prudence, if not of doubtful morality.

Mr. Douglas closed the debate, reiterating and enforcing the views set forth in his Report already referred to; and at last the vote was taken, and the bill passed: Yeas, 37; Nays, 14; as follows:

Yeas—For the Kansas-Nebraska bill:

Messrs.	
Adams,	Hunter,
Atchison,	Johnson,
Badger,	Jones, of Iowa,
Bayard,	Jones, of Tenn.,
Benjamin,	Mason,
Brodhead,	Morton,
Brown,	Norris,
Butler,	Pettit,
Cass,	Pratt,
Clay, of Ala.,	Rusk,
Dawson,	Sebastian,
Dixon,	Shields,
Dodge, of Iowa,	Slidell,
Douglas,	Stuart,
Evans,	Thompson, of Ky.
Fitzpatrick,	Thomson, of N. J.,
Geyer,	Toucey,
Gwin,	Weller,
	Williams—37.

Nays—Against the said bill:

Messrs.	
Bell,	Houston,
Chase,	James,
Dodge, of Wisc.,	Seward,
Fessenden,	Smith,
Fish,	Sumner,
Foot,	Wade,
Hamlin,	Walker—14.

So the bill was passed, and its title declared to be "An Act to organize the Territories of Nebraska and Kansas," and the Senate adjourned over to the Tuesday following.

In the House, a bill to organize the Territory of Nebraska had been noticed on the first day of the session, by Mr. John G. Miller, of Mo., who introduced it December 22d.

Jan. 24th.—Mr. Giddings gave notice of a bill to organize said Territory.

Jan. 30.—Mr. Pringle, of N. Y., endeavored to have the bill passed at the last session (leaving the Missouri Restriction intact), reported by the Committee on Territories; but debate arose, and his resolution lay over.

Jan. 31.—Mr. Richardson, of Ill., chairman of the Committee on Territories, reported a bill "To organize the Territories of Nebraska and Kansas," which was read twice and committed.

Mr. Richardson's bill was substantially Mr. Douglas's last bill, and was accompanied by no report. Mr. English, of Ind., submitted the views of a minority of said Committee on Territories, proposing, without argument, the two following amendments:

1. Amend the section defining the boundary of Kansas, so as to make "the summit of the Rocky Mountains" the western boundary of said Territory.

2. Strike out of the 14th and 34th sections of said bill all after the words "United States," and insert in each instance (the one relating to Kansas, and the other to Nebraska) as follows:

Provided, That nothing in this act shall be so construed as to prevent the people of said Territory, through the properly constituted legislative authority, from passing such laws, in relation to the institution of Slavery, as they may deem best adapted to their locality, and most conducive to their happiness and welfare; and so much of any existing act of Congress as may conflict with the above right of the people to regulate their domestic institutions in their own way, be, and the same is hereby, repealed.

This appears to have been an attempt to give practical effect to the doctrine of Squatter Sovereignty; but it was not successful.

May 8th.—On motion of Mr. Richardson, the House—Yeas, 109; Nays, 88—resolved itself into a Committee of the Whole, and took up the bill (House No. 236) to organize the Territories of Nebraska and Kansas, and discussed it —Mr. Olds, of Ohio, in the chair.

On coming out of Committee, Mr. George W. Jones, of Tenn., moved that the rules be suspended so as to enable him to move the printing of Senate bill (No. 22, passed the Senate as aforesaid) and the amendment now pending to the House bill. No quorum voted—adjourned.

May 9th.—This motion prevailed. After debate in Committee on the Kansas-Nebraska bill, the Committee found itself without a quorum, and thereupon rose and reported the fact to the House—only 106 Members were found to be present. After several fruitless attempts to adjourn, a call was ordered and a quorum obtained, at 9 P.M. At 10, an adjournment prevailed.

May 10th.—Debate in Committee continued.

May 11th.—Mr. Richardson moved that all debate in Committee close to-morrow at noon.

Mr. English moved a call of the House: Refused; Yeas, 88; Nays, 97.

Mr. Mace moved that Mr. Richardson's motion be laid on the table: Defeated. Yeas, 95; Nays 100.

Mr. Edgerton, of Ohio, moved a call of the House. Refused: Yeas, 45; Nays, 80.

The day was spent in what has come to be called "Filibustering"—that is, the minority moving adjournments, calls of the House, asking to be excused from voting, taking appeals, etc., etc. In the midst of this, Mr. Richardson withdrew his original motion, and moved instead that the debate in Committee be closed in five minutes after the House shall have resumed it.

The hour of noon of the 12th having arrived, Messrs. Dean and Banks raised points of order as to the termination of the legislative day. The Speaker decided that the legislative day could only be terminated by the adjournment of the House, except by constitutional conclusion of the session. Mr. Banks appealed, but at length withdrew his appeal.

Finally, at 11½ o'clock, P.M., of Friday, 12th, after a continuous sitting of thirty-six hours, the House, on motion of Mr. Richardson, adjourned.

May 13th.—The House sat but two hours, and effected nothing.

May 15th.—Mr. Richardson withdrew his demand for the Previous Question on closing the debate, and moved instead that the debate close at noon on Friday the 19th instant. This he finally modified by substituting Saturday the 20th; and in this shape his motion prevailed by a two-thirds majority—Yeas, 137; Nays, 66— the following opponents of the bill voting for the motion, namely:

MAINE.—Thomas J. D. Fuller, Samuel Mayall—2.
NEW-HAMPSHIRE.—Geo. W. Kittredge, Geo. W. Morrison—2.
MASSACHUSETTS.—Nathaniel P. Banks, jr.—1.
CONNECTICUT.—Origen S. Seymour—1.
NEW-YORK.—Gilbert Dean, Charles Hughes—2.
PENNSYLVANIA.—Michael C. Trout—1.
OHIO.—Alfred P. Edgerton, Harvey H. Johnson, Andrew Ellison, William D. Lindsley, Thomas Richey—5.
INDIANA.—Andrew J. Harlan, Daniel Mace—2.
ILLINOIS.—John Wentworth—1.
MICHIGAN.—David A. Noble, Hestor L. Stevens—2.
WISCONSIN.—John B. Macy—1
VIRGINIA.—John S. Millson—1.
Total—21.

Mr. Richardson, having thus got in his resolution to close the debate, put on the previous question again, and the House—Yeas, 113; Nays, 59—agreed to close the debate on the 20th.

Debate having been closed, the opponents of the measure expected to defeat or cripple it by moving and taking a vote in Committee on various propositions of amendment, kindred to those moved and rejected in the Senate; some of which it was believed a majority of the House would not choose (or dare) to vote down; and, though the names of those voting on one side or the other in Committee of the Whole are not recorded, yet any proposition moved and rejected there, may be renewed in the House after taking the bill out of committee, and is no longer cut off by the Previous Question, as it formerly was. But, when the hour for closing debate in Committee had arrived, Mr. Alex. H. Stephens moved that *the enacting clause of the bill be stricken out;* which was carried by a rally of the friends of the bill, and of course cut off all amendments. The bill was thus reported to the House with its head off; when, after a long struggle, the House *refused to agree to the report of the Committee of the Whole*—Yeas, (for agreeing) 97; Nays, 117—bringing the House to a direct vote on the engrossment of the bill.

Mr. Richardson now moved an amendment, which was a substitute for the whole bill, being substantially the Senate's bill, with the clause admitting aliens, who have declared their intention to become citizens, to the right of suffrage. He thereupon called the Previous Question, which the House sustained—Yeas, 116; Nays, 90—when the House adopted his amendment—Yeas, 115; Nays, 95—and proceeded to engross the bill—Yeas, 112; Nays, 99—when he put on the Previous Question again, and passed the bill finally—Yeas, 113; Nays, 100— as follows:

A POLITICAL TEXT-BOOK FOR 1860.

YEAS—113.

FROM THE FREE STATES.

MAINE.—Moses McDonald—1.
NEW-HAMPSHIRE—Harry Hibbard—1.
CONNECTICUT.—Colin M. Ingersoll—1.
VERMONT.—*None.* MASSACHUSETTS.—*None.*
RHODE ISLAND.—*None.*
NEW-YORK.—Thomas W. Cumming, Francis B. Cutting, Peter Rowe, John J. Taylor, William M. Tweed, Hiram Walbridge, William a Walker, Mike Walsh, Theo. R. Westbrook—9.
PENNSYLVANIA.—Samuel A. Bridges, John L. Dawson, Thomas B. Florence, J. Clancy Jones, William H. Kurtz, John McNair, Asa Packer, John Robbins, jr., Christian M. Straub, William H. Witte, Hendrick B. Wright—11.
NEW-JERSEY—Samuel Lilly, George Vail—2.
OHIO.—David T. Disney, Frederick W. Green, Edson B. Olds, Wilson Shannon—4.
INDIANA.—John G. Davis, Cyrus L. Dunham, Norman Eddy, William H. English, Thomas A. Hendricks, James H. Lane, Smith Miller—7.
ILLINOIS.—James C. Allen, Willis Allen, Wm. A. Richardson—3.
MICHIGAN.—Samuel Clark, David Stuart—2.
IOWA.—Bernhart Henn—1.
WISCONSIN.—*None.*
CALIFORNIA.—Milton S. Latham, J. A. McDougall—2.
Total—44.

FROM THE SLAVE STATES.

DELAWARE.—George R. Riddle—1.
MARYLAND.—William T. Hamilton, Henry May, Jacob Shower, Joshua Vansant—4.
VIRGINIA.—Thomas H. Bayly, Thomas S. Bocock, John S. Caskie, Henry A. Edmundson, Charles J. Faulkner, William O. Goode, Zedekiah Kidwell, John Letcher, Paulus Powell, William Smith, John F. Snodgrass—11.
NORTH CAROLINA.—William S. Ashe, Burton Craige, Thomas L. Clingman, *John Kerr*, Thos. Ruffin, Henry M. Shaw—6.
SOUTH CAROLINA.—William W. Boyce, President S. Brooks, James L. Orr—3.
GEORGIA.—David J. Bailey, Elijah W. Chastain, Alfred H. Colquitt, Junius Hillyer, *David A. Reese*, Alex. H. Stephens—6.
ALABAMA.—*James Abercrombie*, Williamson R. W. Cobb, James F. Dowdell, Sampson W. Harris, George S. Houston, Philip Phillips, William R. Smith—7.
MISSISSIPPI.—William S. Barry, William Barksdale, Otho R. Singleton, Daniel B. Wright—4.
LOUISIANA.—William Dunbar, Roland Jones, John Perkins, jr.—8
KENTUCKY.—John C. Breckinridge, James S. Chrisman, *Leander M. Cox, Clement S. Hill*, John M. Elliot, *Benj. E. Grey, William Preston*, Richard H. Stanton—8.
TENNESSEE.—William M. Churchwell, George W. Jones, *Charles Ready*, Samuel A. Smith, Frederick P. Stanton, *Felix Zollicoffer*—6.
MISSOURI.—Alfred W. Lamb, *James J. Lindley, John G. Miller, Mordecai Oliver*, John S. Phelps—5.
ARKASNAS.—Alfred B. Greenwood, Edwin A. Warren—2.

FLORIDA.—Augustus E. Maxwell—1.
TEXAS.—Peter H. Bell, Geo. W. Smyth—2. Total—69.

Total, Free and Slave States—113.

NAYS—100.

FREE STATES.

MAINE.—*Samuel P. Benson, E. Wilder Farley*, Thomas J. D. Fuller, Samuel Mayall, *Israel Washburn, jr.*—5.
NEW HAMPSHIRE.—George W. Kittredge, George W. Morrison—2.
MASSACHUSETTS.—Nathaniel P. Banks, jr., *Samuel L. Crocker*, ALEX. DE WITT, *Edward Dickinson, J. Wiley Edmunds, Thomas D. Eliot*, John Z. Goodrich, *Charles W. Upham, Samuel H. Walley, Tappan Wentworth*—10.
RHODE ISLAND.—Thomas Davis, Benjamin B. Thurston—2.
CONNECTICUT.—Nathan Belcher, James T. Pratt, Origen S. Seymour—3.
VERMONT.—*James Meacham, Alvah Sabin, Andrew Tracy*—3.
NEW YORK.—*Henry Bennett, Davis Carpenter*, Gilbert Dean, Caleb Lyon, Reuben E. Fenton, *Thomas T. Flagler*, George Hastings, *Solomon G. Haven*, Charles Hughes, Daniel T. Jones, *Orsamus B. Matteson, Edwin B. Morgan*, William Murray, Andrew Oliver, Jared V. Peck, Rufus W. Peckham, Bishop Perkins, *Benjamin Pringle, Russell Sage, George A. Simmons*, GERRIT SMITH, John Wheeler—22.
NEW-JERSEY.—*Alex. C. M. Pennington*, Charles Skelton, Nathan T. Stratton—3.
PENNSYLVANIA.—*Joseph R. Chandler*, Carlton B. Curtis, *John Dick*, Augustus Drum, *William Everhart*, James Gamble, Galusha A. Grow, *Isaac E. Hiester, Thomas M. Howe*, John McCulloch, *Ner Middleswarth, David Ritchie, Samuel L. Russell*, Michael C. Trout—14.
OHIO.—*Edward Ball, Lewis D. Campbell*, Alfred P. Edgerton, Andrew Ellison, JOSHUA R. GIDDINGS, *Aaron Harlan, John Scott Harrison*, H. H. Johnson, William D. Lindsey, M. H. Nichols, Thomas Richey, *William R. Sapp*, Andrew Stuart, *John L. Taylor*, EDWARD WADE—15.
INDIANA.—Andrew J. Harlan, Daniel Mace, *Samuel W. Parker*—3.
ILLINOIS.—*James Knox, Jesse O. Norton, Elihu B. Washburne*, John Wentworth, *Richard Yates*—5.
MICHIGAN.—David A. Noble, Hestor L. Stevens—2.
WISCONSIN.—Benjamin C. Eastman, Daniel Wells, jr.—2.
IOWA.—*None.*
CALIFORNIA.—*None.* Total—91.

SOUTHERN STATES.

VIRGINIA.—John S. Millson—1.
NORTH CAROLINA.—*Richard C. Puryear, Sion H. Rogers*—2.
TENNESSEE.—*Robert M. Bugg, William Cullom, Emerson Etheridge, Nathaniel G. Taylor*—4.
LOUISIANA.—*Theodore G. Hunt*—1.
MISSOURI.—Thomas H. Benton—1.
OTHER SOUTHERN STATES.—*None.* Total—9.

Total, Free and Slave States—100.

Absent, or not voting—21.

N. ENGLAND STATES.—*William Appleton*, of Mass.—1.
NEW-YORK.—*Geo. W. Chase*, James Maurice—2.
PENNSYLVANIA.—*None.*
NEW-JERSEY.—*None.*
OHIO.—George Bliss, *Moses B. Corwin*—2.
ILLINOIS.—Wm. H. Bissell—1.
CALIFORNIA.—*None.*
INDIANA.—Eben M. Chamberlain—1.
MICHIGAN.—*None.*
IOWA.—*John P. Cook*—1.
WISCONSIN.—John B. Macy—1.

Total from Free States—9.

MARYLAND.—*John R. Franklin, Augustus R. Sollers*—2.
VIRGINIA.—Fayette McMullen—1.
NORTH CAROLINA.—*None.*
DELAWARE.—*None.*
SOUTH CAROLINA.—Wm. Aiken, Lawrence M. Keitt, John McQueen—3.
GEORGIA.—Wm. B. W. Dent, James L. Seward—2.
ALABAMA.—*None.*
MISSISSIPPI.—Wiley P. Harris—1.
KENTUCKY.—Linn Boyd, (Speaker,) *Presley Ewing*—2.
MISSOURI.—*Samuel Caruthers*—1.
ARKANSAS.—*None.* FLORIDA.—*None.*
TEXAS.—*None.* TENNESSEE.—*None.*
LOUISIANA.—*None.*

Total from Slave States—12.

Whigs in *Italics*. Abolitionists in SMALL CAPITALS. Democrats in Roman.

May 23d.—The bill being thus sent to the Senate (not as a Senate but as a House bill), was sent at once to the Committee of the Whole, and there briefly considered.

May 24th.—Mr. Pearce, of Maryland, moved to strike out the clause in section 5, which extends the right of suffrage to

those who shall have declared on oath their intention to become such, [citizens] and shall have taken an oath to support the Constitution of the United States, and the provisions of this act.

Negatived—Yeas: Bayard, Bell, Brodhead, Brown, Clayton, Pearce, and Thompson of Kentucky. Nays, 41.

The bill was then ordered to be engrossed

for a third reading—Yeas, 35; Nays, 13, as follows:

Yeas—For Engrossing:

Messrs. Atchison, Mo., Mason, Va., *Badger*, N. C., *Morton*, Fla., *Benjamin*, La., Norris, N. H., Brodhead, Pa., *Pearce*, Md., Brown, Miss., Pettit, Ind., Butler, S. C., *Pratt*, Md., Cass, Mich., Rusk, Texas, Clay, Ala., Sebastian, Ark., *Dawson*, Ga., Shields, Ill., Douglas, Ill., Slidell, La., Fitzpatrick, Ala., Stuart, Mich., Gwin, Cal., *Thompson*, Ky., Hunter, Va., Thomson, N. J., Johnson, Ark., Toombs, Ga., Jones, Iowa, Toucey, Ct., *Jones*, Tenn., Weller, Cal., Mallory, Fla., Williams, N. H., Wright, N. J.,—35.

Nays—Against Engrossing:

Messrs. Allen, R. I., GILLETTE, Ct., *Bell*, Tenn., Hamlin, Me., CHASE, Ohio, James, R. I., *Clayton*, Del., *Seward*, N. Y., *Fish*, N. Y., SUMNER, Mass., *Foot*, Vt., *Wade*, Ohio. Walker, Wis.—13.

Democrats in Roman; Whigs in *Italics*; Free Democrats in SMALL CAPS.

The bill was then passed without further division, and, being approved by the President, became a law. The clause in the 14th section, which repealed the Missouri Compromise, with the Badger *proviso*, is as follows:

That the Constitution and all the laws of the United States which are not locally inapplicable, shall have the same force and effect within the said territory of Nebraska, as elsewhere within the United States, except the eighth section of the act preparatory to the admission of Missouri into the Union, approved March sixth, eighteen hundred and twenty, which being inconsistent with the principles of non-intervention by Congress with Slavery in the States and Territories, as recognized by the legislation of eighteen hundred and fifty, commonly called the Compromise Measures, is hereby declared inoperative and void; it being the true intent and meaning of this act not to legislate Slavery into any Territory or State, nor to exclude it therefrom, but to leave the people thereof perfectly free to form and regulate their domestic institutions in their own way, subject only to the Constitution of the United States; *Provided*, That nothing herein contained shall be construed to revive or put in force any law or regulation which may have existed prior to the act of sixth of March, eighteen hundred and twenty, either protecting, establishing, prohibiting or abolishing Slavery.

Dec. 3, 1855.—The XXXIVth Congress convened at the Capitol, in Washington.—Jesse D. Bright, of Ind., holding over as President *pro tempore* of the Senate, in place of Vice-President William R. King, of Alabama, deceased. A quorum of either House was found to be present.

But the House found itself unable to organize by the choice of a Speaker, until after an unprecedented struggle of nine weeks' duration. Finally, on Saturday, Feb. 20, 1856, the plurality-rule was adopted—Yeas, 113; Nays, 104 —and the House proceeded under it to its *one hundred and thirty-third* ballot for speaker, when Nathaniel P. Banks, jr. (anti-Nebraska) of Massachusetts, was chosen, having 103 votes to 100, for William Aiken, of South Carolina. Eleven votes scattered on other persons did not count against a choice. It was therefore resolved—Yeas, 155; Nays, 40—that Mr. Banks was duly elected Speaker.

But, during the pendency of this election, the President had transmitted to both Houses, first (Dec. 31st) his Annual Message, and next (Jan. 24th) a special message with regard to the condition of Kansas, in which he thus alludes to those who think Slavery not the best institution to make a prosperous and happy State, and to those who opposed the repeal of the Missouri restriction:

This interference, in so far as concerns its primary causes and its immediate commencement, was one of the incidents of that pernicious agitation on the subject of the condition of the colored persons held to service in some of the States, which has so long disturbed the repose of our country, and excited individuals, otherwise patriotic and law-abiding, to toil with misdirected zeal in the attempt to propagate their social theories by the perversion and abuse of the powers of Congress.

The persons and parties whom the tenor of the act to organize the Territories of Nebraska and Kansas thwarted in the endeavor to impose, through the agency of Congress, their particular views of social organization on the people of the future new States, now perceiving that the policy of leaving the inhabitants of each State to judge for themselves in this respect was ineradicably rooted in the convictions of the people of the Union, then had recourse, in the pursuit of their general object, to the extraordinary measure of propagandist colonization of the Territory of Kansas, to prevent the free and natural action of its inhabitants in its internal organization and thus to anticipate or to force the determination of that question in this inchoate State.

The President makes the following reference to the action of the people of Kansas, who, claiming the right "peaceably to assemble and petition for a redress of grievances," did so assemble, and sent a petition to Congress, to permit them to form a State Government, with the Constitution submitted:

Following upon this movement was another and more important one of the same general character. Persons confessedly not constituting the body politic, or all the inhabitants, but merely a party of the inhabitants, and without law, have undertaken to summon a convention for the purpose of transforming the Territory into a State, and have framed a constitution, adopted it, and under it elected a governor and other officers, and a representative to Congress.

March 12.—In Senate, Mr. Douglas, of Illinois, from the Committee on Territories, made a report on matters relating to Kansas affairs, in which he says:

The act of Congress for the organization o the Territories of Kansas and Nebraska, was designed to conform to the spirit and letter of the Federal Constitution, by preserving and maintaining the fundamental principle of equality among all the States of the Union, notwithstanding the restriction contained in the 8th section of the act of March 6, 1820, (preparatory to the admission of Missouri into the Union,) which assumed to deny to the people forever the right to settle the question of Slavery for themselves, provided they should make their homes and organize States north of thirty-six degrees and thirty minutes north latitude. Conforming to the cardinal principles of State equality and self-government, in obedience to the Constitution, the Kansas-Nebraska act declared, in the precise language of the Compromise Measures of 1850, that, " when admitted as a State, the said Territory, or any portion of the same, shall be received into the Union, with or without Slavery, as their constitutions may prescribe at the time of their admission."

He then refers to the formation of the " Emigrant Aid Company,"* which had been organized on the principle of " State equality " by the people of Massachusetts. This proceeding he calls " a perversion of the plain provisions " of the Kansas-Nebraska Act—that the only

---

* " The Emigrant Aid Company," with five millions dollars, to which Mr. Douglas alludes, and from the existence of which he makes a special plea for the Border Ruffians, was never organized: See Report of Special Committee of Congress, (page 100.)

kind of lawful emigration was "such as has filled up our new States and Territories, when each individual has gone on his own account, to improve his condition and that of his family." The report then states that the people of Missouri were greatly alarmed at the rapid filling up of Kansas by people opposed to Slavery—that **this** might endanger the existence of Slavery in Missouri—and that, as the people of Missouri had a right to defend their own institutions, they might properly resist the formation of an Anti-Slavery State in their neighborhood. The report continues:

For the successful prosecution of such a scheme, the Missourians who lived in the immediate vicinity possessed peculiar advantages over their rivals from the more remote portions of the Union. Each family could send one of its members across the line to mark out his claim, erect a cabin, and put in a small crop, sufficient to give him as valid a right to be deemed an actual settler and qualified voter as those who were being imported by the Emigrant Aid Societies. In an unoccupied Territory, where the lands have not been surveyed, and where there were no marks or lines to indicate the boundaries of sections and quarter-sections, and where no legal title could be had until after the surveys should be made, disputes, quarrels, violence, and bloodshed might have been expected as the natural and inevitable consequences of such extraordinary systems of emigration, which divided and arrayed the settlers into two great hostile parties, each having an inducement to claim more than was his right, in order to hold it for some new-comer of his own party, and at the same time prevent persons belonging to the opposite party from settling in the neighborhood. As a result of this state of things, the great mass of emigrants from the northwest and from other States who went there on their own account, with no other object, and influenced by no other motives than to improve their condition and secure good homes for their families, were compelled to array themselves under the banner of one of these hostile parties, in order to insure protection to themselves and their claims against the aggressions and violence of the other.

On the 29th of November, 1854, the first election in the Territory was held for a delegate to Congress. This was a very short time after the arrival of the Free State emigrants in sufficient bodies to protect themselves. At this election, according to the returns, J. W. Whitfield had received 2,268 votes; other persons, 575. Whitfield, of course, received the Governor's certificate, but great dissatisfaction was expressed by the Free State settlers, charging that many of the votes received by Whitfield were given by men living in Missouri; and it afterward appeared that at the time of the first election there were but 1,114 legal voters in the Territory. Nevertheless, the report continues:

Certain it is, that there could not have been a system of fraud and violence such as has been charged by the agents and supporters of the emigrant aid societies, unless the Governor and judges of election were parties to it; and your committee are not prepared to assume a fact so disreputable to them, and so improbable upon the state of facts presented, without specific charges and direct proof. In the absence of all proof and probable truth, the charge that the Missourians had invaded the Territory and controlled the congressional election by fraud and violence was circulated throughout the Free States, and made the basis of the most inflammatory appeals to all men opposed to the principles of the Kansas-Nebraska act to emigrate or send emigrants to Kansas, for the purpose of repelling the invaders, and assisting their friends who were then in the Territory in putting down the slave-power, and prohibiting Slavery in Kansas, with the view of making it a Free State. Exaggerated accounts of the large number of emigrants on their way under the auspices of the emigrant aid companies, with the view of controlling the election for members of the Territorial Legislature, which was to take place on the 30th of March, 1855, were published and circulated. These accounts, being republished and believed in Missouri, where the excitement had already been inflamed to a fearful intensity, induced a corresponding effort to send at least an equal number, to counteract the apprehended result of the new importation.

The report then gives a history of the Legislature elected March 30th, 1855, its removal from Pawnee City to the Shawnee Mission, its subsequent quarrel with Gov. Reeder, and continues:

A few days after, Governor Reeder dissolved his official relations with the legislature, on account of the removal of the seat of government, and while that body was still in session, a meeting was called by "many voters," to assemble at Lawrence, on the 14th or 15th of August, 1855, "to take into consideration the propriety of calling a Territorial Convention, preliminary to the formation of a State Government, and other subjects of public interest." At that meeting, the following preamble and resolutions were adopted with but one dissenting voice:

" *Whereas*, the people of Kansas Territory have been since the settlement, and now are, without any law-making power ; therefore

" *Be it resolved*, That we, the people of Kansas Territory, in mass meeting assembled, irrespective of party distinctions, influenced by a common necessity, and greatly desirous of promoting the common good, do hereby call upon and request all *bona fide* citizens of Kansas Territory, of whatever political views and predilections, to consult together in their respective election districts, and in mass convention or otherwise, elect three delegates for each representative in the legislative assembly, by proclamation of Governor Reeder of date 10th March, 1855 ; said delegates to assembly in convention at the town of Topeka, on the 19th day of September, 1855, then and there to consider and determine upon all subjects of public interest, and particularly upon that having reference to the speedy formation of a State Constitution, with an intention of an immediate application to be admitted as a State into the Union of the United States of America."

This meeting, so far as your Committee have been able to ascertain, was the first step in that series of proceedings which resulted in the adoption of a Constitution and State Government, to be put in operation on the 4th of the present month, in subversion of the Territorial Government established under the authority of Congress. The right to set up the State Government in defiance of the constituted authorities of the Territory, is based on the assumption "that the people of Kansas Territory have been since its settlement, and now are, without any law-making power ;" in the face of the well-known fact, that the Territorial Legislature was then in session, in pursuance of the proclamation of Governor Reeder, and the organic law of the Territory.

The report then proceeds to narrate the circumstances attending the formation of a State Government in Michigan, Arkansas, Florida and California, and states that "in every instance the proceeding has originated with, and been conducted in subordination to, the authority of the local governments established or recognized by the Government of the United States." It then refers to the case of the effort to change the organic law, made in Rhode Island some years ago, from which it says the "insurgents" (as the Free-State party in Kansas is called) "can derive no aid or comfort."

The following concludes the Report ; the words in Italics below perhaps explain in what sense the people of a Territory are "perfectly free to form their own institutions, in their own way :"

Without deeming it necessary to express any opinion on this occasion, in reference to the merits of that controversy, [referring to Rhode Island,] it is evident that the principles upon which it was conducted are not involved in the revolutionary struggle now going on in Kansas; for the reason, that *the sovereignty of a Territory remains in abeyance, suspended in the United States, in trust for the people, until they shall be admitted into the Union as a State. In the meantime, they are entitled to enjoy and exercise all the privileges and rights of self-government, in subordination to the Constitution of the United States, and in obedience to their organic law passed by Congress in pursuance of that instrument.* These rights and privileges are all derived from the Constitution, through the act of Congress, and must be exercised and enjoyed in subjection to all the limitations and restrictions which that Constitution imposes. Hence, it is clear that the people of the Territory have no inherent sovereign right, under the Constitution of the United States, to annul the laws and resist the authority of the Territorial government which Congress has established in obedience to the Constitution.

In tracing, step by step, the origin and history of these Kansas difficulties, your Committee have been profoundly impressed with the significant fact, that each one has resulted from an attempt to violate or circumvent the principles and provisions of the act of Congress for the organization of Kansas and Nebraska. The leading idea and fundamental principle of the Kansas-Nebraska act, as expressed in the law itself, was *to leave the actual settlers and bona-fide inhabitants of each Territory "perfectly free to form and regulate their domestic institutions in their own way, subject only to the Constitution of the United States."* While this is declared to be the "true intent and meaning of the act," those who were opposed to allowing the people of the Territory, preparatory to their admission into the Union as a State, to decide the Slavery question for themselves, failing to accomplish their purpose in the halls of Congress, and under the authority of the Constitution, immediately resorted, in their respective States, to unusual and extraordinary means to control the political destinies and shape the domestic institutions of Kansas, in defiance of the wishes, and regardless of the rights, of the people of that Territory, as guaranteed by their organic law. Combinations, in one section of the Union, to stimulate an unnatural and false system of emigration, with the view of controlling the elections, and forcing the domestic institutions of the Territory to assimilate to those of the non-slaveholding States, were followed, as might have been foreseen, by the use of similar means in the slaveholding States, to produce directly the opposite result. To these causes, and to these alone, in the opinion of your Committee, may be traced the origin and progress of all the controversies and disturbances with which Kansas is now convulsed.

If these unfortunate troubles have resulted, as natural consequences, from unauthorized and improper schemes of foreign interference with the internal affairs and domestic concerns of the Territory, it is apparent that the remedy must be sought in a strict adherence to the principles and rigid enforcement of the provisions of the organic law. In this connection, your Committee feel sincere satisfaction in commending the messages and proclamation of the President of the United States, in which we have the gratifying assurance that the supremacy of the laws will be maintained; that rebellion will be crushed; that insurrection will be suppressed; that aggressive intrusion for the purpose of deciding elections, or any other purpose, will be repelled; that unauthorized intermeddling in the local concerns of the Territory, both from adjoining and distant States, will be prevented; that the federal and local laws will be vindicated against all attempts at organized resistance; and that the people of the Territory will be protected in the establishment of their own institutions, undisturbed by encroachments from without, and in the full enjoyment of the rights of self-government assured to them by the Constitution and the organic law.

In view of these assurances, given under the conviction that the existing laws confer all the authority necessary to the performance of these important duties, and that the whole available force of the United States will be exerted to the extent required for their performance, your Committee repose in entire confidence that peace, and security, and law, will prevail in Kansas. If any further evidence were necessary to prove that all the collisions and difficulties in Kansas have been produced by the schemes of foreign interference which have been developed in this report, in violation of the principles and in evasion of the provisions of the Kansas-Nebraska act, it may be found in the fact that in Nebraska, to which the emigrant-aid societies did not extend their operations, and into which the stream of emigration was permitted to flow in its usual and natural channels, nothing has occurred to disturb the peace and harmony of the Territory, while the principle of self-government, in obedience to the Constitution, has had fair play, and is quietly working out its legitimate results.

It now only remains for your Committee to respond to the two specific recommendations of the President, in his special message. They are as follows:

"This, it seems to me, can be best accomplished by providing that, when the inhabitants of Kansas may desire it, and shall be of sufficient numbers to constitute a State, a convention of delegates, duly elected by the qualified voters, shall assemble to frame a Constitution, and thus prepare, through regular and lawful means, for its admission into the Union as a State. I respectfully recommend the enactment of a law to that effect.

"I recommend, also, that a special appropriation be made to defray any expense which may become requisite in the execution of the laws, or the maintenance of public order in the Territory of Kansas."

In compliance with the first recommendation, your Committee ask leave to report a bill authorizing the Legislature of the Territory to provide by law for the election of delegates by the people, and the assembling of a Convention to form a Constitution and State Government preparatory to their admission into the Union on an equal footing with the original States, so soon as it shall appear, by a census to be taken under the direction of the Governor, by the authority of the Legislature, that the Territory contains ninety-three thousand, four hundred and twenty inhabitants—that being the number required by the present ratio of representation for a member of Congress.

In compliance with the other recommendation, your Committee propose to offer to the appropriation bill an amendment appropriating such sum as shall be found necessary, by the estimates to be obtained, for the purpose indicated in the recommendation of the President.

All of which is respectfully submitted to the Senate by your Committee.

Mr. Collamer, of Vermont, the Republican member of same Committee, submitted a minority report, in which he says:

Thirteen of the present prosperous States of this Union passed through the period of apprenticeship or pupilage of territorial training, under the guardianship of Congress, preparatory to assuming their proud rank of manhood as sovereign and independent States. This period of their pupilage was, in every case, a period of the good offices of parent and child, in the kind relationship sustained between the National and the Territorial Government, and may be remembered with feelings of gratitude and pride. We have fallen on different times. A territory of our government is now convulsed with violence and discord, and the whole family of our nation is in a state of excitement and anxiety. The National Executive power is put in motion, the army in requisition, and Congress is invoked for interference.

In this case, as in all others of difficulty, it becomes necessary to inquire what is the true *cause* of existing trouble, in order to apply effectual cure. It is but a temporary palliative to deal with the external and more obvious manifestations and developments, while the real, procuring cause lies unattended to, and uncorrected, and unremoved.

It is said that organized opposition to law exists in Kansas. That, if existing, may probably be suppressed by the President, by the use of the army; and so, too, may invasions by armed bodies from Missouri, if the Executive be sincere in its efforts; but when this is done, while the cause of trouble remains, the results will continue with renewed and increased developments of danger.

Let us, then, look fairly and undisguisedly at this subject, in its true character and history. Wherein does this Kansas Territory differ from all our other Territories which have been so peacefully and successfully carried through, and been developed into the manhood of independent States? Can that difference account for existing troubles? Can that difference, as a cause of trouble, be removed?

The first and great point of difference between the Territorial government of Kansas and that of the thirteen Territorial governments before mentioned, consists in the subject of Slavery—the undoubted cause of present trouble.

The action of Congress in relation to all these *thirteen Territories was conducted on a uniform and prudent principle, to wit: To settle, by a clear provision, the law in relation to the subject of Slavery to be operative in the Territory, while it remained such;* not leaving it in any one of those cases to be a subject of controversy within the same, while in the plastic gristle of its youth. This was done by Congress in the exercise of the same power which molded the form of their organic laws, and appointed their executive and judiciary, and sometimes their legislative officers; it was the power provided in the Constitution, in these words: "Congress shall have power to dispose of and make all needful rules and regulations respecting the territory or other property belonging to the United States." Settling the subject of Slavery while the country remained a Territory, was no higher exercise of power in Congress, than the regulation of the functions of the territorial government, and actually appointing its principal functionaries. This practice commenced with this National Government, and was continued, with uninterrupted uniformity, for more than *sixty* years. This practical contemporaneous construction of the constitutional *power* of this government is too clear to leave room for doubt, or opportunity for skepticism. The peace, prosperity, and success which attended this course, and the results which have ensued, in the formation and admission of the thirteen States therefrom, are most conclusive and satisfactory evidence, also, of the wisdom and prudence with which this *power* was *exercised*. Deluded must be that people who, in the pursuit of plausible theories, become deaf to the lessons, and blind to the results of their own experience.

Let us next inquire by what rule of uniformity Congress was governed, in the exercise of this power of determining the condition of each Territory as to Slavery, while remaining a Territory, as manifested in those thirteen instances. An examination of our history will show that this was not done from time to time by agitation and local or party triumphs in Congress. The rule pursued was uniform and clear; and, whoever may have lost by it, peace and prosperity have been gained. That rule was this:

Where Slavery was actually existing in a country to any considerable or general extent, it was (though somewhat modified as to further importation in some instances, as in Mississippi and Orleans Territories) suffered to remain. The fact that it had been taken and existed there, was taken as an indication of its adaptation and local utility. Where Slavery did not in fact exist to any appreciable extent, the same was, by Congress, expressly prohibited; so that in either case the country was settled up without difficulty or doubt as to the character of its institutions. In no instance was this difficult and disturbing subject left to the people who had and who might settle in the Territory, to be there an everlasting bone of contention, so long as the Territorial government should continue. It was ever regarded, too, as a subject in which the whole country had an interest, and, therefore, improper for local legislation.

And though, whenever the people of a Territory come to form their own organic law, as an independent State, they would, either before or after their admission as a State, form and mold their institutions, as a Sovereign State, in their own way, yet it must be expected, and has always proved true, that the State has taken the character her pupilage has prepared her for, as well in respect to Slavery as in other respects. Hence, six of the thirteen States are Free States, because Slavery was prohibited in them by Congress, while Territories, to wit: Ohio, Indiana, Illinois, Michigan, Wisconsin, and Iowa. Seven of the thirteen are slaveholding States, because Slavery was allowed in them by Congress while they were Territories, to wit: Tennessee, Alabama, Mississippi, Florida, Louisiana, Arkansas and Missouri.

On the 6th of March, A.D. 1820, was passed by Congress the act preparatory to the admission of the State of Missouri into the Union. Much controversy and discussion arose on the question whether a prohibition of Slavery within said State should be inserted, and it resulted in this: that said State should be admitted without such prohibition, but that Slavery should be *forever prohibited* in the rest of that country ceded to us by France lying north of 36° 30′ north latitude, and it was so done. This contract is known as the *Missouri Compromise*. Under this arrangement, Missouri was admitted as a slaveholding State, the same having been a slaveholding Territory. Arkansas, south of the line, was formed into a Territory, and Slavery allowed therein, and afterward admitted as a slaveholding State. Iowa was made a Territory north of the line, and, under the operation of the law, was settled up without slaves, and admitted as a free State. The country now making the Territories of Kansas and Nebraska, in 1820, was almost or entirely uninhabited, and lay north of said line, and whatever settlers entered the same before 1854, did so under that law, forever forbidding Slavery therein.

In 1854, Congress passed an act establishing two new Territories—Nebraska and Kansas—in this region of country, where Slavery had been prohibited for more than thirty years; and, instead of leaving said law against Slavery in operation, or prohibiting or expressly allowing or establishing Slavery, Congress left the subject in said Territories, to be discussed, agitated, and legislated on, from time to time, and the elections in said Territories to be conducted with reference to that subject, from year to year, so long as they should remain Territories; for, whatever laws might be passed by the Territorial legislatures on this subject, must be subject to change or repeal by those of the succeeding years. In most former Territorial governments, it was provided by law that their laws were subject to the revision of Congress, so that they would be made with caution. In these Territories, that was omitted.

The provision in relation to Slavery in Nebraska and Kansas is as follows: "The eighth section of the act preparatory to the admission of Missouri into the Union (which being inconsistent with the *principle* of non-intervention by Congress with Slavery in the States and Territories, as required by the legislation of 1850, commonly called the Compromise Measures) is hereby declared *inoperative and void;* it being the true intent and meaning of this act not to legislate Slavery into said Territory or State, nor to exclude it therefrom, but to leave the people thereof *perfectly free* to form and regulate their domestic institutions in their own way, subject only to the Constitution of the United States: *Provided,* That nothing herein contained shall be construed to

revive or put in force any law or regulation which may have existed prior to the act of 6 March, 1820, either protecting, establishing, prohibiting, or abolishing Slavery."

Thus it was promulgated to the people of this whole country that here was a clear field for competition—an open course for the race of rivalship; the goal of which was, the ultimate establishment of a sovereign State; and the prize, the reward of everlasting liberty and its institutions on the one hand, or the perpetuity of Slavery and its concomitants on the other. It is the obvious duty of this government, while this law continues, to see this manifesto faithfully, and honorably, and honestly performed, even though its particular supporters may see cause of a result unfavorable to their hopes.

It is further to be observed that, in the performance of this novel experiment, it was provided that all white men who became inhabitants in Kansas were entitled to vote without regard to their *time of residence*, usually provided in other Territories. Nor was this right of voting confined to American citizens, but included all such aliens as had declared, or would declare, on oath, their intention to become citizens. Thus was the proclamation to the world to become inhabitants of Kansas, and enlist in this great enterprise, by the force of numbers, by vote, to decide for it the great question. Was it to be expected that this great proclamation for the political tournament would be listened to with indifference and apathy? Was it prepared and presented in that spirit? Did it relate to a subject on which the people were cool or indifferent? A large part of the people of this country look on domestic Slavery as " only evil, and that continually," alike to master and to slave, and to the community; to be left alone to the management or enjoyment of the people of the States where it exists, but not to be extended, more especially as it gives, or may give, political supremacy to a minority of the people of this country in the United States government. On the other hand, many of the people of another part of the United States regard Slavery, if not in the abstract a blessing, at least as now existing, a condition of society best for both white and black, while they exist together; while others regard it as no evil, but as the highest state of social condition. These consider that they cannot, with safety to their interests, permit political ascendency to be largely in the hands of those unfriendly to this *peculiar institution*. From these conflicting views, long and violent has been the controversy, and experience seems to show it interminable. . . . .

A succinct statement of the exercise and progress of the material events in Kansas is this: After the passage of this law, establishing the Territory of Kansas, a large body of settlers rapidly entered into said Territory with a view to permanent inhabitancy therein. Most of these were from the Free States of the West and North, who probably intended by their votes and influence to establish there a Free State, agreeably to the law which invited them. Some part of those from the Northern States had been encouraged and aided in this enterprise by the Emigrant Aid Society formed in Massachusetts, which put forth some exertions in this laudable object, by open and public measures, in providing facilities for transportation to all peaceable citizens who desired to become permanent settlers in said Territory, and providing therein hotels, mills, etc., for the public accommodation of that new country.   . •

The Governor of Kansas, having, in pursuance of law, divided the territory into districts, and procured a census thereof, issued his proclamation for the election of a Legislative Assembly therein, to take place on the 30th day of March, 1855, and directed how the same should be conducted, and the returns made to him agreeable to the law establishing said Territory. On the day of election, large bodies of armed men from the State of Missouri, appeared at the polls in most of the districts, and, by most violent and tumultuous carriage and demeanor, overawed the defenseless inhabitants, and by their own votes elected a large majority of the members of both Houses of said Assembly. On the returns of said election being made to the Governor, protests and objections were made to him in relation to a part of said districts; and as to them, he set aside such, and such only, as by the returns appeared to be bad. In relation to others, covering, in all, a majority of the two Houses, equally vicious in fact, but apparently good by formal returns, the inhabitants thereof, borne down by said violence and intimidation, scattered and discouraged, and laboring under apprehensions of personal violence, refrained and desisted from presenting any protest to the Governor in relation thereto; and he, then uninformed in relation thereto, issued certificates to the members who appeared by said formal returns to have been elected.

In relation to those districts which the Governor so set aside, orders were by him issued for new elections. In one of these districts, the same proceedings were repeated by men from Missouri, and in others not, and certificates were issued to the persons elected.

This legislative assembly, so elected, assembled at Pawnee, on the second day of July, 1855, that being the time and place for holding said meeting, as fixed by the Governor, by authority of law. On assembling, the said houses proceeded to set aside and reject those members so elected on said second election, except in the district where the men from Missouri had, at said election, chosen the same persons they had elected at the said first election, and they admitted all of the said first-elected members.

A legislative assembly, so created by military force, by a foreign invasion, in violation of the organic law, was but a usurpation. No act of its own, no act or neglect of the Governor, could legalize or sanctify it. Its own decisions as to its own legality are like its laws, but the fruits of its own usurpation, which no Governor could legitimate. . . . .

The people of Kansas, thus invaded, subdued, oppressed and insulted, seeing their Territorial Government (such only in form) perverted into an engine to crush them in the dust, and to defeat and destroy the professed object of their organic law, by depriving them of the "*perfect freedom*" therein provided; and finding no ground to hope for rights in that organization, they proceeded, under the guaranty of the United States Constitution, "peaceably to assemble to petition the Government for the redress of (their) grievances." They saw no earthly source of relief but in the formation of a State Government by the people, and the acceptance and ratification thereof by Congress.

It is true that, in several instances in our political history, the people of a Territory have been authorized by an act of Congress to form a State Constitution, and, after so doing, were admitted by Congress. It is quite obvious that no such authority could be given by the act of the Territorial Government. *That* clearly has no power to create another Government, paramount to itself. It is equally true that, in numerous instances in our history, the people of a Territory have, without any previous act of Congress, proceeded to call a Convention of the people by their delegates; have formed a State Constitution, which has been adopted by the people, and a State Legislature assembled under it, and chosen Senators to Congress, and then have presented said Constitution to Congress, which has approved the same, and received the Senators and members of Congress who were chosen under it before Congress had approved the same. Such was the case of Tennessee; such was the case of Michigan, where the people not only formed a State Constitution without an act of Congress, but they actually put their State Government into full operation and passed laws, and it was approved by Congress by receiving it as a State. The people of Florida formed their Constitution without any act of Congress therefor, six years before they were admitted into the Union. When the people of Arkansas were about forming a State Constitution without a previous act of Congress, in 1835, the Territorial Governor applied to the President on the subject, who referred the matter to the Attorney-General, and his opinion, as then expressed and published, contained the following:

"It is not in the power of the general assembly of Arkansas to pass any law for the purpose of electing members to a Convention to form a Constitution and State government, nor to do any other act, directly or indirectly, to create such government. Every such law, even though it were approved by the governor of the Territory, would be null and void; if passed by them notwithstanding his veto, by a vote of two-thirds of each branch, it would still be equally void."

He further decided that it was not rebellious, or insurrectionary, or even unlawful, for the people peaceably to proceed, even without an act of Congress, in forming a Constitution, and in so forming a State Constitution and so far organizing under the same as to choose the officers necessary for its representation in Congress, with a view to present the same to Congress for admission, was a power which fell clearly within the right of the people to assemble and petition for redress. The people of Arkansas proceeded without an act of Congress, and were received into the Union accordingly. If any rights were derived to the people of Arkansas from the terms of the French treaty of cession, they equally extended to the people of Kansas, it being a part of the same cession.

In this view of the subject, in the first part of August, 1855, a call was published in the public papers, for a meeting of the citizens of Kansas, irrespective of party, to meet at Lawrence, in said Territory, on the 15th of said August, to take into consideration the propriety of calling a Convention of the people of the whole Territory, to consider that subject. That meeting was held on the 15th day of August last, and it proceeded to call such Convention of delegates to be elected, and to assemble at Topeka in said Territory, on the 19th day of September, 1855, not to form a Constitution, but to consider the propriety of calling, formally, a Convention for that purpose.

Delegates were elected agreeably to the proclamation so issued, and they met at Topeka on the fourth Tuesday in October, 1855, and formed a constitution, which was submitted to the people, and was ratified by them by vote in the districts. An election of State officers and members of the State legislature has been had, and a representative to Congress elected, and it is intended to proceed to the election of senators, with the view to present the same, with the constitution, to Congress for admission into the Union.

Whatever views individuals may at times, or in meetings, have expressed, and whatever ultimate determination may have been entertained in the result of being spurned by Congress, and refused redress, is now entirely immaterial. That cannot condemn or give character to the proceedings thus far pursued.

Many have honestly believed usurpation could make no law, and that if Congress made no further provisions they were well justified in forming a law for themselves; but it is not now necessary to consider that matter, as it is to be hoped that Congress will not leave them to such a necessity.

Thus far, this effort of the people for redress is peaceful, constitutional, and right. Whether it will succeed, rests with Congress to determine; but clear it is that it should not be met and denounced as revolutionary, rebellious, insurrectionary, or unlawful, nor does it call for or justify the exercise of any force by any department of this government to check or control it.

It now becomes proper to inquire what should be done by Congress; for we are informed by the President, in substance, that he has no power to correct a usurpation, and that the laws, even though made by usurped authority, must be by him enforced and executed, even with military force. The measures of redress should be applied to the true cause of the difficulty. This obviously lies in the repeal of the clause for freedom in the act of 1820, and therefore, the true remedy lies in the entire repeal of the act of 1854, which effected it. Let this be done with frankness and magnanimity, and Kansas be organized anew as a Free Territory, and all will be put right.

But, if Congress insist on proceeding with the experiment, then declare all the action by this spurious, foreign legislative assembly utterly inoperative and void, and direct a reorganization, providing proper safeguards for legal voting and against foreign force.

There is, however, another way to put an end to all this trouble there, and in the nation, without retracing steps or continuing violence, or by force compelling obedience to tyrannical laws made by foreign force; and that is, by admitting that Territory as a State, with her free constitution. True, indeed, her numbers are not such as give her a right to demand admission, being, as the President informs us, probably only about twenty-five thousand. The Constitution fixes no number as necessary, and the importance of *now* settling this question may well justify Congress in admitting her as a State, *at this time*, especially as we have good reason to believe that, if admitted as a State, and controversy ended, it will immediately fill up with a numerous and successful population.

At any rate, it seems impossible to believe that Congress is to leave that people without redress, to have enforced upon them by the army of the nation these measures and laws of violence and oppression. Are they to be dragooned into submission; Is that an experiment pleasant to execute on our own free people?

The true character of this transaction is matter of extensive notoriety. Its essential features are too obvious to allow of any successful disguise or palliation, however complicated or ingenious may be the statements, or however special the pleadings, for that purpose. The case requires some quieting, kind and prudent treatment by the hand of Congress to do justice and satisfy the nation. The people of this country are peacefully relying on Congress to provide the competent measures of redress which they have the undoubted power to administer.

The Attorney-General, in the case of Arkansas, says: "Congress may at pleasure repeal or modify the laws passed by the Territorial Legislature, and may at any time abrogate and remodel the legislature itself, and all the other departments of the Territorial Government."

Treating this grievance in Kansas with ingenious excuses, with neglect or contempt, or riding over the oppressed with an army, and dragooning them into submission, will make no satisfactory termination. Party success may at times be temporarily secured by adroit devices, plausible pretenses, and partisan address; but the permanent preservation of this Union can be maintained only by frankness and integrity. Justice may be denied where it ought to be granted; power may perpetuate that vassalage which violence and usurpation have produced; the subjugation of white freemen may be necessary, that African Slavery may succeed; but such a course must not be expected to produce peace and satisfaction in our country, so long as the people retain any proper sentiment of justice, liberty, and law.

J. COLLAMER.

The majority and minority Reports being received, various matters relating to Kansas were debated until the 19th of March, the House was brought to a vote on the proposition of the committee of elections to empower said committee to send to Kansas for persons and papers, which was modified on motion of Mr. Dunn, of Ind., so as to raise a special committee of three members, to be appointed by the Speaker. The resolutions raising this committee gave it ample powers

To inquire into and collect evidence in regard to the troubles in Kansas generally, and particularly in regard to any fraud or force attempted or practiced in reference to any of the elections which have taken place in said Territory, either under the law organizing said Territory, or under any pretended law which may be alleged to have taken effect there since. That they shall fully investigate and take proof of all violent and tumultuous proceedings in said Territory, at any time since the passage of the Kansas Nebraska act, whether engaged in by the residents of said Territory, or by any person or persons from elsewhere going into said Territory, and doing, or encouraging others to do, any act of violence or public disturbance against the laws of the United States, or the rights, peace, and safety of the residents of said Territory; and for that purpose, said Committee shall have full power to send for, and examine, and take copies of, all such papers, public records, and proceedings, as in their judgment will be useful in the premises; and also, to send for persons and examine them on oath, or affirmation, as to matters within their knowledge, touching the matters of said investigation; and said Committee, by their chairman, shall have power to administer all necessary oaths or affirmations connected with their aforesaid duties. That said Committee may hold their investigations at such places and times as to them may seem advisable, and that they have leave of absence from the duties of this House until they shall have completed such investigation. That they be authorized to employ one or more clerks, and one or more assistant sergeants-at-arms, to aid them in their investigation; and may administer to them an oath, or affirmation, faithfully to perform the duties assigned to them, respectively, and to keep secret all matters which may come to their knowledge touching such investigation, as said Committee may direct, until the Report of the same shall be submitted to this House; and said Committee may discharge any such clerk or assistant sergeant-at-arms for neglect of duty or disregard of instructions in the premises, and employ others under like regulations. . . . . . .

The vote of the Slave States was unanimous against the investigation, 17 from the Free States voting with them. Yeas 101; Nays 93.

The following are the negatives from the Free States:

Nays—Against the Investigation:

MAINE—Thomas J. D. Fuller—1.

NEW-YORK—John Kelly, *William W. Valk*, John Wheeler, *Thomas R. Whitney*—4.

NEW-JERSEY—George Vail—1.

PENNSYLVANIA—John Cadwalader, Thomas B. Florence, J. Glancy Jones—3.

INDIANA—William H. English, Smith Miller—2.

MICHIGAN—George W. Peck—1.

ILLINOIS—James C. Allen, Thomas L. Harris, Samuel S Marshall, William A. Richardson—4.

CALIFORNIA—Philemon T. Herbert—1.

So the resolution prevailed, and Messrs. William A. Howard, of Michigan, John Sherman, of Ohio, and Mordecai Oliver, of Missouri, were appointed the Committee of Investigation thereby required.

These gentlemen proceeded to Kansas, and spent several weeks there in taking testimony as to the elections, etc., which had taken place in that Territory. The testimony thus taken forms a volume of nearly twelve hundred large and closely-printed pages, the substance of which was summed up on their return by the majority (Messrs. Howard and Sherman), in the following

REPORT ON THE OUTRAGES IN KANSAS.

A journal of proceedings, including sundry communications made to and by the Committee was kept, a copy of which is herewith submitted. The testimony also is herewith submitted; a copy of it has been made and arranged not according to the order in which it was taken, but so as to present, as clearly as possible, a consecutive history of events in the Territory, from its organization to the 19th day of March, A. D. 1856.

Your Committee deem it their duty to state, as briefly as possible, the principal facts proven before them. When the act to organize the Territory of Kansas was passed on the 24th day of May, 1854, the greater portion of its eastern border was included in Indian reservations not open for settlement; and there were but few white settlers in any portion of the Territory. Its Indian population was rapidly decreasing, while many emigrants from different parts of our country were anxiously waiting the extinction of the Indian title, and the establishment of a Territorial Government, to seek new homes on its fertile prairies. It cannot be doubted that, if its condition as a free Territory had been left undisturbed by Congress, its settlement would have been rapid, peaceful, and prosperous. Its climate, soil, and its easy access to the older settlements, would have made it the favored course for the tide of emigration constantly flowing to the West, and by this time it would have been admitted into the Union as a Free State, without the least sectional excitement. If so organized, none but the kindest feeling could have existed between it and the adjoining State. Their mutual interests and intercourse, instead of, as now, endangering the harmony of the Union, would have strengthened the ties of national brotherhood. The testimony clearly shows, that before the proposition to repeal the Missouri Compromise was introduced into Congress, the people of western Missouri appeared indifferent to the prohibition of Slavery in the Territory, and neither asked nor desired its repeal.

When, however, the prohibition was removed by the action of Congress, the aspect of affairs entirely changed. The whole country was agitated by the reopening of a controversy which conservative men in different sections hoped had been settled, in every State and Territory, by some law beyond the danger of repeal. The excitement which has always accompanied the discussion of the Slavery question was greatly increased, by the hope on the one hand of extending Slavery into a region from which it had been excluded by law, and on the other by a sense of wrong done by what was regarded as a dishonor of a national compact. This excitement was naturally transferred into the border counties of Missouri and the Territory, as settlers favoring free or slave institutions moved into it. A new difficulty soon occurred. Different constructions were put upon the organic law. It was contended by the one party that the right to hold slaves in the Territory existed, and that neither the people nor the Territorial Legislature could prohibit Slavery—that that power was alone possessed by the people when they were authorized to form a State government. It was contended that the removal of the restriction virtually established Slavery in the Territory. This claim was urged by many prominent men in western Missouri, who actively engaged in the affairs of the Territory. Every movement, of whatever character, which tended to establish free institutions, was regarded as an interference with their rights.

Within a few days after the organic law passed, and as soon as its passage could be known on the border, leading citizens of Missouri crossed into the Territory, held squatter meetings, and then returned to their homes. Among their resolutions are the following:

"That we will afford protection to no Abolitionist as a settler of this Territory."

"That we recognize the institution of Slavery as already existing in this Territory, and advise slaveholders to introduce their property as early as possible."

Similar resolutions were passed in various parts of the Territory, and by meetings in several counties of Missouri. Thus the first effect of the repeal of the restriction against Slavery was to substitute the resolves of squatter meetings, composed almost exclusively of Missourians, for the deliberate action of Congress, acquiesced in for 35 years.

This unlawful interference has been continued in every important event in the history of the Territory: *every election* has been controlled, not by the actual settlers, but by citizens of Missouri; and, as a consequence, every officer in the Territory, from constables to legislators, except those appointed by the President, owe their positions to non-resident voters. None have been elected by the settlers; and your Committee have been unable to find that any political power whatever, however unimportant, has been exercised by the people of the Territory

In October A. 1854, Governor A. H. Reeder and the other officers appointed by the President arrived in the Territory. Settlers from all parts of the country were moving in in great numbers, making their claims and building their cabins. About the same time, and before any election was or could be held in the Territory, a secret political society was formed in the State of Missouri. It was known by different names, such as "Social Band," "Friends' Society," "Blue Lodge," "The Sons of the South." Its members were bound together by secret oaths, and they had passwords, signs, and grips, by which they were known to each other. Penalties were imposed for violating the rules and secrets of the Order. Written minutes were kept of the proceedings of the Lodges, and the different Lodges were connected together by an effective organization. It embraced great numbers of the citizens of Missouri, and was extended into other Slave States and into the Territory. Its avowed purpose was not only to extend Slavery into Kansas, but also into other territory of the United States; and to form a union of all the friends of that institution. Its plan of operating was to organize and send men to vote at the elections in the Territory, to collect money to pay their expenses, and, if necessary, to protect them in voting. It also proposed to induce Pro-Slavery men to emigrate into the Territory, to aid and sustain them while there, and to elect none to office but those friendly to their views. This dangerous society was controlled by men who avowed their purpose to extend Slavery into the Territory at all hazards, and was altogether the most effective instrument in organizing the subsequent armed invasions and forays. In its Lodges in Missouri, the affairs of Kansas were discussed, the force necessary to control the election was divided into bands, and leaders selected; means were collected, and signs and badges were agreed upon. While the great body of the actual settlers of the Territory were relying upon the rights secured to them by the organic law, and had formed no organization or combination whatever, this conspiracy against their rights was gathering strength in Missouri, and would have been sufficient at their first election to have overpowered them, if they had been united to a man.

Your Committee had great difficulty in eliciting the proof of the details in regard to this secret society. One witness, member of the legislative council, refused to answer questions in reference to it. Another declined to answer fully, because to do so would result to his injury. Others could or would only answer as to the general purposes of the Society, but sufficient is disclosed in the testimony to show the influence it had in controlling the elections in the Territory.

The first election was for a Delegate to Congress. It was appointed for the 29th of November, 1854. The Governor divided the Territory into seventeen Election-Districts; appointed Judges and prescribed proper rules for the election. In the Ist, IIId, VIIIth, IXth, Xth, XIIth, XIIIth, and XVIIth Districts there appears to have been but little if any fraudulent voting.

The election in the IId District was held at the village of Douglas, nearly fifty miles from the Missouri line. On the day before the election, large companies of men came into the district in wagons and on horseback, and declared that they were from the State of Missouri, and were going to Douglas to vote. On the morning of the election, they gathered around the house where the election was to be held. Two of the judges appointed by the Governor did not appear, and other judges were elected by the crowd. All then voted. In order to make a pretense of right to vote, some persons of the company kept a pretended register of squatter claims, on which any one could enter his name and then assert he had a claim in the Territory. A citizen of the district who was himself a candidate for Delegate to Congress, was told by one of the strangers, that he would be abused and probably killed if he challenged a vote. He was seized by the collar, called a d—d Abolitionist, and was compelled to seek protection in the room with the judges. About the time the polls were closed, these strangers mounted their horses and got into their wagons and c ied out:

"All aboard for Westport and Kansas City." A number were recognized as residents of Missouri, and among them was Samuel H. Woodson, a leading lawyer of Independence. Of those whose names are on the poll-books, 35 were resident settlers and 226 were not.

The election in the IVth District was held at Dr. Chapman's, over 40 miles from the Missouri State line. It was a thinly-settled region, containing but 47 voters in February, 1855, when the census was taken. On the day before the election, from 100 to 150 citizens of Cass and Jackson Counties, Mo., came into this district, declaring their purpose to vote, and that they were bound to make Kansas a Slave State, if they did it at the point of the sword. Persons of the party on the way drove each a stake in the ground and called it a claim—and in one case several names were put on one stake. The party of strangers camped all night near where the election was to be held, and in the morning were at the election-polls and voted. One of their party got drunk, and, to get rid of Dr. Chapman, a judge of the election, they sent for him to come and see a sick man, and in his absence filled his place with another judge, who was not sworn. They did not deny nor conceal that they were residents of Missouri, and many of them were recognized as such by others. They declared that they were bound to make Kansas a Slave State. They insisted upon their right to vote in the Territory if they were in it one hour. After the election, they again returned to their homes in Missouri, camping over night on the way.

We find upon the poll-books 161 names; of these not over 30 resided in the Territory; 131 were non-residents.

But few settlers attended the election in the Vth District, the district being large and the settlement scattered. 82 votes were cast; of these between 20 and 30 were settlers, and the residue were citizens of Missouri. They passed into the Territory by way of the Santa Fe road and by the residence of Dr. Westfall, who then lived on the western line of Missouri. Some little excitement arose at the polls as to the legality of their voting, but they did vote for General Whitfield, and said they intended to make Kansas a Slave State, and that they had claims in the Territory. Judge Teazle, judge of the court in Jackson County, Missouri, was present, but did not vote. He said he did not intend to vote, but came to see that others voted. After the election, the Missourians returned the way they came.

The election in the VIth District was held at Fort Scott, in the southeast part of the Territory, and near the Missouri line. A party of about one hundred men, from Cass and the counties in Missouri south of it, went into the Territory, traveling about 45 miles, most of them with their wagons and tents, and camping out. They appeared at the place of election. Some attempts were made to swear them, but two of the judges were prevailed upon not to do so, and none were sworn, and as many as chose voted. There were but few resident voters at the polls. The settlement was sparse—about 25 actual settlers voted out of 105 votes cast, leaving 80 illegal votes. After the voting was over, the Missourians went to their wagons and commenced leaving for home.

The most shameless fraud practiced upon the rights of the settlers at this election was in the VIIth District. It is a remote settlement, about 75 miles from the Missouri line, and contained in February, A.D. 1855, three months afterward, when the census was taken, but 53 voters, and yet the poll-books show that 604 votes were cast. The election was held at the house of Frey McGee, at a place called "110." But few of the actual settlers were present at the polls. A witness who formerly resided in Jackson County, Missouri, and was well acquainted with the citizens of that county, says that he saw a great many wagons and tents at the place of election, and many individuals he knew from Jackson County. He was in their tents, and conversed with some of them, and they told him they had come with the intention of voting. He went to the polls intending to vote for Flenniken, and his ticket being of a different color from the rest, his vote was challenged by Frey McGee, who had been appointed one of the judges, but did not serve. Lemuel Ralstone, a citizen of Missouri, was acting in his place. The witness then challenged the vote of a young man by the name of Nolan, whom he knew to reside in Jackson County. Finally, the thing was hushed up, as the witness had a good many friends there from that county, and it might lead to a fight if he challenged any more votes. Both voted, and he then went down to their camp. He there saw many of his old acquaintances, whom he knew had voted at the election in August previous in Missouri, and who still resided in that State. By a careful comparison of the poll-lists with the census-rolls, we find but 12 names on the poll-book who were voters when the census was taken three months afterward, and we are satisfied that not more than 20 legal votes could have been polled at that election. The only residents who are known to have voted are named by the witness, and are 13 in number—thus leaving 584 illegal votes cast in a remote district, where the settlers within many miles were acquainted with each other.

The total number of white inhabitants in the XIth District, in the month of February, A.D. 1855, including men, women and children, was 36, of whom 24 were voters—yet the poll-lists in this District show that 245 votes were cast at this election. For reasons stated hereafter in regard to the election on the 30th of March, your Committee were unable to procure the attendance of witnesses from this District. From the records, it clearly appears that the votes cast could not have been by lawful resident voters. The best test, in the absence of direct proof, by which to ascertain the number of legal votes cast, is by a comparison of the census-roll with the poll-book—by which it appears that but 7 resident settlers voted, and 238 votes were illegally and fraudulently cast.

The election in the XIVth District was held at the house of Benjamin Harding, a few miles from the town of St. Joseph, Missouri. Before the polls were opened, a large number of citizens of Buchanan County, Missouri, and among them many of the leading citizens of St. Joseph, were at the place of voting, and made a majority of the company present. At the time appointed by the Governor for opening the polls, two of the Judges were not there, and it became the duty of the legal voters present to select other judges The judge who was present * suggested the name of Mr. Waterson as one of the Judges —but the crowd voted down the proposition. Some discussion then arose as to the right of non-residents to vote 'or judges, during which Mr. Bryant was nominated and elected by the crowd. Some one nominated Col. John Scott as the other judge, who was then and is now a resident of St. Joseph. At that time, he was the City Attorney at that place, and so continued until this spring, but he claimed that the night before he had come to the house of Mr. Bryant, and had engaged boarding for a month, and considered himself a resident of Kansas on that ground. The judges appointed by the Governor refused to put the nomination of Col. Scott to vote, because he was not a resident. After some discussion, Judge Leonard, a citizen of Missouri, stepped forward and put the vote himself; and Mr. Scott was declared by him as elected by the crowd, and served as a judge of election that day. After the election was over, he returned to St. Joseph, and never since has *resided* in the Territory. It is manifest that this election of a non-resident lawyer as a judge was imposed upon the settlers by the citizens of the State. When the board of judges was thus completed, the voting proceeded ; but the effect of the rule adopted by the judges allowed many, if not a majority of the non-residents, to vote. They claimed that their presence on the ground, especially when they had a *claim* in the Territory, gave them a right to vote—under that construction of the law, they readily, when required, swore they were " residents," and then voted. By this evasion, as nearly as your Committee can ascertain from the testimony, as many as 50 illegal votes were cast in this District out of 153, the whole number polled.

The election in the XVth District was held at Penseman's, on Stranger Creek, a few miles from Weston,

Missouri. On the day of the election, a large number of citizens of Platte County, but chiefly from Weston and Platte City, came in small parties, in wagons and on horseback, to the polls. Among them were several leading citizens of that town, and the names of many of them are given by the witnesses. They generally insisted upon their right to vote, on the ground that every man having a claim in the Territory could vote, no matter where he lived. All voted who chose. No man was challenged or sworn. Some of the residents did not vote. The purpose of the strangers in voting was declared to be to make Kansas a Slave State. We find by the poll-books that 306 votes were cast—of these we find but 57 are on the census-rolls as legal voters in February following. Your Committee is satisfied from the testimony that not over 100 of those who voted had any right so to do, leaving at least 2 6 illegal votes cast.

The election in the XVIth District was held at Leavenworth. It was then a small village of three or four houses, located on the Delaware Reservation. There were but comparatively few settlers then in the district, but the number rapidly increased afterward. On the day before and on the day of the election, a great many citizens of Platte, Clay and Ray counties crossed the river—most of them camping in tents and wagons about the town, " like a camp-meeting." They were in companies or messes of ten to fifteen in each, and numbered in all several hundred. They brought their own provision and cooked it themselves, and were generally armed. Many of them were known by the witnesses, and their names given, and their names are found upon the poll-books. Among them were several persons of influence where they resided in Missouri, who held, or had held, high official positions in that State. They claimed to be residents of the Territory, from the fact that they were then present, and insisted upon the right to vote, and did vote. Their avowed purpose in doing so was to make Kansas a Slave State. These strangers crowded around the polls, and it was with great difficulty that the settlers could get to the polls. One resident attempted to get to the polls in the afternoon, but was crowded and pulled back. He then went outside of the crowd and hurrahed for Gen. Whitfield, and some of those who did not know him said, " that's a good Pro-Slavery man," and lifted him over their heads so that he crawled on their heads and put in his vote. A person who saw from the color of his ticket that it was not for Gen. Whitfield, cried out, " He is a damned Abolitionist—let him down ;" and they dropped him. Others were passed to the polls in the same way, and others crowded up in the best way they could. After this mockery of an election was over, the non-residents returned to their homes in Missouri. Of the 312 votes cast, not over 150 were by legal voters.

The following abstract exhibits the whole number of votes at this election, for each candidate ; the number of legal and illegal votes cast in each district ; and the number of legal votes in each district in February following:

ABSTRACT OF CENSUS AND ELECTION NOV. 29, 1854.

Districts.	Place of Voting.	Whitfield	Wakefield.	Flenniken.	Scattering.	Total.	Number Votes by Census.	Legal Vote	Illegal Votes.
	Lawrence....................	46	188	51	15	300	369	300	—
II	Douglas.....................	235	20	6	—	261	199	35	226
III	Stinson's..................	40	—	7	—	47	101	47	—
IV	Dr. Chapman's...............	140	21	—	—	161	47	30	131
	H. Sherman's...............	63	4	15	—	82	442	30	52
VI	Fort Scott..................	105	—	—	—	105	253	25	80
VII	" 116 "............	597	—	7	—	604	58	20	584
II	Council Grove..............	16	—	—	—	16	39	16	—
IX	Reynold's	9	—	31	—	40	36	40	—
X	Big Blue Cross.............	2	6	29	—	37	63	37	—
XI	Marysville.................	237	–	3	5	245	24	7	238
XII	Warton's Store.............	81	9	—	1	41	78	41	—
XI	Osawkie....................	69	1	1	—	71	96	71	—
XIV	Harding's..................	130	—	23	—	153	334	103	50
	Penseno....................	267	—	39	—	306	308	100	206
XVI	Leavenworth	232	—	80	—	312	385	150	162
VII	Shawnee Agency.	49	—	13	—	62	50	62	—
III		—	—	—	—	28	—	—	—
	Total................ ...	2268	249	805	21	2871	—	1114	1729

* Benjamin Harding.

Thus your Committee find that in this, the first election in the Territory, a very large majority of the votes were cast by citizens of the State of Missouri, in violation of the organic law of the Territory. Of the legal votes cast, Gen. Whitfield received a plurality. The settlers took but little interest in the election, not one-half of them voting. This may be accounted for, from the fact that the settlements were scattered over a great extent—that the term of the Delegate to be elected was short—and that the question of Free and Slave institutions was not generally regarded by them as distinctly at issue. Under these circumstances, a systematic invasion from an adjoining State, by which large numbers of illegal votes were cast in remote and sparse settlements for the avowed purpose of extending Slavery into the Territory, even though it did not change the result of the election, was a crime of great magnitude. Its immediate effect was to further excite the people of the Northern States—induce acts of retaliation, and exasperate the actual settlers against their neighbors in Missouri.

In January and February, A.D. 1855, the Governor caused an enumeration to be taken of the inhabitants and qualified voters in the Territory, an abstract of which is here given:

Total population	8501
Total voters	2905
Natives of the United States	7161
Of foreign birth	409
Slaves	242
Free negroes	151

On the same day the census was completed, the Governor issued his proclamation for an election to be held on the 30th of March, A.D. 1855, for members of the Legislative Assembly of the Territory. It prescribed the boundaries of districts, the places for polls, the names of judges, the appointment of members, and recited the qualification of voters. If it had been observed, a just and fair election would have reflected the will of the people of the Territory. Before the election, false and inflammatory rumors were busily circulated among the people of Western Missouri. The number and character of the emigration then passing into the Territory were grossly exaggerated and misrepresented. Through the active exertions of many of its leading citizens, aided by the secret societies before referred to, the passions and prejudices of the people of that State were greatly excited. Several residents there have testified to the character of the reports circulated among and credited by the people. These efforts were successful. By an organized movement, which extended from Andrew County in the north to Jasper County in the south, and as far eastward as Boone and Cole counties, companies of men were arranged in regular parties and sent *into every council district in the Territory, and into every representative district* but one. The numbers were so distributed as to control the election in each district. They went to vote, and with the avowed design to make Kansas a Slave State. They were generally armed and equipped, carried with them their own provisions and tents, and so marched into the Territory. The details of this invasion from the mass of the testimony taken by your committee are so voluminous that we can here state but the leading facts elicited.

Ist District—March 30, 1855.—Lawrence.

The company of persons who marched into this district collected in Ray, Howard, Carroll, Boone, La Fayette, Randolph, Saline, and Cass counties, in the State of Missouri. Their expenses were paid—those who could not come contributing provisions, wagons, etc. Provisions were deposited for those who were expected to come to Lawrence, in the house of William Lykins, and were distributed among the Missourians after they arrived there. The evening before and the morning of the day of election, about 1000 men from the above counties arrived at Lawrence, and encamped in a ravine a short distance from town, near the place of voting. They came in wagons—of which there were over one hundred—and on horseback, under the command of Colonel Samuel Young, of Boone County, Missouri, and Claiborne F. Jackson, of Missouri. They were armed with guns, rifles, pistols, and bowie-knives, and had tents, music, and flags with them. They brought with them two pieces of artillery, loaded with musket-balls. On their way to Lawrence, some of them met Mr. N. B. Blanton, who had been appointed one of the judges of election by Governor Reeder; and, after learning from him that he considered it his duty to demand an oath from them as to their place of residence, first attempted to bribe, and then threatened him with hanging, in order to induce him to dispense with that oath. In consequence of these threats, he did not appear at the polls the next morning to act as judge.

The evening before the election, while in camp, the Missourians were called together at the tent of Captain Claiborne F. Jackson, and speeches were made to them by Colonel Young and others, calling for volunteers to go to other districts where there were not Missourians enough to control the election, as there were more at Lawrence than were needed there. Many volunteered to go, and the morning of the election several companies, from 150 to 200 men each, went off to Tecumseh, Hickory Point, Bloomington, and other places. On the morning of the election, the Missourians came over to the place of voting from their camp, in bodies of one hundred at a time. Mr. Blanton not appearing, another judge was appointed in his place—Colonel Young claiming that, as the people of the Territory had two judges, it was nothing more than right that the Missourians should have the other one, to look after their interests; and Robert E. Cummins was elected in Blanton's stead, because he considered that every man had a right to vote if he had been in the Territory but an hour. The Missourians brought their tickets with them; but, not having enough, they had three hundred more printed in Lawrence on the evening before and the day of election. They had white ribbons in their button-holes to distinguish themselves from the settlers.

When the voting commenced, the question of the legality of the vote of a Mr. Page was raised. Before it was decided, Colonel Samuel Young stepped up to the window where the votes were received, and said he would settle the matter. The vote of Mr. Page was withdrawn, and Colonel Young offered to vote. He refused to take the oath prescribed by the Governor, but swore he was a resident of the Territory, upon which his vote was received. He told Mr. Abbott, one of the judges, when asked if he intended to make Kansas his future home, that it was none of his business; that if he were a resident then he should ask no more. After his vote was received, Colonel Young got up in the window-sill and announced to the crowd that he had been permitted to vote, and they could all come up and vote. He told the judges that there was no use in swearing the others, as they would all swear as he had done. After the other judges concluded to receive Colonel Young's vote, Mr. Abbott resigned as judge of election, and Mr. Benjamin was elected in his place.

The polls were so much crowded until late in the evening, that, for a time, when the men had voted, they were obliged to get out by being hoisted up on the roof of the building where the election was being held, and pass out over the house. Afterward, a passage-way through the crowd was made, by two lines of men being formed, through which the voters could get up to the polls. Colonel Young asked that the old men be allowed to go up first and vote, as they were tired with the traveling, and wanted to get back to camp.

The Missourians sometimes came up to the polls in procession, two by two, and voted.

During the day, the Missourians drove off the ground some of the citizens, Mr. Stevens, Mr. Bond, and Mr. Willis. They threatened to shoot Mr. Bond, and a crowd rushed after him, threatening him; and, as he ran from them, some shots were fired at him as he jumped off the bank of the river and made his escape. The citizens of the town went over in a body, late in the afternoon, when the polls had become comparatively clear, and voted. . . .

The whole number of names appearing upon the poll-lists is 1,034. After full examination, we are satisfied that not over 232 of these were legal voters, and 802 were non-resident and illegal voters. This District is strongly in favor of making Kansas a Free State, and there is no doubt that the Free-State candidates for the legislature would have been elected by large majorities, if none but the actual settlers had voted. At the preceding election in November, 1854, where none but legal voters were polled, General Whitfield, who received the full strength of the Pro-Slavery party, got but 46 votes.

IId District—Bloomington.

On the morning of election, the judges appointed by the Governor appeared and opened the polls. Their names were Harrison Burson, Nathaniel Ramsay, and Mr. Ellison. The Missourians began to come in early in the morning, some 500 or 600 of them, in wagons and carriages, and on horseback, under the lead of Samuel J. Jones, then Postmaster of Westport, Missouri, Claiborne F. Jackson, and Mr. Steely, of Independence, Missouri. They were armed with double-barreled guns, rifles, bowie-knives, and pistols, and had flags hoisted. They held a sort of informal election, off at one side, at first for Governor of Kansas, and shortly afterward announced Thomas Johnson, of Shawnee Mission, elected Governor. The polls had been opened but a short time, when Mr. Jones marched with the crowd up to the window, and demanded that they should be allowed to vote without swearing as to their residence. After some noisy and threatening talk, Claiborne F. Jackson addressed the crowd, saying they had come there to vote, that they had a right to vote if they had been there but five minutes, and he was not willing to go home without voting; this was received with cheers. Jackson then called upon them to form into little bands of fifteen or twenty, which they did, and went to an ox-wagon filled with guns, which were distributed among them, and proceeded to load some of them on the ground. In pursuance of Jackson's request, they tied white tape or ribbons in their buttonholes, so as to distinguish them from the "Abolitionists." They again demanded that the Judges should resign, and upon their refusing to do so, smashed in the window, sash and all, and presented their pistols and guns to them, threatening to shoot them. Some one on the outside cried out to them not to shoot, as there were Pro-Slavery men in the room with the judges. They then put a pry under the corner of the house, which was a log house, and lifted it up a few inches and let it fall again, but desisted upon being told there were Pro-Slavery men in the house. During this time, the crowd repeatedly demanded to be allowed to vote without being sworn, and Mr. Ellison, one of the judges, expressed himself willing, but the other two judges refused; thereupon a body of men, headed by "Sheriff Jones," rushed into the judges' room with cocked pistols and drawn bowie-knives in their hands, and approached Burson and Ramsay. Jones pulled out his watch, and said he would give them five minutes to resign in, or die. When the five minutes had expired and the judges *did not* resign, Jones said he would give them another minute, and no more. Ellison told his associates that if they did not resign, there would be one hundred shots fired in the room in less than fifteen minutes; and then, snatching up the ballot-box, ran out into the crowd, holding up the ballot-box and hurrahing for Missouri. About that time Burson, and Ramsay were called out by their friends, and not suffered to return. As Mr. Burson went out, he put the ballot poll-books in his pocket, and took them with him; and as he was going out, Jones snatched some papers away from him, and shortly afterward came out himself holding them up, crying "Hurrah for Missouri!" After he discovered they were not the poll-books, he took a party of men with him and started off to take the poll-books from Burson. Mr. Burson saw them coming, and he gave the books to Mr. Umberger, and told him to start off in another direction, so as to mislead Jones and his party. Jones and his party caught Mr. Umberger, took the poll-books away from him, and Jones took him up behind him on a horse, and carried him back a prisoner. After Jones and his party had taken Umberger back, they went to the house of Mr. Ramsay and took Judge John A. Wakefield prisoner, and carried him to the place of election, and made him get up on a wagon and make them a speech; after which they put a white ribbon in his button-hole and let him go. They then chose two new judges, and proceeded with the election.

They also threatened to kill the judges if they did not receive their votes without swearing them, or else resign. They said no man should vote who would submit to be sworn—that they would kill any one that would offer to do so—"shoot him," "cut his guts out," etc. They said no man should vote this day unless he voted an open ticket, and was "all right on the goose," and that if they could not vote by fair means, they would by foul means. They said they had as much right to vote, if they had been in the Territory two minutes, as if they had been there for two years, and they would vote. Some of the citizens who were about the window, but had not voted when the crowd of Missourians marched up there, upon attempting to vote, were driven back by the mob, or driven off. One of them, Mr. J. M. Macey, was asked if he would take the oath, and upon his replying that he would if the judges required it, he was dragged through the crowd away from the polls, amid cries of "Kill the d—d nigger-thief," "Cut his throat," "Tear his heart out," etc. After they had got him to the outside of the crowd, they stood around him with cocked revolvers and drawn bowie-knives, one man putting a knife to his heart so that it touched him, another holding a cocked pistol to his ear, while another struck at him with a club. The Missourians said they had a right to vote if they had been in the Territory but five minutes. Some said they had been hired to come there and vote, and get a dollar a day, and, by G—d, they would vote or die there.

They said the 30th day of March was an important day, as Kansas would be made a Slave State on that day. They began to leave in the direction of Missouri in the afternoon, after they had voted, leaving some thirty or forty around the house where the election was held, to guard the polls until after the election was over. The citizens of the Territory were not around, except those who took part in the mob, and a large portion of them did not vote: 341 votes were polled there that day, of which but some thirty were citizens. A protest against the election was made to the Governor. The

returns of the election made to the Governor were lost by the Committee of Elections of the Legislature at Pawnee. The duplicate returns left in the ballot-box were taken by F. E. Laley, one of the judges elected by the Missourians, and were either lost or destroyed in his house, so that your Committee have been unable to institute a comparison between the poll-lists and census returns of this district. The testimony, however, is uniform, that not even thirty of those who voted there that day were entitled to vote, leaving 311 illegal votes. We are satisfied from the testimony that, had the actual settlers alone voted, the Free-State candidates would have been elected by a handsome majority.

IIId District—Tecumseh.

For some days prior to the election, companies of men were organized in Jackson, Cass, and Clay counties, Mo., for the purpose of coming to the Territory and voting in this Vth district. The day previous to the election, some 400 or 500 Missourians, armed with guns, pistols, and knives, came into the Territory and camped, some at Bull Creek, and others at Potawatamie Creek. Their camps were about sixteen miles apart. On the evening before the election, Judge Hamilton of the Cass County Court, Mo., came from the Potawatamie Creek camp to Bull Creek for sixty more Missourians, as they had not enough there to render the election certain, and about that number went down there with him. On the evening before the election, Dr. B. C. Westfall was elected to act as one of the Judges of Election in the Bull Creek precinct, in place of one of the judges appointed by the Governor, who, it was said, would not be there the next day. Dr. Westfall was at that time a citizen of Jackson County, Mo. On the morning of the election, the polls for Bull Creek precinct were opened, and, without swearing the judges, they proceeded to receive the votes of all who offered to vote. For the sake of appearance, they would get some one to come to the window and offer to vote, and when asked to be sworn he would pretend to grow angry at the judges and would go away, and his name would be put down as having offered to vote, but "rejected, refusing to be sworn." This arrangement was made previously and perfectly understood by the judges. But few of the residents of the district were present at the election, and only thirteen voted. The number of votes cast in the precinct was 393.

One Missourian voted for himself and then voted for his little son, but 10 or 11 years old. Col. Coffer, Henry Younger and Mr. Lykins, who were voted for and elected to the Legislature, were residents of Missouri at the time. Col. Coffer subsequently married in the Territory. After the polls were closed, the returns were made, and a man, claiming to be a magistrate, certified on them that he had sworn the judges of election before opening the polls. In the Potawatamie precinct, the Missourians attended the election, and after threatening Mr. Chesnut, the only judge present appointed by the Governor, to induce him to resign, they proceeded to elect two other judges—one a Missourian and the other a resident of another precinct of that district. The polls were then opened, and all the Missourians were allowed to vote without being sworn.

After the polls were closed, and the returns made out for the signature of the judges, Mr. Chesnut refused to sign them, as he did not consider them correct returns of legal voters.

Col. Coffer, a resident of Missouri, but elected to the Kansas Legislature from that district at that election, endeavored with others to induce Mr. Chesnut by threats to sign the returns, which he refused to do, and left the house. On his way home, he was fired at by some Missourians, though not injured. There were three illegal to one legal vote given there that day. At the Big Layer precinct, the judges appointed by the Governor met at the time appointed, and proceeded to open the polls, after being duly sworn. After a few votes had been received, a party of Missourians came into the yard of the house where the election was held, and, unloading a wagon filled with arms, stacked their guns in the yard, and came up to the window and demanded to be admitted to vote. Two of the judges decided to receive their votes, whereupon the third judge, Mr. J. M. Arthur, resigned, and another was chosen in his place. Col. Young, a citizen of Missouri, but a candidate for, and elected to, the Territorial Legislative Council, was present and voted in the precinct. He claimed that all Missourians who were present on the day of election were entitled to vote. But thirty or forty of the citizens of the precinct were present, and many of them did not vote. At the Little Sugar precinct, the election seemed to have been conducted fairly, and there a Free-State majority was polled. From the testimony, the whole district appears to have been largely Free-State, and, had none but actual settlers voted, the Free-State candidates would have been elected by a large majority. From a careful examination of the testimony and the records, we find that from 200 to 225 legal votes were polled out of 885, the total number given in the precincts of the Vth District. Of the legal votes cast, the Free-State candidates received 152.

VITH DISTRICT—FORT SCOTT.

A company of citizens from Missouri, mostly from Bates County, came into this District the day before the election, some camping and others putting up at the public-house. They numbered from 100 to 200, and came in wagons and on horseback, carrying their provisions and tents with them, and were generally armed with pistols. They declared their purpose to vote, and claimed the right to do so. They went to the polls generally in small bodies, with tickets in their hands, and many, if not all, voted. In some cases, they declared that they had voted, and gave their reasons for so doing. Mr. Anderson, a Pro-Slavery candidate for the Legislature, endeavored to dissuade the non-residents from voting, because he did not wish the election contested. This person, however, insisted upon voting, and upon his right to vote, and did so. No one was challenged or sworn, and all voted who desired to. Out of 350 votes cast, not over 100 were legal, and but 64 of these named in the census taken one month before by Mr. Barber, the candidate for Council, voted. Many of the Free-State men did not vote, but your Committee is satisfied that, of the legal votes cast, the Pro-Slavery candidates received a majority. Mr. Anderson, one of these candidates, was an unmarried man, who came into the District from Missouri a few days before the election, and boarded at the public-house until the day after the election. He then took with him the poll-lists, and did not return to Fort Scott until the occasion of a barbacue the week before the election of October 1, 1855. He voted at that election, and after it left, and has not since been in the District. S. A. Williams, the other Pro-Slavery candidate, at the time of the election had a claim in the Territory, but his legal residence was not there until after the election.

VIITH DISTRICT.

From two to three hundred men, from the State of Missouri, came in wagons or on horseback, to the election ground at Switzer's Creek, in the VIIth District, and encamped near the polls, on the day preceding the election. They were armed with pistols and other weapons, and declared their purpose to vote, in order to secure the election of Pro-Slavery members. They said they were disappointed in not finding more Yankees there, and that they had brought more men than were necessary to counterbalance their vote. A number of them wore badges of blue ribbon, with a motto, and the company were under the direction of leaders. They declared their intention to conduct themselves peacefully, unless the residents of the Territory attempted to stop them from voting. Two of the judges of election appointed by Governor Reeder refused to serve, whereupon two others were appointed in their stead by the crowd of Missourians who surrounded the polls. The newly-appointed judges refused to take the oath prescribed by Governor Reeder, but made one to suit themselves. Andrew Johnson requested each voter to swear if he had a claim in the Territory, and if he had voted in another district. The judges did not take the oath prescribed, but were sworn to receive all legal votes. The Missourians voted without being sworn. They supported H. J. Stickler for Council, and M. W. McGee for Representative. They left the evening of the election. Some of them started on horseback for Lawrence, as they said they could be there before night, and all went the way they came. The census-list shows 53 legal voters in the District. 253 votes were cast; of these 25 were residents, 17 of whom were in the District when the census was taken. Some of the residents present at the polls did not vote, declaring it useless. Candidates declined to run on the Free-State ticket because they were unwilling to run the risk of so unequal a contest—it being known that a great many were coming up from Missouri to vote. Nearly all the settlers were Free-State men, and 23 of the 25 legal votes given were cast for the only Free-State candidate running. Mobiller McGee, who was declared elected Representative, had a claim—a saw-mill and a house in the Territory—and he was there part of the time. But his legal residence is now, and was then, near Westport, in Missouri, where he owns and conducts a valuable farm, and where his family resides.

VIIITH DISTRICT.

This was attached to the VIIth District for member of

the Council and a Representative, and its vote was controlled by the illegal vote cast there. The census shows 39 votes in it—37 votes were cast, of whom a majority voted the Free-State ticket.

IXTH DISTRICT.

Fort Riley and Pawnee are in this District. The latter place was selected by the Governor as the temporary capital, and he designed there to expend the sums appropriated by Congress in the construction of suitable houses for the Legislature. A good deal of building was then being done at the fort near by. For these reasons, a number of mechanics, mostly from Pennsylvania, came into this district in March, 1855, to seek employment. Some of these voted at the election. The construction of the capital was first postponed, then abandoned, and finally the site of the town was declared by the Secretary of War to be within the military reservation of Fort Riley. Some of the inhabitants returned to the States, and some went to other parts of the Territory. Your Committee find that they came as settlers, intending to remain as such, and were entitled to vote.

XTH DISTRICT.

In this district, ten persons belonging to the Wyandot tribe of Indians voted. They were of that class who under the law were entitled to vote; but their residence was in Wyandot Village, at the mouth of Kansas River, and they had no right to vote in this district. They voted the Pro-Slavery ticket. Eleven men recently from Pennsylvania voted the Free-State Ticket. From the testimony, they had not, at the time of the election, so established their residence as to have entitled them to vote. In both these classes of cases, the judges examined the voters under oath and allowed them to vote. and in all respects the election seems to have been conducted fairly. The rejection of both would not have changed the result. This and the VIIIth Election District formed one representative district, and was the only one to which the invasion from Missouri did not extend.

XITH DISTRICT.

The IXth, Xth, XIth and XIIth Election Districts, being all sparsely settled, were attached together as a Council District, and the XIth and XIIth as a Representative District. This Election District is 60 miles north from Pawnee, and 150 miles from Kansas City. It is the northwest settlement in the Territory, and contained, when the census was taken, but 36 inhabitants, of whom 24 were voters. There was on the day of election no white settlement about Marysville, the place of voting, for 40 miles, except that Marshall and Bishop kept a store and ferry at the crossing of the Big Blue and the California road. Your Committee were unable to procure witnesses from this district. Persons who were present at the election were duly summoned by an officer, and among them was F. J. Marshall, the member of the House from that district. On his return, the officer was arrested and detained, and persons bearing the names of some of the witnesses summoned were stopped near Lecompton, and did not appear before the Committee. The returns show that, in defiance of the Governor's proclamation, the voting was *viva voce*, instead of by ballot. 328 names appear upon the poll-books as voting, and by comparing these names with those on the census rolls, we find that but seven of the latter voted. The person voted for as Representative, F. J. Marshall, was chief owner of the store at Marysville, and was there sometimes, but his family lived in Weston. John Donaldson, the candidate voted for the Council, then lived in Jackson County, Missouri.

On the day after the election, Mr. Marshall, with 25 or 30 men from Weston, Mo., was on the way from Marysville to the State. Some of the party told a witness who had formerly resided at Weston, that they were up at Marysville and carried the day for Missouri, and that they had voted about 150 votes. Mr. Marshall paid the bill at that point for the party.

There does not appear to have been any emigration into that district in March, 1855, after the census was taken, and, judging from the best test in the power of your Committee, there were but seven legal votes cast in the district, and 321 illegal.

XIITH DISTRICT.

The election in this district was conducted fairly. No complaint was made that illegal votes were cast.

XIIITH DISTRICT.

Previous to the day of election, several hundreds of Missourians from Platte, Clay, Boone, Clinton, and Howard counties, came into the district in wagons and on horseback, and camped there. They were armed with guns, revolvers, and bowie-knives, and had badges of hemp in their button-holes and elsewhere about their persons. They claimed to have a right to vote, from the fact that they were there on the ground, and had, or intended to make, claims in the Territory, although their families were in Missouri.

The judges appointed by the Governor opened the polls, and some persons offered to vote, and when their votes were rejected on the ground that they were not residents of the district, the crowd threatened to tear the house down if the judges did not leave. The judges then withdrew, taking the poll-books with them. The crowd then proceeded to select other persons to act as judges, and the election went on. Those persons voting who were sworn were asked if they considered themselves residents of the district, and if they said they did, they were allowed to vote. But few of the residents were present and voted, and the Free-State men, as a general thing, did not vote. After the Missourians got through voting, they returned home. A formal return was made by the judges of election setting out the facts, but it was not verified. The number of legal voters in this district was 96, of whom a majority were Free-State men. Of these — voted. The total number of votes cast was 296.

XIVTH DISTRICT.

It was generally rumored in this district, for some days before the election, that the Missourians were coming over to vote. Previous to the election, men from Missouri came into the district, and electioneered for the Pro-Slavery candidates. Gen. David R. Atchison and a party controlled the nominations in one of the primary elections.

BURR OAK PRECINCT.

Several hundred Missourians from Buchanan, Platte, and Andrew counties, Mo., including a great many of the prominent citizens of St. Joseph, came into this precinct the day before, and on the day of election, in wagons and on horses, and encamped there. Arrangements were made for them to cross the ferry at St. Joseph free of expense to themselves. They were armed with bowie-knives and pistols, guns and rifles. On the morning of the election, the Free-State candidates resigned in a body, on account of the presence of the large number of armed Missourians, at which the crowd cheered and hurrahed. Gen. B. F. Stringfellow was present, and was prominent in promoting the election of the Pro-Slavery ticket, as was also the Hon. Willard P. Hall, and others of the most prominent citizens of St. Joseph, Mo. But one of the judges of election, appointed by the Governor, served on that day, and the crowd chose two others to supply the vacancies.

The Missourians said they came there to vote for, and secure the election of, Major Wm. P. Richardson. Major Richardson, elected to the Council, had a farm in Missouri, where his wife and daughter lived with his son-in-law, Willard P. Hall, he himself generally going home to Missouri every Saturday night. The farm was generally known as the Richardson farm. He had a claim in the Territory, upon which was a saw-mill, and where he generally remained during the week.

Some of the Missourians gave as their reason for voting that they had heard that eastern emigrants were to be at that election, though no eastern emigrants were there. Others said they were going to vote for the purpose of making Kansas a Slave State.

Some claimed that they had a right to vote, under the provisions of the Kansas-Nebraska bill, from the fact that they were present on the ground on the day of election. The Free-State men generally did not vote, and those who did vote, voted generally for John H. Whitehead, Pro-Slavery, for Council, against Major Wm. P. Richardson, and did not vote at all for members of the Lower House.

The parties were pretty nearly equally divided in the district, some being of opinion that the Free-State party had a small majority, and others that the Pro-Slavery party had a small majority. After the election was over and the polls were closed, the Missourians returned home. During the day, they had provisions and liquor served out, free of expense, to all.

DONIPHAN PRECINCT.

The evening before the election, some 200 or more Missourians from Platte, Buchanan, Saline, and Clay counties, Missouri, came into this precinct, with tents, music, wagons, and provisions, and armed with guns, rifles, pistols, and bowie-knives, and encamped about two miles from the place of voting. They said they came to vote, to make Kansas a Slave State, and intended to return to Missouri after they had voted.

On the morning of the election, the Judges appointed by the Governor would not serve, and others were appointed by the crowd. The Missourians were allowed to vote without being sworn—some of them voting as many as eight or nine times; changing their hats and coats, and giving in different names each time. After they had voted, they returned to Missouri. The Free-State men generally did not vote, though constituting a majority in the precinct. Upon counting the ballots in the box and the names on the poll-lists, it was found that there were too many ballots, and one of the judges of election took out ballots enough to make the two numbers correspond.

WOLF RIVER PRECINCT.

The number of voters in the district by the census was 334—of these 124 voted. The testimony shows that quite a number of persons whose legal residence was in the populous county of Buchanan, Mo., on the opposite side of the river, had claims in the Territory. Some ranged cattle, and others marked out their claim and built a cabin, and sold this incipient title where they could. They were not residents of the Territory in any just or legal sense. A number of settlers moved into the district in the month of March. Your Committee are satisfied, after a careful analysis of the records and testimony, that the number of legal votes cast did not exceed 200—out of 727.

XVTH DISTRICT.

The election in this district was held in the house of a Mr. Hayes. On the day of election, a crowd of from 400 to 500 men collected around the polls, of which the great body were citizens of Missouri. One of the judges of election, in his testimony, states that the strangers commenced crowding around the polls, and that then the residents left. Threats were made before and during the election day that there should be no Free-State candidates, although there were nearly or quite as many Free-State as Pro-Slavery men resident in the district. Most of the crowd were drinking and carousing, cursing the Abolitionists and threatening the only Free-State judge of election. A majority of those who voted wore hemp in their button-holes, and their password was, "all right on the hemp." Many of the Missourians were known and are named by the witnesses. Several speeches were made by them at the polls, and among those who spoke were Major Oliver, one of your Committee, Col. Burns, and Lalan Williams, of Platte County. Major Oliver urged upon all present to use no harsh words, and expressed the hope that nothing would be said or done to harm the feelings of the most sensitive on the other side. He gave some grounds, based on the Missouri Compromise, in regard to the right of voting, and was understood to excuse the Missourians for voting. Your Committee are satisfied that he did not vote. Col. Burns recommended all to vote, and he hoped none would go home without voting. Some of the Pro-Slavery residents were much dissatisfied at the interference with their rights by the Missourians, and for that reason—because reflection convinced them that it would be better to have Kansas a Free-State—they "fell over the fence." The judges requested the voters to take an oath that they were actual residents. They objected at first, some saying they had a claim, or "I am here." But the Free-State judge insisted upon the oath, and his associates, who at first were disposed to waive it, coincided with him, and the voters all took it after some grumbling. One said he cut him some poles and laid them in the shape of a square, and that made him a claim; and another said that he had cut him a few sticks of wood, and that made him a claim. The Free-State men did not vote, although they believed their numbers to be equal to the Pro-Slavery settlers, and some claimed that they had the majority. They were deterred by threats throughout by the Missourians, before and on the day of election, from putting up candidates, and no candidates were run, for this reason—that there was a credited rumor previously that the Missourians would control the election. The Free-State judge was threatened with expulsion from the polls, and a young man thrust a pistol into the window through which the votes were received. The whole number of votes cast was 417; of the names on the poll-book, but 62 are in the census-rolls, and the testimony shows that a small portion, estimated by one witness at one-quarter of the legal voters, voted. Your Committee estimate the number of legal voters at 80. One of the judges referred to, certified to the Governor that the election was fairly conducted. It was not contested, because no one would take the responsibility of doing it, as it was not considered safe, and that if another election was held, the residents would fare no better.

XVITH DISTRICT.

For some time previous to the election, meetings were held and arrangements made in Missouri to get up companies to come over to the Territory and vote, and the day before, and on the day of election, large bodies of Missourians from Platte, Clay, Ray, Charlton, Carrol, Clinton, and Saline counties, Missouri, came into this district and camped there. They were armed with pistols and bowie-knives, and some with guns and rifles, and had badges of hemp in their button-holes and elsewhere about their persons.

On the morning of the election, there were from 1,000 to 1,400 persons present on the ground. Previous to the election, the Missourians endeavored to persuade the two Free-State judges to resign, by making threats of personal violence to them, one of whom resigned on the morning of election, and the crowd chose another to fill his place. But one of the judges, the Free-State judge, would take the oath prescribed by the Governor, the other two deciding that they had no right to swear any one who offered to vote, but that all on the ground were entitled to vote. The only votes refused were some Delaware Indians, some 30 Wyandot Indians being allowed to vote. . . . . .

The Free-State men generally did not vote at that election; and no newly-arrived Eastern emigrants were there. The Free-State judge of election refused to sign the returns until the words " by lawful resident voters" were stricken out, which was done, and the returns made in that way. The election was contested, and a new election ordered by Gov. Reeder, for the 22d of May.

The testimony is divided as to the relative strength of parties in this district. The whole number of voters in the district, according to the census returns, was 385; and, according to a very carefully prepared list of voters, prepared for the Pro-Slavery candidates and other Pro-Slavery men, a few days previous to the election, there were 305 voters in the district, including those who had claims but did not live on them. The whole number of votes cast was 964. Of those named in the census 106 voted. Your Committee, upon careful examination, are satisfied that there were not over 150 legal votes cast, leaving 814 illegal votes.

XVIITH DISTRICT.

The election in this district seems to have been fairly conducted, and not contested at all. In this district, the Pro-Slavery party had the majority.

XVIIITH DISTRICT.

Previous to the election, Gen. David R. Atchison of Platte City, Missouri, got up a company of Missourians, and passing through Weston, Missouri, went over into the Territory. He remained all night at the house of —— and then exhibited his arms, of which he had an abundance. He proceeded to the Nemaha (XVIIIth) district. On his way, he and his party attended a Nominating Convention in the XIVth District, and proposed and caused to be nominated a set of candidates in opposition to the wishes of the Pro-Slavery residents of the district. At that Convention, he said that there were 1,100 men coming over from Platte County, and if that wasn't enough, they could send 5,000 more—that they came to vote, and would vote or kill every G—d d—d Abolitionist in the Territory.

On the day of election, the Missourians, under Atchison, who were encamped there, came up to the polls in the XVIIIth District, taking the oath that they were residents of the district. The Missourians were all armed with pistols or bowie-knives, and said there were 60 in their company. But 17 votes given on that day were given by residents of the district. The whole number of votes was 62.

R. L. Kirk, one of the candidates, came into the district from Missouri about a week before the election, and boarded there. He left after the election, and was not at the time a legal resident of the district in which he was elected. No protest was sent to the Governor on account of threats made against any who should dare to contest the election.

The following tables embody the result of the examination of your Committee in regard to this election. In some of the districts, it was impossible to ascertain the precise number of the legal votes cast, and especially in the XIVth, XVth, and XVIth Districts. In such cases, the number of legal and illegal votes cast is stated, after a careful reëxamination of all the testimony and records concerning the election:

ABSTRACT OF CENSUS, AND RETURNS OF ELECTION OF MARCH 30, 1855, BY ELECTION DISTRICTS.

Number of District.	Places of Voting.	Pro-Slavery Votes.	Free-State Votes.	Scattering.	Total.	Total of Legal Votes.	Total of Illegal Votes.	Census. No. persons resd'ts	Census. No. of Voters	Council. No. of District	Council. of Members.	House. No. of District.	House. of Members.
	Lawrence	781	253	—	1034	232	802	962	369	1	2	2	3
	Bloomington	318	12	11	341	30	316	519	199	2	1	3	2
	Stinson's, or Tecumseh	366	4	2	372	82	333	252	101	3	1	4	1
	Dr. Chapman's.	78	2	—	80	15	65	177	47	1	—	1	1
	Bull Creek	377	9	—	386	13	380	—	—	—	—	—	—
	Potawatamie	199	65	—	264	75	191	—	—	—	—	—	—
	Big Sugar Creek	74	17	—	98	32	59	1407	442	4	2	7	4
	Little Sugar Creek	34	70	—	104	104	—	—	—	—	—	—	—
	Fort Scott	315	35	—	350	100	250	810	253	5	1	6	2
7	Isaac B. Titus	211	23	—	234	25	209	118	58	3	—	5	1
	Council Grove	17	17	3	37	37	—	83	39	3	—	5	—
	Pawnee	23	52	—	75	75	—	86	36	6	1	8	1
10	Big Blue	27	42	—	69	48	21	151	63	10	—	8	—
	Rock Creek	2	21	—	23	23	—	—	—	8	—	8	—
11	Marysville	328	—	—	328	7	321	36	24	9	—	9	1
12	St. Mary's	4	7	—	11	11	—	—	—	10	—	9	—
	Silver Lake	12	19	2	33	33	—	144	78	1	—	9	—
13	Hickory Point	233	6	—	239	12	230	284	96	10	—	10	1
	Doniphan	313	30	3	346	—	—	—	—	7	—	11	—
14	Wolf Creek	57	15	6	78	200	530	1167	334	7	1	11	2
	Burr-Oak, Hodge's	256	2	48	306	—	—	—	—	8	—	12	2
15	Hayes	412	—	5	417	80	337	873	208	9	1	13	2
16	Leavenworth	899	60	5	964	150	814	1283	385	10	2	14	3
	Gum Springs	43	16	—	59	59	—	150	50	1	—	—	—
18	Moorestown	48	14	—	62	17	45	99	28	7	1	—	—
	Total	5427	791	92	6320	1310	4968	8501	2892	—	13	—	26

By the election, as conducted, the Pro-Slavery candidates in every district but the VIIIth representative district, received a majority of the votes; and several of them, in both the Council and the House, did not " reside in " and were not "inhabitants of" the district for which they were elected, as required by the organic law.

By that act it was declared to be the true intent and meaning of this act to leave the people thereof perfectly free to form and regulate their domestic institutions in their own way, subject to the Constitution of the United States.

So careful was Congress of the right of popular sovereignty, that to secure it to the people, without a single petition from any portion of the country, they removed the restriction against Slavery imposed by the Missouri Compromise. And yet this right, so carefully secured, was thus by force and fraud overthrown by a portion of the people of an adjoining State.

The striking difference between this Republic and other Republics on this Continent, is not in the provisions of constitutions and laws, but that here changes in the administration of those laws have been made peacefully and quietly through the ballot-box. This invasion is the first and only one in the history of our Government, by which an organized force from one State has elected a Legislature for another State or Territory, and as such it should have been resisted by the whole executive power of the National Government.

Your Committee are of the opinion that the Constitution and laws of the United States have invested the President and Governor of the Territory with ample power for this purpose. They could only act after receiving authentic information of the facts; but when received, whether before or after the certificates of election were granted, this power should have been exercised to its fullest extent. It is not to be tolerated that a legislative body thus selected should assume or exercise any legislative functions; and their enactments should be regarded as null and void; nor should the question of its legal existence as a legislative body be determined by itself, as that would be allowing the criminal to judge of his own crime. In section twenty-two of the organic act it is provided, that " the persons having the highest number of legal votes in each of said Council-districts for members of the Council, shall be declared by the Governor to be duly elected to the Council, and the persons having the highest number of legal votes for the House of Representatives, shall be declared by the Governor duly elected members of said House " The proclamation of the Governor required a verified notice of a contest when one was made, to be filed with him within four days after the election. Within that time, he did not obtain information as to force or fraud in any except the following districts, and in these there were material defects in the returns of election. Without deciding upon his power to set aside elections for force and fraud, they were set aside for the following reasons:

In the Ist District, because the words " by lawful resident voters," were stricken from the return.

In the IId District, because the oath was administered by G. W. Taylor, who was not authorized to administer an oath.

In the IIId District, because material erasures from the printed form of the oath were purposely made.

In the IVth District, for the same reason.

In the VIIth District, because the Judges were not sworn at all.

In the XIth District, because the returns show the election to have been held *viva voce* instead of by ballot.

In the XVIth District, because the words " by lawful residence" were stricken from the returns.

ABSTRACT OF THE RETURNS OF ELECTION OF MAY 22, 1855.

of District.	PLACES OF VOTING.	'ro-Slavery Votes.	Free-State Votes.	Scattering.	Total.
	Lawrence..............................	—	288	18	306
	Douglas	—	127	—	127
	Stinson's.............................	—	148	1	149
	" 110 "..............................	—	66	13	79
	Council Grove.......................	—	33	—	33
16	Leavenworth....	56	140	15	715
	Total.....................	560	802	——	1409

Although the fraud and force in other districts were equally great as in these, yet, as the Governor had no information in regard to them, he issued certificates according to the returns.

Your Committee here felt it to be their duty not only to inquire into and collect evidence in regard to force and fraud attempted and practiced at the elections in the Territory, but also into the facts and pretexts by which this force and fraud has been excused and justified; and for this purpose your Committee have allowed the declarations of non-resident voters to be given as evidence in their own behalf, also the declarations of all who came up the Missouri River as emigrants in March, 1855, whether they voted or not, and whether they came into the Territory at all or not; and also the rumors which were circulated among the people of Missouri previous to the election. The great body of the testimony taken at the instance of the sitting Delegate is of this character.

When the declarations of parties passing up the river were offered in evidence, your Committee received them upon the distinct statement that they would be excluded unless the persons making the declarations were by other proof shown to have been connected with the elections. This proof was not made, and therefore much of this class of testimony is incompetent by the rules of law, but is allowed to remain as tending to show the cause of the action of the citizens of Missouri.

The alleged causes of the invasion of March, 1855, are included in the following charges:

I. That the New-England Aid Society of Boston was then importing into the Territory large numbers of men, merely for the purpose of controlling the elections. That they came without women, children, or baggage, went into the Territory, voted, and returned again.

II. That men were hired in the Eastern or Northern States, or induced to go into the Territory, solely to vote, and not to settle, and by so doing to make it a Free State.

III. That the Governor of the Territory purposely postponed the day of election to allow this emigration to arrive, and notified the Emigrant Aid Society, and persons in the Eastern States, of the day of election, before he gave notice to the people of Missouri and the Territory.

That these charges were industriously circulated; that grossly exaggerated statements were made in regard to them; that the newspaper press and leading men in public meetings in Western Missouri, aided in one case by a Chaplain of the United States Army, gave currency and credit to them, and thus excited the people, and induced many well-meaning citizens of Missouri to march into the Territory to meet and repel the alleged Eastern paupers and Abolitionists, is fully proven by many witnesses.

But these charges are not sustained by the proof.

In April, 1854, the General Assembly of Massachusetts passed an act entitled " An act to incorporate the Massachusetts Emigrant Aid Society." The object of the Society, as declared in the first section of this act, was " for the purpose of assisting emigrants to settle in the West." The moneyed capital of the corporation was not to exceed five millions of dollars; but no more than four per cent. could be assessed during the year 1854 and no more than ten per cent. in any one year thereafter. No organization was perfected, or proceedings had, under this law.

On the 24th day of July, 1854, certain persons in Boston, Massachusetts, concluded articles of agreement and association for an Emigrant Aid Society. The purpose of this association was declared to be " assisting emigrants to settle in the West." Under these articles of association, each stockholder was individually liable. To avoid this difficulty, an application was made to the General Assembly of Massachusetts for an act of incorporation, which was granted. On the 21st day of February, 1855, an act was passed to incorporate the New England Emigrant Aid Company. The purposes of this act were declared to be " directing emigration westward, and aiding and providing accommodation for emigrants after arriving at their place of destination." The capital stock of the corporation was not to exceed one million of dollars. Under this charter, a company was organized.

Your Committee have examined some of its officers, and a portion of its circulars and records, to ascertain what has been done by it. The public attention at that time was directed to the Territory of Kansas, and emigration naturally tended in that direction. To ascertain its character and resources, this Company sent its agent into it, and the information thus obtained was published. The Company made arrangements with various lines of transportation to reduce the expense of emigration into the Territory, and procured tickets at the reduced rates. Applications were made to the Company by persons desiring to emigrate; and when they were numerous enough to form a party of convenient size, tickets were sold to them at the reduced rates. An agent acquainted with the route was selected to accompany them. Their baggage was checked, and all trouble and danger of loss to the emigrant in this way avoided.

Under these arrangements, companies went into the Territory in the Fall of 1854, under the articles of association referred to. The company did not pay any portion of the fare, nor furnish any personal or real property to the emigrant. The company, during 1855, sent into the Territory from eight to ten saw-mills, purchased one hotel in Kansas City, which they subsequently sold, built one hotel at Lawrence, and owned one other building in that place. In some cases, to induce them to make improvements, town lots were given to them by town associations in this Territory. They held no property of any other kind or description. They imposed no condition upon their emigrants, and did not inquire into their political, religious, or social opinions. The total amount expended by them, including the salaries of their agents and officers, and the expenses incident to all organizations, was less than $100,000.

Their purposes, so far as your Committee can ascertain, were lawful, and contributed to supply those wants most experienced in the settlement of a new country.

The only persons or company who emigrated into the Territory under the auspices of the Emigrant Aid Society in 1855, prior to the election in March, was a party of 159 persons, who came under the charge of Charles Robinson.

In this party, there were 67 women and children. They came as actual settlers, intending to make their homes in the Territory, and for no other purpose. They had about their persons but little baggage; usually sufficient clothing in a carpet-sack for a short time. Their personal effects, such as clothing, furniture, etc., were put into trunks and boxes; and for convenience in selecting, and cheapness in transporting, was marked "Kansas party baggage, care B. Slater, St. Louis." Generally, this was consigned as freight, in the usual way, to the care of a commission merchant. This party had, in addition to the usual allowance of one hundred pounds to each passenger, a large quantity of baggage on which the respective owners paid the usual extra freight. Each passenger or party paid his or their own expenses; and the only benefit they derived from the Society, not shared by all the people of the Territory, was the reduction of about $7 in the price of the fare, the convenience of traveling in a company instead of alone, and the cheapness and facility of transporting their freight through regular agents. Subsequently, many emigrants, being either disappointed with the country or its political condition, or deceived by the statements made by the newspapers and by the agents of the Society, became dissatisfied, and returned, both before and after the election, to their old homes. Most of them are now settlers in the Territory. Some few voted at the election in Lawrence, but the number was small. The names of these emigrants have been ascertained, and —— of them were found upon the poll-books. This company of peaceful emigrants, moving with their household goods, was distorted into an invading horde of pauper Abolitionists, who were, with others of a similar character, to control the domestic institutions of the Territory, and then overturn those of a neighboring powerful State.

In regard to the second charge: There is no proof that any man was either hired or induced to come into the Territory from any Free State, merely to vote. The entire emigration in March, 1855, is estimated at 500 persons, including men, women, and children. They came on steamboats up the Missouri River, in the ordinary course of emigration. Many returned for causes similar to those before stated; but the body of them are now residents. The only persons of those who were connected by proof with the election, were some who voted at the Big Blue Precinct in the Xth District, and at Pawnee, in the IXth District. Their purpose and character are stated in a former part of this report.

The third charge is entirely groundless. The organic law requires the Governor to cause an enumeration of the inhabitants and legal voters to be made; and that he apportion the members of the Council and House, according to this enumeration. For reasons stated by persons engaged in taking the census, it was not completed until the early part of March, 1855. At that time, the day of holding the election had not been, and could not have been, named by the Governor. So soon as practicable after the returns were brought in, he issued his proclamation for an election, and named the earliest day, consistent with due notice, as the day of election. The day on which the election was to be held was a matter of conjecture all over the country; but it was generally known that it would be in the latter part of March. The precise day was not known by any one until the proclamation issued. It was not known to the agents of the Emigrant Aid Society in Boston on the 13th of March, 1855, when the party of emigrants before referred to, left.

Your Committee are satisfied that these charges were made the mere pretext to induce an armed invasion into the Territory, as a means to control the election and establish Slavery there.

The real purpose is avowed and illustrated by the testimony and conduct of Colonel John Scott, of St. Joseph's, Missouri, who acted as the attorney for the sitting delegate before your Committee. The following are extracts from his deposition:

"Prior to the election in Burr-Oak precinct, in the XIVth District, on the 29th of November, 1854, I had been a resident of Missouri, and I then determined, if I found it necessary, to become a resident of Kansas Territory. On the day previous to that election, I settled up my board at my boarding-house, in St. Joseph's, Missouri, and went over to the Territory, and took boarding with Mr. Bryant, near whose house the polls were held the next day, for one month, so that I might have it in my power, by merely determining to do so, to become a resident of the Territory on the day of election.

"When my name was proposed as a Judge of Election, objections were made by two persons only. . . . . I then publicly informed those present, that I had a claim in the Territory; that I had taken board in the Territory for a month; and that I could, at any moment, become an actual resident and legal voter in the Territory, and that I would do so, if I concluded at any time during the day that my vote would be necessary to carry that precinct in favor of the Pro-Slavery candidate for delegate to Congress. . . . . I did not during the day consider it necessary to become a resident of the Territory for the purpose mentioned, and did not vote nor offer to vote at that election.

"I held the office of City-Attorney for St. Joseph's at that time, and had held it for two or three years previously, and continued to hold it until this spring. . . . . I voted at an election in St. Joseph's, in the spring of 1855, and was re-appointed City-Attorney. The question of Slavery was put in issue at the election of November, 1854, to the same extent as in every election in this Territory. Gen. Whitfield was regarded as the Pro-Slavery candidate for the Pro-Slavery party. I regarded the question of Slavery as the primarily prominent issue at that election, and, so far as I know, all parties agreed in making that question the issue of that election.

"*It is my intention, and the intention of a great many other Missourians now resident in Missouri, whenever the Slavery issue is to be determined upon by the people of this Territory in the adoption of the State Constitution, to remove to this Territory in time to acquire the right to become legal voters upon that question. The leading purpose of our intended removal to the Territory is to determine the domestic institutions of this Territory, when it comes to be a State, and we would not come only for that purpose, and would never think of coming here but for that purpose. I believe there are a great many in Missouri who are so situated.*"

The invasion of March 30th left both parties in a state of excitement, tending directly to produce violence. The successful party was lawless and reckless while assuming the name of the "Law and Order" party. The other party, at first surprised and confounded, was greatly irritated, and some resolved to prevent the success of the invasion. In some districts, as before stated, protests were sent to the Governor; in others, this was prevented by threats; in others, by the want of time, only four days being allowed by the proclamation for this purpose; and in others, by the belief that a new election would bring a new invasion. About the same time, all classes of men commenced bearing deadly weapons about the person, a practice which has continued to this time. Under these circumstances, a slight or accidental quarrel produced unusual violence, and lawless acts became frequent. This evil condition of the public mind was further increased by acts of violence in Western Missouri, where, in April, a newspaper press, called *The Parksville Luminary*, was destroyed by a mob.

About the same time, Malcolm Clark assaulted Cole McCrea at a squatter meeting in Leavenworth, and was shot by McCrea in alleged self-defense.

On the 17th day of May, William Phillips, a lawyer of Leavenworth, was first notified to leave; and upon his refusal, was forcibly seized, taken across the river, and carried several miles into Missouri, and then tarred and feathered, and one side of his head shaved, and other gross indignities put upon his person.

Previous to this outrage, a public meeting was held, at which resolutions were unanimously passed, looking to unlawful violence, and grossly intolerant in their character. The right of free speech upon the subject of Slavery was characterized as a disturbance of the peace and quiet of the community, and as "circulating incendiary sentiments." They say "to the peculiar friends of northern fanatics," "Go home and do your treason where you may find sympathy." Among other resolves is the following:

"*Resolved*, That the institution of Slavery is known and recognized in this Territory; and we repel the doctrine that it is a moral and political evil, and we hurl back with scorn upon its slanderous authors the charge of inhumanity; and we warn all persons not to come to our peaceful firesides to slander us, and sow the seeds of discord between the master and the servant; for, as much as we deprecate the necessity to which we may be driven, we cannot be responsible for the consequences."

A Committee of Vigilance of 30 men was appointed "to observe and report all such persons as shall . . . by the expression of abolition sentiments, produce disturbance to the quiet of the citizens, or danger to their domestic relations; and all such persons so offending shall be notified, and made to leave the Territory."

The meeting was "ably and eloquently addressed by Judge Lecompte, Colonel J. N. Burns of Western Missouri, and others." Thus the head of the judiciary in the Territory not only assisted at a public and bitterly partisan meeting, whose direct tendency was to produce violence and disorder, but, before any law is passed in the Territory, he prejudges the character of the domestic institutions which the people of the Territory were, by their organic law, "left perfectly free to form and regulate in their own way."

On this committee were several of those who held certificates of election as members of the legislature; some of the others were then and still are residents of Missouri; and many of the committee have since been appointed to the leading offices in the Territory, one of which is the sheriffalty of the county. Their first act was that of mobbing Phillips.

Subsequently, on the 25th of May, A.D. 1855, a public meeting was held, at which R. R. Rees, a member elect of the council, presided. The following resolutions, offered by Judge Payne, a member elect of the house, were unanimously adopted:

" _Resolved_, That we heartily indorse the action of the committee of citizens that shaved, tarred and feathered, rode on a rail, and had sold by a negro, William Phillips, the moral perjurer.

" _Resolved_, That we return our thanks to the committee for faithfully performing the trust enjoined upon them by the Pro-Slavery party."

" _Resolved_, That the committee be now discharged.

" _Resolved_, That we severely condemn those Pro-Slavery men who, from mercenary motives, are calling upon the Pro-Slavery party to submit without further action.

" _Resolved_, That in order to secure peace and harmony to the community, we now solemnly declare that the Pro-Slavery party will stand firmly by and carry out the resolutions reported by the committee appointed for that purpose on the memorable 30th."

The act of moral perjury here referred to is the swearing by Phillips to a truthful protest in regard to the election of March 30, in the XVIth District.

The members receiving their certificates of the Governor as members of the General Assembly of the Territory, met at Pawnee, the place appointed by the Governor, on the 2d of July, A.D. 1855. Their proceedings are stated in three printed books, herewith submitted, entitled respectively, "The Statutes of the Territory of Kansas," "The Journal of the Council of the Territory of Kansas," and "The Journal of the House of Representatives of the Territory of Kansas."

Your Committee do not regard their enactments as valid laws. A legislature thus imposed upon a people cannot affect their political rights. Such an attempt to do so, if successful, is virtually an overthrow of the organic law, and reduces the people of the Territory to the condition of vassals to a neighboring State. To avoid the evils of anarchy, no armed or organized resistance to them should be made, but the citizens should appeal to the ballot-box at public elections, to the federal judiciary, and to Congress, for relief. Such, from the proof, would have been the course of the people, but for the nature of these enactments and the manner in which they are enforced. Their character and their execution have been so intimately connected with one branch of this investigation—that relating to " violent and tumultuous proceedings in the Territory "—that we were compelled to examine them.

The " laws " in the statute-books are general and special; the latter are strictly of a local character, relating to bridges, roads, and the like. The great body of the general laws are exact transcripts from the Missouri code. To make them in some cases conform to the organic act, separate acts were passed, defining the meaning of words. Thus the word " State " is to be understood as meaning " Territory ;" the words " County Court" shall be construed to mean the board of commissioners transacting county business, or the Probate Court, according to the intent thereof. The words " Circuit Court " to mean " District Court."

The material differences in the Missouri and Kansas statutes are upon the following subjects: The qualifications of voters and of members of the legislative assembly; the official oath of all officers, attorneys, and voters; the mode of selecting officers and their qualifications; the slave code, and the qualifications of jurors.

Upon these subjects, the provisions of the Missouri code are such as are usual in many of the States. But by the " Kansas Statutes " every office in the Territory, executive and judicial, was to be appointed by the legislature, or by some officer appointed by it. These appointments were not merely to meet a temporary exigency, but were to hold over two regular elections, and until after the general election in October, 1857, at which the members

of the new council were to be elected. The new legislature is required to meet on the first Monday in January, 1858. Thus, by the terms of these "laws," the people have no control whatever over either the legislature, the executive, or the judicial departments of the Territorial government until a time before which, by the natural progress of population, the Territorial government will be superseded by a State government.

No session of the legislature is to be held during 1856, but the members of the House are to be elected in October of that year. A candidate, to be eligible at this election, must swear to support the fugitive slave law; and each judge of election, and each voter, if challenged, must take the same oath. The same oath is required of every officer elected or appointed in the Territory, and of every attorney admitted to practice in the courts.

A portion of the militia is required to muster on the day of election. "Every free white male citizen of the United States, and every free male Indian who is made a citizen by treaty or otherwise, and over the age of twenty-one years, and who shall be an _inhabitant_ of the Territory and of the county and district in which he offers to vote, and shall have paid a Territorial tax, shall be a qualified elector for all elective offices." Two classes of persons were thus excluded, who, by the organic act, were allowed to vote, viz.: those who would not swear to the oath required, and those of foreign birth who had declared on oath their intention to become citizens. Any man of proper age who was in the Territory on the day of election, and who had paid one dollar as a tax to the sheriff, who was required to be at the polls to receive it, could vote as an "inhabitant," although he had breakfasted in Missouri, and intended to return there for supper. There can be no doubt that this unusual and unconstitutional provision was inserted to prevent a full and fair expression of the popular will in the election of members of the house, or to control it by non-residents.

All jurors are required to be selected by the sheriff, and " no person who is conscientiously opposed to the holding of slaves, or who does not admit the right to hold slaves in the Territory, shall be a juror in any cause " affecting the right to hold slaves, or relating to slave property.

The Slave Code, and every provision relating to slaves, are of a character intolerant and unusual even for that class of legislation. The character and conduct of the men appointed to hold office in the Territory contributed very much to produce the events which followed. Thus Samuel J. Jones was appointed sheriff of the county of Douglas, which included within it the Ist and IId Election Districts. He had made himself peculiarly obnoxious to the settlers by his conduct on the 30th of March in the IId District, and by his burning the cabins of Joseph Oakley and Samuel Smith.

An election for delegate to Congress, to be held on the 1st day of October, 1855, was provided for, with the same rules and regulations as were applied to other elections. The Free-State men took no part in this election, having made arrangements for holding an election on the 9th of the same month. The citizens of Missouri attended at the election of the 1st of October, some paying the dollar tax, and others not being required to pay it. They were present and voted at the voting places of Atchison and Doniphan, in Atchison County; at Greene Springs, Johnson County; at Willow Springs, Franklin, and Lecompton, in Douglas County; at Fort Scott, Bourbon County; at Baptiste Paola, Lykins County, where some Indians voted, some whites paying the $1 tax for them; at Leavenworth City, and at Kickapoo City, Leavenworth County; at the latter place, under the lead of Gen. B. F. Stringfellow and Col. Lewis Barnes of Missouri. From two of the election precincts at which it was alleged there was illegal voting —viz., Delaware and Wyandotte—your Committee failed to obtain the attendance of witnesses. Your Committee did not deem it necessary, in regard to this election, to enter into details, as it was manifest that, from there being but one candidate—Gen. Whitfield—he must have received a majority of the votes cast. This election, therefore, depends not on the number or character of the votes received, but upon the validity of the laws under which it was held. Sufficient testimony was taken to show that the voting of citizens of Missouri was practiced at this election, as at all former elections in the Territory. The following table will exhibit the result of the testimony as regards the number of legal and illegal votes at this election. The county of Marshall embraces the same territory as was included in the XIth District; and the reasons before stated indicate that the great majority of the votes then cast were either illegal or fictitious. In the counties to which our examination extended, there were —— illegal votes cast as near as the proof will enable us to determine.

ABSTRACT OF POLL-BOOKS OF OCTOBER 1, 1855.

COUNTIES.	TOWNSHIPS.	No. of Votes cast for J. W. Whitfield.	Scattering.	Total Votes cast.	No. of Legal Votes	No. of Illegal Vote
Atchison.	Grasshopper	7	—	—	—	—
	Shannon	131	4	219	—	—
Bourbon		242	—	242	50	192
Brown		4	—	4	4	—
Calhoun		29	—	29	29	—
Davis		8	4	12	12	—
Doniphan	Burr Oak	42	—	—	41	1
	Iowa	31	—	—	31	—
	Wayne	66	—	—	62	4
	Washington	59	—	—	59	—
	Wolf River	53	—	251	53	—
Douglas.	Franklin	86	—	—	23	63
	Lawrence	42	—	—	42	—
	Lecompton	101	—	—	—	—
	Willow Springs	103	—	332	53	50
Franklin		15	—	15	15	—
Jefferson		42	3	45	—	—
Johnson		190	—	190	90	100
Leavenworth	Alexandria	42	—	—	—	—
	Delaware	239	—	—	—	—
	Kickapoo	150	1	—	—	50
	Leavenworth	212	—	—	—	100
	Wyandott	246	5	895	—	—
Lykins		220	—	220	70	150
Lynn		67	—	67	—	—
Madison	(See Wise Co.)					
Marshall		171	—	171	24	47
Nemaha		6	—	6	6	—
Riley		28	—	28	28	—
Shawnee	One Hundred and Ten	23	—	—	23	—
	Tecumseh	52	—	75	52	—
Wise	Council Grove	14	—	14	14	—

While these enactments of the alleged legislative assembly were being made, a movement was instituted to form a State government, and apply for admission into the Union as a State. The first step taken by the people of the Territory, in consequence of the invasion of March 30, 1855, was the circulation for signature of a graphic and truthful memorial to Congress. Your Committee find that every allegation in this memorial has been sustained by the testimony. No further step was taken, as it was hoped that some action by the General Government would protect them in their rights. When the alleged legislative assembly proceeded to construct the series of enactments referred to, the settlers were of opinion that submission to them would result in depriving them of the rights secured to them by the organic law. Their political condition was freely discussed in the Territory during the summer of 1855. Several meetings were held in reference to holding a convention to form a State government, and to apply for admission into the Union as a State. Public opinion gradually settled in favor of such an application to the Congress to meet in December, 1855. The first general meeting was held in Lawrence on the 15th of August, 1855.

The following preamble and resolutions were then passed :

"*Whereas*, The people of Kansas have been, since its settlement, and now are, without any law-making power, therefore be it

"*Resolved*, That we, the people of Kansas Territory, in mass meeting assembled, irrespective of party distinctions, influenced by common necessity, and greatly desirous of promoting the common good, do hereby call upon and request all *bona fide* citizens of Kansas Territory, of whatever political views or predilections, to consult together in their respective Election Districts and in mass convention or otherwise, elect three delegates for each representative to which said Election District is entitled in the House of Representatives of the Legislative Assembly, by proclamation of Governor Reeder, of date 19th of March, 1855 ; said delegates to assemble in convention, at the town of Topeka, on the 19th day of September, 1855, then and there to consider and determine upon all subjects of public interest, and particularly upon that having reference to the speedy formation of a State Constitution, with an intention of an immediate application to be admitted as a State into the Union of the United States of America."

Other meetings were held in various parts of the Territory, which indorsed the action of the Lawrence meeting, and delegates were selected in compliance with its recommendations.

They met at Topeka, on the 19th day of September, 1855. By their resolutions, they provided for the appointment of an Executive Committee, to consist of seven persons, who were required to "keep a record of their proceedings, and shall have a general superintendence of the affairs of the Territory so far as regards the organization of the State Government." They were required to take steps for an election to be held on the second Tuesday of the October following, under regulations imposed by that Committee, "for members of a Convention to form a Constitution, adopt a Bill of Rights for the people of Kansas, and take all needful measures for organizing a State Government, preparatory to the admission of Kansas into the Union as a State." The rules prescribed were such as usually govern elections in most of the States of the Union, and in most respects were similar to those contained in the proclamation of Gov. Reeder for the election of March 30, 1855.

The Executive Committee appointed by that Convention accepted their appointment, and entered upon the discharge of their duties by issuing a proclamation addressed to the legal voters of Kansas, requesting them to meet at their several precincts, at the time and places named in the proclamation, then and there to cast their ballots for members of a Constitutional Convention, to meet at Topeka on the 4th Tuesday of October then next.

The proclamation designated the places of elections, appointed judges, recited the qualifications of voters and the apportionment of members of the Convention.

After this proclamation was issued, public meetings were held in every district in the Territory, and in nearly every precinct. The State movement was a general topic of discussion throughout the Territory, and there was but little opposition exhibited to it. Elections were held at the time and places designated, and the returns were sent to the Executive Committee.

The result of the election was proclaimed by the Executive Committee, and the members elect were required to meet on the 23d day of October, 1855, at Topeka. In pursuance of this proclamation and direction, the Constitutional Convention met at the time and place appointed, and formed a State Constitution. A memorial to Congress was also prepared, praying for the admission of Kansas into the Union under that Constitution. The Convention also provided that the question of the adoption of the Constitution and other questions be submitted to the people, and required the Executive Committee to take the necessary steps for that purpose.

Accordingly, an election was held for that purpose on the 15th day of December, 1855, in compliance with the proclamation issued by the Executive Committee. The returns of this election were made by the Executive Committee, and an abstract of them is contained in the following table:

ABSTRACT OF THE ELECTION ON THE ADOPTION OF THE STATE CONSTITUTION, DEC. 15, 1855.

District.	PRECINCTS.	Constitution.		General Banking Law.		Exclusion of Negroes and Mulattoes.		No. Votes cast.
		Yes.	No.	Yes.	No.	Yes.	No.	
1	Lawrence	348	1	225	83	133	223	356
	Blanton	72	2	59	14	48	20	76
	Palmyra	11	1	9	3	12	—	12
	Franklin	48	4	31	15	48	2	53
2	Bloomington	137	—	122	11	113	15	137
	East Douglas	18	—	13	4	14	4	18
3	Topeka	135	—	125	9	69	64	136
	Washington	42	—	41	1	42	—	42
	Brownsville	24	—	22	2	22	2	24
	Tecumseh	85	—	23	11	85	—	85
4	Prairie City	72	—	39	38	69	3	72
5	Little Osage	21	7	16	12	23	7	31
	Big Sugar	18	2	5	16	20	—	21
	Neosho	12	—	6	6	12	—	12
	Potawatamie	39	3	21	19	25	18	43
	Little Sugar	42	18	33	13	42	2	60
	Stanton	32	—	4	33	33	5	37
	Osawatomie	56	1	33	20	38	17	59
7	Titus	39	5	32	7	25	15	44
	Juniata	30	—	23	6	10	19	31
8	Ohio City	21	—	16	5	20	1	21
	Mill Creek	20	—	—	20	20	—	20
	St. Mary's	14	—	—	14	14	—	14
	Waubaunsee	19	—	17	1	7	11	19
9	Pawnee	45	—	15	29	40	5	45
	Grasshopper Falls	54	—	19	34	50	3	54
10	Doniphan	22	—	5	14	21	—	22
	Burr Oak	23	—	7	16	22	1	23
	Jesse Padur's	12	—	1	11	12	—	12
11	Ocena	28	—	8	20	28	—	28
	Kickapoo	20	—	7	13	16	4	20
13	Pleasant Hill	47	—	87	6	45	1	47
	Indiana	19	—	—	18	19	—	19
	Whitfield	7	—	3	4	6	—	7
14	Wolf River	24	—	11	12	18	6	24
	St. Joseph's Bottom	15	—	4	9	14	1	15
15	Mt. Pleasant	32	—	32	1	30	2	83
16	Easton	71	2	53	19	71	—	73
17	Mission	7	—	3	—	1	2	7
	Total	1731	46	1120	564	1287	453	1778

N. B.—Poll-Book at Leavenworth was destroyed.

The Executive Committee then issued a proclamation reciting the results of the election of the 15th of December, and at the same time provided for an election to be held on the 15th day of January, 1856, for State officers and members of the General Assembly of the State of Kansas. An election was accordingly held in the several election-precincts, the returns of which were sent to the Executive Committee.

The result of this election was announced by a proclamation by the Executive Committee.

In accordance with the Constitution thus adopted, the members of the State Legislature and most of the State officers met on the day and at the place designated by the State Constitution, and took the oath therein prescribed.

After electing United States Senators, passing some preliminary laws, and appointing a Codifying Committee and preparing a Memorial to Congress, the General Assembly adjourned to meet on the 4th day of July, 1856.

The laws passed were all conditional upon the admission of Kansas as a State into the Union. These proceedings were regular, and, in the opinion of your Committee, the Constitution thus adopted fairly expresses the will of the majority of the settlers. They now await the action of Congress upon their memorial.

These elections, whether they were conducted in pursuance of law or not, were not illegal.

Whether the result of them is sanctioned by the action of Congress, or they are regarded as the mere expression of popular will, and Congress should refuse to grant the prayer of the memorial, that cannot affect their legality. The right of the people to assemble and express their political opinion in any form, whether by means of an election or a convention, is secured to them by the Constitution of the United States. Even if the elections are to be regarded as the act of a party, whether political or otherwise, they were proper, in accordance with examples, both in States and Territories.

The elections, however, were preceded and followed by acts of violence on the part of those who opposed them, and those persons who approved and sustained the invasion from Missouri were peculiarly hostile to these peaceful movements preliminary to the organization of a State government. Instances of this violence will be referred to hereafter.

To provide for the election of delegates to Congress, and at the same time do it in such a manner as to obtain the judgment of the House of Representatives upon the validity of the alleged legislative assembly sitting at Shawnee Mission, a convention was held at Big Springs on the 5th and 6th days of September, 1855. This was a party convention, and a party calling itself the Free-State party was then organized. It was in no way connected with the State movement, except that the election of a delegate to Congress was fixed by it on the same day as the election of members of a constitutional convention, instead of the day prescribed by the alleged legislative assembly. Andrew H. Reeder was put in nomination as Territorial delegate to Congress, and an election was provided for under the regulations prescribed for the election of March 30, 1855, excepting as to the appointment of officers, and the persons to whom the returns of the elections should be made. The election was held in accordance with these regulations, and A. H. Reeder received 2,827 votes.

The resolutions passed by this convention indicate the state of feeling which existed in the Territory in consequence of the invasion from Missouri, and the enactments of the alleged legislative assembly. The language of some of the resolutions is violent, and can only be justified either in consequence of the attempt to enforce the grossest acts of tyranny, or for the purpose of guarding against a similar invasion in future.

In the fall of 1855, there sprang out of the existing discords and excitement in the Territory, two secret Free-State societies. They were defensive in their character, and were designed to form a protection to their members against unlawful acts of violence and assault. One of the societies was purely of a local character, and was confined to the town of Lawrence. Very shortly after its organization, it produced its desired effect, and then went out of use and ceased to exist. Both societies were cumbersome, and of no utility except to give confidence to the Free-State men, and enable them to know and aid each other in contemplated danger. So far as the evidence shows, they led to no act of violence in resistance to either real or alleged laws.

On the 21st day of November, 1855, F. M. Coleman, a Pro-Slavery man, and Charles W. Dow, a Free-State man, had a dispute about the division line between their respective claims. Several hours afterward, as Dow was passing from a blacksmith shop toward his claim, and by the cabin of Coleman, the latter shot Dow with a double-barreled gun loaded with slugs. Dow was unarmed. He fell across the road and died immediately. This was about 1 o'clock, P.M. His dead body was allowed to lie where it fell until after sundown, when it was conveyed by Jacob Branson to his house, at which Dow boarded. The testimony in regard to this homicide is voluminous, and shows clearly that it was a deliberate murder by Coleman, and that Harrison Bulkley and a Mr. Hargous were accessories to it. The excitement caused by it was very great among all classes of the settlers. On the 26th, a large meeting of citizens was held at the place where the murder was committed, and resolutions passed that Coleman should be brought to justice. In the meantime, Coleman had gone to Missouri, and then to Gov. Shannon, at Shawnee Mission, in Johnson County. He was there taken into custody by S. J. Jones, then acting as Sheriff. No warrant was issued or examination had. On the day of the meeting at Hickory Point, Harrison Bradley procured a peace warrant against Jacob Branson, which was placed in the hands of Jones. That same evening, after Branson had gone to bed, Jones came to his cabin with a party of about 25 persons, among whom were Hargous and Buckley—burst open the door, and saw Branson in bed. He then drew his pistol, cocked it, and presented it to Branson's breast, and said, "You are my prisoner, and if you move I will blow you through." The others cocked their guns and gathered round him, and took him prisoner. They all mounted and went to Buckley's house. After a time, they went on a circuitous route toward Blanton's Bridge, stopping to "drink" on the way. As they approached the bridge, there were thirteen in the party, several having stopped. Jones rode up to the prisoner and, among other things, told him that he had "heard there were one hundred men at your house to-day," and "that he regretted they were not there, and that they were cheated out of their sport." In the meantime, the alarm had been given in the neighborhood of Branson's arrest, and several of the settlers, among whom were some who had attended the meeting at Hickory Point that day, gathered together. They were greatly excited; the alleged injustice of such an arrest of a quiet settler, under a peace warrant by "Sheriff Jones," aided by two men believed to be accessory to a murder, and who were allowed to be at large, exasperated them, and they proceeded as rapidly as possible by a nearer route than that taken by Jones, and stopped near the house of J. S. Abbott, one of them. They were on foot as Jones's party approached on a canter. The rescuers suddenly formed across the road in front of Jones and his party. Jones halted, and asked, "What's up?" The reply was, "That's what we want to know. What's up?" Branson said, "They have got me a prisoner." Some one in the rescuing party told him to come over to their side. He did so, and dismounted, and the mule he rode was driven over to Jones's party; Jones then left. Of the persons engaged in this rescue, three were from Lawrence, and

had attended the meeting. Your Committee have deemed it proper to detail the particulars of this rescue, as it was made the groundwork of what is known as the Wakerusa War. On the same night of the rescue, the cabins of Coleman and Buckley were burned, but by whom, is left in doubt by the testimony.

On the morning of the rescue of Branson, Jones was at the village of Franklin, near Lawrence. The rescue was spoken of in the presence of Jones, and more conversation passed between two others in his presence, as to whether it was most proper to send for assistance to Col. Boone, in Missouri, or to Gov. Shannon. Jones wrote a dispatch and handed it to a messenger. As soon as he started, Jones said: "That man is taking my dispatch to Missouri, and by G—d I'll have revenge before I see Missouri." A person present, who was examined as a witness, complained publicly that the dispatch was not sent to the Governor; and within half an hour one was sent to the Governor by Jones, through Hargous. Within a few days, large numbers of men from the State of Missouri gathered and encamped on the Wakerusa. They brought with them all the equipments of war. To obtain them, a party of men under the direction of Judge T. V. Thompson broke into the United States arsenal and armory at Liberty, Missouri, and after a forcible detention of Captain Leonard (then in charge), they took the cannon, muskets, rifles, powder, harness, and indeed all the materials and munitions of war they desired, some of which have never been returned or accounted for.

The chief hostility of this military foray was against the town of Lawrence, and this was especially the case with the officers of the law.

Your Committee can see in the testimony no reason, excuse, or palliation for this feeling. *Up to this time, no warrant or proclamation of any kind had been in the hands of any officer against any citizen of Lawrence.* No arrest had been attempted, and no writ resisted in that town. The rescue of Branson sprang out of a murder committed thirteen miles from Lawrence, in a detached settlement, and neither the town nor its citizens extended any protection to Branson's rescuers. On the contrary, two or three days after the rescue, S. N. Wood, who claimed publicly to be one of the rescuing party, wished to be arrested for the purpose of testing the Territorial laws, and walked up to Sheriff Jones and shook hands with him, and exchanged other courtesies. He could have been arrested without difficulty, and it was his design, when he went to Mr. Jones, to be arrested; but no attempt was made to do so.

It is obvious that the only cause of this hostility is the known desire of the citizens of Lawrence to make Kansas a Free State, and their repugnance to laws imposed upon them by non-residents.

Your Committee do not propose to detail the incidents connected with this foray. Fortunately for the peace of the country, a direct conflict between the opposing forces was avoided by an amicable arrangement. The losses sustained by the settlers in property taken and time and money expended in their own defense, added much to the trials incident to a new settlement. Many persons were unlawfully taken and detained—in some cases, under circumstances of gross cruelty. This was especially so in the arrest and treatment of Dr. G. A. Cutter and G. F. Warren. They were taken, without cause or warrant, sixty miles from Lawrence, and when Dr. Cutter was quite sick. They were compelled to go to the camp at Lawrence, were put into the custody of "Sheriff Jones," who had no process to arrest them—they were taken into a small room kept as a liquor shop, which was open and very cold. That night, Jones came in with others, and went to "playing poker at twenty-five cents ante." The prisoners were obliged to sit up all night, as there was no room to lie down, when the men were playing. Jones insulted them frequently, and told one of them he must either "tell or swing." The guard then objected to this treatment of prisoners, and Jones desisted. . . .

While we remained in the Territory, repeated acts of outrage were committed upon the quiet, unoffending citizens, of which we received authentic intelligence. Men were attacked on the highway, robbed, and subsequently imprisoned. Men were seized and searched, and their weapons of defense taken from them without compensation. Horses were frequently taken and appropriated. Oxen were taken from the yoke while plowing, and butchered in the presence of their owners. One young man was seized in the streets of the town of Atchison, and, under circumstances of gross barbarity, was tarred and cottoned, and in that condition was sent to his family. All the provisions of the Constitution of the United States, securing persons and property, are utterly disregarded. The officers of the law, instead of protecting the people, were in some instances engaged in these outrages, and in no instance did we learn that any man was arrested, indicted, or punished for any of these crimes. While such offenses were committed with impunity, the laws were used as a means of indicting men for holding elections, preliminary to framing a Constitution and applying for admission into the Union as the State of Kansas. Charges of high treason were made against prominent citizens upon grounds which seem to your Committee absurd and ridiculous, and under these charges they are now held in custody and are refused the privilege of bail. In several cases, men were arrested in the State of Missouri, while passing on their lawful business through that State, and detained until indictments could be found in the Territory,

These proceedings were followed by an offense of still greater magnitude. Under color of legal process, a company of about 700 armed men, the great body of whom, your Committee are satisfied, were not citizens of the Territory, marched into the town of Lawrence, under Marshal Donaldson and S. J. Jones, officers claiming to act under the law, and bombarded and then burned to the ground a valuable hotel and one private house; destroyed two printing presses and material; and then, being released by the officers, whose posse they claimed to be, proceeded to sack, pillage, and rob houses, stores, trunks, etc., even to the clothing of women and children. Some of the letters thus unlawfully taken were private ones, written by the contesting Delegate, and they were offered in evidence. Your Committee did not deem that the persons holding them had any right thus to use them, and refused to be made the instruments to report private letters thus obtained.

This force was not resisted, because it was collected and marshaled under the forms of law. But this act of barbarity, unexampled in the history of our Government, was followed by its natural consequences. All the restraints which American citizens are accustomed to pay even to the appearance of law, were thrown off; one act of violence led to another; homicides became frequent. A party under H. C. Pate, composed chiefly of citizens of Missouri, were taken prisoners by a party of settlers; and while your Committee were at Westport, a company chiefly of Missourians, accompanied by the acting Delegate, went to relieve Pate and his party, and a collision was prevented by the United States troops. Civil war has seemed impending in the Territory. Nothing can prevent so great a calamity but the presence of a large force of United States troops, under a commander who will with prudence and discretion quiet the excited passions of both parties, and expel with force the armed bands of lawless men coming from Missouri and elsewhere, who with criminal pertinacity infest that Territory.

In some cases, and as to one entire election district, the condition of the country prevented the attendance of witnesses, who were either arrested or detained while obeying our process, or deterred from so doing. The Sergeant-at-Arms, who served the process upon them, was himself arrested or detained for a short time by an armed force, claiming to be a part of the posse of the Marshal, but was allowed to proceed upon an examination of his papers, and was furnished with a pass, signed by "Warren D. Wilkes, of South Carolina." John Upton, another officer of the Committee, was subsequently stopped by a lawless force on the borders of the Territory, and after being detained and treated with great indignity, was released. He also was furnished with a pass signed by two citizens of Missouri, and addressed to "Pro-Slavery men." By reason of these disturbances, we were delayed in Westport, so that while in session there, our time was but partially occupied.

But the obstruction which created the most serious embarrassment to your Committee, was the attempted arrest of Gov. Reeder, the contesting Delegate, upon a writ of attachment issued against him by Judge Lecompte, to compel his attendance as a witness before the Grand Jury of Douglas County. William Fane, recently from the State of Georgia, and claiming to be the Deputy Marshal, came into the room of the Committee, while Gov. Reeder was examining a witness before us, and producing the writ required Gov. Reeder to attend him. Subsequent events have only strengthened the conviction of your Committee, that this was a wanton and unlawful interference by the Judge who issued the writ, tending greatly to obstruct a full and fair investigation. Gov. Reeder and Gen. Whitfield alone were fully possessed of that local information which would enable us to elicit the whole truth, and it was obvious to every one that any event which would separate either of them from the Committee, would necessarily hinder, delay, and embarrass it. Gov. Reeder claimed that, under the circumstances in which he was placed, he was privileged from arrest except for treason, felony, or breach of the peace. As this was a question of privilege, proper for the Courts, or for the privileged person alone to deter-

mine on his peril, we declined to give him any protection or take any action in the matter. He refused to obey the writ, believing it to be a mere pretense to get the custody of his person, and fearing, as he alleged, that he would be assassinated by lawless bands of men then gathering in and near Lecompton. He then left the Territory.

Subsequently, H. Miles Moore, an attorney in Leavenworth City, but for several years a citizen of Weston, Mo., kindly furnished the Committee information as to the residence of persons voting at the elections, and in some cases examined witnesses before us. He was arrested on the streets of that town by an armed band of about thirty men, headed by W. D. Wilkes, without any color of authority, confined, with other citizens, under a military guard for twenty-four hours, and then notified to leave the Territory. His testimony was regarded as important, and upon his sworn statement that it would endanger his person to give it openly, the majority of your Committee deemed it proper to examine him ex-parte, and did so.

By reason of these occurrences, the contestant and the party with and for whom he acted, were unrepresented before us during a greater portion of the time, and your Committee were required to ascertain the truth in the best manner they could.

Your Committee report the following facts and conclusions as established by the testimony :

First. That each election in the Territory, held under the organic or alleged Territorial law, has been carried by organized invasions from the State of Missouri, by which the people of the Territory have been prevented from exercising the rights secured to them by the organic law.

Second. That the alleged Territorial Legislature was an illegally-constituted body, and had no power to pass valid laws, and their enactments are, therefore, null and void.

Third. That these alleged laws have not, as a general thing, been used to protect persons and property and to punish wrong, but for unlawful purposes.

Fourth. That the election under which the sitting Delegate, John W. Whitfield, holds his seat, was not held in pursuance of any valid law, and that it should be regarded only as the expression of the choice of those resident citizens who voted for him.

Fifth. That the election under which the contesting Delegate, Andrew H. Reeder, claims his seat, was not held in pursuance of law, and that it should be regarded only as the expression of the choice of the resident citizens who voted for him.

Sixth. That Andrew H. Reeder received a greater number of votes of resident citizens than John W. Whitfield, for Delegate.

Seventh. That in the present condition of the Territory, a fair election cannot be held without a new census, a stringent and well-guarded election law, the selection of impartial Judges, and the presence of United States troops at every place of election.

Eighth. That the various elections held by the people of the Territory preliminary to the formation of the State Government have been as regular as the disturbed condition of the Territory would allow; and that the Constitution passed by the Convention, held in pursuance of said elections, embodies the will of a majority of the people.

As it is not the province of your Committee to suggest remedies for the existing troubles in the Territory of Kansas, they content themselves with the foregoing statement of facts.

All of which is respectfully submitted.

Wm. A. Howard,
John Sherman.

The Free-State Constitution framed at Topeka for Kansas, by the Convention called by the Free-State party, (as set forth in the foregoing documents,) was in due season submitted to Congress—Messrs. Andrew H. Reeder (the Free-State Territorial delegate) and James H. Lane having been chosen by the first Free-State Legislature, Senators of the United States, and Mr. M. W. Delahay elected Representative in the House, by the Free-State men of Kansas. Of course, these were not entitled to their seats until the aforesaid instrument (known as the "Topeka Constitution") should be accepted by Congress, and the State thereupon admitted into the Union. This Constitution, being formally presented in either House, was received and referred to their respective Committees on Territories; but the accompanying Memorial from the Free-State Legislature, setting forth the grounds of the application, and praying for admission as a State, was, after having been received by the Senate, reconsidered, rejected, and returned to Col. Lane, on the allegation that material changes had been made in it since it left Kansas. The Senate, in like manner, rejected repeated motions to accept the Constitution, and thereupon admit Kansas as a Free State—there never being more than Messrs. Hamlin and Fessenden, of Maine, Hale and Bell, of New-Hampshire, Collamer and Foot, of Vermont, Sumner and Wilson, of Mass., Foster, of Connecticut, Seward and Fish, of New-York, Wade, of Ohio, Durkee and Dodge, of Wisconsin, Trumbull, of Illinois, and Harlan, of Iowa, (16) Senators in favor of such admission, and these never all present at the same time.

In the House—the aforesaid Constitution and Memorial having been submitted to the Committee on Territories—its Chairman, Mr. Grow, of Penna., from a majority of said Committee, reported in favor of the admission of Kansas under such Constitution, as a Free State; and after debate the Previous Question thereon was ordered (June 28th) by a vote of 98 Ayes to 63 Noes. Previous to this, however, Mr. Stephens, of Georgia, had proposed, as an amendment or substitute, a radically different bill, contemplating the appointment by the President and Senate of five Commissioners, who should repair to Kansas, take a census of the inhabitants and legal voters, and thereupon proceed to apportion, during the month of September, 1856, the delegates (52) to form a Constitutional Convention, to be elected by the legal voters aforesaid; said delegates to be chosen on the day of the Presidential election (Tuesday, Nov. 4th, 1856), and to assemble in Convention on the first Monday in December, 1856, to form a State Constitution. The bill proposed, also, penalties for illegal voting at said election.

To this substitute-bill, Mr. Dunn, of Indiana, proposed the following amendment, to come in at the end as an additional section:

SEC. 18.—*And be it further enacted,* That so much of the fourteenth section and of the thirty-second section of the act passed at the first session of the Thirty-Third Congress, commonly called the Kansas and Nebraska act, as reads as follows: " Except the eighth section of the act preparatory to the admission of Missouri into the Union, approved March 6, 1820, which, being inconsistent with the principle of non-intervention by Congress with Slavery in the States and Territories, as recognized by the legislation of 1850, commonly called the Compromise Measures, is hereby declared inoperative and void; it being the true intent and meaning of this act not to legislate Slavery into any State or Territory, or to exclude it therefrom, but to leave the people thereof perfectly free to form and regulate their domestic institutions in their own way, subject only to the Constitution of the United States: *Provided,* That nothing herein contained shall be construed to revive or put in force any law or regulation which may have existed prior to the act of 6th of March, 1820, either protecting, establishing, prohibiting, or abolishing Slavery," be, and the same is hereby, repealed. *Provided,* That any person or persons lawfully held to service within either of the Territories named in said act shall be discharged from such service, if they shall not be removed and kept out of said Territories within twelve months from the passage of this act.

Mr. Dunn's amendment to the Stephens amendment or substitute, was carried: Yeas, 109; Nays, 102.

Mr. Stephens's substitute, as thus amended by its adversaries, was abandoned by its original friends, and received but *two* votes—those of Messrs. George G. Dunn, of Indiana, and John Scott Harrison, of Ohio—Nays, 210.

Mr. Dunn had previously moved a reference of the bill to the Committee of the Whole on the state of the Union. This was now defeated: Yeas, 101; Nays, 109.

Mr. Jones, of Tennessee, now moved that the bill do lie on the table, which was defeated. Yeas, 106; Nays, 107; (Barclay of Pennsylvania, Dunn of Indiana, Haven and Williams, of New-York.—*Yeas :* Bayard Clarke, of New-York, Hickman and Millward, of Pennsylvania, Moore, of Ohio, and Scott, of Indiana.—*Nays :* Scott Harrison, of Ohio, not voting, Wells of Wisconsin, absent). The House now refused to adjourn by 106 to 102; and, after a long struggle, the final question was reached, and the bill *rejected :* Yeas, 106; Nays, 107.

So the bill was lost.

July 1st.—Mr. Barclay, (Dem.) of Pennsylvania rose to a privileged motion. He moved a reconsideration of the preceding vote, by which the Free-Kansas bill had been rejected. A stormy debate ensued, in the midst of which Mr. Howard, of Michigan, rose to a question of higher privilege (as affecting the right of a member [delegate] to his seat) and submitted the report of the Kansas Investigating Committee (already given). The Speaker sustained the motion, and the House sustained the Speaker. The report was thereupon presented and read, consuming a full day.

July 3rd.—The question of reconsidering the vote defeating the Free-Kansas bill was again reached. Mr. Houston, of Alabama, moved that it do lie on the table; defeated: Yeas, 97; Nays, 102. The main question was then ordered: Yeas, 101; Nays, 98; and the reconsideration carried: Yeas, 101; Nays, 99. The previous question on the passage of the bill was now ordered: Yeas, 99; Nays, 96; a motion by Mr. McQueen, of South Carolina, to lay the bill on the table was defeated: Yeas, 97; Nays, 100; and then the bill was finally *passed :* Yeas, 99; Nays, 97.

Mr. Grow, of Pennsylvania, moved the reconsideration of this vote, and that the motion to reconsider do lie on the table, which was permitted, without further division.

June 30th.—Mr. Douglas reported to the Senate on several bills submitted by Messrs. Clayton, Tombs, and others, for the pacification of the Kansas troubles, as also decidedly against Gov. Seward's proposition to admit Kansas as a Free State, under her Topeka Constitution. Mr. Collamer, being the minority of the Territorial Committee, made a brief and pungent counter-report. Mr. Douglas gave notice that he would ask for a final vote on the day after the next.

July 1st.—Bill debated by Messrs. Thompson of Ky., Hale of N H., Bigler of Pa., Adams of Miss., and Crittenden of Ky.

July 2d.—Debate continued through the day and following night, the majority resisting all motions to adjourn. Messrs. Wade, Pugh, Briggs, Bigler, Toombs, Clayton, Crittenden, Bell, Seward, Hale, and nearly half the Senate participated. An amendment moved by Mr. Adams, of Miss., the day before, striking out so much of the bill as secures the Right of Suffrage, in the proposed reorganization of Kansas, to alien residents who shall have declared their intention to become citizens, and renounced all allegiance to foreign governments, was adopted: Yeas, 22; Nays, 16.

Some time in the morning of July 3d, the following amendment, reduced to shape by Mr. Geyer, of Mo., was added to the 18th section of the bill—only Brown, of Miss., Fitzpatrick, of Ala., and Mason, of Va., voting against it: Yeas, 40. It provides that

No law shall be made or have force or effect in said Territory [of Kansas] which shall require any attestation or oath to support any act of Congress or other legislative act, as a qualification for any civil office, public trust, or for any employment or profession, or to serve as a juror, or vote at an election, or which shall impose any tax upon, or condition to, the exercise of the right of suffrage, by any qualified voter, or which shall restrain or prohibit the free discussion of any law or subject of legislation in the said Territory, or the free expression of opinion thereon by the people of said Territory.

Mr. Trumbull, of Ill., moved the following:

And be it further enacted, That it was the true intent and meaning of the " act to organize the Territories of Nebraska and Kansas," not to legislate Slavery into Kansas, nor to exclude it therefrom, but to leave the people thereof perfectly free through their Territorial Legislature to regulate the institution of Slavery in their own way, subject to the Constitution of the United States; and that, until the Territorial Legislature acts upon the subject, the owner of a slave in one of the States has no right or authority to take such slave into the Territory of Kansas, and there hold him as a slave; but every slave taken to the Territory of Kansas by his owner for purposes of settlement is hereby declared to be free, unless there is some valid act of a duly constituted Legislative Assembly of said Territory, under which he may be held as a slave.

The Yeas and Nays being ordered, the proposition was voted down—Yeas, 9; Nays, 34—as follows:

YEAS.—Messrs. Durkee, Fessenden, Foot, Foster, Hale, Seward, Trumbull, Wade, and Wilson—9.

NAYS.—Messrs. Adams, Allen, Bayard, Bell of Tennessee, Benjamin, Biggs, Bigler, Bright, Brodhead, Brown, Cass, Clay, Crittenden, Dodge, Douglas, Evans, Fitzpatrick, Geyer, Hunter, Iverson, Johnson, Jones of Iowa, Mallory, Pratt, Pugh, Reid, Sebastian, Slidell, Thompson of Kentucky, Toombs, Toucey, Weller Wright, and Yulee—34.

Mr. Trumbull then proposed that the Kansas-Nebraska act

was intended to, and does, confer upon, or leave to, the people of the Territory of Kansas full power, at any time, through its Territorial Legislature, to exclude Slavery from said Territory, or to recognize and regulate it therein.

This, too, was voted down. Mr. Trumbull then proposed the following:

And be it further enacted, That all the acts and proceedings of all and every body of men heretofore assembled in said Territory of Kansas, and claiming to be a Legislative Assembly thereof, with authority to pass laws for the government of said Territory, are hereby declared to be utterly null and void. And no person shall hold any office, or exercise any authority or jurisdiction in said Territory, under or by virtue of any power or authority derived from such Legislative Assembly; nor shall the members thereof exercise any power or authority as such.

This, too, was voted down, as follows:

YEAS.—Messrs. Bell of New-Hampshire, Collamer, Durkee, Fessenden, Foot, Foster, Hale, Seward, Trumbull, Wade, and Wilson—11.

NAYS.—Messrs. Adams, Allen, Bayard, Bell of Tennessee, Benjamin, Biggs, Bigler, Bright, Brodhead, Brown, Cass, Clay, Crittenden, Dodge, Douglas, Evans, Fitz-

patrick, Geyer, Hunter, Iverson, Johnson, Jones of Iowa, Mallory, Mason, Pratt, Pugh, Reid, Sebastian, Slidell, Stuart, Thompson of Kentucky, Toombs, Toucey, Weller, Wright, and Yulee—36.

Mr. Foster, of Connecticut, moved the following amendment:

SEC.—*And be it further enacted*, That, until the inhabitants of said Territory shall proceed to hold a Convention to form a State Constitution according to the provisions of this act, and so long as said Territory remains a Territory, the following sections contained in chapter one hundred and fifty-one, in the volume transmitted to the Senate, by the President of the United States, as containing the laws of Kansas, be, and the same are hereby, declared to be utterly null and void, viz. :

"§ 12. If any free person, by speaking or by writing, assert or maintain that persons have not the right to hold slaves in this Territory, or shall introduce into this Territory any book, paper, magazine, pamphlet, or circular, containing any denial of the right of persons to hold slaves in this Territory, such persons shall be deemed guilty of felony, and punished by imprisonment at hard labor for a term of not less than two years.

"§ 13. No person who is conscientiously opposed to holding slaves, or who does not admit the right to hold slaves in this Territory, shall sit as a juror on the trial of any prosecution for the violation of any one of the sections of this act."

This was rejected [as superfluous, or covered by a former amendment,] as follows:

YEAS.—Messrs. Allen, Bell of New-Hampshire, Clayton, Collamer, Durkee, Fessenden, Foot, Foster, Hale, Seward, Trumbull, Wade, and Wilson—13.

NAYS.—Messrs. Bayard, Benjamin, Biggs, Bigler, Bright, Brodhead, Brown, Cass, Clay, Dodge, Douglas, Evans, Fitzpatrick, Geyer, Hunter, Iverson, Johnson, Jones of Iowa, Mallory, Mason, Pratt, Pugh, Reid, Sebastian, Slidell, Stuart, Thompson of Kentucky, Toombs, Toucey, Weller, Wright, and Yulee—32.

Mr. Wilson, of Massachusetts, moved that the whole bill be stricken out and another inserted instead, repealing all the Territorial laws of Kansas.

Rejected: Yeas, 8, (Bell, of New-Hampshire, Collamer, Durkee, Fessenden, Foster, Seward, Wade, and Wilson ;) Nays, 35.

Mr. Seward moved to strike out the whole bill, and insert instead one admitting Kansas as a Free State, under the Topeka Constitution: Defeated—Yeas, 11; Nays, 36—as follows:

YEAS.—Messrs. Bell of New-Hampshire, Collamer Durkee, Fessenden, Foot, Foster, Hale, Seward, Trumbull, Wade, and Wilson—11.

NAYS.—Messrs. Allen, Bayard, Bell of Tennessee, Benjamin, Biggs, Bigler, Bright, Brodhead, Brown, Cass, Clay, Clayton, Crittenden, Dodge, Douglas, Evans, Fitzpatrick, Geyer, Hunter, Iverson, Johnson, Jones of Iowa, Mallory, Mason, Pratt, Pugh, Reid, Slidell, Stuart, Thompson of Kentucky, Toombs, Toucey, Weller, Wright, and Yulee—36.

The bill was now reported as amended, and the amendment made in Committee of the Whole concurred in. The bill was then (8 A. M.) ordered to be engrossed and read a third time; and, on the question of its final passage, the vote stood—Yeas, 33; Nays, 12—as follows:

YEAS.—Messrs. Allen, Bayard, Bell of Tennessee, Benjamin, Biggs, Bigler, Bright, Brodhead, Brown, Cass, Clay, Crittenden, Douglas, Evans, Fitzpatrick, Geyer, Hunter, Iverson, Johnson, Jones of Iowa, Mallory, Pratt, Pugh, Reid, Sebastian, Slidell, Stuart, Thompson of Kentucky, Toombs, Toucey, Weller, Wright, and Yulee—33.

NAYS.—Messrs. Bell of New-Hampshire, Collamer, Dodge, Durkee, Fessenden, Foot, Foster, Hale, Seward, Trumbull, Wade, and Wilson—12.

The bill was then sent to the House. It provides that five competent persons appointed by the President, shall take a census of the legal voters of the Territory on the 4th of July, 1856, these to be apportioned into 52 districts, for the purpose of electing delegates to form a State Constitution; it imposes penalties for using force or threats to influence any qualified voter in giving his vote, or to deter him from going to the polls; the delegates elected under this act to assemble in Convention on the 1st Monday of December, 1856, to first determine by vote whether it is expedient to form a State Constitution and Government, and if it is decided to be expedient, to proceed to form a Constitution and Government for the State of Kansas, with the boundaries defined in this act.

The bill was never acted on in the House, but lay on the Speaker's table, untouched, when the session terminated by adjournment, Monday, Aug. 18th.

July 8th.—In Senate, Mr. Douglas reported back from the Committee on Territories the House bill to admit Kansas as a State, with an amendment striking out all after the enacting clause, and inserting instead the Senate bill (No. 356) just referred to.

Mr. Hale, of N. H., moved to amend this substitute by providing that all who migrate to the Territory prior to July 4th, 1857, shall be entitled to a vote in determining the character of the institutions of Kansas. Lost: Yeas, 13; Nays, 32.

Mr. Trumbull, of Ill., moved that all the Territorial laws of Kansas be repealed and the Territorial officers dismissed. Rejected: Yeas, 12; Nays, 32.

Mr. Collamer, of Vt., proposed an amendment, prohibiting Slavery in all that portion of the Louisiana purchase north of 36° 30' not included in the Territory of Kansas. Rejected— Yeas, 12; Nays, 30—as follows:

YEAS—Messrs. Bell of N. H., Collamer, Dodge, Fessenden, Fish, Foot, Foster, Hale, Hamlin, Seward, Trumbull and Wade.

NAYS—Messrs. Adams, Bayard, Benjamin, Biggs, Bright, Brodhead, Butler, Cass, Clay, Crittenden, Douglas, Fitzpatrick, Geyer, Hunter, Iverson, Johnson, Jones of Iowa, Jones of Tenn., Mallory, Mason, Pearce, Pugh, Reid, Sebastian, Slidell, Stuart, Thompson of Ky., Toombs, Weller, and Yulee.

The substitute reported by Mr. Douglas was then agreed to—Yeas, 32; Nays, 13—and the bill in this shape passed.

[This amendment was not concurred in nor ever acted on by the House.]

July 29th.—Mr. Dunn, of Ind., called up a bill "To reorganize the Territory of Kansas and for other purposes," which he had originally (July 7th) proposed as a substitute for the Senate bill (No 356) aforesaid. Its length, and the substantial identity of many of its provisions with those of other bills organizing Territories contained in this volume, dissuade us from quoting it entire. It provides for a legislative election on the first Tuesday in November next; and section 15 proceeds:

§ 15. *And be it further enacted,* That all suits, processes, and proceedings, civil and criminal, at law and in chancery, and all indictments and informations which shall be pending and undetermined in the courts of the Territory of Kansas or of New-Mexico, when this act shall take effect, shall remain in said courts where pending, to be heard, tried, prosecuted, and determined in such courts as though this act had not been passed: *Provided, nevertheless,* That all criminal prosecutions now pending in any of the courts of the Territory of Kansas imputing to any person or persons the crime of treason against the United States, and all criminal prosecutions, by information or indictment, against any person or persons for any alleged violation or disregard whatever of what are usually known as the laws of the Legislature of Kansas, shall be forthwith dismissed by the courts where such prosecutions may be pending, and every person

who may be restrained of his liberty by reason of said prosecutions, shall be released therefrom without delay. Nor shall there hereafter be instituted any criminal prosecution, in any of the courts of the United States, or of said Territory, against any person or persons for any such charge of treason in said Territory prior to the passage of this act, or any violation or disregard of said Legislative enactments at any time.

§ 23 grants to every actual settler a right of preëmption to the quarter-section of public land improved and occupied by him in said Territory of Kansas, prior to Jan. 1st, 1858.

The two last and most important sections of Mr. Dunn's bill are *verbatim* as follows:

§ 24. *And be it further enacted,* That so much of the fourteenth section, and also so much of the thirty-second section, of the act passed at the first session of the thirty-third Congress, commonly known as the Kansas-Nebraska act, as reads as follows, to wit: "Except the eighth section of the act preparatory to the admission of Missouri into the Union, approved March 6, 1820, which being inconsistent with the principle of non-intervention by Congress with Slavery in the States and Territories as recognized by the legislation of 1850, commonly called the Compromise Measures, is hereby declared inoperative and void; it being the true intent and meaning of this act not to legislate Slavery into any Territory or State, nor to exclude it therefrom, but to leave the people thereof perfectly free to form and regulate their domestic institutions in their own way, subject only to the Constitution of the United States: *Provided,* That nothing herein contained shall be construed to revive or put in force any law or regulation which may have existed prior to the act of 6th March, 1820, either protecting, establishing, prohibiting or abolishing slavery"—be and the same is hereby repealed, and the said eighth section of said act of the 6th of March, 1820, is hereby revived and declared to be in full force and effect within the said Territories of Kansas and Nebraska: *Provided, however,* That any person lawfully held to service in either of said Territories shall not be discharged from such service by reason of such repeal and revival of said eighth section, if such person shall be permanently removed from such Territory or Territories prior to the 1st day of January, 1858: and any child or children born in either of said Territories, of any female lawfully held to service, if in like manner removed without said Territories before the expiration of that date, shall not be, by reason of anything in this act, emancipated from any service it might have owed had this act never been passed: *And provided further,* That any person lawfully held to service in any other State or Territory of the United States, and escaping into either the Territory of Kansas or Nebraska, may be reclaimed and removed to the person or place where such service is due, under any law of the United States which shall be in force upon the subject.

§ 25. *And be it further enacted,* That all other parts of the aforesaid Kansas-Nebraska act which relate to the said Territory of Kansas, and every other law or usage having, or which is pretended to have, any force or effect in said Territory in conflict with the provisions or the spirit of this act, except such laws of Congress and treaty stipulations as relate to the Indians, are hereby repealed and declared void.

Mr. Dunn, having carried a reference to the Committee of the Whole, of a bill introduced by Mr. Grow, repealing all the acts of the alleged Territorial Legislature of Kansas, now moved and carried a reconsideration of that vote, and proceeded to the striking out of Mr. Grow's bill and the insertion of his own as a substitute. The motion prevailed. Whereupon Mr. Dunn moved the previous question on ordering this bill to be engrossed and read a third time, which prevailed—Yeas, 92; Nays, 86 —and then the bill passed—Yeas, 88; Nays, 74.

This bill was not acted on by the Senate.

The House, in the course of its action on the several Annual Appropriation bills, affixed to several of them, respectively, provisos, abolishing, repealing or suspending the various obnoxious acts of the Territorial Legislature; but all these were resisted by the Senate and were ultimately given up by th. House, save one appropriating $20,000 for the pay and expenses of the *next* Territorial Legislature, which the Senate gave up, on finding itself in serious disagreement with the House, and thus secured the passage of the Civil Appropriation bill. Finally, the two Houses were at odds, on a proviso forbidding the employment of the Army to enforce the acts of the Shawnee Mission assemblage, claiming to be a Territorial Legislature of Kansas, when at noon on the 18th of August the speaker's hammer fell, anouncing the termination of the session, leaving the Army bill unpassed. But President Pierce immediately issued a proclamation convening an extra session on the 21st (Thursday), when the two Houses reconvened accordingly,and a full quorum of each was found to be present. The House promptly repassed the army bill, again affixing a proviso forbiding the use of the army to enforce the disputed Territorial laws, which proviso the Senate as promptly struck out, and the House as promptly reinserted. The Senate insisted on its disagreement, but asked no conference, and the House (Aug. 22d) by a close vote decided to adhere to its proviso: Yeas, 97; Nays, 93; but one of the yeas (Bocock of Va.) was so given in order to be able to move a reconsideration; so that the true division was 96 to 94, which was the actual division on a motion by Mr. Cobb of Ga. that the House recede from its position. Finally, a motion to reconsider was made and laid on the table; Yeas, 97; Nays, 96; and the House thereupon adjourned.

Aug. 23d.—The Senate also voted to adhere: Yeas, 35; Nays, 9.

Mr. Clayton proposed a committee of Conference, to which Mr. Seward objected. No action.

In the House, Mr. Campbell, of Ohio, proposed a similiar Committee of Conference. Objected to.

Mr. Cobb, of Ga., moved that the House recede from its Kansas proviso. Defeated: Yeas, 97; Nays, 100. Adjourned.

The struggle for the passage of the bill with or without the proviso continued until Saturday, August 30th, when, several members, hostile to the proviso, and hitherto absent, unpaired, having returned, the House again passed the Army bill with the proviso modified as follows:

Provided, however, that no part of the military force of the United States, for the support of which appropriations are made by this act, shall be employed in aid of the enforcement of any enactments heretofore made by the body claiming to be the Territorial Legislature of Kansas.

The bill passed as reported (under the Previous Question): Yeas, 99; Nays, 79; and was sent to the Senate, where the above proviso was stricken out: Yeas, 26; Nays, 7; and the bill thus returned to the House, when the Senate's amendment was concurred in: Yeas, 101; Nays, 97.

So the proviso was beaten at last, and the bill passed, with no restriction on the President's discretion in the use of the Army in Kansas; just as all attempts of the House to direct the President to have a *nolle prosequi* entered in the case of the Free-State prisoners in Kansas charged with aiding the formation and

adoption of the Free-State constitution as aforesaid, had been previously beaten, after prevailing in the House—the Senate striking them out and the House (by union of nearly all the supporters of Fillmore with nearly or quite all those supporting Buchanan) finally acquiescing.

The 34th Congress reassembled on the 1st of December. Since the adjournment from the last session the presidential election had taken place, resulting in the election of James Buchanan as President. The popular vote gave neither of the three candidates a majority. In the Free States the election was hotly contested and a very large vote polled. In the Southern States the vote was small, as no issue was presented to the people, it being claimed by their respective partisans, that both the candidates (Buchanan and Fillmore) voted for in that section were equally Pro-Slavery. But the pro-slavery leaders had declared in favor of Buchanan, and he consequently received large majorities in nearly every Slave State.

On the first day of the session, Kansas affairs came up in the House on an objection to admit J. W. Whitfield to a seat as a delegate, the objection being that the border ruffian laws under which he had been elected were "null and void."

Mr. Grow spoke against admitting Whitfield, and quoted from a speech of Mr. Clayton (a short time before his decease) in the Senate. Mr. Clayton, in speaking of these laws, said:

Now, sir, let me allude to that subject which is the great cause of all this discord between the two Houses. The *unjust, iniquitous, oppressive and infamous laws* enacted by the Kansas Legislature, as it is called, ought to be repealed before we adjourn." . . . . . . What are these laws? One of them sends a man to hard labor for not less than two years for daring to discuss the question whether Slavery exists, or does not exist, in Kansas: not less than two years—it may be fifty; and if a man could live as old as Methuselah, it might be over nine hundred years. That act prohibits all freedom of discussion in Kansas on the great subject directly referred to the exclusive decision of the people in that Territory; strikes down the liberty of the press too; and is an act egregiously tyrannical as ever was attempted by any of the Stuarts, Tudors or Plantagenets of England, and this Senate persists in declaring that we are not to repeal that!

Sir, let us tender to the House of Representatives the repeal of that and all other objectionable and infamous laws that were passed by that Legislature. I include in this denunciation, without any hesitation, those acts which prescribe that a man shall not even practice law in the Territory unless he swears to support the Fugitive Slave Law; that he shall not vote at any election, or be a member of the Legislature, unless he swears to support the Fugitive Slave Law; that he shall not hold any office of honor or trust there, unless he swears to support the Fugitive Slave Law; and you may as well impose just such a test oath for any other and every other law. . . I will not go through the whole catalogue of the oppressive laws of this Territory. I have done that before today. There are others as bad as these to which I have now referred. . . . . I will not, on the other hand, ever degrade myself by standing for an instant by those *abominable* and *infamous* laws which I denounced here this morning. What I desire now is, that the Senate of the United States shall wash its hands of all participation in these iniquities by repealing those laws.

On Dec. 2nd, President Pierce sent his annual message to the two Houses of Congress. In referring to the late election, the President says:

It is impossible to misapprehend the great principles which, by their recent political action, the people of the United States have sanctioned and announced.

They have asserted the Constitutional equality of each and all of the States of the Union as States; they have affirmed the constitutional equality of each and all of the citizens of the United States as citizens, whatever their religion, wherever their birth, or their residence; they have maintained the inviolability of the constitutional rights of the different sections of the Union; and they have proclaimed their devoted and unalterable attachment to the Union and the Constitution, as objects of interest superior to all subjects of local or sectional controversy, as the safeguard of the rights of all as the spirit and true essence of the liberty, peace, and greatness of the Republic.

In doing this, they have, at the same time, emphatically condemned the idea of organizing in these United States mere geographical parties; of marshalling in hostile array towards each other the different parts of the country, North or South, East or West.

Schemes of this nature, fraught with incalculable mischief, and which the considerate sense of the people has rejected, could have had countenance in no part of the country, had they not been disguised by suggestions plausible in appearance, acting upon an excited state of the public mind, induced by causes temporary in their character, and it is to be hoped transient in their influence.

Perfect liberty of association for political objects and the widest scope of discussion are the received and ordinary conditions of government in our country. Our institutions, framed in the spirit of confidence in the intelligence and integrity of the people, do not forbid citizens, either individually or associated together, to attack by writing, speech, or any other methods short of physical force, the Constitution and the very existence of the Union. Under the shelter of this great liberty, and protected by the laws and usages of the government they assail, associations have been formed in some of the States, of individuals who, pretending to seek only to prevent the spread of the institution of Slavery into the present or future inchoate States of the Union, are really inflamed with desire to change the domestic institutions of existing States. To accomplish their objects, they dedicate themselves to the odious task of depreciating the Government organization which stands in their way, and of calumniating, with indiscriminating invective, not only the citizens of particular States, with whose laws they find fault, but all others of their fellow-citizens throughout the country, who do not participate with them in their assaults upon the Constitution, framed and adopted by our fathers, and claiming for the privileges it has secured, and the blessings it has conferred, the steady support and grateful reverence of their children. They seek an object which they well know to be a revolutionary one. They are perfectly aware that the change in the relative condition of the white and black races in the slaveholding States, which they would promote, is beyond their lawful authority; that to them it is a foreign object; that it cannot be effected by any peaceful instrumentality of theirs; that for them, and the States of which they are citizens, the only path to its accomplishment is through burning cities, and ravaged fields, and slaughtered populations, and all there is most terrible in foreign, complicated with civil and servile war; and that the first step in the attempt is the forcible disruption of a country embracing in its broad bosom a degree of liberty, and an amount of individual and public prosperity to which there is no parallel in history, and substituting in its place hostile governments, driven at once and inevitably into mutual devastation and fratricidal carnage, transforming the now peaceful and felicitous brotherhood into a vast permanent camp of armed men, like the rival monarchies of Europe and Asia. Well knowing that such, and such only, are the means and the consequences of their plans and purposes, they endeavor to prepare the people of the United States for civil war by doing everything in their power to deprive the Constitution and the laws of moral authority, and to undermine the fabric of the Union by appeals to passion and sectional prejudice, by indoctrinating its people with reciprocal hatred, and by educating them to stand face to face as enemies, rather than shoulder to shoulder as friends.

It is by the agency of such unwarrantable interference, foreign and domestic, that the minds of many, otherwise good citizens, have been so inflamed into the passionate condemnation of the domestic institutions of the Southern States, as at length to pass insensibly to almost equally passionate hostility toward their fellow-citizens of those States, and thus, finally, to fall into the temporary fellowship with the avowed and active enemies of the Constitution. Ardently attached to liberty in the abstract, they do not stop to consider practically how the objects they would attain can be accomplished, nor to reflect that, even if the evil were as great as they deem it, they have no remedy to apply, and that it can be only aggravated by their violence and unconstitutional action. A question which is one of the most difficult of all the problems of social institutions, political economy, and statesmanship, they treat with unreasonable intemperance of thought and language. Extremes beget extremes. Violent attack from the North finds its inevitable consequence in the growth of a spirit of angry defiance at the South. Thus, in the progress of events, we had reached the consummation which the voice of the people has now so pointedly rebuked, of the attempt of a portion of the States, by a sectional organization and movement, to usurp the control of the Government of the United States.

I confidently believe that the great body of those who inconsiderately took this fatal step are sincerely attached to the Constitution and the Union. They would, upon deliberation, shrink with unaffected horror from any conscious act of disunion or civil war. But they have entered into a path which leads nowhere, unless it be to civil war and disunion, and which has no other possible outlet. They have proceeded thus far in that direction in consequence of the successive stages of their progress having consisted of a series of secondary issues, each of which professed to be confined within constitutional and peaceful limits, but which attempted indirectly what few men were willing to do directly; that is, to act aggressively against the constitutional rights of nearly one-half of the thirty-one States.

In the long series of acts of indirect aggression, the first was the strenuous agitation, by citizens of the Northern States, in Congress and out of it, of the question of negro emancipation in the Southern States.

In reference to the repeal of the Missouri Compromise, and the legislative power of Congress over the Territories, the President says:

The enactment which established the restrictive geographical line, was acquiesced in, rather than approved, by the States of the Union. It stood on the statute-book, however, for a number of years; and the people of the respective States acquiesced in the reënactment of the principle as applied to the State of Texas; and it was proposed to acquiesce in its further application to the territory acquired by the United States from Mexico. But this proposition was successfully resisted by the representatives from the Northern States, who, regardless of the statute line, insisted upon applying restriction to the new territory generally, whether lying north or south of it, thereby repealing it as a legislative compromise, and, on the part of the North, persistently violating the compact, if compact there was.

Thereupon, this enactment ceased to have binding virtue in any sense, whether as respects the North or the South; and so in effect it was treated on the occasion of the admission of the State of California, and the organization of the Territories of New Mexico, Utah and Washington.

Such was the state of this question when the time arrived for the organization of the Territories of Kansas and Nebraska. In the progress of constitutional inquiry and reflection, it had now at length come to be seen clearly that Congress does not possess constitutional power to impose restrictions of this character upon any present or future State of the Union. In a long series of decisions, on the fullest argument, and after the most deliberate consideration, the Supreme Court of the United States had finally determined this point in every form under which the question could arise, whether as affecting public or private rights—in questions of the public domain, of religion, of navigation, and of servitude.

The several States of the Union are, by force of the Constitution, coequal in domestic legislative power. Congress cannot change a law of domestic relation in the State of Maine: no more can it in the State of Missouri. Any statute which proposes to do this is a mere nullity; it takes away no right, it confers none. If it remains on the statute-book unrepealed, it remains there only as a monument of error, and a beacon of warning to the legislator and the statesman. To repeal it will be only to remove imperfection from the statutes, without affecting, either in the sense of permission or of prohibition, the action of the States, or of their citizens.

Still, when the nominal restriction of this nature, already a dead letter in law, was in terms repealed by the last Congress, in a clause of the act organizing the Territories of Kansas and Nebraska, that repeal was made the occasion of a wide spread and dangerous agitation.

It was alleged that the original enactment being a compact of perpetual moral obligation, its repeal constituted an odious breach of faith.

On the motion to print the Message and accompanying documents, Mr. Hale, of N. H., said:

I look on the message of the President as a most unfortunate one. I have no desire to say anything which shall be construed into a want of courtesy, kindness, or respect for him. I mean all due courtesy, kindness and respect. His situation is certainly such as to appeal to the magnanimity rather than provoke the hostility of his opponents. If he had been content to submit to it, and go out, as it seemed to be the wish of his friends and foes that he should, without attempting to make such a charge as this against his political opponents, I should certainly have been content.

But, sir, this message of the President is an arraignment of a vast majority of the people of eleven States of this Union of want of fidelity to their constitutional obligations, and of hostility to the Union and Constitution of these States. I deny it totally. More than that ; the President of the United States, by virtue of the privileges conferred on him by the Constitution, charges upon the majority of the people of these States, in the exercise of their constitutional prerogative of voting for whom they please, the high offense of endeavoring to " usurp "—this is his very language—" the control of the Government of the United States." "Usurp," if lexicographers understand the meaning of the word, is " to seize by force without right." I have observed in the history of the past few months no attempt in any section of the country, last and least in that section which the President arraigns, to seize upon power in this Government except by the regular constitutional discharge of the people's obligations and duties as citizens going to the polls in the exercise of their elective franchise. Again, sir, I have not heard from a single citizen of those States an intimation, that if they should fail in the canvass upon which they had entered and in which they were striving to secure a majority in the councils of this Government, they were to do anything else but submit quietly and peaceably to the constitutionally expressed will of a majority.

Mr. Seward, of N. Y., said :

The President, I think, has departed from a customary course which was well established by his predecessors ; that was to confine the annual message of the Executive to legitimate matters of legislation which must necessarily occupy the attention of Congress, and leave partisan disputes, occurring among the people, to the consideration and reflection of the people themselves. This President of the United States was the first one, I think, to depart from that course in his Inaugural Address ; and, if I remember aright, he continued this departure in his first message and second message. He has been uncorrected, or rather unreformed in his erroneous course ; he goes through to the end in the same course. I am willing, for my own part, that he, like all the rest of us, shall have his speech—shall assign his reasons and his vindication for his policy. I do not ·question his right ; I do not dispute it. Whatever I have thought necessary to submit to any portion of my countrymen in regard to the canvass which is past, has been submitted in the right time, in the right place, and I trust, in the right spirit. I am willing to allow the President of the United States the same opportunity which you and I and all others have enjoyed.

Mr. Mason, of Va., said :

Mr. President: the constant and obstinate agitation of questions connected with the institution of Slavery, has brought, I am satisfied, the public mind in those States where the institution prevails, to the conviction that the preservation of that institution rests with themselves and with themselves only. Therefore, at this day, when it is the pleasure of Senators again to bring that institution under review upon this floor, in any connection whatever, as one of the Representatives of the South, I take no further interest in the discussion, or in the opinion which is entertained at the North in relation to it, than as it may confirm the hope that there is a public sentiment at the North yet remaining, which unites with the South in the desire to perpetuate the Union, and that, by the aid of that public sentiment at the North, the Union will be preserved. But further than that, as a statesman, and as one representing a Southern State, where that institution prevails m re largely than in any other, the public sentiment of the North is a matter indifferent to me, because I say again, we have attained the conviction that the safety of that institution will rest, must rest, and should rest, with the people of the States only where it prevails.

Mr. Wilson, of Mass., said :

The party to which reference has been made in this message—for I take it this assault of the President of the United States is upon the Republican party, and the people who supported that organization in the last election—stands before the country with its opinions clearly expressed and openly avowed. It has a right to claim from the President of the United States—it has a right to claim from honorable Senators here—it has a right to claim before the country that it shall stand upon its broad and open declarations of principle. How does it stand? It accepts the Declaration of Independence and the Constitution of the United States as its fundamental creed of doctrine. It claims that Congress has a right to legislate for the Territories of the United States, and to exclude Slavery from them. It avows its determination to exercise that power. It has a right to ask of the President, and the country, that it shall be judged by its open and avowed declarations, and shall not be misrepresented, as it has been misrepresented in this document by the President of the United States. The declaration is broadly made here, not only that these men are sectionalists—not only that they have gotten up a sectional warfare, but that they are maintaining doctrines hostile to the perpetuity of the Union. Now, sir, let me say here to-day, that I do not know a man in the Free States who supported John C. Fremont in the last presidential election, not one ●f the one million three hundred thousand intelligent freemen who supported that nomination, that ever avowed his intention to go for a dissolution of this Union ; but at all times, on all occasions, in public and in private, they have avowed their devotion to the Union, and their intention to maintain and defend it.

Let me say further, that the men in this country, who avow themselves to be disunionists, that squad, which, during the last thirty years, on all fit and unfit occasions, in moments of excitement and moments of calm, have avowed themselves disunionists, have, as a body, *en masse*, supported the Democratic party. The whole southern heavens have been darkened during the last four months by the black banners of disunion that have floated in the breeze.

Mr. Pugh, of Ohio, defended the President against the construction put on certain parts of the message by other Senators. He said :

My colleague (Mr. Wade) asserts that the President has employed libellous terms in speaking of a large number of our common constituents, who voted for Col. Fremont at the last election. If the charges were true in any sense, I should unite with my colleague in the condemnation which he has pronounced ; for although I would have deplored the election of Col. Fremont as the greatest calamity that could befall the American people, I feel bound to render my tribute of respect to those honest, patriotic, but as I think, misguided, citizens of Ohio, who voted for him. The paragraph upon which my colleague based this accusation, is the one which I now send to the secretary's desk. (Here the secretary read the part of the message quoted above, beginning, " Our institutions framed" and down to " rather than shoulder to shoulder as friends.") It is (continued Mr. Pugh) impossible that this paragraph should apply to the members of the Republican party, if, as now asserted, they do not aim at the abolition by Congress of Slavery within the States. It is directed against those who hold that doctrine. It refers to the men whom the Senator from Mass. (Mr. Wilson) and the Senator from Maine (Mr. Fessenden) themselves have denounced on the floor.

THE LECOMPTON CONSTITUTION.

On the 8th December, 1857, President Buchanan transmitted to Congress his first annual message. He devotes considerable space to the subject of Slavery, giving a history of the formation of the Lecompton Constitution for Kansas, and announcing the doctrine that the Constitution of its own force carries Slavery into all the Territories. Speaking of this subject, he says : " In emerging from the condition of Territorial dependence into that of a sovereign State, it was their duty, in my opinion, to make known their will by the votes of the majority, on the direct question, whether this important domestic institution should or should not *continue to exist :*" and that the slaves now in Kansas " were brought into the Territory under the Constitution of the United States."

The following is the part of the message referring to Kansas affairs :

It is unnecessary to state in detail the alarming condition of the Territory of Kansas at the time of my inauguration. The opposing parties then stood in hostile array against each other, and any accident might have relighted the flames of civil war. Besides, at this critical moment, Kansas was left without a governor by the resignation of Governor Geary.

On the 19th of February previous, the Territorial legislature had passed a law providing for the election of delegates on the third Monday of June, to a convention to meet on the first Monday in September, for the purpose of framing a constitution preparatory to admission into the Union. This law was in the main fair and just; and it is to be regretted that all the qualified electors had not registered themselves and voted under its provisions.

At the time of the election for delegates, an extensive organization existed in the Territory, whose avowed object it was, if need be, to put down the lawful government by force, and to establish a government of their own under the so-called Topeka Constitution. The persons attached to this revolutionary organization abstained from taking any part in the election.

The act of the Territorial legislature had omitted to provide for submitting to the people the constitution which might be framed by the Convention; and in the excited state of public feeling throughout Kansas, an apprehension extensively prevailed that a design existed to force upon them a constitution, in relation to Slavery, against their will. In this emergency it became my duty, as it was my unquestionable right, having in view the union of all good citizens in support of the Territorial laws, to express an opinion on the true construction of the provisions concerning Slavery contained in the organic act of Congress of the 30th May, 1854. Congress declared it to be "the true intent and meaning of this act not to legislate Slavery into any Territory or State, nor to exclude it therefrom, but to leave the people thereof perfectly free to form and regulate their domestic institutions in their own way." Under it Kansas, "when admitted as a State," was to "be received into the Union with or without Slavery as their constitution may prescribe at the time of their admission."

Did Congress mean by this language that the delegates elected to frame a constitution, should have authority finally to decide the question of Slavery, or did they intend, by leaving it to the people, that the people of Kansas themselves should decide this question by a direct vote? On this subject I confess I had never entertained a serious doubt, and, therefore, in my instructions to Governor Walker of the 28th March last, I merely said that when "a constitution shall be submitted to the people of the Territory, they must be protected in the exercise of their right of voting for or against that instrument, and the fair expression of the popular will must not be interrupted by fraud or violence."

In expressing this opinion it was far from my intention to interfere with the decision of the people of Kansas, either for or against Slavery. From this I have always carefully abstained. Intrusted with the duty of "taking care that the laws be faithfully executed," my only desire was that the people of Kansas should furnish to Congress the evidence required by the organic act, whether for or against Slavery; and in this manner smooth their passage into the Union. In emerging from the condition of Territorial dependence into that of a sovereign State, it was their duty, in my opinion, to make known their will by the votes of the majority, on the direct question, whether this important domestic institution should or *should not continue to exist.* Indeed this was the only possible mode in which their will could be authentically ascertained.

The election of delegates to a convention must necessarily take place in separate districts. From this cause it may readily happen, as has often been the case, that a majority of the people of a State or Territory are on one side of a question, whilst a majority of the representatives from the several districts into which it is divided may be upon the other side. This arises from the fact that in some districts delegates may be elected by small majorities, whilst in others those of different sentiments may receive majorities sufficiently great not only to overcome the votes given for the former, but to leave a large majority of the whole people in direct opposition to a majority of the delegates. Besides, our history proves that influences may be brought to bear on the representative sufficiently powerful to induce him to disregard the will of his constituents. The truth is, that no other authentic and satisfactory mode exists of ascertaining the will of a majority of the people of any State or Territory on an important and exciting question like that of Slavery in Kansas, except by leaving it

to a direct vote. How wise, then, was it for Congress to pass over all subordinate and intermediate agencies, and proceed directly to the source of all legitimate power under our institutions!

How vain would any other principle prove in practice! This may be illustrated by the case of Kansas. Should she be admitted into the Union with a constitution either maintaining or abolishing Slavery, against the sentiment of the people, this could have no other effect than to continue and to exasperate the existing agitation during the brief period required to make the constitution conform to the irresistible will of the majority.

The friends and supporters of the Nebraska and Kansas act, when struggling on a recent occasion to sustain its wise provisions before the great tribunal of the American people, never differed about its true meaning on this subject. Everywhere throughout the Union they publicly pledged their faith and their honor that they would cheerfully submit the question of Slavery to the decision of the *bona fide* people of Kansas, without any restriction or qualification whatever. All were cordially united upon the great doctrine of popular sovereignty, which is the vital principle of our free institutions. Had it, then, been insinuated from any quarter that it would be a sufficient compliance with the requisitions of the organic law for the members of a convention, thereafter to be elected, to withhold the question of slavery from the people, and to substitute their own will for that of a legally-ascertained majority of all their constituents, this would have been instantly rejected. Everywhere they remained true to the resolution adopted on a celebrated occasion recognizing "the right of the people of all the Territories—including Kansas and Nebraska, acting through the legally and fairly expressed will of a majority of actual residents, and whenever the number of their inhabitants justified it—to form a constitution with or without Slavery, and be admitted into the Union upon terms of perfect equality with the other States."

The Convention to frame a constitution for Kansas met on the first Monday of September last. They were called together by virtue of an act of the Territorial legislature, whose lawful existence had been recognized by Congress in different forms and by different enactments. A large proportion of the citizens of Kansas did not think proper to register their names and to vote at the election for delegates; but an opportunity to do this having been fairly afforded, their refusal to avail themselves of their right could in no manner affect the legality of the convention.

This Convention proceeded to frame a constitution for Kansas, and finally adjourned on the 7th day of November. But little difficulty occurred in the Convention, except on the subject of Slavery. The truth is, that the general provisions of our recent State constitutions are so similar, and, I may add, so excellent, that the difference between them is not essential. Under the earlier practice of the Government, no constitution framed by the convention of a Territory preparatory to its admission into the Union as a State had been submitted to the people. I trust, however, the example set by the last Congress, requiring that the constitution of Minnesota "should be subject to the approval and ratification of the people of the proposed State," may be followed on future occasions. I took it for granted that the Convention of Kansas would act in accordance with this example, founded as it is, on correct principles; and hence my instructions to Governor Walker, in favor of submitting the constitution to the people, were expressed in general and unqualified terms.

In the Kansas-Nebraska act, however, this requirement, as applicable to the whole constitution, had not been inserted, and the Convention were not bound by its terms to submit any other portion of the instrument to an election, except that which relates to the "domestic institution" of Slavery. This will be rendered clear by a simple reference to its language. It was "not to legislate Slavery into any Territory or State, nor to exclude it therefrom, but to leave the people thereof perfectly free to form and regulate their domestic institutions in their own way." According to the plain construction of the sentence, the words "domestic institutions" have a direct as they have an appropriate reference to Slavery. "Domestic institutions" are limited to the family. The relation between master and slave and a few others are "domestic institutions," and are entirely distinct from institutions of a political character. Besides, there was no question then before Congress, nor indeed has there since been any serious question before the people of Kansas or the country, except that which relates to the "domestic institution" of Slavery.

The Convention, after an angry and excited debate, finally determined, by a majority of only two, to submit the question of Slavery to the people, though at the last forty-three of the fifty delegates present affixed their signatures to the constitution.

A large majority of the Convention were in favor of establishing Slavery in Kansas. They accordingly inserted an article in the constitution for this purpose similar in form to those which had been adopted by other Territorial conventions. In the schedule, however, providing for the transition from a Territorial to a State government, the question has been fairly and explicitly referred to the people, whether they will have a constitution " with or without Slavery." It declares that, before the constitution adopted by the Convention " shall be sent to Congress for admission into the Union as a State," an election shall be held to decide this question, at which all the white male inhabitants of the Territory above the age of 21 are entitled to vote. They are to vote by ballot ; and "the ballots cast at said election shall be indorsed 'constitution with Slavery,' and 'constitution with no Slavery.'" If there be a majority in favor of the the "constitution with Slavery," then it is to be transmitted to Congress by the president of the Convention in its original form. If, on the contrary, there shall be a majority in favor of the "constitution with no Slavery," "then the article providing for Slavery shall be stricken from the constitution by the president of this Convention ;" and it is expressly declared that " no Slavery shall exist in the State of Kansas, except that the right of property in slaves now in the Territory shall in no manner be interfered with ;" and in that event it is made his duty to have the constitution thus ratified, transmitted to the Congress of the United States, for the admission of the State into the Union.

At this election, every citizen will have an opportunity of expressing his opinion by his vote "whether Kansas shall be received into the Union with or without Slavery," and thus this exciting question may be peacefully settled in the very mode required by the organic law. The election will be held under legitimate authority, and if any portion of the inhabitants shall refuse to vote, a fair opportunity to do so having been presented, this will be their own voluntary act, and they alone will be responsible for the consequences.

Whether Kansas shall be a free or a slave State, must eventually, under some authority, be decided by an election ; and the question can never be more clearly or distinctly presented to the people than it is at the present moment. Should this opportunity be rejected, she may be involved for years in domestic discord, and possibly in civil war, before she can again make up the issue now so fortunately tendered, and again reach the point she has already attained.

Kansas has for some years occupied too much of the public attention. It is high time this should be directed to far more important objects. When once admitted into the Union, whether with or without Slavery, the excitement beyond her own limits will speedily pass away, and she will then, for the first time, be left, as she ought to have been long since, to manage her own affairs in her own way. If her constitution on the subject of Slavery, or on any other subject, be displeasing to a majority of the people, no human power can prevent them from changing it within a brief period. Under these circumstances, it may well be questioned whether the peace and quiet of the whole country are not of greater importance than the mere temporary triumph of either of the political parties in Kansas.

Should the constitution without Slavery be adopted by the votes of the majority, the rights of property in slaves now in the Territory are reserved. The number of these is very small ; but if it were greater the provision would be equally just and reasonable. The slaves were brought into the Territory under the Constitution of the United States, and are now the property of their masters. This point has at length been finally decided by the highest judicial tribunal of the country—and this upon the plain principle that when a confederacy of sovereign States acquire a new territory at their joint expense, both equality and justice demand that the citizens of one and all of them thall have the right to take into it whatsoever is recognized as property by the common Constitution. To have summarily confiscated the property in slaves already in the Territory would have been an act of gross injustice, and contrary to the practice of the older States of the Union which have abolished Slavery.

MR. DOUGLAS ON LECOMPTON.

Mr. Douglas, who very early joined in the debate on the President's Message, at first said he dissented from the views of the President in regard to Kansas, but afterward endeavored to show that the President did not mean to " recommend" the Lecompton Constitution, but that he only

referred that document to the Congress of the United States—as the Constitution of the United States refers it—for us to decide upon it under our own responsibility. "It is proper," said Mr. D., " that he should have thus referred it to us as a matter for congressional action, and not as an administrative or executive measure, for the reason that the Constitution of the United States says, ' Congress may admit new States into the Union.' Hence we find the Kansas question before us now, not as an Administrative measure, not as an Executive measure, but as a measure coming before us for our free action, without any recommendation or interference, directly or indirectly, by the Administration now in possession of the Federal Government." . . . . .

Mr. President, I am not going to stop and inquire how far the Nebraska bill, which said the people should be left perfectly free to form their constitution for themselves, authorized the President, or the Cabinet, or Governor Walker, or any other Territorial officer, to interfere and tell the Convention of Kansas whether they should or should not submit the question to the people. I am not going to stop to inquire how far they were authorized to do that, it being my opinion that the spirit of the Nebraska bill required it to be done. It is sufficient for my purpose that the Administration of the Federal Government unanimously—that the administration of the Territorial government, in all its parts, unanimously—understood the Territorial law under which the Convention was assembled to mean that the constitution to be formed by that Convention should be submitted to the people for ratification or rejection, and, if not confirmed by a majority of the people, should be null and void, without coming to Congress for approval.

Not only did the National Government and the Territorial government so understand the law at the time, but, as I have already stated, the people of the Territory so understood it. As a further evidence on that point, a large number, if not a majority, of the delegates were instructed in the nominating conventions to submit the constitution to the people for ratification. I know that the delegates from Douglas County, eight in number, Mr. Calhoun, President of the Convention, being among them, were not only instructed thus to submit the question, but they signed and published, while candidates, a written pledge that they would submit it to the people for ratification. I know that men high in authority, and in the confidence of the Territorial and National Government, canvassed every part of Kansas during the election of delegates, and each one of them pledged himself to the people that no snap judgment was to be taken ; that the constitution was to be submitted to the people for acceptance or rejection : that it would be void unless that was done ; that the Administration would spurn and scorn it as a violation of the principles on which it came into power, and that a Democratic Congress would hurl it from their presence as an insult to the Democrats who stood pledged to see the people left free to form their domestic institutions for themselves.

Not only that, sir, but up to the time when the Convention assembled, on the 1st of September, so far as I can learn, it was understood everywhere that the constitution was to be submitted for ratification or rejection. They met, however, on the 1st of September, and adjourned until after the October election. I think that it was wise and prudent that they should thus have adjourned. They did not wish to bring any question into that election which would divide the Democratic party, and weaken our chances of success in the election. I was rejoiced when I saw that they did adjourn, so as not to show their hand on any question that would divide and distract the party until after the election. During that recess, while the Convention was adjourned, Governor Ransom, the Democratic candidate for Congress, running against the present Delegate from that Territory, was canvassing every part of Kansas, in favor of the doctrine of submitting the constitution to the people, declaring that the Democratic party were in favor of such submission, and that it was a slander of the Black Republicans to intimate the charge that the Democratic party did not intend to carry out that pledge in good faith. Thus, up to the time of the Convention, in October last, the pretense was kept up, the profession was openly made, and believed by me, and I thought believed by them, that the Convention intended to submit a constitution to the people, and not to attempt to put a government in operation without such submission. The election being over, the Democratic party being defeated by an overwhelming vote, the Opposition having triumphed, and got possession of both branches of the legislature, and having elected their Territorial

Delegate, the Convention assembled, and then proceeded to complete their work.

Now let us stop to inquire how they redeemed the pledge to submit the constitution to the people. They first go on to make a constitution. Then they make a schedule, in which they provide that the constitution, on the 21st of December—the present month—shall be submitted to all the *bona fide* inhabitants of the Territory on that day, for their free acceptance or rejection, in the following manner, to wit: Thus acknowledging that they were bound to submit it to the will of the people; conceding that they had no right to put it into operation without submitting it to the people; providing in the instrument that it should take effect from and after the date of its ratification, and not before; showing that the Constitution derives its vitality, in their estimation, not from the authority of the Convention, but from that vote of the people, to which it was to be submitted for their free acceptance or rejection. How is it to be submitted? It shall be submitted in this form: "Constitution with Slavery, or constitution with no Slavery?" All men must vote for the constitution, whether they like it or not, in order to be permitted to vote for or against Slavery. Thus a constitution made by a convention that had authority to assemble and petition for a redress of grievances, but not to establish a government—a constitution made under a pledge of honor that it should be submitted to the people before if took effect—a constitution which provides on its face, that it shall have no validity except what it derives from such submission—is submitted to the people at an election where all men are at liberty to come forward freely, without hindrance, and vote for it, but no man is permitted to record a vote against it!

That would be as fair an election as some of the enemies of Napoleon attributed to him when he was elected First Consul. He is said to have called out his troops and had them reviewed by his officers, with a speech, patriotic and fair in its professions, in which he said to them: "Now, my soldiers, you are to go to the election and vote freely, just as you please. If you vote for Napoleon, all is well; vote against him, and you are to be instantly shot!" That was a fair election. (Laughter.) This election is to be equally fair. All men in favor of the constitution may vote for it, all men against it shall not vote at all. Why not let them vote against it? I presume you have asked many a man this question. I have asked a very large number of the gentlemen who framed the constitution, quite a number of delegates, and a still larger number of persons who are their friends, and I have received the same answer from every one of them. I never received any other answer, and I presume we never shall get any other answer. What is that? They say, if they had allowed a negative vote, the constitution would have been voted down by an overwhelming majority; and hence the fellows shall not be allowed to vote at all. (Laughter.)

Mr. President, that may be true. It is no part of my purpose to deny the proposition that that constitution would have been voted down if submitted to the people. I believe it would have been voted down by a majority of four to one. I am informed by men well posted there —Democrats—that it would be voted down ten to one; some say by twenty to one.

But is it a good reason why you should declare it in force, without being submitted to the people, merely because it would have been voted down by five to one if you had submitted it? What does that fact prove? Does it not show undeniably that an overwhelming majority of the people of Kansas are unalterably opposed to that constitution? Will you force it on them against their will, simply because they would have voted it down if you had consulted them? If you will, are you going to force it upon them under the plea of leaving them perfectly free to form and regulate their domestic institutions in their own way? Is that the mode in which I am called upon to carry out the principle of self-government and popular sovereignty in the Territories—to force a constitution on the people against their will, in opposition to their protest, with a knowlege of the fact, and then to assign as a reason for my tyranny, that they would be so obstinate and so perverse as to vote down the constitution if I had given them an opportunity to be consulted about it?

Sir, I deny your right, or mine, to inquire of these people what their objections to that constitution are. They have a right to judge for themselves whether they like or dislike it. It is no answer to tell me that the constitution is a good one, and unobjectionable. It is not satisfactory to me to have the President say, in his message, that that constitution is an admirable one, like all the constitutions of the new States that have been recently framed. Whether good or bad, whether obnoxious or not, is none of my business, and none of yours.

It is their business, and not ours. I care not what they have in their constitution, so that it suits them and does not violate the Constitution of the United States and the fundamental principles of liberty upon which our institutions rest. I am not going to argue the question whether the banking system established in that constitution is wise or unwise. It says there shall be no monopolies, but there shall be one bank of issue in the State, with two branches. All I have to say on that point is, if they want a banking system, let them have it; if they do not want it, let them prohibit it. If they want a bank with two branches, be it so; if they want twenty, it is none of my business; and it matters not to me whether one of them shall be on the north side and the other on the south side of the Kaw River, or where they shall be.

While I have no right to expect to be consulted on that point, I do hold that the people of Kansas have the right to be consulted and to decide it, and you have no rightful authority to deprive them of that privilege. It is no justification, in my mind, to say that the provision for the eligibility for the officers of Governor and Lieut.-Governor requires twenty years' citizenship in the United States. If men think that no person should vote or hold office until he has been here twenty years, they have a right to think so; and if a majority of the people of Kansas think that no man of foreign birth should vote or hold office unless he has lived there twenty years, it is their right to say so, and I have no right to interfere with them; it is their business, not mine; but if I lived there I should not be willing to have that provision in the constitution without being heard upon the subject, and allowed to record my protest against it.

I have nothing to say about their system of taxation, in which they have gone back and resorted to the old exploded system which we tried in Illinois, but abandoned because we did not like it. If they wish to try it and get tired of it and abandon it, be it so; but if I were a citizen of Kansas I would profit by the experience of Illinois on that subject, and defeat it if I could. Yet I have no objection to their having it if they want it; it is their business, not mine.

So it is in regard to the free negroes. They provide that no free negro shall be permitted *to live* in Kansas. I suppose they have a right to say so if they choose; but if I lived there I should want to vote on the question. We, in Illinois, provide that no more shall come there. We say to the other States, "Take care of your own free negroes and we will take care of ours." But we do not say that the negroes now there shall not be permitted to live in Illinois; and I think the people of Kansas ought to have the right to say whether they will allow them to live there, and if they are not going to do so, how they are to dispose of them.

So you may go on with all the different clauses of the Constitution. They may be all right; they may be all wrong. That is a question on which my opinion is worth nothing. The opinion of the wise and patriotic Chief Magistrate of the United States is not worth anything as against that of the people of Kansas, for they have a right to judge for themselves; and neither President, nor Senates, nor Houses of Representatives, nor any other power outside of Kansas, has a right to judge for them. Hence it is no justification, in my mind, for the violation of the great principle of self-government, to say that the Constitution you are forcing on them is not particularly obnoxious, or is excellent in its provisions.

Perhaps, sir, the same thing might be said of the Topeka Constitution. I do not recollect its peculiar provisions. I know one thing: we Democrats, we Nebraska men, would not even look into it to see what its provisions were. Why? Because we said it was made by a political party, and not by the people; that it was made in defiance of the authority of Congress; that if it was as pure as the Bible, as holy as the Ten Commandments, yet we would not touch it until it was submitted to and ratified by the people of Kansas, in pursuance of the forms of law. Perhaps the Topeka Constitution, but for the mode of making it, would have been unexceptionable. I do not know; I do not care. You have no right to force an unexceptionable constitution on a people. It does not mitigate the evil, it does not diminish the insult, it does not ameliorate the wrong, that you are forcing a good thing upon them. I am not willing to be forced to do that which I would do if I were left free to judge and act for myself. Hence I assert that there is no justification to be made for this flagrant violation of popular rights in Kansas, on the plea that the constitution which they have made is not particularly obnoxious.

But, sir, the President of the United States is really and sincerely of the opinion that the Slavery clause has been fairly and impartially submitted to the free acceptance or rejection of the people of Kansas, and that, inasmuch as that was the exciting and paramount question, if they get the right to vote as they please on that subject, they ought to be satisfied; and possibly it might be better if we would accept it, and put an end to the question. Let me ask, sir, is the Slavery clause fairly submitted, so that the people can vote for or against it? Suppose I were a citizen of Kansas, and should go up to the polls and say, " I desire to vote to make Kansas a Slave State; here is my ballot." They reply to me, "Mr. Douglas, just vote for that constitution first, if you please." " Oh, no!" I answer, "I cannot vote for that constitution conscientiously—I am opposed to the clause by which you locate certain railroads in such a way as to sacrifice my county and my part of the State. I am opposed to that banking system. I am opposed to this Know-Nothing or American clause in the constitution about the qualifications for office. I cannot vote for it." Then they answer, "You shall not vote on making it a Slave State." I then say, "I want to make it a Free State." They reply, " Vote for that constitution first, and then you can vote to make it a Free State; otherwise you cannot." Thus they disqualify every Free-State man who will not first vote for the constitution; they disqualify every Slave-State man who will not first vote for the constitution. No matter whether or not the voters state that they cannot conscientiously vote for those provisions, they reply, " You cannot vote for or against Slavery here. Take the constitution as we have made it, take the Elective Franchise as we have established it, take the Banking System as we have dictated it, take the Railroad lines as we have located them, take the Judiciary System as we have formed it, take it all as we have fixed it to suit ourselves, and ask no questions, but vote for it, or you shall not vote either for a Slave or Free State." In other words, the legal effect of the schedule is this: all those who are in favor of this constitution may vote for or against Slavery, as they please; but all those who are against this constitution are disfranchised, and shall not vote at all. That is the mode in which the Slavery proposition is submitted. Every man opposed to the constitution is disfranchised on the Slavery clause. How many are they? They tell you there is a majority, for they say the constitution will be voted down instantly, by an overwhelming majority, if you allow a negative vote. This shows that a majority are against it. They disqualify and disfranchise every man who is against it, thus referring the Slavery clause to a minority of the people of Kansas, and leaving that minority free to vote for or against the Slavery clause as they choose.

Let me ask you if that is a fair mode of submitting the Slavery clause? Does that mode of submitting that particular clause leave the people perfectly free to vote for or against Slavery as they choose? Am I free to vote as I choose on the Slavery question, if you tell me I shall not vote on it until I vote for the Maine Liquor Law? Am I free to vote on the Slavery question, if you tell me I shall not vote either way until I vote for a Bank? Is it freedom of election to make your right to vote upon one question depend upon the mode in which you are going to vote on some other question which has no connection with it? Is that freedom of election? Is that the great fundamental principle of Self-Government, for which we combined and struggled, in this body and throughout the country, to establish as a rule of action in all time to come? . . . . . .

Let me ask you, why force this Constitution down the throats of the people of Kansas, in opposition to their wishes and in violation of our pledges? What great object is to be attained? *Cui bono?* What are you to gain by it? Will you sustain the party by violating its principles? Do you propose to keep the party united by forcing a division? Stand by the doctrine that leaves the people perfectly free to form and regulate their institutions for themselves in their own way, and your party will be united and irresistible in power. Abandon that great principle, and the party is not worth saving, and cannot be saved, after it shall be violated. I trust we are not to be rushed upon this question. Why shall it be done? Who is to be benefited? Is the South to be the gainer? Neither the North nor the South has the right to gain a sectional advantage by trickery or fraud.

But I am beseeched to wait till I hear from the election on the 21st of December. I am told that perhaps that will put it all right, and will solve the whole difficulty. How can it? Perhaps there may be a large vote. There may be a large vote returned. (Laughter.) But I deny that it is possible to have a fair vote on the Slavery Clause; and I say that it is not possible to have any vote on the Constitution. Why wait for the mockery of an election, when it is provided, unalterably, that the people cannot vote—when the majority are disfranchised?

But I am told on all sides, "Oh, just wait; the Pro-Slavery clause will be voted down." That does not obviate any of my objections; it does not diminish any of them. You have no more right to force a Free-State Constitution on Kansas than a Slave-State Constitution.

If Kansas wants a Slave-State Constitution, she has a right to it; if she wants a Free-State Constitution, she has a right to it. It is none of my business which way the Slavery clause is decided. *I care not whether it is voted down or voted up.* Do you suppose, after pledges of my honor, that I would go for that principle, and leave the people to vote as they choose, that I would now degrade myself by voting one way if the Slavery clause be voted down, and another way if it be voted up? I care not how that vote may stand. I take it for granted that it will be voted out. I think I have seen enough in the last three days to make it certain that it will be returned out, no matter how the vote may stand. (Laughter.)

Sir, I am opposed to that concern, because it looks to me like a system of trickery and jugglery to defeat the fair expression of the will of the people. There is no necessity for crowding this measure, so unfair, so unjust, as it is in all its aspects, upon us.

On the 2nd of Feb., 1858, the President transmitted to Congress the Lecompton Constitution, accompanied by a special Message strongly urging the admission of Kansas as a State under this constitution. (The following is a brief statement in regard to the origin of the Lecompton Constitution:)

The first Territorial Legislature passed an act in 1855 to take the sense of the people on the call of a Convention to form a State Constitution, at the election in Oct., 1856. Accordingly, an election was held at which about 2,500 votes were polled, the Free-State men not voting. At this election, a new legislature was elected, all Pro-Slavery, which met in Jan., 1857, and in conformity with the vote of 2,500 at the preceding October election, passed an act providing for the election of delegates on the 15th of June, to meet in convention in September following. Soon after this, Gov. Walker went to Kansas, and published an address to the people in which he assured them of his determination to use every means in his power to prevent all disorder and violence. He persuaded the Free-State men to go to the polls and vote. An objection which they urged was, that in 19 out of the 38 counties no registry had been made, and that in 15 out of the 19 no census had been taken, so that it was impossible for the people to vote in those counties. These facts are confirmed by Gov. Walker and Secretary Stanton.

The election for delegates to the Convention was held on the 15th of June. The Free-State men did not vote, for the reason just mentioned, and also (as they stated,) that they had no confidence in the officers who were to hold the election, and because the Constitution which might be formed, must, in the opinion of Gov. Walker, be submitted to a vote of all the people for ratification or rejection, whether they voted at this election or not. The entire vote for delegates was only about 2,200.

The delegates elected assembled in Convention at Lecompton, Sept. 5th, but soon adjourned over to October, to await the result of the Territorial Election on the first Monday of that month. At this Territorial Election, both parties nominated candidates. At the request of Gov. Walker, 2,000 U. S. troops were in the Territory, and they were stationed so as to protect the polls as much as possible. Over eleven thousand votes were po'led, after rejecting 2,800 as fraudulent and irregular, 1,600 of which were returned from the Oxford precinct, where, according to the census, there were but 43 voters, and twelve hundred from McGee County, where no poll was opened. The result of this election was, the Free-State party carried the legislature and the delegate to Congress.

The Convention reassembled in October, according to adjournment, and formed the Constitution now so famous as the Lecompton Constitution. When it became known that the Convention had refused to submit the entire constitution to a vote of the people for ratification or rejection, and had submitted only a proposition in regard to Slavery, and that in a form and under a test oath which would prevent the Free-State people from voting, there was great excitement in the Territory, threatening bloodshed. Under these circumstances, Acting Gov. Stanton called (Gov. Walker had resigned) an extra session of the Territorial Legislature. The legislature assembled Dec. 17th, and passed an act to submit the Lecompton Constitution fairly to a vote of the people on the 4th of January next, following, the time fixed by the Lecompton convention for the election of State officers under that constitution.

On the 21st of Dec., the vote was taken in the manner prescribed by the Convention, and resulted as follows :

"For the constitution with Slavery " 6,266
" For the constitution without Slavery " . . . 567

Total vote 6,793

Jan. 4th, 1858, in accordance with the act of the Territorial Legislature, the people voted as follows :

For the Lecompton Constitution with Slavery . 138
" " " without " . 24
Against the Lecompton Constitution 10,226

Being over ten thousand majority against the Lecompton Constitution.

PRESIDENT BUCHANAN'S LECOMPTON MESSAGE.

The following is the President's special Message, of Feb. 2nd, 1858.

I have received from J. Calhoun, Esq., President of the late Constitutional Convention of Kansas, a copy duly certified by himself, of the Constitution framed by that body, with the expression of the hope that I would submit the same to the consideration of Congress " with the view of the admission of Kansas into the Union as an independent State." In compliance with this request, I herewith transmit to Congress for their action the Constitution of Kansas, with the ordinance respecting the public lands, as well as the letter of Mr. Calhoun, dated at Lecompton, on the 14th ult., by which they were accompanied. Having received but a single copy of the Constitution and ordinance, I send this to the Senate.

A great delusion seems to pervade the public mind in relation to the condition of parties in Kansas. This arises from the difficulty of inducing the American people to realize the fact that any portion of them should be in a state of rebellion against the Government under which they live. When we speak of the affairs of Kansas, we are apt to refer merely to the existence of two violent political parties in that Territory, divided on the question of Slavery, just as we speak of such parties in the States. This presents no adequate idea of the true state of the case. The dividing line there is not between two political parties, both acknowledging the lawful existence of the Government, but between those who are loyal to this Government and those who have endeavored to destroy its existence by force and by usurpation—between those who sustain, and those who have done all in their power to overthrow, the Territorial Government established by Congress. This Government they would long since have subverted had it not been protected from their assaults by the troops of the United States. Such has been the condition of affairs since my inauguration. Ever since that period, a large portion of the people of Kansas have been in a state of rebellion against the Government, with a military leader at their head, of most turbulent and dangerous character. They have never acknowledged, but have constantly renounced and defied, the Government

to which they owe allegiance, and have been all the time in a state of resistance against its authority. They have all the time been endeavoring to subvert it and to establish a revolutionary Government, under the so-called Topeka Constitution, in its stead. Even at this very moment, the Topeka Legislature are in session. Whoever has read the correspondence of Gov. Walker with the State Department, recently communicated to the Senate, will be convinced that this picture is not overdrawn. He always protested against the withdrawal of any portion of the military force of the United States from the Territory, deeming its presence absolutely necessary for the preservation of the regular Government and the execution of the laws. In his very first dispatch to the Secretary of State, dated June 2, 1857, he says :

"The most alarming movement, however, proceeds from the assembling, on the 9th of June, of the so-called Topeka Legislature, with a view to the enactment of an entire code of laws. Of course, it will be my endeavor to prevent such a result, as it would lead to inevitable and disastrous collision, and in fact renew the civil war in Kansas."

This was with difficulty prevented by the efforts of Governor Walker ; but soon thereafter, on the 14th of July, we find him requesting General Harney to furnish him a regiment of dragoons to proceed to the city of Lawrence, and this for the reason that he had received authentic intelligence, verified by his own actual observation, that a dangerous rebellion had occurred, involving an open defiance of the laws, and the establishment of an insurgent government in that city. In the Governor's dispatch of July 15, he informs the Secretary of State that

"This movement at Lawrence was the beginning of a plan, originating in that city, to organize insurrection throughout the Territory, and especially in all towns, cities and counties where the Republican party have a majority. Lawrence is the hotbed of all the Abolition movements in this Territory. It is the town established by the Abolition Societies of the East, and, while there are respectable people there, it is filled by a considerable number of mercenaries, who are paid by Abolition Societies to perpetuate and diffuse agitation throughout Kansas, and prevent a peaceful settlement of this question. Having failed in inducing their own so-called Topeka State Legislature to organize this insurrection, Lawrence has commenced it herself, and, if not arrested, the rebellion will extend throughout the Territory."

And again :

" In order to send this communication immediately by mail, I must close, assuring you that the spirit of rebellion pervades the great mass of the Republican party of this Territory, instigated, as I entertain no doubt they are, by Eastern Societies, having in view results most disastrous to the Government and the Union ; and that the continued presence of Gen. Harney is indispensable, as was originally stipulated by me, with a large body of dragoons and several batteries."

On the 20th of July, 1857, Gen. Lane, under the authority of the Topeka Convention, undertook, as Gen. Walker informs us,

"To organize the whole Free-State party into volunteers, and to take the names of all who refuse enrolment. The professed object was to protect the polls at the elections, in August, of a new insurgent Topeka State Legislature. The object in taking the names of all who refuse enrollment is to terrify the Free-State Conservatives into submission. This is proved by the recent atrocities committed on such men by the Topekaites. The speedy location of large bodies of regular troops here with two batteries is necessary. The Lawrence insurgents await the developments of this new military organization."

In the Governor's dispatch of July 27, he says that

" Gen. Lane and his staff everywhere deny the authority of the Territorial laws, and counsel a total disregard of these enactments."

Without making further quotations of a similar character from other dispatches of Governor Walker, it appears, by reference to Secretary Stanton's communication to Gen. Cass on the 9th of December last, that

" The important step of calling the legislature together was taken after I (he) had become satisfied that the election ordered by the Convention on the 21st of December could not be conducted without collision and bloodshed." .

So intense was the disloyal feeling among the enemies of the Government established by Congress, that an election which afforded them opportunities, if in the majority, of making Kansas a Free State according to their own expressed desire, could not be conducted without collision and bloodshed. The truth is that, up to the present moment, the enemies of the existing government still adhere to their Topeka revolutionary constitution and government. The very first paragraph of the message of Gov. Robinson, dated the 7th of December, to the Topeka Legislature, now assembled at Lawrence, contains an open defiance of the laws and Constitution of the United States. The Governor says :

" The Convention which framed the Topeka Constitution originated with the people of Kansas Territory. They have adopted and ratified the same twice by a direct vote, also indirectly through two elections for State officers and members of the State Legislature ; yet it has pleased the Administration to regard the whole proceeding as revolutionary."

This Topeka Government, adhered to with such treasonable pertinacity, is a government in direct opposition to the existing government prescribed and recognized by Congress.

It is usurpation of the same character as it would be for a portion of the people of any State to undertake to establish a separate government within its limits for the purpose of redressing any grievance, real or imaginary, of which they might complain against the legitimate State Government. Such a principle, if carried into execution, would destroy all lawful authority and produce universal anarchy. From this statement of facts, the reason becomes palpable why the enemies of the government authorized by Congress have refused to vote for the delegates to the Kansas Constitutional Convention, and also, afterward, on the question of Slavery submitted by it to the people. It is because they have ever refused to sanction or recognize any other Constitution than that framed at Topeka. Had the whole Lecompton Constitution been submitted to the people, the adherents of this organization would doubtless have voted against it, because, if successful, they would thus have removed the obstacles out of the way of their own revolutionary Constitution ; they would have done this, not upon the consideration of the merits of the whole or part of the Lecompton Constitution, but simply because they have ever resisted the authority of the government authorized by Congress from which it emanated. Such being the unfortunate condition of affairs in the Territory, what was the right as well as the duty of the law-abiding people? Were they silently and patiently to submit to the Topeka usurpation, or to adopt the necessary measure to establish a Constitution under the authority of the organic law of Congress ? That this law recognized the right of the people of the Territory, without an enabling act of Congress, to form a State Constitution, is too clear for argument. For Congress "to leave the people of the Territory perfectly free" in framing their Constitution " to form and regulate their domestic institutions in their own way, subject only to the Constitution of the United States," and then to say that they shall not be permitted to proceed and frame the Constitution in their own way, without express authority from Congress, appears to be almost a contradiction in terms. It would be much more plausible to contend that Congress had no power to pass such an enabling act, than to argue that the people of a Territory might be kept out of the Union for an indefinite period, and until it might please Congress to permit them to exercise the right of self-government. This would be to adopt, not their own way, but the way which Congress might prescribe. It is impossible that any people could have proceeded with more regularity in the formation of a Constitution than the people of Kansas have done. It was necessary, first, to ascertain whether it was the desire of the people to be relieved from their Territorial dependence and establish a State Government. For this purpose, the Territorial Legislature, in 1855, passed a law for taking the sense of the people of the Territory upon the expediency of calling a Convention to form a State Constitution at the general election to be held in October, 1856. The "sense of the people" was accordingly taken, and they decided in favor of a Convention.

It is true that at this election the enemies of the Territorial Government did not vote, because they were then engaged at Topeka, without the slightest pretext of lawful authority, in framing a Constitution of their own for subverting the Territorial Government. In pursuance of this decision of the people in favor of a Convention, the Territorial Legislature, on the 27th of February, 1857, passed an act for the election of delegates on the third Monday of June, 1857, to frame a State Constitution. This law is as fair in its provisions as any that ever passed a legislative body for a similar purpose. The right of suffrage at this election is clearly and justly defined. Every bona fide citizen of the United States, above the age of twenty-one, and who had resided therein for three months previous to that date, was entitled to a vote. In order to avoid all interference from neighboring States and Territories with the freedom and fairness of the election, a provision was made for the registry of qualified voters, and in pursuance thereof, nine thousand two hundred and fifty-one voters were registered. Gov. Walker did his whole duty in urging all qualified citizens of Kansas to vote at this election. In his Inaugural Address on the 27th of May, he informed them that—

" Under our practice, the preliminary act of framing a State Constitution is uniformly performed through the instrumentality of a Convention of delegates chosen by the people themselves. That Convention is now about to be elected by you, under the call of the Territorial Legislature created, and still recognized, by the authority of Congress and clothed by it, in the comprehensive language of the organic law, with full power to make such an enactment. The Territorial Legislature, then, in assembling this Convention, were fully sustained by the act of Congress, and the authority of the Convention is distinctly recognized in my instructions from the President of the United States."

The Governor also clearly and distinctly warns them what would be the consequences if they did not participate in the election. The people of Kansas, then, he says,

" Are invited by the highest authority known to the Constitution to participate freely and fairly in the election of delegates to frame a Constitution and State Government. The law has performed its entire appropriate function, when it extends to the people the right of suffrage ; but it cannot compel the performance of that duty. Throughout the whole Union, however, and wherever free government prevails, those who abstain from the exercise of the right of suffrage authorize those who do vote to act for them in that contingency, and absentees are as much bound, under the law and Constitution, where there is no fraud or violence, by the act of the majority of those who do vote, as if all had participated in the election. Otherwise, as voting must be voluntary, self-government would be impracticable, and monarchy or despotism would remain as the only alternative."

It may also be observed that at this period any hope, if such had existed, that the Topeka Constitution would ever be recognized by Congress must have been abandoned. Congress had adjourned on the third of March previous, having recognized the legal existence of the Territorial Legislature in a variety of forms, which I need not enumerate. Indeed, the Delegate elected to the House of Representatives under a Territorial law had been admitted to a seat and had just completed his term of service the day previous to my inauguration. This was the propitious moment for settling all the difficulties of Kansas. This was the time for abandoning the revolutionary Topeka organization, and for the enemies of the existing government to conform to the laws and unite with its friends in framing a State Constitution. But this they refused to do, and the consequences of their refusal to submit to the lawful authority, and vote at the election of delegates, may yet prove to be of the most deplorable character. Would that the respect for the laws of the land, which so eminently distinguished the men of the past generation, could be revived ! It is a disregard and violation of law which has for years kept the Territory of Kansas in a state of almost open rebellion against its Government—it is the same spirit which has produced actual rebellion in Utah. Our only safety consists in obedience and conformity to the law. Should a general spirit against its enforcement prevail, this will prove fatal to us as a nation.

We acknowledge no master but law, and should we cut loose from its restraints and every one do what seemeth good in his own eyes, our case would indeed be hopeless. The enemies of the Territorial Government determined still to resist the authority of Congress. They refused to vote for delegates to the Convention, not because, from circumstances which I need not detail, there was an omission to register the comparatively few voters who were inhabitants of certain counties in Kansas in the early spring of 1857, but because they had determined, at all hazards, to adhere to their revolutionary organization, and defeat the establishment of any other constitution than that which they had framed at Topeka. The election was therefore suffered to pass by default, but of this result the qualified electors who refused to vote can never justly complain.

From this review, it is manifest that the Lecompton Convention, according to every principle of constitutional law, was legally constituted and invested with power to frame a Constitution. The sacred principle of Popular Sovereignty has been invoked in favor of the enemies of Law and Order in Kansas ; but in what manner is Popular Sovereignty to be exercised in this country if not through the instrumentality of established law ? In certain small republics of ancient times, the people did assemble in primary meeting, passed laws and directed public affairs. In our country, this is manifestly impossible. Popular Sovereignty can be exercised here only through the ballotbox ; and if the people will refuse to exercise it in this manner, as they have done in Kansas at the election of Delegates, it is not for them to complain that their rights have been violated.

The Kansas Convention, thus lawfully constituted, proceeded to frame a Constitution, and, having completed their work, finally adjourned on the 7th of November last. They did not think proper to submit the whole of this Constitution to a popular vote, but they did submit the question whether Kansas should be a Free or Slave State to the people. This was the question which had convulsed the Union and shaken it to the very center. This was the question which had lighted the flames of civil war in Kansas and had produced dangerous sectional parties throughout the confederacy. It was of a character so paramount in respect to the condition of Kansas, as to rivet the anxious attention of the people of the whole country upon it and it alone—no person thought of any other question. For my own part, when I instructed Governor Walker in general terms in favor of submitting the constitution to the people, I had no object in view except the all-absorbing question of Slavery. In what manner the people of Kansas might regulate their other concerns, was not the subject which attracted my attention. In fact, the general provisions of our recent State constitutions, after an experience of eighty years, are so similar and excellent that it would be difficult to go far wrong at the present day in framing a new constitution. I then believed, and still believe, that, under the organic act, the Kansas Convention were bound to submit this all-important question of Slavery to the people. It was never, however, my opinion that, independently of this act, they would have been bound to submit any portion of the constitution to a popular vote in order to give it validity. Had I entertained such an opinion, this would have been in opposition to many precedents in our history, commencing in the very best age of our Republic. It would have been in opposition to the principle which pervades our institutions, and which is every day carried into practice, that the people have a right to delegate to the representatives chosen by themselves their sovereign power to frame constitutions, enact laws, and perform many other important acts, without requiring that these should be subjected to their subsequent approbation. It would be a most inconvenient limitation of their own power, imposed by the people upon themselves, to exclude them from exercising their sovereignty in any lawful manner which they think proper.

It is true that the people of Kansas might, if they had pleased, have required the Convention to submit the constitution to a popular vote, but this they have not done.

The only remedy, therefore, in this case is that which exists in all other similar cases. If the delegates who framed the Kansas Constitution have in any manner violated the will of their constituents, the people always possess the power to change their constitution or laws according to their own pleasure. The question of Slavery was submitted to an election of the people on the 21st of December last, in obedience to the mandate of the Convention. Here, again, a fair opportunity was presented to the adherents of the Topeka Constitution, if they were the majority, to decide this exciting question " in their own way," and thus restore peace to the distracted Territory ; but they again refused to exercise the right of Popular Sovereignty, and again suffered the election to pass by default. I heartily rejoice that a wiser and better spirit prevailed among a large majority of these people on the first Monday in January, and that they did on that day vote under the Lecompton Constitution for a Governor and other State officers, a member of Congress, and for members of the Legislature. This election was warmly contested by the parties, and a larger vote polled than at any previous election in the Territory. We may now reasonably hope that the revolutionary Topeka organization will be speedily and finally abandoned, and this will go far toward a final settlement of the unhappy differences in Kansas. If frauds have been committed at this election by one or both parties, the legislature and people of Kansas, under their constitution, will know how to redress themselves and punish these detestable but too common crimes without outside interference.

The people of Kansas have, then, " in their own way," and in strict accordance with the organic act, framed a Constitution and State Government, have submitted the all-important question of Slavery to the people, and have elected a Governor, a member to represent them in Congress, members of the State Legislature and other State officers ; and they now ask admission into the Union under this constitution, which is republican in its form. It is for Congress to decide whether they will admit or reject the State which has thus been created.

For my own part, I am decidedly in favor of its admission, and thus terminating the Kansas question. This will carry out the great principle of Non-Intervention recognized and sanctioned by the organic act, which declares in express language in favor of the non-intervention of Congress with Slavery in the States and Territories, leaving the people " perfectly free to form and regulate their domestic institutions in their own way, subject only to the Constitution of the United States." In this manner, by localizing the question of Slavery and confining it to the people who it immediately concerned, every patriot anxiously expected that this question would

be banished from the halls of Congress, where it has always exerted a baneful influence throughout the whole country.

It is proper that I should briefly refer to the election held under the act of the Territorial Legislature on the first Monday of January last on the Lecompton Constitution. This election was held after the Territory had been prepared for admission into the Union as a Sovereign State, and when no authority existed in the Territorial Legislature which could possibly destroy its existence or change its character. The election, which was peaceably conducted under my instructions, involved strange inconsistencies. A large majority of the persons who voted against the Lecompton Constitution were at the same time and place recognizing its valid existence in the most solid and authentic manner by voting under its provisions. I have yet received no official information of the result of this election.

As a question of expediency, after right has been maintained, it may be wise to reflect upon the benefits to Kansas and the whole country that will result from its immediate admission into the Union, as well as the disasters that may follow its rejection. Domestic peace will be the happy consequence of the admission, and that fine Territory, which has hitherto been torn by dissensions, will rapidly increase in population and wealth, and speedily realize the blessings and comforts which follow in the train of agricultural and mechanical industry. The people, then, will be sovereign, and can regulate their affairs in their own way. If the majority of them desire to abolish domestic Slavery within the State, there is no other possible mode by which it can be effected so speedily as by prompt admission. The will of the majority is supreme and irresistible, when expressed in an orderly and lawful manner. It can make and unmake constitutions at pleasure. It would be absurd to say that they can impose fetters upon their own power which they cannot afterward remove. If they could do this, they might tie their own hands just as well for a hundred as for ten years. These are the fundamental principles of American freedom, and are recognized, I believe, in some form or other by every State constitution ; and if Congress, in the act of admission, should think proper to recognize them, I can perceive no objection.

This has been done emphatically in the constitution of Kansas. It declares in its bill of rights that " All political power is inherent in the people," and all free governments are founded on their authority and instituted for their benefit, and therefore have at all times an inalienable and indefeasible right to alter, reform and abolish their form of government, in such manner as they may think proper. The great State of New-York is at this moment governed under a constitution framed and established in direct opposition to a mode prescribed by the previous constitution. If, therefore, a provision changing the constitution of Kansas after the year 1864, could by possibility be construed into a prohibition to make such change previous to that period, this prohibition would be wholly unavailing. The legislature already elected may, at its very first session, submit the question to a vote of the people, whether they will or not have a convention, to amend their constitution, and adopt all necessary means for giving effect to the popular will. It has been solemnly adjudged, by the highest judicial tribunal known to our laws, that Slavery exists in Kansas by virtue of the Constitution of the United States. Kansas is therefore at this moment as much a Slave State as Georgia or South Carolina. Without this, the equality of the Sovereign States composing the Union would be violated, and the use and enjoyment of a Territory acquired by the common treasure of all the States, would be closed against the people and property of nearly half the members of the Confederacy. Slavery can, therefore, never be prohibited in Kansas, except through the means of a constitutional provision ; and in no other manner can this be obtained so promptly, if the majority of the people desire it, as by admitting her into the Union under her present constitution. On the other hand, should Congress reject the constitution, under the idea of affording the disaffected in Kansas a third opportunity to prohibit Slavery in the State, which they might have done twice before if in the majority, no man can foretell the consequences. If Congress, for the sake of those men who refused to vote for delegates to the convention, when they might have excluded Slavery from the constitution, and who afterward refused to vote on the 21st of December, when they might, as they claim, have stricken Slavery from the constitution, should now reject the State because Slavery remains in the constitution, it is manifest that the agitation upon this dangerous subject will be renewed in a more alarming form than it has ever yet assumed. Every patriot in the country had indulged the hope that the Kansas-Nebraska Act would have put a final end to the Slavery agitation, at least in Congress, which had for more than twenty years convulsed the country and endangered the Union. This act involved great and fundamental principles, and, if fairly carried into effect, will settle the question. Should agitation be again revived—should the people of sister States be again estranged from each other with more than their former bitterness—this will arise from a cause, so far as the interests of Kansas are concerned, more trifling and insignificant than has ever stirred the elements of a great people into commotion. To the people of Kansas, the only practical difference between admission or rejection, depends simply upon the fact whether they can themselves more speedily change their present Constitution if it does not accord with the will of the majority, or frame a second Constitution to be submitted to Congress hereafter.

Even if this were a question of mere expediency and not of right, a small difference of time one way or the other, is not of the least importance, when contrasted with the evils which must necessarily result to the whole country from the revival of the Slavery agitation.

In considering this question, it should never be forgotten that in proportion, to its insignificance, let the decision be what it may, so far as it may affect a few thousand inhabitants of Kansas, who have from the beginning resisted the Constitution and the laws, for this very reason the rejection of the Constitution will be so much the more keenly felt by the people of fourteen States of the Union where Slavery is recognized under the Constitution of the United States.

Again the speedy admission of Kansas into the Union will restore peace and quiet to the whole country. Already the affairs of this Territory have engrossed an undue proportion of public attention. They have sadly affected the friendly relations of the people of the States with each other and alarmed the fears of patriots for the safety of the Union. Kansas once admitted into the Union, the excitement becomes localized and would soon die away for want of outside aliment, and then every difficulty could be settled by the ballot-box. Besides, and no trifling consideration, I shall then be enabled to withdraw the troops from Kansas, and employ them on a service where they are much needed. They have been kept there on the earnest importunity of Governor Walker, to maintain the existence of the Territorial Government, and secure the execution of the laws. He considered at least two thousand regular troops, under the command of General Harney, were necessary for this purpose. Acting upon his reliable information, I have been obliged in some degree, to interfere with the expedition to Utah in order to keep down the rebellion in Kansas. This has involved very heavy expenses to the Government. Kansas once admitted, it is believed there will no longer be occasion there for the troops.

I have thus performed my duty on this important question under a deep sense of my responsibility to God and to the country. My public life will terminate in a brief period, and I have no other object of earthly ambition than to leave my country in a peaceful and prosperous condition, and to live in the affections and respect of my countrymen. The dark and ominous clouds now impending over the Union I conscientiously believe will be dissipated with honor to every portion of it by the admission of Kansas during the present session of Congress; whereas, if she should be rejected, I greatly fear these clouds will become darker and more ominous than any which have ever yet threatened the Constitution and the Union. (Signed) JAMES BUCHANAN.

The Lecompton Constitution contains a provision on the subject of Slavery, as follows:

SLAVERY.

§ 1. The right of property is before and higher than any constitutional sanction, and the right of the owner of a slave to such a slave and its increase is the same, and is inviolable, as the right of the owner of any property whatever.

§ 2. The Legislature shall have no power to pass laws for the emancipation of slaves without the consent of their owners, or without paying their owners, previous to emancipation, a full equivalent in money for the slaves so emancipated. They shall have no power to prevent emigrants to the State from bringing with them such persons as are deemed slaves by the laws of any one of the United States or Territories so long as any persons of the same age or description shall be continued slaves by the laws of this State; *provided*, that such person or slave be the *bona fide* property of such emigrant; and *provided, also*, that laws may be passed to prohibit the introduction of slaves into this State who have committed high crimes in other States or Territories.

They shall have power to permit the owners of slaves to emancipate them, saving the rights of creditors, and preventing them from becoming a public charge. They shall have power to oblige the owners of slaves to treat them with humanity—to provide for their necessary food and clothing—to abstain from all injuries to them, extending to life or limb—and, in case of neglect or refusal to comply with the direction of such laws, to have such slave or slaves sold for the benefit of the owner or owners.

§ 3. In the prosecution of slaves for crimes of higher grade than petit larceny, the Legislature shall have no power to deprive them of an impartial trial by a petit jury.

§ 4. Any person who shall dismember or deprive a slave of life shall suffer such punishment as would be inflicted in case the like offense had been committed on a free white person, and on the like proof, except in case of insurrection of such slave.

This provision, and this provision alone, it was finally determined by a close vote to submit to the registered electors. For this purpose, by the terms of a schedule annexed to the Constitution, an election was to be held on the 21st of December. The ballots cast were to be indorsed either "Constitution with Slavery," or "Constitution with No Slavery." Thus to have the privilege of voting No Slavery, it was still made necessary to vote for the Constitution, beside which, all persons offering to vote must, if challenged, "take an oath to support the Constitution if adopted."·

If the number of votes "for the Constitution without Slavery" should be a majority, then the schedule provides, that "The rights of property in slaves now in the Territory, shall in no manner be interfered with." Making it impossible to abolish Slavery.

This schedule, as if with a direct view of superseding the Territorial Legislature and Congressional delegate elect, further provided that the Constitution shall be in force "after its ratification by the people" (without waiting for the approval of Congress) a State election to be held on the first Monday in January, 1858, for the choice of a Governor, Lieutenant-Governor, Secretary of State, Auditor, State Treasurer, and members of the Legislature, and also a member of Congress. It also provided (as if to deprive the Territorial Legislature of all power of acting) that all laws in force not repugnant to the Constitution shall continue until altered, amended or repealed by a Legislature assembled under the provisions of this Constitution; and that all officers, civil or military, under the authority of the Territory of Kansas, shall continue to hold and exercise their respective offices until superseded by the authority of the State: the first meeting of the State Legislature to take place upon the issue of a proclamation by the President of the Convention, upon the receipt of official information that Congress has admitted Kansas into the Union. A provision is also inserted intended to prevent any amendment previous to the year 1864, and then only upon the concurrence of two-thirds of the members of both houses, and "a majority of all the citizens of the State."

LECOMPTON AND ENGLISH BILLS.

The following record of the action of Congress on the admission of Kansas under the Lecompton Constitution, will be interesting for future reference.

The original bill, as it passed the Senate under the lead of Senator Green (March 23, 1858), was as follows:

THE LECOMPTON BILL.

A Bill for the Admission of the State of Kansas into the Union, presented in the Senate by Mr. Green, of Missouri, from the Committee on Territories, February 17, 1858.

Whereas, The people of the Territory of Kansas did, by a Convention of Delegates called and assembled at Lecompton, September 4, 1857, form for themselves a Constitution and State Government, which said Convention having asked the admission of the Territory into the Union as a State on an equal footing with the original States,

Be it enacted by the Senate and House of Representatives of the United States of America in Congress assembled, That the State of Kansas shall be, and is hereby declared to be, one of the United States of America, and admitted into the Union on an equal footing with the original States, in all respects whatever; and the said State shall consist of all the territory included within the following boundaries, to wit: Beginning at a point on the western boundary of the State of Missouri where the thirty-seventh parallel of latitude crosses the same; thence west on said parallel to the eastern boundary of New Mexico; thence north on said boundary to latitude thirty-eight; thence following said boundary westward to the eastern boundary of the Territory of Utah, on the summit of the Rocky Mountains; thence northward on said summit to the fortieth parallel of latitude; thence east on said parallel to the western boundary of the State of Missouri; thence south with the westward boundary of said State, to the place of beginning: . . .

§ 2. *And be it further enacted,* That the State of Kansas is admitted into the Union upon the express condition that said State shall never interfere with the primary disposal of the public lands, or with any regulations which Congress may find necessary for securing the title in said lands to the bona fide purchasers and grantees thereof, or impose or levy any tax, assessment, or imposition of any description whatsoever upon them, or other property of the United States, within the limits of said State; and that nothing in this act shall be construed to abridge or infringe any right of the people asserted in the Constitution of Kansas, at all times, to alter, reform or abolish their form of government in such manner as they may think proper, Congress hereby disclaiming any authority to intervene or declare the construction of the Constitution of any State, except to see that it is republican in form and not in conflict with the Constitution of the United States; and nothing in this act shall be construed as an assent by Congress to all or to any of the propositions or claims contained in the ordinance annexed to the Constitution of the people of Kansas, nor to deprive the said State of Kansas of the same grants which were contained in said act of Congress, entitled, "An act to authorize the people of the Territory of Minnesota to form a Constitution and State Government, preparatory to admission into the Union on an equal footing with the original States," approved February 26, 1858.

§ 3. *And be it further enacted,* That until the next general census shall be taken, and an apportionment of representation made, the State of Kansas shall be entitled to one Representative in the House of Representatives of the United States.

The bill passed, 33 to 25, as follows:

YEAS—FOR LECOMPTON.

ALABAMA.—Fitzpatrick, Clay. ARKANSAS.—Sebastian, Johnson. CALIFORNIA.—Gwin. DELAWARE.—Bayard. FLORIDA.—Mallory, Yulee. GEORGIA.—Iverson, Toombs. INDIANA.—Fitch, Bright. IOWA.—Jones. KENTUCKY.—THOMPSON. LOUISIANA.—Benjamin, Slidell. MARYLAND.—Pearce, KENNEDY. MISSISSIPPI—Brown. MISSOURI.—Green, Polk. NEW-JERSEY.—Wright, Thomson. NORTH CAROLINA—Biggs. PENNSYLVANIA—Bigler. RHODE ISLAND.—Allen. SOUTH CAROLINA.—Evans, Hammond. TENNESSEE.—Johnson. TEXAS.—Henderson, HOUSTON. VIRGINIA.—Mason, Hunter. Total, 33,

NAYS—AGAINST LECOMPTON.

CALIFORNIA.—Broderick. CONNECTICUT.—*Foster, Dixon.* ILLINOIS.—Douglas, *Trumbull.* IOWA.—*Harlan.* KENTUCKY.—CRITTENDEN. MAINE.—*Fessenden, Hamlin.* MASSACHUSETTS.—*Wilson, Sumner.* MICHIGAN.—Stuart, *Chandler.* NEW-HAMPSHIRE.—*Hale, Clark.* NEW-YORK.—*Seward, King.* OHIO.—Pugh, *Wade.* RHODE ISLAND.—*Simmons.* TENNESSEE.—BELL. VERMONT.—*Collamer, Foot.* WISCONSIN.—*Durkee, Doolittle.* Total, 25.

ABSENT OR NOT VOTING.—Messrs. Bates (Del.), Reid (N. C.), Davis (Mi.), *Cameron* (Pa.) Mr. Cameron paired off with Mr. Davis.

Previous to taking this vote, Mr. Crittenden moved a substitute for the bill, in substance, that the Constitution be submitted to the people at once, and, if approved, the President to admit Kansas by proclamation. If rejected, the people to call a Convention and frame a Constitution. The substitute made special provision against frauds at the election.

This substitute was lost: Yeas, 24; Nays, 34.

On the first of April, the bill was taken up in the House and read once, when, its second reading having been objected to by Mr. Giddings, the question recurred under the rule, Shall the bill be rejected? A vote was taken and resulted, Yeas, 95; Nays, 137.

Mr. Montgomery, of Pa., offered as a substitute, with slight alterations, the bill which Mr. Crittenden had offered in the Senate. Mr. Quitman, of Mississippi, also offered a substitute, which was the same as the Senate bill, with the omission of the declaratory clause, " that the people shall have the right at all times to alter or amend the Constitution in such manner as they think proper," etc.

Mr. Quitman's substitute was lost—Yeas, 72; Nays, 160, the yeas being all from the Slave States, and Mr. Montgomery's was adopted, 120 to 112.

The Crittenden-Montgomery substitute, as it passed the House, was in the following words:

§ 1. *Be it enacted, etc.,* That the State of Kansas be, and is hereby, admitted into the Union on an equal footing with the original States in all respects whatever; but inasmuch as it is greatly disputed whether the Constitution framed at Lecompton on the 7th day of November last, and now pending before Congress, was fairly made, or expressed the will of the people of Kansas, this admission of her into the Union as a State is here declared to be upon this fundamental condition precedent, namely: That the said constitutional instrument shall be first submitted to a vote of the people of Kansas, and assented to by them, or a majority of the voters, at an election to be held for the purpose; and as soon as such assent shall be given, and duly made known, by a majority of the Commissioners herein appointed, to the President of the United States, he shall announce the same by proclamation, and thereafter, without any further proceedings on the part of Congress, the admission of the said State of Kansas into the Union upon an equal footing with the original States, in all respects whatever, shall be complete and absolute. At the said election the voting shall be by ballot, and by indorsing on his ballot as each voter may please, " for the Constitution," or " against the Constitution." Should the said Constitution be rejected at the said election by a majority of votes being cast against it, then, and in that event, the inhabitants of said Territory are hereby authorized and empowered to form for themselves a Constitution and State Government by the name of the State of Kansas, according to the Federal Constitution, and to that end may elect delegates to a convention as hereinafter provided.

§ 2. *And be it further enacted,* That the said State of Kansas shall have concurrent jurisdiction on the Missouri and all other rivers and waters bordering on the said State of Kansas, so far as the same shall form a common boundary to said State and any other State or States now or hereafter to be formed or bounded by the same; and said rivers and waters, and all the navigable waters of said State, shall be common highways and forever free, as well to the inhabitants of said State as to all other citizens of the United States, without any tax, duty, impost, or toll therefor.

§ 3. *And be it further enacted,* That for the purpose of insuring, as far as possible, that the elections authorized by this act may be fair and free, the Governor and the Secretary of the Territory of Kansas, and the presiding officers of the two branches of its Legislature, namely the President of the Council and Speaker of the House of Representatives, are hereby constituted a board of commissioners to carry into effect the provisions of this act, and to use all the means necessary and proper to that end. Any three of them shall constitute a Board; and the board shall have power and authority, in respect to each and all of the elections hereby authorized or provided for, to designate and establish precincts for voting, or to adopt those already established; to cause polls to be opened at such places as it may deem proper in the respective counties and election precincts of said Territory; to appoint, as judges of election at each of the several places of voting, three discreet and respectable persons, any two of whom shall be competent to act; to require the Sheriffs of the several counties, by themselves or deputies, to attend the judges at each of the places of voting, for the purpose of preserving peace and good order, or the said Board may, instead of said Sheriffs and their deputies, appoint, at their discretion, and in such instances as they may choose, other fit persons for the same purpose; and when the purpose of the election is to elect delegates to a Convention to form a Constitution, as hereinbefore provided for, the number of delegates shall be sixty, and they shall be apportioned by said Board among the several counties of said Territory, according to the number of voters; and in making this apportionment, the Board may join two or more counties together to make an election or representative district, where neither of the said counties has the requisite number of voters to entitle it to a delegate, or to join a smaller to a larger county having a surplus population, where it may serve to equalize the representation. The elections hereby authorized shall continue one day only, and shall not be continued later than sundown on that day. The said Board shall appoint the day of election for each of the elections hereby authorized, as the same may become necessary. The said Governor shall announce, by proclamation, the day appointed for any one of said elections, and the day shall be as early a one as is consistent with due notice thereof to the people of said Territory, subject to the provisions of this act. The said Board shall have full power to prescribe the time, manner and places of each of said elections, and to direct the time and manner of the returns thereof, which returns shall be made to the said Board, whose duty it shall be to announce the result by proclamation, and to appoint therein as early a day as practicable for the delegates elected (where the election has been for delegates) to assemble in Convention at the seat of Government of said Territory. When so assembled, the Convention shall first determine, by a vote, whether it is the wish of the proposed State to be admitted into the Union at that time; and if so, shall proceed to form a Constitution, and take all necessary steps for the establishment of a State Government, in conformity with the Federal Constitution, subject to the approval and ratification of the people of the proposed State. And the said Convention shall accordingly provide for its submission to the vote of the people for approval or rejection; and if the majority of votes shall be given for the Constitution so framed as aforesaid, the Governor of the Territory shall, within twenty days after the result is known, notify the President of the United States of the same. And thereupon the President shall announce the same by proclamation, and thereafter, and without any further proceedings whatever on the part of Congress, the admission of the said State of Kansas into the Union, upon an equal footing with the original States in all respects whatever, shall be complete and absolute.

§ 4. *And be it further enacted*, That in the elections hereby authorized, all white male inhabitants of said Territory over the age of twenty-one years, who are legal voters under the laws of the Territory of Kansas, and none others, shall be allowed to vote; and this shall be the only qualification required to entitle the voter to the right of suffrage in said elections. And if any person not so qualified shall vote or offer to vote, or if any person shall vote more than once at either of said elections, or shall make, or cause to be made, any false, fictitious or fraudulent returns, or shall alter or change any returns of either of said elections, such person shall, upon conviction thereof before any court of competent jurisdiction, be kept at hard labor not less than six months, and not more than three years.

§ 5. *And be it further enacted*, That the members of the aforesaid Board of Commissioners, and all persons appointed by them to carry into effect the provisions of this act, shall, before entering upon their duties, take an oath to perform faithfully the duties of their respective offices; and on failure thereof, they shall be liable and subject to the same charges and penalties as are provided in like cases under the Territorial laws.

§ 6. *And be it further enacted*, That the officers mentioned in the preceding section shall receive for their services the same compensation as is given for like services under the Territorial laws.

§ 7. *And be it further enacted*, That the said State of Kansas, when her admission as a State becomes complete and absolute, shall be entitled to one member in the House of Representatives, in the Congress of the United States, till the next census be taken by the Federal Government.

§ 8. *And be it further enacted*, That the following propositions be, and the same are hereby offered to the said people of Kansas for their free acceptance or rejection, which, if accepted, shall be obligatory on the United States and upon the said State of Kansas, to wit: *First*, That the sections numbered sixteen and thirty-six in every township of public lands in said State, and where either of said sections, or any part thereof has been sold or otherwise disposed of, other lands equivalent thereto, and as contiguous as may be, shall be granted to said State for the use of schools. *Second*, That seventy-two sections of land shall be set apart and reserved for the use and support of a State University, to be selected by the Governor of said State, subject to the approval of the Commissioner of the General Land Office, and to be appropriated and applied in such manner as the Legislature of said State may prescribe for the purpose aforesaid, but for no other purposes. *Third*, That ten entire sections of land, to be selected by the Governor of said State, in legal subdivisions, shall be granted to said State for the purpose of completing the public buildings, or for the erection of others at the seat of government, under the direction of the Legislature thereof. *Fourth*, That all salt springs within said State, not exceeding twelve in number, with six sections of land adjoining, or as contiguous as may be to each, shall be granted to said State for its use; the same to be selected by the Governor thereof within one year after the admission of said State, and when so selected, to be used or disposed of on such terms, conditions and regulations as the Legislature shall direct: *Provided*, That no salt springs or land the right whereof is now vested in any individual or individuals, or which may be hereafter be confirmed or adjudged to any individual or individuals, shall by this article be granted to said State. *Fifth*, That five per centum of the net proceeds of sales of all public lands lying within said States, which shall be sold by Congress after the admission of said State into the Union, after deducting all the expenses incident to the same, shall be paid to said State, for the purpose of making public roads and internal improvements, as the Legislature shall direct: *Provided*, The foregoing propositions hereinbefore offered are on the condition that the people of Kansas shall provide, by an ordinance, irrevocable without the consent of the United States, that said State shall never interfere with the primary disposal of the soil within the same, by the United States, or with any regulations Congress may find necessary for securing the title in said soil to *bona fide* purchasers thereof, and that no tax shall be imposed on lands belonging to the United States, and that in no case shall non-resident proprietors be taxed higher than residents. *Sixth:* And that the said S ate shall never tax the lands or the property of the United States in that State : *Provided however*, That nothing in this act of admission shall be so construed as to ratify or accept the ordinance attached to said Constitution; but said ordinance is hereby rejected by the Government of the United States.

The following are the Yeas and Nays:

YEAS—TO AMEND OR SUBSTITUTE.

CALIFORNIA.—McKibbin—1.
CONNECTICUT.—*Clark, Dean*—2.
ILLINOIS.—*Elihu Washburne, Farnsworth, Lovejoy, Kellogg*, Morris, Harris, Shaw, Robert Smith, Sam. S. Marshall—9.
INDIANA.—English, Foley, *Kilgore*, J. G. Davis, *Wilson, Colfax, Case, Pettit*—8.
IOWA.—*Curtis, T. Davis*—2.
KENTUCKY.—UNDERWOOD, HUMPHREY MARSHALL—2.
MAINE.—*Wood, Gilman, Abbott, Morse, I. Washburne, Foster*—6.
MARYLAND.—RICAUD, J. M. HARRIS, H. WINTER DAVIS—3.
MASSACHUSETTS.—*Hall, Buffinton, Damrell, Comins, Burlingame, Davis, Gooch, Knapp, Thayer, Chaffee, Dawes*—11.
MICHIGAN.—*Howard, Waldron, Walbridge, Leach*—4.
MISSOURI.—*Blair*—1.
NEW-HAMPSHIRE.—*Pike, Tappan, Cragin*—3.
NEW-JERSEY.—*Clawson, Robbins*, Adrain—3.
NORTH CAROLINA.—GILMER—1.
NEW-YORK.—Haskin, H. F. Clark, *Murray, Thompson, Olin, Dodd, Palmer, Spinner, Clark B. Cochrane, Morse, Matteson, Bennett, Goodwin, Hoard, Granger*

Morgan, Pottle, Parker, Kelsey, Andrews, Sherman, Burroughs, Fenton—23.

OHIO.—Pendleton, Groesbeck, *Campbell, Nichols, Mott*, Cockerill, *Harlan, Stanton*, Hall, *Horton*, Cox, *Sherman, Bliss, Tompkins*, Lawrence, *Leiter, Wade, Giddings, Bingham*—19.

PENNSYLVANIA.—*E. J. Morris*, Owen Jones, Hickman, *Roberts, Kunkel, Grow, Edie, Covode*, Montgomery, *Ritchie, Purviance, Stewart, Dick*, Chapman.—14.

RHODE ISLAND.—*Durfee, Brayton*—2.

VERMONT.—*Walton, Morrill, Royce*—3.

WISCONSIN.—*Potter, C. C. Washburne, Billinghurst*—3.—Total, 120.

NAYS.

ALABAMA.—Stallworth, Shorter, Dowdell, Moore, Houston, Cobb, Curry—7.

ARKANSAS.—Greenwood, Warren—2.

CALIFORNIA.—Scott—1.

CONNECTICUT.—Arnold, Bishop—2.

DELAWARE.—Whiteley—1.

FLORIDA.—Hawkins—1.

GEORGIA.—Seward, Crawford, TRIPPE, Gartrell, Wright, Jackson, HILL, Stephens—8.

INDIANA.—Niblack, Hughes, Gregg—3.

KENTUCKY.—Burnett, Peyton, Talbott, Jewett, Elliott, Clay, Mason, Stevenson—8.

LOUISIANA.—EUSTIS, Taylor, Davidson, Sandidge—4.

MARYLAND.—Stewart, Kunkel, Bowie—3.

MISSOURI.—ANDERSON, Clark, Craig, WOODSON, Phelps—5.

MISSISSIPPI.—Lamar, R. Davis, Barksdale, Singleton, Quitman—5.

NEW-JERSEY.—Huyler, Wortendyke—2.

NORTH CAROLINA.—Shaw, Ruffin, Winslow, Branch, Scales, Craige, Clingman—7.

NEW-YORK.—Searing, Taylor, Sickles, Kelly, Maclay, John Cochrane, Ward, Russell, Corning, Hatch—10.

OHIO.—Miller, Burns—2.

PENNSYLVANIA.—Florence, Landy, Phillips, Glancy Jones, Leidy, Dimmick, White, Ahl, Gillis, Reilly, Dewart—11.

SOUTH CAROLINA.—McQueen, Miles, Keitt, Bonham, Boyce—5.

TENNESSEE.—Watkins, MAYNARD, S. A. Smith, Savage, READY, Jones, Wright, ZOLLICOFFER, Atkins, Avery—10.

TEXAS.—Bryan, Reagan—2.

VIRGINIA.—Garnet, Millson, Caskie, Goode, Bocock, Powell, Smith, Faulkner, Letcher, Clemens, Jenkins, Edmundson, Hopkins—13. Total, 112.

Absent—Caruthers (Mo.)

RECAPITULATION.

Yeas.

Republicans, 92; Democrats, 22; Americans, 6. Total—120.

Nays.

Democrats, 104; Americans, 8. Total—112.

The bill having been returned to the Senate on the second day of April, Mr. Green moved to disagree to the House amendment which motion was adopted: Yeas, 34, Nays, 22.

The following are the Nays:

Messrs. Broderick, Cameron, Chandler, Clark, Collamer, Crittenden, Dixon, Doolittle, Douglas, Fessenden, Foot, Foster, Hale, Hamlin, Harlan, King, Seward, Simmons, Stuart, Trumbull, Wade, Wilson.

In the House of Representatives, on the 7th of April, Mr. Montgomery, of Pennsylvania, moved that the House adhere to its amendment, which motion was carried, Yeas, 119, Nays 111—the vote being the same as on the adoption of the amendment, with the exception of Messrs. Marshall and Bowie, who paired off and did not vote.

On the 13th of April, the Senate voted to insist and ask for a conference committee, Yeas, 30, Nays, 24—the Nays being the same as the Nays on Mr. Green's motion to disagree, with the addition of Messrs. Bell and Sumner. On the following day, the House received a message from the Senate insisting on its disagreement and asking a committee of conference, when Mr. Montgomery, of Pa., moved that the House insist on its adherence, on which he de-

manded the previous question. The call for the previous question was lost by the casting vote of the Speaker: 108 to 108. Very much to the surprise of the House, Mr. English, of Indiana, who had acted with the Anti-Lecompton party up to this time, moved that the House agree to a Conference Committee, and that a committee of three be appointed by the Speaker to meet a similar committee of the Senate, and on this he called for the previous question, which was ordered. The Yeas and Nays were called, and the vote stood 108 to 108: the Speaker voting in the affirmative, Mr. English's proposition was agreed to. The Yeas and Nays were as follows:

YEAS.—Messrs. Ahl, Anderson, Atkins, Avery, Barksdale, Bishop, Bocock, Bonham, Bowie, Boyce, Branch, Bryan, Burnett, Burns, Caruthers, Caskie, Clark (Mo.), Clay, Clemens, Clingman, Cobb, John Cochrane, Craig (Mo.), Craige (N. C.), Crawford, Curry, Davidson, Davis (Miss.), Dewart, Dowdell, Edmundson, Elliot, *English*, Eustis, Faulkner, Florence, Garnett, Gartrell, Goode, Greenwood, Gregg, *Hall* (Ohio), Hatch, Hawkins, Hill, Hopkins, Houston, Hughes, Jackson, Jenkins, Jewett, Jones (Tenn.), J. Glancy Jones, *Owen Jones*, Keitt, Kelly, Kunkel (Md.), Lamar, Landy, Leidy, Letcher, Maclay, McQueen, Mason, Maynard, Miles, Miller, Millson, Moore, Niblack, Orr, *Pendleton*, Peyton, Phelps, Phillips, Powell, Quitman, Ready, Reagan, Ruffin, Russell, Sandidge, Savage, Scales, Scott, Searing, Seward, Shaw (N. C.), Shorter, Singleton, Smith (Tenn.), Smith (Va.), Stallworth, Stephens, Stevenson, Stewart (Md.), Talbott, Taylor (N. Y.), Trippe, Ward, Warren, Watkins, White, Winslow, Woodson, Wortendyke, Wright (Ga.), Wright (Tenn.), Zollicoffer—109.

[The four in *italics* had hitherto voted anti-Lecompton.]

NAYS.—Messrs. Abbott, Andrews, Bennett, Billinghurst, Bingham, Blair, Bliss, Brayton, Buffinton, Burlingame, Burroughs, Campbell, Case, Chaffee, Chapman, Clark (Conn.), Clark (N. Y.), Clawson, Cockerill, Colfax, Comins, Covode, Cox, Cragin, Curtis, Damrell, Davis (Md.), Davis (Ind.), Davis (Mass.), Davis (Iowa), Dawes, Dean, Dick, Dodd, Durfee, Edie, Farnsworth, Fenton, Foley, Foster, Giddings, Gilman, Gooch, Goodwin, Granger, Groesbeck, Grow, Hall (Mass.), Harlan, Harris (Md.), Harris, (Ill.), Haskin, Hickman, Hoard, Horton, Howard, Kellogg, Kelsey, Knapp, Lawrence, Leiter, Lovejoy, Marshall (Ky.) Marshall (Ill.), Matteson, Montgomery, Morgan, Morrill, Morris (Penn.) Morris (Ill.), Morse (Me.), Morse (N. Y.), Mott, Murray, Nichols, Palmer, Pettit, Pike, Potter, Pottle, Purviance, Ricaud, Ritchie, Robbins, Royce, Shaw (Ill.), Sherman (Ohio), Sherman (N. Y.), Smith (Ill.), Spinner, Stanton, Stewart (Penn.), Tappan, Thompson, Tompkins, Underwood, Wade, Walbridge, Waldron, Walton, Washburne (Ill.), Washburne (Me.), Wilson, Wood—108.

The following, not voting, had paired off:

Adrain with Huyler, Dimmick with McKibbin, Gillis with Roberts, Clark B. Cochrane with Sickles, Reilly with Thayer, Taylor (La.) with Kunkel (Pa.), Washburne (Wis.) with Arnold, Olin with Corning. Whiteley, absent.

The Committee of Conference was composed of Messrs. James S. Green, (Mo.), Robert M. T. Hunter, (Va.), and William H. Seward, (N. Y.), of the Senate; and Messrs. William H. English, (Ind.), Alexander H. Stephens, (Ga.), and William A. Howard, (Mich.), on the part of the House.

On the 23d of April, the Committee made their report (susceptible of various interpretations), Messrs. Seward of the Senate, and Howard, of the House, dissenting. After a running fight of a week between the friends and opponents of the new scheme, on the 30th of April, the report of the Committee was adopted by both branches of Congress. It was as follows:

An Act for the Admission of the State of Kansas into the Union.—Whereas, the people of the Territory of Kansas did, by a convention of delegates assembled at Lecompton on the 7th day of Nov., 1857, for that purpose, form for themselves a constitution and State government, which constitution is republican; and *whereas*, at the same time and place, said convention did adopt an ordinance, which said ordinance asserts that Kansas, when admitted as a State, will have an undoubted right to tax the lands within her limits belonging to the United States, and proposes to relinquish said asserted right if certain conditions set forth in said ordinance be accepted and agreed to by the Congress of the United States; and *whereas*, the said constitution and ordinance have been presented to Congress by order of said convention, and admission of said Territory into the Union thereon as a State requested; and *whereas*, said ordinance is not acceptable to Congress, and it is desirable to ascertain whether the people of Kansas concur in the changes in said ordinance, hereinafter stated, and desire admission into the Union as a State as herein proposed: Therefore,

Be it enacted, etc., That the State of Kansas be, and is hereby admitted into the Union on an equal footing with the original States, in all respects whatever, but upon this fundamental condition precedent, namely: That the question of admission with the following proposition, in lieu of the ordinance framed at Lecompton, be submitted to a vote of the people of Kansas, and assented to by them or a majority of the voters voting at an election to be held for that purpose, namely: That the following propositions be, and the same are hereby offered to the people of Kansas for acceptance or rejection, which, if accepted, shall be obligatory on the United States and upon the said State of Kansas, to wit: *First*, That sections number sixteen and thirty-six in every township of public lands in said State, or where either of said sections or any part thereof has been sold or otherwise disposed of, other lands equivalent thereto, and as contiguous as may be, shall be granted to said State for the use of schools. *Second*, That seventy-two sections of land shall be set apart and reserved for the support of a State University, to be selected by the Governor of said State, subject to the approval of the Commissioners of the General Land-Office, and to be appropriated and applied in such manner as the legislature of said State may prescribe for the purpose aforesaid, but for no other purpose. *Third*, That ten entire sections of land, to be selected by the Governor of said State, in legal subdivisions, shall be granted to said State for the purpose of completing the public buildings, or for the erection of others at the seat of government, under the direction of the legislature thereof. *Fourth*, That all salt springs within said State, not exceeding twelve in number, with six sections of land adjoining, or as contiguous as may be to each, shall be granted to said State for its use, the same to be selected by the Governor thereof, within one year after the admission of said State; and, when so selected, to be used or disposed of on such terms, conditions and regulations as the legislature may direct: *Provided*, That no salt spring or land, the right whereof is now vested in any individual or individuals, or which may hereafter be confirmed or adjudged to any individual or individuals, shall by this article be granted to said State. *Fifth*, That five per centum of the net proceeds of sales of all public lands lying within said State which shall be sold by Congress after the admission of said State into the Union, after deducting all the expenses incident to the same, shall be paid to said State for the purpose of making public roads and internal improvements, as the legislature shall direct: *Provided*, The foregoing propositions herein offered are on the condition that said State of Kansas shall never interfere with the primary disposal of the lands of the United States, or with any regulations which Congress may find necessary for securing the title in said soil to *bona fide* purchasers thereof, and that no tax shall be imposed on lands belonging to the United States, and that in no case shall non-resident proprietors be taxed higher than residents. *Sixth*, And that said State shall never tax the lands or property of the United States in that State.

At the said election the voting shall be by ballot, and by indorsing on his ballot, as each voter may be pleased, "Proposition accepted," or "Proposition rejected." Should a majority of the votes cast be for "Proposition accepted," the President of the United States, as soon as the fact is duly made known to him, shall announce the same by proclamation; and thereafter, and without any further proceedings on the part of Congress, the admission of the State of Kansas into the Union upon an equal footing with the original States in all respects whatever shall be complete and absolute; and said State shall be entitled to one member in the House of Representatives in the Congress of the United States until the next census be taken by the Federal Government. But should a majority of the votes cast be for "Proposition rejected," it shall be deemed and held that the people of Kansas do not desire admission into the Union with said Constitution under the conditions set forth in said proposition: and in that event the people of said Territory are hereby authorized and empowered to form for themselves a Constitution and State Government, by the name of the State of Kansas, according to the Federal Constitution, and may elect delegates for that purpose whenever, and not before, it is ascertained by a census duly and legally taken, that the population of said Territory equals or exceeds the ratio of representation required for a member of the House of Representatives of the Congress of the United States; and whenever thereafter such delegates shall assemble in Convention, they shall first determine by a vote whether it is the wish of the people of the proposed State to be admitted into the Union at that time; and, if so, shall proceed to form a Constitution, and take all necessary steps for the establishment of a State Government, in conformity with the Federal Constitution, subject to such limitations and restrictions as to the mode and manner of its approval or ratification by the people of the proposed State as they may have prescribed by law, and shall be entitled to admission into the Union as a State under such Constitution, thus fairly and legally made, with or without Slavery, as said Constitution may prescribe.

§ 2. *And be it further enacted*, That for the purpose of insuring, as far as possible, that the elections authorized by this act may be fair and free, the Governor, United States District Attorney, and Secretary of the Territory of Kansas, and the presiding officers of the two branches of its Legislature, namely, the President of the Council and the Speaker of the House of Representatives, are hereby constituted a board of Commissioners to carry into effect the provisions of this act, and to use all the means necessary and proper to that end. And three of them shall constitute a board; and the board shall have power and authority to designate and establish precincts for voting or to adopt those already established; to cause polls to be opened at such places as it may deem proper in the respective counties and election precincts of said Territory; to appoint as judges of election at each of the several places of voting, three discreet and respectable persons, any two of whom shall be competent to act; to require the sheriffs of the several counties, by themselves or deputies, to attend the judges at each of the places of voting, for the purpose of preserving peace and good order; or the said board may, instead of said sheriffs and their deputies, appoint at their discretion, and in such instances as they may choose, other fit persons for the same purpose. The election hereby authorized shall continue one day only, and shall not be continued later than sun down on that day. The said board shall appoint the day for holding said election, and the said Governor shall announce the same by proclamation; and the day shall be as early a one as is consistent with due notice thereof to the people of said Territory, subject to the provisions of this act. The said board shall have full power to prescribe the time, manner, and place of said election, and to direct the time (within) which returns shall be made to the said board, whose duty it shall be to announce the result by proclamation, and the said Governor shall certify the same to the President of the United States without delay.

§ 3. *And be it further enacted*, That in the election hereby authorized, all white male inhabitants of said Territory, over the age of twenty-one years, who possess the qualifications which were required by the laws of said Territory for a legal voter at the last general election for the members of the Territorial Legislature, and none others, shall be allowed to vote; and this shall be the only qualification required to entitle the voter to the right of suffrage in said election. And if any person not so qualified shall vote or offer to vote, or if any person shall vote more than once at said election, or shall make, or cause to be made, any false, fictitious, or fraudulent returns, or shall alter or change any returns of said election, such person shall, upon conviction thereof before any court of competent jurisdiction, be kept at hard labor not less than six months and not more than three years.

§ 4. *And be it further enacted*, That the members of the aforesaid board of commissioners, and all persons appointed by them to carry into effect the provisions of this act, shall, before entering upon their duties, take an oath to perform faithfully the duties of their respective offices: and on failure thereof, they shall be liable and subject to the same charges and penalties as are provided in like cases under the Territorial laws.

§ 5. *And be it further enacted*, That the officers mentioned in the preceding section shall receive for their services the same compensation as is given for like services under the Territorial laws.

The vote in the Senate, on agreeing to the Conference Committee's Report, stood—Yeas, 30; Nays, 22; as follows:

YEAS.—Messrs. Allen, Bayard, Benjamin, Bigler, Biggs, Bright, Brown, Clay, Davis, Evans, Fitzpatrick, Green,

Gwin, Hammond, Houston, Hunter, Iverson, Johnson (Ark) Johnson (Tenn.), Jones, Kennedy, Mallory, Mason, Polk, Pugh, Sebastian, Thompson (N.J.), Toombs, Wright, Yulee.

NAYS.—Messrs. Broderick, Cameron, Chandler, Collamer, Crittenden, Dixon, Doolittle, Douglas, Durkee, Fessenden, Foot, Foster, Hale, Hamlin, Harlan, King, Seward, Simmons, Stuart, Trumbull, Wade, Wilson.

PAIRED.—Bell with Pearce, Fitch with Sumner.

ABSENT.—Clark, Bates, Henderson, Reid, Thompson (Ky.), Slidell.

In the House, on the final vote, among those who had voted against the original Lecompton Bill and who now supported the English scheme, were Gilmer, Am., of N. C., and the following Democrats, viz.: English and Foley, of Ind ; Cockerill, Cox, Groesbeck, Hall, Lawrence and Pendleton, of Ohio ; and Owen Jones, of Pa. Gen. Quitman, of Mississippi, and Mr. Bonham, of S. C., fire eaters, voted No, and the following members "paired off," viz.: Washburn (Wis.) with Arnold ; Matteson with Reuben Davis ; Purviance with Dimmick ; Morrill with Faulkner ; Horton with Hill ; J. C. Kunkel with Miles Taylor ; Montgomery with Warren ; Thompson with Stewart (Md.) ; and Wood with George Taylor.

In accordance with this act of Congress, the people of Kansas went into an election on the 3d of August, 1858. Notwithstanding the liberal offers in regard to donations to Kansas of public lands, in this bill, and the threat that if the people did not accept a State Government with the Lecompton Constitution, they should not be permitted to come in as a State with any Constitution, till they should have a full population of 93,340, still, the Lecompton Constitution was again rejected by more than ten thousand majority. This may be regarded as the *final* disposition of this famous Constitution. From first to last, it had been the cause or the subject of more speeches in Congress than any measure ever brought before that body.

THE WYANDOT CONSTITUTION.

The Territorial Legislature passed an act (Feb. 11, 1859) to refer the question to the people of a new Constitutional Convention, the election to be held on the first Tuesday in March, 1859. The election was held, and resulted in a majority of 3,881 in favor of a Convention. This result being ascertained, the Governor issued his proclamation for an election of delegates. The old party organizations were now abandoned, and those of Republicans and Democrats substituted, and it was on this basis that the canvass for the election of delegates proceeded. The Convention was to consist of fifty-two delegates. The Democrats proclaimed themselves disciples of Mr. Douglas and his Territorial Sovereignty doctrine, and decidedly opposed to making Kansas a Slave State. The Leavenworth district, where, through its contractors for army supplies, the Government exercised a great influence, and which from its population was entitled to ten delegates, elected the Democratic ticket, not, however, without the aid of fraudulent votes. But the Republicans, by their predominance in other parts of the Territory, succeeded in securing a majority in the Convention of thirty-five to seventeen.

The Convention met at Wyandot on the 5th of July, and adjourned on the 27th of the same month, after adopting a Constitution by a vote of thirty-four to thirteen, all the Democrats present voting against it and refusing to sign it. They had strenuously contended, in the Convention, for the annexation to Kansas of that part of Nebraska south of the Platte ; for retaining as a part of the new State the western gold region about Pike's Peak, which was beginning to attract great numbers of immigrants ; for the exclusion from the State of free negroes, and for the prohibition of bank issues, but had been defeated as to all these points.

By the Constitution, as adopted, the boundaries of the new State were declared to be the State of Missouri on the east, the 37th parallel of north latitude on the south, the 41st parallel of north latitude on the north, and the 23d meridian of longitude west from Washington on the west. The western boundary cuts off the Pike's Peak region and the desert which bounds it on the east, and limits the new State to the habitable eastern portion of the Territory, embracing an area of some sixty thousand square miles. The Executive is to consist of a Governor, Secretary of State, Auditor, Attorney-General, and Superintendent of Public Schools, to be chosen by the people, and to serve for two years. The House of Representatives is to consist of seventy-five members, to serve one year, and the Senate of twenty-five Senators, to serve two years, the numbers to be regulated by law, but never to exceed one hundred Representatives, and thirty-three Senators. The pay is to be three dollars a day and fifteen cents per mile travel. All bills must originate with the House, and no act can include more than one subject. The Supreme Court is to consist of three Judges, to be chosen by the people, to hold office for six years, one to go out every two years. There are to be five District Judges, to be chosen by the people of their respective districts, and to serve for four years. Each county is to choose a Judge of Probate, to serve for two years, and each township is to choose Justices of the Peace, to serve also for two years. Elections are to be by ballot. Every white male adult who is a citizen of the United States, or who has declared his intention to become one, having been a resident in the State for six months, and in the precinct for thirty days, is entitled to vote.

The State is prohibited from becoming a party in carrying on any work of internal improvement, nor can any debt, to exceed a million of dollars, be contracted, unless the question be previously submitted to, and the debt authorized by, a popular vote ; and in all cases a special tax must be levied sufficient to pay the interest and provide a sinking fund adequate to meet the principal when it becomes due. All corporations, banks included, must be established under general laws only, and the corporators made liable to twice the amount of their stock. The sale of lottery tickets is prohibited. The schedule annexed to the Constitution claimed of Congress $500,000, or in lieu thereof 500,000 acres of land, to meet the claims audited to nearly that amount for losses incurred by citizens of Kansas during the late troubles. The Commissioners had declined to entertain the claim of the New-England Emigrant Aid Society, to the amount of $25,000, for the destruction of their hotel at Lawrence, on the ground that they had no authority to act on any claims except those presented by citizens of Kansas, and the Convention declined to go beyond the report of the Commissioners.

A grant is asked from Congress of 4,550,000 acres of land for internal improvements, also the swamp lands of the State to be appropriated as a school fund.

Prefixed to the Constitution is a Bill of Rights, which includes a prohibition of Slavery. This Bill of Rights also provides that no person shall be incompetent to testify on account of his religious belief.

By a provision of the schedule, this Constitution was submitted to a popular vote on the first Tuesday in October, which resulted in its ratification by the people by a majority of some f ur thousand. The Territorial election in November attracted but little interest from the general expectation of the admission of the State under the new Constitution. The Republicans, however, succeeded in electing their delegate to Congress and a majority of the Legislature.

The first State Election under this Constitution was held December 6, 1859, and resulted in the election of Charles Robinson (Rep.) as Governor by 2513 majority. Martin F. Conway (Rep.) for Congress by 2107 majority, and the entire Republican ticket for State officers by majorities ranging from 2000 to 2,500, also a Legislature which was Republican in both branches by very decided majorities.

Feb. 15—Mr. Grow introduced in the House, a bill to admit Kansas under the Wyandot Constitution. Referred to Committee on Territories, which (March 29th) reported (majority) through Mr. Grow in favor of admission.

April 11.—Mr. Grow demanded the Previous Question on the passage of the Bill, which was seconded, and the main question ordered.

Mr. Barksdale, demanded the Yeas and Nays —ordered.

The question was then taken, and decided in the affirmative : Yeas, 134 ; Nays, 73, as follows :

YEAS—Messrs. Chas. F. Adams, A d r a i n, Aldrich, *Allen,* Alley, Ashley, Babbitt, *Barr, Barrett,* Beale, Bingham, Blair (Pa.), Blake, Brayton, BRIGGS, Buffinton, *Burch,* Burlingame, Burnham, Butterfield, Campbell, Carey, Carter, Case, H o r a c e F. C l a r k, Clark B. Cochrane, *John Cochrane,* Colfax, Conkling, *Cooper,* Corwin, Covode, *Cox,* Curtis, Dawes, Delano, Duell, Dunn, Edgerton, Edwards, Elliot, Ely, ETHERIDGE, Farnsworth, Fenton, Ferry, *Florence* Foster, *Fouke,* Frank, French, Gooch, Grow, Gurley, Hale, Hall, H a s k i n, Helmick, H i c k m a n, Hoard, *Holman, Howard* (Ohio), Humphry, Hutchins, Irvine, Junkin, Francis W. Kellogg, William Kellogg, Kenyon, Kilgore, Killinger, *Larrabee,* De Witt C. Leach, Lee, *Logan,* Longnecker, Loomis, Lovejoy, Marston, *Chas. D. Martin, McClernand,* McKean, McKnight, McPherson, *Wm. Montgomery,* Moorehead, Morrill, Edward Joy Morris, *Isaac N. Morris,* Morse, *Niblack,* Nixon, Olin, Palmer, *Pendleton,* Perry, Pettit, Porter, Potter, Pottle, Rice, R i g g s, Christopher Robinson, *James C. Robinson,* Royce, S c h w a r t z, Scranton, Sedgwick, Spaulding, Spinner, Stanton, Stevens, Wm. Stewart, *Stout,* Stratton, Tappan, Thayer, Theaker, Tompkins, Train, Trimble, *Vallandigham,* Vandever, Verree, Waldron, Walton, C. C. Washburn, E. B. Washburne, Israel Washburn, WEBSTER, Wells, Wilson, Windom, Wood, Woodruff.

Republicans, in Roman, ... 103
Democrats (from Free States.), in *Italics,* . . 22
Anti-Lecompton Democrats, Roman spaced, . . 6
Americans, in SMALL CAPS, ... 3
———
Total, ... 134

NAYS—Messrs. GREEN ADAMS, *Thos. L. Anderson,* WM. C. ANDERSON. *Ashmore, Avery Barksdale, Bocock, Bonham,* BOTELER, *Boyce,* BRABSON *Branch,* BRISTOW, *Burnett, John B. Clark. Clopton, Cobb, James Craig Burton Craige, Crawford, Curry, Davidson,* HENRY W.

DAVIS, *Edmundson. English* (Indiana), *Garnett, Gartrell,* GILMER, *Hamilton* HARDEMAN, *John T Harris, Hawkins,* HILL. *Hindman, Houston, Hughes Jackson, Jenkins, Jones. Keitt. Lamar,* JAMES M. LEACH, *Leake, Love,* MALLORY, MAYNARD, *McQueen, McRae, Miles, Millson,* LABAN T. MOORE, *Sydenham Moore,* NELSON, *Noell, Pugh.* QUARLES, *Reagan Ruffin, Scott* (Cal.), *Sickles* (N. Y.), *Simms, Singleton, Wm. Smith.* W. N. H. SMITH. *Stallworth, Stevenson,* STOKES, *Thomas,* VANCE, *Whitely, Winslow, Woodson.*

Democrats, in *Italics,* (3 from Free States), . . 55
Americans, in SMALL CAPS (all from Slave States), 18
———
Total, ... 73

PAIRED—D a v i s (Indiana), with *Phelps.*
  Sherman with HARRIS, of Md.
  Wade with *Peyton.*
  Somes with *McClay* (N.Y.)
  Van Wyck with *Underwood.*
  Burroughs with *Dejarnette.*
ABSENT UNPAIRED—*Davis* (Mis.), *Landrum, Martin,* (Va.), *Kunkel.*

Senate, Feb. 21st.—Mr. Seward introduced a bill for the admission of Kansas under the Wyandotte Constitution.

On the 5th June, this bill being under consideration,

Mr Wigfall, of Tex., explained his views. He declared he would not vote for the admission of this so-called State, under any circumstances. He objected to their moral character, and was not willing Texas should associate with such a State.

Mr. Greene's amendment, to change the boundary (taking in Pike's Peak), was discussed by Mr. Wade, who said the effect of the amendment would be to defeat the bill.

Mr. Hunter moved to postpone the subject, and take up the Army bill.

Mr. Trumbull opposed the motion. He should keep the Kansas bill before the Senate till it was finally disposed of. It was more important than the appropriation bills, which appeared to be kept back in order to interrupt other important business.

Mr. Seward hoped the friends of Kansas would let a vote be taken, so that the responsibility might lie where it belonged.

The vote was taken by yeas and nays, and resulted, Yeas, 32 ; Nays, 27. It was a strict party vote, except that Messrs Pugh (Dem., Ohio) and Latham (Dem., Cal.) voted with the Republicans not to postpone. Mr. Kennedy (S. Am., Md.) voted with the Democrats. Messrs. Crittenden (S. Am., Ky.), Douglas, Clay, (Dem. Ala.), and Nicholson (Dem., Tenn) we.e absent. Messrs. Douglas and Clay were paired.

So the motion to postpone, and take up the Army bill prevailed.

Mr. Trumbull called attention to the fact that the Senator from Pennsylvania (Bigler) desired to postpone the Kansas bill because the Senate was not full. The vote showed that sixty votes had been cast, with two paired off, showing the fullest vote of the session.

He said the effect of the vote just taken was equivalent to the defeat of the Kansas bill. and the Senator from Pennsylvania must have known the effect of his vote.

Mr. Wigfall desired to call attention to the fact that the House had once defeated the Army bill, because it did not want the army used against the Black Republican thieves and murderers in Kansas.

June 7.—Mr. Wade, of Ohio, moved to take up the Kansas bill, which was lost—as follows :

YEAS—Messrs. Anthony, Bigler, Bingham, Cameron, Chandler, Clark, Collamer, Dixon, Doolittle, Durkee, Fessenden, Foot, Foster, Grimes, Hale, Hamlin, Harlan, King, Pugh, Seward, Simmons, Sumner, Ten Eyck. Trumbull, Wade, Wilkinson, Wilson, Republicans, 25 ; Democrats, (Bigler and Pugh) 2—27.

NAYS—Messrs. Bayard, Benjamin, Bragg, Bright, Brown, Chesnut, Clingman, Davis, Fitch, Fitzpatrick, Greene, Gwin, Hammond, Hemphill, Hunter, Iverson, Johnson, (Tenn.) Lane, Latham, Mallory, Mason, Nicholson, Pearce, Polk, Powell, Rice, Sebastian, Slidell, Thomson, Toombs, Wigfall, Yulee.—32. [All Democrats.]

Mr. Douglas was paired with Mr. Clay ; Crittenden (Am.), with Johnson, of Ark., Kennedy and Saulsbury absent.

So both Houses adjourned and left Kansas still in the condition of a Territory.

THE NEBRASKA DOCTRINE

AND

THE DRED SCOTT DECISION REVIEWED,

SPEECH OF THE HON. ABRAHAM LINCOLN,

At Springfield, Ill., June 17, 1858.

MR. PRESIDENT, AND GENTLEMEN OF THE CONVENTION: If we could first know where we are, and whither we are tending, we could better judge what to do, and how to do it. We are now far into the fifth year, since a policy was initiated with the avowed object, and confident promise, of putting an end to Slavery agitation. Under the operation of that policy, that agitation has not only not ceased, but has constantly augmented. In my opinion, it will not cease, until a crisis shall have been reached and passed. "A house divided against itself cannot stand." I believe this government cannot endure permanently half slave and half free. I do not expect the Union to be dissolved—I do not expect the house to fall—but I do expect it will cease to be divided. It will become all one thing, or all the other. Either the opponents of slavery will arrest the further spread of it, and place it where the public mind shall rest in the belief that it is in the course of ultimate extinction; or its advocates will push it forward, till it shall become alike lawful in all the States, old as well as new—North as well as South.

Have we no tendency to the latter condition?

Let any one who doubts, carefully contemplate that now almost complete legal combination—piece of machinery, so to speak—compounded of the Nebraska doctrine, and the Dred Scott Decision. Let him consider not only what work the machinery is adapted to do, and how well adapted; but also, let him study the history of its construction, and trace, if he can, or rather fail, if he can, to trace the evidence of design, and concert of action, among its chief architects, from the beginning.

The new year of 1854 found Slavery excluded from more than half the States by State Constitutions, and from most of the national territory by Congressional prohibition. Four days later, commenced the struggle which ended in repealing that Congressional prohibition. This opened all the national territory to Slavery, and was the first point gained.

But, so far, Congress only had acted: and an indorsement by the people, real or apparent, was indispensable, to save the point already gained, and give chance for more.

This necessity had not been overlooked; but had been provided for, as well as might be, in the notable argument of "squatter sovereignty," otherwise called "sacred right of self-government," which latter phrase, though expressive of the only rightful basis of any government, was so perverted in this attempted use of it as to amount to just this: That if any *one* man choose to enslave *another*, no *third* man shall be allowed to object. That argument was incorporated into the Nebraska bill itself, in the language which follows: "It being the true intent and meaning of this act not to legislate Slavery into any Territory or State, nor to exclude it therefrom; but to leave the people thereof perfectly free to form and regulate their domestic institutions in their own way, subject only to the Constitution of the United States." Then opened the roar of loose declamation in favor of "Squatter Sovereignty," and "sacred right of self-government." "But," said opposition members, "let us amend the bill so as to expressly declare that the people of the Territory may exclude Slavery." "Not we," said the friends of the measure; and down they voted the amendment.

While the Nebraska bill was passing through Congress, a *law case* involving the question of a negro's freedom, by reason of his owner having voluntarily taken him first into a Free State and then into a Territory covered by the Congressional prohibition, and held him as a slave for a long time in each, was passing through the United States Circuit Court for the District of Missouri; and both Nebraska bill and law suit were brought to a decision in the same month of May, 1854. The negro's name was "Dred Scott," which name now designates the decision finally made in the case. Before the then next Presidential Election, the law case came to, and was argued in, the Supreme Court of the United States; but the decision of it was deferred until after the election. Still, before the election, Senator Trumbull, on the floor of the Senate, requested the leading advocate of the Nebraska bill to state *his opinion* whether the people of a Territory can constitutionally exclude Slavery from their limits; and the latter answers: "That is a question for the Supreme Court."

The election came. Mr. Buchanan was elected, and the indorsement, such as it was, secured. That was the second point gained. The indorsement, however, fell short of a clear popular majority by nearly four hundred thousand votes, and so, perhaps, was not overwhelmingly reliable and satisfactory. The outgoing President, in his last annual message, as impressively as possible, echoed back upon the people the weight and authority of the indorsement. The Supreme Court met again; did not announce their decision, but ordered a re-argument. The Presidential inauguration came, and still no decision of the court; but the incoming President in his inaugural address, fervently exhorted the people to abide by the forthcoming decision, whatever it might be. Then in a few days, came the decision.

The reputed author of the Nebraska bill finds an early occasion to make a speech at this capital, indorsing the Dred Scott decision, and vehemently denouncing all opposition to it. The new President, too, seizes the early occasion of the Silliman letter to indorse and strongly construe that decision, and to express his astonishment that any different view had ever been entertained!

At length a squabble springs up between the President and the author of the Nebraska bill, on the mere question of *fact*, whether the Lecompton Constitution was or was not, in any just sense, made by the people of Kansas; and in that quarrel the latter declares that all he wants is a fair vote for the people, and that he cares not whether Slavery be voted *down* or voted *up*. I do not understand his declaration that he cares not whether Slavery be voted down or voted up, to be intended by him other than as an apt definition of the policy he would impress upon the public mind—the principle for which he declares he has suffered so much, and is ready to suffer to the end. And well may he cling to that principle. If he has any parental feeling, well may he cling to it. That principle is the only shred left of his original Nebraska doctrine. Under the Dred Scott decision "squatter sovereignty" squatted out of existence, tumbled down like temporary scaffolding—like the mold at the foundry served through one blast and fell back into loose sand—helped to carry an election, and then was kicked to the winds. His late joint struggle with the Republicans, against the Lecompton Constitution, involves nothing of the original Nebraska doctrine. That struggle was made on a point—the right of a people to make their own constitution—upon which he and the Republicans have never differed.

The several points of the Dred Scott decision, in connection with Senator Douglas's "care not" policy, constitute the piece of machinery, in its present state of advancement. This was the third point gained. The working points of that machinery are:

First, That no negro slave, imported as such from Africa, and no descendant of such slave, can ever be a citizen of any State, in the sense of that term as used in the Constitution of the United States. This point is made in order to deprive the negro, in every possible event, of the benefit of that provision of the United States Constitution, which declares that "The citizens of each State shall be entitled to all privileges and immunities of citizens in the several States."

Secondly, That "subject to the Constitution of the United States," neither Congress nor a Territorial Legislature can exclude Slavery from any United States Territory. This point is made in order that individual men may fill up the Territories with slaves, without danger of losing them as property, and thus to enhance the chances of permanency to the institution through all the future.

Thirdly, That whether the holding a negro in actual slavery in a Free State, makes him free, as against the holder, the United States courts will not decide, but will leave to be decided by the courts of any Slave State the negro may be forced into by the master. This point is made, not to be pressed immediately ; but, if acquiesced in for awhile, and apparently indorsed by the people at an election, then to sustain the logical conclusion that what Dred Scott's master might lawfully do with Dred Scott, in the free State of Illinois, every other master may lawfully do with any other one, or one thousand slaves, in Illinois, or in any other Free State.

Auxiliary to all this, and working hand in hand with it, the Nebraska doctrine, or what is left of it, is to educate and mold public opinion, at least Northern public opinion, not to care whether Slavery is voted down or voted up. This shows exactly where we now are; and partially, also, whither we are tending.

It will throw additional light on the latter, to go back, and run the mind over the string of historical facts already stated. Several things will now appear less dark and mysterious than they did when they were transpiring. The people were to be left "perfectly free," subject only to the Constitution. What the Constitution had to do with it, outsiders could not then see. Plainly enough now, it was an exactly fitted niche, for the Dred Scott decision to afterward come in, and declare the perfect freedom of the people to be just no freedom at all. Why was the amendment, expressly declaring the right of the people, voted down? Plainly enough now: the adoption of it would have spoiled the niche for the Dred Scott decision. Why was the court decision held up? Why even a Senator's individual opinion withheld, till after the Presidential election? Plainly enough now: the speaking out then would have damaged the perfectly free argument upon which the election was to be carried. Why the outgoing President's felicitation on the indorsment? Why the delay of a reargument? Why the incoming President's advance exhortation in favor of the decision? These things look like the cautious patting and petting of a spirited horse preparatory to mounting him, when it is dreaded that he may give the rider a fall. And why the hasty after-indorsement of the decision by the President and others?

We cannot absolutely know that all these exact adaptations are the result of preconcert. But when we see a lot of framed timbers, different portions of which we know have been gotten out at different times and places, and by different workmen—Stephen, Franklin, Roger and James, for instance—and when we see these timbers joined together, and see they exactly make the frame of a house or a mill, all the tenons and mortices exactly fitting, and all the lengths and proportions of the different pieces exactly adapted to their respective places, and not a piece too many or too few—not omitting even scaffolding—or, if a single piece be lacking, we see the place in the frame exactly fitted and prepared yet to bring such piece in—in such a case, we find it impossible not to believe that Stephen and Franklin and Roger and James all understood one another from the beginning, and all worked upon a common plan or draft drawn up before the first blow was struck.

It should not be overlooked that, by the Nebraska bill, the people of a *State* as well as a Territory, were to be left "perfectly free," "subject only to the Constitution." Why mention a State? They were legislating for Territories, and not for or about States. Certainly the people of a State are and ought to be subject to the Constitution of the United States; but why is mention of this lugged into

this merely Territorial law? Why are the people of a Territory and the people of a State therein lumped together, and their relation to the Constitution therein treated as being precisely the same ? While the opinion of the court, by Chief Justice Taney, in the Dred Scott case, and the separate opinions of all the concurring Judges, expressly declare that the Constitution of the United States neither permits Congress nor a Territorial Legislature to exclude Slavery from any United States Territory, they all omit to declare whether or not the same Constitution permits a State, or the people of a State, to exclude it. *Possibly*, this is a mere omission ; but who can be quite sure, if McLean or Curtis had sought to get into the opinion a declaration of unlimited power in the people of a State to exclude Slavery from their limits, just as Chase and Mace sought to get such declaration, in behalf of the people of a territory, into the Nebraska bill—I ask, who can be quite sure that it would not have been voted down in the one case as it had been in the other? The nearest approach to the point of declaring the power of a State over Slavery, is made by Judge Nelson. He approaches it more than once, using the precise idea, and almost the language, too, of the Nebraska act. On one occasion, his exact language is, "except in cases where the power is restrained by the Constitution of the United States, the law of the State is supreme over the subject of Slavery within its jurisdiction." In what cases the power of the States is so restrained by the United States Constitution, is left an open question, precisely as the same question, as to the restraint on the power of the Territories, was left open in the Nebraska act. Put this and that together, and we have another nice little niche, which we may, ere long, see filled with another Supreme Court decision, declaring that the Constitution of the United States does not permit a *State* to exclude Slavery from its limits. And this may especially be expected if the doctrine of " care not whether Slavery be voted down or voted up," shall gain upon the public mind sufficiently to give promise that such a decision can be maintained when made.

Such a decision is all that Slavery now lacks of being alike lawful in all the States. Welcome, or unwelcome, such decision is probably coming, and will soon be upon us, unless the power of the present political dynasty shall be met and overthrown. We shall lie down pleasantly dreaming that the people of Missouri are on the verge of making their State free, and we shall awake to the reality instead, that the Supreme Court has made Illinois a Slave State. To meet and overthrow the power of that dynasty, is the work now before all those who would prevent that consummation. This is what we have to do. How can we best do it?

There are those who denounce us openly to their own friends, and yet whisper us softly, that Senator Douglas is the aptest instrument there is with which to effect that object. They wish us to *infer* all, from the fact that he now has a little quarrel with the present head of the dynasty ; and that he has regularly voted with us on a single point, upon which he and we have never differed. They remind us that he is a great man, and that the largest of us are very small ones. Let this be granted. But "a living dog is better than a dead lion." Judge Douglas, if not a dead lion, for this work, is at least a caged and toothless one. How can he oppose the advances of Slavery? He don't care anything about it. His avowed mission is impressing the " public heart " to *care nothing about it*. A leading Douglas Democratic newspaper thinks Douglas's superior talent will be needed to resist the revival of the African slave-trade. Does Douglas believe an effort to revive that trade is approaching? He has not said so. Does he really think so? But if it is, how can he resist it? For years he has labored to prove it a sacred right of white men to take negro slaves into the new Territories. Can he possibly show that it is less a sacred right to buy them where they can be bought cheapest? And unquestionably they can be bought cheaper in Africa than in Virginia. He has done all in his power to reduce the whole question of Slavery to one of a mere right of property ; and as such, how can he oppose the foreign slave-trade—how can he refuse that trade in that " property " shall be " perfectly free "— unless he does it as a protection to the home production? And as the home producers will probably not ask the protection, he will be wholly without a ground of opposition.

Senator Douglas holds, we know, that a man may rightfully be wiser to-day than he was yesterday—that he may rightfully change when he finds himself wrong. But can we, for that reason, run ahead, and infer that he will make any particular change, of which he, himself, has given no intimation? Can we safely base our action upon any such vague inference? Now, as ever, I wish not to misrepresent Judge Douglas's position, question his motives, or do aught that can be personally offensive to him. Whenever, if ever, he and we can come together on principle so that our cause may have assistance from his great ability, I hope to have interposed no adventitious obstacle. But clearly, he is not now with us—he does not pretend to be—he does not promise ever to be.

Our cause, then, must be intrusted to, and conducted by, its own undoubted friends—those whose hands are free, whose hearts are in the work—who *do care* for the result. Two years ago the Republicans of the nation mustered over thirteen hundred thousand strong. We did this under the single impulse of resistance to a common danger, with every external circumstance against us. Of strange, discordant, and even hostile elements, we gathered from the four winds, and formed and fought the battle through, under the constant hot fire of a disciplined, proud and pampered enemy. Did we brave all them to falter now?—now, when that same enemy is wavering, dissevered and belligerent? The result is not doubtful. We shall not fail—if we stand firm, we *shall not fail*. Wise counsels may accelerate, or mistakes delay it, but, sooner or later, the victory is sure to come.

SLAVERY DISCUSSED BY LINCOLN AND DOUGLAS.

QUESTIONS AND ANSWERS.

MR. LINCOLN'S SPEECH.

At the second Joint Debate, between Mr. Douglas and Mr. Lincoln, at Freeport, Illinois, August 27th, 1858, Mr. Lincoln spoke as follows :

LADIES AND GENTLEMEN: On Saturday last, Judge Douglas and myself first met in public discussion. He spoke one hour, I an hour and a half, and he replied for half and hour. The order is now reversed. I am to speak an hour, he an hour and a half, and then I am to reply for half an hour. I propose to devote myself during the first hour to the scope of what was brought within the range of his half-hour speech at Ottawa. Of course there was brought within the scope in that half-hour's speech something of his own opening speech, In the course of that opening argument, Judge Douglas proposed to me seven distinct interrogatories. In my speech of an hour and a half, I attended to some other parts of his speech, and incidentally, as I thought, answered one of the interrogatories then. I then distinctly intimated to him that I would answer the rest of his interrogatories on condition only that he should agree to answer as many for me. He made no intimation at the time of the proposition, nor did he in his reply allude at all to that suggestion of mine. I do him no injustice in saying that he occupied at least half of his reply in dealing with me as though I had *refused* to answer his interrogatories. I now propose that I will answer any of the interrogatories, upon condition that he will answer questions from me not exceeding the same number. I give him an opportunity to respond. The Judge remains silent. I now say that I will answer his interrogatories, whether he answers mine or not; and that after I have done so, I shall propound mine to him.

I have supposed myself, since the organization of the Republican party at Bloomington, in May, 1856, bound as a party man by the platforms of the party, then and since. If in any interrogatories which I shall answer I go beyond the scope of what is within these platforms, it will be perceived that no one is responsible but myself.

Having said thus much, I will take up the Judge's interrogatories as I find them printed in the Chicago *Times*, and answer them *seriatim*. In order that there may be no mistake about it, I have copied the interrogatories in writing, and also my answers to them. The first of these interrogatories is in these words :

Question 1. "I desire to know whether Lincoln to-day stands, as he did in 1854, in favor of the unconditional repeal of the Fugitive Slave law ?"

Answer. I do not now, nor ever did, stand in favor of the unconditional repeal of the Fugitive Slave law.

Q. 2. "I desire him to answer whether he stands pledged to-day, as he did in 1854, against the admission of any more Slave States into the Union, even if the people want them ?"

A. I do not now, or ever did, stand pledged against the admission of any more Slave States into the Union.

Q. 3. "I want to know whether he stands pledged against the admission of a new State into the Union with such a Constitution as the people of that State may see fit to make ?"

A. I do not stand pledged against the admission of a new State into the Union, with such a Constitution as the people of that State may see fit to make.

Q. 4. "I want to know whether he stands to-day pledged to the abolition of Slavery in the District of Columbia ?"

A. I do not stand to-day pledged to the abolition of Slavery in the District of Columbia.

Q. 5. "I desire him to answer whether he stands pledged to the prohibition of the slave-trade between the different States ?"

A. I do not stand pledged to the prohibition of the slave-trade between the different States.

Q. 6. "I desire to know whether he stands pledged to prohibit Slavery in all the Territories of the United States, North as well as South of the Missouri Compromise line ?"

A. I am impliedly, if not expressly, pledged to a belief in the *right* and *duty* of Congress to prohibit Slavery in all the United States Territories.

Q. 7. "I desire him to answer whether he is opposed to the acquisition of any new territory unless Slavery is first prohibited therein ?"

A. I am not generally opposed to honest acquisition of territory ; and, in any given case, I would or would not oppose such acquisition, accordingly as I might think such acquisition would or would not aggravate the Slavery question among ourselves.

Now, my friends, it will be perceived upon an examination of these questions and answers, that so far I have only answered that I was not *pledged* to this, that or the other. The Judge has not framed his interrogatories to ask me anything more than this, and I have answered in strict accordance with the interrogatories, and have answered truly that I am not *pledged* at all upon any of the points to which I have answered. But I am not disposed to hang upon the exact form of his interrogatory. I am rather disposed to take up at least some of these questions, and state what I really think upon them.

As to the first one, in regard to the Fugitive Slave Law, I have never hesitated to say, and I do not now hesitate to say, that I think, under the Constitution of the United States, the people of the Southern States are entitled to a Congressional Fugitive Slave Law. Having said that, I have had nothing to say in regard to the existing Fugitive Slave Law, further than that I think it should have been framed so as to be free from some of the objections that pertain to it, without lessening its efficiency. And inasmuch as we are not now in an agitation in regard to an alteration or modification of that law, I would not be the man to introduce it as a new subject of agitation upon the general question of Slavery.

In regard to the other question, of whether I am pledged to the admission of any more Slave States into the Union, I state to you very frankly that I would be exceedingly sorry ever to be put in a position of having to pass upon that question. I should be exceedingly glad to know that there would never be another Slave State admitted into the Union ; but I must add, that if Slavery shall be kept out of the Territories during the territorial existence of any one given Territory, and then the people shall, having a fair opportunity and a clear field, when they come to adopt the Constitution, do such an extraordinary thing as adopt a Slave Constitution, uninfluenced by the actual presence of the institution among them, I see no alternative, if we own the country, but to admit them into the Union.

The third interrogatory is answered by the answer to the second, it being, as I conceive, the same as the second.

The fourth one is in regard to the abolition of Slavery in the District of Columbia. In relation to that, I have my mind very distinctly made up. I should be exceedingly glad to see Slavery abolished in the District of Columbia. I believe that Congress possesses the constitutional power to abolish it. Yet, as a member of Congress, I should not, with my present views, be in favor of *endeavoring* to abolish Slavery in the District of Columbia, unless it would be upon these conditions: *First*, that the abolition should be gradual. *Second*, that it should be on a vote of the majority of qualified voters in the District; and *Third*, that compensation should be made to unwilling owners. With these three conditions, I confess I would be exceedingly glad to see Congress abolish Slavery in the District of Columbia, and, in the language of Henry Clay, " sweep from our Capital that foul blot upon our nation."

In regard to the fifth interrogatory, I must say here, that as to the question of the abolition of the slave-trade between the different States, I can truly answer, as I have, that I am *pledged* to nothing about it. It is a subject to which I have not given that mature consideration that would make me feel authorized to state a position so as to hold myself entirely bound by it. In other words, that question has never been prominently enough before me to induce me to investigate whether we really have the constitutional power to do it. I could investigate it if I had sufficient time, to bring myself to a conclusion upon that subject; but I have not done so, and I say so frankly to you here, and to Judge Douglas. I must say, however, that if I should be of opinion that Congress does possess the constitutional power to abolish the slave-trade among the different States, I should still not be in favor of the exercise of that power unless upon some conservative principle as I conceive it, akin to what I have said in relation to the abolition of Slavery in the District of Columbia.

My answer as to whether I desire that Slavery should be prohibited in all the Territories of the United States, is full and explicit within itself, and cannot be made clearer by any comments of mine. So I suppose in regard to the question whether I am opposed to the acquisition of any more territory unless Slavery is first prohibited therein, my answer is such that I could add nothing by way of illustration, or making myself better understood, than the answer which I have placed in writing.

Now in all this, the Judge has me, and he has me on the record. I suppose he had flattered himself that I was really entertaining one set of opinions for one place and another set for another place—that I was afraid to say at one place what I uttered at another. What I am saying here I suppose I say to a vast audience as strongly tending to Abolitionism as any audience in the State of Illinois, and I believe I am saying that which, if it would be offensive to any persons and render them enemies to myself, would be offensive to persons in this audience.

I now proceed to propound to the Judge the interrogatories, so far as I have framed them. I will bring forward a new installment when I get them ready. I will bring them forward now, only reaching to number four.

The first one is:

Question 1. If the people of Kansas shall, by means entirely unobjectionable in all other respects, adopt a State Constitution, and ask admission into the Union under it, *before* they have the requisite number of inhabitants according to the English bill—some ninety-three thousand—will you vote to admit them?

Q. 2. Can the people of a United States Territory, in any lawful way, against the wish of any citizen of the United States, exclude Slavery from its limits prior to the formation of a State Constitution?

Q. 3. If the Supreme Court of the United States shall decide that States cannot exclude Slavery from their limits, are you in favor of acquiescing in, adopting and following such decision as a rule of political action?

Q. 4. Are you in favor of acquiring additional territory, in disregard of how such acquisition may affect the nation on the Slavery question?

As introductory to these interrogatories which Judge Douglas propounded to me at Ottawa, he read a set of resolutions which he said Judge Trumbull and myself had participated in adopting, in the first Republican State Convention, held at Springfield, in October, 1854. He insisted that I and Judge Trumbull, and perhaps the entire Republican party, were responsible for the doctrines contained in the set of resolutions which he read, and I understand that it was from that set of resolutions that he deduced the interrogatories which he propounded to me, using these resolutions as a sort of authority for propounding those questions to me. Now I say here to-day that I do not answer his interrogatories because of their springing at all from that set of resolutions which he read. I answered them because Judge Douglas thought fit to ask them. I do not now, nor never did, recognize any responsibility upon myself in that set of resolutions. When I replied to him on that occasion, I assured him that I never had anything to do with them. I repeat here to-day, that I never, in any possible form, had anything to do with that set of resolutions. It turns out, I

believe, that those resolutions were never passed in any Convention held in Springfield. It turns out that they were never passed at any Convention or any public meeting that I had any part in. I believe it turns out in addition to all this, that there was not, in the fall of 1854, any Convention holding a session at Springfield calling itself a Republican State Convention; yet it is true there was a Convention, or assemblage of men calling themselves a Convention, at Springfield, that did pass *some* resolutions. But so little did I really know of the proceedings of that Convention, or what set of resolutions they had passed, though having a general knowledge that there had been such an assemblage of men there, that when Judge Douglas read the resolutions, I really did not know but they had been the resolutions passed then and there. I did not question that they were the resolutions adopted. For I could not bring myself to suppose that Judge Douglas could say what he did upon this subject without *knowing* that it was true. I contented myself, on that occasion, with denying, as I truly could, all connection with them, not denying or affirming whether they were passed at Springfield. Now it turns out that he had got hold of some resolutions passed at some Convention or public meeting in Kane County. I wish to say here, that I don't conceive that in any fair and just mind this discovery relieves me at all. I had just as much to do with the Convention in Kane County as that at Springfield. I am just as much responsible for the resolutions at Kane County as those at Springfield, the amount of the responsibility being exactly nothing in either case: no more than there would be in regard to a set of resolutions passed in the moon.

I allude to this extraordinary matter in this canvass for some further purpose than anything yet advanced. Judge Douglas did not make his statement upon that occasion as matters that he believed to be true, but he stated them roundly as *being true*, in such form as to pledge his veracity for their truth. When the whole matter turns out as it does, and when we consider who Judge Douglas is—that he is a distinguished Senator of the United States—that he has served nearly twelve years as such—that his character is not at all limited as an ordinary Senator of the United States, but that his name has become of world-wide renown—it is *most extraordinary* that he should so far forget all the suggestions of justice to an adversary, or of prudence to himself, as to venture upon the assertion of that which the slightest investigation would have shown him to be wholly false. I can only account for his having done so upon the supposition that that evil genius which has attended him through his life, giving to him an apparent astonishing prosperity, such as to lead very many good men to doubt there being any advantage in virtue over vice—I say I can only account for it on the supposition that that evil genius has at last made up its mind to forsake him.

And I may add that another extraordinary feature of the Judge's conduct in this canvass—made more extraordinary by this incident—is, that he is in the habit, in almost all the speeches he makes, of charging falsehood upon his adversaries, myself and others. I now ask whether he is able to find in anything that Judge Trumbull, for instance, has said, or in anything that I have said, a justification at all compared with what we have, in this instance, for that sort of vulgarity.

MR. DOUGLAS' REPLY.

LADIES AND GENTLEMEN: I am glad that at last I have brought Mr. Lincoln to the conclusion that he had better define his position on certain political questions to which I called his attention at Ottawa. He there showed no disposition, no inclination, to answer them. I did not present idle questions for him to answer merely for my gratification. I laid the foundation for those interrogatories by showing that they constituted the platform of the party whose nominee he is for the Senate. I did not presume that I had the right to catechise him as I saw proper, unless I showed that his party, or a majority of it, stood upon the platform and were in favor of the propositions upon which my questions were based. I desired simply to know, inasmuch as he had been nominated as the first, last, and only choice of his party, whether he concurred in the platform which that party had adopted for its government. In a few moments I will proceed to review the answers which he has given to these interrogatories; but in order to relieve his anxiety I will first respond to these which he has presented to me. Mark you, he has not presented interrogatories which have ever received the sanction of the party with which I am acting, and hence he has no other foundation for them than his own curiosity.

First, he desires to know if the people of Kansas shall form a Constitution by means entirely proper and unebjectionable and ask admission into the Union as a State, before they have the requisite population for a member of Congress, whether I will vote for that admission. Well now, I regret exceedingly that he did not answer that interrogatory himself before he put it to me, in order that we might understand, and not be left to infer on which side he is. Mr. Trumbull, during the last session of Congress, voted from the beginning to the end against the admission of Oregon, although a free State, because she had not the requisite population for a member of Congress. Mr. Trumbull would not consent, under any circumstances, to let a State, free or slave, come into the Union until it had the requisite population. As Mr. Trumbull is in the field, fighting for Mr. Lincoln, I would like to have Mr. Lincoln answer his own question and tell me whether he is fighting Trumbull on that issue or not. But I will answer his question. In reference to Kansas, it is my opinion, that as she has population enough to constitute a slave State, she has people enough for a Free State. I will not make Kansas an exceptionable case to the other States of the Union. I hold it to be a sound rule of universal application to require a Territory to contain the requisite population for a member of Congress, before it is admitted as a State into the Union. I made that proposition in the Senate in 1856, and I renewed it during the last session, in a bill providing that no Territory of the United States should form a Constitution and apply for admission until it had the requisite population. On another occasion I proposed that neither Kansas, or any other Territory, should be admitted until it had the requisite population. Congress did not adopt any of my propositions containing this general rule, but did make an exception of Kansas. I will stand by that exception. Either Kansas must come in as a Free State, with whatever population she may have, or the rule must be applied to all the other territories alike. I therefore answer at once, that it having been decided that Kansas has people enough for a Slave State, I hold that she has enough for a Free State. I hope Mr. Lincoln is satisfied with my answer; and now I would like to get his answer to his own interrogatory—whether or not he will vote to admit Kansas before she has the requisite population. I want to know whether he will vote to admit Oregon before that Territory has the requisite population. Mr. Trumbull will not, and the same reason that commits Mr. Trumbull against the admission of Oregon, commits him against Kansas, even if she should apply for admission as a Free State. If there is any sincerity, any truth, in the argument of Mr. Trumbull in the Senate, against the admission of Oregon because she had not 93,420 people, although her population was larger than that of Kansas, he stands pledged against the admission of both Oregon and Kansas until they have 93,420 inhabitants. I would like Mr. Lincoln to answer this question. I would like him to take his own medicine. If he differs with Mr. Trumbull let him answer his argument against the admission of Oregon, instead of poking questions at me.

The next question propounded to me by Mr. Lincoln is, can the people of the Territory in any lawful way, against the wishes of any citizen of the United States, exclude Slavery from their limits prior to the formation of a State constitution? I answer emphatically, as Mr. Lincoln has heard me answer a hundred times from every stump in Illinois, that in my opinion the people of a Territory can, by lawful means, exclude Slavery from their limits prior to the formation of a State constitution. Mr. Lincoln knew that I had answered that question over and over again. He heard me argue the Nebraska bill on that principle all over the State in 1854, in 1855, and in 1856; and he has no excuse for pretending to be in doubt as to my position on that question. It matters not what way the Supreme Court may hereafter decide as to the abstract question whether Slavery may or may not go into a Territory under the Constitution; the people have the lawful means to introduce it or exclude it as they please, for the reason that Slavery cannot exist a day or an hour anywhere, unless it is supported by local police regulations. Those police regulations can only be established by the local legislature; and if the people are opposed to Slavery they will elect representatives to that body who will by unfriendly legislation effectually prevent the introduction of it into their midst. If, on the contrary, they are for it, their legislation will favor its extension. Hence, no matter what the decision of the Supreme Court may be on that abstract question, still the right of the people to make a slave Territory or a free Territory is perfect and complete under the Nebraska bill. I hope Mr. Lincoln deems my answer satisfactory on that point.

In this connection, I will notice the charge which he has introduced in relation to Mr. Chase's amendment. I thought that I had chased that amendment out of Mr. Lincoln's brain at Ottawa; but it seems that still haunts his imagination, and he is not yet satisfied. I had sup-

posed that he would be ashamed to press that question further. He is a lawyer, and has been a member of Congress, and has occupied his time and amused you by telling you about parliamentary proceeding. He ought to have known better than to try to palm off his miserable impositions upon this intelligent audience. The Nebraska bill provided that the legislative power and authority of the said Territory should extend to all rightful subjects of legislation, consistent with the organic act and the Constitution of the United States. It did not make any exception as to Slavery, but gave all the power that it was possible for Congress to give, without violating the Constitution, to the Territorial Legislature, with no exception or limitation on the subject of Slavery at all. The language of that bill which I have quoted, gave the full power and the full authority over the subject of Slavery, affirmatively and negatively, to introduce it or exclude it, so far as the Constitution of the United States would permit. What more could Mr. Chase give by his amendment? Nothing. He offered his amendment for the identical purpose for which Mr. Lincoln is using it, to enable demagogues in the country to try and deceive the people.

His amendment was to this effect. It provided that the Legislature should have the power to exclude Slavery: and General Cass suggested, "why not give the power to introduce as well as exclude?" The answer was, they have the power already in the bill to do both. Chase was afraid his amendment would be adopted if he put the alternative proposition and so make it fair both ways, but would not yield. He offered it for the purpose of having it rejected. He offered it, as he has himself avowed over and over again, simply to make capital out of it for the stump. He expected that it would be capital for small politicans in the country, and that they would make an effort to deceive the people with it; and he was not mistaken, for Lincoln is carrying out the plan admirably. Lincoln knows that the Nebraska bill, without Chase's amendment, gave all the power which the Constitution would permit. Could Congress confer any more? Could Congress go beyond the Constitution of the country? We gave all a full grant with no exception in regard to Slavery one way or the other. We left that question, as we left all others, to be decided by the people for themselves, just as they pleased. I will not occupy my time on this question. I have argued it before all over Illinois. I have argued it in this beautiful city of Freeport; I have argued it in the North, the South, the East, and the West, avowing the same sentiments and the same principles. I have not been afraid to avow my sentiments up here for fear I would be trotted down into Egypt.

The third question which Mr. Lincoln presented is, if the Supreme Court of the United States shall decide that a State of this Union cannot exclude Slavery from its own limits, will I submit to it? I am amazed that Lincoln should ask such a question. ("A school-boy knows better.") Yes, a school-boy does know better.) Mr. Lincoln's object is to cast an imputation upon the Supreme Court. He knows that there never was but one man in America, claiming any degree of intelligence or decency, who ever for a moment pretended such a thing. It is true that the Washington *Union*, in an article published on the 17th of last December, did put forth that doctrine, and I denounced the article on the floor of the Senate, in a speech which Mr. Lincoln now pretends was against the President. The *Union* had claimed that Slavery had a right to go into the free States, and that any provision in the Constitution or laws of the Free States to the contrary were null and void. I denounced it in the Senate, as I said before, and I was the first man who did. Lincoln's friends, Trumbull, and Seward, and Hale, and Wilson, and the whole Black Republican side of the Senate, were silent. They left it to me to denounce it. And what was the reply made to me on that occasion? Mr. Toombs, of Georgia, got up and undertook to lecture me on the ground that I ought not to have deemed the article worthy of notice, and ought not to have replied to it; that there was not one man, woman, or child south of the Potomac, in any Slave State, who did not repudiate any such pretension. Mr. Lincoln knows that that reply was made on the spot, and yet now he asks this question. He might as well ask me, Suppose Mr. Lincoln should steal a horse, would I sanction it; and it would be as genteel in me to ask him, in the event he stole a horse, what ought to be done with him. He casts an imputation upon the Supreme Court of the United States, by supposing that they would violate the Constitution of the United States. I tell him that such a thing is not possible. It would be an act of moral treason that no man on on the bench could ever descend to. Mr. Lincoln himself, would never, in his partisan feelings, so far forget what was right as to be guilty of such an act.

The fourth question of Mr. Lincoln is, are you in favor of acquiring additional territory, in disregard as to how such acquisition may affect the Union on the Slavery question ? This question is very ingeniously and cunningly put.

The Black Republican creed lays it down expressly, that under no circumstances shall we acquire any more territory unless Slavery is first prohibited in the country. I ask Mr. Lincoln whether he is in favor of that proposition. Are you (addressing Mr. Lincoln) opposed to the acquisition of any more territory, under any circumstances, unless Slavery is prohibited in it ? That he does not like to answer. When I ask him whether he stands up to that article in the platform of his party, he turns, Yankee-fashion, and without answering it, asks me whether I am in favor of acquiring territory without regard to how it may affect the Union on the Slavery question. I answer that whenever it becomes necessary, in our growth and progress, to acquire more territory, that I am in favor of it, without reference to the question of Slavery, and when we have acquired it, I will leave the people free to do as they please, either to make it slave or free territory, as they prefer. It is idle to tell me or you that we have territory enough. Our fathers supposed that we had enough when our territory extended to the Mississippi River, but a few years' growth and expansion satisfied them that we needed more, and the Louisiana territory, from the west branch of the Mississippi to the British possessions, was acquired. Then we acquired Oregon, then California and New Mexico. We have enough now for the present, but this is a young and a growing nation. It swarms as often as a hive of bees, and as new swarms are turned out each year, there must be hives in which they can gather and make their honey. In less than fifteen years, if the same progress that has distinguished this country for the last fifteen years continues, every foot of vacant land between this and the Pacific Ocean, owned by the United States, will be occupied. Will you not continue to increase at the end of fifteen years as well as now ? I tell you, increase, and multiply, and expand, is the law of this nation's existence. You cannot limit this great Republic by mere boundary lines, saying, " thus far shalt thou go, and no further." Any one of you gentlemen might as well say to a son twelve years old that he is big enough, and must not grow any larger, and in order to prevent his growth put a hoop around him to keep him to his present size. What would be the result ? Either the hoop must burst and be rent asunder, or the child must die. So it would be with this great nation. With our natural increase, growing with a rapidity unknown in any other part of the globe, with the tide of emigration that is fleeing from despotism in the old world to seek refuge in our own, there is a constant torrent pouring into this country that requires more land, more territory upon which to settle, and just as fast as our interests and our destiny require additional territory in the North, in the South, or on the Islands of the ocean, I am for it, and when we acquire it, will leave the people, according to the Nebraska bill, free to do as they please on the subject of Slavery and every other question.

I trust now that Mr. Lincoln will deem himself answered on his four points. He racked his brain so much in devising these four questions that he exhausted himself, and had not strength enough to invent the others. As soon as he is able to hold a council with his advisers, Lovejoy, Farnsworth, and Fred Douglass, he will f ame and propound others. (" Good, good.") You Black Republicans who say good, I have no doubt think that they are all good men. I have reason to recollect that some people in this country think that Fred Douglass is a very good man. The last time I came here to make a speech, while talking from the stand to you, people of Freeport, as I am doing to-day, I saw a carriage, and a magnificent one it was, drive up and take a position on the outside of the crowd ; a beautiful young lady was sitting on the box-seat, whilst Fred Douglass and her mother reclined inside, and the owner of the carriage acted as driver. I saw this in your own town. (" What of it ?") All I have to say of it is this, that if you, Black Republicans, think that the negro ought to be on a social equality with your wives and daughters, and ride in a carriage with your wife, whilst you drive the team, you have perfect right to do so. I am told that one of Fred Douglass's kinsmen, another rich black negro, is now traveling in this part of the State making speeches for his friend Lincoln as the champion of black men. (" What have you to say against it ?") All I have to say on that subject is, that those of you who believe that the negro is your equal and ought to be on an equality with you socially, politically, and legally, have a right to entertain those opinions, and of course will vote for Mr. Lincoln.

POPULAR SOVEREIGNTY IN THE TERRITORIES.

BY STEPHEN A. DOUGLAS.

From Harper's Magazine, 1859.

UNDER our complex system of government it is the first duty of American statesmen to mark distinctly the dividing line between Federal and Local Authority. To do this with accuracy involves an inquiry, not only into the powers and duties of the Federal Government under the Constitution, but also into the rights, privileges, and immunities of the people of the Territories, as well as of the States composing the Union. The relative powers and functions of the Federal and State governments have become well understood and clearly defined by their practical operation and harmonious action for a long series of years ; while the disputed question—involving the right of the people of the Territories to govern themselves in respect to their local affairs and internal polity— remains a fruitful source of partisan strife and sectional controversy. The political organization which was formed in 1854, and has assumed the name of the Republican Party, is based on the theory that African Slavery, as it exists in this country, is an evil of such magnitude— social, moral, and political—as to justify and require the exertion of the entire power and influence of the Federal Government to the full extent that the Constitution, according to their interpretation, will permit for its ultimate extinction. In the platform of principles adopted at Philadelphia by the Republican National Convention in 1856, it is affirmed :

" That the Constitution confers upon Congress sovereign power over the Territories of the United States for their government, and that in the exercise of this power it is both the right and the duty of Congress to prohibit in the Territories those twin relics of barbarism, polygamy and Slavery."

According to the theory of the Republican party there is an irrepressible conflict between Freedom and Slavery, free labor and slave labor, Free States and Slave States, which is irreconcilable, and must continue to rage with increasing fury until the one shall become universal by the annihilation of the other. In the language of the most eminent and authoritative expounder of their political faith,

" It is an irrepressible conflict between opposing and enduring forces ; and it means that the United States must and will, sooner or later, become either entirely a slave holding nation or entirely a free-labor nation. Either the cotton and rice fields of South Carolina, and the sugar plantations of Louisiana will ultimately be tilled by free labor, and Charleston and New-Orleans become marts for legitimate merchandise alone, or else the rye fields and wheat fields of Massachusetts and New-York must again be surrendered by their farmers to slave culture and to the production of slaves, and Boston and New-York become once more markets for trade in the bodies and souls of men."

In the Illinois canvass of 1858 the same proposition was advocated and defended by the distinguished Republican standard-bearer in these words :

" In my opinion it (the Slavery agitation) will not cease until a crisis shall have been reached and passed. ' A House divided against itself cannot stand.' I believe this government cannot endure permanently half slave and half free. I do not expect the House to fall, but I do expect it will cease to be divided. It will become all one thing or all the other. Either the opponents of Slavery will arrest the further spread of it, and place it where the public mind shall rest in the belief that it is in the course of ultimate extinction, or its advocates will push forward till it shall become alike lawful in all the States —old as well as new, North as well as South."

Thus it will be seen, that under the auspices of a political party, which claims sovereignty in Congress over the subject of Slavery, there can be no peace on the

Slavery question—no truce in the sectional strife—no fraternity between the North and South, so long as this Union remains as our fathers made it—divided into free and slave States, with the right on the part of each to retain Slavery so long as it chooses, and to abolish it whenever it pleases.

On the other hand, it would be uncandid to deny that, while the Democratic party is a unit in its irreconcilable opposition to the doctrines and principles of the Republican party, there are radical differences of opinion in respect to the powers and duties of Congress, and the rights and immunities of the people of the Territories under the Federal Constitution, which seriously disturb its harmony and threaten its integrity. These differences of opinion arise from the different interpretations placed on the Constitution by persons who belong to one of the following classes:

First.—Those who believe that the Constitution of the United States neither establishes nor prohibits Slavery in the States or Territories beyond the power of the people legally to control it, but " leaves the people thereof perfectly free to form and regulate their domestic institutions in their own way, subject only to the Constitution of the United States."

Second.—Those who believe that the Constitution establishes Slavery in the Territories, and withholds from Congress and the Territorial Legislature the power to control it ; and who insist that, in the event the Territorial Legislature fails to enact the requisite laws for its protection, it becomes the imperative duty of Congress to interpose its authority and furnish such protection.

Third.—Those who, while professing to believe that the Constitution establishes Slavery in the Territories beyond the power of Congress or the Territorial Legislature to control it, at the same time protest against the duty of Congress to interfere for its protection ; but insist that it is the duty of the Judiciary to protect and maintain slavery in the Territories without any law upon the subject.

By a careful examination of the second and third propositions, it will be seen that the advocates of each agree on the theoretical question, that the Constitution establishes Slavery in the Territories, and compels them to have it whether they want it or not ; and differ on the practical point, whether a right secured by the Constitution shall be protected by an act of Congress when all other remedies fail. The reason assigned for not protecting by law a right secured by the Constitution is, that it is the duty of the Courts to protect Slavery in the Territories without any legislation upon the subject. How the Courts are to afford protection to slaves or any other property, where there is no law providing remedies and imposing penalties and conferring jurisdiction upon the courts to hear and determine the cases as they arise, remains to be explained

The acts of Congress, establishing the several Territories of the United States, provide that : " The jurisdiction of the several Courts herein provided for, both appellate and original, and that of the Probate Courts and Justices of the Peace shall be limited by law"—meaning such laws as the Territorial Legislatures shall from time to time enact. It will be seen that the judicial tribunals of the Territories have just such jurisdiction, and only such, in respect to the rights of persons and property pertaining to the citizens of the Territory as the Territorial Legislature shall see fit to confer ; and consequently, that the Courts can afford protection to persons and property no further than the Legislature shall, by law, confer the jurisdiction, and prescribe the remedies, penalties, and modes of proceeding.

It is difficult to conceive how any person who believes that the Constitution confers the right of protection in the enjoyment of slave property in the Territories, regardless of the wishes of the people and of the action of the Territorial Legislature, can satisfy his conscience and his oath of fidelity to the Constitution in withholding such Congressional legislation as may be essential to the enjoyment of such right under the Constitution. Under this view of the subject it is impossible to resist the conclusion that, if the Constitution does establish Slavery in the Territories, beyond the power of the people to control it by law, it is the imperative duty of Congress to supply all the legislation necessary to its protection ; and if this proposition is not true, it necessarily results that the Constitution neither establishes nor prohibits Slavery anywhere, but leaves the people of each State and Territory entirely free to form and regulate their domestic affairs to suit themselves, without the intervention of Congress or any other power whatsoever.

But it is urged with great plausibility by those who have entire faith in the soundness of the proposition, that Territory is the mere creature of Congress ; that the creature cannot be clothed with any powers not possessed by the creator ; and that Congress, not possessing the power to legislate in respect to African Slavery in the Territories, cannot delegate to a Territorial Legislature any power which it does not itself possess."

This proposition is as plausible as it is fallacious. But the reverse of it is true as a general rule. Congress cannot delegate to a Territorial Legislature, or to any other body of men whatsoever, any power which the Constitution has vested in Congress. In other words : *Every power conferred on Congress by the Constitution must be exercised by Congress in the mode prescribed in the Constitution.*

Let us test the correctness of this proposition by reference to the powers of Congress as defined in the Constitution :

" The Congress shall have power—
" To lay and collect taxes, duties, imposts, and excises," etc. ;
" To borrow money on the credit of the United States ;"
" To regulate commerce and foreign nations," etc. ;
" To establish a uniform rule of naturalization," etc. ;
" To coin money, and regulate the value thereof ;"
" To establish post-offices and post-roads ;"
" To constitute tribunals inferior to the Supreme Court ;"
" To declare war," etc. ;
" To provide and maintain a navy."

This list might be extended so as to embrace all the power conferred on Congress by the Constitution ; but enough has been cited to test the principle. Will it be contended that Congress can delegate any one of these powers to a Territorial Legislature, or to any tribunal whatever ? Can Congress delegate to Kansas the power to " regulate commerce," or to Nebraska the power " to establish uniform rules of naturalization," or to Illinois the power " to coin money and regulate the value thereof," or to Virginia the power " to establish post-offices and post-roads ?"

The mere statement of the question carries with it the emphatic answer, that Congress cannot delegate any power which it does not possess ; but that every power conferred on Congress by the Constitution must be exercised by Congress in the manner prescribed in that instrument.

On the other hand, there are cases in which Congress may establish tribunals and local governments, and invest them with powers which Congress does not possess, and cannot exercise under the Constitution. For instance, Congress may establish courts inferior to the Supreme Court, and confer upon them the power to hear and determine cases, and render judgments affecting the life, liberty, and property of the citizen, without itself having the power to hear and determine such causes, render judgments, or revise or annul the same. In like manner Congress may institute governments for the Territories, composed of an executive, judicial, and legislative department ; and may confer upon the Governor all the executive powers and functions of the Territory, without having the right to exercise any one of those powers or functions itself.

Congress may confer upon the judicial department all the judicial powers and functions of the Territory, without having the right to hear and determine a cause, or render a judgment, or to revise or annul any decision made by the courts so established by Congress. Congress may also confer upon the legislative department of the Territory certain legislative powers which it can not itself exercise, and only such as Congress cannot exercise under the Constitution. The powers which Congress may thus *confer*, but cannot *exercise*, are such as relate to the domestic affairs and internal polity of the Territory, and do not affect the general welfare of the Republic.

This dividing line between Federal and Local authority was familiar to the framers of the Constitution. It is clearly defined and distinctly marked on every page of history which records the great events of that immortal struggle between the American Colonies and the British Government, which resulted in the establishment of our national independence. In the beginning of that struggle the Colonies neither contemplated nor desired independence. In all their addresses to the Crown, and to the Parliament, and to the people of Great Britain, as well as to the people of America, they averred that as loyal British subjects they deplored the causes which impelled their separation from the parent country. They were strongly and affectionately attached to the Constitution, civil and political institutions and jurisprudence of Great Britain, which they proudly claimed as the birthright of all Englishmen ; and desired to transmit them unimpaired as a precious legacy to their posterity. For a long series of years they remonstrated against the violation of their inalienable rights of self-government under the British Constitution, and humbly petitioned for the redress of their grievances.

They acknowledged and affirmed their allegiance to the Crown, their affection for the people, and their devotion to the Constitution of Great Britain; and their only complaint was that they were not permitted to enjoy the rights and privileges of self-government, in the management of their internal affairs and domestic concerns, in accordance with the guaranties of that Constitution and of the colonial charters granted by the Crown in pursuance of it. They conceded the right of the Imperial Government to make all laws and perform all acts concerning the Colonies, which were in their nature *Imperial* and not *Colonial*—which affected the general welfare of the Empire, and did not interfere with the "internal polity" of the Colonies. They recognized the right of the Imperial Government to declare war and make peace; to coin money and determine its value; to make treaties and conduct intercourse with foreign nations; to regulate commerce between the several colonies, and between each colony and the parent country, and with foreign countries; and in general they recognized the right of the Imperial Government of Great Britain to exercise all the powers and authority which, under our Federal Constitution, are delegated by the people of the several States to the Government of the United States.

Recognizing and conceding to the Imperial Government all these powers, *including the right to institute governments for the colonies*, by granting charters under which the inhabitants residing within the limits of any specified territory might be organized into a political community, with a government consisting of its appropriate departments, executive, legislative, and judicial; conceding all these powers, the Colonies emphatically denied that the Imperial Government had any rightful authority to impose taxes upon them without their consent, or to interfere with their internal polity; claiming that it was the birthright of all Englishmen—inalienable when formed into a political community—to exercise and enjoy all the rights, privileges, and immunities of self-government in respect to all matters and things which were local and not general—internal and not external—colonial and not imperial—as fully as if they were inhabitants of England, with a fair representation in Parliament.

Thus it appears that our fathers of the Revolution were contending, not for independence in the first instance, but for the inestimable right of local self-government under the British Constitution; the right of every distinct political community — dependent colonies, territories, provinces, as well as sovereign States—to make their own local laws, form their own domestic institutions, and manage their own internal affairs in their own way, subject only to the Constitution of Great Britain as the paramount law of the empire.

The government of Great Britain had violated this inalienable right of local self-government by a long series of acts on a great variety of subjects. The first serious point of controversy arose on the Slavery question as early as 1699, which continued a fruitful source of irritation until the Revolution, and formed one of the causes for the separation of the Colonies from the British crown.

For more than forty years the provincial legislature of Virginia had passed laws for the protection and encouragement of African Slavery within her limits. This policy was steadily pursued until the white inhabitants of Virginia became alarmed for their own safety, in view of the numerous and formidable tribes of Indian savages which surrounded and threatened the feeble white settlements, while ship-loads of African savages were being daily landed in their midst. In order to check and restrain a policy which seemed to threaten the very existence of the colony, the provincial legislature enacted a law imposing a tax upon every slave who should be brought into Virginia. The British merchants, who were engaged in the African slave-trade, regarding this legislation as injurious to their interests and in violation of their rights, petitioned the King of England and his majesty's ministers to annul the obnoxious law, and protect them in their right to carry their slaves into Virginia and all other British colonies which were the common property of the empire — acquired by the common blood and common treasure—and from which a few adventurers, who had settled on the imperial domain by his majesty's sufferance, had no right to exclude them, or discriminate against their property by a mere provincial enactment. Upon a full consideration of the subject, the king graciously granted the prayer of the petitioners; and accordingly issued peremptory orders to the royal governor of Virginia, and to the governors of all the other British colonies in America, forbidding them to sign or approve any colonial or provincial enactment injurious to the African slave-trade, unless such enactment should contain a clause suspending its operation until his majesty's pleasure should be made known in the premises.

Judge Tucker, in his Appendix to Blackstone, refers to thirty-one acts of the provincial legislature of Virginia, passed at various periods from 1662 to 1772, upon the subject of African Slavery, showing conclusively that Virginia

always considered this as one of the questions affecting her "internal polity," over which she, in common with the other colonies, claimed "the right of exclusive legislation in their provincial legislatures" within their respective limits. Some of these acts, particularly those which were enacted prior to the year 1699, were evidently intended to foster and encourage, as well as to regulate and control, African Slavery, as one of the domestic institutions of the colony. The act of 1699, and most of the enactments subsequent to that date, were as obviously designed to restrain and check the growth of the institution, with the view of confining it within the limit of the actual necessities of the community, or its ultimate extinction, as might be deemed most conducive to the public interests, by a system of unfriendly legislation, such as imposing a tax on all slaves introduced into the colony, which was increased and renewed from time to time, as occasion required, until the period of the Revolution. Many of these acts never took effect, in consequence of the king withholding his assent, even after the governor had approved the enactment, in cases where it contained a clause suspending its operation until his majesty's pleasure should be made known in the premises.

In 1772, the provincial legislature of Virginia, after imposing another tax of five per cent. on all slaves imported into the colony, petitioned the king to remove all those restraints which inhibited his majesty's governors assenting to such laws as might check so very pernicious a commerce as Slavery. Of this petition Judge Tucker says:

"The following extract from a petition to the Throne, presented from the House of Burgesses of Virginia, April 1st, 1772, will show the sense of the people of Virginia on the subject of Slavery at that period:

"'The importation of slaves into the colony from the coast of Africa hath long been considered as a trade of great inhumanity; and under its present encouragement we have too much reason to fear will endanger the very existence of your Majesty's American dominions.'"

Mark the ominous words! Virginia tells the king of England in 1772, four years prior to the Declaration of Independence, that his Majesty's American dominions are in danger: not because of the Stamp duties—not because of the tax on tea—not because of his attempts to collect revenue in America! These have since been deemed sufficient to justify rebellion and revolution. But none of these are referred to by Virginia in her address to the Throne—there being another wrong which in magnitude and enormity, so far exceeded these and all other causes of complaint, that the very existence of his Majesty's American dominions depended upon it! That wrong consisted in forcing African Slavery upon a dependent colony without her consent, and in opposition to the wishes of her own people!

The people of Virginia at that day did not appreciate the force of the argument used by the British merchants, who were engaged in the African slave-trade, and which was afterward indorsed, at least by implication, by the king and his ministers; that the Colonies were the common property of the empire—acquired by the common blood and treasure—and therefore all British subjects had the right to carry their slaves into the colonies, and hold them in defiance of the local law and in contempt of the wishes and safety of the Colonies.

The people of Virginia not being convinced by th's process of reasoning, still adhered to the doctrine which they held in common with their sister colonies, that it was the birthright of all freemen—inalienable when formed into political communities—to exercise exclusive legislation in respect to all matters pertaining to their internal polity—Slavery not excepted; and rather than surrender this great right, they were prepared to withdraw their allegiance from the crown.

Again referring to this petition to the king, the same learned judge adds:

"This petition produced no effect, as appears from the first clause of our (Virginia) Constitution, where, among other acts of misrule, the inhuman use of the royal negative in refusing us (the people of Virginia) permission to exclude Slavery from us by law, is enumerated among the reasons or separating from Great Britain."

This clause in the Constitution of Virginia, referring to the inhuman use of the royal negative, in refusing the Colony of Virginia permission to exclude Slavery from her limits by law, as one of the reasons for separating from Great Britain, was adopted on the 12th day of June, 1776, three weeks and one day previous to the Declaration of Independence by the Continental Congress; and after remaining in force as a part of the Constitution for a period of fifty-four years, was re-adopted, without alteration, by the Convention which framed the new Constitution in 1830, and then ratified by the people as a part of the new Constitution; and was again re-adopted by the Convention which amended the Constitution in 1850, and again ratified by the people as a part of the amended Constitution, and at this day remains a portion of the fundamental law of Virginia—proclaiming to the world and to posterity that one of the reasons for separating from Great Britain was "the inhuman use of the royal negative in refusing us (the Colony of Virginia) permission to exclude Slavery from us by law!"

The legislation of Virginia on this subject may be taken as a fair sample of the legislative enactments of each of the thirteen Colonies, showing conclusively that slavery was regarded by them all as a domestic question to be regarded and determined by each colony to suit itself, without the intervention of the British Parliament or "the inhuman use of the royal negative." Each colony passed a series of enactments, beginning at an early period of its history and running down to the commencement of the Revolution, either protecting, regulating, or restraining African Slavery within its respective limits, and in accordance with their wishes and supposed interests. North and South Carolina, following the example of Virginia, at first encouraged the introduction of slaves, until the number increased beyond their wants and necessities, when they attempted to check and restrain the further growth of the institution, by imposing a high rate of taxation upon all slaves which should be brought into those colonies; and finally, in 1764, South Carolina passed a law imposing a penalty of one hundred pounds (or five hundred dollars) for every negro slave subsequently introduced into that colony.

The colony of Georgia was originally founded on strict anti-slavery principles, and rigidly maintained this policy for a series of years, until the inhabitants became convinced by experience that, with their climate and productions, slave labor, if not essential to their existence, would prove beneficial and useful to their material interests. Maryland and Delaware protected and regulated African Slavery as one of their domestic institutions. Pennsylvania, under the advice of William Penn, substituted fourteen years' service and perpetual adscript to the soil for hereditary Slavery, and attempted to legislate, not for the total abolition of Slavery, but for the sanctity of marriage among slaves, and for their personal security. New-Jersey, New-York, and Connecticut recognized African Slavery as a domestic institution lawfully existing within their respective limits, and passed the requisite laws for its control and regulation.

Rhode Island provided by law that no slave should serve more than ten years, at the end of which time he was to be set free; and if the master should refuse to let him go free, or sold him elsewhere for a longer period of service, he was subject to a penalty of forty pounds, which was supposed at that period to be nearly double the value of the slave.

Massachusetts imposed heavy taxes upon all slaves brought into the colony, and provided in some instances for sending the slaves back to their native land; and finally prohibited the introduction of any more slaves into the colony under any circumstances.

When New-Hampshire passed laws which were designed to prevent the introduction of any more slaves, the British Cabinet issued the following order to Governor Wentworth: "You are not to give your assent to, or pass any law imposing duties upon negroes imported into New-Hampshire."

While the legislation of the several colonies exhibits dissimilarity of views, founded on a diversity of interests, on the merits and policy of Slavery, it shows conclusively that they all regarded it as a domestic question affecting their internal polity in respect to which they were entitled to a full and exclusive power of legislation in the several provincial legislatures. For a few years immediately preceding the American Revolution, the African slave-trade was encouraged and stimulated by the British Government, and carried on with more vigor by the English merchants, than at any other period in the history of the Colonies; and this fact, taken in connection with the extraordinary claim asserted in the memorable preamble to the act repealing the stamp duties, that "Parliament possessed the right to bind the Colonies in all cases whatever," not only in respect to all matters affecting the general welfare of the empire, but also in regard to the domestic relations and internal polity of the Colonies—produced a powerful impression upon the minds of the colonists, and imparted peculiar prominence to the principle involved in the controversy.

Hence the enactments by the several colonial legislatures calculated and designed to restrain and prevent the increase of slaves; and, on the other hand, the orders issued by the Crown, instructing the colonial governors not to sign or permit any legislative enactment prejudicial or injurious to the African slave-trade, unless such enactment should contain a clause suspending its operation until the royal pleasure should be made known in the premises; or, in other words, until the king should have an

opportunity of annulling the acts of the colonial legislatures by the "inhuman use of the royal negative."

Thus the policy of the Colonies on the Slavery question had assumed a direct antagonism to that of the British Government; and this antagonism not only added to the importance of the principle of local self-government in the Colonies, but produced a general concurrence of opinion and action in respect to the question of Slavery in the proceedings of the Continental Congress, which assembled at Philadelphia for the first time on the 5th of September, 1774.

On the 14th of October the Congress adopted a Bill of Rights for the Colonies, in the form of a series of resolutions, in which, after conceding to the British Government the power to regulate commerce and do such other things as affected the general welfare of the empire, without interfering with the internal polity of the Colonies, they declared "That they are entitled to a free and exclusive power in their several provincial legislatures, where their right of representation can alone be preserved in all cases of taxation and internal polity." Having thus defined the principle for which they were contending, the Congress proceeded to adopt the following "Peaceful Measures," which they still hoped would be sufficient to induce compliance with their just and reasonable demands. These "Peaceful Measures" consisted of addresses to the king, to the Parliament, and to the people of Great Britain, together with an association of non-intercourse to be observed and maintained so long as their grievances should remain unredressed.

The second article of this association, which was adopted without opposition, and signed by the delegates from all the Colonies, was in these words:

"That we will neither import nor purchase any slave imported after the first day of December next; after which time we will wholly discontinue the slave-trade, and will neither be concerned in it ourselves, nor will we hire our vessels, nor sell our commodities or manufactures to those who are engaged in it"

This Bill of Rights, together with these articles of association, were subsequently submitted to and adopted by each of the thirteen Colonies in their respective provincial Legislatures.

Thus was distinctly formed between the Colonies and the parent country that issue upon which the Declaration of Independence was founded, and the battles of the Revolution were fought. It involved the specific claim on the part of the Colonies—denied by the King and Parliament—to the exclusive right of legislation touching all local and internal concerns, *Slavery included.* This being the principle involved in the contest, a majority of the Colonists refused to permit their delegates to sign the Declaration of Independence except upon the distinct condition and express reservation to each colony of the exclusive right to manage and control its local concerns and police regulations without the intervention of any general Congress which might be established for the United Colonies.

Let us cite one of these reservations as a specimen of all, showing conclusively that they were fighting for the inalienable right of local self-government, with the clear understanding that when they had succeeded in throwing off the despotism of the British Parliament, no Congressional despotism was to be substituted for it:

"We, the Delegates of Maryland, in Convention assembled, do declare that the King of Great Britain has violated his compact with this people, and that they owe no allegiance to him. We have therefore thought it just and necessary to empower our Deputies in Congress to join with a majority of the United Colonies in declaring them free and independent States, in framing such further confederation between them, in making foreign alliances, and in adopting such other measures as shall be judged necessary for the preservation of their liberties:

"*Provided,* The sole and exclusive right of regulating the internal polity and government of this Colony be reserved to the people thereof.

"We have also thought proper to call a new Convention for the purpose of establishing a government in this Colony.

"No ambitious views, no desire of independence, induced the people of Maryland to form a union with the other Colonies. To procure an exemption from Parliamentary taxation, and to continue to the Legislatures of these Colonies the sole and exclusive right of regulating their Internal Polity, was our original and only motive. To maintain, inviolate our liberties, and to transmit them unimpaired to posterity, was our duty and first wish; our next, to continue connected with and dependent on Great Britain. For the truth of these assertions we appeal to that Almighty Being who is emphatically styled the Searcher of hearts, and from whose omniscience none is concealed. Relying on this Divine protection and assistance, and trusting to the justice of our cause, we exhort and conjure every virtuous citizen to join cordially in defense of our common rights and in maintenance of the freedom of this and her sister colonies."

The first plan of Federal Government adopted for the United States was formed during the Revolution, and is usually known as "The Articles of Confederation." By these Articles it was provided that "Each State retains its Sovereignty, Freedom, and Independence, and every power, jurisdiction, and right which is not by this Confederation expressly delegated to the United States in Congress assembled."

At the time the Articles of Confederation were adopted—July 9, 1778—the United States held no lands or territory in common. The entire country—including all the waste and unappropriated lands—embraced within or pertaining to the Confederacy, belonged to and was the property of the several States within whose limits the same was situated.

On the 6th day of September, 1780, Congress "recommended to the several States in the Union having claims to waste and unappropriated lands in the Western country, a liberal cession to the United States of a portion of their respective claims for the common benefit of the Union."

On the 20th day of October, 1783, the Legislature of Virginia passed an act authorizing the Delegates in Congress from that State to convey to the United States "the territory or tract of country within the limits of the Virginia Charter, lying and bearing to the northwest of the river Ohio "—which grant was to be made upon the "condition that the territory so ceded shall be laid out and formed into States;" and that "the States so formed shall be distinct republican States, and admitted members of the Federal Union, having the same rights of Sovereignty, Freedom, and Independence as the other States."

On the 1st day of March, 1784, Thomas Jefferson and his colleagues in Congress executed the deed of cession in pursuance of the act of the Virginia Legislature, which was accepted and ordered to "be recorded and enrolled among the acts of the United States in Congress assembled." This was the first territory ever acquired, held, or owned, by the United States. On the same day of the deed of cession, Mr. Jefferson, as chairman of a committee which had been appointed, consisting of Mr. Jefferson of Virginia, Mr. Chase of Maryland, and Mr. Howell of Rhode Island, submitted to Congress "a plan for the temporary government of the territory ceded or to be ceded by the individual States to the United States."

It is important that this Jeffersonian plan of government for the Territories should be carefully considered for many obvious reasons. It was the first plan of government for the Territories ever adopted in the United States. It was drawn by the author of the Declaration of Independence, and revised and adopted by those who shaped the issues which produced the Revolution, and formed the foundations upon which our whole American system of government rests. It was not intended to be either local or temporary in its character, but was designed to apply to all "territory ceded or to be ceded," and to be universal in its application and eternal in its duration, wherever and whenever we might have territory requiring a government. It ignored the right of Congress to legislate for the people of the Territories, without their consent, and recognized the inalienable right of the people of the Territories, when organized into political communities, to govern themselves in respect to their local concerns and internal polity. It was adopted by the Congress of the Confederation on the 23d day of April, 1784, and stood upon the Statute Book as a general and permanent plan for the government of all territory which we then owned or should subsequently acquire, with a provision declaring it to be a "Charter of Compact," and that its provisions should "stand as fundamental conditions between the thirteen original States and those newly described, unalterable but by the joint consent of the United States in Congress assembled, and of the particular State within which such alteration is proposed to be made." Thus this Jeffersonian plan for the government of the Territories—this "Charter of Compact" —"these fundamental conditions," which were declared to be "unalterable" without the consent of the people of "the particular State [territory] within which such alteration is proposed to be made," stood on the Statute Book when the Convention assembled at Philadelphia in 1787, and proceeded to form the Constitution of the United States.

Now let us examine the main provisions of the Jefferson Plan :

First.—"That the territory ceded or to be ceded by the individual States to the United States, whenever the same shall have been purchased of the Indian inhabitants and offered for sale by the United States, shall be formed into *additional States,*" etc., etc.

The Plan proceeds to designate the boundaries and territorial extent of the proposed "additional States," and then provides :

Second.—"That the settlers within the Territory so to be purchased and offered for sale shall, either on their own petition or on the order of Congress, receive authority from them, with appointments of time and place, for their free males of full age to meet together for the purpose of establishing a temporary government to adopt a Constitution and laws of any one of these States (the original States), so that such laws nevertheless shall be subject to alteration by their ordinary Legislature ; and to erect, subject to like alteration, counties or townships for the election of members for their Legislature."

Having thus provided a mode by which the first inhabitants or settlers of the territory may assemble together and choose for themselves the Constitution and laws of some one of the original thirteen States, and declare the same in force for the government of their territory temporarily, with the right on the part of the people to change the same, through their local Legislature, as they may see proper, the Plan then proceeds to point out the mode in which they may establish for themselves " a permanent Constitution and government" whenever they shall have twenty thousand inhabitants, as follows :

Third.—"That such temporary government only shall continue in force in any *State* until it shall have acquired twenty thousand free inhabitants, when, giving due proof thereof to Congress, they shall receive from them authority, with appointments of time and place, to call a Convention of Representatives to establish a permanent Constitution and government for themselves."

Having thus provided for the first settlers "a temporary government" in these " additional States," and for a "permanent Constitution and government" when they shall have acquired twenty thousand inhabitants, the Plan contemplates that they shall continue to govern themselves *as States,* having, as provided in the Virginia deed of session, "the same rights of sovereignty, freedom, and independence," in respect to their domestic affairs and internal polity, "as the other States," until they shall have a population equal to the least numerous of the original thirteen States ; and in the meantime shall keep a sitting member in Congress, with a right of debating but not of voting, when they shall be admitted into the Union on an equal footing with the other States, as follows :

Fourth.—"That whenever any of the said States shall have of free inhabitants as many as shall then be in any one of the least numerous of the thirteen original States, such *State* shall be admitted by its delegates into the Congress of the United States on an equal footing with the said original States." . . . .

And—

" Until such admission by their delegates into Congress any of the said *States,* after the establishment of their temporary government, shall have authority to keep a sitting member in Congress, with the right of debating, but not of voting."

Attached to the provision which appears in this paper under the "third" head is a proviso, containing five propositions, which, when agreed to and accepted by the people of said additional States, were "to be formed into a charter of compact," and to remain forever " unalterable," except by the consent of such States as well as of the United States—to wit :

" *Provided,* That both the temporary and permanent governments be established on these principles as their basis :"

1st.—" That they shall forever remain a part of the United States of America."

2d.—" That in their persons, property, and Territory they shall be subject to the government of the United States in Congress assembled, and to the Articles of Confederation in all those cases in which the original States shall be so subject."

3d.—" That they shall be subject to pay a part of the federal debts contracted, or to be contracted—to be apportioned on them by Congress according to the same common rule and measure by which apportionments thereof shall be made on the other States."

4th.—" That their respective government shall be in republican form, and shall admit no person to be a citizen who holds any hereditary title."

The fifth article, which relates to the prohibition of Slavery, after the year 1800, having been rejected by Congress, never became a part of the Jeffersonian Plan of Government for the Territories, as adopted April 23, 1784.

The concluding paragraph of this Plan of Government, which emphatically ignores the right of Congress to bind the people of the Territories without their consent, and recognizes the people therein as the true source of all legitimate power in respect to their internal polity, is in these words :

" That all the preceding articles shall be formed into a *charter of compact,* shall be duly executed by the President of the United States in Congress assembled, under his hand and the seal of the United States, shall be promulgated, and shall stand as fundamental conditions between the thirteen original States and those newly described, unalterable but by the joint consent of the United States in Congress assembled, and of the particular State within which such alteration is proposed to be made."

This Jeffersonian Plan of Government embodies and carries out the ideas and principles of the fathers of the Revolution—that the people of every separate political community (dependent Colonies, Provinces, and Territories as well as sovereign States) have an inalienable right to govern themselves in respect to their internal polity, and repudiates the dogma of the British Ministry and the Tories of that day, that all Colonies, Provinces and Territories were the property of the empire, acquired with the common blood and common treasure, and that the inhabitants thereof have no rights, privileges, or immunities except such as the Imperial Government should graciously condescend to bestow upon them. This Plan recognizes by law and irrevocable "compact" the existence of two distinct classes of States under our American system of government—the one being members of the Union, and consisting of the original thirteen and such other States, having the requisite population, as Congress should admit into the Federal Union, with an equal vote in the management of Federal affairs as well as the exclusive power in regard to their internal polity respectively—the other, not having the requisite population for admission into the Union, could have no vote or agency in the control of the Federal relations, but possessed the same exclusive power over their domestic affairs and internal policy respectively as the original States, with the right, while they have less than twenty thousand inhabitants, to choose for their government the Constitution and laws of any one of the original States; and when they should have more than twenty thousand, but less than the number required to entitle them to admission into the Union, they were authorized to form for themselves "a permanent Constitution and government;" and in either case they were entitled to keep a delegate in Congress with the right of debating, but not of voting. This "Charter of Compact," with its "fundamental conditions," which were declared to be "unalterable" without "the joint consent" of the people interested in them, as well as of the United States, thus stood on the statute book unrepealed and unrepealable—furnishing a complete system of government for all "the territory ceded or to be ceded" to the United States, without any other legislation upon the subject, when, on the 14th day of May, 1787, the Federal Convention assembled in Philadelphia and proceeded to form the Constitution under which we now live. Thus it will be seen that the dividing line between Federal and Local authority, in respect to the rights of those political communities which, for the sake of convenience and in contradistinction to the States represented in Congress, we now call Territories, but which were then known as "States," or "new States," was so distinctly marked at that day that no intelligent man could fail to perceive it.

It is true that the government of the Confederation had proved totally inadequate to the fulfillment of the ends for which it was devised; not because of the relations between the Territories, or new States, and the United States, but in consequence of having no power to enforce its decrees on the Federal questions which were clearly within the scope of its expressly delegated powers. The radical defects in the Articles of Confederation were found to consist in the fact that it was a mere league between sovereign States, and not a Federal Government with its appropriate departments—Executive, Legislative, and Judicial—each clothed with authority to perform and carry into effect its own peculiar functions. The Confederation having no power to enforce compliance with the resolves, "the consequence was, that though in theory its resolutions of Congress were equivalent to laws, yet in practice they were found to be mere recommendations, which the States, like other sovereignties, observed or disregarded, according to their own good-will and gracious pleasure." Congress could not impose duties, collect taxes, raise armies, or do any other act essential to the existence of government, without the voluntary consent and coöperation of each of the States. Congress could resolve, but could not carry its resolutions into effect—could recommend to the States to provide a revenue for the necessities of the Federal Government, but could not use the means necessary to the collection of the revenue when the States failed to comply—could recommend to the States to provide an army for the general defense, and apportion among the States their respective quotas, but could not enlist the men and order them into the Federal service. For these reasons a Federal Government, with its appropriate departments, acting directly upon the individual citizens, with authority to enforce its decrees to the extent of its delegated powers, and not dependent upon the voluntary action of the several States in their corporate capacity, became indispensable as a substitute for the government of the Confederation.

In the formation of the Constitution of the United States the Federal Convention took the British Constitution, as interpreted and expounded by the Colonies during their controversy with Great Britain, for their model—making such modifications in its structure and principles as the change in our condition had rendered necessary. They entrusted the Executive functions to a President in the place of a King; the Legislative functions to a Congress, composed of a Senate and House of Representatives, in lieu of the Parliament consisting of the Houses of Lords and Commons; and the Judicial functions to a Supreme Court and such inferior courts as Congress should from time to time ordain and establish.

Having thus divided the powers of government into the three appropriate departments, with which they had always been familiar, they proceeded to confer upon the Federal Government substantially the same powers which they as colonies had been willing to concede to the British Government; and to reserve to the States and to the people the same rights and privileges which they as colonies had denied to the British Government during the entire struggle which terminated in our Independence, and which they had claimed for themselves and their posterity as the birthright of all freemen, inalienable when organized into political communities, and to be enjoyed and exercised by colonies, territories, and provinces as fully and completely as by sovereign States. Thus it will be seen that there is no organic feature or fundamental principle embodied in the Constitution of the United States which had not been familiar to the people of the Colonies from the period of their earliest settlement, and which had not been repeatedly asserted by them when denied by Great Britain during the whole period of their colonial history.

Let us pause at this point for a moment, and inquire whether it be just to those illustrious patriots and sages who formed the Constitution of the United States, to assume that they intended to confer upon Congress that unlimited and arbitrary power over the people of the American Territories, which they had resisted with their blood when claimed by the British Parliament over British colonies in America? Did they confer upon Congress the right to bind the people of the American Territories in all cases whatsoever, after having fought the battles of the Revolution against a "Preamble" declaring the right of Parliament "to bind the Colonies in all cases whatsoever?"

If, as they contended before the Revolution, it was the birthright of all Englishmen, inalienable when formed into political communities, to exercise exclusive power of legislation in their local legislatures in respect to all things affecting their internal polity—Slavery not excepted—did not the same right, after the Revolution, and by virtue of it, become the birthright of all Americans, in like manner inalienable when organized into political communities—no matter by what name, whether Colonies, Territories, Provinces, or new States?

Names often deceive persons in respect to the nature and substance of things. A single instance of this kind is to be found in that clause of the Constitution which says:

"Congress shall have power to dispose of, and make all needful rules and regulations respecting the territory or other property belonging to the United States."

This being the only clause of the Constitution in which the word "Territory" appears, that fact alone has doubtless led many persons to suppose that the right of Congress to establish temporary governments for the Territories, in the sense in which the word is now used, must be derived from it, overlooking the important and controlling facts that at the time the Constitution was formed the word "Territory" had never been used or understood to designate a political community or government of any kind in any law, compact, deed of cession, or public document; but had invariably been used either in its geographical sense to describe the superficial area of a State or district of country, as in the Virginia deed of cession of the "Territory or *tract of country*" northwest of the river Ohio; or as meaning land in its character as property, in which latter sense it appears in the clause of the Constitution referred to, when providing for the disposition of the "Territory or other property belonging to the United States." These facts, taken in connection with the kindred one that during the whole period of the Confederation and the formation of the Constitution the temporary governments which we now call "Territories," were invariably referred to in the deeds of cession, laws, compacts, plans of government, resolutions of Congress, public records, and authentic documents as "States," or "new States," conclusively show that the words "Territory and other property" in the Constitution were used to designate the unappropriated lands and other property which the United States owned, and not the people who might become residents on those lands, and be organized into political communities after the United States had parted with their title.

It is from this clause of the Constitution alone that Congress derives the power to provide for the surveys and sale of the public lands and all other property belonging to the United States, not only in the Territories, but also in the several States of the Union. But for this provision Congress would have no power to authorize the sale of the public lands, military sites, old ships, cannon, muskets, or other property, real or personal, which belong to the United States, and are no longer needed for any public purpose. It refers exclusively to property in contradistinction to persons and communities. It confers the same power "to make all needful rules and regulations" in the States as in the Territories, and extends wherever there may be any land or other property belonging to the United States to be regulated or disposed of; but does not authorize Congress to control or interfere with the domestic institutions and internal polity of the people (either in the States or the Territories) who may reside upon lands which the United States once owned. Such a power, had it been vested in Congress, would annihilate the sovereignty and freedom of the States as well as the great principle of self-government in the Territories, wherever the United States happen to own a portion of the public lands within their respective limits, as, at present, in the States of Alabama, Florida, Mississippi, Louisiana, Arkansas, Missouri, Illinois, Indiana, Ohio, Michigan, Wisconsin, Iowa, Minnesota, California, and Oregon, and in the Territories of Washington, Nebraska, Kansas, Utah, and New-Mexico. The idea is repugnant to the spirit and genius of our complex system of Government; because it effectually blots out the dividing line between Federal and Local authority which forms an essential barrier for the defense of the independence of the States and the liberties of the people against Federal invasion. With one anomalous exception, all the powers conferred on Congress are *Federal*, and not *Municipal*, in their character—affecting the general welfare of the whole country without interfering with the internal polity of the people—and can be carried into effect by laws which apply alike to States and Territories. The exception, being in derogation of one of the fundamental principles of our political system (because it authorizes the Federal Government to control the municipal affairs and internal polity of the people in certain specified, limited localities), was not left to vague inference or loose construction, nor expressed in dubious or equivocal language; but is found plainly written in that Section of the Constitution which says:

"Congress shall have power to exercise exclusive legislation in all cases whatsoever, over such district (not exceeding ten miles square) as may, by cession of particular States, and the acceptance of Congress, become the seat of the government of the United States, and to exercise like authority over all places purchased by the consent of the Legislature of the State in which the same shall be, for the erection of forts, magazines, arsenals, dock-yards and other needful buildings."

No such power "to exercise exclusive legislation in all cases whatsoever," nor indeed any legislation in any case whatsoever, is conferred on Congress in respect to the municipal affairs and internal polity, either of the States or of the Territories. On the contrary, after the Constitution had been finally adopted, with its Federal powers delegated, enumerated, and defined, in order to guard in all future time against any possible infringement of the reserved rights of the States, or of the people, an amendment was incorporated into the Constitution which marks the dividing line between Federal and Local authority so directly and indelibly that no lapse of time, no partisan prejudice, no sectional aggrandizement, no frenzied fanaticism can efface it. The amendment is in these words:

"The powers not delegated to the United States by the Constitution, nor prohibited by it to the States, are reserved to the States respectively, or to the people."

This view of the subject is confirmed, if indeed any corroborative evidence is required, by reference to the proceedings and debates of the Federal Convention, as reported by Mr. Madison. On the 18th of August, after a series of resolutions had been adopted as the basis of the proposed Constitution and referred to the Committee of Detail for the purpose of being put in proper form, the record says:

"Mr. Madison submitted, in order to be referred to the Committee of Detail, the following powers, as proper to be added to those of the general Legislature (Congress):

"To dispose of the unappropriated lands of the United States.

"To institute temporary governments for the new States arising therein.

"To regulate affairs with the Indians, as well within as without the limits of the United States.

"To exercise exclusively legislative authority at the seat of the General Government, and over a district around the same not exceeding —— square miles, the consent of the legislature of the State or States comprising the same being first obtained."

Here we find the original and rough draft of these several powers as they now exist, in their revised form, in the Constitution. The provision empowering Congress " to dispose of the unappropriated lands of the United States" was modified and enlarged, so as to include "other property belonging to the United States," and to authorize Congress to "make all needful rules and regulations" for the preservation, management, and sale of the same.

The provision empowering Congress " to institute temporary governments for the new States arising in the unappropriated lands of the United States," taken in connection with the one empowering Congress "to exercise exclusively Legislative authority at the seat of the General Government, and over a district of country around the same," clearly shows the difference in the extent and nature of the powers intended to be conferred in the new States or Territories on the one hand, and in the District of Columbia on the other. In the one case it was proposed to authorize Congress " to institute temporary governments for the new States," or Territories, as they are now called, just as our Revolutionary fathers recognized the right of the British crown to institute local governments for the Colonies, by issuing charters under which the people of the Colonies were "entitled (according to the Bill of Rights adopted by the Continental Congress) to a free and exclusive power of legislation, in their several Provincial Legislatures, where their right of representation can alone be preserved, in all cases of taxation and internal polity;" while, in the other case, it was proposed to authorize Congress to exercise, exclusively, legislative authority over the municipal and internal polity of the people residing within the district which should be ceded for that purpose as the seat of the General Government.

Each of these provisions was modified and perfected by the Committee of Detail and Revision, as will appear by comparing them with the corresponding clauses as finally incorporated into the Constitution. The provision to authorize Congress to institute temporary governments for the new States or Territories, and to provide for their admission into the Union, appears in the Constitution in this form:

New States may be admitted by the Congress into this Union."

The power to admit " *new States*," and " to make all laws which shall be necessary and proper " to that end, may fairly be construed to include the right to institute temporary governments for such new States or Territories, the same as Great Britain could rightfully institute similar governments for the Colonies; but certainly not to authorize Congress to legislate in respect to their municipal affairs and internal concerns, without violating that great fundamental principle in defense of which the battles of the Revolution were fought.

If judicial authority were deemed necessary to give force to principles so eminently just in themselves, and which form the basis of our entire political system, such authority may be found in the opinion of the Supreme Court of the United States, in the Dred Scott case. In that case the Court say:

"This brings us to examine by what provision of the Constitution the present Federal Government, under its delegated and restricted powers, is authorized to acquire territory outside of the original limits of the United States, and what powers it may exercise therein over the person or property of a citizen of the United States, while it remains a territory, and until it shall be admitted as one of the States of the Union.

"There is certainly no power given by the Constitution to the Federal Government to establish or maintain colonies, bordering on the United States or at a distance, to be ruled and governed at its own pleasure; nor to enlarge its territorial limits in any way except by the admission of new States. . . . .

"The power to expand the territory of the United States by the admission of new States is plainly given; and in the construction of this power by all the departments of the Government, it has been held to authorize the acquisition of territory, not fit for admission at the time, but to be admitted as soon as its population and situation would entitle it to admission. It is acquired to become a State, and not to be held as a colony and governed by Congress with absolute authority; and as the propriety of admitting a new State is committed to the sound discretion of Congress, the power to acquire territory for that purpose, to be held by the United States until it is in a suitable condition to become a State upon an equal footing with the other States, must rest upon the same discretion."

Having determined the question that the power to acquire territory for the purpose of enlarging our territorial limits and increasing the number of States, is included within the power to admit new States and conferred by the same clause of the Constitution, the Court proceed to say that " the power to acquire necessarily carries with it the power to preserve and apply to the purposes for which it was acquired." And again, referring to a former decision of the same court in respect to the power of Congress to institute governments for the Territories, the Court say:

"The power stands firmly on the latter alternative put by

the Court—that is, as the 'inevitable consequence of the right to acquire territory.'"

The power to acquire territory, as well as the right, in the language of Mr. Madison, "to institute temporary governments for the new States arising therein" 'or Territorial governments, as they are now called), having been traced to that provision of the Constitution which provides for the admission of "new States," the Court proceed to consider the nature and extent of the power of Congress over the people of the Territories:

"All we mean to say on this point is, that, as there is no express regulation in the Constitution defining the power which the General Government may exercise over the person or property of a citizen in a territory thus acquired, the Court must necessarily look to the provisions and principles of the Constitution, and its distribution of powers, or the rules and principles by which its decision must be governed.

"Taking this rule to guide us, it may be safely assumed that citizens of the United States, who emigrate to a territory belonging to the people of the United States, cannot be ruled as mere colonists, dependent upon the will of the General Government, and to be governed by any laws it may think proper to impose. . . . . The Territory being a part of the United States, the Government and the citizen both enter it under the authority of the Constitution, with their respective rights defined and marked out; and the Federal Government can exercise no power over his person or property beyond what that instrument confers, nor lawfully deny any right which it has reserved."

Hence, inasmuch as the Constitution has conferred on the Federal Government no right to interfere with the property, domestic relations, police regulations, or internal polity of the people of the Territories, it necessarily follows, under the authority of the Court, that Congress can rightfully exercise no such power over the people of the Territories. For this reason alone, the Supreme Court were authorized and compelled to pronounce the eighth section of the Act approved March 6, 1820 (commonly called the Missouri Compramise), inoperative and void—there being no power delegated to Congress in the Constitution authorizing Congress to prohibit Slavery in the Territories.

In the course of the discussion of this question the Court gave an elaborate exposition of the structure, principles, and powers of the Federal Government; showing that it possesses no powers except those which are delegated, enumerated, and defined in the Constitution; and that all other powers are either *prohibited* altogether or are *reserved* to the States, or to the people. In order to show that the prohibited, as well as the delegated powers are enumerated and defined in the Constitution, the Court enumerated certain powers which cannot be exercised either by Congress or by the Territorial Legislatures, or by any other authority whatever, for the simple reason that they are forbidden by the Constitution.

Some persons who have not examined critically the opinion of the Court in this respect have been induced to believe that the *slavery question* was included in this class of prohibited powers, and that the Court had decided in the Dred Scott case that the Territorial Legislature could not legislate in respect to slave property the same as all other property in the Territories. A few extracts from the opinion of the Court will correct this error, and show clearly the class of powers to which the Court referred, as being forbidden alike to the Federal Government, to the States, and to the Territories. The Court say:

"A reference to a few of the provisions of the Constitution will illustrate this proposition. For example, no one, we presume, will contend that Congress can make any law in a Territory respecting the establishment of religion, or the free exercise thereof, or abridging the freedom of speech or of the the press, or the right of the people of the territory peaceably to assemble, and to petition the Government for the redress of grievances.

"Nor can Congress deny to the people the right to keep and bear arms, nor the right to trial by jury, nor compel any one to be a witness against himself in a criminal proceeding. . . . So too, it will hardly be contended that Congress could by law quarter a soldier in a house in a territory without the consent of the owner in a time of peace; nor in time of war but in a manner prescribed by law. Nor could they by law forfeit the property of a citizen in a territory who was convicted of treason, for a longer period than the life of the person convicted, nor take private property for public use without just compensation."

"The powers over persons and property, of which we speak, are not only not granted to Congress, but are in express terms denied, and they are forbidden to exercise them. And this prohibition is not confined to the States, but the words are general, and extend to the whole territory over which the Constitution gives it power to legislate, including those portions of it remaining under Territorial governments, as well as that covered by States.

"It is a total absence of power, everywhere within the dominion of the United States, and places the citizens of a Territory, so far as these rights are concerned, on the same

footing with citizens of the States, and guards them as firmly and plainly against any inroads which the General Government might attempt under the plea of implied or incidental powers.

And if Congress itself cannot do this—if it is beyond the powers conferred on the Federal Government—it will be admitted, we presume, that it could not authorize a Territorial government to exercise them. It could confer no power on any local government, established by its authority, to violate the provisions of the Constitution."

Nothing can be more certain than that the Court were here speaking only of *forbidden powers*, which were denied alike to Congress, to the State Legislatures, and to the Territorial Legislatures, and that the prohibition extends "everywhere within the dominion of the United States," applicable equally to States and Territories, as well as to the United States.

If this sweeping prohibition—this just but inexorable restriction upon the powers of Government—Federal, State, and Territorial—shall ever be held to include the Slavery question, thus negativing the right of the people of the States and Territories, as well as the Federal Government, to control it by law (and it will be observed that in the opinion of the Court "the citizens of a Territory, so far as these rights are concerned, are on the same footing with the citizens of the States.") then, indeed, will the doctrine become firmly established that the principles of law applicable to African Slavery are *uniform throughout the dominion of the United States*, and that there "is an irrepressible conflict between opposing and enduring forces, which means that the United States must and will, sooner or later, become either entirely a slaveholding nation or entirely a free labor nation."

Notwithstanding the disastrous consequences which would inevitably result from the authoritative recognition and practical operation of such a doctrine, there are those who maintain that the Court referred to and included the Slavery question within that class of forbidden powers which (although the same in the Territories as in the States) could not be exercised by the people of the Territories.

If this proposition were true, which fortunately for the peace and welfare of the whole country it is not, the conclusion would inevitably result, which they logically deduce from the premises—that the Constitution by the recognition of Slavery establishes it in the Territories beyond the power of the people to control it by law, and guarantees to every citizen the right to go the e and be protected in the enjoyment of his slave property; and when all other remedies fail for the protection of such rights of property, it becomes the imperative duty of Congress (to the performance of which every member is bound by his conscience and his oath, and from which no consideration of political policy or expediency can release him) to provide by law such adequate and complete protection as is essential to the enjoyment of an important right secured by the Constitution. If the proposition be true, that the Constitution establishes Slavery in the Territories beyond the power of the people legally to control it, another result no less startling, and from which there is no escape, must inevitably follow. The Constitution is uniform "everywhere within the dominions of the United States"—is the same in Pennsylvania as in Kansas—and if it be true, as stated by the President in a special message to Congress, "that Slavery exists in Kansas by virtue of the Constitution of the United States," and that "Kansas is therefore at this moment as much a Slave State as Georgia or South Carolina," why does it not exist in Pennsylvania by virtue of the same Constitution?

If it be said that Pennsylvania is a sovereign State, and therefore has a right to regulate the Slavery question within her own limits to suit herself, it must be borne in mind that the sovereignty of Pennsylvania, like that of every other State, is limited by the Constitution, which provides that:

"This Constitution, and all laws of the United States which shall be made in pursuance thereof, and all treaties made, or which shall be made, under the authority of the United States, shall be the *supreme law of the land*, and the judges in every State shall be bound thereby, *anything in the Constitution or laws of any State to the contrary notwithstanding*."

Hence, the State of Pennsylvania, with her Constitution and laws, and domestic institutions, and internal policy, is subordinate to the Constitution of the United States, in the same manner and to the same extent as the Territory of Kansas. The Kansas-Nebraska Act says that the Territory of Kansas shall exercise legislative power over "all rightful subjects of legislation consistent with the Constitution," and that the people of said Territory shall be left "perfectly free to form and regulate their domestic institutions in their own way, subject only to the Constitution of the United States." The provisions of this act are believed to be in entire harmony with the Constitution, and under them the people of Kansas possess every right, privilege, and immunity, in respect to their internal polity and domestic relations, which the people of Pennsylvania can exercise under their Constitution and laws. Each is invested with full, complete, and exclusive powers in this respect, "subject only to the Constitution of the United States."

The question recurs, then, if the Constitution does establish Slavery in Kansas or any other Territory beyond the power of the people to control it by law, how can the conclusion be resisted that Slavery is established in like manner and by the same authority in all the States of the Union? And if it be the imperative duty of Congress to provide by law for the protection of slave property in the Territories upon the ground that "Slavery exists in Kansas" (and consequently in every other Territory) "by virtue of the Constitution of the United States," why is it not also the duty of Congress, for the same reason, to provide similar protection to slave property in all the States of the Union, when the legislatures fail to furnish such protection?

Without confessing or attempting to avoid the inevitable consequences of their own doctrine, its advocates endeavor to fortify their position by citing the Dred Scott decision to prove that the Constitution recognizes property in slaves—that there is no legal distinction between this and every other description of property—that slave property and every other kind of property stand on an equal footing—that Congress has no more power over the one than over the other—and, consequently, cannot discriminate between them.

Upon this point the Court say:

"Now as we have already said in an earlier part of this opinion, upon a different point, the right of property in a slave is distinctly and expressly affirmed in the Constitution. . . . And if the Constitution recognizes the right of property of the master in a slave, and makes no distinction between that description of property and other property owned by a citizen, no tribunal acting under the authority of the United States, whether it be legislative, executive or judicial, has a right to draw such a distinction, or deny to it the benefit of the provisions and guaranties which have been provided for the protection of private property against the encroachments of the government. . . . . . And the government in express terms is pledged to protect it in all future time, *if the slave escapes from his owner.* This is done in plain words—too plain to be understood. And no word can be found in the Constitution which gives Congress a *greater* power over slave property, or which entitles property of that kind to *less* protection than property of any other description. The only power conferred is the power coupled w.th the duty of guarding and protecting the owner in his rights."

The rights of the owner, which it is thus made the duty of the Federal Government to guard and protect, are those expressly provided for in the Constitution, and defined in clear and explicit language by the Court—that " the government, in express terms, is pledged to protect it (slave property) in all future time, *if the slave escapes from his owner.*" This is the only contingency, according to the plain reading of the Constitution, as authoritatively interpreted by the Supreme Court, in which the Federal Government is authorized, required, or permitted to interfere with Slavery in the States or Territories; and in that case only for the purpose "of guarding and protecting the owner in his rights" to reclaim his slave property. In all other respects slaves stand on the same footing with all other property—"the Constitution makes no distinction between that description of property and other property owned by a citizen;" and "no word can be found in the Constitution which gives Congress a greater power over slave property, or which entitles property of that kind to less protection than property of any other description." This is the basis upon which all rights pertaining to slave property, either in the States or the Territories, stand under the Constitution as expounded by the Supreme Court in the Dred Scott case.

Inasmuch as the Constitution has delegated no power to the Federal Government in respect to any other kind of property belonging to the citizen—neither introducing, establishing, prohibiting, nor excluding it anywhere within the dominion of the United States, but leaves the owner thereof perfectly free to remove into any State or Territory, and carry his property with him, and hold the same subject to the local law, and relying upon the local authorities for protection, it follows, according to the decision of the Court, that slave property stands on the same footing, is entitled to the same rights and immunities, and, in like manner, is dependent upon the local authorities and laws for protection.

The Court refer to that clause of the Constitution which provides for the rendition of fugitive slaves as their authority for saying that "the right of property in slaves is distinctly and expressly affirmed in the Constitution." By reference to that provision, it will be seen that, while the word "slaves" is not used, still the Constitution not only recognizes the right of property in slaves, as stated by the Court, but explicitly states what class of persons shall be deemed slaves, and under what laws or authority they may be held to servitude, and under what circumstances fugitive slaves shall be restored to their owners, all in the same section, as follows:

" No person held to service or labor in one State, *under the laws thereof,* escaping into another, shall, in consequence of any law or regulation therein, be discharged from such service or labor, but shall be delivered up on claim of the party to whom such service or labor may be due."

Thus it will be seen that a slave, within the meaning of the Constitution, is a "person held to service or labor in one State, *under the laws thereof*"—not under the Constitution of the United States, nor by the laws thereof, nor by virtue of any federal authority whatsoever, but under the laws of the particular State where such service or labor may be due.

It was necessary to give this exact definition of Slavery in the Constitution in order to satisfy the people of the South as well as of the North. The slaveholding States would never consent for a moment that their domestic relations—and especially their right of property in their slaves—should be dependent upon Federal authority, or that Congress should have any power over the subject—either to extend, confine, or restrain it, much less to protect or regulate it—lest, under the pretense of protection and regulation, the Federal Government, under the influence of the strong and increasing anti-slavery sentiment which prevailed at that period, might destroy the institution, and divest those rights of property in slaves which were sacred under the laws and constitutions of their respective States so long as the Federal Government had no power to interfere with the subject.

In like manner, the non-slaveholding States, while they were entirely willing to provide for the surrender of all fugitive slaves—as is conclusively shown by the unanimous vote of all the States in the Convention for the provision now under consideration—and to leave each State perfectly free to hold slaves under its own laws, and by virtue of its own separate and exclusive authority, so long as it pleased, and to abolish it when it chose, were unwilling to become responsible for its existence by incorporating it into the Constitution as a national institution, to be protected and regulated, extended and controlled by Federal authority, regardless of the wishes of the people, and in defiance of the local laws of the several States and Territories. For these opposite reasons, the Southern and Northern States united in giving a unanimous vote in the Convention for that provision of the Constitution which recognizes Slavery as a local institution in the several States where it exists, "under the laws thereof," and provides for the surrender of fugitive slaves.

It will be observed that the term "State" is used in this provision, as well as in various other parts of the Constitution, in the same sense in which it was used by Mr. Jefferson in his plan for establishing governments for the new States in the territory ceded and to be ceded to the United States; and by Mr. Madison in his proposition to confer on Congress power " to institute temporary governments for the *new States* arising in the unappropriated lands of the United States," to designate the political communities, Territories as well as States, within the dominion of the United States. The word "States" is used in the same sense in the ordinance of the 13th July, 1787, for the government of the Territory northwest of the river Ohio, which was passed by the remnant of the Congress of the Confederation, sitting in New York while its most eminent members were at Philadelphia, as delegates to the Federal Convention, aiding in the formation of the Constitution of the United States.

In this sense the word "States" is used in the clause providing for the rendition of fugitive slaves, applicable to all political communities under the authority of the United States, including the Territories as well as the several States of the Union. Under any other construction, the right of the owner to recover his slave would be restricted to the *States* of the Union, leaving the Territories a secure place of refuge for all fugitives. The same remark is applicable to the clause of the Constitution which provides that "a person charged in any *State* with treason, felony, or other crime, who shall flee from justice, and be found in *another State,* shall, on the demand of the executive authority of the *State* from which he fled, be delivered up to be removed to the State having jurisdiction of the crime." Unless the term State, as used in these provisions of the Constitution, shall be construed to include every distinct political community under the jurisdiction of the United States, and to apply to Territories as well as to the States of the Union, the Territories must become a sanctuary for all the fugitives from service and justice, for all the felons and criminals who shall escape from the several *States* and seek refuge and immunity in the *Territories.*

If any other illustration were necessary to show that the political communities which we now call Territories (but which, during the whole period of the Confederation and the formation of the Constitution, were always referred to as "States" or "new States'), are recognized as "States" in *some* of the provisions of the Constitution, they may be found in those clauses which declare that "no *State*" shall enter into any "treaty, alliance, or confederation; grant letters of marque and reprisal; coin money; emit bills of credit; make anything but gold and silver coin a tender in payment of debts; pass any bill of attainder, *ex post facto* law, or law impairing the obligation of contracts, or grant any title of nobility."

It must be borne in mind that in each of these cases where the power is not expressly delegated to Congress the prohibition is not imposed upon the Federal Government, but upon the *States*. There was no necessity for any such prohibition upon Congress or the Federal Government, for the reason that the omission to delegate any such powers in the Constitution was of itself a prohibition, and so declared in express terms by the 10th amendment, which declares that "the powers not delegated to the United States by the Constitution, nor prohibited by it to the States, are reserved to the States respectively, or to the people."

Hence it would certainly be competent for the States and Territories to exercise these powers but for the prohibition contained in those provisions of the Constitution; and inasmuch as the prohibition only extends to the "States," the people of the "Territories" are still at liberty to exercise them, unless the Territories are included within the term *States*, within the meaning of these provisions of the Constitution of the United States.

It only remains to be shown that the Compromise Measures of 1850 and the Kansas-Nebraska Act of 1854 are in perfect harmony with, and a faithful embodiment of, the principles herein enforced. A brief history of these measures will disclose the principles upon which they are founded.

On the 29th of January, 1850, Mr. Clay introduced into the Senate a series of resolutions upon the Slavery question which were intended to form the basis of the subsequent legislation upon that subject. Pending the discussion of these resolutions, the chairman of the Committee on Territories prepared and reported to the Senate, on the 25th of March, two bills—one for the admission of California into the Union of States, and the other for the organization of the Territories of Utah and New Mexico, and for the adjustment of the disputed boundary with the State of Texas, which were read twice and printed for the use of the Senate. On the 19th of April a select committee of thirteen was appointed, on motion of Mr. Foote, of Mississippi, of which Mr. Clay was made chairman, and to which were referred all pending propositions relating to the slavery question. On the 8th of May, Mr. Clay, from the select committee of thirteen, submitted to the Senate an elaborate report covering all the points in controversy, accompanied by a bill which is usually known as the "Omnibus Bill." By reference to the provisions of this bill, as it appears on the files of the Senate, it will be seen that it is composed of the two printed bills which had been reported by the Committee on Territories on the 25th of March previous; and that the only material change in its provisions, involving an important and essential principle, is to be found in the tenth section, which prescribes and defines the powers of the Territorial Legislature. In the bill, as reported by the Committee on Territories, the legislative power of the Territories extended to "all rightful subjects of legislation consistent with the Constitution of the United States," *without excepting African Slavery;* while the bill, as reported by the committee of thirteen, conferred the same power on the Territorial Legislature, *with the exception of African Slavery.* This portion of the section in its original form read thus:

"*And be it further enacted* that the Legislative power of the Territory shall extend to all rightful subjects of legislation consistent with the Constitution of the United States and the provisions of this act; but no law shall be passed interfering with the primary disposition of the soil."

To which the committee of thirteen added these words: "*Nor in respect to African Slavery.*" When the bill came up for action on the 15th of May, Mr. Davis, of Mississippi, said:

"I offer the following amendment. To strike out, in the sixth line of the tenth section, the words '*in respect to African Slavery.*' and insert the words, '*with those rights of property growing out of the institution of African Slavery as it exists in any of the States of the Union.*' The object of the amendment is to prevent the Territorial Legislature from legislating against the rights of property growing out of the institution of Slavery. . . . . . It will leave to the Territorial Legislatures those rights and powers which are essentially necessary, not only to the preservation of property, but to the peace of the Territory. It will leave the right to make such police regulations as are necessary to prevent disorder, and which will be absolutely necessary with such property as that to secure its beneficial use to its owner. With this brief explanation I submit the amendment."

Mr. Clay, in reply to Mr. Davis, said

"I am not perfectly sure that I comprehend the full meaning of the amendment offered by the Senator from Mississippi. If I do, I think he accomplishes nothing by striking out the clause now in the bill and inserting that which he proposes to insert. The clause now in the bill is, that the Territorial legislation shall not extend to anything respecting African Slavery within the Territory. The effect of retaining the clause as reported by the Committee will be this: That if in any of the Territories Slavery now exists, it shall not be abolished by the Territorial Legislature; and if in any of the Territories Slavery does not now exist, it cannot be introduced by the Territorial Legislature. The clause itself was introduced into the bill by the Committee for the purpose of tying up the hands of the Territorial Legislature in respect to legislating at all, one way or the other, upon the subject of African Slavery. It was intended to leave the legislation and the law of the respective Territories in the condition in which the Act will find them. I stated on a former occasion that I did not, in Committee, vote for the amendment to insert the clause, though it was proposed to be introduced by a majority of the Committee. I attached very little consequence to it at the time, and I attach very little to it at present. It is perhaps of no particular importance whatever. Now, sir, if I understand the measure proposed by the Senator from Mississippi, it aims at the same thing. I do not understand him as proposing that if any one shall carry slaves into the Territory—although by the laws of the Territory he cannot take them there—the Legislative hands of the Territorial government should be so tied as to prevent it saying he shall not enjoy the fruits of their labor. If the Senator from Mississippi means to say that—"

Mr. Davis:

"I do mean to say it."

Mr. Clay:

"If the object of the Senator is to provide that slaves may be introduced into the Territory contrary to the *lex loci*, and, being introduced, nothing shall be done by the Legislature to impair the rights of owners to hold the slaves thus brought contrary to the local laws, *I certainly cannot vote for it.* In doing so I shall repeat again the expression of opinion which I announced at an early period of the session."

Here we find the line distinctly drawn between those who contended for the right to carry slaves into the Territories and hold them in defiance of the local law, and those who contended that such right was subject to the local law of the Territory. During the progress of the discussion on the same day, Mr. Davis, of Mississippi, said:

"We are giving, or proposing to give, a government to a Territory, which act rests upon the basis of our right to make such provision. We suppose we have a right to confer power. If so, we may mark out the limit to which they may legislate, and are bound not to confer power beyond that which exists in Congress. If we give them power to legislate beyond that, we commit a fraud or usurpation, as it may be done openly, covertly, or indirectly."

To which Mr. Clay replied:

Now, sir, I only repeat what I have had occasion to say before, that while I am willing to stand aside and make no legislative enactment one way or the other—to lay off the Territories without the Wilmot Proviso, on the one hand, with which I understand we are threatened, or without an attempt to introduce a clause for the introduction of Slavery into the Territories—while I am for rejecting both the one and the other, I am content that the law as it exists shall prevail; and if there be any diversity of opinion as to what it means, I am willing that it shall be settled by the highest judicial authority of the country. While I am content thus to abide the result, I must say that I cannot vote for any express provision recognizing the right to carry slaves there."

To which Mr. Davis rejoined, that—

"It is said our Revolution grew out of a preamble; and I hope we have something of the same character of the hardy men of the Revolution who first commenced the war with the mother country—something of the spirit of that bold Yankee who said he had a right to go to Concord, and that go he would; and who, in the maintenance of that right, met his death at the hands of a British sentinel. Now, sir, if our right to carry slaves into these Territories be a constitutional right, it is our first duty to maintain it."

Pending the discussion which ensued, Mr. Davis, at the suggestion of friends, modified his amendment from time to time, until it assumed the following shape:

"Nor to introduce or exclude African Slavery. Provided that nothing herein contained shall be construed so as to prevent said Territorial Legislature from passing such laws as may be necessary for the protection of the rights of property of every kind which may have been, or may be hereafter, conformably to the Constitution of the United States, held in or introduced into said Territory"

To which, on the same day, Mr. Chase, of Ohio, offered the following amendment:

"Provided further, That nothing herein contained shall be construed as authorizing or permitting the introduction of

Slavery or the holding of persons as property within said Territory."

Upon these amendments—the one affirming the Pro-Slavery, and the other the Anti-Slavery position, in opposition to the right of the people of the Territories to decide the Slavery question for themselves—Mr. Douglas said:

"The position that I have ever taken has been, that this, and all other questions relating to the domestic affairs and domestic policy of the Territories, ought to be left to the decision of the people themselves; and that we ought to be content with whatever way they may decide the question, because they have a much deeper interest in these matters than we have, and know much better what institutions suit them than we, who have never been there, can decide for them. I would therefore have much preferred that that portion of the bill should have remained as it was reported from the Committee on Territories, with no provision on the subject of Slavery, the one way or the other. And I do hope yet that that clause will be stricken out. I am satisfied, sir, that it gives no strength to the bill. I am satisfied, even if it did give strength to it, that it ought not to be there, *because it is a violation of principle*—a violation of that principle upon which we have all rested our defense of the course we have taken on this question. I do not see how those of us who have taken the position we have taken—that of *non-intervention*—and have argued in favor of the right of the people to legislate for themselves on this question, can support such a provision without abandoning all the arguments which we used in the Presidential campaign in the year 1848, and the principles set forth by the honorable Senator from Michigan (Mr. Cass) in that letter which is known as the 'Nicholson Letter.' We are required to abandon that platform; we are required to abandon those principles, and to stultify ourselves, and to adopt the opposite doctrine—and for what? In order to say that *the people of the Territories shall not have such institutions as they shall deem adapted to their condition and their wants.* I do not see, sir, how such a provision can be acceptable either to the people of the North or the South."

Upon the question of how many inhabitants a Territory should contain before it should be formed into a political community with the rights of self-government, Mr. Douglas said:

"The Senator from Mississippi puts the question to me as to what number of people there must be in a Territory before this right to govern themselves accrues. Without determining the precise number, I will assume that the right ought to accrue to the people at the moment they have enough to constitute a government; and, sir, the bill assumes that there are people enough there to require a government, and enough to authorize the people to govern themselves. . . . . . Your bill concedes that a representative government is necessary—a government founded upon the principles of popular sovereignty and the right of a people to enact their own laws; and for this reason you give them a Legislature composed of two branches, like the Legislatures of the different States and Territories of the Union. You confer upon them the right to legislate on 'all rightful subjects of legislation,' except negroes. Why except negroes? Why except African Slavery? If the inhabitants are competent to govern themselves upon all other subjects, and in reference to all other descriptions of property—if they are competent to make laws and determine the relations between husband and wife, and parent and child, and municipal laws affecting the rights and property of citizens generally, they are competent also to make laws to govern themselves in relation to Slavery and negroes."

With reference to the protection of property in slaves, Mr. Douglas said:

"I have a word to say to the honorable Senator from Mississippi (Mr. Davis). He insists that I am not in favor of protecting property, and that his amendment is offered for the purpose of protecting property under the Constitution. Now, sir, I ask you what authority he has for assuming that? Do I not desire to protect property because I wish to allow the people to pass such laws as they deem proper respecting their rights to property without any exception? He might just as well say that I am opposed to protecting property in merchandise, in steamboats, in cattle, in real estate, as to say that I am opposed to protecting property of any other description; for I desire to put them all on an equality, and allow the people to make their own laws in respect to the whole of them."

Mr. Cass said (referring to the amendments offered by Mr. Davis and Mr. Chase):

"Now, with respect to the amendments. I shall vote against them both; and then I shall vote in favor of striking out the restriction in the bill upon the power of the Territorial governments. I shall do so upon this ground. I was opposed, as the honorable Senator from Kentucky has declared he was, to the insertion of this prohibition by the Committee. I consider it inexpedient and unconstitutional. I have already stated my belief that the rightful power of internal legislation in the Territories belongs to the people."

After further discussion the vote was taken by yeas and nays on the amendment of Mr. Chase, and decided in the negative: Yeas, 25; Nays, 30. The question recurring on the amendment of Mr. Davis, of Mississippi, it was also rejected: Yeas, 25; Nays, 30. Whereupon Mr. Seward offered the following amendment:

"Neither Slavery nor involuntary servitude, otherwise than by conviction for crime, shall ever be allowed in either of said Territories of Utah and New Mexico.'

Which was rejected—Yeas, 23; Nays, 33.

After various other amendments had been offered and voted upon—all relating to the power of the Territorial Legislature over Slavery—Mr. Douglas moved to strike out all relating to African Slavery, so that the Territorial Legislature should have the same power over that question as over all other rightful subjects of legislation consistent with the Constitution—which amendment was rejected. After the rejection of this amendment, the discussion was renewed with great ability and depth of feeling in respect to the powers which the Territorial Legislature should exercise upon the subject of Slavery. Various propositions were made, and amendments offered and rejected—all relating to this one controverted point—when Mr. Norris, of New-Hampshire, renewed the motion of Mr. Douglas, to strike out the restriction on the Territorial Legislature in respect to African Slavery. On the 31st of July this amendment was adopted by a vote of 32 to 19—restoring this section of the bill to the form in which it was reported from the Committee on Territories on the 25th of March, and conferring on the Territorial Legislature power over "all rightful subjects of legislation consistent with the Constitution of the United States," *without excepting African Slavery.*

Thus terminated this great struggle in the affirmance of the principle, as the basis of the Compromise Measures of 1850, so far as they related to the organization of the Territories, *that the people of the Territories should decide the Slavery question for themselves through the action of their Territorial Legislature.*

This controverted question having been definitely settled, the Senate proceeded on the same day to consider the other portions of the bill, and after striking out all except those provisions which provided for the organization of the Territory of Utah, ordered the bill to be engrossed for a third reading, and on the next day—August 1, 1850—the bill was read a third time, and passed.

On the 14th of August the bill for the organization of the Territory of New-Mexico was taken up, and amended so as to conform fully to the provisions of the Utah Act in respect to the power of the Territorial Legislature over "all rightful subjects of legislation consistent with the Constitution," without excepting African Slavery, and was ordered to be engrossed for a third reading without a division; and on the next day the bill was passed—Yeas, 27; Nays, 10.

These two bills were sent to the House of Representatives, and passed that body without any alteration in respect to the power of the Territorial Legislatures over the subject of Slavery, and were approved by President Fillmore, September 9, 1850.

In 1852, when the two great political parties—Whig and Democratic—into which the country was then divided, assembled in National Convention at Baltimore for the purpose of nominating candidates for the Presidency and Vice-Presidency, each Convention adopted and affirmed the principles embodied in the Compromise Measures of 1850 as rules of action by which they would be governed in all future cases in the organization of Territorial governments and the admission of new States.

On the 4th of January, 1854, the Committee on Territories, of the Senate, to which had been referred a bill for the organization of the Territory of Nebraska, reported the bill back, with an amendment, in the form of a substitute for the entire bill, which, with some modifications, is now known on the statute book as the "Kansas-Nebraska Act," accompanied by a Report explaining the principles upon which it was proposed to organize those Territories, as follows:

"The principal amendments which your Committee deem it their duty to commend to the favorable action of the Senate, in a special report, are those in which the principles established by the Compromise Measures of 1850, so far as they are applicable to territorial organizations, are proposed to be affirmed and carried into practical operation within the limits of the new Territory. The wisdom of those measures is attested, not less by their salutary and beneficial effects in allaying sectional agitation and restoring peace and harmony to an irritated and distracted people, than by the cordial and almost universal approbation with which they have been received and sanctioned by the whole country.

"In the judgment of your Committee, those measures were intended to have a far more comprehensive and enduring effect than the mere adjustment of the difficulties arising out of the recent acquisition of Mexican territory. They were designed to establish certain great principles, which would not only furnish adequate remedies for existing evils, but, in all time to come, avoid the perils of a similar agitation, by withdrawing the question of Slavery from the Halls of Congress and the political arena, and committing it to the arbitrament of those who were immediately interested in and alone responsible for its consequences. With a view of conforming their action to the settled policy of the Government, sanctioned by the approving voice of the American people, your Committee have deemed it their duty to incorporate and perpetuate, in their territorial bill, the principles and spirit of those measures."

After presenting and reviewing certain provisions of the bill, the Committee conclude as follows:

" From these provisions it is apparent that the Compromise Measures of 1850 affirm and rest upon the following propositions:

" ' *First.*—That all questions pertaining to Slavery in the Territories, and in the new States to be formed therefrom, are to be left to the decision of the people residing therein, by their appropriate representatives to be chosen by them for that purpose.

" ' *Second.*—That all cases involving title to slaves and questions of personal freedom, are referred to the adjudication of the local tribunals, with the right of appeal to the Supreme Court of the United States.

" ' *Third.*—That the provision of the Constitution of the United States in respect to fugitives from service, is to be carried into faithful execution in all the organized Territories, the same as in the States. The substitute for the bill which your Committee have prepared, and which is commended to the favorable action of the Senate, proposes to carry these propositions and principles into practical operation, in the precise language of the Compromise Measures of 1850.' "

By reference to that section of the " Kansas-Nebraska Act " as it now stands on the statute book, which prescribed and defined the power of the Territorial Legislature, it will be seen that it is, " in the precise language of the Compromise Measures of 1850," extending the legislative power of the Territory " to all rightful subjects of legislation consistent with the Constitution," without excepting African Slavery.

It having been suggested, with some plausibility, during the discussion of the bill, that the act of Congress of March 6, 1820, prohibiting Slavery north of the parallel of 36' 30' would deprive the people of the Territory of the power of regulating the Slavery question to suit themselves while they should remain in a Territorial condition, and before they should have the requisite population to entitle them to admission into the Union as a State, an amendment was prepared by the Chairman of the Committee, and incorporated into the bill to remove this obstacle to the free exercise of the principle of popular sovereignty in the Territory, while it remained in a Territorial condition, by repealing the said act of Congress, and declaring the true intent and meaning of all the friends of the bill in these words:

" That the Constitution and all laws of the United States which are not locally inapplicable, shall have the same force and effect within the Territory as elsewhere within the United States, except the eighth section of the act preparatory to the admission of Missouri into the Union, approved March 6, 1820, which being inconsistent with the principle of non-intervention by Congress with Slavery in the States and Territories, as recognized by the legislation of 1850, commonly called the ' Compromise Measures,' is hereby declared inoperative and void—*it being the true intent and meaning of this act not to legislate Slavery into any Territory or State, nor to exclude it therefrom, but to leave the people thereof perfectly free to form and regulate their domestic institutions in their own way, subject only to the Constitution of the United States.*

To which was added, on motion of Mr. Badger, the following:

" *Provided,* That nothing herein contained shall be construed to revive or put in force any law or regulation which may have existed prior to the act of the sixth of March, 1820, either protecting, establishing, of abolishing slavery."

In this form, and with this distinct understanding of its " true intent and meaning," the bill passed the two houses of Congress, and became the law of the land by the approval of the President, May 30, 1854.

In 1856, the Democratic party, assembled in National Convention at Cincinnati, declared by a unanimous vote of the delegates from every State in the Union, that—

" The American Democracy recognize and adopt the principles contained in the organic laws establishing the Territories of Kansas and Nebraska as embodying the only sound and safe solution of the 'Slavery question,' upon which the great national idea of the people of this whole country can repose in its determined conservatism of the Union—noninterference by Congress with Slavery in State and Territory, or in the District of Columbia ;

" That this was the basis of the Compromises of 1850, confirmed by both the Democratic and Whig parties in National Conventions—ratified by the people in the election of 1852—and rightly applied to the organization of the Territories in 1854 ; That by the uniform application of this Democratic principle to the organization of Territories and to the admission of new States, with or without domestic Slavery as they may elect, the equal rights of all will be preserved intact—the original compacts of the Constitution maintained inviolate—and the perpetuity and expansion of this Union insured to its utmost capacity of embracing in peace and harmony any future American State that may be constituted or annexed with a Republican form of government."

In accepting the nomination of this Convention, Mr. Buchanan, in a letter dated June 16, 1856, said:

" The agitation on the question of domestic Slavery has too long distracted and divided the people of this Union, and alienated their affections from each other. This agitation has assumed many forms since its commencement, but it now seems to be directed chiefly to the Territories ; and judging from its present character, I think we may safely anticipate that it is rapidly approaching a 'finality.' The recent legislation of Congress respecting domestic Slavery, derived, as it has been, from the original and pure fountain of legitimate political power, the will of the majority, promises, ere long, to allay the dangerous excitement. This legislation is founded upon principles as ancient as free government itself, and in accordance with them has simply declared that the people of a Territory, like those of a State, *shall decide for themselves whether Slavery shall or shall not exist within their limits.*"

This exposition of the history of these measures shows conclusively that the authors of the Compromise Measures of 1850, and of the Kansas-Nebraska Act of 1854, as well as the members of the Continental Congress of 1774, and the founders of our system of government subsequent to the Revolution, regarded the people of the Territories and Colonies as political communities which were entitled to a free and exclusive power of legislation in their Provincial Legislatures, where their representation could alone be preserved, in all cases of taxation and internal polity. This right pertains to the people collectively as a law-abiding and peaceful community, and not to the isolated individuals who may wander upon the public domain in violation of law. It can only be exercised where there are inhabitants sufficient to constitute a government, and capable of performing its various functions and duties—a fact to be ascertained and determined by Congress. Whether the number shall be fixed at ten, fifteen or twenty thousand inhabitants does not affect the principle.

The principle, under our political system, is *that every distinct political Community, loyal to the Constitution and the Union, is entitled to all the rights, privileges, and immunities of self-government in respect to their local concerns and internal polity, subject only to the Constitution of the United States.*

NATIONAL POLITICS.

SPEECH OF ABRAHAM LINCOLN, OF ILLINOIS,

Delivered at the Cooper Institute, Monday, Feb. 27, 1860.

Mr. President and Fellow-Citizens of New-York: The facts with which I shall deal this evening are mainly old and familiar; nor is there anything new in the general use I shall make of them. If there shall be any novelty, it will be in the mode of presenting the facts, and the inferences and observations following that presentation.

In his speech, last autumn, at Columbus, Ohio, as reported in "The New York Times," Senator Douglas said:

"Our fathers, when they framed the Government under which we live, understood this question just as well, and even better than we do now."

I fully indorse this, and I adopt it as a text for this discourse. I so adopt it because it furnishes a precise and an agreed starting point for a discussion between Republicans and that wing of Democracy headed by Senator Douglas. It simply leaves the inquiry: "What was the understanding those fathers had of the question mentioned?"

What is the frame of Government under which we live?

The answer must be: "The Constitution of the United States." That Constitution consists of the original, framed in 1787 (and under which the present Government first went into operation), and twelve subsequently framed amendments, the first ten of which were framed in 1789.

Who were our fathers that framed the Constitution? I suppose the "thirty-nine" who signed the original instrument may be fairly called our fathers who framed that part of the present Government. It is almost exactly true to say they framed it, and it is altogether true to say they fairly represented the opinion and sentiment of the whole nation at that time. Their names, being familiar to nearly all, and accessible to quite all, need not now be repeated.

I take these "thirty-nine," for the present, as being "our fathers who framed the Government under which we live."

What is the question which, according to the text, those fathers understood just as well, and even better than we do now?

It is this: Does the proper division of local from federal authority, or anything in the Constitution, forbid our Federal Government to control as to Slavery in our Federal Territories?

Upon this, Douglas holds the affirmative, and Republicans the negative. This affirmative and denial form an issue; and this issue—this question—is precisely what the text declares our fathers understood better than we.

Let us now inquire whether the "thirty-nine," or any of them, ever acted upon this question; and if they did, how they acted upon it—how they expressed that better understanding.

In 1784—three years before the Constitution—the United States then owning the Northwestern Territory, and no other—the Congress of the Confederation had before them the question of prohibiting Slavery in that Territory; and four of the "thirty-nine," who afterward framed the Constitution were in that Congress, and voted on that question. Of these, Roger Sherman, Thomas Mifflin, and Hugh Williamson voted for the prohibition—thus showing that, in their understanding, no line dividing local from federal authority, nor anything else, properly forbade the Federal Government to control as to Slavery in Federal Territory. The other of the four—James McHenry—voted against the prohibition, showing that, for some cause, he thought it improper to vote for it.

In 1787, still before the Constitution, but while the Convention was in session framing it, and while the Northwestern Territory still was the only Territory owned by the United States—the same question of prohibiting Slavery in the Territory again came before the Congress of the Confederation; and three more of the "thirty-nine" who afterward signed the Constitution, were in that Congress, and voted on the question. They were William Blount, William Few and Abraham Baldwin; and they all voted for the prohibition—thus showing that, in their understanding, no line dividing local from federal authority, nor anything else, properly forbids the Federal Government to control as to Slavery in federal territory. This time the prohibition became a law, being part of what is now well known as the Ordinance of '87.

The question of federal control of Slavery in the Territories, seems not to have been directly before the Convention which framed the original Constitution; and hence it is not recorded that the "thirty-nine," or any of them, while engaged on that instrument, expressed any opinion on that precise question.

In 1789, by the first Congress which sat under the Constitution, an act was passed to enforce the Ordinance of '87, including the prohibition of Slavery in the Northwestern Territory. The bill for this act was reported by one of the "thirty-nine," Thomas Fitzsimmons, then a member of the House of Representatives from Pennsylvania. It went through all its stages without a word of opposition, and finally passed both branches without yeas and nays, which is equivalent to a unanimous passage. In this Congress there were sixteen of the "thirty-nine" fathers who framed the original Constitution. They were John Langdon, Nicholas Gilman, Wm. S. Johnson, Roger Sherman, Robert Morris, Thomas Fitzsimmons, William Few, Abraham Baldwin, Rufus King, William Patterson, George Clymer, Richard Bassett, George Read, Pierce Butler, Daniel Carroll, James Madison.

This shows that, in their understanding, no line dividing local from federal authority, nor anything in the Constitution, properly forbade Congress to prohibit Slavery in the federal territory; else both their fidelity to correct principle, and their oath to support the Constitution, would have constrained them to oppose the prohibition.

Again, George Washington, another of the "thirty-nine," was then President of the United States, and, as such, approved and signed the bill, thus completing its validity as a law, and thus showing that, in his understanding, no line dividing local from federal authority, nor anything in the Constitution, forbade the Federal Government, to control as to Slavery in federal territory.

No great while after the adoption of the original Constitution, North Carolina ceded to the Federal Government the country now constituting the State of Tennessee; and a few years later Georgia ceded that which now constitutes the States of Mississippi and Alabama. In both deeds of cession it was made a condition by the ceding States that the Federal Government should not prohibit Slavery in the ceded country. Besides this, Slavery was then actually in the ceded country. Under these circumstances, Congress, on taking charge of these countries, did not absolutely prohibit Slavery within them. But they did interfere with it—take control of it—even there, to a certain extent. In 1798, Congress organized the Territory of Mississippi. In the act of organization they prohibited the bringing of Slaves into the Territory, from any place without the United States, by fine, and giving freedom to slaves so brought. This act passed both branches of Congress without yeas and nays. In that Congress were three of the "thirty-nine" who framed the original Constitution. They were John Langdon, George Read and Abraham Baldwin. They all, probably voted for it. Certainly they would have placed their opposition to it upon record, if, in their understanding, any line dividing local from federal authority, or anything in the Constitution, properly forbade the Federal Government to control as to Slavery in federal territory.

In 1803, the Federal Government purchased the Louisiana country. Our former territorial acquisitions came from certain of our own States; but this Louisiana country was acquired from a foreign nation. In 1804, Congress gave a Territorial organization to that part of it which now constitutes the State of Louisiana. New Orleans, lying within that part, was an old and comparatively large city. There were other considerable towns and settlements, and Slavery was extensively and thoroughly intermingled with the people. Congress did not, in the Territorial Act, prohibit Slavery; but they did interfere with it—take control of it—in a more marked and extensive way than they did in the case of Mississippi. The substance of the provision therein made, in relation to slaves, was:

First. That no slave should be imported into the Territory from foreign parts.

Second. That no slave should be carried into it who had been imported into the United States since the first day of May, 1798.

Third. That no slave shall be carried into it except by the owner, and for his own use as a settler; the penalty in all the cases being a fine upon the violator of the law, and freedom to the slave.

This act also was passed without yeas and nays. In the Congress which passed it, there were two of the "thirty-nine." They were Abraham Baldwin and Jonathan Dayton. As stated in the case of Mississippi, it is probable they both voted for it. They would not have allowed it to pass without recording their opposition to it, if, in their understanding, it violated either the line proper dividing local from federal authority or any provision of the Constitution.

In 1819-20, came and passed the Missouri question. Many votes were taken, by yeas and nays, in both branches of Congress, upon the various phases of the general question. Two of the "thirty-nine"—Rufus King and Charles Pinckney—were members of that Congress. Mr. King steadily voted for Slavery prohibition and against all compromises, while Mr. Pinckney as steadily voted against Slavery prohibition and against all compromises. By this Mr. King showed that, in his understanding, no line dividing local from federal authority, nor anything in the Constitution, was violated by Congress prohibiting Slavery in federal territory; while Mr. Pinckney, by his votes, showed that in his understanding there was sufficient reason for opposing such prohibition in that case.

The cases I have mentioned are the only acts of the "thirty-nine," or of any of them, upon the direct issue, which I have been able to discover.

To enumerate the persons who thus acted, as being four in 1784, three in 1787, seventeen in 1789, three in 1798, two in 1804, and two in 1819-20—there would be thirty-one of them. But this would be counting John Langdon, Roger Sherman, William Few, Rufus King, and George Read, each twice, and Abraham Baldwin four times. The true number of those of the "thirty-nine" whom I have shown to have acted upon the question, which, by the text they understood better than we, is twenty-three, leaving sixteen not shown to have acted upon it in any way.

Here, then, we have twenty-three out of our "thirty-nine" fathers who framed the Government under which we live, who have, upon their official responsibility and their corporal oaths, acted upon the very question which the text affirms they "understood just as well, and even better than we do now;" and twenty-one of them—a clear majority of the whole "thirty-nine"—so acting upon it as to make them guilty of gross political impropriety, and willful perjury, if, in their understanding, any proper division between local and federal authority, or anything in the Constitution they had made themselves, and sworn to support, forbade the Federal Government to control as to Slavery in the federal territories. Thus the twenty-one acted; and, as actions speak louder than words, so actions under such responsibility speak still louder.

Two of the twenty-three voted against Congressional prohibition of Slavery in the federal Territories in the instances in which they acted upon the question. But for what reason they so voted is not known. They may have done so because they thought a proper division of local

from federal authority, or some provision or principle of the Constitution, stood in the way; or they may, without any such question, have voted against the prohibition, on what appeared to them to be sufficient grounds of expediency. No one who has sworn to support the Constitution, can conscientiously vote for what he understands to be an unconstitutional measure, however expedient he may think it; but one may and ought to vote against a measure which he deems constitutional, if, at the same time, he deems it inexpedient. It, therefore, would be unsafe to set down even the two who voted against the prohibition, as having done so because, in their understanding, any proper division of local from federal authority, or anything in the Constitution forbade the Federal Government to control as to Slavery in federal territory.

The remaining sixteen of the "thirty-nine," so far as I have discovered, have left no record of their understanding upon the direct question of the control of Slavery in the federal territories. But there is much reason to believe that their understanding upon that question would not have appeared different from that of their twenty-three compeers, had it been manifested at all.

For the purpose of adhering rigidly to the text, I have purposely omitted whatever understanding may have been manifested, by any person, however distinguished, other than the thirty-nine fathers who framed the original Constitution; and, for the same reason, I have also omitted whatever understanding may have been manifested by any of the "thirty-nine" even, on any other phase of the general question of Slavery. If we should look into their acts and declarations on those other phases, as the foreign slave-trade, and the morality and policy of Slavery generally, it would appear to us that on the direct question of federal control of Slavery in federal territories, the sixteen, if they had acted at all, would probably have acted just as the twenty-three did. Among that sixteen were several of the most noted anti-slavery men of those times—as Dr. Franklin, Alexander Hamilton, and Gouverneur Morris—while there was not one now known to have been otherwise, unless it may be John Rutledge, of South Carolina.

The sum of the whole is, that of our "thirty-nine" fathers who framed the original Constitution, twenty-one—a clear majority of the whole—certainly understood that no proper division of local from federal authority nor any part of the Constitution, forbade the Federal Government to control Slavery in the federal territories, while all the rest probably had the same understanding. Such, unquestionably, was the understanding of our fathers who framed the original Constitution; and the text affirms that they understood the question better than we.

But, so far, I have been considering the understanding of the question manifested by the framers of the original Constitution. In and by the original instrument, a mode was provided for amending it; and, as I have already stated, the present frame of Government under which we live consists of that original, and twelve amendatory articles framed and adopted since. Those who now insist that federal control of Slavery in federal territories violates the Constitution, point us to the provisions which they suppose it thus violates; and, as I understand, they all fix upon provisions in these amendatory articles, and not in the original instrument. The Supreme Court, in the Dred Scott case, plant themselves upon the fifth amendment, which provides that " no person shall be deprived of property without due process of law;" while Senator Douglas and his peculiar adherents plant themselves upon the tenth amendment, providing that " the powers not granted by the Constitution, are reserved to the States respectively, and to the people."

Now, it so happens that these amendments were framed by the first Congress which sat under the Constitution—the identical Congress which passed the act already mentioned, enforcing the prohibition of Slavery in the north-western Territory. Not only was it the same Congress, but they were the identical, same individual men, who, at the same session, and at the same time within the session, had under consideration, and in progress toward maturity, these Constitutional amendments, and this act prohibiting Slavery in all the Territory the nation owned. The Constitutional amendments were introduced before, and passed after the act enforcing the Ordinance, of '87; so that during the whole pendency of the act to enforce the ordinance, the Constitutional amendments were also pending.

That Congress, consisting in all of seventy-six members, including sixteen of the framers of the original Constitution, as before stated, were preëminently our fathers who framed that part of the Government under which we live, which is now claimed as forbidding the Federal Government to control Slavery in the Federal Territories.

It is not a little presumptuous in any one at this day to affirm that the two things which that Congress deliberately framed, and carried to maturity at the same time, are absolutely inconsistent with each other? And does not such affirmation become impudently absurd when coupled with the other affirmation, from the same mouth, that those who did the two things alleged to be inconsistent understood whether they really were inconsistent better than we—better than he who affirms that they are inconsistent?

It is surely safe to assume that the "thirty-nine" framers of the original Constitution, and the seventy-six members of the Congress which framed the amendments thereto, taken together, do certainly include those who may be fairly called "our fathers who framed the Government under which we live." And so assuming, I defy any man to show that any one of them ever, in his whole life, declared that, in his understanding, any proper division of local from federal authority, or any part of the Constitution, forbade the Federal Government to control as to Slavery in the federal territories. I go a step further. I defy any one to show that any living man in the whole world ever did, prior to the beginning of the present century (and I might almost say prior to the beginning of the last half of the present century) declare that, in his understanding, any proper division of local from federal authority, or any part of the Constitution, forbade the Federal Government to control as to Slavery in the federal territories. To those who now so declare, I give, not only " our fathers who framed the Government under which we live." but with them all other living men within the century in which it was framed, among whom to search, and they shall not be able to find the evidence of a single man agreeing with them.

Now, and here, let me guard a little against being misunderstood. I do not mean to say we are bound to follow implicitly in whatever our fathers did. To do so, would be to discard all the lights of current experience—to reject all progress—all improvement. What I do say is, that if we would supplant the opinions and policy of our fathers in any case, we should do so upon evidence so conclusive, and argument so clear, that even their great authority, fairly considered and weighed, cannot stand; and most surely not in a case whereof we ourselves declare they understood the question better than we.

If any man, at this day, sincerely believes that a proper division of local from federal authority, or any part of the Constitution, forbids the Federal Government to control as to Slavery in the federal territories, he is right to say so, and to enforce his position by all truthful evidence and fair argument which he can. But he has no right to mislead others, who have less access to history and less leisure to study it, into the false belief that " our fathers, who framed the Government under which we live," were of the same opinion—thus substituting falsehood and deception for truthful evidence and fair argument. If any man at this day sincerely believes " our fathers, who framed the Government under which we live," used and applied principles, in other cases, which ought to have led them to understand that a proper division of local from federal authority or some part of the Constitution, forbids the federal government to control as to Slavery in the Federal Territories, he is right to say so. But he should, at the same time, brave the responsibility of declaring that, in his opinion, he understands their principles better than they did themselves ; and especially should he not shirk that responsibility by asserting that they " understood the question just as well, and even better, than we do now."

But enough. Let all who believe that " our fathers, who framed the Government under which we live, understood the question just as well, and even better, than we do now," speak as they spoke, and act as they acted upon it. This is all Republicans ask—all Republicans desire—in relation to Slavery. As those fathers marked it. so let it be again marked, as an evil not to be extended, but to be tolerated and protected only because of and so far as its actual presence among us makes that, toleration and protection a necessity. Let all the guaranties those fathers gave it, be not grudgingly, but fully and fairly, maintained. For this Republicans contend, and with this, so far as I know or believe, they will be content.

And now, if they would listen, as I suppose they will not, I would address a few words to the southern people.

I would say to them : You consider yourselves a reasonable and a just people ; and I consider that in the general qualities of reason and justice you are not inferior to any other people. Still, when you speak of us Republicans, you do so only to denounce us as reptiles, or, at the best, as no better than outlaws. You will grant a hearing to pirates or murderers, but nothing like it to " Black Republicans." In all your contentions with one another, each of you deems an unconditional condemnation of "Black Republicanism" as the first thing to be attended to. Indeed such condemnation of us seems to be an indispensable prerequisite—license, so to speak, among you to be admitted or permitted to speak at all.

Now, can you, or not, be prevailed upon to pause and to consider whether this is quite just to us, or even to yourselves?

Bring forward your charges and specifications, and then be patient long enough to hear us deny or justify.

You say we are sectional. We deny it. That makes an issue: and the burden of proof is upon you. You produce your proof; and what is it? Why, that our party has no existence in your section—gets no votes in your section. The fact is substantially true ; but does it prove the issue? If it does, then in case we should, without change of principle, begin to get votes in your section, we should thereby cease to be sectional. You cannot escape this conclusion; and yet, are you willing to abide by it? If you are, you will probably soon find that we have ceased to be sectional, for we shall get votes in your section this very year. You will then begin to discover, as the truth plainly is, that your proof does not touch the issue. The fact that we get no votes in your section is a fact of your making, and not of ours. And if there be fault in that fact, that fault is primarily yours, and remains so until you show that we repel you by some wrong principle or practice. If we do repel you by any wrong principle or practice, the fault is ours ; but this brings you to where you ought to have started—to a discussion of the right or wrong of our principle. If our principle, put in practice, would wrong your section for the benefit of ours, or for any other object, then our principle, and we with it, are sectional, and are justly opposed and denounced as such. Meet us, then, on the question of whether our principle, put in practice, would wrong your section ; and so meet it as if it were possible that something may be said on our side. Do you accept the challenge? No? Then you really believe that the principle which our fathers who framed the Government under which we live thought so clearly right as to adopt it, and indorse it again and again, upon their official oaths, is, in fact, so clearly wrong as to demand your condemnation without a moment's consideration.

Some of you delight to flaunt in our faces the warning against sectional parties given by Washington in his Farewell Address. Less than eight years before Washington gave that warning he had, as President of the United States, approved and signed an act of Congress enforcing the prohibition of Slavery in the northwestern Territory, which act embodied the policy of the Government upon that subject, up to and at the very moment he penned that warning; and about one year after he penned it he wrote Lafayette, that he considered that prohibition a wise measure, expressing in the same connection his hope that we should sometime have a confederacy of free States.

Bearing this in mind, and seeing that sectionalism has since arisen upon this same subject, is that warning a weapon in your hands against us, or, in our hands, against you? Could Washington himself speak, would he cast the blame of that sectionalism upon us, who sustain his policy, or upon you, who repudiate it? We respect that warning of Washington, and we commend it to you, together with his example pointing to the right application of it.

But you say you are conservative—eminently conservative—while we are revolutionary, destructive, or something of the sort. What is conservatism? Is it not adherence to the old and tried, against the new and untried? We stick to, contend for, the identical old policy on the point in controversy which was adopted by our fathers who framed the Government under which we live; while you, with one accord, reject, and scout, and spit upon that old policy, and insist upon substituting something new. True, you disagree among yourselves as to what that substitute shall be. You have considerable variety of new propositions and plans, but you are unanimous in rejecting and denouncing the old policy of the fathers. Some of you are for reviving the foreign slave-trade ; some for a congressional slave-code for the Territories ; some for Congress forbidding the Territories to prohibit Slavery within their limits ; some for maintaining Slavery in the Territories through the judiciary ; some for the " gur-reat pur-rinciple" that " if one man would enslave another, no third person should object," fantastically called " Popular Sovereignty ;" but never a man among you in favor of federal prohibition of Slavery in Federal Territories, according to the practice of our fathers who framed the Government under which we live. Not one of all your various plans can show a precedent or an advocate in the century within which our Government originated. Consider, then, whether your claim of conservatism for yourselves, and your charge of destructiveness against us, are based on the most clear and stable foundations.

Again, you say we have made the Slavery question more prominent than it formerly was. We deny it. We admit that it is more prominent, but we deny that we made it so. It was not we, but you, who discarded the old policy of the fathe.s. We resisted, and still resist, your innovation; and thence comes the greater prominence of the question. Would you have that question reduced to its former proportions? Go back to that old policy. What has been will be again, under the same conditions. If you would have the peace of the old times, re-adopt the precepts and policy of the old times.

You charge that we stir up insurrections among your slaves. We deny it; and what is your proof? Harper's Ferry! John Brown! John Brown was no Republican; and you have failed to implicate a single Republican in his Harper's Ferry enterprise. If any member of our party is guilty in that matter, you know it, or you do not know it. If you do know it, you are inexcusable to not designate the man, and prove the fact. If you do not know it, you are inexcusable to assert it, and especially to persist in the assertion after you have tried and failed to make the proof. You need not be told that persisting in a charge which one does not know to be true, is simply a malicious slander.

Some of you admit that no Republican designedly aided or encouraged the Harper's Ferry affair; but still insist that our doctrines and declarations necessarily lead to such results. · We do not believe it. We know we hold to no doctrine, and make no declarations, which were not held to and made by our fathers who framed the Government under which we live. You never dealt fairly by us in relation to this affair. When it occurred, some important State elections were near at hand, and you were in evident glee with the belief that, by charging the blame upon us, you could get an advantage of us in those elect.ons. The elections came, and your expectations were not quite fulfilled. Every Republican man knew that, as to himself at least, your charge was a slander, and he was not much inclined by it to cast his vote in your favor. Republican doctrines and declarations are accompanied with a continual protest against any interference whatever with your slaves, or with you about your slaves. Surely, this does not encourage them to revolt. True, we do, in common with our fathers, who framed the Government under which we live, declare our belief that Slavery is wrong; but the slaves do not hear us declare even this. For anything we say or do, the slaves would scarcely know there is a Republican party. I believe they would not, in fact, generally know it but for your misrepresentations of us, in their hearing. In your political contests among yourselves, each faction charges the other with sympathy with Black Republicanism; and then, to give point to the charge, defines Black Republicanism to simply be insurrection, blood and thunder among the slaves.

Slave insurrections are no more common now than they were before the Republican party was organized. What induced the Southampton insurrection, twenty-eight years ago, in which, at least, three times as many lives were lost as at Harper's Ferry? You can scarcely stretch your very elastic fancy to the conclusion that Southampton was got up by Black Republicanism. In the present state of things in the United States, I do not think a general, or even a very extensive slave insurrection, is possible. The indispensable concert of action cannot be attained. The slaves have no means of rapid communication; nor can incendiary free men, black or white, supply it. The explosive materials are everywhere in parcels; but there neither are, nor can be supplied, the indispensable connecting trains.

Much is said by Southern people about the affection of slaves for their masters and mistresses; and a part of it, at least, is true. A plot for an uprising could scarcely be devised and communicated to twenty individuals before some one of them, to save the life of a favorite master or mistress, would divulge it. This is the rule; and the slave-revolution in Hayti was not an exception to it, but a case occurring under peculiar circumstances. The gunpowder plot of British history, though not connected with slaves, was more in point. In that case, only about twenty were admitted to the secret; and yet one of them, in his anxiety to save a friend, betrayed the plot to that friend, and, by consequence, averted the calamity. Occasional poisonings from the kitchen, and open or stealthy assassinations in the field, and local revolts extending to a score or so, will continue to occur as the natural results of Slavery; but no general insurrection of slaves, as I think, can happen in this country for a long time. Whoever much fears, or much hopes, for such an event, will be alike disappointed.

In the language of Mr. Jefferson, uttered many years ago, "it is still in our power to direct the process of emancipation, and deportation, peaceably, and in such slow degrees, as that the evil will wear off insensibly; and their places be, *pari passu,* filled up by free white laborers. If, on the contrary, it is left to force itself on, human nature must shudder at the prospect held up."

Mr. Jefferson did not mean to say, nor do I, that the power of emancipation is in the Federal Government. He spoke of Virginia; and, as to the power of emancipation, I speak of the slaveholding States only.

The Federal Government, however, as we insist, has the power of restraining the extension of the institution—the power to insure that a slave insurrection shall never occur on any American soil which is now free from Slavery.

John Brown's effort was peculiar. It was not a slave insurrection. It was an attempt by white men to get up a revolt among slaves, in which the slaves refused to participate. In fact, it was so absurd that the slaves, with all their ignorance, saw plainly enough it could not succeed. That affair, in its philosophy, corresponds with many attempts related in history, at the assassination of Kings and Emperors. An enthusiast broods over the oppression of a people till he fancies himself commissioned by Heaven to liberate them. He ventures the attempt, which ends in little else than in his own execution. Orsini's attempt on Louis Napoleon, and John Brown's attempt at Harper's Ferry, were, in their philosophy, precisely the same. The eagerness to cast blame on old England in the one case, and on New England in the other, does not disprove the sameness of the two things.

And how much would it avail you, if you could, by the use of John Brown, Helper's book, and the like, break up the Republican organization? Human action can be modified to some extent, but human nature cannot be changed. There is a judgment and a feeling against Slavery in this nation, which cast at least a million and a half of votes. You cannot destroy that judgment and feeling—that sentiment—by breaking up the political organization which rallies around it. You can scarcely scatter and disperse an army which has been formed into order in the face of your heaviest fire, but if you could, how much would you gain by forcing the sentiment which created it out of the peaceful channel of the ballot box, into some other channel? What would that other channel probably be? Would the number of John Browns be lessened or enlarged by the operation?

But you will break up the Union rather than submit to a denial of your constitutional rights.

That has a somewhat reckless sound; but it would be palliated, if not fully justified, were we proposing, by the mere force of numbers, to deprive you of some right, plainly written down in the Constitution. But we are proposing no such thing.

When you make these declarations, you have a specific and well-understood allusion to an assumed constitutional right of yours, to take slaves into the federal territories, and to hold them there as property. But no such right is specifically written in the Constitution. That instrument is literally silent about any such right. We, on the contrary, deny that such a right has any existence in the Constitution, even by implication.

Your purpose, then, plainly stated, is, that you will destroy the Government, unless you be allowed to construe and enforce the Constitution as you please, on all points in dispute between you and us. You will rule or ruin in all events.

This, plainly stated, is your language to us. Perhaps you will say the Supreme Court has decided the disputed Constitutional question in your favor. Not quite so. But waiving the lawyer's distinction between *dictum* and decision, the Courts have decided the question for you in a sort of way. The Courts have substantially said, it is your Constitutional right to take slaves into the federal territories, and to hold them there as property.

When I say the decision was made in a sort of way, I mean it was made in a divided Court by a bare majority of the Judges, and they not quite agreeing with one another in the reasons for making it; that it is so made as that its avowed supporters disagree with one another about its meaning, and that it was mainly based upon a mistaken statement of fact—the statement in the opinion that " the right of property in a slave is distinctly and expressly affirmed in the Constitution."

An inspection of the Constitution will show that the right of property in a slave is not distinctly and expressly affirmed in it. Bear in mind the Judges do not pledge their judicial opinion that such is right is impliedly affirmed in the Constitution; but they pledge their veracity that it is distinctly and expressly affirmed there—" distinctly," that is, not mingled with anything else—" expressly," that is, in words meaning just that, without the aid of any inference, and susceptible of no other meaning.

If they had only pledged their judicial opinion that

such right is affirmed in the instrument by implication, it would be open to others to show that neither the word "slave" nor "Slavery" is to be found in the Constitution, nor the word "property" even, in any connection with the language alluding to the things slave, or Slavery, and that wherever in that instrument the slave is alluded to, he is called a "person;" and wherever his master's legal right in relation to him is alluded to, it is spoken of as "service or labor due," as a "debt" payable in service or labor. Also, it would be open to show, by contemporaneous history, that this mode of alluding to slaves and Slavery, instead of speaking of them, was employed on purpose to exclude from the Constitution the idea that there could be property in man.

To show all this is easy and certain.

When this obvious mistake of the Judges shall be brought to their notice, it is not reasonable to expect that they will withdraw the mistaken statement, and reconsider the conclusion based upon it?

And then it is to be remembered that "our fathers, who framed the Government under which we live"—the men who made the Constitution—decided this same Constitutional question in our favor, long ago—decided it without a division among themselves, when making the decision; without division among themselves about the meaning of it after it was made, and so far as any evidence is left, without basing it upon any mistaken statement of facts.

Under all these circumstances, do you really feel yourselves justified to break up this Government, unless such a court decision as yours is shall be at once submitted to as a conclusive and final rule of political action?

But you will not abide the election of a Republican President. In that supposed event, you say, you will destroy the Union; and then, you say, the great crime of having destroyed it will be upon us?

That is cool. A highwayman holds a pistol to my ear, and mutters through his teeth, "stand and deliver, or I shall kill you, and then you will be a murderer!"

To be sure, what the robber demanded of me—my money—was my own; and I had a clear right to keep it; but it was no more my own than my vote is my own; and the threat of death to me to extort my money, and the threat of destruction to the Union, to extort my vote, can scarcely be distinguished in principle.

A few words now to Republicans. It is exceedingly desirable that all parts of this great Confederacy shall be at peace, and in harmony, one with another. Let us Republicans do our part to have it so. Even though much provoked, let us do nothing through passion and ill temper. Even though the southern people will not so much as listen to us, let us calmly consider their demands, and yield to them if, in our deliberate view of our duty, we possibly can. Judging by all they say and do, and by the subject and nature of their controversy with us, let us determine, if we can, what will satisfy them?

Will they be satisfied if the Territories be unconditionally surrendered to them? We know they will not. In all their present complaints against us, the Territories are scarcely mentioned. Invasions and insurrections are the rage now. Will it satisfy them if, in the future, we have nothing to do with invasions and insurrections? We know it will not. We so know because we know we never had anything to do with invasions and insurrections; and yet this total abstaining does not exempt us from the charge and the denunciation.

The question recurs, what will satisfy them? Simply this: We must not only let them alone, but we must, somehow, convince them that we do let them alone. This, we know by experience, is no easy task. We have been so trying to convince them, from the very beginning of our organization, but with no success. In all our platforms and speeches we have constantly protested our purpose to let them alone; but this has had no tendency to convince them. Alike unavailing to convince them is the fact that they have never detected a man of us in any attempt to disturb them.

These natural, and apparently adequate means all failing, what will convince them? This, and this only: cease to call Slavery *wrong*, and join them in calling it *right*. And this must be done thoroughly—done in *acts* as well as in *words*. Silence will not be tolerated—we must place ourselves avowedly with them. Douglas's new sedition law must be enacted and enforced, suppressing all declarations that Slavery is wrong, whether made in politics, in presses, in pulpits, or in private. We must arrest and return their fugitive slaves with greedy pleasure. We must pull down our Free State constitutions. The whole atmosphere must be disinfected from all taint of opposition to Slavery, before they will cease to believe that all their troubles proceed from us.

I am quite aware they do not state their case precisely in this way. Most of them would probably say to us, "Let us alone, do nothing to us, and say what you please about Slavery." But we do let them alone—have never disturbed them—so that, after all, it is what we say, which dissatisfies them. They will continue to accuse us of doing, until we cease saying.

I am also aware they have not, as yet, in terms, demanded the overthrow of our Free State Constitutions. Yet those constitutions declare the wrong of Slavery, with more solemn emphasis, than do all other sayings against it; and when all these other sayings shall have been silenced, the overthrow of these constitutions will be demanded, and nothing be left to resist the demand. It is nothing to the contrary, that they do not demand the whole of this just now. Demanding what they do, and for the reason they do, they can voluntarily stop nowhere short of this consummation. Holding, as they do, that Slavery is morally right, and socially elevating, they cannot cease to demand a full national recognition of it, as a legal right, and a social blessing.

Nor can we justifiably withhold this, on any ground save our conviction that Slavery is wrong. If Slavery is right, all words, acts, laws, and constitutions against it, are themselves wrong, and should be silenced, and swept away. If it is right, we cannot justly object to its nationality—its universality; if it is wrong, they cannot justly insist upon its extension—its enlargement. All they ask, we could readily grant, if we thought Slavery right; all we ask, they could as readily grant, if they thought it wrong. Their thinking it right, and our thinking it wrong, is the precise fact upon which depends the whole controversy. Thinking it right, as they do, they are not to blame for desiring its full recognition, as being right; but, thinking it wrong, as we do, can we yield to them? Can we cast our votes with their view, and against our own? In view of our moral, social, and political responsibilities, can we do this?

Wrong as we think Slavery is, we can yet afford to let it alone where it is, because that much is due to the necessity arising from its actual presence in the nation; but can we, while our votes will prevent it, allow it to spread into the National Territories, and to overrun us here in these Free States?

If our sense of duty forbids this, then let us stand by our duty, fearlessly and effectively. Let us be diverted by none of those sophistical contrivances wherewith we are so industriously plied and belabored—contrivances such as groping for some middle ground between the right and the wrong, vain as the search for a man who should be neither a living man nor a dead man—such as a policy of "don't care" on a question about which all true men do care—such as Union appeals beseeching true Union men to yield to Disunionists, reversing the divine rule, and calling, not the sinners, but the righteous to repentance—such as invocations to Washington, imploring men to unsay what Washington said, and undo what Washington did.

Neither let us be slandered from our duty by false accusations against us, nor frightened from it by menaces of destruction to the Government, nor of dungeons to ourselves. Let us have faith that right makes might, and in that faith, let us, to the end, dare to do our duty, as we understand it.

MR. BRECKINRIDGE ON NATIONAL POLITICS.

SPEECH AT FRANKFORT, KY.

THE HON. JOHN C. BRECKINRIDGE delivered the following speech on the general political topics of the day before the Legislature of Kentucky at Frankfort in Dec. 1859. Mr. Breckinridge had been recently elected to the United States Senate, by the Kentucky Legislature; and after returning his thanks for the distinguished honor, and promising to serve the State to the best of his ability, he continued as follows:

The election took place on Monday. The day before I received a letter signed by a number of gentlemen in the Legislature, asking my opinion in reference to the DRED SCOTT decision, in reference to Territorial Sovereignty, and the power of Congress to protect the property of citizens within the Territories. I received that letter with profound respect, and only regret it did not come to my hands in time, that I might answer it before the election. But yet I am glad that I could not answer it before that day, for your choice is a sort of indorsement of my soundness upon those questions. I confess I was somewhat gratified that the election took place before I had those questions to answer. It was utterly impossible for me to have returned an answer before the time fixed by your law for the election, but, I never intended to fail in this answer. I never should have failed. Had it been one who signed it, instead of twenty, the result would have been precisely the same.

Besides this, it would have been of but little consequence, be the answer before or after. I belong to that school of politics that believes in instruction, and whenever I am not ready to receive the instructions of the State, I stand ready to give back the trust confided in my hands.

THE DRED SCOTT DECISION.

Gentlemen, I bow to the decision of the Supreme Court of the United States upon every question within its proper jurisdiction, whether it corresponds with my private opinion or not; only, I bow a trifle lower when it happens to do so, as the decision in the Dred Scott case does. I approve it in all its parts as a sound exposition of the law and constitutional rights of the States, and citizens that inhabit them. (Applause.) It may not be improper for me here to add that so great an interest did I take in that decision, and in its principles being sustained and understood in the commonwealth of Kentucky, that I took the trouble, at my own cost, to print or have printed a large edition of that decision to scatter it over the State. and unless the mails have miscarried, there is scarcely a member elected to the Legislature who has not received a copy with my frank.

To approve the decision of the Supreme Court in the Dred Scott case would seem to settle the whole question of Territorial Sovereignty, as I think will presently appear; but, in order that no one may misunderstand my views on that question, I will, with your leave, detain you with a brief review of what was done as to the Slavery question up to the time of that decision, referring also to the duties imposed by it.

THE MISSOURI LINE.

I was in the Congress of the United States when that Missouri line was repealed. I never would have voted for any bill organizing the Territory of Kansas as long as that odious stigma upon our institutions remained upon the statute-book. I voted cheerfully for its repeal, and in doing that I cast no reflection upon the wise patriots who acquiesced in it at the time it was established. It was re-

pealed, and we passed the act known as the Kansas-Nebraska bill. The Abolition, or *quasi* Abolition party of the United States were constantly contending that it was the right of Congress to prohibit Slavery in the common Territories of the Union. The Democratic party, aided by most of the gentlemen from the South, took the opposite view of the case. Our object was, if possible, to withdraw that question from the Halls of Congress, and place it where it could no longer risk the public welfare and the public interest. In the Congress of the United States it had been agitated all the time, to the disadvantage of the South; accordingly (I have not a copy of the bill before me now, but I remember its leading provisions), a bill was passed, repealing the Missouri line, and leaving those Territories upon the contract and the assertion that the bill made. Did we intend by it to legislate Slavery into Kansas and Nebraska? We denied that, and denied it upon the face of the bill itself. The settlement thus made, afterward received the approval of the people of the whole country. The bill said within itself, not that we intend to legislate Slavery into the Territories, but to leave the people free to form their own domestic institutions, subject only to the Constitution of the United States. That was as much as we could agree upon. There was a point upon which we could not agree. A considerable portion of the Northern Democracy held that Slavery was in derogation of common right, and could only exist by force of positive law. They contended that the Constitution did not furnish that law, and that the slaveholder could not go into the Territories with his slaves with the Constitution to authorize him in holding his slaves as property, or to protect him. The South, generally, without distinction of party, held the opposite view. They held that the citizens of all the States may go with whatever was recognized by the Constitution as property, and enjoy it. That did not seem to be denied to any article of property except slaves. Accordingly, the bill contained the provision, that any question in reference to Slavery should be referred to the court of the United States, and the understanding was, that whatever the judicial decision should be, it would be binding upon all parties, not only by virtue of the agreement, but under the obligation of the citizens to respect the authority of the legally constituted courts of the country.

WHAT HE SAID IN 1856.

It was under these circumstances, while the Territory of Kansas was in a state of commotion, and when that question had not been determined by the courts, that the canvass of 1856 came on. It became my duty, by the request of my friends, to visit the States of Ohio, Indiana, Michigan and Pennsylvania. In all those States I made speeches. In all those States I uttered the same opinions and declared the same principles that I have ever done in the commonwealth of Kentucky, and am ready to do again. None other!

It has been charged that the Democratic party of the country, and particularly of the South, desired to employ the Federal Government for the purpose of propagating Slavery and slave legislation in the Territories. I denied that the Democratic party desired to use the Federal Government for the propagation of Slavery, and I never conceded what we believed to be our constitutional right to its protection, and what the decision of the Supreme Court has allowed to be our right, I said—yes! I did say that the Democratic party of this country, in its federal aspect, was neither a Pro-Slavery nor an Anti-Slavery party, but a constitutional party, and I repeat it here to-night. (Applause.) I do not believe it is. I do not believe that the Federal Government was organized for either purpose, but to protect the rights adjudicated by the courts. All these belong to the States themselves.

These were the declarations that I made, of which something has been heard in all the States. I made the declarations that I am willing to make before my own constituents ; I made the declarations that I am willing to stand here and repeat. (Applause.) We had confidence in our own view of our own rights. Our northern friends had their views. It was a paradoxical question, and we gave it to the Courts.

Well, the Courts did decide the very question, which had been submitted to them, not upon a case from Kansas, but in another case. Without going into the argument, for time does not permit of that, let me give you the conclusion. In the opinion of the Court in the case of Dred Scott, it is said :

"Upon these considerations, it is the opinion of the Court that the act of Congress which prohibits a citizen from holding and owning property of this kind in the Territory of the United States, north of the line herein mentioned, is not warranted by the Constitution, and is therefore void ; and that neither Dred Scott himself nor any of his family were made free by being carried into this Territory, even if they had been carried there by the owner, with the intention of becoming a permanent resident."

Again :

"The powers over person and property of which we speak, are not only not granted to Congress, but are in express terms denied, and they are forbidden to exercise them. And this prohibition is not confined to the States, but the words are general, and extend to the whole territory over which the Constitution gives it power to legislate, including those portions of it remaining under Territorial government, as well as that covered by States. It is a total absence of power everywhere within the dominion of the United States, and places the citizen of a Territory, so far as those rights are concerned, on the same footing with citizens of the States, and guards them as firmly and plainly against any inroads which the General Government might attempt, under the plea of implied or incidental power. And if Congress itself cannot do this— if it is beyond the powers conferred on the Federal Government—it will be admitted, we presume, that it could not authorize a Territorial government to exercise them. It could confer no power on any local government, established by its authority, to violate the provisions of the Constitution."

Thus the highest court in the United States settled the very question referred to it as the disputed point, not legislative in its character, on which Congress could not agree when the Kansas-Nebraska bill passed. The view that we in the Southern States took of it was sustained, that in the Territories, the common property of the Union, pending their Territorial condition, Congress itself nor the Territorial Government had the power to confiscate any description of property recognized in the States of the Union. The Court drew no distinction between slaves and other property. It is true some foreign philanthropists and some foreign writers do undertake to draw this distinction, but these distinctions have nothing to do with our system of Government. Our Government rests not upon the speculations of philanthropic writers, but upon the plain understanding of a written constitution which determines it, and upon that alone. It is the result of positive law ; therefore we are not to look to the analogy of the supposed law of nations, but to regard the Constitution itself, which is the written expression of the respective powers of the Government and the rights of the States.

UNFRIENDLY LEGISLATION.

Well, that being the case, and it having been authoritatively determined by the very tribunal to which it was referred that Congress had no power to exclude slave property from the Territory, and judiciously determined that the Territorial Legislatures, authorities created by Congress, had not the power to exclude or confiscate slave property, I confess that I had not anticipated that the doctrines of unfriendly legislation would be set up. Hence, I need not say to you that I do not believe in the doctrine of unfriendly legislation ; that I do not believe in the authority of Territorial Legislatures to do by indirection what they cannot do directly. I repose upon the decision of the Supreme Court of the United States, as to the point that neither Congress nor the Territorial Legislature has the right to obstruct or confiscate the property of any citizen, slaves included, pending the territorial condition. (Applause.)

I do not see any escape from that decision, if you admit that the question was a judicial one ; if you admit the decision of the Supreme Court, and if you stand by the decision of the highest Court of the country.

The Supreme Court seems to have recognized it as the duty—as the duty of the Courts of this Union in their proper sphere to execute this constitutional right, thus adjudicated by the Supreme Court, in the following language. In speaking of the acquisition of territory, they pronounce it a political question for Congress to determine what territory they acquire and how many. Now mark the words of the Court :

"And whatever the political department of the Government shall recognize as within the limits of the United States, the Judicial Department is also bound to recognize, and to administer in it the laws of the United States, so far as they apply, and to maintain in the territory the authority and rights of the Government, and also the political right and rights of property of individual citizens as secured by the Constitution. All we mean to say on this point is, that as there is no express regulation in the Constitution defining the power which the General Government may exercise over the person or property of a citizen in a territory thus acquired, the Court must necessarily look to the provisions and principles of the Constitution and its distribution of powers, for the rules and principles by which its decision must be governed."

So that in regard to slave property, as in regard to any other property recognized and guarded by the Constitution, it is the duty, according to the Supreme Court, of all the Courts of the country to protect and guard it by their decision, whenever the question is brought before them. To which I will only add this, that the judicial decisions in our favor must be maintained—these judicial decisions in our favor must be sustained. (Applause.)

SLAVE CODE.

If present remedies are adequate to sustain these decisions, I would have nothing more done. I, with many other public men in the country, believe they are able If they are not—if they cannot be enforced for want of the proper legislation to enforce them, sufficient legislation must be passed, or our Government is a failure. (Applause.) Gentlemen, I see no escape from that conclusion.

At the same time, fellow-citizens, I make no hesitation in saying to you that I trust the time will never come— I trust the time will never come when it may be deemed necessary for the Congress of the United States in any form to interfere with this question in the Territories. So far it has been only productive of evil to us, and it would portend only evil in the future. At present there is no question before Congress. No Southern Representative or Senator proposes legislation on that point—no complaint comes from any territory—there is no evidence that the existing laws and decisions of the Courts are not adequate to protect every description of property recognized by the several States. None whatever. Therefore, in my opinion, and I submit it humbly and with deference, our true policy is not to anticipate trouble, but to let the matter rest upon the Executive, upon the existing laws, and upon the decisions of the Courts. (Applause.) I will add this : we must never give up the principle, we must never give up the question that has been judiciously decided, that this constitutional right exists. We must stand by that decision. We must hold to our constitutional rights, but I would never prematurely raise the question to distract the country, when there is no voice calling for it, North, East, South or West. (Applause.) I say we must hold to the principle—we must stand by it. We stand in a good position. We have the Executive, we have the laws, we have the decisions of the Courts, and that is a great advance from where we stood ten years ago.

I am glad—although we did not succeed as we desired in Kansas—I am glad that the territorial question is nearly fought out. It is nearly fought out. I know of no existing Territory where this question can arise. As to the territory south of the line, where slave labor is really profitable, I have not a doubt but that the climate and interest, and the proximity of slaveholders, and the Constitution and laws, and the decision of the Court, will sustain and protect us there in the full enjoyment of our rights, and in making Southern territory out of Southern soil. While I would not give up the principle, I never have believed, and I do not believe now, in the possibility of Slavery planting itself in a territory against the determined opposition of the inhabitants, any more than I believe the institution of Slavery could continue in existence in Kentucky for three years against the desire of the voters of the Commonwealth, even with the constitutional restictions that are here thrown around it.

Still, I would save the question and the principle, and never let go the constitutional right, because our protection in the Union consists in a strict adherence to the provisions of the Constitution. When we allow an infraction of the Constitution on any one point, we lose our claim to the observance of the whole. We should insist to the last that the Constitution of the country shall be sustained in every particular. (A voice—" Good.")

THE PERIL OF THE COUNTRY.

Fellow-citizens, if you will allow me, I will offer you some observations upon another aspect of public affairs. We have been talking of things that concern us no more than they concern others, but we have questions to determine that come nearer home—questions that come to our firesides. According to my humble judgment, the condition of our country was never so perilous as it is at this hour; and if things go drifting on as they have of late, we shall have to determine questions of far nearer vitality than the territorial question.

I hope I do not speak in the spirit of an alarmist or a demagogue, but since I have been acquainted with public affairs (and men older and wiser than myself say the same thing) there never was a time when the interests of this Union were in so much peril, and when the feelings of our people were so much alienated as at this hour. Certainly if the aspect of affairs at Washington is in the slightest degree indicative of the feeling elsewhere, that remark is truth.

ITS CAUSE.

Fellow-citizens, the danger arises, in the opinion of our wisest and best men, from the character and purpose and aim of an organization in the country called the Republican party.

I do not think we fully realize what are the objects, purposes and aims of the Republican party, what it intends, and what would be the consequences to us of their success and dominion in the United States. If you will allow me, therefore, I have gathered together three or four facts—mere expressions—mere illustrations or examples, from many thousands of kindred characters, for the purpose of showing what its objects are—to show what we may expect to follow their success.

HIS VIEWS OF REPUBLICANISM.

First is their platform, made three years ago, but beyond which they have far advanced. Like all aggressive organizations, the rear rank of the Republican party marches up and comes upon the ground that the advanced guard occupied months before, while the advanced guard is going ahead. The Republicans are far in advance of their platform, but we have there enough to put us on our guard.

What are our rights? Have we not a right to have our fugitives returned? If there is a plainer provision than that in the instrument, what is it? Have we not a right to live in peace in this Union? What was the Constitution formed for? When the Constitution was made, was it not made by brethren? Was it not made that this political organization should be carried on in peace and harmony? Have we not a right to demand of our sister States, that we may live together in peace with our respective State institutions, with our whole domestic policy? And is it not a gross violation of the Constitution not to allow us to live in peace, as to refuse to return our fugitives from labor that have escaped into other States? Do they intend to do it? No, they do not. They begin by declaring the Declaration of Independence is a rule of our political action. Here is the declaration of the Republican platform, adopted three years ago, beyond which they have now far advanced:

"*Resolved*, That with our Republican fathers we hold it to be a self-evident truth that all men are endowed with the inalienable right of life, liberty and the pursuit of happiness, and that the primary object and ulterior design of our Federal Government were to secure these rights to all persons under its exclusive jurisdiction; that as our Republican fathers, when they had abolished Slavery in all our national territory, ordained that no person should be deprived of life, liberty and property, without due process of law, it becomes our duty to maintain this provision of the Constitution against all attempts to violate it for the purpose of establishing Slavery in the Territories of the United States by positive legislation, prohibiting its existence or extension therein.

This is a positive pledge, that as soon as that party obtains power, it will recognize the equality of the negro with the white man. Its object will be to give him those rights to life, liberty, and the pursuit of happiness. To maintain that equality what follows? Everybody knows that when they obtain the power in the District of Columbia, they will abolish Slavery there; when they obtain the power, they will undertake to abolish it in the forts, arsenals, and dock-yards of the United States throughout the South; they will undertake to abolish the internal slave-trade. Already they declare that not another Slave State shall be admitted into the Union, and they will go beyond that. How can we expect to live in peace and harmony, when declarations of this sort are uttered?

"*Resolved*, That the Constitution confers upon Congress sovereign power over the Territories of the United States for their government, and that, in the exercise of this power, it is both the right and the imperative duty of Congress, to prohibit in the Territories those twin relics of barbarism—polygamy and Slavery."

Is that in the spirit of our revolutionary ancestors? Is it in the spirit of our revolutionary ancestors for a great and growing party, that now claims, and perhaps have, dominance in the Northern States of the Union, to say of an institution of their Southern relatives they are harboring a relic of barbarism? That shows you, fellow-citizens, their indomitable purpose, their deep-seated hate. I am sorry that it exists, but it is true. How can you expect a great political organization that obtains power, to fail to exercise that power when in its opinion this Union is stained or defiled as to one-half, perhaps, of its inhabitants, by a relic of barbarism, which it classes with the crime of polygamy.

SEWARD QUOTED.

This is not all. I could have brought here the declarations of its representative and leading men from all parts of the Northern States, going infinitely further than is contained there. Allow me, however, to read one or two of the most striking from the most eminent of their leaders. I beg you, fellow-citizens, though they may be familiar, not to weary with a few extracts, for these utterances are the rallying cry of millions of men. I hold in my hand a speech delivered by a Senator of the State of New-York, who is to-day the most influential public man in this Union, on whose words millions hang, and by whose direction millions move. Is this the Constitution and Union that our fathers founded?

Last year, in a speech delivered at Rochester, that gentleman uttered the following language:

"Our country is a theatre which exhibits, in full operation, two radically different political systems; the one resting on the basis of servile or slave labor, the other on the basis of voluntary labor of freemen.

"The two systems are at once perceived to be incongruous. But they are more than incongruous. They are incompatible. They never have permanently existed together in one country, and they never can.

"Hitherto the two systems have existed in different States, but side by side within the American Union. This has happened because the Union is a confederation of States. But on another aspect the United States constitute only one nation. Increase of population which is filling the States out to their very borders, together with a new and extended net-work of railroads and other avenues, and an internal commerce which daily becomes more intimate, is rapidly bringing the States into a higher and more perfect social unity or consolidation. Thus these antagonistic systems are constitutionally coming into close contact and collision results."

Yes, "collision ensues," and his prophecy was fulfilled in less than twelve months after it was made.

"Shall I tell you what this collision means? It is an irrepressible conflict between opposing and enduring forces; and it means that the United States must and will, sooner or later, become entirely a slaveholding nation, or entirely a free-labor nation. Either the cotton and rice fields of South Carolina, and the sugar plantations of Louisiana will ultimately be tilled by free labor, and Charleston and New-Orleans become marts for legitimate merchandise alone; or else the rye-fields and wheat-fields of Massachusetts and New-York must again be surrendered by their farmers to slave culture, and to the production of slaves, and Boston and New-York become once more markets for trade in the bodies and souls of men. It is the failure to apprehend this great truth that induces so many unsuccessful attempts at final compromise between the Slave and Free States, and it is the existence of this great fact that renders all such pretended compromises, when made, vain and ephemeral."

These things would have no consequence if they were the individual opinions of their author, but they are the opinions of a large and formidable and growing party in this Union; of a party that now claims a majority in the House of Representatives, and which looks, at no very distant day, to have a majority in the Senate. I ask you if that was the Union formed by our fathers? Did they anticipate such a political party would arise to declare that there "is an irrepressible conflict between opposing and enduring forces" in the United States?

It is not my purpose to characterize or stigmatize this doctrine now, but to set forth what we are to expect and what we are to meet.

At a later period, in the Senate of the United States, that same distinguished Senator uttered the following language, (I well remember the occasion and the speech:)

"A free Republican Government like this, notwithstanding all its constitutional checks, cannot long resist and counteract the progress of society."

They don't expect the provisions of the Constitution and its checks to prevent them from taking their onward progress. Indeed, they have a facility of construing that instrument, which makes it as dust in the balance. They construe it to authorize them not to return fugitive slaves; to authorize them to make a war upon one half of the nation. There is no provision of the Constitution which has stood in their way as to any right of ours that we have claimed upon this great question. Not only did he announce in the Senate of the United States, that constitutional checks cannot stand for any time against the progress of Northern opinion, but,

"Free labor," says Mr. Seward, "has at last apprehended its rights and its destiny, and is organizing itself to assume the government of the Republic. It will henceforth meet you boldly and resolutely here (Washington ;) it will meet you everywhere, in the Territories and out of them, wherever you may go to extend Slavery. It has driven you back in California and in Kansas ; it will invade you soon in Delaware, Maryland, Virginia, Missouri and Texas. It will meet you in Arizona, in Central America, and even in Cuba."

Not content with confining it to the Territories, he adds :

"You may, indeed, get a start under or near the tropics. and seem safe for a time, but it will be only a short time, Even there you will found States only for free labor to maintain and occupy. The interest of the white race demands the ultimate emancipation of all men. Whether that consummation shall be allowed to take effect, with needful and wise precautions against sudden change and disaster, or be hurried on by violence, is all that remains for you to decide. The white man needs this continent to labor upon. His head is clear, his arm is strong, and his necessaries are fixed. It is for yourselves and not for us to decide how long and through what further mortifications and disasters the contest shall be protracted, before freedom shall enjoy her already assured triumph ! You may refuse to yield it now, and for a short period, but your refusal will only animate the friends of freedom with the courage and the resolution, and produce the union among them, which alone are necessary on their part, to attain the position itself, simultaneously with the impending overthrow of the exciting Federal Administration, and the Constitution of a new and more independent Congress,"—and they think they have that Congress.

I tell you again, fellow-citizens, this is not the opinion of Mr. Seward alone. It is Mr. Seward and, with one or two exceptions, the other Republican Senators in the Senate of the United States, and nine-tenths of the Republican members of the House of Representatives. Could that language have been uttered with impunity or been sustained at the epoch of 1779, when the Constitution was formed ? Did not the Constitution languish and stop just because there was some question about inserting these checks about the institution of the Southern States ? Were they not put into the Constitution by the great men who formed it, and are not all the citizens of all the States bound to respect the relations that exist between them, and to give the Southern States peace in this Union ? How do you receive the declaration that there is an irrepressible conflict waging—that there shall be no peace ? There is no use attempting to turf over the volcano, there is no use crying peace when there is no peace. It is the avowed purpose of the Republican party to agitate, agitate ; to overturn the Constitution itself, until they succeed not only in drawing a *cordon* around you, and shutting you within your present limits, but to put you in a position where you were about, for peace sake, to emancipate your slaves.

Well might we say, as was once said in France, " Oh, Constitution ! what crimes are committed in thy sacred name !"

HELPER'S CRISIS.

But, gentlemen, I hold in my hand another book, which is of no consequence as the opinions of its individual author, but is of consequence as indorsed by the distinguished gentleman from whose productions I have read, and as indorsed also by sixty-eight or nine Republicans of the House of Representatives, who represent a constituency of seven millions of people. This, then, may be considered as the declaration of near seven millions of men. What is it ? It is a book called the "Impending Crisis of the South," by a person called Helper, who professes to be a North Carolinian. Whether he is or not I am unable to say. (I will read very little, gentlemen. In this book, thus indorsed nearly seventy members of the House of Representatives, representing nearly seven millions of the people, this sentiment is declared :

The slaveholding oligarchy say we cannot abolish Slavery without infringing on the right of property. Again we tell them we do not recognize property in men.

But the Constitution does ; the bond of our Union does, and the Supreme Court of the United States has decided that it does. Our fathers so considered it. It has been so admitted all the time, until the apostles of the new doctrine spoke. At another point he says :

For the services of the blacks from the 20th of August, 1620, up to the 4th of July, 1869—an interval of precisely two hundred and forty-eight years, ten months and fourteen days—their masters, if unwilling, ought, in our judgment, to be compelled to grant them their freedom, and to pay each and every one of them at least sixty dollars cash in hand.

He goes on to remark that it would only take two

crops of cotton, and a trifle over, to do it. That was indorsed, I tell you again, by sixty-eight or sixty-nine members of the House of Representatives, and the very gentleman who they are running for Speaker of that body indorsed it. It is true, his friends say that he indorsed it without having read it. Admit that to be true, he has again and again, when called upon, refused to disavow those sentiments, hence the excuse is paltry.

HARPER'S FERRY.

That is the condition of affairs, and that is the condition of the Republican organization of this country, if any reliance is to be placed in their record, in their declarations, in their public attitude, in the attitude which they defiantly assume before the country. Their purpose is to make war, eternal war, upon the institutions of one half of the States of the Union. Gradually we approach the crisis until at last is not the legitimate result of the irrepressible conflict of which they speak, of the crime of which they say we are guilty, to put down these relics of barbarism? The ignorant and fanatical throw off the obligations of the Constitution and invade by violence the Southern States of the Union, and although I am far from holding the Republican party of the North, or any large portion of them, responsible for the late atrocious proceedings in Virginia, I do say that that proceeding was the carrying out of the logical result of their teachings—carrying it into execution. How did they receive it? Why gentlemen, the conservative portion of the North abhors it; but, in the Senate and House, in the great body of their public press, what do they say of it? That they regret it—they deplore it—they even condemn it—they say, because it was against law, and they stand for law. These are the honeyed and qualified phrases with which they characterize the most atrocious act of treason, rapine, and murder combined, that was ever known in the Republic, and then, as though afraid of what they have said, they immediately go on to eulogize the man and his motives, much as they regret the act.

A VOLLEY OF COMPLAININGS.

Gentlemen, have we no complaints in other respects ? Are laws passed for the purpose of punishing those who make inroads into the border States and rob us of our property ? Suppose a Kentuckian should go into the State of Ohio and rob a citizen of that State, does any one doubt that we would pass a law to punish him and to prevent the recurrence of the outrage ? So far from this being their course, they are encouraged, and we are subject to constant secret predatory incursions by which we lose annually hundreds of thousands of dollars, these people availing themselves of the bond of amity between us, to perpetrate the outrage.

That is not all ! About one half of the Northern States have passed laws and made it a criminal and penal offence for their citizens to give any assistance in the rendition of fugitive slaves. Massachusetts has passed laws closing her jails to us, and making it a penal offence to aid in the enforcement of the Fugitive Slave law, or to appear as council to try such a case, thus nullifying the laws of Congress, and of the United States, distinctly, and some seven or eight States have passed similar laws refusing all remedy and making it penal in their citizens to obey the behests of the Constitution.

I have not uttered these things for the purpose of arousing any spirit of disloyalty to the Constitution and the Union. I hope I love them as reverently as any man within the sound of my voice, but let us look and see the facts as they are. What may be set down as the unquestioned purpose of this organization? It is avowed that it is to exclude all and any Slave States from the Union hereafter. It is to give us no fugitive slave law, declaring that the States under the Constitution must provide for that, and then to give no remedy in the States ; it is to pass no laws for the purpose of preventing the robbery of our property but, on the contrary, in many States to make it penal to enforce the law ; it is to abolish Slavery in the District of Columbia ; to abolish the internal slave-trade and the coastwise slave-trade, and then to agitate and agitate, giving us no peace as long as we retain this ' relic of barbarism " and crime, as they call it.

This is the purpose. Are you ready for it? Are you ready to say we will make no stand in any form for your Constitutional rights? I think you are not ! Yet that is the present condition of affairs—but what are we to do ?

PRACTICAL REMEDIES.

I know they will consider the consequences, and carefully consider the consequences of any serious collisions

In this Union. I know we duly appreciate the position of our own State, not only a border State, but an interior border State having no ocean outlet. I know that we have read history to some purpose, and that we have seen what have been the consequences of the disruption of amicable relations between those who have banded themselves together as a confederation of States. We need but go back and see the consequence upon the Greeks when they carried on the Peloponnesian war, until at last exhausted, they fell into the lap of despotism. The same fate might meet us. What would be our condition? War! War! Inevitable war, in all human probability, would be our position, and then in time we might be driven into degrading alliances with foreign powers—the most degrading position for American citizens.

Then the spectacle would be presented of America falling back under the control of Europe, and American liberty sinking down under European despotism. Besides this, could we ever hope that a fairer state of things would arise? Could we ever hope that Providence itself would ever exercise its omnipotent power to create a State, or Union of States, under more favorable auspices than in these? Would it not be worse than impiety itself, to presume that the Almighty would ever attempt to sustain a confederation of Free States under circumstances more bright or favorable than in our system? I know that the State of Kentucky is devoted to the Union, not only because of her interests, but from that feeling of affection and of loyalty, and that sentiment of love that have always marked her people from the earliest period of her history. I do not believe there is a man under the sound of my voice who would not view as the last, the greatest of all evils, the wreck of the Union. I do not believe there is the man in the State that would compete to enjoy the highest honors within the State, purchased at such a price.

WHAT IS TO BE DONE.

At the same time steps must be taken, something must be done. I do not believe that if the Constitution is allowed to remain permanently violated in its important provisions, we can have hope under it. None whatever! Broken in one particular, it will soon fall to pieces in all. I recollect when I was a boy, to have read that great speech of Demosthenes, for the crown, where the real question at issue was the charge that he was the author of the public misfortunes, because he had advised the Greeks to make a last stand for their country, against Philip of Macedon. He was arraigned, and on trial and in his great defence, he says: "What, though we did fail? We did our duty. We responded in the temper and character of our forefathers." The result is such as God gives to each; and even those degenerate Greeks acquitted him, and crowned the world's great orator as a benefactor; debased as they were in national character, they did this, and from that day have never known or read of the success of him who would be deterred from the assertion of fundamental rights for fear of offence.

Gentlemen, the condition of affairs existing here, and existing generally, I am happy to say, throughout the Commonwealth of Kentucky, is not a fair indication of the feeling in many parts of the Union. I have seen the evidence growing within a few years, and culminating during the last few weeks, of a determined purpose in the South to attain and maintain the complete power in Union, and I have seen, upon the other hand, in the representatives of the lower Southern States, a most resolute and determined spirit of resistance. The representatives from Georgia—from Alabama—from South Carolina—from Mississippi, not to speak of other Southern States, say that they represent their constituents—nay, say that they do not go so far as their constituents—and they declare that they are ready at any moment for a separate organization. God forbid that such a thing should take place. God forbid the overt act should ever be done; but we know enough of our political institutions, that when once done the subject becomes involved in inexplicable distress. If one were to fall upon Washington and see the state of feeling there, he would think that the President of your country was the Executive of two hostile countries. The feeling of alienation seems to be almost complete from the expression of the public press and public men. (I mean not your inflammatory, furious speakers, but men of thought and reflection.) They are alarmed, other men are alarmed, we all are alarmed. It is not a craven fear, but it is the ennobled fear that patriots feel for an imperilled country. Suppose this should occur—do you not remember, in 1832 when South Carolina arrayed herself against the Federal Government, upon a mere question of policy connected with the collection of taxes, that it did shake the Union to its centre. Such is the nature of our system, that did shake the Union to the very centre. What were the circumstances then? Andrew Jackson was President of the United States, and he was a native of South Carolina; the question was a mere question of policy; few of the other States sympathized with the movement of that little State. Henry Clay was alive, and Calhoun was ready to give the benefit of his influence to peace and harmony, and yet that little question, when Jackson, a native son of that State, was President, and Clay and Calhoun were in the Senate, brought on a struggle that shook this Union to its centre, and imperilled it in the estimation of the wisest and best of men. Look at it as it may be, with disaffection spread all over the South, with a very different state of feelings in the North to what existed then, with Clay dead, and Calhoun dead, and none to take their places, with such a man as Seward, not only not native, but hostile to the South, in the Chair of State. Cannot a child read the result? Cannot we see that one State falling away, our Union will be like an arch with two or three stones dropped out, the whole fabric may fall in pieces.

These are facts which it becomes the people of Kentucky, with all their loyalty to the Union, to observe, to know, to see, to think of, and then to act upon, with the dignity and moderation which marks and so well becomes them.

But, gentlemen, what is the mode that occurs to any man—because no man, I take it, in Kentucky, will back on this subject, except as a friend of the Union of the States—what is the mode? I see none, except it be the union of all the conservative elements of the country, North and South. The South must first be united, and I am sure she will, for I take it there is not a citizen of Kentucky that would associate himself with an organization whose march to triumph would be over the ruins of our rights.

MEND OUR MANNERS DOWN SOUTH.

Ought we not first to put ourselves right in Court? Some little there is to complain of us. I say to you, in my opinion, those who appeal to the Constitution and the laws should obey the Constitution and the laws. I would have the South, if I might venture, as one of her humblest but truest sons, to advise her to obey the laws of our country. (Applause.) I would have the South first obey the laws of the Union which prohibit the foreign slave-trade. (Applause.) That is the law of the land. It rests not with us to complain of the violation of law by others, when in a portion of our States the citizens violate the laws themselves. Let us frown down any attempt to violate those laws upon the part of our States. Let us do more. Let us do more, by preventing the fitting out of filibustering expeditions upon our shores, to invade feeble sister countries. That is the law, and we live by the Constitution and the law, and let us obey it, and whatever expansion of territory we make, let us make it in a manner becoming the dignity of this glorious Confederacy under our own flag. Then let us call to our aid the pure elements of conservatism and truth that we can find in the northern States. What are they? I did not intend to introduce any party question to-night, but the largest organization I see is the Democratic Party of the North. As a historical fact, it is undisputed; as a current fact of the day, it is undisputed, that you do not find these declarations of hostility issuing from the Northern Democracy; you do not find these attempts to overturn the laws coming from Democratic sources; you do not find these denunciations of you and your institutions coming from Democratic lips and Democratic Presses. On the contrary, you find them at home, and in most cases in the minority, sustaining with unfaltering courage your rights and institutions, at odds and risks that you little think of.

I want them all. We need them all. We need every Southern State, and every honest man everywhere not willing to enter into the crusade against us.

There is another element North, not large but noble and true. They are the scattered and wandering cohorts of the old Whig party, who have refused to ally themselves with the Republicans of the North—men of whom Everett and Choate and others are illustrious examples. There are thousands of them in the Northern States. When this great crisis comes upon us, I have confidence that men like these will be found to unite with the Democratic party in maintaining the laws and the Constitution. These are the elements upon which we are to rely. When you get them together, let us see if there cannot be a general revolt of the intelligence, virtue, and loyalty of the country, against these pernicious *isms*, and if not, let us see how far these pernicious *isms* control society.

Besides these, there are many thousands of men in the Northern States who, silent, are not heard in the midst of the clamor that surrounds them—men who seldom attend the polls. Let us hope that that feeling will be in our favor.

Fellow-citizens, I have uttered these things because I

believe we are standing to-day not in the presence of spectres and shadows, but in the presence of terrible realities. There is a mode by which we can have peace—a permanent peace—and that is by an utter and absolute surrender of all our rights upon the subject to which I have referred, at the call of this Republican Party. If we do not make this surrender, we will have no peace until the Republican Party is destroyed, which can only be done by producing a reaction upon the public mind of the North. As it is, without our being aware of it, things are getting worse every day. I had almost intended to say, that we were absolutely dissolving month by month, and year by year. I see no mode—wiser men than I see no mode to avoid this, except to produce a reaction in the public mind, and to bring up sharply, in some form, the question, Can we not, North and South, live in peace with our several State institutions, after the manner of our fathers? For myself, I yet believe in, and I have an abounding hope of, the ultimate destiny of our common country. I believe a reaction will take place; and I believe that out of this commotion is destined to come for us an era of tranquillity and peace. Of this I am quite certain, that this Commonwealth of Kentucky will pursue   course answerable to her

character and history; she will stand by the union of the States as long as there is a thread of the Constitution to hold it together. We know that if madness, and folly, and fanaticism shall succeed in tearing down the fairest fabric ever erected to liberty among men—we know that our honored State will conduct herself with so much moderation and prudence that she shall stand justified for her acts before men and in the eye of Heaven.

Fellow-citizens, I do not propose to detain you by more extended observations. I have trespassed too far upon your time already. I think, if you will allow me to say so, that I know something of the temper, and spirit, and interest of this people; and, as far as my humble abilities extend, I propose, in the sphere to which you have devoted me, to serve you with all the fidelity of a grateful heart. At all times, and under all circumstances, I owe my allegiance to the State, and I am ready, and willing, and anxious to devote whatever faculties of mind and body I possess to serve you, and to serve you with the uncalculating devotion of a man who loves the green mountains and smiling plains, the clear running streams and the generous people of the State, and with one who loves all her infirmities with the affection of a son.

KANSAS—THE MORMONS—SLAVERY.

SPEECH OF SENATOR DOUGLAS.

Delivered at Springfield, Ill., June 12, 1857.

MR. PRESIDENT, LADIES AND GENTLEMEN: I appear before you to-night, at the request of the grand jury in attendance upon the United States Court, for the purpose of submitting my views upon certain topics upon which they have expressed a desire to hear my opinion. It was not my purpose when I arrived among you, to have engaged in any public or political discussion; but when called upon by a body of gentlemen so intelligent and respectable, coming from all parts of the State, and connected with the administration of public justice, I do not feel at liberty to withhold a full and frank expression of my opinion upon the subjects to which they have referred, and which now engrosses so large a share of the public attention.

The points which I am requested to discuss are:

1st. The present condition and prospects of Kansas.

2d. The principles affirmed by the Supreme Court of the United States in the Dred Scott case.

3d. The condition of things in Utah, and the appropriate remedies for existing evils.

KANSAS.

Of the Kansas question but little need be said at the present time. You are familiar with the history of the question, and my connection with it. Subsequent reflection has strengthened and confirmed my convictions in the soundness of the principles and the correctness of the course I have felt it my duty to pursue upon that subject. Kansas is about to speak for herself through her delegates assembled in Convention to form a Constitution, preparatory to her admission into the Union on an equal footing with the original States. Peace and prosperity now prevail throughout her borders. The law under which her delegates are about to be elected, is believed to be just and fair in all its objects and provisions. There is every reason to hope and believe that the law will be fairly interpreted and impartially executed, so as to insure to every *bona fide* inhabitant the free and quiet exercise of the elective franchise. If any portion of the inhabitants, acting under the advice of political leaders in distant States, shall choose to absent themselves from the polls, and withhold their votes, with a view of leaving the Free State Democrats in a minority, and thus securing a Pro-Slavery Constitution in opposition to the wishes of a majority of the people living under it, let the responsibility rest on those who, for partisan purposes, will sacrifice the principles they profess to cherish and promote. Upon them, and upon the political party for whose benefit and under the direction

of whose leaders they act, let the blame be visited of fastening upon the people of a new State, institutions repugnant to their feelings and in violation of their wishes. The organic act secures to the people of Kansas the sole and exclusive right of forming and regulating their domestic institutions to suit themselves, subject to no other limitation than that which the Constitution of the United States imposes. The Democratic party is determined to see the great fundamental principles of the organic act carried out in good faith. The present election law in Kansas is acknowledged to be fair and just—the rights of the voters are clearly defined—and the exercise of those rights will be efficiently and scrupulously protected. Hence, if the majority of the people of Kansas desire to have it a Free State (and we are told by the Republican party that nine-tenths of the people of that Territory are Free State men), there is no obstacle in the way of bringing Kansas into the Union as a Free State, by the votes and voice of her own people, and in conformity with the principles of the Kansas-Nebraska act; provided all the Free State men will go to the polls, and vote their principles in accordance with their professions. If such is not the result let the consequences be visited upon the heads of those whose policy it is to produce strife, anarchy and bloodshed in Kansas, that their party may profit by Slavery agitation in the Northern States of this Union. That the Democrats in Kansas will perform their duty fearlessly and nobly, according to the principle they cherish, I have no doubt, and that the result of the struggle will be such as will gladden the heart and strengthen the hopes of every friend of the Union, I have entire confidence.

The Kansas question being settled peacefully and satisfactorily, in accordance with the wishes of her own people, Slavery agitation should be banished from the halls of Congress, and cease to be an exciting element in our political struggles. Give fair play to that principle of self-government which recognizes the right of the people of each State and Territory, to form and regulate their own domestic institutions, and sectional strife will be forced to give place to that fraternal feeling which animated the fathers of the Revolution, and made every citizen of every State of this glorious confederacy a member of a common brotherhood.

That we are steadily and rapidly approaching that result, I cannot doubt, for the Slavery issue has already dwindled down to the narrow limits covered by the decisions of the Supreme Court of the United States in the Dred Scott case. The moment that decision was pronounced, and before the opinions of the Court could be published and read by the people, the newspaper press in the interest of a powerful political party in this country, began to pour forth torrents of abuse and misrepresentations, not only upon the decision, but upon the character and motives of the venerable Chief Justice and his illustrious associates on the bench. The character of Chief Justice Taney and the associate Judges who concurred with him, require no eulogy—no vindication from me. They are endeared to the people of the United States by their eminent public services—venerated for their great learning, wisdom and experience—and beloved for the spotless purity of their characters and their exemplary lives. The poisonous shafts of partisan malice will fall harmless at their feet, while their judicial decisions will stand in all future time, a proud monument to their greatness, the admiration of the good and wise, and a rebuke to the partisans of faction and lawless violence. If, unfortunately, any considerable portion of the people of the United States shall so far forget their obligations to society as to allow partisan leaders to array them in violent resistance to the final decision of the highest judicial tribunal on earth, it will become the duty of all the friends of order and constitutional government, without reference to past political differences, to organize themselves and marshal their forces under the glorious banner of the Union, in vindication of the Constitution and the supremacy of the laws over the advocates of faction and the champions of violence. To preserve the Constitution inviolate, and vindicate the supremacy of the laws, is the first and highest duty of every citizen of a free Republic. The peculiar merit of our form of government over all others, consists in the fact that the law, instead of the arbitrary will of a hereditary prince, prescribes, defines and protects all our rights. In this country the law is the will of the people, embodied and expressed according to the forms of the Constitution. The Courts are the tribunals prescribed by the Constitution, and created by the authority of the people to determine, expound and enforce the law. Hence, whoever resists the final decision of the highest judicial tribunal, aims a deadly blow to our whole republican system of government—a blow which, if successful, would place all our rights and liberties at the mercy of passion, anarchy and violence. I repeat, therefore, that if resistance to the decisions of the Supreme Court of the United States, in a matter like the points decided in the Dred Scott case, clearly within their jurisdiction as defined by the Constitution, shall be forced upon the country as a political issue, it will become a distinct and naked issue between the friends and the enemies of the Constitution—the friends and the enemies of the supremacy of the laws.

HE RED SCOTT ECISION

The case of Dred Scott was an action of trespass, *vi et armis*, in the Circuit Court of the United States for the District of Missouri, for the purpose of establishing his claim to be a free man, and was taken by writ of error on the application of Scott to the Supreme Court of the United States, where the final decision was pronounced by Chief Justice Taney. The facts of the case were agreed upon and admitted to be true by both parties, and were in substance, that Dred Scott was a negro slave in Missouri, that he went with his master, who was an officer in the army, to Fort Armstrong, on Rock Island, and thence to Fort Snelling on the west bank of the Mississippi River, and within the country covered by the act of Congress known as the Missouri Compromise: and then he reaccompanied his master to the State of Missouri, where he has since remained a slave. Upon this statement of facts two important and material questions arose, besides several incidental and minor ones, which it was incumbent upon the Court to take notice of and decide. The Court did not attempt to avoid responsibility by disposing of the case upon technical points without touching the merits, nor did they go out of their way to decide questions not properly before them and directly presented by the record. Like honest and conscientious judges, as they are, they met and decided each point as it arose, and faithfully performed their whole duty and nothing but their duty to the country by determining all the questions in the case, and nothing but what was essential to the decision of the case upon its merits. The State Courts of Missouri had decided against Dred Scott, and declared him and his children slaves, and the Circuit Court of the United States for the district of Missouri had decided the same thing in this very case which had thus been removed to the Supreme Court of the United States by Scott, with the hope of reversing the decision of the Circuit Court and securing his freedom. If the Supreme Court had dismissed the writ of error for want of jurisdiction, without first examining into and deciding the merits of the case, as they are now denounced and abused for not having done, the result would have been to remand Dred Scott and his children to perpetual Slavery under the decisions which had already been pronounced by the Supreme Court of Missouri, as well as by the Circuit Court of the United States, without obtaining a decision on the merits of his case by the Supreme Court of the United States. Suppose Chief Justice Taney and his associates had thus remanded Dred Scott and his children back to Slavery on a plea in abatement or any mere technical point, not touching the merits of the question, and without deciding whether under the Constitution and laws as applied to the facts of the case Dred Scott was a free man or a slave, would they not have been denounced with increased virulence and bitterness on the charge of having remanded Dred Scott to perpetual Slavery without first examining the merits of his case and ascertaining whether he was a slave or not?

If the case had been disposed of in that way, who can doubt that such would have been the character of the denunciations which would have been hurled upon the devoted heads of those illustrious Judges with much more plausibility and show of fairness than they are now denounced for having decided the case fairly and honestly upon its merits?

The material and controlling points of the case—those which have been made the subject of unmeasured abuse and denunciation—may be thus stated:

1. The Court decided that under the Constitution of the United States a negro descended from slave parents is not and cannot be a citizen of the United States.

2. That the act of the 6th of March, 1820, commonly called the Missouri Compromise act, was unconstitutional and void before it was repealed by the Nebraska act, and consequently did not and could not have the legal effect of extinguishing a master's right to his slave in that Territory. While the right continues in full force under the guaranty of the Constitution, and cannot be divested or alienated by an act of Congress, it necessarily remains a barren and a worthless right, unless sustained, protected and enforced by appropriate police regulations and local legislation, prescribing adequate remedies for its violation. These regulations and remedies must necessarily depend entirely upon the will and wishes of the people of the Territory, as they can only be prescribed by the local Legislatures. Hence the great principle of popular sovereignty and self-government is sustained and firmly established by the authority of this decision. Thus it appears that the only sin involved in the passage of the Kansas-Nebraska act consists in the fact of having removed from the statute-book an act of Congress which was unauthorized by the Constitution of the United States, and void because passed without constitutional authority, and constituted in lieu of it the great fundamental principle of self-government, which recognizes the rights of the people of such State and Territory to control their own domestic concerns.

I will direct attention to the question involved in the first proposition, to wit: That the negro is not and cannot be a citizen of the United States.

We are told by a certain political organization that that decision is cruel—is inhuman and infamous, and should neither be respected nor obeyed. What is the objection to that decision? Simply that the negro is not a citizen. What is the object of making him a citizen? Of course to give him the rights, privileges and immunities of a citizen, it being the great fundamental law in our Government, that under the law, citizens are equal in their rights and privileges. It is said to be inhuman—to be infamous—to deprive an African negro of these privileges of citizenship, which would put him on an equality with the other citizens of the country.

Now, let me ask my fellow-citizens, are you prepared to resist the constituted authorities of this country, in order to secure citizenship, and, through citizenship, equality with the white man. (Voices, "No! no!") If you are, you must reverse the whole policy of this State—the organic law of our own State. In order to carry out that principle of negro citizenship and negro equality under the law, you must not only reverse the organic law in our own State, but of every other State in this Union. But you have not accomplished it then; you must make furious war upon the slaveholding States, to compel them to emancipate and set at liberty their three millions of slaves. When that shall be done, before you have secured that great principle of equality to the son of Africa, you must strike out of the constitution of Illinois that provision which prevents a negro, whether free or slave, from crossing the Ohio or the Mississippi, and coming into Illinois to reside. When you shall have made that change in our organic law, and turned loose all the Africans that may choose to come from the slaveholding States to settle upon our prairies, and turn Illinois into a negro colony, rather than into a State of white men, still you have not secured to the negro the rights of citizenship on an equality with the white man. You must then strike the word "white" out of the constitution of our own State, and allow the negro to come to our polls and vote on an equality with yourselves. You must also change the Constitution in that respect that declares, that a negro shall not be eligible to office, and declare that a negro shall be eligible to your Legislature, to the bar, bench, and gubernatorial chair. And still you have not reached that point to which we are told we must go, of placing the negro on an equality with other citizens. You must admit him to the jury-box, and license him by law to marry a white woman. And then you will have secured nearly all the privileges that the decision of the Supreme Court has denied him. (Applause.)

I submit to you, fellow-citizens, whether any man can pronounce the decision inhuman and infamous, without resorting to that great principle, which, carried out, puts the negro on an equality with other citizens. But listen to the speeches of any one of those who sympathize so much with the poor African that they are not willing to allow him to occupy an inferior position, and you will find that they all adhere to the position of negro equality. For instance, did you ever hear any of them make a public speech in which he did not quote the Declaration of Independence, that "we hold all men are born free and equal," and then appeal to you to know whether Slavery could be justified or palliated by any man who believed in the Declaration of Independence. Do they not argue that by this instrument negroes were declared to be born equal to white men; and hence, any man who is opposed to carrying out that great dear principle of theirs, of negro equality with the white man, is opposed to the Declaration of Independence.

Now, my friends, permit me to reply to this assumption, that the Declaration of Independence declared the negro to be equal with white men, by a few historical facts recorded in our school-books, and familiar to our children. By reference to the History of the United States, you will find that on the Fourth of July, 1776, when the Declaration of Independence was put forth, the thirteen colonies were then, each and all of them, slaveholding colonies. Each signer of the Declaration, without an exception, represented a slaveholding constituency. Every battle of the Revolutionary War, from Lexington and Bunker Hill to King's Mountain and Yorktown, was fought in a slaveholding constituency. The treaty of peace with Great Britain which acknowledged our independence, was made on the part of Great Britain on the one side and the thirteen original slaveholding States on the other. Passing from that to the formation of the Constitution of the United States, you will find that instrument was framed, and adopted, and put into operation with the immortal Washington at the head, by twelve slaveholding States and one free State, or one State about to become free. In view of these facts, I submit to you whether any sane man can assert that the founders of our institutions intended to put the negro and the white man on an equality in the system of government which they adopted? If the signers of the Declaration had intended to declare the negro equal to the white man, would not they, on that very day, have abolished Slavery in every one of the States of the Union in order to have conformed to that Declaration? If any one of these States had thus understood the Declaration of Independence, would not that State then immediately have abolished Slavery, and put the negro on an equality with the white man in conformity with that Declaration? Did they do so? I have already shown you that no one of those States abolished Slavery during the whole period of the Revolutionary war. I have already stated, and I challenge contradiction, that to this day no one of them has put the negro on an equality with the white man in all the laws touching on the relations of life. And yet, if they honestly believed the Declaration of Independence meant negroes as well as white men, they were bound to advocate every law so as to carry out their principle. Their position on this subject would charge the signers of that Declaration with hypocrisy in making it to the world, and going on to fight battles on the principle thus asserted. But no vindication is needed from me of those immortal men who drafted, and signed, and proclaimed to the world the Declaration of Independence. They did what they professed. They had reference to the white man, and to him only, when they declared all men were created equal. They were in a struggle with Great Britain. The principle they were asserting was that a British subject, born on American soil was equal to a British subject born in England—that a British subject here was entitled to all the rights, and privileges, and immunities, under the British Constitution, that a British subject in England enjoyed; that their rights were inalienable, and hence that Parliament, whose power was omnipotent, had no power to

alienate them. They did not mean the negroes and Indians—they did not say we white men and negroes were born equal; but they were speaking of the race of people who colonized America, who ruled America, and who were declaring the liberties of Americans, when they proclaimed the self-evident truth that those men were born free and equal. And if you will examine the journal of the Continental Congress you will find this great principle carried out. No one of the colonies would then consent to the Declaration of Independence until they had placed on the record the express reservation, that each colony reserved and retained to itself the sole and exclusive right of regulating its own domestic concerns and police regulations. It was made a fundamental condition of the Declaration, that this right should be forever reserved beyond the power of Congress or other Confederation or power on earth, except the free will of their own people. The articles of confederation were based upon the same great fundamental principle, and the Constitution of the United States was adopted for the purpose of preserving and carrying into effect the same grand principle that made us one people for one specified object, but reserved to each State and each locality the sole and exclusive privilege of managing its own domestic concerns.

At that day the negro was looked upon as a being of an inferior race. All history had proved that in no part of the world, or of the world's history, had the negro ever shown himself capable of self-government, and it was not the intention of the founders of this Government to violate that great law of God, which made the distinction between the white and the black man. That distinction is plain and palpable, and it has been the rule of civilization and of Christianity the world over, that whenever any one man, or set of men, were incapable of taking care of themselves, they should consent to be governed by those who were capable of managing their affairs for them. It is on that principle that your courts of justice appoint guardians to take charge of the idiot, the lunatic, the insane, blind, dumb, the unfortunate, whatever may be his condition. And if history had proved that the negro race, as a race, were incapable of self-government, it was not only the right but the duty of those who were capable to provide for them. It did not necessarily follow that they were to be reduced to Slavery. The true principle is that the inferior race should be allowed to enjoy all their rights, which their nature is capable of exercising and enjoying, consistently with the good of society. I would not advocate that the negro should be treated harshly or unkindly. Far from it. I would extend and secure to him every right, privilege and immunity he was capable of enjoying consistent with the highest welfare of society. The Constitution is founded on that great principle, and leaves to each State, as the articles of confederation did to each colony, the right to determine for itself what these principles were, and the extent of them, in order that they might adopt their laws to their actual condition. Under that great provision, Illinois has chosen to say, that the negro shall not come here to reside—that a negro shall not vote—shall not hold office—shall not serve in the jury-box—shall not marry white women—and I think that the Constitution of Illinois is wisely framed as to this provision. On the other hand, Kentucky goes further, and deprives the negro of his right over his person. Kentucky, under the Constitution, had a right to make that provision. We have no right to complain of her, nor can she complain of us. Each has the right to do as it pleases, and each must mind its own business and not interfere with its neighbor's concerns. (Applause.)

Our fathers, when they framed this Government, had witnessed the sad and melancholy results of the mixture of the races in Mexico, South America and Central America, where the Spanish, from motives of policy, had admitted the negro and other inferior races to citizenship, and, consequently, to political and social amalgamation. The demoralization and degradation which prevailed in the Spanish and French colonies, where no distinctions on account of color or race were tolerated, operated as a warning to our revolutionary fathers to preserve the purity of the white race, and to establish their political, social and domestic institutions upon such a basis as would forever exclude the idea of negro citizenship and negro equality. (Applause.)

They understood that great natural law which declares that amalgamation between superior and inferior races brings their posterity down to the lower level of the inferior, but never elevates them to the high level of the superior race. I appeal to each of those gallant young men before me, who won immortal glory on the bloody fields of Mexico, in vindication of their country's right and honor, whether their information and observation in that country does not fully sustain the truth of the proposition that amalgamation is degradation, demoralization, disease and death? Is it true that the negro is our equal and our brother? The history of the times clearly show that our fathers did not regard the African race as any kin to them, and determined so to lay the foundation of society and government that they should never be of kin to their posterity. (Immense applause.)

But, when you confer upon the African race the privileges of citizenship, and put them on an equality with white men at the polls, in the jury-box, on the bench, in the Executive chair, and in the councils of the nation, upon what principle will you deny their equality at the festive board and in the domestic circle?

The Supreme Court of the United States have decided that, under the Constitution, a negro is not and cannot be a citizen.

The Republican Abolition party pronounce that decision cruel, inhuman and infamous, and appeal to the American people to disregard and refuse to obey it. Let us join issue with them, and put ourselves upon the country for trial. (Cheers and applause.)

CONDITION OF AFFAIRS IN UTAH, AND THE REMEDY.

Mr. President, I will now respond to the call which has been made upon me for my opinions of the condition of things in Utah, and the appropriate remedies for existing evils.

The Territory of Utah was organized under one of the acts known as the Compromise Measures of 1850, on the supposition that the inhabitants were American citizens, owing and acknowledging allegiance to the United States, and consequently entitled to the benefits of self-government while a Territory, and to admission in the Union on an equal footing with the original States, as soon as they should number the requisite population. It was conceded on all hands, and by all parties, that the peculiarities of their religious faith and ceremonies interposed no valid and constitutional objection to their reception into the Union, in conformity with the Federal Constitution, so long as they were in all other respects entitled to admission. Hence, the great political parties of the country indorsed and approved the Compromise Measures of 1850, including the act for the organization of the Territory of Utah, with the hope and in the confidence that the inhabitants would conform to the Constitution and laws, and prove themselves worthy, respectable and law-abiding citizens. If we are permitted to place credence in the rumors and reports from that country (and it must be admitted that they have increased and strengthened and assumed consistency and plausibility by each successive mail), seven years' experience has disclosed a state of facts entirely different from that which was supposed to exist when Utah was organized. These rumors and reports would seem to justify the belief that the following facts are susceptible of proof.

1. That nine-tenths of the inhabitants are aliens by birth, who have refused to become naturalized, or to take the oath of allegiance, or to do any other act recognizing the Government of the United States as the paramount authority in that Territory.

2. That all the inhabitants, whether native or alien born, known as Mormons, (and they constitute the whole people of the Territory), are bound by horrid oaths and terrible penalties, to recognize and maintain the authority of Brigham Young, and the government of which he is the head, as paramount to that of the United States, in civil as well as in religious affairs; and that they will, in due time, and under the direction of their leaders, use all means in their power to subvert the government of the United States, and resist its authority.

3. That the Mormon government, with Brigham Young at its head, is now forming alliance with Indian tribes in Utah and adjoining territories—stimulating the Indians to acts of hostility—and organizing bands of his own followers under the name of "Danites, or Destroying Angels," to prosecute a system of robbery and murders upon American citizens, who support the authority of the United States, and denounce the infamous and disgusting practices and institutions of the Mormon Government.

If, upon a full investigation, these representations shall prove true, they will establish the fact that the Mormon inhabitants of Utah, as a community, are outlaws and alien enemies, unfit to exercise the right of self-government under the organic act, and unworthy to be admitted into the Union as a State, when their only object in seeking admission is to interpose the sovereignty of the State, as an invincible shield to protect them in their treason and crime, debauchery and infamy. (Applause.)

Under this view of the subject, I think it is the duty of the President, as I have no doubt it is his fixed purpose to remove Brigham Young and all his followers from office, and to fill their places with bold, able, and true men, and to cause a thorough and searching investigation into all the crimes and enormities which are alleged to be perpetrated daily in that Territory, under the direction of Brigham Young and his confederates and to use all the military force necessary to protect the officers in the discharge of their duties, and to enforce the laws of the land. (Applause.)

When the authentic evidence shall arrive, if it shall establish the facts which are believed to exist, it will become the duty of Congress to apply the knife and cut out this loathsome, disgusting ulcer. (Applause.) No temporizing policy—no halfway measures will then answer. It has been supposed by those who have not thought deeply upon the subject, that an act of Congress prohibiting murder, robbery, polygamy, and other crimes, with appropriate penalties for those offences, would afford adequate remedies for all the enormities complained of. Suppose such a law to be on the statute book, and I believe they have a criminal code, providing the usual punishment for the entire catalogue of crimes, according to the usages of all civilized and Christian countries, with the exception of polygamy, which is practised under the sanction of the Mormon Church, but is neither prohibited nor authorized by the laws of the Territory.

Suppose, I repeat, that Congress should pass a law prescribing a criminal code, and punishing polygamy among other offences, what other effect would it have—what good would it do? Would you call on twenty-three grand jurymen, with twenty-three wives each, to find a bill of indictment against a poor miserable wretch for having two wives? (Cheers and laughter.) Would you call upon twelve petit jurors, with twelve wives each, to convict the same loathsome wretch for having two wives? (Continued applause.) Would you expect a grand jury composed of twenty-three "Danites" to find a bill of indictment against a brother "Danite" for having murdered a Gentile, as they call all American citizens, under their direction? Much less would you expect a jury of twelve "destroying angels" to find another "destroying angel" guilty of the crime of murder, and cause him to be hanged for no other offence than taking the life of a Gentile? No! If there is any truth in the reports we receive from Utah, Congress may pass whatever laws it chooses; but you can never rely upon the local tribunals and juries to punish crimes committed by Mormons in that Territory. Some other and more effectual remedy must be devised and applied. In my opinion, the first step should be the absolute and unconditional repeal of the organic act—blotting the Territorial Government out of existence—upon the ground that they are outlaws, denying their allegiance and defying the authorities of the United States. (Immense applause.)

The Territorial Government once abolished, the country would revert to its primitive condition prior to the act of 1850, "under the sole and exclusive jurisdiction of the United States," and should be placed under the operation of the act of Congress of the 30th of April, 1790, and the various acts supplemental thereto and amendatory thereof, "providing for the punishment of crimes against the United States within any fort, arsenal dockyard, magazine, OR ANY OTHER PLACE OR DISTRICT OF COUNTRY, UNDER THE SOLE AND EXCLUSIVE *jurisdiction of the United States.*" All offenses against the provisions of these acts are required by law to be tried and punished by the United States Courts in the States or Territories where the offenders shall be "FIRST APPREHENDED OR BROUGHT FOR TRIAL." Thus it will be seen that under the plan proposed, BRIGHAM YOUNG and his confederates could be "apprehended and brought for trial," to Iowa or Missouri, California or Oregon, or to any other adjacent State or Territory, where a fair trial could be had, and justice administered impartially—where the witnesses could be protected and the judgment of the court could be carried into execution, without violence or intimidation. I do not propose to introduce any new principles into our jurisprudence, nor to change the modes of proceeding or the rules of practice in our Courts. I only propose to place the district of country embraced within the Territory of Utah under the operation of the same laws and rules of proceeding, that Kansas, Nebraska, Minnesota and our other Territories were placed before they became organized Territories. The whole country embraced within these Territories was under the operation of that same system of laws, and all the offenses committed within the same were punished in the manner now proposed, so long as the country remained "under the sole and exclusive jurisdiction of the United States;" but the moment the country was organized into Territorial Governments, with legislative, executive and judicial departments, it ceased to be under the sole and exclusive jurisdiction of the United States, within the meaning of the act of Congress, for the reason that it had passed under another and a different jurisdiction. Hence, if we abolish the Territorial Government of Utah, preserving all existing rights, and place the country under the sole and exclusive jurisdiction of the United States, offenders can be apprehended and brought into the adjacent States or Territories for punishment, in the same manner and under the same rules and regulations which obtained and have been uniformly practiced under like circumstances since 1790.

If the plan proposed shall be found an effective and adequate remedy for the evils complained of in Utah, no one, no matter what his political creed or partisan associations, need be apprehensive that it will violate any cherished theory or constitutional right in regard to the government of the Territories. It is a great mistake to suppose that all the territory or land belonging to the United States must necessarily be governed by the same laws and under the same clause of the Constitution, without reference to the purpose to which it is dedicated or the use which it is proposed to make of it; while all that portion of the country which is or shall be set apart to become new States, must necessarily be governed under and consistent with that clause of the Constitution which authorizes Congress to admit new States, it does not follow that other territory, not intended to be organized and admitted into the Union as States, must be governed under the same clause of the Constitution, with all the rights of self-government and State equality. For instance, if we should purchase Vancouver's Island from Great Britain for the purpose of removing all the Indians from our Pacific territories and locating them on that island as their permanent home, with guaranties that it should never be occupied or settled with white men, will it be contended that the purchase should be made and the island governed under the power to admit new States when it was not acquired for that purpose, nor intended to be applied to that object? Being acquired for Indian purposes and applied to Indian purposes, it is not more reasonable to assume that the power to acquire was derived from the Indian clause, and the island must necessarily be governed under and consistent with that clause of the Constitution which relates to Indian affairs. Again, suppose we should deem it expedient to buy a small island in the Mediterranean or the Carribean Sea for a naval station, can it be said with any force or plausibility that the purchase should be made or the island governed under the power to admit new States? On the contrary, is it not obvious that the right to acquire and govern in that case is derived from the power " to provide and maintain a navy," and must be exercised consistently with that power. So, if we purchase land for forts, arsenals, or other military purposes, or set apart and dedicate any territory which we now own for a military reservation, it immediately passes under the military power and must be governed in harmony with it. So if the land be purchased for a mint, it must be governed under the power to coin money; or, if purchased for a post-office, it must be governed under the power to establish post-offices and post-roads; or, for a custom-house, under the power to regulate commerce; or for a court-house, under the judiciary power. In short, the clause in the Constitution under which any land or territory belonging to the United States must be governed, is indicated by the object for which it was acquired and the purpose for which it is dedicated. So long, therefore, as the organic act of Utah shall remain in force, setting apart that country for a new State, and pledging the faith of the United States to receive it into the Union as soon as it should have the requisite population, we are bound to extend to it all the rights of self-government, agreeably to the clause in the Constitution providing for the admission of new States. Hence the necessity of repealing the organic act—withdrawing the pledge of admission, and placing it under the sole and exclusive jurisdiction of the United States, in order that persons and property may be protected, and justice administered, and crimes punished under the laws prescribed by Congress in such cases.

While the power of Congress to repeal this organic act and abolish the Territorial Government cannot be denied, the question may arise whether we possess the moral right of exercising the power, after the charter has been once granted and the local government organized under its provisions. This is a grave question—one which should not be decided hastily, nor under the influence of passion or prejudice. I am free to say that in my opinion there is no moral right to repeal the organic act of a Territory, and abolish the government organized under it, unless the inhabitants of that Territory, as a community, have done such acts as amount to a forfeiture of all rights under it—such as becoming alien enemies, outlaws, disavowing their allegiance, or resisting the authority of the United States. These, and kindred acts, which we have every reason to believe are daily perpetrated in that Territory, would not only give us the moral right, but make it our imperative duty to abolish the Territorial Government, and place the inhabitants under the sole and exclusive jurisdiction of the United States, to the end that justice may be done and the dignity and authority of the Government vindicated.

I have thus presented plainly and frankly my views of the Utah question—the evils and the remedy—upon the facts as they have reached us, and are supposed to be substantially correct. If official reports and authentic information shall change or modify these facts, I shall be ready to conform my notion to the real facts as they shall be found to exist. I have no such pride of opinion as will induce me to persevere in an error one moment after my judgment is convinced. If, therefore, a better plan can be devised—one more consistent with justice and sound policy, or more effective as a remedy for acknowledged evils, I shall take great pleasure in adopting it, in lieu of the one I have presented to you to-night.

In conclusion, permit me to express my grateful acknowledgments for your patient attention and the kind and respectful manner in which you have received my remarks.

INVASION OF STATES--SEDITION LAW PROPOSED.

SPEECH OF MR. DOUGLAS.

On the 16th of January, 1860, Mr. Douglas submitted to the United States Senate the following Resolution :

Resolved, That the Committee on the Judiciary be instructed to report a bill for the protection of each State and Territory of the Union, against invasion by the authorities or inhabitants of any other State or Territory ; and for the suppression and punishment of conspiracies or combinations in any State or Territory with intent to invade, assail, or molest the government, inhabitants, property, or institutions of any other State or Territory of the Union.

This Resolution, coming up as a special order on the 23d of January,

Mr. Douglas said: Mr. President, on the 25th of November last, the Governor of Virginia addressed on official communication to the President of the United States, in which he said :

" I have information from various quarters, upon which I rely, that a conspiracy of formidable extent, in means and numbers, is formed in Ohio, Pennsylvania, New-York, and other States, to rescue John Brown and his associates, prisoners at Charleston, Virginia. The information is specific enough to be reliable " . . . . .

" Places in Maryland, Ohio, and Pennsylvania, have been occupied as depots and rendezvous by these desperadoes, unobstructed by guards or otherwise, to invade this State, and we are kept in continual apprehension of outrage from fire and rapine. I apprise you of these facts in order that you may take steps to preserve peace between the States."

To this communication, the President of the United States, on the 28th of November, returned a reply, from which I read the following sentence :

" I am at a loss to discover any provision in the Constitution or laws of the United States which would authorize me to ' take steps for this purpose.' " [That is, to preserve the peace between the States.]

Mr. Douglas argued at considerable length, to prove that the Constitution does provide for the protection, by the Federal Government, of each State against invasion from any and all sources, and continued:

The question then remaining is, what legislation is necessary and proper to render this guaranty of the Constitution effectual? I presume there will be very little difference of opinion that it will be necessary to place the whole military power of the Government at the disposal of the President, under proper guards and restrictions against abuse, to repel and suppress invasion when the hostile force shall be actually in the field. But, sir, that is not sufficient. Such legislation would not be a full compliance with this guaranty of the Constitution. The framers of that instrument meant more when they gave the guaranty. Mark the difference in language between the provision for protecting the United States against invasion and that for protecting the States. When it provided for protecting the United States, it said Congress shall have power to "*repel* invasion." When it came to make this guaranty to the States, it changed the language, and said the United States shall "*protect*" each of the States against invasion. In the one instance, the duty of the Government is to repel; in the other, the guaranty is that they will protect. In other words, the United States are not permitted to wait until the enemy shall be upon your borders; until the invading army shall have been organized and drilled and placed in march with a view to the invasion; but they must pass all laws necessary and proper to insure protection and domestic tranquillity to each State and Territory of this Union against invasion or hostilities from other States and Territories.

Then, sir, I hold that it is not only necessary to use the military power when the actual case of invasion shall occur, but to authorize the judicial department of the Government to suppress all conspiracies and combinations in the several States with intent to invade a State, or molest or disturb its government, its peace, its citizens, its property or its institutions. You must punish the conspiracy, the combination with intent to do the act, and then you will suppress it in advance. There is no principle more familiar to the legal profession than that wherever it *is* proper to declare an act to be a crime, it is proper to punish a conspiracy or combination with intent to perpetrate the act. Look upon your statute-books, and I presume you will find an enactment to punish the counterfeiting of the coin of the United States; and then another section to punish a man for having counterfeit coin in his possession *with intent* to pass it; and another section to punish him for having the molds or dies or instruments for counterfeiting, *with intent* to use them. This is a familiar principle in legislative and judicial proceedings. If the act of invasion is criminal, the conspiracy to invade should also be made criminal. If it be unlawful and illegal to invade a State, and run off fugitive slaves, why not make it unlawful to form conspiracies and combinations in the several States with intent to do the act? We have been told that a notorious man who has recently suffered death for his crimes upon the gallows, boasted in Cleveland, Ohio, in a public lecture, a year ago, that he had then a body of men employed in running away horses from the slaveholders of Missouri, and pointed to a livery stable in Cleveland which was full of the stolen horses at that time.

I think it is within our competency, and consequently our duty, to pass a law making every conspiracy or combination in any State or Territory of this Union to invade another with intent to steal or run away property of any kind, whether it be negroes, or horses, or property of any other description, into another State, a crime, and punish the conspirators by indictment, in the United States courts and confinement in the prisons and penitentiaries of the State or Territory where the conspiracy may be formed and quelled. Sir, I would carry these provisions of law as far as our constitutional powers will reach. *I would make it a crime to form conspiracies with a view of invading States or Territories to control elections, whether they be under the garb of Emigrant Aid Societies of New England or Blue Lodges of Missouri.* (Applause in the galleries.) In other words, this provision of the Constitutions means more than the mere repelling of an invasion when the invading army shall reach the border of a State. The language is, it shall protect the State against invasion; the meaning of which is, to use the language of the preamble to the Constitution, to insure to each State domestic tranquillity against external violence. There can be no peace, there can be no prosperity, there can be no safety in any community, unless it is secured against violence from abroad. Why, sir, it has been a question seriously mooted in Europe, whether it was not the duty of England, a power foreign to France, to pass laws to punish conspiracies in

England against the lives of the princes of France. I shall not argue the question of comity between foreign States. I predicate my argument upon the Constitution by which we are governed, and which we have sworn to obey, and demand that the Constitution be executed in good faith so as to punish and suppress every combination, every conspiracy, either to invade a State or to molest its inhabitants, or to disturb its property, or to subvert its institutions and its government. I believe this can be effectually done by authorizing the United States courts in the several States to take jurisdiction of the offense, and punish the violation of the law with appropriate punishments.

It cannot be said that the time has not yet arrived for such legislation. It cannot be said with truth that the Harper's Ferry case will not be repeated, or is not in danger of repetition. It is only necessary to inquire into the causes which produced the Harper's Ferry outrage, and ascertain whether those causes are yet in active operation, and then you can determine whether there is any ground for apprehension that that invasion will be repeated. Sir, what were the causes which produced the Harper's Ferry outrage? Without stopping to adduce evidence in detail, I have no hesitation in expressing my firm and deliberate conviction that *the Harper's Ferry crime was the natural, logical, inevitable result of the doctrines and teachings of the Republican party, as explained and enforced in their platform, their partisan presses, their pamphlets and books, and especially in the speeches of their leaders in and out of Congress.* (Applause in the galleries.) . . . .

And, sir, inasmuch as the Constitution of the United States confers upon Congress the power coupled with the duty of protecting each State against external aggression, and inasmuch as that includes the power of suppressing and punishing conspiracies in one State against the institutions, property, people, or government of every other State, I desire to carry out that power vigorously. Sir, give us such a law as the Constitution contemplates and authorizes, and I will show the Senator from New York that there is a constitutional mode of *repressing* the "irrepressible conflict." *I will open the prison doors to allow conspirators against the peace of the Republic and the domestic tranquillity of our States to select their cells wherein to drag out a miserable life as a punishment for their crimes against the peace of society.* . . . .

Mr. President, the mode of preserving peace is plain. This system of sectional warfare must cease. The Constitution has given the power, and all we ask of Congress is to give the means, and we, by indictments and convictions in the Federal courts of our several States, will make such examples of the leaders of these conspiracies as will strike terror into the hearts of the others, and there will be an end of this crusade. Sir, you must check it by crushing out the conspiracy, the combination, and then there can be safety.

[A special committee of the Senate, of which Mr. Mason, of Va., was chairman, appointed to investigate the Harper's Ferry affair, ascertain the cause of the raid, and report what laws, if any, were necessary to prevent a repetition, reported near the close of the session, that the committee were unable to discover that any persons were either directly or indirectly engaged in the invasion, other than John Brown and those who accompanied him to Harper's Ferry.]

WHAT POPULAR SOVEREIGNTY HAS DONE.

From Mr. Douglas' Speech in the Senate, May 16, 1860.

But, we are told that the necessary result of this doctrine of non-intervention, which, gentlemen, by way of throwing ridicule upon it, call squatter sovereignty, is to deprive the South of all participation in what they call the common Territories of the United States. That was the ground on which the Senator from Mississippi (Mr. Davis), predicated his opposition to the Compromise Measures of 1850. He regarded a refusal to repeal the Mexican law as equivalent to the Wilmot Proviso; a refusal to recognize by an act of Congress the right to carry a slave there as equivalent to the Wilmot Proviso; a refusal to deny to a Territorial Legislature the right to exclude Slavery as equivalent to an exclusion. He believed at that time that this doctrine did amount to a denial of southern rights; and he told the people of

Mississippi so; but they doubted it. Now let us see how far his theory and suppositions have been verified. I infer that he told the people of Mississippi so, for he makes it a charge in his bill of indictment against me, that I am hostile to southern rights because I gave those votes.

Now, what has been the result? My views were incorporated into the Compromise Measures of 1850, and his were rejected. Has the South been excluded from all the territory acquired from Mexico? What says the bill from the House of Representatives now on your table, repealing the slave code in New Mexico, established by the people themselves? *It is part of the history of the country that under this doctrine of non-intervention, this doctrine that you delight to call squatter sovereignty, the people of New Mexico have introduced and protected Slavery in the whole of that Territory. Under this doctrine, they have converted a tract of Free Territory into Slave Territory, more than five times the size of the State of New-York. Under this doctrine, Slavery has been extended from the Rio Grande to the Gulf of California, and from the line of the Republic of Mexico, not only up to 36 deg. 30 min., but up to 38 deg.*—GIVING YOU A DEGREE AND A HALF MORE SLAVE TERRITORY THAN YOU EVER CLAIMED. In 1848 and 1849 and 1850, you only asked to have the line of 36 deg. 30 min. The Nashville convention fixed that as its ultimatum. I offered it in the Senate in August, 1848 and it was adopted here but rejected in the House of Representatives. You asked only up to 36 deg. 30 min., *and non-intervention has given you Slave Territory up to 38 deg.*, A DEGREE AND A HALF MORE THAN YOU ASKED; and yet you say that this is a sacrifice of Southern rights!

These are the fruits of this principle which the Sena-tor from Mississippi regards as hostile to the rights of the South. Where did you ever get any other fruits that were more palatable to your taste or more refreshing to your strength? What other inch of Free Territory has been converted into Slave Territory on the American continent, since the Revolution, except in New Mexico and Arizona, under the principle of non-intervention affirmed at Charleston? If it be true that this principle of non-intervention has given to Slavery all New Mexico, which was surrounded on nearly every side by Free Territory, will not the same principle protect you in the northern states of Mexico when they are acquired, since they are now surrounded by Slave Territory; are several hundred miles further South; have many degrees of greater heat; and have a climate and soil adapted to Southern products? Are you not satisfied with these practical results? Do you desire to appeal from the people of the Territories to the Congress of the United States to settle this question in the Territories? When you distrust the people and appeal to Congress, with both houses largely against you on this question, what sort of protection will you get? Whenever you ask a Slave code from Congress to protect your institutions in a Territory where the people do not want it, you will get that sort of protection which the wolf gives to the lamb; you will get that sort of friendly hug that the grizzly bear gives to the infant. Appealing to an Anti-Slavery Congress to pass laws of protection, with a view of forcing Slavery upon an unwilling and hostile people! Sir, of all the mad schemes that ever could be devised by the South, or by the enemies of the South, that which recognizes the right of Congress to touch the institution of Slavery either in States or Territories, beyond the single case provided in the Constitution for the rendition of fugitive Slaves, is the most fatal.—*Appendix to Congressional Globe, page 314.*

THE IRREPRESSIBLE CONFLICT.

A SPEECH BY WILLIAM H. SEWARD,

Delivered at Rochester, Monday, Oct. 25, 1858.

FELLOW-CITIZENS: The unmistakable outbreaks of zeal which occur all around me, show that you are earnest men —and such a man am I. Let us, therefore, at least for a time, pass by all secondary and collateral questions, whether of a personal or of a general nature, and consider the main subject of the present canvass. The Democratic party, or, to speak more accurately, the party which wears that attractive name, is in possession of the Federal Government. The Republicans propose to dislodge that party, and dismiss it from its high trust.

The main subject, then, is, whether the Democractic party deserves to retain the confidence of the American people. In attempting to prove it unworthy, I think that I am not actuated by prejudices against that party, or by prepossessions in favor of its adversary; for I have learned, by some experience, that virtue and patriotism, vice and selfishness, are found in all parties, and that they differ less in their motives than in the policies they pursue.

Our country is a theatre, which exhibits in full operation, two radically different political systems; the one resting on the basis of servile or slave labor, the other on the basis of voluntary labor of freemen.

The laborers who are enslaved are all negroes, or persons more or less purely of African derivation. But this is only accidental. The principle of the system is, that labor in every society, by whomsoever performed, is necessarily unintellectual, groveling, and base; and that the laborer, equally for his own good and for the welfare of the State, ought to be enslaved. The white laboring man, whether native or foreigner, is not enslaved, only because he cannot, as yet, be reduced to bondage.

You need not be told now that the slave system is the older of the two, and that once it was universal.

The emancipation of our own ancestors, Caucasians and Europeans as they were, hardly dates beyond a period of five hundred years. The great melioration of human society which modern times exhibit, is mainly due to the incomplete substitution of the system of voluntary labor for the old one of servile labor, which has already taken place. This African slave system is one which, in its origin and in its growth, has been altogether foreign from the habits of the races which colonized these States, and established civilization here. It was introduced on this new continent as an engine of conquest, and for the establishment of monarchical power, by the Portuguese and the Spaniards, and was rapidly extended by them all over South America, Central America, Louisiana, and Mexico. Its legitimate fruits are seen in the poverty, imbecility, and anarchy, which now pervade all Portuguese and Spanish America. The free-labor system is of German extraction, and it was established in our country by emigrants from Sweden, Holland, Germany, Great Britain, and Ireland. We justly ascribe to its influences the strength, wealth, greatness, intelligence, and freedom which the whole American people now enjoy. One of the chief elements of the value of human life is freedom in the pursuit of happiness. The slave system is not only intolerant, unjust, and inhuman toward the laborer, whom, only because he is a laborer, it loads down with chains and converts into merchandise, but is scarcely less severe upon the freeman, to whom, only because he is a laborer from necessity, it denies facilities for employment, and whom it expels from the community because it cannot enslave and convert him into merchandise also. It is necessarily improvident and ruinous, because, as a general truth, communities prosper and flourish or droop and decline in just the degree that they practice or neglect to practice the primary duties of justice and humanity. The free-labor system conforms to the divine law of equality, which is written in the hearts and consciences of men, and therefore is always and everywhere beneficent.

The slave system is one of constant danger, distrust, suspicion, and watchfulness. It debases those whose toil alone can produce wealth and resources for defense, to the lowest degree of which human nature is capable, to guard against mutiny and insurrection, and thus wastes energies which otherwise might be employed in national development and aggrandizement.

The free-labor system educates all alike, and by opening all the fields of industrial employment, and all the departments of authority, to the unchecked and equal rivalry of all classes of men, at once secures universal contentment, and brings into the highest possible activity all the physical, moral, and social energies of the whole State. In States where the slave system prevails, the masters, directly or indirectly, secure all political ɔower, and constitute a ruling aristocracy. In States where the free-labor system prevails, universal suffrage necessarily obtains, and the State inevitably becomes, sooner or later, a republic or democracy.

Russia yet maintains Slavery, and is a despotism. Most of the other European States have abolished Slavery, and adopted the system of free labor. It was the antagonistic political tendencies of the two systems which the first Napoleon was contemplating when he predicted that Europe would ultimately be either all Cossack or all Republican. Never did human sagacity utter a more pregnant truth. The two systems are at once perceived to be incongruous. But they are more than incongruous—they are incompatible. They never have permanently existed together in one country, and they never can. It would be easy to demonstrate this impossibility, from the irreconcilable contrast between their great principles and characteristics. But the experience of mankind has conclusively established it. Slavery, as I have already intimated, existed in every state in Europe. Free labor has supplanted it everywhere except in Russia and Turkey. State necessities developed in modern times, are now obliging even those two nations to encourage and employ free labor; and already, despotic as they are, we find them engaged in abolishing Slavery. In the United States, Slavery came into collision with free labor at the close of the last century, and fell before it in New-England, New-York, New-Jersey, and Pennsylvania, but triumphed over it effectually, and excluded it for a period yet undetermined, from Virginia, the Carolinas, and Georgia. Indeed, so incompatible are the two systems, that every new State which is organized within our ever-extending domain makes its first political act a choice of the one and an exclusion of the other, even at the cost of civil war, if necessary. The Slave States, without law, at the last national election, successfully forbade, within their own limits, even the casting of votes for a candidate for President of the United States supposed to be favorable to the establishment of the free-labor system in new States.

Hitherto, the two systems have existed in different States, but side by side within the American Union. This has happened because the Union is a confederation of States. But in another aspect the United States constitute only one nation. Increase of population, which is filling the States out to their very borders, together with a new and extended net-work of railroads and other avenues, and an internal commerce which daily becomes more intimate, is rapidly bringing the States into a higher and more perfect social unity or consolidation. Thus, these antagonistic systems are continually coming into closer contact, and collision results.

Shall I tell you what this collision means? They who think that it is accidental, unnecessary, the work of interested or fanatical agitators, and therefore ephemeral, mistake the case altogether. It is an irrepressible conflict between opposing and enduring forces, and it means that the United States must and will, sooner or later, become either entirely a slaveholding nation, or entirely a free-labor nation. Either the cotton and rice fields of South Carolina and the sugar plantations of Louisiana will ultimately be tilled by free labor, and Charleston and New Orleans become marts for legitimate merchandise alone, or else the rye-fields and wheat-fields of Massachusetts and New-York must again be surrendered by their farmers to slave culture and to the production of slaves, and Boston and New-York become once more markets for trade in the bodies and souls of men. It is the failure to apprehend this great truth that induces so many unsuccessful attempts at final compromise between the Slave and Free States, and it is the existence of this great fact that renders all such pretended compromises, when made, vain and ephemeral. Startling as this saying may appear to you, fellow-citizens, it is by no means an original or even a modern one. Our forefathers knew it to be true, and unanimously acted upon it when they framed the Constitution of the United States. They regarded the existence of the servile system in so many of the States with sorrow and shame, which they openly confessed, and they looked upon the collision between them, which was then just revealing itself, and which we are now accustomed to deplore, with favor and hope. They knew that either the one or the other system must exclusively prevail.

Unlike too many of those who in modern times invoke their authority, they had a choice between the two. They preferred the system of free labor, and they determined to organize the Government, and so to direct its activity, that that system should surely and certainly prevail. For this purpose, and no other, they based the whole structure of Government broadly on the principle that all men are created equal, and therefore free—little dreaming that, within the short period of one hundred years, their descendants would bear to be told by any orator, however popular, that the utterance of that principle was merely a rhetorical rhapsody; or by any judge however venerated, that it was attended by mental reservations, which rendered it hypocritical and false. By the Ordinance of 1787, they dedicated all of the national domain not yet polluted by Slavery to free labor immediately, thenceforth and forever; while by the new Constitution and laws they invited foreign free labor from all lands under the sun, and interdicted the importation of African Slave Labor, at all times, in all places, and under all circumstances whatsoever. It is true that they necessarily and wisely modified this policy of Freedom, by leaving it to the several States, affected as they were by differing circumstances, to abolish Slavery in their own way and at their own pleasure, instead of confiding that duty to Congress, and that they secured to the Slave States, while yet retaining the system of Slavery, a three-fifths representation of slaves in the Federal Government, until they should find themselves able to relinquish it with safety. But the very nature of these modifications fortifies my position that the fathers knew that the two systems could not endure within the Union, and expected that within a short period Slavery would disappear forever. Moreover, in order that these modifications might not altogether defeat their grand design of a Republic maintaining universal equality, they provided that two-thirds of the States might amend the Constitution.

It remains to say on this point only one word, to guard against misapprehension. If these States are to again become universally slaveholding, I do not pretend to say with what violations of the Constitution that end shall be accomplished. On the other hand, while I do confidently believe and hope that my country will yet become a land of universal Freedom, I do not expect that it will be made so otherwise than through the action of the several States coöperating with the Federal Government, and all acting in strict conformity with their respective Constitutions.

The strife and contentions concerning Slavery, which gently-disposed persons so habitually deprecate, are nothing more than the ripening of the conflict which the fathers themselves, not only thus regarded with favor, but which they may be said to have instituted.

It is not to be denied, however, that thus far the course of that contest has not been according to their humane anticipations and wishes. In the field of federal politics, Slavery, deriving unlooked-for advantages from commercial changes, and energies unforeseen from the facilities of combination between members of the slaveholding class and between that class and other property classes, early rallied, and has at length made a stand, not merely to retain its original defensive position, but to extend its sway throughout the whole Union. It is certain that the slaveholding class of American citizens indulge this high ambition, and that they derive encouragement for it from the rapid and effective political successes which they have already obtained. The plan of operation is this: By continued appliances of patronage and threats of disunion, they will keep a majority favorable to these designs in the Senate, where each State has an equal representation. Through that majority they will defeat, as they best can, the admission of Free States, and secure the admission of Slave States. Under the protection of the Judiciary, they will, on the principle of the Dred Scott case, carry Slavery into all the Territories of the United States now existing, and hereafter to be organized. By the action of the President and the Senate, using the treaty-making power, they will annex foreign slaveholding States. In a favorable conjuncture they will induce Congress to repeal the act of 1808, which prohibits the foreign slave-trade, and so they will import from Africa, at the cost of only $20 a head, slaves enough to fill up the interior of the continent. Thus relatively increasing the number of Slave States, they will allow no amendment to the Constitution prejudicial to their interest; and so, having permanently established their power, they expect the Federal Judiciary to nullify all State laws which shall interfere with internal or foreign commerce in slaves. When the Free States shall be sufficiently demoralized to tolerate these designs, they reasonably conclude that Slavery will be accepted by those States themselves. I shall not stop to show how speedy or how complete would be the ruin which the accomplishment of these slaveholding schemes would bring upon the country. For one, I should not remain in the country to test the sad experiment. Having spent my manhood, though not my whole life, in a Free State, no aristocracy of any kind, much less an aristocracy of slaveholders, shall ever make the laws of the land in which I shall be content to live. Having seen the society around me universally engaged in agriculture, manufactures and trade, which were innocent and beneficent, I shall never be a denizen of a State where men and women are reared as cattle, and bought and sold as merchandise. When that evil day shall come, and all further effort at resistance shall be impossible, then, if there shall be no better hope for redemption than I can now foresee, I shall say with Franklin, while looking abroad over the whole earth for a new and more congenial home, "Where liberty dwells, there is my country."

You will tell me that these fears are extravagant and chimerical. I answer, they are so; but they are so only because the designs of the slaveholders must and can be defeated. But it is only the possibility of defeat that renders them so. They cannot be defeated by inactivity. There is no escape from them, compatible with non-resistance. How, then, and in what way, shall the necessary resistance be made? There is only one way. The Democratic party must be permanently dislodged from the Government. The reason is, that the Democratic party is inextricably committed to the designs of the slaveholders, which I have described. Let me be well understood. I do not charge that the Democratic candidates for public office now before the people are pledged to, much less that the Democratic masses who support them really adopt, those atrocious and dangerous designs. Candidates may, and generally do, mean to act justly, wisely, and patriotically, when they shall be elected; but they become the ministers and servants, not the dictators, of the power which elects them. The policy which a party shall pursue at a future period is only gradually developed, depending on the occurrence of events never fully foreknown. The motives of men, whether acting as electors, or in any other capacity, are generally pure. Nevertheless, it is not more true that "Hell is paved with good intentions," than it is that earth is covered with wrecks resulting from innocent and amiable motives.

The very constitution of the Democratic party commits it to execute all the designs of the slaveholders, whatever they may be. It is not a party of the whole Union, of all the Free States and of all the Slave States; nor yet is it a party of the Free States in the North and in the Northwest; but it is a sectional and local party, having practically its seat within the Slave States, and counting its constituency chiefly and almost exclusively there. Of all its representatives in Congress and in the Electoral College, two-thirds uniformly come from these States. Its great element of strength lies in the vote of the slaveholders, augmented by the representation of three-fifths of the slaves. Deprive the Democratic party of this strength, and it would be a helpless and hopeless minority, incapable of continued organization. The Democratic party, being thus local and sectional, acquires new strength from the admission of every new Slave State, and loses relatively by the admission of every new Free State into the Union.

A party is, in one sense, a joint-stock association, in which those who contribute most direct the action and management of the concern. The slaveholders contributing in an overwhelmning proportion to the capital strength of the Democratic party, they necessarily dictate and prescribe its policy. The inevitable caucus system enables them to do so with a show of fairness and justice. If it were possible to conceive for a moment that the Democratic party should disobey the behests of the slaveholders, we should then see a withdrawal of the slaveholders, which would leave the party to perish. The portion of the party which is found in the Free States is a mere appendage, convenient to modify its sectional character, without impairing its sectional constitution, and is less effective in regulating its movement than the nebulous tail of the comet is in determining the appointed though apparently eccentric course of the fiery sphere from which it emanates.

To expect the Democratic party to resist Slavery and favor Freedom, is as unreasonable as to look for Protestant missionaries to the Catholic Propaganda of Rome. The history of the Democratic party commits it to the policy of Slavery. It has been the Democratic party, and no other agency, which has carried that policy up to its present alarming culmination. Without stopping to ascertain, critically, the origin of the present Democratic party, we may concede its claim to date from the era of good feeling which occurred under the Administration of President Monroe. At that time, in this State, and about that time in many others of the Free States, the Democratic party deliberately disfranchised the free colored, or African citizen, and it has pertinaciously continued this disfranchisement ever since. This was an effective aid to Slavery; for while the slaveholder votes for his slaves against Freedom, the freed slave in the Free States is prohibited from voting against Slavery.

In 1824, the Democracy resisted the election of John Quincy Adams—himself before that time an acceptable Democrat—and in 1828, it expelled him from the Presidency, and put a slaveholder in his place, although the office had been filled by slaveholders thirty-two out of forty years.

In 1836, Martin Van Buren—the first non-slaveholding citizen of a Free State to whose election the Democratic party ever consented—signalized his inauguration into the Presidency, by a gratuitous announcement, that under no circumstances would he ever approve a bill for the abolition of Slavery in the District of Columbia. From 1838 to 1844, the subject of abolishing Slavery in the District of Columbia and in the national dock-yards and arsenals, was brought before Congress by repeated popular appeals. The Democratic party thereupon promptly denied the right of petition, and effectually suppressed the freedom of speech in Congress, so far as the institution of Slavery was concerned.

From 1840 to 1843, good and wise men counselled that Texas should remain outside of the Union until she should consent to relinquish her self-instituted slavery; but the Democratic party precipitated her admission into the Union, not only without that condition, but even with a covenant that the State might be divided and reorganized so as to constitute four Slave States instead of one.

In 1846, when the United States became involved in a war with Mexico, and it was apparent that the struggle would end in the dismemberment of that republic, which was a non-slaveholding power, the Democratic party rejected a declaration that Slavery should not be established within the territory to be acquired. When, in 1850, governments were to be instituted in the Territories of California and New-Mexico the fruits of that war, the Democratic party refused to admit New-Mexico as a Free State, and only consented to admit California as a Free State on the condition, as it has since explained the transaction, of leaving all of New-Mexico and Utah open to Slavery, to which was also added the concession of perpetual Slavery in the District of Columbia, and the passage of an unconstitutional, cruel, and humiliating law, for the recapture of fugitive slaves, with a further stipulation that the subject of Slavery should never again be agitated in either chamber of Congress. When, in 1854, the slaveholders were contentedly reposing on these great advantages, then so recently won, the Democratic party, unnecessarily, officiously, and with superserviceable liberality, awakened them from their slumber, to offer and force on their acceptance the abrogation of the law which declared that neither Slavery nor involuntary servitude should ever exist within that part of the ancient territory of Louisiana which lay outside of the State of Missouri, and north of the parallel of 36 deg. 30 min. of north latitude—a law which, with the exception of one other, was the only statute of Freedom then remaining in the Federal code.

In 1856, when the people of Kansas had organized a new State within the region thus abandoned to Slavery, and applied to be admitted as a Free State into the Union, the Democratic party contemptuously rejected their petition and drove them, with menaces and intimidations, from the halls of Congress, and armed the President with military power to enforce their submission to a slave code, established over them by fraud and usurpation. At every subsequent stage of the long contest which has since raged in Kansas, the Democratic party has lent its sympathies, its aid, and all the powers of the Government which it controlled, to enforce Slavery upon that unwilling and injured people. And now, even at this day, while it mocks us with the assurance that Kansas is free, the Democratic party keeps the State excluded from her just and proper place in the Union, under the hope that she may be dragooned into the acceptance of Slavery.

The Democratic party, finally, has procured from a Supreme Judiciary, fixed in its interest, a decree that Slavery exists by force of the Constitution in every Territory of the United States, paramount to all legislative authority either within the Territory, or residing in Congress.

Such is the Democratic party. It has no policy, State or Federal, for finance or trade, or manufacture, or commerce, or education, or internal improvements, or for the protection or even the security of civil or religious liberty. It is positive and uncompromising in the interest of Slavery—negative, compromising and vacillating, in regard to everything else. It boasts its love of equality and wastes its strength, and even its life, in fortifying the only aristocracy known in the land. It professes fraternity, and, so often as Slavery requires, allies itself with proscription. It magnifies itself for conquests in foreign lands, but it sends the national eagle forth always with chains, and not the olive branch, in his fangs.

This dark record shows you, fellow citizens, what I was unwilling to announce at an earlier stage of this argument, that of the whole nefarious schedule of slaveholding designs which I have submitted to you, the Democratic party has left only one yet to be consummated—the abrogation of the law which forbids the African slave trade.

Now, I know very well that the Democratic party has, at every stage of these proceedings, disavowed the motive and the policy of fortifying and extending Slavery, and has excused them on entirely different and more plausible grounds. But the inconsistency and frivolity of these pleas prove still more conclusively the guilt I charge upon that party. It must, indeed, try to excuse such guilt before mankind, and even to the consciences of its own adherents. There is an instinctive abhorrence of Slavery, and an inborn and inhering love of Freedom in the human heart, which renders palliation of such gross misconduct indispensable. It disfranchised the free African on the ground of a fear that, if left to enjoy the right of suffrage, he might seduce the free white citizen into amalgamation with his wronged and despised race. The Democratic party condemned and deposed John Quincy Adams, because he expended $12,000,000 a year, while it justifies his favored successor in spending $70,000,000, $80,000,000, and even $100,000,000, a year. It denies emancipation in the District of Columbia, even with compensation to masters and the consent of the people, on the ground of an implied constitutional inhibition, although the Constitution expressly confers upon Congress sovereign legislative power in that District, and although the Democratic party is tenacious of the principle of strict construction. It violated the express provisions of the Constitution in suppressing petition and debate on the subject of Slavery, through fear of disturbance of the public harmony, although it claims that the electors have a right to instruct their representatives, and even demand their resignation in cases of contumacy. It extended Slavery over Texas, and connived at the attempt to spread it across the Mexican territories, even to the shores of the Pacific Ocean, under a plea of enlarging the area of Freedom. It abrogated the Mexican slave law and the Missouri Compromise prohibition of Slavery in Kansas, not to open the new Territories to Slavery, but to try therein the new and fascinating theories of Non-intervention and Popular Sovereignty; and, finally, it overthrew both these new and elegant systems by the English Lecompton bill and the Dred Scott decision, on the ground that the Free States ought not to enter the Union without a population equal to the representative basis of one member of Congress, although Slave States might come in without inspection as to their numbers.

Will any member of the Democratic party now here claim that the authorities chosen by the suffrages of the party transcended their partisan platforms, and so misrepresented the party in the various transactions I have recited? Then I ask him to name one Democratic statesman or legislator, from Van Buren to Walker, who either timidly or cautiously like them, or boldly or defiantly like Douglas, ever refused to execute a behest of the slaveholders, and was not therefor, and for no other cause, immediately denounced, and deposed from his trust, and repudiated by the Democratic party for that contumacy.

I think, fellow-citizens, that I have shown you that it is high time for the friends of Freedom to rush to the rescue of the Constitution, and that their very first duty is to dismiss the Democratic party from the administration of the Government.

Why shall it not be done? All agree that it ought to be done. What, then, shall prevent its being done? Nothing but timidity or division of the opponents of the Democratic party.

Some of these opponents start one objection, and some another. Let us notice these objections briefly. One class say that they cannot trust the Republican party; that it has not avowed its hostility to Slavery boldly enough, or its affection for Freedom earnestly enough.

I ask in reply, is there any other party which can be more safely trusted? Every one knows that it is the Republican party or none, that shall displace the Democratic party. But I answer further, that the character and fidelity of any party are determined, necessarily, not by its pledges, programmes, and platforms, but by the public exigencies, and the temper of the people when they call it into activity. Subserviency to Slavery is a law written not only on the forehead of the Democratic party, but also in its very soul—so resistance to Slavery, and devotion to Freedom, the popular elements now actively working for the Republican party among the people, must and will be the resources for its ever-renewing strength and constant invigoration.

Others cannot support the Republican party, because it it has not sufficiently exposed its platform, and determined what it will do, and what it will not do, when triumphant. It may prove too progressive for some, and too conservative for others. As if any party ever foresaw so clearly the course of future events as to plan a universal scheme for future action, adapted to all possible emergencies. Who would ever have joined even the Whig party of the Revolution, if it had been obliged to answer, in 1775, whether it would declare for Independence in 1776, and for this noble Federal Constitution of ours in 1787, and not a year earlier or later?

The people of the United States will be as wise next year, and the year afterward, and even ten years hence, as we are now. They will oblige the Republican party to act as the public welfare and the interests of justice and humanity shall require, through all the stages of its career, whether of trial or triumph.

Others will not venture an effort, because they fear that the Union would not endure the change. Will such objectors tell me how long a Constitution can bear a strain directly along the fibres of which it is composed? This is a Constitution of Freedom. It is being converted into a Constitution of Slavery. It is a republican Constitution. It is being made an aristocratic one. Others wish to wait until some collateral questions concerning temperance, or the exercise of the elective franchise are properly settled. Let me ask all such persons, whether time enough has not been wasted on these points already, without gaining any other than this single advantage, namely, the discovery that only one thing can be effectually done at one time, and that the one thing which must and will be done at any one time is just that thing which is most urgent, and will no longer admit of postponement or delay. Finally, we are told by faint-hearted men that they despond; the Democratic party, they say, is unconquerable, and the dominion of Slavery is consequently inevitable. I reply to them, that the complete and universal dominion of Slavery would be intolerable enough when it should have come after the last possible effort to escape should have been made. There would, in that case, be left to us the consoling reflection of fidelity to duty.

But I reply, further, that I know—few, I think, know better than I—the resources and energies of the Democratic party, which is identical with the Slave Power. I do ample prestige to its traditional popularity. I know further—few, I think, know better than I—the difficulties and disadvantages of organizing a new political force like the Republican party, and the obstacles it must encounter in laboring without prestige and without patronage. But, notwithstanding all this, I know that the Democratic party must go down, and that the Republican party must rise into its place. The Democratic party derived its strength, originally, from its adoption of the principles of equal and exact justice to all men. So long as it practiced this principle faithfully, it was invulnerable. It became vulnerable when it renounced the principle, and since that time it has, maintained itself, not by virtue of its own strength, or even of its traditional merits, but because there as yet had appeared in the political field no other party that had the conscience and the courage to take up, and avow, and practice the life-inspiring principles which the Democratic party had surrendered. At last, the Republican party has appeared. It avows now, as the Republican party of 1800 did, in one word, its faith and its works, " Equal and exact justice to all men." Even when it first entered the field, only half organized, it struck a blow which only just failed to secure complete and triumphant victory. In this, its second campaign, it has already won advantages which render that triumph now both easy and certain.

The secret of its assured success lies in that very characteristic which, in the mouth of scoffers, constitutes its great and lasting imbecility and reproach. It lies in the fact that it is a party of one idea; but that idea is a noble one—an idea that fills and expands all generous souls ; the idea of equality—the equality of all men before human tribunals and human laws, as they all are equal before the Divine tribunal and Divine laws.

I know, and you know, that a revolution has begun. I know, and all the world knows, that revolutions never go backward. Twenty Senators and a hundred Representatives proclaim boldly in Congress to-day sentiments and opinions and principles of Freedom which hardly any many men, even in this free State, dared to utter in their own homes twenty years ago. While the Government of the United States, under the conduct of the Democratic party, has been all that time surrendering one plain and castle after another to Slavery, the people of the United States have been no less steadily and perseveringly gathering together the forces with which to recover back again all the fields and all the castles which have been lost, and to confound and overthrow, by one decisive blow, the betrayers of the Constitution and Freedom forever.

"NEGRO SLAVERY NOT UNJUST."

A SPEECH BY CHARLES O'CONOR,

At the Union Meeting at the Academy of Music, New York City, Dec. 19, 1859.

MR. MAYOR AND GENTLEMEN: I cannot express to you the delight which I experience in beholding in this great city so vast an assembly of my fellow citizens, convened for the purpose stated in your resolutions. I am delighted beyond measure to behold at this time so vast an assembly responding to the call of a body so respectable as the twenty thousand New Yorkers who have convened this meeting. If anything can give assurance to those who doubt, and confidence to those who may have had misgivings as to the permanency of our institutions, and the solidity of the support which the people of the North are prepared to give them, it is that in the queen city of the New World, in the capital of North America, there is assembled a meeting so large, so respectable, and so unanimous as this meeting has shown itself to be in receiving sentiments which, if observed, must protect our Union from destruction, and even from danger. (Applause.) Gentlemen, is it not a subject of astonishment that the idea of danger, and the still more dreadful idea of dissolution, should be heard from the lips of an American citizen, at this day, in reference to, or in connection with, the sacred name of this most sacred Union? (Applause.) Why gentlemen, what is our Union? What are its antecedents? What is its present condition? If we ward off the evils which threaten it, what its future hope for us and for the great family of mankind? Why gentlemen, it may well be said of this Union as a government, that as it is the last offspring, so is it Time's most glorious and beneficent production. Gentlemen, we are created by an Omniscient Being. We are created by a Being not only All-Seeing, but All-Powerful and All-Wise. And in the benignity and the farseeing wisdom of His power, He permitted the great family of mankind to live on, to advance, to improve, step by step, and yet permitted five thousand years and upward to elapse ere He laid the foundation of a truly free, a truly happy, and a truly independent empire. It was not, gentlemen, until that great length of time had elapsed, that the earth was deemed mature for laying the foundations of this mighty and prosperous State. It was then that He inspired the noble-minded and chivalrous Genoese to set forth upon the trackless ocean and discover the empire that we now enjoy. But a few years, comparatively, had elapsed when there was raised up in this blessed land a set of men whose like had never before existed upon the face of this earth. Men unequalled in their perceptions of the true principles of justice, in their comprehensive benevolence, in their capacity to lay safely, justly, soundly, and with all the qualities which should insure permanency, the foundations of an empire. It was in 1776, and in this country, that there assembled the first, the very first, assembly of rational men who ever proclaimed, in clear and undeniable form, the immutable principles of liberty, and consecrated, to all time I trust, in the face of tyrants, and in opposition to their power, the rights of nations and the rights of men. (Applause.) These patriots, as soon as the storm of war had passed away, sat down and framed that instrument upon which our Union rests, the Constitution of the United States of America. (Applause.) And the question now before us is neither more nor less than this: whether that Constitution, consecrated by the blood shed in that glorious Revolution, consecrated by the signature of the most illustrious man who ever lived, George Washington (applause)—whether that instrument, accepted by the wisest and by the best of that day, and accepted in convention, one by one, in each and every State of this Union—that instrument from which so many blessings have flown—whether that instrument was conceived in crime, is a chapter of abominations (cries of "No, no,") is a violation of justice, is a league between strong-handed but wicked-hearted white men to oppress, and impoverish, and plunder their fellow-creatures, contrary to rectitude, honor and justice. (Applause.) This is the question, neither more nor less. We are told from pulpits, we are told from the political rostrum, we are

told in the legislative assemblies of our Northern States, not merely by speakers, but by distinct resolutions of the whole body—we are told by gentlemen occupying seats in the Congress of the Union through the votes of Northern people—that the Constitution seeks to enshrine, to protect, to defend a monstrous crime against justice and humanity, and that it is our duty to defeat its provisions, to outwit them, if we cannot otherwise get rid of their effect, and to trample upon the rights which it has declared shall be protected and insured to our brethren of the South. (Applause.) That is now the doctrine advocated. And I ask whether that doctrine, necessarily involving the destruction of our Union, shall be permitted to prevail as it has hitherto prevailed? Gentlemen, I trust you will excuse me for deliberately coming up to and meeting this question—not seeking to captivate your fancies by a trick of words—not seeking to exalt your imaginations by declamation or by any effort at eloquence—but meeting this question gravely, sedately, and soberly, and asking you what is to be our course in relation to it? Gentlemen, the Constitution guarantees to the people of the Southern States the protection of their slave property. In that respect it is a solemn compact between the North and the South. As a solemn compact are we at liberty to violate it? (Cries of "No, no!") Are we at liberty to seek or take any mean, petty advantage of it? (Cries of "No, no!") Are we at liberty to con over its particular words, and to restrict and to limit its operation, so as to acquire, under such narrow construction, a pretence of right by hostile and adverse legislation? ("No, no!")—to interfere with the interests, wound the feelings, and trample on the political rights of our Southern fellow-citizens? ("No, no, no!") No, gentlemen. If it be a compact, and has anything sacred in it, we are bound to observe it in good faith, honestly and honorably, not merely to the letter, but fully to the spirit, and not in any mincing, half-way, unfair, or illiberal construction, seeking to satisfy the letter, to give as little as we can, and thereby to defeat the spirit. (Applause.) That may be the way that some men keep a contract about the sale of a house or of a chattel, but it is not the way honest men observe contracts, even in relation to the most trivial things. (" True," and applause.) What has been done, having a tendency to disturb harmony under this Constitution, and to break down and destroy the union now existing between these States? Why, gentlemen, at an early period the subject of Slavery, as a mere philosophical question, was discussed by many, and its justice or injustice made the subject of argument leading to various opinions. It mattered little how long this discussion should last, while it was confined within such limits. If it had only led to the formation of societies like the Shakers, who do not believe in matrimony; societies like the people of Utah, destined to a short career, who believe in too much of it (laughter); or societies of people like the strong-minded women of our country, who believe that women are much better qualified than men to perform the functions and offices usually performed by men (laughter)—and who probably would, if they had their way, simply change the order of proceedings, and transfer the husband to the kitchen, and themselves to the field or the cabinet. (Laughter and applause.) So long, I say, as this sentimentality touching Slavery confined itself to the formation of parties and societies of this description, it certainly could do no great harm, and we might satisfy ourselves with the maxim that "Error can do little harm as long as truth is left free to combat it." But unfortunately gentlemen, this sentimentality has found its way out of the meeting-houses—from among pious people, assemblies of speculative philosophers, and societies formed to benefit the inhabitants of Barioboola-gha—it has found its way into the heart of the selfish politician; it has been made the war-cry of party; it has been made the instrument whereby to elevate not merely to personal distinction and social rank, but to political power throughout the non-slaveholding States of this Union, men have been thus elevated who advocate a course of conduct necessarily exasperating the South, and the natural effect of whose teachings renders the Southern people insecure in their property and their lives, making it a matter of doubt each night whether they can safely retire to their numbers without sentries and guards to protect them against incursions from the North. I say the effect has been to elevate, on the strength of this sentiment, such men to power. And what is the result—the condition of things at this day? Why, gentlemen, the occasion that calls us together is the occurrence of a raid upon the state of Virginia by a few misguided fanatics—followers of these doctrines, with arms in their hands, and bent upon rapine and murder. I called them followers, but they should be deemed leaders. They were the best, the bravest, and the most virtuous of all the abolition party. (Applause.) On the Lord's day, at the hour of still repose, they armed the bondman with pikes brought from the North, that he might slay his master, his master's wife, and his master's little children. And immediately succeeding to it—at this very instant—what is the political question pending before Congress?

A book substantially encouraging the same course of provocation toward the South which has been long pursued, is openly recommended to circulation by sixty-eight members of your Congress. (Cries of "Shame, on them," applause, and hisses.)—Recommended to circulation by sixty-eight members of your Congress, all elected in Northern States (hisses and applause)—every one, I say, elected from non-slaveholding States. And with the assistance of their associates, some of whom hold their offices by your votes, there is great danger that they will elect to the highest office in that body, where he will sit as a representative of the whole North, a man who united in causing that book to be distributed through the South, carrying poison and death in its polluted leaves. ("Hang him!" and applause.) Is it not fair to say that this great and glorious Union is menaced when such a state of things is found to exist? when such an act is attempted? Is it reasonable to expect that our brethren of the South will calmly sit down (No") and submit quietly to such an outrage? (Cries of " No, no.") Why, gentlemen, we greatly exceed them in numbers. The non-slaveholding States are by far the more populous; they are increasing daily in numbers and in population, and we may soon overwhelm the Southern vote. If we continue to fill the halls of legislation with abolitionists, and permit to occupy the executive chair men who declare themselves to be enlisted in a crusade against Slavery, and against the provisions of the Constitution which secure that species of property, what can we reasonably expect from the people of the South but that they will pronounce the Constitution, with all its glorious associations, with all its sacred memories—this Uuion, with its manifold present and promised blessings—an unendurable evil, threatening to crush and to destroy their most vital interests—to make their country a wilderness. Why should we expect them to submit to such a line of conduct on our part, and recognize us as brethren, or unite with us in perpetuating the Union?

For my part I do not see anything unjust or unreasonable in the declaration often made by Southern members on this subject. They tell us : "If you will thus assail us with incendiary pamphlets, if you will thus create a spirit in your country which leads to violence and bloodshed among us, if you will assail the institution upon which the prosperity of our country depends, and will elevate to office over us men who are pledged to aid in such transactions, and to oppress us by hostile legislation, we cannot—much as we revere the Constitution, greatly as we estimate the blessings which would flow from its faithful enforcement—we cannot longer depend on your compliance with its injunctions, or adhere to the Union." For my part, gentlemen, if the North continues to conduct itself in the selection of representatives to the Congress of the United States as, from, perhaps a certain degree of negligence and inattention, it has heretofore conducted itself, the South is not to be censured if it withdraws from the Union. (Hisses and applause. A voice—"that's so." Three cheers for the Fugitive Slave Law.) We are not, gentlemen, to hold a meeting to say that " We love this Union ; we delight in it ; we are proud of it ; it blesses us, and we enjoy it ; but we shall fill all its offices with men of our own choosing, and, our brethren of the South, you shall enjoy its glorious past ; you shall enjoy its mighty recollections ; but it shall trample your institutions in the dust." We have no right to say it. We have no right to exact so much, and an opposite and entirely different course, fellow-citizens, must be ours—must be the course of the great North, if we would preserve this Union. (Applause, and cries of " Good.")

And, gentlemen, what is this glorious Union? What must we sacrifice if we exasperate our brethren of the South, and compel them, by injustice and breach of

compact, to separate from us and to dissolve it ? Why gentlemen, the greatness and glory of the American name will then be a thing of yesterday. The glorious Revolution of the thirteen States will be a Revolution not achieved by us, but by a nation that has ceased to exist. The name of Washington will be, to us at least at the North (cheers), but as the name of Julius Cæsar, or of some other great hero who has lived in times gone by, whose nation has perished and exists no more. The Declaration of Independence, what will that be? Why, the declaration of a State that no longer has place among the nations. All these bright and glorious recollections of the past must cease to be our property, and become mere memorials of a by-gone race and people. A line must divide the North from the South. What will be the consequences? Will this mighty city—growing as it now is, with wealth pouring into it from every portion of this mighty empire—will it continue to flourish as it has done? (Cries of " No, no !") Will your marble palaces that line Broadway, and raise their proud tops toward the sky, continue to increase, until, as is now promised under the Union, it shall present the most glorious picture of wealth, prosperity, and happiness, that the world has ever seen? (Applause.) No ! gentlemen, no ! such things cannot be. I do not say that we will starve, that we will perish, as a people, if we separate from the South. I admit, that if the line be drawn between us, they will have their measure of prosperity, and we will have ours ; but meagre, small in the extreme, compared with what is existing and promised under our Union, will be the prosperity of each.

Truly has it been said here to-night, that we were made for each other ; separate us, and although you may not destroy us, you reduce each to so low a scale that well might humanity deplore the evil courses that brought about the result. True, gentlemen, we would have left, to boast of, our share of the glories of the Revolution. The Northern States sent forth to the conflict their bands of heroes, and shed their blood as freely as those of the South. But the dividing line would take away from us the grave of Washington. It is in his own beloved Virginia. (Applause and cheers.) It is in the State and near the spot where this treason that has been growing up in the North, so lately culminated in violence and bloodshed. We would lose the grave—we would lose all connection with the name of Washington. But our philanthropic and pious friends who fain would lead us to this result, would, of course, comfort us with the consoling reflection that we had the glorious memory of John Brown in its place. (Great laughter and cheers.) Are you, gentlemen, prepared to make the exchange? (Cries of " No, no.") Shall the tomb of Washington, that rises upon the bank of the Potomac, receiving its tribute from every nation of the earth—shall that become the property of a foreign State—a State hostile to us in its feelings, and we to it in ours? Shall we erect a monument among the arid hills at North Elba, and deem the privilege of making pilgrimages thither a recompense for the loss of every glorious recollection of the past, and for our severance from the name of Washington? He who is recognized as the Father of his Country ? (Cries of " No, no," and cheers.) No, gentlemen, we are not prepared, I trust, for this sad exchange, this fatal severance. We are not prepared, I trust, either to part with our glorious past or to give up the advantages of our present happy condition. We are not prepared to relinquish our affection for the South, nor to involve our section in the losses, the deprivation of blessings and advantages necessarily resulting to each from dis union. Gentlemen, we never would have attained the wealth and prosperity as a nation which is now ours, but for our connection with these very much reviled and injured slaveholders of the Southern States. And, gentlemen, if dissolution is to take place, we must part with the trade of the South, and thereby surrender our participation in the wealth of the South. Nay, more—we are told from good authority that we must not only part with the slaveholding States, but that our younger sister with the golden crown—rich, teeming California, she who added the final requisite to our greatness as a nation— will not come with us. She will remain with the South.

Gentlemen, if we allow this course of injustice toward the South to continue, these are to be the consequences— evil to us, evil also to them. Much of all that we are most proud of ; much of all that contributes to our prosperity and greatness as a nation, must pass away from us.

The question is—should we permit it to be continued, and submit to all these evils? Is there any reason to justify such a course? There is a reason preached to us for permitting it. We are told that Slavery is unjust ; we are told that it is a matter of conscience to put it down ;

and that whatever treaties or compacts, or laws, or constitutions, have been made to sanction and uphold it, it is still unholy, and that we are bound to trample upon treaties, compacts, laws, and constitutions, and to stand by what these men arrogantly tell us is the law of God and a fundamental principle of natural justice. Indeed, gentlemen, these two things are not distinguishable. The law of God and natural justice, as between man and man, are one and the same. The wisest philosopher of ancient times—heathen philosophers—said, The rule of conduct between man and man is, to live honestly, to injure no man, and to render to every man his due. In words far more direct and emphatic, in words of the most perfect comprehensiveness, the Saviour of the world gave us the same rule in one short sentence—" Love thy neighbor as thyself." (Applause.) Now, speaking between us, people of the North and our brethren of the South, I ask you to act upon this maxim—the maxim of the heathen—the command of the living God : " Render to every man his due," " Love thy neighbor as thyself." (Applause.) Thus we should act and feel toward the South. Upon that maxim which came from Him of Nazareth we should act toward the South, but without putting upon it any new-fangled, modern interpretation. We should neither say nor think that any Gospel minister of this day is wiser than God himself—than He who gave us the Gospel. These maxims should govern between us and our brethren of the South. But, gentlemen, the question is this: Do these maxims justify the assertion of those who seek to invade the rights of the South, by proclaiming negro Slavery unjust ? That is the point to which this great argument, involving the fate of our Union, must now come. Is negro Slavery unjust ? If it be unjust, it violates the first rule of human conduct, " Render to every man his due." If it be unjust, it violates the law of God, which says, " Love thy neighbor as thyself," for that law requires that we should perpetrate no injustice. Gentlemen, if it could be maintained that negro Slavery is unjust, is thus in conflict with the law of nature and the law of God, perhaps I might be prepared—perhaps we all ought to be prepared to go with that distinguished man to whom allusion is frequently made, and say, there is a " higher law " which compels us to trample beneath our feet, as a wicked and unholy compact, the Constitution established by our fathers, with all the blessings it secures to their children. But I insist—and that is the argument which we must meet, and on which we must come to a conclusion that shall govern our action in the future selection of representatives in the Congress of the United States—*I insist that negro Slavery is not unjust.* (Long continued applause.) *It is not unjust; it is just, wise, and beneficent.* (Hisses, followed by applause, and cries of " Put him out.") Let him stay, gentlemen.

PRESIDENT.—Let him stay there. Order.

MR. O'CONOR.—Serpents may hiss, but good men will hear. (Cries again of " Put him out ;" calls to order ; confusion for a time.)

THE PRESIDENT.—If anybody hisses here, remember that every one has his own peculiar way of expressing himself, and as some birds only understand hissing, they must hiss. (Applause.)

MR. O'CONOR.—Gentlemen, there is an animal upon this earth that has no faculty of making its sentiments known in any other way than by a hiss. I am for equal rights. (Three cheers were here given for Mr. O'Conor, three for Gov. Wise, and three groans for John Brown.) I beg of you, gentlemen, all of you who are of my mind at least, to preserve silence, and leave the hissing animal in the full enjoyment of his natural privileges. (Cries of " Good, good," laughter and applause.) The first of our race that offended was taught to do so by that hissing animal. (Laughter and applause.) The first human society that was ever broken up through sin and discord, had its happy union dissolved by the entrance of that animal. (Applause.) Therefore I say it is his privilege to hiss. Let him hiss on. (Cries of " Good, good," laughter and applause.) Gentlemen, I will not detain you much longer. (Cries of " Go on, go on.") I maintain that negro Slavery is not unjust—(a voice—" No, sir," applause,) that it is benign in its influence upon the white man and upon the black. (Voices—" That's so, that's so," applause.) I maintain that it is ordained by nature; that it is a necessity of both races ; that, in climates where the black race can live and prosper, nature herself enjoins correlative duties on the black man and on the white, which cannot be performed except by the preservation, and, if the hissing gentleman please, the perpetuation of negro Slavery.

I am fortified in this opinion by the highest tribunal in our country, that venerable exponent of our institutions, and of the principles of justice—the Supreme Court of the United States. That court has held, on this subject, what wise men will ever pronounce to be sound and just doctrine. There are some principles well known, well understood, universally recognized and universally acknowledged among men, that are not to be found written in constitutions or in laws. The people of the United States, at the formation of our Government, were, as they still are, in some sense, peculiarly and radically distinguishable from other nations. We were white men, of—what is commonly called, by way of distinction—the Caucasian race. We were a monogamous people ; that is to say, we were not Mohammedans, or followers of Joe Smith—with half a dozen wives apiece. (Laughter.) It was a fundamental principle of our civilization that no State could exist or be tolerated in this Union, which should not, in that respect, resemble all the other States of the Union. Some other distinctive features might be stated which serve to mark us as a people distinct from others, and incapable of associating on terms of perfect political equality, or social equality, as friends and fellow-citizens, with some kinds of people that are to be found upon the face of the earth. As a white nation, we made our Constitution and our laws, vesting all political rights in that race. They, and they alone, constituted, in every political sense, the American people. (Applause.) As to the negro, why, we allowed him to live under the shadow and protection of our laws. We gave him, as we were bound to give him, protection against wrong and outrage ; but we denied to him political rights, or the power to govern, · We left him, for so long a period as the community in which he dwelt should so order, in the condition of a bondsman. (Applause.) Now, gentlemen, to that condition the negro is assigned by nature. (Cries of " Bravo," and " That's so," and applause.) Experience shows that this race cannot prosper—that they become extinct in any cold, or in any very temperate clime ; but in the warm, the extremely warm regions, his race can be perpetuated, and with proper guardianship, may prosper. He has ample strength, and is competent to labor, but nature denies to him either the intellect to govern or the willingness to work. (Applause.) Both were denied him. That same power which deprived him of the will to labor, gave him, in our country, as a recompense, a master to coerce that duty, and convert him into a useful and valuable servant. (Applause.) I maintain that it is not injustice to leave the negro in the condition in which nature placed him, and for which alone he is adapted. Fitted only for a state of pupilage, our slave system gives him a master to govern him and to supply his deficiencies : in this there is no injustice. Neither is it unjust in the master to compel him to labor, and thereby afford to that master a just compensation in return for the care and talent employed in governing him. In this way alone is the negro enabled to render himself useful to himself and to the society in which he is placed.

These are the principles, gentlemen, which the extreme measures of abolitionism compel us to enforce. This is the ground that we must take, or abandon our cherished Union. We must no longer favor political leaders who talk about negro Slavery being an evil ; nor must we advance the indefensible doctrine that negro Slavery is a thing which, although pernicious, is to be tolerated merely because we have made a bargain to tolerate it. We must turn away from the teachings of fanaticism. We must look at negro slavery as it is, remembering that the voice of inspiration, as found in the sacred volume, nowhere condemns the bondage of those who are fit only for bondage. Yielding to the clear decree of nature, and the dictates of sound philosophy, we must pronounce that institution just, benign, lawful and proper. The Constitution established by the fathers of our Republic, which recognized it, must be maintained. And that both may stand together, we must maintain that neither the institution itself, nor the Constitution which upholds it, is wicked or unjust ; but that each is sound and wise, and entitled to our fullest support.

We must visit with our execration any man claiming our suffrages, who objects to enforcing, with entire good faith, the provisions of the Constitution in favor of negro Slavery, or who seeks, by any indirection, to withhold its protection from the South, or to get away from its obligations upon the North. Let us henceforth support no man for public office whose speech or action tends to induce assaults upon the territory of our Southern neighbors, or to generate insurrection within their borders. (Loud applause.) These are the principles upon which we must act. This is what we must say to our brethren of the South. If we have sent men into Congress who are false to these views, and are seeking to violate the compact which binds us together, we must ask to be forgiven until we have another chance to manifest our will at the ballot-boxes. We must tell them that these men shall be consigned to privacy (applause), and that true men, men faithful to the Constitution, men loving all portions of the country alike, shall be elected in their stead And, gentlemen, we must do more than promise this—we must perform it. (Loud applause, followed by three cheers for Mr. O'Conor, and a tiger.) But a word more, gentlemen, and I have done. (Cries of " Go on.") I have no doubt at all that what I have said to you this evening will be greatly misrepresented. It is very certain that I have not had time enough properly to enlarge upon and fully to explain the interesting topics on which I have ventured to express myself thus boldly and distinctly, taking upon myself the consequences, be they what they may. (Applause.) But I will say a few words by way of explanation. I have maintained the justice of Slavery ; I have maintained it, because I hold that the negro is decreed by nature to a state of pupilage under the dominion of the wiser white man, in every clime where God and nature meant the negro should live at all. (Applause.) I say a state of pupilage ; and, that I may be rightly understood, I say that it is the duty of the white man to treat him kindly ; that is the interest of the white man to treat him kindly. (Applause.) And further, it is my belief that if the white man, in the States where Slavery exists, is not interfered with by the fanatics who are now creating these disturbances, whatever laws, whatever improvements, whatever variations in the conduct of society are necessary for the purpose of enforcing in every instance the dictates of interest and humanity, as between the white man and the black, will be faithfully and fairly carried out in the progress of that improvement in all these things in which we are engaged. It is not pretended that the master has a right to slay his slave ; it is not pretended that he has a right to be guilty of harshness and inhumanity to his slave. The laws of all the Southern States forbid that ; we have not the right here at the North to be guilty of cruelty toward a horse. It is an indictable offence to commit such cruelty. The same laws exist in the South, and if there is any failure in enforcing them to the fullest extent, it is due to this external force, which is pressing upon the Southern States, and compels them to abstain perhaps from many acts beneficent toward the negro which otherwise would be performed. (Applause.) In truth, in fact, in deed, the white man in the slaveholding States has no more authority by law of the land over his slave than our laws allow to a father over his minor children. He can no more violate humanity with respect to them, than a father in any of the free States of this Union can exercise acts violative of humanity toward his own son under the age of twenty-one. So far as the law is concerned, you own your boys, and have a right to their services until they are twenty-one. You can make them work for you ; you have the right to hire out their services and take their earnings ; you have the right to chastise them with judgment and reason if they violate your commands ; and they are entirely without political rights. Not one of them at the age of twenty years and eleven months even, can go to the polls and and give a vote. Therefore, gentlemen, before the law, there is but one difference between the free white man of twenty years of age in the Northern States, and the negro bondman in the Southern States. The white man is to be emancipated at twenty-one, because his God-given intellect entitles him to emancipation and fits him for the duties to devolve upon him. The negro, to be sure, is a bondman for life. He may be sold from one master to another, but where is the ill in that ?—one may be as good as another. If there be laws with respect to the mode of sale, which by separating man and wife do occasionally lead to that which shocks humanity, and may be said to violate all propriety and all conscience—if such things are done, let the South alone and they will correct the evil. Let our brethren of the South take care of their own domestic institutions and they will do it. (Applause.) They will so govern themselves as to suppress acts of this description, if they are occasionally committed, as perhaps they are, and we must all admit that they are contrary to just conceptions of right and humanity. I have never yet heard of a nation conquered from evil practices, brought to the light of civilization, brought to the light of religion or the knowledge of the Gospel by the bayonet, by the penal laws, or by external persecutions of any kind. It is not by declamation and outcry against a people from those abroad and outside of their territory that you can improve their manners or their morals in any respect. No ; if, standing outside of their territory, you attack the errors of a people, you make them cling to their faults. From a sentiment somewhat excusable—somewhat akin to self-respect and patriotism—they will resist their nation's enemy. Let our brethren of the South alone, gentlemen, and if there be any errors of this kind, they will correct them.

There is but one way in which you can thus leave them to the guidance of their own judgment—by which you can retain them in this Union as our brethren, and perpetuate this glorious Union ; and that is, by resolving—without reference to the political party or faction to which any one of you may belong, without reference to the name, political or otherwise, which you may please to bear—resolving that the man, be he who he may, who advocates the doctrine that negro Slavery is unjust, and ought to be assailed or legislated against, or who agitates the subject of extinguishing negro Slavery in any of its forms as a political hobby, that that man shall be denied your suffrages, and not only denied your suffrages, but that you will select from the ranks of the opposite party, or your own, if necessary, the man you like least, who entertains opposite sentiments, but through whose instrumentality you may be enabled to defeat his election, and to secure in the councils of the nation men who are true to the Constitution, who are lovers of the Union—men who cannot be induced by considerations of imaginary benevolence for a people who really do not desire their aid, to sacrifice or to jeopard in any degree the blessings we enjoy under this Union. May it be perpetual.

(Great and continued cheering.)

◄►

THE REAL QUESTION STATED.

•••

LETTER FROM CHARLES O'CONOR TO A COMMITTEE OF MERCHANTS.

New York, Dec. 20, 1859.

Chas. O'Conor, Esq. : The undersigned, being desirous of circulating as widely as possible, both at the North and at the South, the proceedings of the Union Meeting held at the Academy of Music last evening, intend publishing in pamphlet form, for distribution, a correct copy of the same.

Will you be so kind as to inform us whether this step meets your approval ; and if so, furnish us with a corrected report of your speech delivered by you on that occasion. Yours respectfully

LEITCH, BURNET & CO.,
GEO. W. & JEHIAL READ,
BRUFF, BROTHER & SEAVER,
C. B. HATCH & CO.,
DAVIS, NOBLE & CO.,
(Formerly Furman, Davis & Co.,)
WESSON & COX,
CRONIN, HURXTHAL & SEARS,
ATWATER, MULFORD CO.

Gentlemen : The measure you propose meets my entire approval.

I have long thought that our disputes concerning negro Slavery would soon terminate, if the public mind could be drawn to the true issue, and steadily fixed upon it. To effect this object was the sole aim of my address.

Though its ministers can never permit the law of the land to be questioned by private judgment, there is, nevertheless, such a thing as natural justice. Natural justice has the Divine sanction ; and it is impossible that any human law which conflicts with it should long endure.

Where mental enlightenment abounds, where morality is professed by all, where the mind is free, speech is free, and the press is free, is it possible, in the nature of things, that a law which is *admitted* to conflict with natural justice, and with God's own mandate, should long endure ?

You all will admit that, within certain limits, at least, our Constitution does contain positive guaranties for the preservation of negro Slavery in the old States through all time, unless the local legislatures shall think fit to abolish it. And, consequently, if negro Slavery, however humanely administered or judiciously regulated, be an institution which conflicts with natural justice and with God's law, surely the most vehement and extreme admirers of

John Brown's sentiments are right; and their denunciations against the Constitution, and against the most hallowed names connected with it, are perfectly justifiable.

The friends of truth—the patriotic Americans who would sustain their country's honor against foreign rivalry, and defend their country's interests against all assailants, err greatly when they contend with these men on any point but one. Their general principles cannot be refuted; their logic is irresistible; the error, if any there be, is in their premises. They assert that negro Slavery is unjust. This, and this alone, of all they say, is capable of being fairly argued against.

If this proposition cannot be refuted, our Union cannot endure, and it ought not to endure.

Our negro bondmen can neither be exterminated nor transported to Africa. They are too numerous for either process, and either, if practicable, would involve a violation of humanity. If they were emancipated, they would relapse into barbarism, or a set of negro States would arise in our midst, possessing political equality, and entitled to social equality. The division of parties would soon make the negro members a powerful body in Congress—would place some of them in high political stations, and occasionally let one into the executive chair.

It is in vain to say that this could be endured; it is simply impossible.

What, then, remains to be discussed?

The negro race is upon us. With a Constitution which held them in bondage, our Federal Union might be preserved; but if so holding them in bondage be a thing forbidden by God and Nature, we cannot lawfully so hold them, and the Union must perish.

This is the inevitable result of that conflict which has now reached its climax.

Among us at the north, the sole question for reflection, study, and friendly interchange of thought should be—Is negro Slavery unjust? The rational and dispassionate inquirer will find no difficulty in arriving at my conclusion. It is fit and proper; it is, in its own nature, as an institution, beneficial to both races; and the effect of this assertion is not diminished by our admitting that many faults are practised under it. Is not such the fact in respect to all human laws and institutions?

I am, gentlemen, with great respect, yours truly,
CHARLES O'CONOR.

To Messrs. Leitch, Burnet & Co.; Geo. W. & Jehial Read; Bruff, Brother & Seaver ; C. B. Hatch & Co. ; Davis, Noble & Co. ; Wesson & Cox ; Cronin, Hurxthal & Sears ; Atwater, Mulford & Co.

HERSCHEL V. JOHNSON

ON SLAVERY IN THE TERRITORIES.

On the 7th of July, 1848, while the bill to establish the Territorial Government of Oregon was under consideration in the United States Senate, the Hon. Herschel V. Johnson, then a member of the Senate, from Georgia, and now a candidate for Vice-President on the ticket with Mr. Douglas, made a lengthy speech from which we extract the following :

It remains now to consider the question involved in the amendment proposed by the Senator from Mississippi (Mr. Davis). That question is, whether it is the duty of Congress to guarantee to the slaveholder, who shall remove with his salves into the territory of the United States, the undisputed enjoyment of his property in them, so long as it continues to be a Territory. Or, in other words, whether the inhabitants of a Territory, during their Territorial condition, have the right to prohibit Slavery therein.

For the purpose of this question, it matters not where the power of legislating for the Territory resides—whether exclusively in Congress, or jointly in Congress and the inhabitants, or exclusively in the inhabitants of the Territory; the power is precisely the same—no greater in the hands of one than the other. In no event, can the slaveholder of the South be excluded from settling in such Territory with his property of every description. If the right of exclusive legislation for the Territories belongs to Congress, then I have shown that they have no Constitutional power, either expressed or implied, to prohibit Slavery therein. But suppose that Congress have the right to establish a Territorial Government only, and that then, all further governmental control ceases ; can the Territorial Legislature pass an act prohibiting Slavery? Surely not. For the moment you admit the right to organize a Territorial Government to exist in Congress, you admit, necessarily the subordination of the people of the Territory—their dependence on this Government for an organic law to give them political existence. Hence all their legislation must be in conformity with the organic law; they can pass no act in violation of it—none but such as permits. Since, therefore, Congress has no power, as I have shown, to prohibit Slavery, they cannot delegate such a power to the inhabitants of the Territory; they cannot authorize the Territorial Legislature to do that which they have no power to do. The stream cannot rise higher than its source. This is as true in governments as in physics.

It is idle, however, to discuss this question in this form. For if Congress possess the power to organize temporary governments, it must then possess the power to legislate for the Territories. If they may perform the greater, they may the less; the major includes the minor proposition.

Hence Congress has, in all cases since the foundation of our government, reserved a veto upon the legislation of the territorial governments; *it is absolutely necessary,* in order to restrain them from violations of the Constitution and infringements of the rights of the States, as joint owners of the public lands. If, therefore, the act of the Territorial Government, prohibiting Slavery, should be sent up to Congress for approval, they would be bound to withhold it, upon the ground of its being an act which Congress themselves could not pass.

But suppose the right of legislation for the Territory be in its inhabitants, can they prohibit Slavery ? *Surely not;* and for reasons similar to those which show that Congress cannot.

The Territories are not independent of, but subordinate to, the United States ; and therefore their legislation must be subordinate. Let us look at some of the limitations which this condition imposes. Under the Constitution, "No title of nobility shall be granted by the United States;" "Congress shall make no law respecting the establishment of religion, or pertaining to the free exercise thereof; no religious test shall be required as a qualification to any office or public trust under the United States," etc. It is true, these restrictions do not apply in terms to the Territories ; but will it be contended for a moment that they would have the right by legislation to lay these impositions upon citizens of the States who emigrate thither for settlement ? . . .

Sovereignty follows the ownership of the domain, and therefore the sovereignty over the Territories is in the States in their confederated capacity; hence the reason that the legislation of Congress, as the agent of the States respecting the Territories, must be limited by the object of the trust, the situation and nature of the property to be administered, and the respective rights of the proper owners. Now, if the sovereignty over the Territories is in the States, and the right of legislation not in Congress, but in the inhabitants of the Territories, it is evident that they can have no higher right of legislation than Congress could have ; they must be bound by limitations just mentioned ; and if the prohibition of Slavery in the Territories by Congress be inconsistent with these limitations, its prohibition by the territorial legislature would be so likewise.

If possessing the right of legislation, the inhabitants of the Territories are bound by the limitations to which I have alluded, it may be asked, who holds the check upon their action ? I reply, that it is indispensable for Congress to exercise the veto upon their legislation. Who else shall prevent their passing laws in violation of the equal rights of the States in the Territory, which is the common property of all ? Without the retention of a veto upon the legislation of the Territorial Governments, it would make the inhabitants of the Territory independent of Congress ; aye, it would establish the proposition, that the moment you conquer a people they rise superior to the government that conquers. New-Mexico and California are ours by tieaty; but for all the purposes of this argument, we have acquired them by conquest. To assert, therefore, that they have the right to legislate over all subjects—to prohibit Slavery, despite the consent of the United States—is to say that, by our conquest of them, they become invested with rights superior to those of Congress. The institution of Slavery is *guaranteed* by the Constitution of the United States, and it has *the same protection* thrown around it which guards our citizens against the granting of titles of nobility or the establishment of religion; *therefore Congress would be as much bound* to veto an act of Territorial legislation prohibiting it, as an act violating these rights of every citizen of the Republic. . . .

Mr. Mangum.—This is a free Territory (New-Mexico) I am now speaking about. Suppose a North Carolinian emigrates to New-Mexico with his slaves? they must either be recognized as property, or not; who has the right to determine that question?

Mr. Johnson.—I think that question has already been decided by the late treaty (with Mexico). . . Now, is not Slavery in the United States a political as well as a municipal institution? It is municipal, in that its entire control and continuance belong to the State in which it exists; and it is political, because it is recognized by the organic law of the Confederacy, and cannot be changed or altered by Congress, without an amendment to the Constitution; and because it is a fundamental law, that three-fifths of the slaves are represented in the National Legislature. Being political, upon the execution of the Treaty of Cession with Mexico, it extended *eo instanti*, over the Territories of New-Mexico and California. Then, I say, if a fellow-citizen of the Senator from North Carolina (Mr. Mangum) were to remove with his slaves into New-Mexico, his right to their use and service is guaranteed by the Constitution of the United States, and no power on earth can deprive him of them, . . It is a misapplication of terms to speak of prohibiting Slavery in the territory of the United States. It already exists in contemplation of law, and the legislation proposed (prohibition) amounts to abolition. . . .

But suppose, Mr. President, you have the right to prohibit Slavery in the Territories of the United States, what high political consideration requires you to exercise it? All must see, that it cannot be effected without producing *a popular convulsion which will probably dissolve this Union.*

"CAPITAL SHOULD OWN LABOR."

Mr. Herschel V. Johnson made a speech at a Democratic meeting in Philadelphia on the 17th of September, 1856, in which the newspapers report him as having said, among other things:

"We believe that capital should own labor; is there any doubt that there must be a laboring class everywhere? In all countries and under every form of social organization there' must be a laboring class—a class of men who get their living by the sweat of their brow; and then there must be another class that controls and directs the capital of the country."

MR. JOHNSON'S VIEWS ON POPULAR SOVEREIGNTY.

After the adjournment of the Democratic National Convention from Charleston to Baltimore a Democratic State Convention met at Milledgeville, Ga., on the 4th of June, to take action in regard to the secession of most of the Georgia delegates at Charleston. It seems that a Business Committee of 24 was appointed, of which Herschel V. Johnson was one. This Committee disagreed as to the propriety of appointing new delegates to Baltimore, the friends of the Seceders opposing and a few who preferred to see Douglas elected to a dissolution of the party, favoring that step; and the consequence was, that two reports were presented—

a majority one by twenty members of the Committee, and a minority one by four members. which latter division included Herschel V. Johnson who, as chairman, introduced the minority report.

The two reports were discussed by various persons, Mr. Johnson defending his, and Howell Cobb, Secretary of the Treasury, acting as pacificator. The latter gentleman stated that there was "no difference in the principles enunciated in both the majority and minority reports. There were only two minor differences; one was, that the majority report indorsed the secession from the Charleston Convention—while the minority neither indorsed nor commended the action of the Georgia delegates there."

The result was, that the majority report was adopted by a vote of 299 to 41, when the minority, under the lead of Mr. Johnson, seceded, organized another Convention and appointed a full delegation to Baltimore, one-half of whom were admitted to seats by the Convention, together with one-half of the other delegation.

The following is the report presented to the regular Convention by Mr. Johnson:

MINORITY REPORT.

Resolved, That we reaffirm the Cincinnati Platform, with the following additional propositions:

1st. That the citizens of the United States have an equal right to settle with *their property of any kind*, in the organized Territories of the United States, and that under the decision of the Supreme Court of the United States in the case of Dred Scott, which we recognize as the correct exposition of the Constitution in this particular, *slave property stands upon the same footing as all other descriptions of property*, and that *neither the General Government*, NOR ANY TERRITORIAL GOVERNMENT, can *destroy* or *impair* the right to *slave property* in the common Territories, any more than the right to *any other description of property;* that property of all kinds, slaves as well as any other species of property, in the Territories, stand upon the same equal and broad Constitutional basis, and subject to like principles of *recognition and protection in the* LEGISLATIVE, *judicial* and *executive departments of the Government.*

2d. That we will support any man who may be nominated by the Baltimore Convention, for the Presidency, who *holds the principles* set forth in the foregoing proposition, and who will give them *his indorsement*, and that we will *not* hold ourselves bound to support any man, who may be the nominee, who entertains principles *inconsistent* with those set forth in the above proposition, or *who denies that slave property* in the Territories does stand on *an equal footing*, and on the *same Constitutional basis* of *other descriptions of property.*

In view of the fact that a large majority of the delegates from Georgia felt it to be their duty to withdraw from the late Democratic Convention at Charleston, thereby depriving this State of her vote therein, according to the decision of said Convention.

Resolved, That this Convention will appoint twenty delegates—four from the State at large, and two from each Congressional District—to represent the Democratic party of Georgia, in the adjourned Convention at Baltimore, on the 18th inst., and that said delegates be and they are hereby instructed to *present the foregoing propositions, and ask their adoption by the National Democratic Convention.* HERSCHEL V. JOHNSON, THOS. P. SAFFOLD, H. K. McCAY, A. COLVARD.

TREASON AND DISUNION AVOWED.

In 1856, as now, many of the leading Statesmen and editors of the Democratic party in the Southern States uttered predictions of Disunion, made arguments for Disunion and very solemn threats of Disunion in case they should be beaten in the Presidential Election. Mr. Slidell, Senator from Louisiana, and the particular friend and champion of Mr. Buchanan, declared in 1856 that "if Fremont should be elected, the Union would be dissolved." Mr. Toombs, of Georgia, said "that in such an event the Union would be dissolved, and ought to be dissolved." Mr. Butler, of S. C., a leading member of the U. S. Senate and chairman of the Judiciary Committee in 1856, said:

> When Fremont is elected, we must rely upon what we have—a good State Government. Every Governor of the South should call the Legislature of his State together, and have measures of the South decided upon. *If they did not, and submit to the degradation, they would deserve the fate of slaves. I should advise my Legislature to go at the tap of the drum.*

Mr. Keitt, of S. C., made a fiery speech at Lynchburgh, Va., in 1856 and in view of the apprehended election of Col. Fremont, exclaimed:

> I tell you now, that if Fremont is elected, *adherence to the Union is treason to liberty.* (Loud cheers.) I tell you now, that the southern man who will submit to his election is a *traitor and a coward.* (Enthusiastic cheers.)

This speech was indorsed as "sound doctrine" by the Hon. John B. Floyd, of Va., now Mr. Buchanan's Secretary of War.

Mr. Preston S. Brooks was complimented for his attempted (and nearly successful) assassination of Senator Sumner, by an ovation at the hands of his constituents at which Senators Butler, S. C., and Toombs, of Georgia, assisted. The hero of the day, Mr. Brooks, made a speech on the occasion from which the following is an extract;

> [We have the issue upon us now; and how are we to meet it? I tell you, fellow-citizens, from the bottom of my heart, that the only mode which I think available for meeting it *is just to tear the Constitution of the United States, trample it under foot, and form a Southern Confederacy every State of which will be a slaveholding State.* (Loud and prolonged cheers) I believe it, as I stand in the face of my Maker; I believe it on my responsibility to you as your honored representative, that *the only hope of the South is in the South, and that the only available means of making that hope effective is to cut asunder the bonds that tie us together, and take our separate position in the family of nations.* [These are my opinions. They have always been my opinions. *I have been a disunionist from the time I could think.* . . .
> Now, fellow-citizens, I have told you very frankly and undisguisedly, that I believe *the only hope of the South is in dissolving the bonds which connect us with the Government—in separating the living body from the dead carcass.* If I was the commander of an army, *I never would post a sentinel who would not swear that Slavery is right."* . . .
> I speak on my individual responsibility: *If Fremont be elected President of the United States, I am for the people in their majesty rising above the law and leaders, taking the power into their own hands, going by concert or not by concert, and laying the strong arm of southern freemen upon the Treasury and archives of the Government.* (Applause.)

[The Charleston "Mercury," the recognized organ of the South Carolina Democracy, in a recent article says:

> *Upon the policy of dissolving the Union, of separating the South from her northern enemies, and establishing a southern Confederacy, parties, presses, politicians, and people, are a unit. There is not a single public man in her limits, not one of her present representatives or senators in Congress who is not pledged to the lips in favor of disunion.* Indeed, we well remember that one of the most prominent leaders of the coöperation party, when taunted with submission, rebuked the thought by saying, "*that in opposing secession, he only took a step backward to strike a blow more deadly against the Union.*"]

In the autumn of 1856, Henry A. Wise, then Governor of Virginia, told the people of that State that—

> The South could not, without degradation, submit to the election of a Black Republican President. To tell me we should submit to the election of a Black Republican, under circumstances like these, is to tell me that Virginia and the fourteen Slave States are already subjugated and degraded, [cheers ;] that the southern people are without spirit, and without purpose to defend the rights they know and dare not maintain. [Cheers] If you submit to the election of Fremont, you will prove what Seward and Burlingame said to be true—that the South cannot be kicked out of the Union.

During the Presidential campaign of 1856, the Washington correspondent of the "New Orleans Delta," a journal high in the confidence of the Pierce administration, wrote:

> It is already arranged, in the event of Fremont's election, or a failure to elect by the people, to call the Legislatures of Virginia, South Carolina and Georgia 'to concert measures to withdraw from the Union before Fremont can get possession of the Army and navy and the purse-strings of government. *Governor Wise is actively at work already in the matter. The South can rely on the President in the emergency contemplated.* The question now is, whether the people of the South will sustain their leaders.

At a Union meeting recently held at Knoxville, Tenn., Judge Daily, formerly of Georgia, made a violent southern speech, in the course of which he said:

> During the Presidential contest, Governor Wise had addressed letters to all the southern governors, and that *the one to the Governor of Florida had been shown him, in which Gov. Wise said he had an army in readiness to prevent Fremont from taking his seat* if elected, and asking the coöperation of those to whom he wrote:

Charles J. Faulkner, formerly a Representative in Congress from Virginia, Chairman of the Democratic Congressional Committee, in 1856, and now Minister to France, at a recent Democratic meeting held in Virginia, over which ho presided, said:

> When that noble and gallant son of Virginia, Henry A. Wise, declared, as was said he did in October, 1856, that if Fremont should be elected, HE WOULD SEIZE THE NATIONAL ARSENAL AT HARPER'S FERRY, how few would, at that time, have justified so bold and decided a measure? *It is the fortune of some great and gifted minds to see far in advance of their contemporaries* Should William H. Seward be elected in 1860, where is the man now in our midst, *who would not call for the impeachment of a Governor of Virginia who would silently suffer*

that armory to pass under the control of such an Executive head?

The *Richmond Enquirer*, long one of the leading exponents of the Southern Democracy, in commenting on the murderous assault on Senator Sumner, said :

Sumner, and Sumner's friends, must be punished and silenced. Either such wretches must be hung or put in the penitentiary, or the South should prepare at once to quit the Union.

If Fremont is elected, the Union will not last an hour after Mr. Pierce's term expires.

If Fremont is elected, it will be the duty of the South to dissolve the Union and form a Southern Confederacy.

Let the South present a compact and undivided front. Let her, if possible, detach Pennsylvania and southern Ohio, southern Indiana, and southern Illinois, from the North, and make the highlands between the Ohio and the lakes the dividing line. Let the South treat with California ; and, if necessary, ally herself with Russia, with Cuba, and Brazil.

Senator Iverson, of Georgia, in a speech made to his constituents previous to the assembling of the second session of the 36th Congress, said :

Slavery must be maintained—in the Union, if possible ; out of it. if necessary : peaceably, if we may, forcibly if we must. . . . .
In a confederated government of their own, the Southern States would enjoy sources of wealth, prosperity, and power, unsurpassed by any nation on earth. No neutrality laws would restrain our adventurous sons. Our expanding policy would stretch far beyond present limits. Central America would join her destiny to ours, and so would Cuba, now withheld from us by the voice and votes of Abolition enemies.

During the late memorable contest for Speaker, the same Senator remarked, as follows :

Sir, I will tell you what I would do, if I had the control of the southern members of this House and the other, when you elect John Sherman. If I had control of the public sentiment, the very moment you elect John Sherman, thus giving to the South the example of insult as well as injury, I would walk, every one of us, out of the Halls of this Capitol, and consult our constituents ; and I would never enter again until I was bade to do so by those who had the right to control me. Sir, I go further than that. I would counsel my constituents instantly to dissolve all political ties with a party and a people who thus trample on our rights. That is what I would do.

In an elaborate speech delivered later in the session by the same Senator, he said :

Sir, there is but one path of safety to the South ; but one mode of preserving her institution of domestic Slavery ; and that is a confederacy of States having no incongruous and opposing elements—a confederacy of Slave States alone, with homogeneous language, laws, interests, and institutions. Under such a confederated Republic, with a Constitution which should shut out the approach and entrance of all incongruous and conflicting elements, which should protect the institution from change, and keep the whole nation ever bound to its preservation, by an unchangeable fundamental law, the fifteen Slave States, with their power of expansion, would present to the world the most free, prosperous, and happy nation on the face of the wide earth.
Sir, with these views, and with the firm conviction which I have entertained for many years, and which recent events have only seemed to confirm, that the " irrepressible conflict " between the two sections must and will go on, and with accumulated speed, and must end, in the Union, with the total extinction of African Slavery in the southern States, that I have announced my determination to approve and urge the southern States to dissolve the Union upon the election of a Black Republican to the Presidency of the United States, by a sectional northern party, and upon a platform of opposition and hostility to southern Slavery.

Senator Brown, of Mississippi, in a recent speech to his constituents, said

want Cuba want Tamaulipas, Potosi, and one or two other Mexican States ; and *I want them all for the same reason—for the planting and spreading of Slavery.* And a footing in Central America will powerfully aid us in acquiring those other States. Yes ; *I want these countries for the spread of Slavery.* I would spread

the blessings of Slavery, *like the religion of our Divine Master*, to the uttermost ends of the earth ; and, rebellious and wicked as the Yankees have been, *I would even extend it to them.* . . . .
Whether we can obtain the Territory while the Union lasts, I do not know ; I fear we cannot. But I would make an honest effort, and if we failed, I would go out of the Union, and try it there. I speak plainly—I would make a refusal to acquire territory, because it was to be slave territory, a cause for disunion, just as I would make the refusal to admit a new State, because it was to be a Slave State, a cause for disunion. . . . .
The election of Mr. Seward, or any other man of his party, is not, *per se,* justifiable ground for dissolving the *Union.* But the *act* of putting the Government in the hands of men who mean to use it for our subjugation, ought to be resisted, even to the disruption of every tie that binds us to the Union.

Jefferson Davis, U. S. Senator from Mississippi, in an address to the people of his State, July 6, 1859, said :

For myself, I say, as I said on a former occasion, in the contingency of the election of a President on the platform of Mr. Seward's Rochester speech, let the Union be dissolved. Let the " great, but not the greatest of evils," come.

Mr. Clay, of Alabama, in a recent speech in the Senate, contemplating the possible defeat of his party in the coming Presidential contest, said :

I make no predictions, no promise for my State ; but, in conclusion, will only say, that if she is faithful to the pledges she has made and principles she has professed—if she is true to her own interest and her own honor—if she is not recreant to all that State pride, integrity and duty demand—she will never submit to your authority. I will add, that unless she and all the southern States of this Union, with perhaps but two, or, at most, three exceptions, are not faithless to the pledges they have given, *they will never submit to the government of a President professing yo r political faith and elected by your sectional majority.*

When Mr. Clay had taken his seat, Mr. Gwin, of California, made a speech in which he declared it as " the inevitable result that the South would prepare for resistance in the event of the election of a Republican President."

On the 24th of January, 1860, the Hon. Robert Toombs, of Georgia, made a violent speech in the Senate, on Mr. Douglas' Resolution directing the Judiciary Committee to report a bill for the protection of each State and Territory against invasion from any other State or Territory. Mr. Toombs commenced his speech by the announcement that the country was in the midst of civil war, adding, " I feel and know that a large body of these Senators are enemies of my country." Mr. Toombs proceeded in an elaborate and vituperative speech to prove that the people of the North had violated the Constitution, by refusing to capture and return fugitive slaves to their masters in the South.

Sir, I have but little more to add—nothing for myself. I feel that I have no need to pledge my poor services to this great cause—to my country. My State has spoken for herself. Nine years ago a convention of her people met and declared that her connection with this government depended upon the faithful execution of this fugitive slave law, and her full enjoyment of equal rights in the common Territories. I have shown that the one contingency has already arrived ; the other waits only the success of the Republican party in the approaching Presidential election. I was a member of that convention, and stood then and now pledged to its action. I have faithfully labored to avert these calamities. I will yet labor until this last contingency happens, faithfully, honestly, and to the best of my poor abilities. When that time comes, freemen of Georgia redeem your pledge ; I am ready to redeem mine. Your honor is involved—your faith is plighted. I know you feel a stain as a wound ; your peace, your social system, your firesides are involved. *Never permit this Federal Government to pass into the traitorous hands of the Black Republican party.* It has already declared war against you and your institutions. It every day commits acts of war against you: it has already compelled you to arm for your defense. Listen to "no vain babblings," to no treacherous jargon about "overt acts;" they have already been committed. Defend yourselves; the enemy is at your door; wait not to meet him at the hearthstone—meet him at the door-sill, and drive him from the temple of liberty, or pull down its pillars and involve him in a common ruin.

Senator Clingman, of North Carolina, in a recent speech, says that "there are hundreds of disunionists in the South now, where there was not one ten years ago," and that in some of the States the men who would willingly see the Union dissolved are in the majority. In considering the proper cause for disunion, Mr. Clingman continues:

In my judgment, the election of the Presidential candidate of the Black Republican party will furnish that cause. . . .

No other "*overt act*" can so imperatively demand resistance on our part as the simple election of their candidate. Their organization is one of avowed hostility, and they come against us as *enemies*. . . .

The objections are not personal merely to this Senator (Mr. Seward), but apply equally to any member of the party elected by it. It has, in fact, been suggested that, as a matter of prudence, for the first election they should choose a southern free-soiler. Would the Colonies have submitted more willingly to Benedict Arnold than to Lord Cornwallis?

Mr. Curry, of Alabama, a member of the House of Representatives, in a recent speech, says:

However distasteful it may be to my friend from New York (Mr. Clark), however much it may revolt the public sentiment or conscience of this country, I am not ashamed or afraid publicly to avow that the election of William H. Seward or Salmon P. Chase, or any such representative of the Republican party, upon a sectional platform, ought to be resisted to the disruption of every tie that binds this Confederacy together. (Applause on the Democratic side of the House.)

Mr. Pugh, of the same State, made a speech in the House, in which he said:

If, with the character of the Government well defined, and the rights and privileges of the parties to the compact clearly asserted by the Democratic party, the Black Republicans get possession of the Government, then the question is fully presented, whether the Southern States will remain in the Union, as subject and degraded colonies, or will they withdraw and establish a Southern Confederacy of coëqual homogeneous sovereigns?

In my judgment, the latter is the only course compatible with the honor, equality, and safety of the South; and the sooner it is known and acted upon the better for all parties to the compact.

The truest conservatism and wisest statesmanship demand a speedy termination of all association with such confederates, and the formation of another Union of States, homogeneous in population, institutions, interests, and pursuits.

Mr. Moore, of the same State, said:

I do not concur with the declaration made yesterday by the gentleman from Tennessee, that the election of a Black Republican to the Presidency was not cause for a dissolution of the Union. Whenever a President is elected by a fanatical majority at the North, those whom I represent, as I believe, and the gallant State which I in part represent, are ready, let the consequences be what they may, to fall back on their reserved rights, and say, "As to this Union, we have no longer any lot or part in it."

Mr. Bonham, a member of the House from South Carolina, said:

As to disunion, upon the election of a Black Republican, I can speak for no one but myself and those I have here the honor to represent; and I say, without hesitation, that, upon the election of Mr. Seward, or any other man who indorses and proclaims the doctrines held by him and his party—call him by what name you please—I am in favor of an immediate dissolution of the Union. And, sir,

I think I speak the sentiments of my own constituents and the State of South Carolina, when I say so.

Mr. Crawford, of Georgia, said:

Now, in regard to the election of a Black Republican President, I have this to say, and I speak the sentiment of every Democrat on this floor from the State of Georgia: we will never submit to the inauguration of a Black Republican President. (Applause from the Democratic benches, and hisses from the Republicans.) I repeat it, sir—and I have authority to say so—that no Democratic representative from Georgia on this floor will ever submit to the inauguration of a Black Republican President. (Renewed applause and hisses.) . . . The most confiding of them all are, sir, for "equality in the Union or independence out of it;" having lost all hope in the former, I am for "INDEPENDENCE NOW AND INDEPENDENCE FOREVER!"

Mr. Gartrell, of the same State, said:

Just so sure as the Republican party succeeds in electing a sectional man, upon their sectional, Anti-Slavery platform, breathing destruction and death to the rights of my people, just so sure, in my judgment, the time will have come when the South must and will take an unmistakable and decided action, and that then, "he who dallies is a dastard, and he who doubts is damned." I need not tell what I, as a Southern man, will do—I think I may safely speak for the masses of the people of Georgia —that when that event happens, they, in my judgment, will consider it an overt act, a declaration of war, and meet immediately in convention, to take into consideration the mode and measure of redress. That is my position; and if that be treason to the Government, make the most of it.

Mr. McRae, formerly Governor of Mississippi, now a member of the House of Representatives, recently spoke in that body as follows:

I said to my constituents, and to the people at the capital of my State, on my way here, that if such an event did occur, while it would be their duty to determine the course which the State would pursue, it would be my privilege to counsel with them as to what I believed to be the proper course; and I said to them, what I say now, and will always say in such an event, that my counsel would be to take independence out of the Union in preference to the loss of constitutional rights, and consequent degradation and dishonor in it. That is my position, and it is the position which I know the Democratic party of the State of Mississippi will maintain.

Mr. De Jarnette, a member of the House from Virginia, says:

Thus William H. Seward stands before the country a perjured traitor; and yet that man, with hands stained with the blood of our citizens, we are asked to elect President of the United States. You may elect him President of the North, but of the South never. Whatever the event may be, others may differ; but Virginia, in view of her ancient renown, in view of her illustrious dead, and in view of her *sic semper tyrannis*, will resist his authority. I have done.

Mr. Leake, also of Virginia, declares:

Virginia has the right, when she pleases, to withdraw from the Confederacy. (Applause from the Democratic benches.) . . . That is her doctrine. We will not fight in the Union, but quit it the instant we think proper to do so.

Mr. Singleton, of Mississippi, says:

You ask me when will the time (for disunion) come; when will the South be united? It will be when you elect a Black Republican—Hale, Seward, or Chase—President of the United States. Whenever you undertake to place such a man to preside over the destinies of the South, you may expect to see us undivided and indivisible friends, and to see all parties of the South arrayed to resist his inauguration.

We can never quietly stand by and permit the control of the army and navy to go into the hands of a Black Republican President.

Gov. Letcher, of Virginia, in his recent message to the Legislature of his State, avows the rankest disunion and revolutionary sentiments. In this document, he declares that if a Republican President is elected in 1860,

It is useless to attempt to conceal the fact that, in the present temper of the Southern people, *it cannot be and will not be submitted to.* The "irrepressible conflict" doctrine, announced and advocated by the ablest and most distinguished leader of the Republican party, is an open declaration of war against the institution of African Slavery, wherever it exists; and I would be disloyal to Virginia and the South if I did not declare that the election of such a man, entertaining such sentiments, and advocating such doctrines, *ought to be resisted by the slaveholding States.* The idea of permitting such a man to have the control and direction of the army and navy of the United States, and the appointment of high judicial and executive officers, postmasters included, *cannot be entertained by the South for a moment.*

The Hon. William L. Yancy, a leading and prominent Democratic politician of Alabama, and formerly member of Congress from that State, wrote the following letter in 1858, which the *Washington States,* a Democratic Journal, recently published under the title of the "Scarlet Letter:"

MONTGOMERY, *June* 15, 1858.

DEAR SIR: Your kind favor of the 15th is received.

I hardly agree with you that a general movement can be made that will clear out the Augean stable. If the Democracy were overthrown, it would result in giving place to a greater and hungrier swarm of flies.

The remedy of the South is not in such a process. It is in a diligent organization of her true men for prompt resistance to the next aggression. It must come in the nature of things. No national party can save us; no sectional party can ever do it. But if we could do as our fathers did—organize committees of safety all over the Cotton States (and it is only in them that we can hope for any effective movement)—we shall fire the Southern heart, instruct the Southern mind, give courage to each other, and at the PROPER MOMENT, *by one organized concerted action, we can precipitate the Cotton States into a revolution.*

The idea has been shadowed forth in the South by Mr. Ruffin; has been taken up and recommended in *The Advertiser* (Published at Montgomery, Alabama), under the name of "League of United Southerners," who, keeping up their old party relations on all other questions, will hold the Southern issue paramount, and will influence parties, legislatures, and statesmen. I have no time to enlarge, but to suggest merely.

In haste, yours, etc., W. L. YANCEY.

To JAMES S. SLAUGHTER, Esq.

The Montgomery (Ala.) *Confederation* thus gives the record of the leading secession delegates from the Charleston Convention from that State. It says:

No one can be deceived as to what are the objects of the Charleston Convention. Listen to what their men say:

" I want the Cotton States precipitated into a revolution."—*Wm. L. Yancey.*

" If I had the power, I would dissolve this Government in two minutes."—*J. T. Morgan.*

" Let us break up this rotten, stinking, and oppressive Government."—*George Gayle.*

" Resistance! Resistance to death against the Government is what we want now."—*David Hubbard.*

AN ANTI-SLAVERY VIEW OF DISUNION.

The following Resolutions, prepared by Wm. Lloyd Garrison, were adopted at a Convention of the non-voting Abolitionists (better known as Garrisonians), at Albany, New-York, on the 2d of February, 1859:

Whereas (to quote the language of John Quincy Adams),

"The bargain between Freedom and Slavery contained in the Constitution of the United States, is morally and politically vicious, inconsistent with the principles on which alone our Revolution can be justified; cruel and oppressive, by riveting the chains of Slavery; and grossly unequal and impolitic, by admitting that Slaves are at once enemies to be kept in subjection, property to be secured and returned to their owners, and persons not to be represented themselves, but for whom their masters are privileged with nearly a double share of representation;" and

Whereas (to quote the language of Wm. Ellery Channing) "We in the Free States cannot fly from the shame or guilt of the Institution of Slavery, while there are provisions of the Constitution binding us to give it support. On this subject our fathers, in framing the Constitution, swerved from the right. We, their children, see the path of duty more clearly than they, and must walk in it. No blessings of the Union can be a compensation for taking part in the enslaving of our fellow-creatures;" and

Whereas (to quote the language of Josiah Quincy, Sen.), "The arm of the Union is the very sinew of the subjection of the Slaves; it is the Slaveholder's main strength; its continuance is his forlorn hope;" and

Whereas (to quote the language of Mr. Underwood, of Kentucky, as uttered on the floor of Congress), "The Dissolution of the Union, making the Ohio River and Mason and Dixon's line the boundary line, is the Dissolution of Slavery. It had been the common practice for Southern men to get up on this floor and say, 'Touch this subject and we will Dissolve the Union as a remedy.' Their remedy was the destruction of the thing which they wished to save, and any sensible man could see it;" and

Whereas (to quote the language of Mr. Arnold, of Tennessee, on the same occasion), "The South has nothing to rely on, if the Union be Dissolved; for, supposing that Dissolution to be effected, a million of Slaves are ready to rise and strike for Freedom at the first tap of the drum:" therefore,

1. *Resolved,* That in advocating the Dissolution of the Union, the Abolitionists are justified by every precept of the Gospel, by every principle of morality, by every claim of humanity; that such a Union is a "Covenant with Death," which ought to be annulled, and " an agreement with Hell," which a just God cannot permit to stand; and that it is the imperative and paramount duty of all who would keep their souls from blood-guiltiness, to deliver the oppressed out of the hand of the spoiler, and usher in the day of Jubilee; to seek its immediate overthrow by all righteous instrumentalities.

2. *Resolved,* That (to quote the language of William H. Seward) " they who think this agitation is accidental, unnecessary, the work of interested or fanatical agitators, and therefore ephemeral, mistake the case altogether: it is an Irrepressible Conflict between opposing and enduring forces · and it means that the United States must and will, sooner or later, become either entirely a Slaveholding Nation or entirely a Free Labor Nation. It is the failure to apprehend this great truth that induces so many unsuccessful attempts at final Compromise between the Free and Slave States; and it is the existence of this great fact that renders all such pretended Compromises, when made, vain and ephemeral." Therefore,

3. *Resolved,* That no matter how sincerely or zealously any Political Party may be struggling with side issues, in relation to Slavery, to prevent its extension, or otherwise cripple its power, while standing within the Union and sanctioning its Pro-Slavery Compromises, and refusing to attack the Institution itself, its position is morally indefensible; it rests upon a sandy foundation; its testimonies are powerless, and its example fatal to the cause of liberty: hence we cannot give it any support.

4. *Resolved,* That "better a thousand times that all North America should be obliterated by a concurrence of the Atlantic and Pacific Oceans, as a dead, revenging sea over buried Cities, than that we, after all our light and Liberty, should live only by removing the truth that gave us being, or should set the example to a terrified and struggling world of a Nation claiming and daring to exist only by sustained and sanctified oppression."

THE POWER OF THE SUPREME COURT.

In view of the Dred Scott *dicta* and other encroachments upon the Liberties of the People and the rights of the States, that may well be apprehended from future decisions of a Federal partisan Judiciary, the opinions of the leaders of the old Jeffersonian Republican party on the powers and duties of the Supreme Court become matter of public interest.

OPINIONS OF THOMAS JEFFERSON.

In a letter to John Adams, dated Sept. 11, 1804, Mr. Jefferson says:

You seemed to think that it devolved on the Judges to decide on the validity of the Sedition Law. But nothing in the Constitution has given them a right to decide for the Executive, more than the Executive to decide for them. Both magistrates are equally independent in the sphere of action assigned to them. The Judges, believing the law constitutional, had a right to pass a sentence of fine and imprisonment, because the power was placed in their hands by the Constitution. But the Executive, believing the law to be unconstitutional, were bound to remit the execution of it, because that power had been confided to them by the Constitution."

Again, in a letter to Judge Roane, dated Poplar Forest, Sept. 6, 1819, Mr. Jefferson remarks:

In denying the right they usurp in exclusively explaining the Constitution, I go further than you do, if I understand rightly your quotation from the *Federalist,* of an opinion that " The Judiciary is the last resort in relation to the other departments of the Government, but not in relation to the rights of the parties to the compact under which the Judiciary is derived." If this opinion be sound, then indeed is our Constitution a complete *felo de se.* For intending to establish three departments, coördinate and independent, that they might check and balance one another, it has given, according to this opinion, to one of them alone the right to prescribe rules for the government of the others, and to that one, too, which is unelected by and independent of the nation. . . . . The Constitution, on this hypothesis, is a mere thing of wax, in the hands of the Judiciary, which they may twist and shape into any form they please. It should be remembered, as an eternal truth in politics, that whatever power in any government is independent, is absolute also ; in theory only at first, while the spirit of the people is up, but in practice as fast as that relaxes. Independence can be trusted nowhere but with the people in mass. They are inherently independent of all but moral law. My construction of the Constitution is very different from that you quote. It is that each department is truly independent of the others, and has an equal right to decide for itself what is the meaning of the Constitution in the cases submitted to its action, and especially where it is to act ultimately and without appeal.

In a letter to Mr. Jarvis, dated Monticello, Sept. 28, 1820, Mr. Jefferson says:

. . . . You seem, in pages 84 and 148, to consider the Judges as the ultimate arbiters of all constitutional questions—a very dangerous doctrine indeed, and one which would place us under the despotism of an oligarchy. Our judges are as honest as other men, and not more so. They have, with others, the same passions for party, for power, and the privilege of their corps. Their maxim is, *" boni judicis est ampliare jurisdictionem,"* and their power the more dangerous as they are in office for life, and not responsible, as the other functionaries are, to the elective control. The Constitution has erected no such single tribunal, knowing that, to whatever hands confided, with the corruptions of time and party, its members would become despots. It has more wisely made all the departments co-equal and co-sovereign within themselves.

Under date of Montecello, Dec. 25, 1820, he writes to Thomas Ritchie as follows:

. . . . The Judiciary of the United States is the subtle corps of sappers and miners constantly working under-ground to undermine the foundations of our confederated fabric. They are construing our Constitution from a coördination of a general and special government to a general and supreme one alone.

On the 18th of August, 1821, Mr. Jefferson writes to Mr. C. Hammond, as follows:

It has long, however, been my opinion, and I have never shrunk from its expression, that the germ of dissolution of our Federal Government is in the constitution of the Federal Judiciary—an irresponsible body, working like gravity by night and by day, gaining a little to-day and a little to-morrow, and advancing its noiseless step, like a thief, over the field of jurisdiction, until all shall be usurped from the States, and the Government of all be consolidated into one. To this I am opposed ; because, when all government, domestic and foreign, in little as in great things, shall be drawn to Washington as the centre of all power, it will render powerless the checks provided of one Government on another, and will become as venal and oppressive as the Government from which we separated. It will be as in Europe, where every man must be either pike or gudgeon, hammer or anvil. Our functionaries and theirs are wares from the same workshop, made of the same materials, and by the same hand. If the States look with apathy on this silent descent of their Government into the gulf which is to swallow all, we have only to weep over the human character, formed uncontrollable but by a rod of iron, and the blasphemers of man as incapable of self-government, become his true historians.

In a letter to Judge Johnson, dated Monticello, March 4, 1820, he says—

I cannot lay down my pen without recurring to one of the subjects of my former letter, for, in truth, there is no danger I apprehend so much as the consolidation of our Government by the noiseless, and therefore unalarming, instrumentality of the Supreme Court. This is the form in which Federalism now arrays itself.

In a letter dated June 12, same year, he says,

The practice of Judge Marshall, of traveling out of his case to prescribe what the law would be in a moot case not before the court is very irregular and very censurable.

In writing to Mr W. H. Torrance, June 11, 1815, Mr. Jefferson says:

The second question, whether the judges are invested with exclusive authority to decide on the constitutionality of a law, has been heretofore a subject of consideration with me in the exercise of official duties. Certainly there is not a word in the Constitution which has given that power to them more than to the Executive or Legislative branches. Questions of property, of character, and of crime, being ascribed to the judges through a definite course of legal proceeding, laws involving such questions, belong, of course, to them ; and as they decide on them ultimately, and without appeal, they, of course, decide for *themselves.* The constitutional validity of the law or laws again prescribing executive action, and to be administered by that branch ultimately, and without appeal, the Executive must decide for *themselves,* also, whether, under the Constitution, they are valid or not. So also, as to laws governing the proceedings of the Legislature, that body must judge *for itself* the constitutionality of the law, and equally without appeal or control from its coördinate branches. And, in general, the branch which is to act ultimately, and without appeal on any law, is the rightful expositor of the validity of the law, uncontrolled by the opinions of the other coördinate authorities.

John Taylor, of Caroline, Va., who used in his day to speak and write "as one having authority" in the old Jeffersonian Republican party, in an essay entitled " New Views of the Constitution," says :

The perseverance of the gentleman in favor of a National Government proves that the subject was thoroughly considered; and the solemn preference of the Federal form demonstrates that no construction by which the preference will be frustrated can be just. Its basis was State sovereignty, compatible with a federal limited Government, but incompatible with a supreme National Government. Hence State Sovereignty was denied by the gentlemen who proposed a National Government. This sovereignty is the foundation of all the powers reserved to the States. Unless they are sustained by it, they are baseless. State legislative, executive, and judicial powers, must all or none flow from this source. All are necessary to sustain the State Republican Governments. Subject either to a master, and the others become subject to the same master. If the State judicial power, as flowing from State sovereignty, is not independent, State legislative and executive power cannot be independent, because all rest upon the same foundation; and because if a supreme federal Judiciary can control State Courts, it can also control State Legislatures and Executives. Thus a federal form of Government would be rejected, though it was established, and a National Government would be established, though it was rejected. . . . .

The legal features of the Constitution, in relation to judges, is expressed in the sixth article: "The Constitution is the *supreme law* of the land, and the judges in *every State* are to be bound thereby." Can the judgments of the Federal court be a supreme law over this supreme law? Is there no difference between the supremacy of a Federal court over inferior Federal courts, and the supremacy of the Constitution over all courts? The supremacy of the Constitution is a guaranty of the independent powers, within their respective spheres, allowed by the Federalist to the State and Federal Governments. A supremacy in the court might abridge or alter these spheres. The State judges are bound by the Constitution and by an oath to obey the supremacy of the Constitution, and not even required to obey the supremacy of the Federal court. Why are all the departments of the State and Federal Governments equally bound to obey the supremacy of the Constitution? Because the State and Federal Governments were considered as checking or balancing departments. Had either been considered as subordinate to a supremacy in the other, it would have been tyrannical to require it by an oath to support the supremacy of the Constitution, and also to break that oath by yielding to the usurped supremacy of the other.

During the administration of John Adams, the Judiciary system was remodeled in such way as to create a large number of Circuit Judgeships, and to make the Supreme Court simply a Court of Appeal from the inferior jurisdictions. After the election of Mr. Jefferson, with a Republican (Democratic) majority in Congress the act was repealed.

During the debate in the Senate, which was protracted, on this repeal bill, Mr. Jackson of Georgia, said :

We have been asked if we are afraid of having an army of judges? For myself, I am more afraid of an army of judges under the patronage of the President, than of an army of soldiers. The former can do us more harm. They may deprive us of our liberties, if attached to the Executive, from their decisions; and from the tenure of office contended for, we cannot remove them; while the soldier, however he may act, is enlisted, or if not enlisted, only subsisted for two years ; whilst the judge is enlisted for life, for his salary cannot be taken from him.—*See Annals of Congress*, 1801-2, *page* 47.

During the same discussion, Mr. Mason, of Virginia, said :

The objects of courts of law, as I understand them, are to settle questions of right between suitors, to enforce obedience to the laws, and to protect the citizens against the oppressive use of power in the Executive offices. Not to protect them against the Legislature,

for that I think I have shown to be impossible, with the powers which the Legislature may safely use and exercise, and because the people have retained in their own hands the power of controlling and directing the Legislature, by their immediate and mediate elections of President, Senate, and House of Representatives.—*See ib.*, *page* 73.

Mr. Cocke, of Tennessee, on the same subject, said :

We have been told that the nation is to look up to these immaculate judges to protect their liberties ; to protect the people against themselves.—*Ib.*, *page* 75.

In the House, Robert Williams, of North Carolina, said :

If this doctrine is to extend to the length gentlemen contend, then is the sovereignty of the Government to be swallowed up in the vortex of the Judiciary. Whatever the other departments of the Government may do, they can undo. You may pass a law, but they can annul it. Will not the people be astonished to hear that their laws depend upon the will of the judges, who are themselves independent of all law?—*Ib.*, *pages* 531, 532.

John Randolph, of Roanoke, said :

But, sir, if you pass the law, the judges are to put their veto upon it by declaring it unconstitutional. Here is a new power, of a dangerous and uncontrollable nature, contended for. The decision of a constitutional question must rest somewhere. Shall it be confided to men immediately responsible to the people, or to those who are irresponsible? for the responsibility by impeachment is little less than a name. From whom is a corrupt decision most to be feared? To me it appears that the power which has the right of passing, without appeal, on the validity of your laws, is your sovereign. . . . But, sir, are we not as deeply interested in the true exposition of the Constitution as the judges can be? With all due deference to their talents, is not Congress as capable of forming a correct opinion as they are? Are not its members acting under a responsibility to public opinion, which can and will check their aberrations from duty? Let a case, not an imaginary one, be stated : Congress violates the Constitution by fettering the press; the judicial corrective is applied to ; far from protecting the liberty of the citizen, or the letter of the Constitution, you find them outdoing the legislature in zeal; pressing the common law of England to their service where the sedition law did not apply. Suppose your reliance had been altogether on this broken staff, and not on the elective principle? Your press might have been enchained till doomsday, your citizens incarcerated for life, and where is your remedy ? But if the construction of the Constitution is left with us, there are no longer limits to our power ; and this would be true, if an appeal did not lie through the elections, from us to the nation, to whom alone, and not a few privileged individuals, it belongs to decide, in the last resort, on the Constitution. . . . .
In their inquisitorial capacity, the Supreme Court, relieved from the tedious labor of investigating judicial points by the law of the last session, may easily direct the Executive, by mandamus, in what mode it is their pleasure that we should execute his functions. They will also have more leisure to attend to the legislature, and forestall, by inflammatory pamphlets, their decisions on all important questions ; whilst, for the amusement of the public, we shall retain the right of debating, but not of voting.—*Ib.*, *pages* 661, 662.

Nathaniel Macon, of North Carolina, said :

We have heard much about the judges, and the necessity of their independence. I will state one fact, to show that they have power as well as independence. Soon after the establishment of the Federal Courts, they issued a writ—not being a professional man, I shall not undertake to give its name—to the Supreme Court of North Carolina, directing a case then depending in the State Court to be brought into the Federal Court. The State judges refused to obey the summons, and laid the whole proceedings before the legislature, who approved their conduct, and, as well as I remember, unanimously ; and this in that day was not called disorganizing.—*Ib.* *page* 711.

John Bacon, of Massachusetts, said :

The Judiciary have no more right to prescribe, direct, or control the acts of the other departments of the Government, than the other departments of the Government have to prescribe or direct those of the Judiciary.—*Ib., page* 983.

THE SEDITION LAW.

When the case of Matthew Lyon was before the United States Senate in 1818, on petition asking indemnity for a fine imposed upon him under the Sedition Law, John J. Crittenden, of Kentucky, said:

The judiciary is a valuable part of the Government, and ought to be highly respected, but is not infallible. The Constitution is our guide—our supreme law. Blind homage can never be rendered by freemen to any power. In all cases of alleged violations of the Constitution, it was for Congress to make a just discrimination. — *Benton's Abridgment, vol.* 6, *page* 184.

Nathaniel Macon, of North Carolina, on the same day said:

According to some gentlemen, we were to regard the Judiciary more than the law, and both more than the Constitution. It was a misfortune the judges were not equal in infallibility to the God who made them. The truth was, if the judge was a party-man out of power, he would be a party-man in. The office would not change human nature. He had no doubt that the Sedition Law, and the proceedings under it, had more effect in revolutionizing the Government than all its other acts. He well remembered the language of the times—pay your taxes, but don't speak against government.—*Ibid., page* 187.

Hon. James Barbour, of Virginia, made a report on the subject of the petition, of which the following is an extract:

The first question that naturally presents itself in the investigation is, was the law constitutional? The committee have no hesitation in pronouncing, in their opinions, it was not. . . .

The committee are aware that, in opposition to this view of the subject, the decision of some of the judges of the Supreme Court, sustaining the constitutionality of the law, has been frequently referred to, as sovereign and conclusive of the question.

The committee entertain a high respect for the purity and intelligence of the Judiciary. But it is a rational respect, limited by a knowledge of the frailty of human nature, and the theory of the Constitution, which declares, not only that Judges may err in opinion, but also may commit crimes, and hence has provided a tribunal for the trial of offenders.

GEORGIA.

In the case of Paddleford, Fay, & Company *v.* the Mayor and Aldermen of the city of Savannah, Judge Benning, in delivering the opinion of the court, recited two or three cases in which the State of Georgia had acted in disregard of the decisions of the Supreme Court of the United States. In the case of Chisholm, executor, against Georgia, the Supreme Court of the United States—

Ordered, that unless the said State shall either in due form appear, or show cause to the contrary, in this court, by the first day of next term, judgment by default shall be entered against the said State.

The reporter adds, in a note, that "in February term, 1794, judgment *was* rendered for the plaintiff, and a writ of inquiry awarded. The writ, however, was not sued out and executed; so that this cause, and all of the other suits against States, were swept at once from the records of the court by the amendment of the Federal Constitution."

Georgia treated the court with contempt in respect to this case. Her position was, that the court had no jurisdiction of *her* as a *party.*—*Georgia Reports*, vol. 14, *page* 479.

The Judge proceeds to say, that "in this position Georgia triumphed," and that the judgment against her "fell dead."

The Judge next cites the case of Worcester and Butler, who had settled on the Cherokee lands in Georgia, contrary to the laws of the State, and for which offense they were sent to the penitentiary. On a writ of error, the Supreme Court of the United States annulled the judgment in the State court, and issued a mandate to the Superior Court of Georgia, to carry its judgment of reversal into execution. Judge Benning proceeds:

Now, what did Georgia do on receipt of this special mandate? Through every department of her government she treated the mandate and the writ of error with contempt the most profound. She did not even protest against jurisdiction, as she had done in the case of Chisholm's executors; but she kept Worcester and Butler in the penitentiary, and she executed, in the Creek nation, the laws, for violating which they had been put in the penitentiary. . . .

Judge Benning, in delivering his opinion, says further:

It was not only in this case that Georgia occupied this position; she did it in two other cases, and those, cases of life and death: the case of Tassels, and that of Graves. One of these happened before those of Worcester and Butler, namely, in 1830; the other afterward, in 1834. The Supreme Court had issued writs of error in each of these cases, on the application of the defendants to the State of Georgia; but, as the cases are not reported, it is to be presumed that these writs never got back to the Supreme Court; or that, if they ever did, it was too late. It is certain that Georgia hung the applicants for the writ.

In the Tassels case, the legislature passed these, among other resolutions:

Resolved, That the State of Georgia will never so far compromit her sovereignty, as an independent State, as to become a party to the case sought to be made before the Supreme Court of the United States by the writ in question.

Resolved, That his excellency the Governor be, and he and every other officer of this State is hereby, requested and enjoined to disregard any and every mandate and process that has been or shall be served on him or them, purporting to proceed from the Chief Justice or any Associate Justice of the Supreme Court of the United States, for the purpose of arresting the execution of any of the criminal laws of this State.

Similar resolutions were passed, as to the case of Graves, by the legislature of 1834.

PENNSYLVANIA.

The Supreme Court of Pennsylvania, in the case of the Commonwealth *v.* Cobbett, gave a unanimous opinion in 1788, from which the following is an extract:

If a State should differ with the United States about the construction of them, there is no common umpire but the people, who should adjust the affair by making amendments in the constitutional way, or suffer from the defect. In such a case, the Constitution of the United States is federal; it is a league or treaty made by the individual States as one party, and all the States as another party. When two nations differ about the meaning of any clause, sentence, or word, in a treaty, neither has an exclusive right to decide it; they endeavor to adjust the matter by negotiation; but if it cannot be thus accomplished, each has a right to retain its own interpretation, until a reference be had to the mediation of other nations, and arbitration, or the fate of war. There is no provision in the Constitution that in such a case the judges of the Supreme Court of the United States shall control and be conclusive; neither can the Congress by a law confer that power.—*Respublica* v. *Cobbett,* 3 *Dallas's Reports, page* 475.

VIRGINIA.

The Court of Appeals of Virginia, in 1814, in the case of Hunter *v.* Martin, devisee of Fairfax, entered the following unanimous opinion, after full argument:

The court is unanimously of opinion that the appellate power of the Supreme Court of the United States does not extend to this court, under a sound construction of the Constitution of the United States; that so much of the twenty-fifth section of the act of Congress to establish the judicial courts of the United States as extends the appellate jurisdiction of the Supreme Court to this court is not in pursuance of the Constitution of the United States; that the writ of error in this case was improvidently allowed under the authority of that act; that the proceedings thereon in the Supreme Court were *coram non judice* in relation to this court; and that obedience to its mandate be declined by this court.

In times of violent party excitement, agitating the whole nation, to expect that judges will be entirely exempt from its influence, argues a profound ignorance of mankind. Although clothed with the ermine, they are still men, and carry into the judgment seat the passions and motives common to their kind. Their decisions on party questions reflect their individual opinions, which frequently betray them unconsciously into error. To balance the judgment of a whole people by that of two or three men, no matter what may be their official elevation, is to exalt the creature of the Constitution above its creator, and to assail the foundation of our political fabric; which is, that the decision of the people is infallible, from which there is no appeal but to Heaven.—*See Benton's Abridgment, vol. 6, pages* 660, 661.

Mahlon Dickerson, of New-Jersey, said:

But I must beg leave to differ from the honorable gentleman (Mr. Walker, of Georgia) when he informs us that our independent Judiciary is the bulwark of the liberties of the people. By which he must mean, defenders of the people against the oppressions of the Government. From what I witnessed in the years 1798, 1799, and 1800, I never shall, I never can, consider our Judiciary as the bulwark of the liberties of the people. The people must look out for other bulwarks for their liberties.—*See ib., page* 701.

RICHARD M. JOHNSON, OF KENTUCKY.

Mr. Johnson, who was elected Vice-President of the United States by the Democratic party, represented Kentucky in the United States Senate in 1822. I find in Benton's Abridgment of the Debates of Congress, vol. 7, page 145, an elaborate speech of Mr. Johnson upon a resolution offered by him, proposing an amendment of the Constitution. His proposition was to amend the Constitution by referring all cases in which a State may be a party to the final adjudication of the Senate. In the course of his remarks, he says:

At this time there is, unfortunately, a want of confidence in the Federal Judiciary, in cases that involve political power; and this distrust my be carried to other cases, such as the lawyers call *meum et tuum.*

Courts also, like cities and villages, or like legislative bodies, will sometimes have their leaders; and it may happen, that a single individual will be the prime cause of a decision to overturn the deliberate act of a whole State, or of the United States; yet, we are admonished to receive their opinions as the ancients did the responses of the Delphic oracle, or the Jews, with more propriety, the communications from Heaven, delivered by *Urim* and *Thummim*, to the High Priest of God's chosen people, from the *sanctum sanctorum.* Other causes of difference might be multiplied to a tedious extent; but enough has been said to show that judges, who, like other men, are subject to the frailties, the passions, the partialities, and antipathies, incident to human nature, should not be exempted from responsibility on account of their superior integrity, learning, and capacity; or that their decisions should be subject to revision by some competent tribunal, responsible to the people. It is believed that this is the opinion of that great and good man who penned the Declaration of Independence, and who now enjoys, in the shades of Monticello, the blessings of the principles which it contains. . . .

It was the judgment of a court that doomed the immortal Socrates to drink the hemlock. When the Roman tyrant could no longer use a hired soldiery to immolate the victims of his jealousy, he resorted to courts of law. When Henry VIII , of England, would exercise cruel despotism under the forms of a free Constitution, the army, the court, and the Parliament, were the potent engines that sustained him. When Mary, his daughter, compelled the Protestants to seal their testimony at the stake, the court gave sanction to the murderous deeds. Her sister and successor, Elizabeth, created the Court of High Commission, and formally invested it with inquisitorial power. She also supported the arbitrary edicts of the Star Chamber. The Puritans, because obnoxious to the free exercise of the prerogatives of the Crown, were imprisoned and dispersed by process of law, and the judges were the supporters of her despotic power. When she would destroy her unfortunate kinswoman,

the Queen of Scots, the judges were instructed to condemn her, and by their sentence she came to the block. This horrid deed was covered by the cloak of judicial proceedings. When Charles I., determined to change the religion of Scotland, he made use of the Court of High Commission to effect the object. By the same judicial power, the advocates for the doctrines of the Reformation have so often been divested of their religious privileges, and doomed to seal with their blood that religion which bore them triumphantly through the vale of death.

The short, though splendid history of this Government furnishes nothing that can induce us to look with a very favorable eye to the Federal Judiciary as a safe depository of our liberties. When a law was enacted in violation of a vital principle of the Constitution, that which was designed to secure the freedom of speech and of the press, the victims of its operation looked in vain to the judges to arrest the progress of usurpation. If this power could ever be exercised to any good purpose, it would be, on such occcasions, to declare the law unconstitutional which aims a deadly blow at the vital principles of freedom; but, so far as the transactions of that day are detailed in our public records, it appears that the Judiciary was a willing instrument of Federal usurpation. That law was executed in all the rigor of the spirit which dictated it. The turbulence of faction found no moderation there; and the people found relief only in their own power. The exercise of their elective franchise removed the evil, and this is their only safe dependence.

GEN. JACKSON.

The following is an extract from Gen. Jackson's message vetoing the bill for rechartering the Bank of the United States. It may be found on page 438 of the Senate Journal for the first session of the Twenty-second Congress, and is in these words:

If the opinion of the Supreme Court covered the whole ground of this act, it ought not to control the co-ordinate authorities of this Government. The Congress, the Executive, and the Court, must each for itself be guided by its own opinion of the Constitution. Each public officer, who takes an oath to support the Constitution, swears that he will support it as he understands it, and not as it is understood by others. It is as much the duty of the House of Representatives, of the Senate, and of the President, to decide upon the constitutionality of any bill or resolution which may be presented to them for passage or approval, as it is of the supreme judges, when it may be brought before them for judicial decision. The opinion of the judges has no more authority over Congress than the opinion of Congress over the judges; and, on that point, the President is independent of both. The authority of the Supreme Court must not, therefore, be permitted to control the Congress or the Executive when acting in their legislative capacities, but to have only such influence as the force of their reasoning may deserve.

THE OTHER SIDE OF THE QUESTION.

MR. WEBSTER'S VIEWS.

The other side of this question was lucidly and ably stated by the late Daniel Webster, in a speech delivered before the U. S. Senate, on the 27th of January, 1830, in the famous debate between Mr. W. and Mr. Hayne, of South Carolina, on Foot's Resolution, as follows:

Mr. Hayne having rejoined to Mr. Webster, especially on the constitutional question, Mr. Webster rose, and, in conclusion, said:

A few words, Mr. President, on this constitutional argument, which the honorable gentleman has labored to reconstruct.

His argument consists of two propositions and an inference. His propositions are:

1st. That the Constitution is a compact between the States.

2d. That a compact between two, with authority reserved to one to interpret its terms, would be a surrender to that one of all power whatever.

3d. Therefore, (such is his inference,) the General Government does not possess the authority to construe its own powers.

Now, sir, who does not see, without the aid of exposition or detection, the utter confusion of ideas involved in this so elaborate and systematic argument.

The Constitution, it is said, is a compact *between* States; the States, then, and the States only, *are parties* to the compact. How comes the General Government itself a *party?* Upon the honorable gentleman's hypothesis, the General Government is the result of the compact, the crea ture of the compact, not one of the parties to it. Yet the argument, as the gentleman has now stated it, makes the Government itself one of its own creators. It makes it a party to that compact to which it owes its own existence.

For the purpose of erecting the Constitution on the basis of a compact, the gentleman considers the States as parties to that compact; but as soon as his compact is made, then he chooses to consider the General Government, which is the offspring of that compact, not its offspring, but one of its parties; and so being a party, without the power of judging on the terms of compact. Pray, sir, in what school is such reasoning as this taught?

If the whole of the gentleman's main proposition were conceded to him, that is to say, if I admit for the sake of the argument, that the Constitution is a compact between States, the inferences which he draws from that proposition are warranted by no just reasoning. If the Constitution be a compact between States, still that Constitution, or that compact, has established a government, with certain powers; and whether it be one of those powers, that it shall construe and interpret for itself the terms of the compact, in doubtful cases, is a question which can only be decided by looking to the compact, and inquiring what provisions it contains on this point. Without any inconsistency with natural reason, the Government even thus created might be trusted with this power of construction. The extent of its powers, therefore, must still be sought for in the instrument itself.

If the Old Confederation had contained a clause, declaring that Resolutions of the Congress should be the supreme law of the land, any State law or Constitution to the contrary notwithstanding, and that a Committee of Congress, or any other body created by it, should possess judicial powers extending to all cases arising under resolutions of Congress, then the power of ultimate decision would have been vested in Congress under the Confederation, although that Confederation was a compact between States; and for this plain reason, that it would have been competent to the States, who alone were parties to the compact, to agree who should decide in cases of dispute arising on the construction of the compact.

For the same reason, sir, if I were now to concede to the gentleman his principal proposition, namely, that the Constitution is a compact between States, the question would still be, what provision is made, in this compact, to settle points of disputed construction, or contested power, that shall come into controversy? And this question would still be answered, and conclusively answered, by the Constitution itself.

While the gentleman is contending against construction, he himself is setting up the most loose and dangerous construction. The Constitution declares, that the *laws of Congress passed in pursuance of the Constitution shall be the supreme law of the land.* No construction is necessary here. It declares, also, with equal plainness and precision, *that the judicial power of the United States shall extend to every case arising under the laws of Congress.* This needs no construction. Here is a law, then, which is declared to be supreme; and here is a power established, which is to interpret that law. Now, sir, how has the gentleman met this? Suppose the Constitution to be a compact, yet here are its terms; and how does the gentleman get rid of them? He cannot argue the *seal off the bond,* nor the word out of the instrument. Here they are; what answer does he give to them? None in the world, sir, except that the effect of this would be to place the States in a condition of inferiority; and that it results from the very nature of things, there being no superior, that the parties must be their own judges! Thus closely and cogently does the honorable gentleman reason on the words of the Constitution. The gentleman says, if there be such a power of final decision in the General Government, he asks for the grant of that power. Well, sir, I show him the grant. I turn him to the very words. I show him that the laws of Congress are made supreme; and that the judicial power extends, by express words, to the interpretation of these laws. Instead of answering this, he retreats into the general reflection, that it must result *from the nature of things,* that the States, being parties, must judge for themselves.

I have admitted, that, if the Constitution were to be considered as the creature of the State Governments, it might be modified, interpreted, or construed according to their pleasure. But, even in that case, it would be necessary that they should *agree.* One alone could not interpret it conclusively; one alone could not construe it; one alone could not modify it. Yet the gentleman's doctrine is, that Carolina alone may construe and interpret that compact which equally binds all, and gives equal rights to all.

So, then, sir, even supposing the Constitution to be a compact between the States, the gentleman's doctrine, nevertheless, is not maintainable; because, first, the General Government is not a party to that compact, but a *government* established by it, and vested by it with the powers of trying and deciding doubtful questions; and secondly, because, if the Constitution be regarded as a compact, not one State only, but all the States, are parties to that compact, and one can have no right to fix upon it her own peculiar construction.

So much, sir, for the argument, even if the premises of the gentleman were granted, or could be proved, But, sir, the gentleman has failed to maintain his leading proposition. He has not shown, it cannot be shown, that the Constitution is a compact between State Governments. The Constitution itself, in its very front, refutes that idea; it declares that it is ordained and established *by the people of the United States.* So far from saying that it is established by the governments of the several States, it does not even say that it is established by the people *of the several States;* but it pronounces that it is established by the people of the United States, in the aggregate. The gentleman says, it must mean no more than the people of the several States. Doubtless, the people of the several States, taken collectively, constitute the people of the United States; but it is in this, their collective capacity, it is as all the people of the United States, that they establish the Constitution. So they declare; and words cannot be plainer than the words used.

When the gentleman says the Constitution is a compact between the States, he uses language exactly applicable to the old Confederation. He speaks as if he were in Congress before 1789. He describes fully that old state of things then existing. The Confederation was, in strictness, a compact; the States, as States, were parties to it. We had no other general government. But that was found insufficient, and inadequate to the public exigencies. The people were not satisfied with it, and undertook to establish a better. They undertook to form a General Government, which should stand on a new basis; not a confederacy, not a league, not a compact between States, but a *Constitution;* a popular government, founded in popular election, directly responsible to the people themselves, and divided into branches with prescribed limits of power, and prescribed duties. They ordained such a government, they gave it the name of a *Constitution,* and therein established a distribution of power between this, their General Government, and their several State governments. When they shall become dissatisfied with this distribution, they can alter it. Their own power over their own instrument remains. But until they shall alter it, it must stand as their will, and is equally binding on the General Government and on the States.

The gentleman, sir, finds analogy where I see none. He likens it to the case of a treaty, in which, there being no common superior, each party must interpret for himself, under its own obligation of good faith. But this is not a treaty, but a constitution of government, with powers to execute itself, and fulfill its duties.

I admit, sir, that this government is a government of checks and balances; that is, the House of Representatives is a check upon the Senate, and the Senate is a check on the House, and the President a check on both. But I cannot comprehend, or, if I do, I totally differ from him, when he applies the notion of checks and balances to the interference of different governments. He argues that if we transgress our constitutional limits, each State, as a State, has a right to check us. Does he admit the converse of the proposition, that we have a right to check the States? The gentleman's doctrines would give us a strange jumble of authorities and powers, instead of governments of separate and defined powers. It is the part of wisdom, I think, to avoid this; and to keep the General Government and the State Government each in its proper sphere, avoiding as carefully as possible every kind of interference.

Finally, sir, the honorable gentleman says, that the States will only interfere, by their power, to preserve the Constitution. They will not destroy it, they will not impair it; they will only save, they will only preserve, they will only strengthen it. Ah! sir, this is but the old story. All regulated governments, all free governments, have been broken by similar disinterested and well disposed interference. It is the common pretence. But I take leave of the subject.

GEN. CASS ON POPULAR SOVEREIGNTY.

LETTER TO A. O. P. NICHOLSON.

WASHINGTON, *Dec.* 24, 1847.

DEAR SIR: I have received your letter, and shall answer it as frankly as it is written.

You ask me whether I am in favor of the acquisition of Mexican territory, and what are my sentiments with regard to the Wilmot Proviso.

I have so often and so explicitly stated my views of the first question, in the Senate, that it seems almost unnecessary to repeat them here. As you request it, however, I shall briefly give them.

I think, then, that no peace should be granted to Mexico, till a reasonable indemnity is obtained for the injuries which she has done us. The territorial extent of this indemnity is, in the first instance, a subject of Executive consideration. There the Constitution has placed it, and there I am willing to leave it; not only because I have full confidence in its judicious exercise, but because, in the ever-varying circumstances of a war, it would be indiscreet, by a public declaration, to commit the country to any line of indemnity, which might otherwise be enlarged, as the obstinate injustice of the enemy prolongs the contest with its loss of blood and treasure.

It appears to me, that the kind of metaphysical magnanimity which would reject all indemnity at the close of a bloody and expensive war, brought on by a direct attack upon our troops by the enemy, and preceded by a succession of unjust acts for a series of years, is as unworthy of the age in which we live, as it is revolting to the common sense and practice of mankind. It would conduce but little to our future security, or, indeed to our present reputation, to declare that we repudiate all expectation of compensation from the Mexican Government, and are fighting, not for any practical result, but for some vague, perhaps philanthropic object, which escapes my penetration, and must be defined by those who assume this new principle of national intercommunication. All wars are to be deprecated, as well by the statesman as by the philanthropist. They are great evils; but there are greater evils than these, and submission to injustice is among them. The nation which should refuse to defend its rights and its honor when assailed, would soon have neither to defend; and, when driven to war, it is not by professions of disinterestedness and declarations of magnanimity that its rational objects can be best obtained, or other nations taught a lesson of forbearance—the strongest security for permanent peace We are at war with Mexico, and its vigorous prosecution is the surest means of its speedy termination, and ample indemnity the surest guaranty against the recurrence of such injustice as provoked it.

The Wilmot Proviso has been before the country some time. It has been repeatedly discussed in Congress and by the public press. I am strongly impressed with the opinion, that a great change has been going on in the public mind upon this subject, in my own as well as others; and that doubts are resolving themselves into convictions, that the principle it involves should be kept out of the National Legislature, and left to the people of the confederacy in their respective local governments.

The whole subject is a comprehensive one, and fruitful of important consequences. It would be ill-timed to discuss it here. I shall not assume that responsible task, but shall confine myself to such general views as are necessary to the fair exhibition of my opinion.

We may well regret the existence of Slavery in the Southern States, and wish they had been saved from its introduction. But then it is, not by the act of the present generation; and we must deal with it as a great practical question, involving the most momentous consequences. We have neither the right nor the power to touch it where it exists; and if we had both, their exercise by any means heretofore suggested, might lead to results which no wise man would willingly encounter, and which no good man could contemplate without anxiety.

The theory of our Government presupposes that its various members have reserved to themselves the regulation of all subjects relating to what may be termed their internal police. They are sovereign within their boundaries, except in those cases where they have surrendered to the General Government a portion of their rights, in order to give effect to the objects of the Union, whether these concern foreign nations or the several States themselves. Local institutions, if I may so speak, whether they have reference to Slavery or to any other relations, domestic or public, are left to local authority, either original or derivative. Congress has no right to say there shall be Slavery in New-York, or that there shall be no Slavery in Georgia; nor is there any other human power, but the people of those States, respectively, which can change the relations existing therein; and they can say, if they will, we will have Slavery in the former, and we will abolish it in the latter.

In various respects, the Territories differ from the States. Some of their rights are inchoate, and they do not possess the peculiar attributes of sovereignty. Their relation to the General Government is very imperfectly defined by the Constitution; and it will be found, upon examination, that in that instrument the only grant of power concerning them is conveyed in the phrase, "Congress shall have the power to dispose of and make all needful rules and regulations respecting the territory and other property belonging to the United States." Certainly this phraseology is very loose, if it were designed to include in the grant the whole power of legislation over persons, as well as things. The expression, the "territory and other property," fairly construed, relates to the public lands, as such; to arsenals, dockyards, forts, ships, and all the various kinds of property which the United States may and must possess.

But surely the simple authority *to dispose of and regulate* these does not extend to the unlimited power of legislation; to the passage of all *laws*, in the most general acceptation of the word, which, by the by, is carefully excluded from the sentence. And, indeed, if this were so, it would render unnecessary another provision of the Constitution, which grants to Congress the power to legislate, with the consent of the States, respectively, over all places purchased for the "erection of forts, magazines, arsenals, dockyards," etc. These being the "*property*" of the United States, if the power to make "needful rules and regulations concerning" them includes the general power of legislation, then the grant of authority to regulate "the territory and other property of the United States" is unlimited, wherever subjects are found for its operation, and its exercise needed no auxiliary provision. If, on the other hand, it does not include such power of legislation over the "other property" of the United States, then it does not include it over their "*territory;*" for the same terms which grant the one grant the other. "*Territory*" is here classed with property, and treated as such; and the object was evidently to enable the General Government, as a property-holder—which, from necessity, it must be—to manage, preserve and "*dispose of*" such property as it might possess, and which authority is essential almost to its being. But the lives and persons of our citizens, with the vast variety of objects connected with them, cannot be controlled by an authority which is merely called into existence for the purpose of making *rules and regulations for the disposition and management of property.*

Such, it appears to me, would be the construction put upon this provision of the Constitution, were this question now first presented for consideration, and not controlled by imperious circumstances. The original ordinance of the Congress of the Confederation, passed in 1787, and which was the only act upon this subject in force at the adoption of the Constitution, provided a complete frame of government for the country north of the Ohio, while in a territorial condition, and for its eventual admission in separate States into the Union. And the persuasion that this ordinance contained within itself all the necessary means of execution, probably prevented any direct reference to the subject in the Constitution, further than vesting in Congress the right to admit the States formed under it into the Union. However, circumstances arose, which required legislation, as well over the territory north of the Ohio, as over other territory, both within and without the original Union, ceded to the General Government, and, at various times, a more enlarged power has been exercised over the *Territories*—meaning thereby the different Territorial Governments — than is conveyed by the limited grant referred to. How far an existing necessity may have operated in producing this legislation, and thus extending, by rather a violent implication, powers not directly given, I know not. But certain it is that the principle of interference should not be carried beyond the necessary implication, which produces it. It should be limited to the creation of proper governments for new countries, acquired or settled, and to the necessary provisions for their eventual admission into the Union; leaving, in the meantime, to the people inhabiting them, to regulate their internal concerns in their own way. They are just as capable of doing so as the people of the States; and they can do so, at any rate as soon as their political independence is recognized by admission into the Union. During this temporary condition, it is hardly expedient to call into exercise a doubtful and invidious authority which questions the intelligence of a respectable portion of our citizens, and whose limitation, whatever it may be, will be rapidly approaching its termination—an authority which would give to Congress despotic power, uncontrolled by the Constitution, over most important sections of our common country. For, if the relation of master and servant may be regulated or annihilated by its legislation, so may the regulation of husband and wife, of parent and child, and of any other condition which our institutions and the habits of our society recognize. What would be thought if Congress should undertake to prescribe the terms of marriage in New-York, or to regulate the authority of parents over their children in Pennsylvania? And yet it would be as vain to seek one justifying the interference of the national legislature in the cases referred to in the original States of the Union. I speak here of the inherent power of Congress, and do not touch the question of such contracts as may be formed with new States when admitted into the confederacy.

Of all the questions which can agitate us, those which are merely sectional in their character are the most dangerous, and the most to be deprecated. The warning voice of him who from his character and services and virtue had the best right to warn us, proclaimed to his countrymen, in his Farewell Address—that monument of wisdom for him, as I hope it will be of safety for them—how much we had to apprehend from measures peculiarly affecting geographical sections of our country. The grave circumstances in which we are now placed make these words words of safety; for I am satisfied, from all I have seen and heard here, that a successful attempt to ingraft the principles of the Wilmot Proviso upon the legislation of this Government, and to apply them to new territory, should new territory be acquired, would seriously affect our tranquillity. I do not suffer myself to foresee or foretell the consequences that would ensue; for I trust and believe there is good sense and good feeling enough in the country to avoid them, by avoiding all occasions which might lead to them.

Briefly, then, I am opposed to the exercise of any jurisdiction by Congress over this matter; and I am in favor of leaving to the people of any Territory, which may be hereafter acquired, the right to regulate it for themselves, under the general principles of the Constitution. Because—

1. I do not see in the Constitution any grant of the requisite power to Congress; and I am not disposed to extend a doubtful precedent beyond its necessity—the establishment of Territorial Governments when needed—leaving to the inhabitants all the rights compatible with the relations they bear to the confederation.

2. Because I believe this measure, if adopted, would weaken, if not impair, the Union of the States; and would sow the seeds of future discord, which would grow up and ripen into an abundant harvest of calamity.

3. Because I believe a general conviction that such a proposition would succeed, would lead to an immediate withholding of the supplies, and thus to a dishonorable termination of the war. I think no dispassionate observer at the seat of Government can doubt this result.

4. If, however, in this I am under a misapprehension, I am under none in the practical operation of this restriction, if adopted by Congress, upon a treaty of peace, making any acquisition of Mexican Territory. Such a treaty would be rejected as certainly as presented to the Senate. More than one-third of that body would vote against it, viewing such a principle as an exclusion of the citizens of the slaveholding States from a participation in the benefits acquired by the treasure and exertions of all, and which should be common to all. I am repeating—neither advancing nor defending these views. That branch of the subject does not lie in my way, and I shall not turn aside to seek it.

In this aspect of the matter, the people of the United States must choose between this restriction and the extension of their territorial limits. They cannot have both; and which they will surrender must depend upon their representatives first, and then, if these fail them, upon themselves.

5 But after all, it seems to be generally conceded that this restriction, if carried into effect could, not operate upon any State to be formed from newly-acquired territory. The well-known attributes of Sovereignty, recognized by us as belonging to the State Governments, would sweep before them any such barrier, and would leave the people to express and exert their will at pleasure. Is the object, then, of temporary exclusion for so short a period as the duration of the Territorial Governments, worth the price at which it would be purchased?—worth the discord it would engender, the trial to which it would expose our Union, and the evils that would be the certain consequence, let the trial result as it might? As to the course, which has been intimated, rather than proposed, of ingrafting such a restriction upon any treaty of acquisition, I persuade myself it would find but little favor in any portion of this country. Such an arrangement would render Mexico a party, having a right to interfere in our internal institutions in questions left by the Constitution to the State Governments, and would inflict a serious blow upon our fundamental principles. Few, indeed, I trust, there are among us who would thus grant to a foreign power the right to inquire into the constitution and conduct of the sovereign States of this Union; and if there are any, I am not among them, nor never shall be. To the people of this country, under God, now and hereafter, are its destinies committed; and we want no foreign power to interrogate us, treaty in hand, and to say, Why have you done this, or why have you left that undone? Our own dignity and the principles of national independence unite to repel such a proposition.

But there is another important consideration, which ought not to be lost sight of, in the investigation of this subject. The question that presents itself is not a question of the increase, but of the diffusion of Slavery. Whether its sphere be stationary or progressive, its amount will be the same. The rejection of this restriction will not add one to the class of servitude, nor will its adoption give freedom to a single being who is now placed therein. The same numbers will be spread over greater territory; and, so far as compression, with less abundance of the necessaries of life, is an evil, so far will that evil be mitigated by transporting slaves to a new country, and giving them a larger space to occupy.

I say this in the event of the extension of Slavery over any new acquisition. But can it go there? This may well be doubted. All the descriptions which reach us of the condition of the Californias and of New-Mexico, to the acquisition of which our efforts seem to be at present directed, unite in representing those countries as agricultural regions, similar in their products to our Middle States, and generally unfit for the production of the great staples which can alone render slave labor valuable. If we are not grossly deceived—and it is difficult to conceive how we can be—the inhabitants of those regions, whether they depend up on their plows or their herds, cannot be slaveholders. In voluntary labor, requiring the investment of large capital, can only be profitable when employed in the production of a few favored articles confined by nature to special districts, and paying larger returns than the usual agricultural products spread over more considerable portions of the earth.

In the able letter of Mr. Buchanan upon this subject, not long since given to the public, he presents similar considerations with great force. "Neither," says the distinguished writer, "the soil, the climate, nor the productions of California, south of 36° 30', nor indeed of any portion of it, North or South, is adapted to slave labor; and beside every facility would be there afforded for the slave to escape from his master. Such property would be entirely insecure in any part of California. It is morally impossible, therefore, that a majority of the emigrants to that portion of the Territory south of 36° 30', which will be chiefly composed of our citizens, will ever reëstablish Slavery within its limits.

"In regard to New-Mexico, east of the Rio Grande, the question has already been settled by the admission of Texas into the Union.

"Should we acquire territory beyond the Rio Grande and east of the Rocky Mountains, it is still more impossible that a majority of the people would consent to *reëstablish* Slavery. They are themselves a colored population, and among them the negro does not belong socially to a degraded race."

With this last remark, Mr Walker fully coincides in his letter written in 1844, upon the annexation of Texas, and which everywhere produced so favorable an impression upon the public mind, as to have conduced very materially to the accomplishment of that great measure. "Beyond the Del Norte," says Mr. Walker, "Slavery will not pass; not only because it is forbidden by law, but because the colored race there preponderates in the ratio of ten to one over the whites; and holding, as they do, the government and most of the offices in their possession, they will not permit the enslavement of any portion of the colored race, which makes and executes the laws of the country."

The question, it will be therefore seen on examination, does not regard the exclusion of Slavery from a region where it now exists, but a prohibition against its introduction where it does not exist, and where, from the feelings of the inhabitants and the laws of nature, "it is morally impossible," as Mr. Buchanan says, that it can ever reëstablish itself.

It augurs well for the permanence of our confederation that during more than half a century, which has elapsed since the establishment of this government, many serious questions, and some of the highest importance, have agitated the public mind, and more than once threatened the gravest consequences; but that they have all in succession passed away, leaving our institutions unscathed, and our country advancing in numbers, power, and wealth, and in all the other elements of national prosperity, with a rapidity unknown in ancient or modern days In times of political excitement, when difficult and delicate questions present themselves for solution, there is one ark of safety for us ; and that is an honest appeal to the fundamental principles of our Union, and a stern determination to abide their dictates. This course of proceeding has carried us in safety through many a trouble ; and I trust will carry us safely through many more, should many more be destined to assail us. The Wilmot Proviso seeks to take from its legitimate tribunal a question of domestic policy, having no relation to the Union, as such, and to transfer it to another, created by the people for a special purpose, and foreign to the subject matter involved in this issue. By going back to our true principles, we go back to the road of peace and safety. Leave to the people, who will be affected by this question, to adjust it upon their own responsibility, and in their own manner, and we shall render another tribute to the original principles of our Government, and furnish another guaranty of its permanence and prosperity. I am, dear sir, respectfully, your obedient servant,   LEWIS CASS.

A. O. P. NICHOLSON, Esq., Nashville, Tenn.

MR. VAN BUREN ON SLAVERY IN THE TERRITORIES.

THE following letter was addressd to the New York City Delegates to the Utica Free Soil Convention, of 1848, in response to a letter to Martin Van Buren, asking his opinion on the subject herein discussed :

) LINDENWOLD, *June* 20, 1848.

GENTLEMEN : . . . . .You desire also my views in regard to the prohibition by Congress of Slavery in territories where it does not now exist, and they shall be given in a few words, and in a manner which will not, I hope, increase, if it does not diminish the existing excitement in the public mind.

The illustrious founders of our Government were not insensible to the apparent inconsistency between the perpetuation of Slavery in the United States, and the principles of the Revolution, as delineated in the Declaration of Independence; and they were too ingenuous in their dispositions to attempt to conceal the impressions by which they were embarrassed. But they knew, also, that its speedy abolition in several of the States, was impossible, and its existence in all, without fault on the part of the present generation. They were also too upright and the fraternal feelings which had carried them through the struggle for independence were too strong to permit them to deal with such a matter upon any other principles than those of liberality and justice. The policy they adopted was to guarantee to the States in which Slavery existed, an exclusive control over the subject within their respective jurisdictions, but to prevent by united efforts, its extension to territories of the United States in which it did not in fact exist.

On all sides the most expedient means to carry out this policy were adopted with alacrity and good feeling. Their first step was to interdict the introduction of Slavery into the Northwestern Territory, now covered by the States of Ohio, Indiana, Illinois, Michigan and Wisconsin. This may justly be regarded, as being in the main, a Southern measure. The subject was first brought forward in Congress by Mr. Jefferson. Virginia made the cession of territory upon which the ordinance was intended to operate, and the Representatives from all the slaveholding States gave it a unanimous support. Doubts have arisen in the minds of some whether the ordinance of 1787 was authorized by the articles of Confederation. A bill was introduced in the new Constitution, recognizing and adapting it to the new organization, and it has ever since been treated and regarded as a valid act. This bill received the Constitutional approbation of President Washington, whose highest and sworn duty it was to support the Constitution under which it was enacted. Nor was the North backward in doing its part to sustain the policy which had been wisely adopted. They assented to the insertion of provisions in the Constitution necessary and sufficient to protect that interest in the States, and they did more.

The trouble apprehended at the commencement of the Government from this source, began to show itself as early as the year 1790, in the form of Petitions presented to Congress upon the subject of Slavery and the slave-trade by the Quakers of Philadelphia and New-York, and by Dr. Franklin as President of a society for the promotion of Abolition. These petitions were in the House of Representatives, referred to a Committee of seven, all but one of whom were Northern members, whose report as amended in Committee of the Whole, affirmed " that Congress have no power to interfere in the emancipation of slaves, or in the treatment of them within any of the States, it remaining with the several States alone to provide any regulation therein which humanity and true policy might require."

The perseverance and good faith with which both branches of policy thus adopted have, until very recently, been recognized and carried out, are highly honorable to the whole country. The peculiarity of the subject to be converted into an element of political agitation, as well in the slaveholding as in the non-slaveholding States, may have led to occasional attempts so to employ it, but these efforts have been very successfully frustrated by the good sense and good feeling of the people in every quarter of the Union. A detailed account of the numerous acts of the Federal Government, sustaining and carrying into full effect the policy of its founders upon the subject of Slavery in the States, and its extension to the Territories, and the steps taken, in the non-slaveholding States, to suppress or neutralize undue agitation in regard to it, would be alike instructive and honorable to the actors in them. But it will be readily perceived that this could not be given within the necessary limits of a communication like the present. It must therefore suffice to say that from 1787, the date of the ordinance for the prevention of Slavery in the Northwestern Territory, down to and including 1838, at least eleven acts of Congress have been passed, organizing Territories which have since become States, in all of which the Constitutional power of Congess to interdict the introduction of Slavery into the Territories of the United States, is either directly exercised, or clearly asserted by enactments which, as matters of authority, are tantamount to its exercise ; and that at the only period when the peace of the slaveholding States was supposed to be seriously endangered by Abolition agitation, there was a spontaneous uprising of the people of the North of both parties, by which agitation was paralyzed, and the South reassured of our fidelity to the compromises of the Constitution.

In the laws for the organization of the Territories, which now constitute the States of Ohio, Indiana, Michigan, Illinois, Wisconsin and Iowa, Slavery was expressly prohibited. The laws for the organization of the Territories of Mississippi, New Orleans, Arkansas, Alabama and Florida, containing enactments fully equivalent in regard to the extent of power in Congress over the subject of Slavery in the Territories to the express exercise of it in other cases. These acts were approved by Presidents Washington, the elder Adams, Jefferson, Madison, Monroe, Jackson and myself, all bound by our oaths of office to withhold our respective approvals from laws which we believed unconstitutional. If in the passage of these laws during a period of half a century, and under the administration of so many Presidents, there was anything like sectional divisions, or a greater or less participation in their enactment on the part of the Representatives of the slaveholding or non-slaveholding States, I am not apprised of it. I believe the plan devised by the founders of the Government, including the Fathers of our Political Church, for the treatment of this great subject, and which has hitherto been so faithfully sustained, and which has proven so successful in preserving the Union of these States, to be not only the wisest which the wit of man could have devised ; but the only one consistent with the safety and prosperity of the whole country. I do, therefore, desire to see it continued so long as Slavery exists in the United States. The extent to which I have sustained it in the various public stations I have occupied is known to the country. I was at the time well aware that I went further in this respect than many of my best friends could approve. But deeply penetrated by the conviction that Slavery was the only subject that could endanger our blessed Union, I was determined that no effort on my part, within the pale of the Constitution, should be wanting to sustain its compromises, as they were then understood, and it is now a source of consolation to me that I pursued the course I then adopted.

The doctrine which the late Baltimore Convention has presented for the sanction of the nation, is, in substance, that the laws I referred to were but so many violations of the Constitution—that this instrument confers no power on Congress to exclude Slavery from the Territories, as has so often been done with the assent of all. This doctrine is set forth in the published opinion of the highly respectable nominee of that Convention, who, it is well known, received that distinction, because he avowed that opinion, and who, it is equally certain, would not have received it if he had not done so. It is proposed to give this doctrine the most solemn sanction known to our political system, by the election of its declared advocate and supporter to the Presidency. If it receives the proposed sanction of the People of the United States, the result cannot be doubtful. The policy in regard to the extension of Slavery to the Territories of the United States into which it has not yet been introduced, which has existed since the commencement of the Government, and the consequences of which have been so salutary, must cease, and every act of Congress designed to carry it into effect be defeated by the Veto of the Executive.

The Territories now owned by the United States, and every acquisition of territory that may hereafter be made to the United States, whether obtained by annexation, by cession for a valuable consideration, or by conquest, must, as long as this opinion is held, and as far as the action of the National Legislature is concerned, be subject to the inroads of Slavery. And this consequence is to be submitted to on the assumption that the framers of the Constitution, with their attention directed to the subject, and with a well understood desire to do so, have failed to clothe Congress with the necessary powers to prevent it. I cannot, with my vote, contribute to this sanction. I cannot do so, because I cannot concur in the opinion which we are called upon to sustain.

The power, the existence of which is at this late day denied, is, in my opinion, fully granted to Congress by the Constitution. Its language, the circumstances under which it was adopted, the recorded explanations which accompanied its formation—the construction it has received from our highest judicial tribunals, and the very solemn and repeated confirmations it has derived from the measures of the Government—leave not the shadow of a doubt in my mind, in regard to the authority of Congress to exercise the power in question. This is not a new opinion on my part, nor the first occasion on which it has been avowed. While the candidate of my friends for the Presidency, I

distinctly announced my opinion in favor of the power of Congress to abolish Slavery in the District of Columbia, although I was, for reasons which were then, and are still satisfactory to my mind, very decidedly opposed to its exercise there. The question of power is certainly as clear in respect to the Territories as it is in regard to that District ; and as to the Territories, my opinion was also made known in a still more solemn form, by giving the Executive approval required by the Constitution to the bill for the organization of the Territorial Government of Iowa, which prohibited the introduction of Slavery into that Territory.

The opinion from which we dissent was given in the face of, and directly contrary to, the views expressed, in forms the most solemn and explicit, by all or nearly all the non-slaveholding States, and we are not at liberty to suspect the sincerity of these expressions. Honest and well-meaning men, as we know the masses of our political friends in those States to be, are incapable of trifling with so grave a subject.

Our ancestors signalized the commencement of this glorious Government of ours, by rescuing from subjection to Slavery a Territory which is now covered by five great States, and peopled by more than four millions of freemen, in the full enjoyment of every blessing which industry and good institutions can confer. They did this when the opinions and conduct of the world in regard to the institution of Slavery were very different from what they are now.

They did so before Great Britain had even commenced those gigantic efforts for the suppression of Slavery by which she has so greatly distinguished herself. After seventy-four years' enjoyment of the sacred and invaluable right of self-government, obtained for us by the valor and discretion of our ancestors, we, their descendants, are called upon to doom, or if that is too strong a word, to expose to the inroad of Slavery, a territory capable of sustaining an equal number of new States to be added to our Confederacy—a territory in a great part of which Slavery has never existed in fact, and from the residue of which it has been expressly abolished by the existing Government. We are called upon to do this at a period when the minds of nearly all mankind have been penetrated by a conviction of the evils of Slavery, and are united in efforts for its suppression—at a moment, too, when the spirit of Freedom and Reform is everywhere far more prevalent than it has ever been, and when our Republic stands proudly forth as the great exemplar of the world in the science of Free Government.

Who can believe that a population like that which inhabits the non-slaveholding States, probably amounting to twelve millions, who by their own acts, or by the foresight of others, have been exempted from the evils of Slavery, can at such a moment be induced, by considerations of any description, to make a retrograde movement of a character so extraordinary and so painful? Such a movement would, in my view of the matter—and I say it with unfeigned deference to the conflicting opinions of others—bring reproach upon the influence of free institutions, which would delight the hearts and excite the hopes of the advocates of arbitrary power throughout the world. . . . . . .

Accept, gentlemen, my warmest acknowledgments for the obliging expressions contained in your letter, and believe me to be

Your friend,   MARTIN VAN BUREN.

To Messrs. Nelson J. Waterbury, David Dudley Field, and others, New York.

LAND FOR THE LANDLESS.

Action of Congress on the Public Lands.

THE Public Domain of the United States is still immense, notwithstanding the millions upon millions of acres which have been squandered or passed over to the hands of speculators and monopolists, by the action of the National Government during the past few years. It is estimated by intelligent persons, who have given their attention to the subject, that lying within the States and Territories of this Government there are now about *one thousand millions of acres* of public lands still unentered. "What shall be done with this immense domain?" is a question which has for years occupied the minds of thoughtful men, who have the best interests of society at heart. At length, the great question of the proper disposition of these lands has become one of party, and may be stated as follows: "Shall the Public Domain be open to monopoly by speculators, leading inevitably to a landed aristocracy ? or shall it be reserved for actual occupants in small quantities, at a nominal price, or without price ?" There would be no difficulty whatever in adjusting this question at any time and in the right way, if the Negro question, which, in the National Administration, absorbs or overrides all others, were not behind it. Although this is an old question, it had never commanded in Congress, the attention to which it is entitled, previous to the organization of the Republican party; because until that time both the great parties into which the country was divided were either controlled, or their action was modified, by the Slaveholding interest of the country. That interest, which is ever vigilant, understands that Slavery cannot well exist were small freeholds prevail, and hence it opposes, with all its great power, all Preëmption and Homestead laws, knowing well that if our new States and Territories are to be occupied in quarter-sections, they will be occupied by working farmers, and not by speculators and great planters.

Since this question has assumed a national importance, a concise record of the proceedings and votes in Congress during the session of 1858-9, and 1859-60, upon the disposition of the Public Domain, will be of interest as a matter of record.

On the 20th of January, 1859, (See *Congressional Globe*, p 492,) bill relating to preemptions, reported from the Committee on Public Lands, was pending before the House. The bill proposed to make some changes in the details of existing preëmption laws, but without affecting the substance of the present system of disposing of the public lands. It was, however, in parliamentary order to propose to amend the bill so as to change the present system, and to bring the House to a direct vote upon such propositions. The friends of such change were prompt to avail themselves of this advantage.

Mr. Grow, of Pennsylvania, moved to amend the bill by adding the following as an additional section:

Be it further enacted, That from and after the passage of this act, no public land shall be exposed to sale by proclamation of the President, unless the same shall have been surveyed, and the return of such survey duly filed in the Land Office, for ten years or more before such sale.

The force and effect of this amendment would be to give the preëmptors ten years the start of the speculators and land monopolists. That is to say: with the addition of Mr. Grow's amendment to the existing laws and regulations touching the Public Lands, they would be open to preëmption ten years before they could come within the grasp of the speculator, thus giving the poor, industrious settler ample time to "clear up" his farm and pay for it from the proceeds of the soil. This was just what the South and the Democracy did not want, as the sequel will sh

The opponents of the bill forthwith resorted to parliamentary tactics to avoid a direct issue upon Mr. Grow's proposition.

Their first movement was a motion to refer the bill and amendment to the Committee of the Whole, familiarly and aptly styled "*the tomb of the Capulets.*" If that reference had been car-

ried, the bill never would have been reached, and would never have been heard of afterward.

The vote upon the motion to refer the bill to the Committee of the Whole, was as follows— the Democrats in Roman, the Republicans in *Italics*, and the Southern Americans in SMALL CAPITALS:

YEAS.

MAINE.—*Wood*—1.
CONNECTICUT.—Arnold, Bishop—2.
NEW-YORK.—*Burroughs*, Maclay, Russell, Taylor—4.
NEW-JERSEY.—Wortendyke—1.
PENNSYLVANIA.—Ahl, Chapman, Dewart, Montgomery, *Morris, Ritchie*, White—7.
MARYLAND.—HARRIS, RICAUD—2.
VIRGINIA.—Bocock, Caskie, Edmundson, Faulkner, Garnett, Millson, Powell—7.
NORTH CAROLINA.—Craige, Ruffin, Scales, Winslow—4.
SOUTH CAROLINA.—Boyce, Branch, Keitt, McQueen, Miles—5.
GEORGIA.—Crawford, Gartrell, Jackson, Seward, Stephens, TRIPPE, Wright—7.
FLORIDA.—Hawkins—1.
ALABAMA.—Curry, Houston, Moore, Shorter—4.
MISSISSIPPI.—Barksdale, Davis, McRae—3.
LOUISIANA.—EUSTIS, Sandidge, Taylor—3.
TEXAS.—Bryan, Reagan—2.
TENNESSEE.—Atkins, Jones, MAYNARD, READY, Savage, Watkins, ZOLLICOFFER—7.
KENTUCKY.—Burnett, Jewett, MARSHALL, Peyton, Stevenson, Talbott, UNDERWOOD—7.
MISSOURI.—ANDERSON, Caruthers, John B. Clark, James Craig, Phelps, WOODSON—6.
OHIO.—Burns, Cockerill, Groesbeck, *Harlan*, Lawrence, *Nichols*, Pendleton, Vallandigham—8.
INDIANA.—Davis, English, Gregg, Hughes, Niblack—5.
ILLINOIS.—Marshall, Morris, Shaw, Smith—4.
Total, 90.

NAYS.

MAINE.—*Foster, Gilman, Morse, I. Washburn*—4.
NEW-HAMPSHIRE.—*Cragin, Tappan*—2.
VERMONT.—*Morrill, Royce, Walton*—3.
MASSACHUSETTS.—*Buffinton, Burlingame, Chaffee, Comins, Dawes, Hall, Knapp, Thayer*—8.
RHODE ISLAND.—*Brayton, Durfee*—2.
CONNECTICUT.—*Clark, Dean*—2.
NEW-YORK.—*Andrews*, Clark, John Cochrane, *Dodd, Fenton, Granger*, Hatch, *Hoard, Kelsey, Matteson, Morgan, Morse, Murray, Olin, Palmer, Parker, Spinner, Thompson*—18.
NEW-JERSEY.—*Clawson*, Huyler—2.
PENNSYLVANIA.—*Covode, Edie*, Florence, *Grow*, Jones, *Keim*, Leidy, *Purviance, Stewart*—9.
MARYLAND.—Bowie, Stewart—2.
VIRGINIA.—Goode, Hopkins—2.
NORTH CAROLINA.—GILMER, VANCE—2.
ALABAMA.—Cobb, Dowdell, Stallworth—3.
MISSISSIPPI.—Singleton—1.
OHIO.—*Bingham, Bliss, Giddings*, Hall, *Leiter, Mott, Sherman, Stanton, Tompkins, Wade*—11.
INDIANA.—*Colfax*, Foley, *Kilgore, Pettit, Wilson*—5.
ILLINOIS.—*Farnsworth, Kellogg, Lovejoy, Washburne*,—4.
MISSOURI.—*Blair*—1.
MICHIGAN.—*Howard, Leach, Walbridge, Waldron*—4.
WISCONSIN.—*Potter, Washburn*—2.
IOWA.—*Curtis, Davis*—2.
CALIFORNIA.—Scott—1.
MINNESOTA.—Cavanaugh, Phelps—2. Total, 92.

The motion to refer the bill to the Committee of the Whole having thus failed, the House was brought to a direct vote upon Mr. Grow's amendment, which was adopted by the following votes:

YEAS.

MAINE.—*Foster, Gilman, Morse, Washburn, Wood*—5.
NEW-HAMPSHIRE.—*Cragin, Pike, Tappan*—3.
VERMONT.—*Morrill, Royce, Walton*—3.
MASSACHUSETTS.—*Buffinton, Burlingame, Chaffee, Comins, Davis, Dawes, Gooch, Hall, Knapp, Thayer*—10.
RHODE ISLAND.—*Brayton, Durfee*—2.
CONNECTICUT.—*Dean*—1.
NEW-YORK.—*Andrews, Bennett, Burroughs*, Clark John Cochrane, *Dodd, Fenton, Granger, Hoard, Kel-*

sey, *Matteson, Morgan, Morse, Murray, Olin, Pal-mer, Parker, Sherman, Spinner, Thompson*— 20.
NEW-JERSEY.—*Robbins*—1.
PENNSYLVANIA.—Chapman, *Covode, Edie,* Florence, *Grow, Keim, Morris,* Phillips, *Purviance, Ritchie, Stewart*—11.
MARYLAND.—Stewart—1.
TENNESSEE.—Atkins, Avery, Jones, Savage—4.
KENTUCKY.—Jewett, Stevenson, Talbott—3.
OHIO—.*Bingham, Bliss,* Cockerill, *Giddings, Harlan, Horton,* Lawrence, *Leiter,* Miller, *Mott, Sherman, Stanton, Tompkins, Wade*—14.
INDIANA.—*Colfax, Kilgore, Pettit, Wilson*—4.
ILLINOIS.—*Farnsworth, Kellogg, Lovejoy, Washburne*—4.
MICHIGAN.—*Howard, Leach, Walbridge, Waldron*—4.
WISCONSIN.—*Billinghurst, Potter, Washburn*—3.
MINNESOTA.—Cavanaugh, Phelps—2.
IOWA.—*Curtis, Davis*—2.
MISSOURI.—*Blair*—1. Total, 98.

NAYS.

CONNECTICUT.—Arnold—1.
NEW-YORK.—Russell, Searing, Taylor—3.
NEW-JERSEY.—Huyler, Wortendyke—2.
PENNSYLVANIA.—Ahl, Dewart, Leidy, Montgomery—4.
DELAWARE—Whiteley—1.
MARYLAND—Bowie—1.
VIRGINIA.—Bocock, Caskie, Edmundson, Garnett, Goode, Hopkins, Millson, Powell—8.
NORTH CAROLINA.—Branch, Craige, GILMER, Ruffin, Scales, Shaw, VANCE, Winslow—8.
SOUTH CAROLINA.—Bonham, Boyce, McQueen, Miles—4.
GEORGIA—Crawford, Gartrell, Jackson, Seward, Stephens, TRIPPE, Wright—7.
FLORIDA.—Hawkins—1.
ALABAMA.—Cobb, Curry, Dowdell, Houston, Moore, Shorter, Stallworth—7.
MISSISSIPPI.—Davis, McRae, Singleton—3,
LOUISIANA.—Eustis, Sandidge—2.
TEXAS.—Reagan—1.
TENNESSEE.—MAYNARD, READY, Smith, Watkins, ZOLLICOFFER—5.
KENTUCKY.—Burnett, Elliott, UNDERWOOD—3.
OHIO.—Burns, Cox, Hall, Pendleton, Vallandigham—5.
INDIANA.—Davis, Foley, Gregg, Hughes—4.
ILLINOIS.—Hodges, Marshall, Shaw, Smith—4.
MISSOURI.—ANDERSON, Caruthers, Clark, Craig, Phelps, WOODSON—6.
CALIFORNIA.—Scott—1. Total, 81.

Upon the adoption of Mr. Grow's amendment, the Republican vote, as will be seen, was unanimously in the affirmative. Of the votes from the Slave States, all but nine were in the negative, and, as we shall presently see, there was only one of that number who was really in favor of it, this one being Mr. Blair, Republican, of Missouri.

Mr. Grow's amendment being incorporated into the bill, the next question was upon the passage of the bill, which was defeated by the following vote :

YEAS.

MAINE.—*Foster, Morse, Washburn, Wood*—4.
NEW-HAMPSHIRE.—*Cragin, Pike, Tappan*—2.
VERMONT.—*Morrill, Royce, Walton*—3.
MASSACHUSETTS.—*Buffinton, Burlingame, Chaffee, Comins, Davis, Dawes, Gooch, Hall, Knapp, Thayer*—10.
RHODE ISLAND.—*Brayton, Durfee*—2.
CONNECTICUT.—*Clark, Dean*—2.
NEW-YORK.—*Andrews, Bennett, Burroughs,* Clark, *J. B. Cochrane,* John Cochrane, *Dodd, Fenton, Granger,* Hatch, *Hoard, Kelsey, Matteson, Morgan, Morse, Murray, Olin, Palmer, Parker, Spinner, Thompson*—21.
NEW-JERSEY.—*Clawson, Robbins*—2.
PENNSYLVANIA.—*Covode, Dick, Edie, Grow, Keim, Morris, Purviance, Ritchie, Stewart*—9.
MARYLAND.—Davis—1.
OHIO.—*Bingham, Bliss,* Cox, *Giddings,* Hall, *Harlan, Horton, Leiter,* Miller, *Mott, Sherman, Stanton, Tompkins, Wade*—14.
MICHIGAN.—*Howard, Leach, Walbridge, Waldron*—4.
INDIANA.—*Colfax, Kilgore, Pettit, Wilson*—4.

ILLINOIS.—*Farnsworth, Kellogg, Lovejoy,* **Morris,** Washburne—5.
WISCONSIN.—*Potter, Washburn*—2.
IOWA.—*Curtis, Davis*—2.
MINNESOTA.—Cavanaugh, Phelps—2.
MISSOURI.—*Blair*—1. Total—91.

NAYS.

CONNECTICUT.—Arnold—1.
NEW-YORK.—Corning, Russell, Searing, Taylor—4.
NEW-JERSEY.—Huyler.—1.
PENNSYLVANIA.—Ahl, Chapman, Dewart, Florence, Jones, Leidy, Montgomery, Phillips, White—9.
DELAWARE.—Whiteley—1.
MARYLAND.—Bowie, RICAUD, Stewart—3.
VIRGINIA.—Bocock, Caskie, Edmundson, Garnett, Goode, Hopkins, Millson, Powell—8.
NORTH CAROLINA.—Craige, GILMER, Ruffin, Scales, Shaw, VANCE, Winslow—7.
SOUTH CAROLINA.—Bonham, Boyce, McQueen—3.
GEORGIA. — Crawford, Gartrel, Jackson, Stephens, TRIPPE, Wright—6.
FLORIDA.—Hawkins—1.
ALABAMA.—Cobb, Dowdell, Houston, Moore, Shorter, Stallworth—6.
MISSISSIPPI.—Barksdale, Davis, McRae, Singleton—4.
LOUISIANA.—Sandidge, Taylor—2.
TEXAS.—Bryan, Reagan—2.
ARKANSAS.—Greenwood—1.
TENNESSEE.—Atkins, Avery, Jones, MAYNARD, READY, Savage, Smith, Watkins, ZOLLICOFFER—9.
KENTUCKY.—Burnett, Clay, Elliott, Jewett, MARSHALL, Mason, Peyton, Stevenson, Talbott, UNDERWOOD—10.
OHIO.—Burns, Cockerill, Groesbeck, Pendleton, Vallandigham—5.
INDIANA.—Davis, Foley, Gregg, Hughes—4.
ILLINOIS.—Marshall, Shaw—2.
MISSOURI.—ANDERSON, Caruthers, Clark, Craig, Phelps, WOODSON. Total—95.

The defeat of the bill, in consequence of the incorporation into it of Mr. Grow's amendment, shows that a majority of the House was really opposed to that amendment, although it had been adopted by a vote of 98 to 81. Certain members, who did not dare to vote directly against the amendment, joined in killing it afterward, by killing the bill, of which it had been made a part by their own votes.

Thus Messrs. Stewart, of Maryland, Atkins, Avery, Jones and Savage, of Tennessee, and Jewett, Stephenson, and Talbot, of Kentucky, who had voted for the amendment, voted afterward against the bill. Only one, Mr. Blair, of the nine Southern supporters of the amendment, proved true to it in the end, and no other Southern member came to its support in the final vote, saving only Mr. Davis, of Maryland, who represents the free-labor interest of the city of Baltimore, rather than the interest of the slaveholding and landed aristocracy of the planting States.

Afterward, on the same day, when these votes upon Mr. Grow's amendment were given, the representatives from Minnesota, both of them members of the Democratic party, delivered speeches, in which they made no secret of their chagrin that a measure so vital to their constituency encountered the nearly unanimous opposition of their political friends. Mr. Cavanaugh, one of the members from Minnesota (*Globe*, p. 505), said :

With reference to the vote on this bill to-day, with an overwhelming majority of this side of the House voting against my colleague and myself, voting against this bill, I say it frankly, I say it in sorrow, that it was to the Republican side of the House to whom we were compelled to look for support of this just and honorable measure. Gentlemen from the South, gentlemen who have broad acres and wide plantations, aided here to-day by their votes more to make Republican States in the North than by any vote which has been cast within the last two years. These gentlemen come here and ask us to support the South; yet they, to a man almost, vote against the free, independent labor of the North and West.

I, sir, have inherited my Democracy; have been attached to the Democratic party from my boyhood; have believed in the great truths as enunciated by the "fathers of the faith," and have cherished them religiously, knowing that, by their faithful application to every department of this Government, this nation has grown up from struggling colonies to prosperous, powerful, and sovereign States. But, sir, when I see Southern gentlemen come up, as I did to-day, and refuse, by their votes, to aid my constituents, refuse to place the actual tiller of the soil, the honest, industrious laborer, beyond the grasp and avarice of the speculator, I tell you, sir, I falter and I hesitate.

The amendment of Mr. Grow, forbidding the public sales of lands for at least ten years after their survey, would secure the great bulk of the lands to preëmptors, and would give them a long pay-day, and thus save them from the enormous usury they are now compelled to pay to money-lenders. It would not reduce the revenue derived by the Treasury from the public lands, but would only postpone it, and this postponement would be far less prejudicial to the Government than it would be beneficial to the settler. The Government can borrow money at four and a half per cent. per annum, while the settler frequently pays five per cent. per month for the money to enter his lands, to prevent their sale at public auction.

On the first of February, the question of the Public Lands was again before the House, the pending bill (House bill No. 72) being a bill to secure Homesteads to actual settlers, and being in the words following

A BILL TO SECURE HOMESTEADS TO ACTUAL SETTLERS ON THE PUBLIC DOMAIN.

§ 1. *Be it enacted by the Senate and House of Representatives of the United States of America in Congress assembled,* That any person who is the head of a family, or who has arrived at the age of twenty-one years, and is a citizen of the United States, or who shall have filed his intention to become such, as required by the naturalization laws of the United States, shall, from and after the passage of this act, be entitled to enter, free of cost, one quarter-section of vacant and unappropriated public lands which may, at the time the application is made, be subject to private entry, at $1 25 per acre, or a quantity equal thereto, to be located in a body, in conformity with the legal subdivisions of public lands, and after the same shall have been surveyed.

§ 2. *And be it further enacted,* That the person applying for the benefit of this act shall, upon application to the register of the land office in which he or she is about to make such entry, make affidavit before the said register that he or she is the head of a family, or is twenty-one years or more of age, and that such application is made for his or her exclusive use and benefit, and those specially mentioned in this act, and not either directly or indirectly for the use or benefit of any other person or persons whomsoever; and upon making the affidavit as above required, and filing the affidavit with the register, he or she shall thereupon be permitted to enter the quantity of land already specified: *Provided, however,* That no certificate shall be given or patent issued therefor until the expiration of five years from the date of such entry; and if, at the expiration of such time, or at any time thereafter, the person making such entry, or, if he be dead, his widow, or, in case of her death, his heirs or devisee, or in case of a widow making such entry, her heirs or devisee, in case of her death, shall prove by two creditable witnesses that he, she, or they, have continued to reside upon and cultivate such land, and still reside upon the same, and have not alienated the same, or any part thereof, then, in such case, he, she, or they, if at that time a citizen of the United States, shall, on payment of ten dollars, be entitled to a patent, as in other cases provided by for law: *And provided, further,* In case of the death of both father and mother, leaving an infant child or children under twenty-one years of age, the right and the fee shall inure to the benefit of said infant child or children, and the executor, administrator or guardian may, at any time within two years after the

death of the surviving parent, and in accordance with the laws of the State in which such children for the time being have their domicil, sell said land for the benefit of said infants, but for no other purpose; and the purchaser shall acquire the absolute title by the purchase, and be entitled to a patent from the United States.

§ 3. *And be it further enacted,* That the register of the land office shall note all such applications on the tract-books and plats of his office, and keep a register of all such entries, and make a return thereof to the General Land Office, together with the proof upon which they have been founded.

§ 4. *And be it further enacted,* That all lands acquired under the provisions of this act shall in no event become liable to the satisfaction of any debt or debts contracted prior to the issuing the patent therefor.

§ 5. *And be it further enacted,* That if, at any time after the filing the affidavit, as required in the second section of this act, and before the expiration of the five years aforesaid, it shall be proven, after due notice to the settler, to the satisfaction of the register of the land office, that the person having filed such affidavit shall have actually changed his or her residence, or abandoned the said entry for more than six months at any time, then, and in that event, the land so entered shall revert back to the Government, and be disposed of as other public lands are now by law, subject to an appeal to the General Land Office.

§ 6. *And be it further enacted,* That no individual shall be permitted to make more than one entry under the provisions of this act; and that the Commissioner of the General Land Office is hereby required to prepare and issue such rules and regulations, consistent with this act, as shall be necessary and proper to carry its provisions into effect; and that the registers and receivers of the several land offices shall be entitled to receive the same compensation for any lands entered under the provisions of this act that they are now entitled to receive when the same quantity of land is entered with money. one-half to be paid by the person making the application, at the time so doing, and the other half on the issue of the certificate by the person to whom it may be issued: *Provided,* That nothing in this act shall be so construed as to impair or interfere in any manner whatever with existing preëmption rights.

The previous question having been ordered, the House was brought to a direct vote upon this bill, without debate.

A motion to lay the bill on the table was lost —Yeas, 77; Nays, 113; and the bill was then passed—Yeas, 120; Nays, 76.

As these two votes were substantially the same, we only give the last one, which was upon the passage of the bill, and which was as follows:

YEAS.

MAINE.—*Abbott, Foster, Gilman, Morse, Washburn* —5.

NEW-HAMPSHIRE.—*Cragin, Pike, Tappan*—3.

VERMONT.—*Morrill, Royce, Walton*—3.

MASSACHUSETTS.—*Buffinton, Burlingame, Chaffee, Comins, Davis, Dawes, Gooch, Hall, Knapp, Thayer* —10.

RHODE ISLAND.—*Brayton, Durfee*—2.

CONNECTICUT.—Bishop, *Clark, Dean*—3.

NEW-YORK.—*Andrews,* Barr, *Burroughs, C. B. Cochrane,* John Cochrane, Corning, *Dodd, Fenton, Goodwin, Granger,* Haskin, Hatch, *Hoard, Kelsey,* Maclay, *Matteson, Morgan, Morse, Murray, Olin, Palmer, Parker, Pottle,* Russell, *Spinner,* Taylor, Ward—27.

NEW-JERSEY.—Adrian, *Clawson, Robbins,* Wortendyke —4.

PENNSYLVANIA.—*Covode, Dick,* Florence, *Grow,* Hickman, *Keim, Morris,* Phillips, *Purviance,* Reilly, *Roberts, Stewart, Kunkel*—13.

TENNESSEE.—Jones—1.

KENTUCKY.—Jewett—1.

OHIO.—*Bingham, Bliss,* Burns, Cockerill, Cox, *Giddings,* Groesbeck, Hall, *Harlan, Horton,* Lawrence, *Leiter,* Miller, Pendleton, *Sherman, Stanton, Tompkins,* Vallandigham, *Wade*—19.

INDIANA.—*Case, Colfax,* Davis, Foley, Gregg, *Kilgore, Pettit, Wilson*—8.

ILLINOIS.—*Farnsworth,* Hodges, *Kellogg, Lovejoy,* Morris, Smith, *Washburne*—7.

MICHIGAN.—*Howard, Leach, Walbridge, Waldron*—4.

WISCONSIN.—*Billinghurst, Potter, Washburn*—3.

MINNESOTA.—Cavanaugh, Phelps—2.

IOWA—*Curtis, Davis*—2.

MISSOURI.—Craig—1.
CALIFORNIA.—McKibbin, Scott—2. Total, 120.

NAYS.

PENNSYLVANIA.—Leidy—1.
DELAWARE.—Whiteley—1.
MARYLAND.—Bowie, DAVIS, HARRIS, Kunkel, RICAUD, Stewart—6.
VIRGINIA.—Bocock, Caskie, Edmundson, Faulkner, Garnett, Goode, Hopkins, Jenkins, Letcher, Millson, Smith—11.
NORTH CAROLINA. — Branch, Craige, GILMER, Ruffin, Scales, Shaw, VANCE, Winslow—8.
SOUTH CAROLINA. — Bonham, Boyce, Keitt, McQueen, Miles—5.
GEORGIA.—Crawford, Gartrell, HILL, Jackson, Seward, Stephens, TRIPPE, Wright—8.
ALABAMA. — Cobb, Curry, Dowdell, Houston, Moore, Shorter, Stallworth—7.
MISSISSIPPI.—Barksdale, Lamar, McRae, Singleton—4.
LOUISIANA.—EUSTIS—1.
TEXAS.—Reagan—1.
ARKANSAS.—Greenwood—1.
TENNESSEE.—Atkins, Avery, MAYNARD, READY, Smith, Watkins, Wright, ZOLLICOFFER—8.
KENTUCKY.—Burnett, MARSHALL, Mason, Peyton, UNDERWOOD—5.
OHIO.—*Nichols*—1.
INDIANA.—English, Hughes, Niblack—3.
ILLINOIS.—Marshall, Shaw—2.
MISSOURI.—ANDERSON, Clark, WOODSON—3. Total, 76.

Only three Southern members—Jones of Tennessee, Jewett of Kentucky, and Craig of Missouri—voted for the bill, thereby marking unmistakably the sectional character of the opposition to it.

The Republican vote, with a solitary exception, was given solid for the bill. Of the Northern members connected with the Democratic party, twenty-nine voted for the bill and six voted against it. Thus, of the entire Democratic party in the House, a large majority was against the bill, but even this is less important than the other fact, that the Southern wing of the vote was almost unanimously against, it being this Southern wing which controls in the party councils, and which, when out-voted in the House, has other departments of the Government, the Senate and the President, with which it is more powerful, and by means of which it has so far rarely failed to defeat measures, however popular and beneficial, which it dislikes.

The Homestead bill had now passed the House by a decisive majority, but it had yet to encounter the more dangerous ordeal of the Senate, in which the Democratic majority was larger, and in which the representation of the slaveholding States is proportionably greater.

No direct vote upon the measure was, in fact, reached in the Senate, because the Southern managers would not permit it.

There are two ways of killing off obnoxious measures. One is, to act upon them and vote them down. Another is, to overslaugh them whenever they are proposed, by proceeding to consider some other business. This latter method is invariably resorted to, where a measure, obnoxious to a majority of the Senate, is supposed to be acceptable to the people. And it was precisely by this method, and for that reason, that the Homestead bill was run over, shoved aside, evaded, and left unacted upon, by the Senate during its late session. The regular appropriation bills and the bill for the purchase of Cuba were being pressed upon the time of the Senate during the last days of the session,

both of them commanding the support of the majority of that body.

On the 17th day of February, Mr. Wade, of Ohio, (*Con. Globe*, page 1074,) moved to postpone all prior orders and take up the Homestead bill, which had passed the House. The following extracts from the debate upon this motion will exhibit the points made :

Mr. Wade.—The Homestead bill, to which I am a good deal attached, has, I believe, twice passed the House and come to this body, but somehow it has had the go-by, and we have never had a direct vote upon it here that I know of. I do not propose to discuss it for a single moment, and I hope none of its friends will debate it, because it has been pending before Congress for several years, and I presume every senator is perfectly well acquainted with all its provisions, and has made up his mind as to the course he will pursue in regard to it. I have no hope that anything I could say would win an opponent of the bill to its support; and I hope every friend of the measure will take no time in debate, but will try to get a vote upon it, for I think it is the great measure of the session. All I want, all I ask, is to have a vote upon it.

Mr. Reid, of North Carolina.—I think it is too late in the session now to take up this bill to be acted upon here, at least until we act upon other great measures upon which there is more unanimity of sentiment in the country, and a higher sense of duty upon us to pass them during the few days of the session that remain.

Mr. Hunter, of Virginia.—I believe that a fortnight from to-day will take us to the 3d of March. Now, it is known that we have nearly all the important appropriation bills, and one that is unfinished, to take up. I hope there will be no effort to press this Homestead bill, so as to displace the appropriation bills. I must appeal to the Senate to consider how little of the session is now left to us, and whether we ought not to take up the appropriation bill and dispose of it.

Mr. Shields, of Minnesota.—The friends of this bill desire nothing but a vote upon it, not to waste time in debate. Let us take it up, and have a fair vote upon it.

Mr. Hunter—I do not conceal the fact that I am very much opposed to it; but I suppose whenever this bill comes up, it must be the subject of debate.

Mr. Wilson, of Massachusetts.—I appreciate the anxiety of the senator from Virginia to take up the appropriation bill; but I would suggest to that senator that he allow us to take up this bill, and have a vote upon it. I do not suppose that anybody, who is in favor of the measure, desires to consume the time of the Senate, at this stage of the session, by discussing it. It has been discussed before the nation. It is well understood. I believe it is sustained by an overwhelming majority of the people of the country.

Mr. Wade.—I have no doubt, from the business before us, that this is the last opportunity we shall have to act upon this great measure, I hope, as I said before, that every friend of it will stand by it until it is either triumphant or defeated, and that, too, in preference to any other business that may be urged upon us. As to the appropriation bills, I have not the least fear but that they will go through. Their gravitation carries them through.

The question was then taken, and Mr. Wade's motion was carried by the following vote, the Republicans being indicated by *italics :*

YEAS—Messrs. Bright, Broderick, *Chandler, Collamer, Dixon, Doolittle, Fessenden, Foot, Foster,* Gwin, *Hale, Hamlin, Harlan,* Johnson, of Tennessee, *King,* Pugh, Rice, *Seward,* Shields, *Simmons,* Smith, Stuart, *Trumbull, Wade,* and *Wilson*—26.

NAYS—Messrs. Allen, Bayard, Benjamin, Bigler, Brown, Chestnut, Clay, Clingman, Davis, Fitch, Fitzpatrick, Green, Hammond, Hunter, Iverson, Lane, Mallory, Mason, Pearce, Reid, Slidell, Toombs, and Ward—23.

Upon an examination of this vote, it will be seen that the Republicans voted unanimously in the affirmative, and that the Slave State Senators were all in the negative, with the solitary exception of Mr. Johnson, of Tennessee. Of the Free State Democrats, Gwin, Bright, Pugh, Rice, Shields, Smith, and Stuart, all being from the new States, voted for Mr. Wade's motion.

The Homestead bill was now up, and, so far

as its friends were concerned, nothing was asked but a vote, which would not have consumed ten minutes. But a vote was precisely what the Southern managers were determined to avoid.

Instantly, therefore, upon the announcement of the success of Mr. Wade's motion, which brought the bill before the Senate, Mr. Hunter took the floor, and moved that it be set aside, so as to take up another bill, viz. : the Diplomatic and Consular Appropriation bill.

No question of order was raised upon this motion of Mr. Hunter, but it was well characterized as "*child's play*," to move to set aside a bill, instantly after a vote to take it up.

Pending some conversational debate upon Mr. Hunter's motion, the hour of twelve o'clock arrived, and the Vice-President decided that the Cuba bill, having been assigned for that hour, was the subject pending before the Senate.

Hereupon, Mr. Wade moved to postpone the twelve o'clock order, and continue the consideration of the Homestead bill, and this motion prevailed by the following vote :

Yeas—Messrs. Bell, Bright, Broderick, *Chandler*, *Clark, Collamer, Dixon, Doolittle,* Douglas, *Durkee, Fessenden, Foot, Foster, Hale, Hamlin, Harlan,* Johnson of Tennessee, *King,* Pugh, Rice, *Seward. Simmons,* Smith, Stuart, *Trumbull, Wade,* and *Wilson* —27.

Nays—Messrs. Allen, Bates, Benjamin, Bigler, Brown, Clay, Clingman, Davis, Fitch, Fitzpatrick, Green, Gwin, Hammond, Hunter, Iversons, Johnson, of Arkansas, Lane, Mallory, Mason, Pearce, Reid, Sebastian, Slidell, Toombs, Ward, and Yulee—26.

On this vote, an additional Southern Senator, Mr. Bell, of Tennessee, ranged himself on the side of Homesteads. But this was offset by the ratting back to the negative side of Mr. Gwin.

The Homestead bill was now again before the Senate, but the question, as stated by the Vice-President, was still upon Mr. Hunter's motion to set it aside, and take up the Consular and Diplomatic Appropriation bill.

Mr. Mason, of Virginia, threatened an "*extended debate*" upon the Homestead bill, if its consideration were insisted upon. He declared, at any rate, for himself that he intended to "*go into it pretty largely, because he had not yet known a bill so fraught with mischief, and mischief of the most demoralizing kind.*"

Mr. Wade and Mr. Seward, in brief and energetic terms, exhorted the friends of the bill to stand firm.

The vote was then taken upon Mr. Hunter's motion, and resulted as follows :

Yeas.—Messrs. Allen, Bates, Bayard, Benjamin, Bigler, Brown, Clay, Clingman, Davis, Fitch, Fitzpatrick, Green, Gwin, Hammond, Hunter, Iverson, Johnson of Arkansas, Kennedy, Lane, Mallory, Mason, Pearce, Reid, Sebastian, Slidell, Toombs, Ward, and Yulee—28.

Nays.—Messrs. Bell, Bright, Broderick, *Chandler, Clark, Collamer, Dixon, Doolittle,* Douglas, *Durkee, Fessenden, Foot, Foster, Hale, Hamlin, Harlan,* Houston, Johnson of Tennessee, *King,* Pugh, Rice, *Seward, Simmons,* Smith, Stuart, *Trumbull Wade,* and *Wilson*—28.

The vote being a tie, the Vice-President, Mr. Breckinridge, voted in the affirmative, and thus, after a long struggle, the Homestead bill was, for that day, overslaughed.

Of the twenty-eight votes for overslaughing it, all but five are from the South, and one of

these five, Mr. Gwin, is only a temporary resident of a Free State.

Of the twenty-eight votes in favor of sustaining the bill, only three are from the South, and only one of the three (Johnson of Tennessee,) is a Democrat.

Two days afterward, on the 19th of February, Mr. Wade again moved to set aside all prior orders and take up the Homestead bill ; but this motion was negatived by the following vote :

Yeas.—Messrs. Broderick, *Chandler, Clark, Collamer, Dixon, Doolittle, Durkee, Fessenden, Foot, Hale Hamlin, Harlan,* Johnson of Tennessee, Jones, *King,* Pugh, Rice, *Seward,* Shields, *Simmons,* Stuart, *Trumbull, Wade,* and *Wilson*—24.

Nays.—Messrs. Allen, Bates, Bayard, Benjamin, Bigler, Bright, Brown, Chestnut, Clay, Clingman, Crittenden, Davis, Fitch, Fitzpatrick, Green, Hammond, Houston, Hunter, Iverson, Kennedy, Mallory, Mason, Pearce, Polk, Reid, Sebastian, Slidell, Smith, Toombs, Ward, and Yulee—31.

Upon these two days, the 17th and 19th of February, the question was made between the consideration of the Homestead bill and the consideration of the appropriation bills, the necessity of passing which last bills did not fail to be insisted upon by the Democratic managers. At a subsequent stage of the session, as will be presently seen, the question was made between considering the Homestead bill and considering the Cuba bill.

Upon the 25th day of February, upon the occasion of a motion by Mr. Slidell to postpone all prior orders and take up the bill for the purchase of Cuba, Mr. Doolittle resisted it, and called upon the friends of Homesteads to vote it down, so that he himself might submit a motion to take up the Homestead bill. Mr. Doolittle said :

I think it would be better to take up this question of the Homestead bill and vote upon it, and then the Cuba bill will come up. I ask the friends of the Homestead bill now to stand by it and give it the preference.

The vote was then taken, and the motion to take up the Cuba bill prevailed, as follows :

Yeas.—Messrs. Allen, Bayard, Bell, Benjamin, Bigler, Brown, Chestnut, Clay, Clingman, Davis, Fitch, Fitzpatrick, Green, Gwin, Hammond, Houston, Hunter, Iverson, Jones, Lane, Mallory, Mason, Polk, Pugh, Reid, Rice, Sebastian, Shields, Slidell, Smith, Stuart, Toombs, Ward, Wright, and Yulee—35.

Nays.—Messrs. Broderick, *Cameron, Chandler, Clark, Collamer, Dixon, Doolittle,* Douglas, *Durkee, Fessenden, Foot, Foster, Hale, Hamlin, Harlan,* Johnson of Tennessee, Kennedy, *King,* Pearce, *Seward, Simmons, Trumbull, Wade,* and *Wilson*—24.

The Cuba bill was now up, and the discussion upon it protracted the session late into the night, and almost into the next morning. It was distinctly seen during the progress of this discussion that it would be without practical result, and that no vote could be reached before the final adjournment of Congress.

Accordingly, at ten o'clock in the evening, Mr. Doolittle felt it to be his duty to renew the attempt to set aside the Cuba bill, the subject-matter of a manifestly idle debate, so as to take up the Homestead bill. His motion to that effect, and the commencement of the debate upon it, will be found on page 1351 of the *Congressional Globe.* Such extracts are made as will exhibit its general character :

Mr. Trumbull.—If there was any assurance that the Homestead bill could be taken up, after the Cuba question was disposed of, I should be willing to see it have the go by on the present occasion ; but we have sought repeatedly to bring up the Homestead bill, and every movement that has been made to bring it up has been met with a counter movement, crowding it out of the way with something else. . . . . If the senator from Virginia will give us an assurance that we shall have a chance to bring up the Homestead bill, and keep it before the Senate until we can get a vote upon it, after the Cuba bill is through, and that he will not interpose an appropriation bill, I would join with gentlemen in asking my friend from Wisconsin to withdraw the motion he has made.

Mr. Hunter.—I certainly will press the appropriation bills. I will give no promise to vote to take up the Homestead bill.

Mr. Trumbull.—That is as I expected. We now have notice that we are to be met with an appropriation bill the moment that the Cuba question is disposed of, and here we are wasting our time at this stage of the session in making long speeches, and debating about the acquisition of a country that does not belong to us, instead of providing for the settlement of the country which we own. There can be no hope of getting up the Homestead bill as against an appropriation bill.

Mr. Seward.—After nine hours yielding to the discussion of the Cuba question, it is time to come back to the great question of the day and the age. The Senate may as well meet face to face the issue which is before them. It is an issue presented by the competition between these two questions. One, the Homestead bill, is a question of homes, of lands for the landless freemen of the United States. The Cuba bill is a question of slaves for the slaveholders of the United States.

Mr. Wade.—I am very glad that this question has at length come up. I am glad, too, that it has antagonized with this nigger question. (Laughter.) I have been trying here for nearly a month to get a straightforward vote upon this great measure of land for the landless. I glory in that measure. It is the greatest that has ever come before the American Senate, and it has now come so that there is no dodging it. The question will be, shall we give niggers to the niggerless, or lands to the landless?

I moved some days ago to take up this subject. It was said then that there was an appropriation bill that stood in the way. The senator from Virginia had his appropriation bills. It was important, then, that they should be settled at once; there was danger that they would be lost, and the Government would stop in consequence; and the appeal was made to gentlemen to give this bill the go-by for the time being, at all events, and the appeal was successful. The appropriation bills lie very easy now behind this nigger operation. (Laughter.) When you come to niggers for the niggerless, all other questions sink into insignificance.

Mr. Doolittle's motion to set aside the Cuba bill for the purpose of taking up the Homestead bill, was lost, by the following vote:

YEAS—Messrs. Broderick, *Cameron, Clark, Chandler, Collamer, Doolittle, Fessenden, Foot, Foster, Hale, Hamlin, Harlan,* Johnson of Tennessee, *King, Seward, Simmons, Trumbull, Wade,* and *Wilson*—19.

NAYS—Messrs. Allen, Benjamin, Bayard, Bigler, Brown, Chestnut, Clay, Clingman, Douglas, Fitch, Fitzpatrick, Green, Gwin, Hunter, Iverson, Johnson of Arkansas, Lane, Mallory, Mason, Polk, Pugh, Reid, Rice, Sebastian, Shields, Slidell, Toombs, Ward and Wright—29.

This was the last attempt made to get up the Homestead bill in the Senate. It had first been overslaughed by the appropriation bills, and now by the Cuba bill, and no expectation remained of reaching it during the few remaining days of the session. The Republicans, who had endeavored to get it up in all forms and on all occasions without success, felt it to be their duty to abandon a manifestly hopeless struggle.

From this review of the votes in the Senate and House, it will be seen that the two great national parties, the one representing the rights and interests of free labor, and the other representing the pretensions of Negro Slavery, have come to a well-defined issue upon this great matter of the disposition of the Public Domain.

———

In the House of Representatives, on the 6th of March, 1860, Mr. Lovejoy, from the Committee on Public Lands, reported the following bill (previously introduced by Mr. Grow), which was read twice, and committed to the Committee of the Whole.

Be it enacted by the Senate and House of Representatives of the United States of America in Congress assembled, That any person who is the head of a family, or who has arrived at the age of twenty-one years, and is a citizen of the United States, or who shall have filed his intention to become such, as required by the naturalization laws of the United States, shall, from and after the passage of this act, be entitled to enter, free of cost, one hundred and sixty acres of unappropriated public lands, upon which said person may have filed a preëmption claim, or which may, at the time the application is made, be subject to preëmption at one dollar and twenty-five cents, or less, per acre; or eighty acres of such unappropriated lands, at two dollars and fifty cents per acre; to be located in a body, in conformity to the legal subdivisions of the public lands, and after the same shall have been surveyed.

§ 2. *And be it further enacted,* That the person applying for the benefit of this act shall, upon application to the register of the land office in which he or she is about to make such entry, make affidavit before the said register or receiver that he or she is the head of a family, or is twenty-one years or more of age, and that such application is made for his or her exclusive use and benefit, and those specially mentioned in this act, and not either directly or indirectly for the use or benefit of any other person or persons whomsoever; and upon filing the affidavit with the register or receiver, he or she shall thereupon be permitted to enter the quantity of land specified: *Provided, however,* That no certificate shall be given or patent issued therefor until the expiration of five years from the date of such entry; and if, at the expiration of such time, or at any time within two years thereafter, the person making such entry—or if he be dead, his widow; or in case of her death, his heirs or devisee; or in case of a widow making such entry, her heirs or devisee, in case of her death—shall prove by two credible witnesses that he, she, or they have resided upon and cultivated the same for the term of five years immediately succeeding the time of filing the affidavit aforesaid; then, in such case, he, she, or they, if at that time a citizen of the United States, shall, on payment of ten dollars, be entitled to a patent, as in other cases provided for by law: *And provided, further,* That in case of the death of both father and mother, leaving an infant child, or children, under twenty-one years of age, the right and fee shall inure to the benefit of said infant child, or children; and the executor, administrator, or guardian may, at any time within two years after the death of the surviving parent, and in accordance with the laws of the State in which such children for the time being have their domicil, sell said land for the benefit of said infants, but for no other purpose; and the purchaser shall acquire the absolute title by the purchase, and be entitled to a patent from the United States, on payment of the office fees and sum of money herein specified.

SEC. 3. *And be it further enacted,* That the register of the land office shall note all such applications on the tract-books and plats of his office, and keep a register of all such entries, and make return thereof to the General Land Office, together with the proof upon which they have been founded.

SEC. 4. *And be it further enacted,* That all lands acquired under the provisions of this act shall in no event become liable to the satisfaction of any debt or debts contracted prior to the issuing of the patent therefor.

SEC. 5. *And be it further enacted,* That if, at any time after the filing of the affidavit, as required in the second section of this act, and before the expiration of the five years aforesaid, it shall be proven, after due notice to the settler, to the satisfaction of the register of the land office, that the person having filed such affidavit shall have actually changed his or her residence, or abandoned the said entry for more than six months at any time, then, and in that event, the land so entered shall revert to the government.

SEC 6. *And be it further enacted,* That no individual shall be permitted to make more than one entry under the provisions of this act; and that the Commissioner of the General Land Office is hereby required to prepare and issue such rules and regulations, consistent with this act, as shall be necessary and proper to carry its provisions into effect; and that the registers and receivers of the several land offices shall be entitled to receive the same compensation for any lands entered under the provisions of this act that they are now entitled to receive when the same quantity of land is entered with money, one-half to be paid by the person making the application at the time of so doing, and the other half on the issue of the certificate, by the person to whom it may be issued: *Provided*, That nothing contained in this act shall be so construed as to impair or interfere in any manner whatever with existing preëmption rights: *And provided, further*, That all persons who may have filed their applications for a preëmption right prior to the passage of this act shall be entitled to all privileges of this act.

Subsequently. a motion was made by Mr. Lovejoy, to reconsider the vote by which the bill had been referred to the Committee of the Whole. On Monday, March 12, Mr. Lovejoy called up this motion, and under the operation of the previous question, it was agreed to, 106 to 67, as follows:

YEAS.—Messrs. A d r a i n, Aldrich, Ashley, Babbitt, Bingham, Blake, Buffinton, Burlingame. Campbell, Carey, Carter, Case, *John Cochrane*, Colfax, Conkling, *Cooper*, Corwin, Covode, *Cox, James Craig*, Curtis, J o h n G, D a v i s, Dawes, Delano, Duell, Dunn, Edgerton, Elliot, Fenton, Ferry, *Florence*, Foster, *Fouke*, Frank, French, Gooch, Graham, Grow, Gurley, Hale, Hall, H a s k i n, Helmick, Hoard, *Holman, Howard*, Hutchins, Junkin, Francis W. Kellogg, William Kellogg, Kilgore, Killinger, *Larrabee*, De Witt C. Leach, Lee, *Logan*, Loomis, Lovejoy. *Maclay*, Marston, *Charles D. Martin, McClernand*, McKean, McKnight, Millward, Moorhead, Morrill, Edward Joy Morris, Morse, Olin, *Pendleton*, Perry, Porter, Potter, Pottle, Rice, R i g g s, Christopher Robinson, *James C. Robinson*, Royce, S c h w a r t z, *Scott*, Scranton, Sedgwick, Sherman, Somes, Spinner, Stanton, *Stout*, Stratton, Tappan, Thayer, Tompkins, Train, Trimble, *Vallandigham*, Vandever, Verree, Waldron, Walton, Cadwalader C. Washburn, Ellihu B Washburne, Israel Washburn, Wells, Windom, and Woodruff—106

NAYS—Messrs. GREEN ADAMS. *Thomas L. Anderson*, WILLIAM C. ANDERSON. *Avery, Barksdale, Bocock, Bonham*, BRABSON, *Branch*, BRISTOW, *Burch, Burnett, Clopton, Cobb, Curry, Reuben Davis, De Jarnette, Edmundson, English*, ETHERIDGE. *Garnett, Gartrell*, GILMER, *Hardeman*, J. MORRISON HARRIS, HATTON, HILL, *Hindman, Houston, Hughes, Jackson, Jenkins, Jones, Keitt. Lamar, Landrum, Leake, Love*, MALLORY, *Elbert S. Martin*, MAYNARD, *McQueen, McRae, Miles, Millson, Montgomery*, NELSON, *Niblack, Noell, Peyton, Pryor, Pugh, Reagan, Ruffin, Sickles, Simms, Singleton, William Smith*, WILLIAM N. H. SMITH, *Stevenson*, STOKES, *Underwood*, VANCE, WEBSTER, *Whiteley, Woodson, and Wright*—67.

Republicans in Roman; Democrats in *Italics*; Americans in SMALL CAPS; Anti-Lecompton Democrats in Roman s p a c e d.

So the motion was reconsidered, and the bill was before the House. Mr. Lovejoy moved that the bill be engrossed and read a third time. Mr. Branch (N. C.) moved to lay the bill on the table. Lost, 62 to 112, the yeas being all from the South, except Mr. Montgomery, Democrat, of Pennsylvania, and the nays all from the North, except Mr. James Craig, Democrat, of Missouri.

So the House refused to lay the bill on the table; and it was read a third time and passed. The vote was as follows—The Republicans in Roman, the Administration Democrats in *Italics*, the Americans in SMALL CAPS, and the Anti-Lecompton Democrats in Roman s p a c e d:

YEAS.

MAINE.—Foster, French, Morse, Perry, Somes, Israel Washburn—6

NEW-HAMPSHIRE.—Marston, Tappan—2.

VERMONT.—Morrill, Royce, Walton—3.

MASSACHUSETTS.—Buffinton, Dawes, Delano, Elliot, Gooch, Rice, Thayer, Train—8.

CONNECTICUT.—Burnham, Ferry, Loomis, Woodruff—4.

RHODE-ISLAND.—Christopher Robinson—1.

NEW-YORK.—*Barr*, BRIGGS, Carter, *John Cochrane*, Conkling, Duell, Fenton, Frank, Graham, H a s k i n, Hoard, Humphrey, Lee, *Maclay*, McKean, Olin, Pottle, *Sickles*, Spinner, Van Wyck, Wells—21.

NEW-JERSEY.—A d r a i n, R i g g s, Stratton—3.

PENNSYLVANIA.—Babbitt, Campbell. Covode, *Florence*, Grow, Hale, Hall, H i c k m a n, Junkin. Killenger, McKnight, McPherson, Millward, E. Joy Morris, S c h w a r t z Scranton, Verree—17.

OHIO.—Ashley, Bingham, Blake, Carey, Corwin, Cox, Edgerton, Gurley, Helmick, *Howard*, Hutchins, *Charles D. Martin, Pendleton*, Sherman, Stanton, Tompkins, Trimble, *Vallandigham*—18.

MICHIGAN.—*Cooper*, Francis W. Kellogg, De Witt C. Leach, Waldron—4.

INDIANA.—Case, Colfax, J o h n G. D a v i s, Dunn, *English, Holman*, Kilgore. *Niblack*, Porter, Wilson—10.

ILLINOIS.—*Fouke*, Wm. Kellogg, *Logan*, Lovejoy. *McClernand, James C. Robinson*, E. B. Washburne—7

WISCONSIN.—*Larrabee*, Potter, C. C. Washburn—3.

IOWA.—Curtis, Vandever—2.

MINNESOTA.—Aldrich, Windom—2.

CALIFORNIA.—*Burch, Scott*—2.

OREGON.—*Stout*—1.

MISSOURI.—*James Craig*—1. Total, 115.

All from the Free States except James Craig, of Missouri.

NAYS.

PENNSYLVAVIA.—*Montgomery*—1.

DELAWARE.—*Whiteley*—1.

MARYLAND.—H. WINTER DAVIS, J. M. HARRIS, *Hughes*, WEBSTER—4.

VIRGINIA.—*Bocock, De Jarnette, Edmundson, Garnett, Jenkins, Leake, Elbert S. Martin, Wilson, Pryor, William Smith*—10.

NORTH CAROLINA.—*Branch*, GILMER, *Ruffin*, WILLIAM N. H. SMITH, VANCE—5.

SOUTH CAROLINA.—*Bonham, Keith, McQueen, Miles*—2.

GEORGIA.—*Gartrell*, HARDEMAN, HILL, *Jackson, Jones, Love, Underwood*—7.

ALABAMA.—*Clopton, Cobb, Curry, Houston, Suydenham Moore, Pugh*—6.

MISSISSIPPI—*Barksdale, Reuben Davis, Lamar, McRea, Singleton*—5.

LOUISIANA.—*Landrum*—1.

ARKANSAS.—*Hindman*—1.

TEXAS.—*Hamilton, Reagan*—2.

MISSOURI.—*Thomas L. Anderson, Noell, Woodson*—3

TENNESSEE.—*Avery*, ETHERIDGE, HATTON, MAYNARD, NELSON, STOKES, *Wright*—7.

KENTUCKY.—GREEN, ADAMS, WILLIAM C. ANDERSON, BRISTOW, *Burnett*, MALLORY, *Peyton, Simms, Stevenson*—8. Total, 65.

All from Slave States except Montgomery, Dem., of Pennsylvania.

This bill was sent to the Senate, where it was referred to the Committee on Public Lands, and on the 17th of April, Mr. Johnson, of Tennessee, the Chairman of that Committee, reported a substitute for the House bill, granting Homesteads to actual settlers, at 25 cents per acre, but not including preëmptors then occupying the Public Lands. When this bill came before the Senate for action, Mr. Wade, of Ohio, moved to amend, by substituting the House bill, which was lost, 26 to 31, as follows:

YEAS—Messrs. Anthony, Bingham, Cameron, Chandler, Clark, Collamer, Dixon, Doolittle, Douglas, Durkee, Foot, Foster, Grimes, Hale, Hamlin, King, Rice, Seward, Simmons, Sumner, Ten Eyck, Toombs, Trumbull, Wade, Wilkinson, and Wilson—26.

NAYS—Messrs. Bayard, Bigler, Bragg, Bright, Brown, Chesnut, Clay, Clingman, Davis. Fitch, Fitzpatrick, Green, Gwin, Hammond, Hemphill, Hunter, Iverson, Johnson, of Arkansas, Johnson, of Tennessee, Lane, Latham, Mason, Nicholson, Polk, Powell, Pugh, Saulsbury, Sebastian, Slidell, Wigfall, and Yulee—31.

Yeas, all Republicans except three, Douglas, Rice, and Toombs. Nays, all Democrats.

The Senate finally, on the 10th May, passed Mr. Johnson's bill, 44 to 8, the Nays being Messrs. Bragg, Clingman, Hamlin, Hunter, Mason, Pearce, Powell and Toombs. The House refused to concur; the Senate refused to recede, and the result was a protracted conference on the part of Committees of the two Houses, which committees finally came to an agreement, on the 19th June, by the House accepting the Senate bill with slight amendments. On that day Mr. Schuyler Colfax reported to the House as follows:

Mr. Colfax.—I rise to a question of privilege. I am instructed by the Committee of Conference on the disagreeing votes of the two Houses on the Homestead bill, to report that, after twelve meetings of the three different Conferences that have been appointed, they this morning finally agreed. I hold in my hand the report of the Committee, which can be read if any gentleman desires it. But perhaps it would render the report clearer and more intelligible if I should briefly state its leading features. The Senate bill all the members of the House are familiar with. The Conferees upon the part of the House finding, after the most earnest efforts, that it would be utterly impossible for them to induce the Senate to agree to the House bill, have been discussing what changes could be made in the Senate bill, so as to render it acceptable enough for the House to accept, rather than the whole should fail. They have finally agreed upon a report as follows: In the first place, I will say that the bill, as it passed the Senate, provided, that the preëmptors now upon the public lands might remain there two years before they should be required to purchase their lands, but should then pay for them at the rate of $1 25 per acre, thus removing them entirely from within the purview of the benefits which would apply to the settlers hereafter upon the public lands. This point the House Conferees refused to accede to, and if persisted in, we should have again reported a disagreement. Finally, however, a compromise was arranged on this point, and to protect the preëmptors now on the Government land, which was to be advertised this fall for sale, we changed the Senate bill so as to protect them for at least two years from land sales, and to allow them then to secure their homes at *one half* the Government price, namely sixty-two and a-half cents per acre. I need scarcely add, that, if the Senate could have been induced to give them the benefit of their twenty-five-cent-per-acre provision, we should have insisted on it inflexibly; but what I have stated is the very lowest point that could be obtained. The second change we have made in the Senate bill is in relation to the scope of land coming under the operations of the law. The House bill embraced all the Government land, offered or unoffered, except such as was specially reserved. The Senate bill confined its provisions to land subject to private entry, exclusively. As I have explained on a former occasion, the expression "subject to private entry" means such as are left after the lands have been once regularly brought into market, exposed to public sale, and the speculators have taken such as they see fit to purchase. The difference between these two bills seemed so radical as to be incapable of adjustment; and the scope of farming land covered by the Senate bill was so limited, there being but little, if any, in Minnesota, Kansas, Nebraska, California, Oregon, and Washington, that the House conferees declined to accept it. But on this, too, we finally effected a compromise. By our report, all the land subject to private entry is included, and, *in addition*, all the odd-numbered sections of the surveyed public lands, which have not been opened to public sale—a most material and beneficent enlargement of the Senate bill. We were offered, after this agreement, whichever half of the unoffered lands we chose, and we took the odd-numbered sections. The reason for this was, that the 16th section of a township, being reserved for school purposes by our land laws, the four *adjoining* sections to it, on the north, west, east, and south, are sections 9, 15, 17, and 21, all odd-numbered sections, which are thus saved for homestead settlers, who have reserved for them 18 out of the 35 disposable sections in each township of six miles square.

On all these lands, actual settlers, who are heads of families, are allowed, after having occupied the land for five years, to purchase at 25 cents per acre, which is about the average cost price of the public lands to the Government. We struggled, of course, to include all young men over 21 who are not heads of families, and to adopt the Free Homestead principle of the House bill; but on these points the Senate was inflexible, and we took what we did because it was the very best we could get. The Senate bill originally provided that the Homestead settler might acquire title to his land at any time by paying full Government prices; but desiring to promote actual settlement, we now provide that he cannot do this till after he has been on the land six months. When he stays, or his family if he deceases, the full five years he obtains it at 25 cents per acre. The Senate have also agreed to strike out the eighth section of their bill, which made it imperative upon the President to ex-

pose all public lands to sale within two years after they shall have been surveyed, which we held would be peculiarly oppressive upon the pioneers who had gone to the frontier to settle upon the public lands, and to which we could never have consented. Now, Mr. Speaker, I desire to state, in conclusion, that the compromise we have made upon the subject is not in accordance with what I should desire to have passed, if I had the power to frame the bill myself; but it is the very utmost we could obtain from the Senate, as now constituted. The Senators who served with us on the Conference have been notified by me, and also by my colleague (Mr. Windom, of Minnesota,) that we regard this as but a single step in advance toward a law which we shall demand from the American Congress, enacting a comprehensive and liberal Homestead policy. This we have agreed to as merely an *avant courrier*. We shall demand it at the next session of Congress, and until it is granted; until all the public lands shall be open to all the people of the United States; and I state this publicly, that no one shall regard us as estopped hereafter, because we accepted this half-way measure rather than to allow the whole to fail. I should have added that all persons, whether citizens or those who have only declared their intentions, are allowed to go on the lands under this bill; but are required to perfect their naturalization before the five years expire, and the patent issues. I now demand the previous question on concurring on the report of the Committee, and passing the bill as thus amended.

Mr. Farnsworth.—I desire to ask the gentleman from Indiana whether this bill confines its benefits to those who are heads of families.

Mr. Colfax.—It does, because we failed, despite our utmost efforts, in procuring its extension to all; but we shall appeal to the young men to demand of those who make and who execute the laws, that the system inaugurated by this bill, shall be widened so as to admit them to its benefits, and I will join them in this demand.

Mr. Grow.—I just desire to say that we have taken this bill, not because it is what we want, but on the principle that "half a loaf is better than no bread."

The House agreed to the Report of the Committee, 115 to 51, as follows:

Yeas.—Messrs. Ashley, Babbitt, Barr, Bingham, Francis P. Blair, Samuel S. Blair, Blake, Brayton, Briggs, Buffinton, Burch, Burlingame, Burnham, Butterfield, Campbell, Carey, Carter, Case, Horace F. Clark, Cobb, Colfax, Corwin, Covode, Cox, Curtis, John G. Davis, Dawes, Delano, Duell, Dunn, Edgerton, Edwards, Elliot, Ely, Ferry, Florence, Foster, Frank, French, Gooch, Graham, Grow, Gurley, Hale, Hall, Haskin, Helmick, Hoard, Wm. Howard, Humphrey, Hutchins, Junkin, Francis W. Kellogg, Wm. Kellogg, Kenyon, Killinger, DeWitt C. Leach, Lee, Longnecker, Loomis, Maclay, Marston, McKean, McKnight, McPherson, Millward, Moorhead, Morrill, Edward Joy Morris, Isaac N. Morris, Morse, Niblack, Nixon, Olin, Palmer, Pendleton, Perry, Pettit, Phelps, Porter, Potter, Rice, Riggs, Christopher Robinson, Royce, Sedgwick, Sherman, Somes, Spaulding, Spinner, Stanton, William Stewart, Stout, Tappan, Taylor, Thayer, Theaker, Tompkins, Train, Trimble, Vandever, Van Wyck, Verree, Wade, Walton, Cadwalader C. Washburn, Elihu B. Washburne, Israel Washburn, Wells, Windom, and Woodruff—115.

Nays—Messrs. Green Adams, William C. Anderson, Ashmore, Avery, Barksdale, Bocock, Bonham, Boyce, Brabson, Branch, Burnett, Clopton, Burton Craige, Crawford, Curry, De Jarnette, Gilmer, Hardeman, J. Morrison Harris, John T. Harris, Hatton, Houston, Jenkins, Jones, Keitt, Landrum, James M. Leach, Leake, Love, Mallory, Maynard, McQueen, Miles, Millson, Sydenham Moore, Nelson, Peyton, Quarles, Reagan, Ruffin, William Smith, William N. H. Smith, Stevenson, Stokes, Thomas, Underwood, Vance, Webster, Winslow, Woodson, and Wright—51.

The nays are all from the Slave States.

The Senate agreed to the report of the Conference Committee, 36 to 2—Messrs. Bragg and Pearce.

The following is the bill as it was finally reported by the Conference Committee and passed both Houses:

AN ACT to secure Homesteads to actual settlers on the Public Domain, and for other purposes.

Be it enacted by the Senate and House of Representatives of the United States of America in Congress assembled, That any person who is the head of a family, and a citizen of the United States, shall, from and after the passage of this act, be entitled to enter one quarter-section of vacant and unappropriated public lands, or any less quantity, to be located in a body, in conformity with the legal subdivisions of the public lands, after the same shall have been surveyed, upon the following conditions : that the person applying for the benefit of this act shall, upon application to the register of the land-office in which he or she is about to make such entry, make affidavit before the said register or receiver of said land-office that he or she is the head of a family, and is actually settled on the quarter-section, or other subdivision not exceeding a quarter-section, proposed to be entered, and that such application is made for his or her use and benefit, or for the use and benefit of those specially mentioned in this section, and not either directly or indirectly for the use or benefit of any other person or persons whomsoever, and that he or she has never at any previous time, had the benefit of this act; and upon making the affidavit as above required, and filing the same with the register, he or she shall thereupon be permitted to enter the quantity of land already specified : *Provided, however,* That no final certificate shall be given, or patent issued therefor, until the expiration of five years from the date of such entry ; and if, at the expiration of such time, the person making such entry, or, if he be dead, his widow, or, in case of her death, his child or children, or in case of a widow making such entry, her child or children, in case of her death, shall prove, by two credible witnesses, that he, she, or they—that is to say, some member or members of the same family—has or have erected a dwelling-house upon said land, and continued to reside upon and cultivate the same for the term of five years, and still reside upon the same (and that neither the said land or any part thereof has been alienated) ; then, in such case, he, she, or they, upon the payment of 25 cents per acre for the quantity entered, shall be entitled to a patent, as in other cases provided by law : *And provided further,* In case of the death of both father and mother, leaving a minor child or children, the right and the fee shall inure to the benefit of said minor child or children, and the guardian shall be authorized to perfect the entry for the beneficiaries, as if there had been a continued residence of the settler for five years. *Provided,* That nothing in this section shall be so construed as to embrace or in any way include any quarter-section or fractional quarter-section of land upon which any preëmption right has been acquired prior to the passage of this act. *And provided further,* That all entries made under the provisions of this section, upon *lands which have not been offered for public sale, shall be confined to and upon sections designated by odd numbers.*

§ 2. *And be it further enacted,* That the register of the Land Office shall note all such applications on the tract books and plats of his office, and keep a register of all such entries, and make return thereof to the General Land Office, together with the proof upon which they have been founded.

§ 3. *And be it further enacted,* That no land acquired under the provisions of this act shall in any event, become liable to the satisfaction of any debt or debts until after the issuing of the patent therefor.

§ 4. *And be it further enacted,* That if, at any time after filing the affidavit, as required in the first section of this act, and before the expiration of the five years aforesaid, it shall be proved, after due notice to the settler, to the satisfaction of the register of the Land Office, that the person having filed such affidavit shall have sworn falsely in any particular, or shall have voluntarily abandoned the possession and cultivation of the said land for more than six months at any time, or sold his right under the entry, then, and in either of those events, the register shall cancel the entry, and the land so entered shall revert to the Government, and be disposed of as other public lands are now by law, subject to an appeal to the Secretary of the Interior. And in no case shall any land, the entry whereof shall have been cancelled, again be subject to occupation, or entry, or purchase, until the same shall have been reported to the General Land Office, and, by the direction of the President of the United States, again advertised and offered at public sale.

§ 5. *And be it further enacted,* That if any person, now or hereafter, a resident of any one of the States or Territories, and not a citizen of the United States, but who at the time of making such application for the benefit of this act, *shall have filed a declaration of intention,* as required by the naturalization laws of the United States, and shall have become a citizen of the same before the issuing of the patent as provided for in this act, such person shall be entitled to all the rights conferred by this act.

§ 6. *And be it further enacted,* That no individual shall be permitted to enter more than one quarter-section or fractional quarter-section, and that in a compact body ; but entries may be made at different times, under the provisions of this act ; and that the Secretary of the Interior is hereby required to prepare and issue, from time to time, such rules and regulations, consistent with this act, as shall be necessary and proper to carry its provisions into effect ; and that the registers and receivers of the several land offices shall be entitled to receive, upon the filing of the first affidavit, the sum of 50 cents each and a like sum upon the issuing of the final certificate. But this shall not be construed to enlarge the maximum of compensation now prescribed by law for any register or receiver : *Provided,* That nothing in this act shall be so construed as to impair the existing preëmption, donation, or graduation laws, or to embrace lands which have been reserved to be sold or entered at the price of $2 50 per acre ; *but no entry, under said graduation act, shall be allowed until after proof of actual settlement and cultivation or occupancy for at least three months,* as provided for in Sec. 3 of the said act.

§ 7. *And be it further enacted,* That each actual settler upon lands of the United States, which have not been offered at public sale, upon filing his declaration or claim, as now required by law, shall be entitled to two years from the commencement of his occupation or settlement ; or, if the lands have not been surveyed, two years from the receipt of the approved plat of such lands at the District Land Office, within which to complete the proofs of his said claim, and to enter and pay for the land so claimed, at minimum price of such lands ; and where such settlements have already been made in good faith, the claimant shall be entitled to the said period of two years from and after the date of this act; *Provided,* That no claim of preëmption shall be allowed for more than 160 acres, or one-quarter section of land, nor shall any such claim be admitted under the provisions of this act, unless there shall have been at least three months of actual and continuous residence upon and cultivation of the land so claimed from the date of settlement, and proof thereof made according to law ; *Provided further,* That any claimant under the preëmption laws may take less than 160 acres by legal subdivisions ; *Provided further,* That all persons who are *preëmptors,* on the date of this act, shall, *upon the payment to the proper authority of 62½ cents per acre, if paid within two years from the passage of this act,* be entitled to a patent from the Government, as now provided by the existing preëmption laws.

§ 8. *And be it further enacted,* That the 5th section of the act entitled "An act in addition to an act more effectually to provide for the punishment of certain crimes against the United States, and for other purposes," approved the 3d of March, in the year 1857, shall extend to all oaths, affirmations, and affidavits required or authorized by this act.

§ 9. *And be it further enacted,* That nothing in this act shall be so construed as to prevent any person who has availed him or herself of the benefit of the first section of this act from paying the minimum price, or the price to which the same may have graduated, for the quantity of land so entered at any time after an actual settlement of six months, and before the expiration of the five years, and obtaining a patent therefor from the Government, as in other cases provided by law.

§ 10. *And be it further enacted,* That all lands lying within the limits of a State which have been subject to sale at private entry, and which remain unsold after the lapse of thirty years, shall be, and the same are hereby, ceded to the State in which the same may be situated ; *Provided,* These cessions shall in no way invalidate any inceptive preëmption right or location, or any entry under this act, nor any sale or sales which may be made by the United States before the lands hereby ceded shall be certified to the State, as they are hereby required to be, under such regulations as may be prescribed by the Secretary of the Interior. *And provided further,* That no cessions shall take effect until after the States, by legislative act, shall have assented to the same.

On the 23d, the President returned the bill to the Senate with his veto, as follows :

THE HOMESTEAD BILL.

VETO MESSAGE OF THE PRESIDENT.

To the Senate of the United States.

I return, with my objections, to the Senate, in which it originated, the bill entitled 'An act to secure Homesteads to actual settlers on the public domain and for other purposes," presented to me on the 20th instant.

This bill gives to every citizen of the United States, "who is the head of a family," and to every person of foreign birth residing in the country, who has declared his intention to become a citizen, though he may not be the head of a family, the privilege of appropriating to himself one hundred and sixty acres of Government land, of settling and residing upon it for five years; and should his residence continue until the end of this period, he shall then receive a patent on the payment of twenty-five cents per acre, or one-fifth of the present Government price. During this period, the land is protected from all the debts of the settler.

This bill also contains a cession to the States of all the public lands within their respective limits "which have been subject to sale at private entry, and which remain unsold after the lapse of thirty years." This provision embraces a present donation to the States of twelve millions two hundred and twenty-nine thousand seven hundred and thirty-one acres, and will, from time to time, transfer to them large bodies of such lands which, from peculiar circumstances, may not be absorbed by private purchase and settlement.

To the actual settler, this bill does not make an absolute donation; but the price is so small that it can scarcely be called a sale. It is nominally twenty-five cents per acre; but considering this is not to be paid until the end of five years, it is, in fact, reduced to about eighteen cents per acre, or one-seventh of the present minimum price of the public lands. In regard to the States, it is an absolute and unqualified gift.

I. This state of the facts raises the question whether Congress, under the Constitution, has the power to give away the public lands, either to States or individuals. On this question, I expressed a decided opinion in my message to the House of Representatives, of the 24th February, 1859, returning the agricultural college bill. This opinion remains unchanged. The argument then used applies, as a constitutional objection, with the greater force to the present bill. There it had the plea of consideration, growing out of a specific beneficial purpose; here, it is an absolute gratuity to the State without the pretext of consideration. I am compelled, for want of time, in these last hours of the session, to quote largely from this message

I presume the general proposition will be admitted, that Congress does not possess the power to make donations of money, already in the Treasury, raised by taxes on the people, either to States or individuals.

But it is contended that the public lands are placed upon a different footing from money raised by taxation, and that the proceeds arising from their sale are not subject to the limitations of the Constitution, but may be appropriated or given away by Congress, at its own discretion, to States, corporations, or individuals, for any purpose they may deem expedient.

The advocates of this bill attempt to sustain their position upon the language of the second clause of the third section of the fourth article of the Constitution, which declares that "the Congress shall have power to dispose of, and make all needful rules and regulations respecting the territory or other property belonging to the United States." They contend that, by a fair interpretation of the words "dispose of" in this clause, Congress possesses the power to make this gift of public lands to the States for purposes of education.

It would require clear and strong evidence to induce the belief that the framers of the Constitution, after having limited the powers of Congress to certain, precise, and specific objects, intended, by employing the words "dispose of," to give that body unlimited power over the vast public domain. It would be a strange anomaly indeed, to have created two funds, the one by taxation, confined to the execution of the enumerated powers delegated to Congress, and the other from the public lands, applicable to all subjects, foreign and domestic, which Congress might designate. That this fund should be "disposed of," not to pay the debts of the United States, nor "to raise and support armies," nor "to provide and maintain a navy," nor to accomplish any one of the other great objects enumerated in the Constitution, but be diverted from them to pay the debts of the States, to educate their people, and to carry into effect any other measure of their domestic policy—this would be to confer upon Congress a vast and irresponsible authority, utterly at war with the well-known jealousy of the Federal power which prevailed at the formation of the Constitution. The natural intendment would be that, as the Constitution confined Congress to well-defined specific powers, the funds placed at their command, whether in land or money, should be appropriated to the performance of the duties corresponding with these powers. If not, a Government has been created, with all its other powers

carefully limited, but without any limitation in respect to the public lands.

But I cannot so read the words "disposed of" as to make them embrace the idea of "giving away." The true meaning of words is always to be ascertained by the subject to which they are applied, and the known general intent of the lawgiver. Congress is trustee under the Constitution for the people of the United States to "dispose of" their public lands, and I think I may venture to assert with confidence that no case can be found in which a trustee in the position of Congress has been authorized to "*dispose of*" property by its owner, where it has ever been held that these words authorized such trustee to give away the fund intrusted to his care. No trustee, when called upon to account for the disposition of the property placed under his management before any judicial tribunal, would venture to present such a plea in his defense. The true meaning of these words is clearly stated by Chief Justice Taney in delivering the opinion of the Court (19 Howard, p. 486). He says, in reference to this clause of the Constitution, "It begins its enumeration of powers by that of disposing; in other words, making sale of the lands, or raising money from them, which, as we have already said, was the main object of the cession (from the States), and which is the first thing provided for in the article." It is unnecessary to refer to the history of the times to establish the known fact that this statement of the Chief Justice is perfectly well founded. That it never was intended by the framers of the Constitution that these lands should be given away by Congress is manifest from the concluding portion of the same clause. By it, Congress has power not only "to dispose of" the territory, but of the "other property of the United States." In the language of the Chief Justice (p. 437), "And the same power of making needful rules respecting the territory is in precisely the same language applied to the other property of the United States, associating the power over the territory, in this respect, with the power over movable or personal property—that is, the ships, arms, or munitions of war, which then belonged in common to the State sovereignties."

The question is still clearer in regard to the public lands in the States and Territories within the Louisiana and Florida purchases. These lands were paid for out of the public Treasury from money raised by taxation. Now, if Congress had no power to appropriate the money with which these lands were purchased, is it not clear that the power over the lands is equally limited? The mere conversion of this money into land could not confer upon Congress new power over the disposition of land which they had not possessed over money. If it could, then a trustee, by changing the character of the fund intrusted to his care for special objects from money into land, might give the land away, or devote it to any purpose he thought proper, however foreign from the trust. The inference is irresistible that this land partakes of the very same character with the money paid for it, and can be devoted to no objects different from those to which the money could have been devoted. If this were not the case, then, by the purchase of a new Territory from a foreign government out of the public Treasury, Congress could enlarge their own powers, and appropriate the proceeds of the sales of the land thus purchased, at their own discretion, to other and far different objects from what they could have applied the purchase money which had been raised by taxation.

II. It will prove unequal and unjust in its operation among the actual settlers themselves.

The first settlers of a new country are a most meritorious class. They brave the dangers of savage warfare, suffer the privations of a frontier life, and, with the hand of toil, bring the wilderness into cultivation. The " old settlers," as they are everywhere called, are public benefactors. This class have all paid for their lands, the government price, or $1 25 per acre. They have constructed roads, established schools, and laid the foundation of prosperous Commonwealths. Is it just, is it equal, that, after they have accomplished all this by their labor, new settlers should come in among them and receive their farms at the price of twenty-five or eighteen cents per acre? Surely the old settlers, as a class, are entitled to at least equal benefits with the new. If you give the new settlers their lands for a comparatively nominal price, upon every principle of equality and justice, you will be obliged to refund out of the common Treasury the difference which the old have paid above the new settlers for their land.

III. This bill will do great injustice to the old soldiers who have received land warrants for their services in fighting the battles of their country. It will greatly reduce the market value of these warrants. Already their value has sunk, for one hundred and sixty acre warrants, to sixty-seven cents per acre, under an apprehension that such a measure as this might become a law. What price would they command, when any head of a family may take possession of a quarter section of land, and not pay for it until the end of five years, and then at the rate of only twenty-five cents per acre? The magnitude of the interest to be affected will appear in the fact that there are outstanding unsatisfied land warrants reaching back to the last war with great Britain, and even Revolutionary times, amounting in round numbers, to seven and a half millions acres.

IV. This bill will prove unequal and unjust in its operation, because, from its nature, it is confined to one class of our people. It is a boon expressly conferred upon the cultivators of the soil. While it is cheerfully admitted that these are the most numerous and useful class of our fellow-citizens, and eminently deserve all the advantages which our laws have already extended to them, yet there should be no new legislation which would operate to the injury or embarrassment of the large body of respectable artisans and laborers. The mechanic who emigrates to the West, and pursues his calling, must labor long before he can purchase a quarter-section of land; while the tiller of the soil who accompanies him obtains a farm at once by the bounty of the Government. The numerous body of mechanics in our large cities cannot, even by emigrating to the West, take advantage of the provisions of this bill without entering upon a new occupation, for which their habits of life have rendered them unfit.

V. This bill is unjust to the old States of the Union in many respects; and among these States, so far as the public lands are concerned, we may enumerate every State east of the Mississippi, with the exception of Wisconsin and a portion of Minnesota.

It is a common belief, within their limits, that the older States of the Confederacy do not derive their proportionate benefit from the public lands. This is not a just opinion. It is doubtful whether they could be rendered more beneficial to these States under any other system than that which at present exists. Their proceeds go into the common Treasury to accomplish the objects of the Government, and in this manner all the States are benefited in just proportion. But to give this common inheritance away would deprive the old States of their just proportion of this revenue, without holding out any, the least, corresponding advantage. While it is our common glory that the new States have become so prosperous and populous, there is no good reason why the old States should offer premiums to their own citizens to emigrate from them to the West. That land of promise presents in itself sufficient allurements to our young and enterprising citizens, without any adventitious aid. The offer of free farms would probably have a powerful effect in encouraging emigration, especially from States like Illinois, Tennessee, and Kentucky, to the west of the Mississippi, and could not fail to reduce the price of property within their limits. An individual in States thus situated would not pay its fair value for land when, by crossing the Mississippi, he could go upon the public lands, and obtain a farm almost without money and without price.

VI. This bill will open one vast field for speculation. Men will not pay $1 25 for lands, when they can purchase them for one-fifth of that price. Large numbers of actual settlers will be carried out by capitalists upon agreements to give them half of the land for the improvement of the other half. This cannot be avoided. Secret agreements of this kind will be numerous. In the entry of graduated lands, the experience of the Land Office justifies this objection.

VII. We ought ever to maintain the most perfect equality between native and naturalized citizens. They are equal, and ought always to remain equal, before the laws. Our laws welcome foreigners to our shores, and their rights will ever be respected. While these are the sentiments on which I have acted through life, it is not, in my opinion, expedient to proclaim to all the nations of the earth that whoever shall arrive in this country from a foreign shore, and declare his intention to become a citizen, shall receive a farm of 160 acres, at a cost of 25 or 20 cents per acre, if he will only reside on it and cultivate it. The invitation extends to all; and if this bill becomes a law, we may have numerous actual settlers from China, and other Eastern nations, enjoying its benefits on the great Pacific slope. The bill makes a distinction in favor of such persons over native and naturalized citizens. When applied to such citizens, it is confined to such as are the heads of families; but when applicable to persons of foreign birth recently arrived on our shores, there is no such restriction. Such persons need not be the heads of families, provided they have filed a declaration of intention to become citizens. Perhaps this dis-

tinction was an inadvertence; but, it is, nevertheless, a part of the bill.

VIII. The bill creates an unjust distinction between persons claiming the benefit of the preëmption laws. While it reduces the price of the land to existing preëmptors to 62½ cents per acre, and gives them a credit on this sum for two years from the present date, no matter how long they may have hitherto enjoyed the land, future preëmptors will be compelled to pay double this price per acre. There is no reason or justice in this discrimination.

IX. The effect of this bill on the public revenue must be apparent to all. Should it become a law, the reduction of the price of lands to actual settlers to 25 cents per acre with a credit of five years, and the reduction of its price to existing preëmptors to 62½ cents per acre, with a credit of two years will so diminish the sale of other public lands as to render the expectation of future revenue from that source beyond the expenses of survey and management illusory. The Secretary of the Interior estimated the revenue from the public lands for the next fiscal year at $4,000,000 on the presumption that the present land system would remain unchanged. Should this bill become a law, he does not believe that $1,000,000 will be derived from this source.

This bill lays the ax at the root of our present admirable land system. The public land is an inheritance of vast value to us and to our descendants. It is a resource to which we can resort in the hour of difficulty and danger. It has been managed heretofore with the greatest wisdom, under existing laws. In this management, the rights of actual settlers have been conciliated with the interests of the Government. The price to all has been reduced from $2 per acre to $1 25 for fresh lands, and the claims of actual settlers have been secured by our preëmption laws. Any man can now acquire a title in fee-simple to a homestead of 80 acres, at the minimum price of $1 25 per acre for $100. Should the present system remain, we shall derive a revenue from the public lands of $10,000,000 per annum, when the bounty land warrants are satisfied, without oppression to any human being. In the time of war, when all other sources of revenue are seriously impaired, this will remain intact. It may become the best security for public loans hereafter, in times of difficulty and danger, as it has been heretofore. Why should we impair or destroy this system at the present moment? What necessity exists for it?

The people of the United States have advanced with steady but rapid strides to their present condition of power and prosperity. They have been guided in their progress by the fixed principle of protecting the equal rights of all, whether they be rich or poor. No agrarian sentiment has ever prevailed among them. The honest poor man, by frugality and industry can, in any part of our country, acquire a competence for himself and his family, and in doing this he feels that he eats the bread of independence. He desires no charity, either from the government or from his neighbors. This bill, which proposes to give him land at an almost nominal price, out of the property of the government, will go far to demoralize the people, and repress this noble spirit of independence. It may introduce among us those pernicious social theories which have proved so disastrous in other countries.   JAMES BUCHANAN.

WASHINGTON, *June* 22, 1860.

In the Senate the question, Shall this bill pass notwithstanding the objections of the President? was put and lost, as follows:

YEAS—Messrs. Anthony, *Brown*, Chandler, Clark, Doolittle, Durkee, Fessenden, *Fitch*, Foot, Foster, *Gwin*, Hale, Hamlin, Harlan, King, *Lane*, *Latham*, *Nicholson*, *Polk*, *Pugh*, *Rice*, Simmons, Sumner, Ten Eyck, Trumbull, Wade, Wilkinson, and Wilson.

Republicans in Roman, 19; Democrats in *Italics*, 9. Total, 28.

NAYS—Messrs. Bragg, Chesnut, CRITTENDEN, Davis, Fitzpatrick, Green, Hemphill, Hunter, Iverson, Johnson (Tenn.), Johnson (Ark.), Mallory, Mason, Pearce, Powell, Sebastian, Wigfall, Yulee—18.

All from the South, and all Democrats, except Mr. Crittenden (Am.), of Kentucky. Several Senators were paired, which accounts for the light vote. So the bill failed, not having received the requisite two-thirds vote necessary to pass it over the Executive Veto.

DEMOCRATIC PLATFORM,

ADOPTED BY THE UNITED STATES SENATE.

On the first of March, 1860, Mr. Davis, of Mississippi, submitted to the Senate the following Resolutions:

1. *Resolved*, that in the adoption of the Federal Constitution, the States adopting the same acted severally as free and independent sovereignties, delegating a portion of their powers to be exercised by the Federal Government for the increased security of each against dangers, *domestic* as well as foreign; and that any intermeddling by any one or more States, or by a combination of their citizens, with the domestic institutions of the others, on any pretext whatever, political, moral, or religious, with a view to their disturbance or subversion, is in violation of the Constitution, insulting to the States so interfered with, endangers their domestic peace and tranquillity—objects for which the Constitution was formed—and by necessary consequence, tends to weaken and destroy the Union itself.

2. *Resolved*, That negro Slavery, as it exists in fifteen States of this Union, composes an important portion of their domestic institutions, inherited from their ancestors, and existing at the adoption of the Constitution, by which it is recognized as constituting an important element in the apportionment of powers among the States; and that no change of opinion or feeling on the part of the non-slaveholding States of the Union, in relation to this institution, can justify them, or their citizens, in open or covert attacks thereon, with a view to its overthrow; and that all such attacks are in manifest violation of the mutual and solemn pledge to protect and defend each other, given by the States respectively on entering into the constitutional compact which formed the Union, and are a manifest breach of faith, and a violation of the most solemn obligations.

3. *Resolved*, That the Union of these States rests on the equality of rights and privileges among its members; and that it is especially the duty of the Senate, which represents the States in their sovereign capacity, to resist all attempts to discriminate either in relation to persons or property in the Territories, which are the common possessions of the United States, so as to give advantages to the citizens of one State which are not equally assured to those of every other State.

4. *Resolved*, That neither Congress nor a Territorial Legislature, whether by direct legislation or legislation of an indirect and unfriendly character, possess power to annul or impair the constitutional right of any citizen of the United States to take his slave property into the common Territories, and there hold and enjoy the same while the Territorial condition remains.

5. *Resolved*, That if experience should at any time prove that the judicial and executive authority do not possess means to insure adequate protection to constitutional rights in a Territory, and if the Territorial Government should fail or refuse to provide the necessary remedies for that purpose, it will be the duty of Congress to supply such deficiency.

6. *Resolved*, That the inhabitants of a Territory of the United States, when they rightfully form a constitution to be admitted as a State into the Union, may then, for the first time, like the people of a State when forming a new Constitution, decide for themselves whether Slavery, as a domestic institution, shall be maintained or prohibited within their jurisdiction; and "they shall be received into the Union with or without Slavery, as their Constitution may prescribe at the time of their admission."

7. *Resolved*, That the provision of the Constitution for the rendition of fugitives from service or labor, without the adoption of which the Union could not have been formed, and that the laws of 1793 and 1850, which were enacted to secure its execution, and the main features of which, being similar, bear the impress of nearly seventy years of sanction by the highest judicial authority, should be honestly and faithfully observed and maintained by all who enjoy the benefits of our compact of Union; and that all acts of individuals or of State Legislatures to defeat the purpose or nullify the requirements of that provision, and the laws made in pursuance of it, are hostile in character, subversive of the Constitution, and revolutionary in their effect.

On the 8th May following, Mr. Clingman, of North Carolina, addressed the Senate at length on these resolutions, maintaining the position that the Constitution does guarantee the right of holding slaves in the Territories of the United States, but that the enforcing of that right, by Congressional action, was inexpedient, and would be of no practical value to the Slave States; also, that the South waived that right in agreeing to the Compromises of 1850 and the Kansas-Nebraska Act (repeal of the Missouri Compromise) of 1854. Mr. C. also reviewed the proceedings of the National Convention at Charleston, and concluded as follows:

Entertaining these views, I have been disposed to abstain as much as possible from the discussion of these questions, and I really hope that we shall not press them. I think no advantage can grow out of it. I greatly fear that I have occupied more of the valuable time of the Senate than I intended. I felt, however, that from me, in my position, some explanation was necessary. I think that the gentlemen on the other side of the Chamber have given us a platform already. We shall have to fight them; we had better make up our minds to go into the contest, and meet them on the great issue they tender us. In ten days, we shall probably have their declaration of war from Chicago, and the clash of arms will commence very soon. It is time for us to close our ranks. I am ready to fight under any flag and any standard-bearer that may be given us. I can adopt any of those platforms that were presented at Charleston. I leave all that to our political friends assembled in convention. I know that they will present a platform, and present a man less objectionable to me than the candidate on the other side. I regard them as the deadly political enemies of my section; as the enemies of the Constitution of the United States. I want to embark in the contest and fight them with closed and serried ranks on our side. I have spoken only in behalf of the Democratic party, of the Constitution, and the country.

MR. BENJAMIN ON POPULAR SOVEREIGNTY.

Senator Benjamin, of Louisiana, followed:

Mr. Benjamin.—Mr. President, I had no intention of joining in this debate, or of uttering one word on the resolutions now before the Senate; but, sir, I have listened with intense surprise to what has fallen from the Senator from North Carolina this morning, and I cannot remain quiescent and by silence appear to give consent to what he has said in relation to the action of certain Southern delegates in the recent Convention at Charleston.

The Senator from North Carolina thinks that political races can best be run without the load of principles. The Senator from North Carolina thinks that the best way to get success in a political contest is not to bother yourself with the baggage of principle, but let your candidate run with nothing on his back, and probably in that way he may run the faster and reach the goal the sooner. And again, the honorable Senator thinks that, because the Cincinnati platform was acceptable to the whole Democracy in 1856, there is and can be no reason why Democrats who stood on that platform at that time should be dissatisfied with it now.

Mr. President, let us look a little back, behind 1856, in relation to that platform, and to the living issue on which we are separated as regards that platform. We all remember, sir—no man can forget—that, in the exciting contest which took place on the Kansas-Nebraska bill, those who were the firmest supporters of the bill differed in principle on that one point which now threatens to divide the Democratic party. They differed openly; they avowed their differences; they provided for the final settlement of those differences. Sir, *when we met in* *caucus, **under the lead of the honorable Senator from Illinois, who introduced the Kansas-Nebraska bill, it was found that the Democrats from the North and the Democrats from the South could not agree in principle.*** The Democrats from the South then took the position that the Constitution of the United States was plain and clear. The rights of the people of the South were placed upon that instrument. I agree with the Senator from Mississippi (Mr. Davis) that we have nothing to do in this controversy with natural rights or natural principles. Those rights and those principles, which lie at the foundation of social organization and civil government, were proper subjects of examination and consideration with the fathers. They did take them into consideration. They decided them. They have given us a chart by which now we are bound all to direct our course; and that chart is the Constitution of our country. Resting the rights of the South upon that Constitution, when the discussions arose upon the Kansas-Nebraska bill, the Senators from the South who met in caucus, or in convention, or in primary meeting, if you choose so to say, all agreed, without a dissenting voice, that, by the true construction of the Constitution of the United States, the Territories belonging to the United States were the common property of all; that each State had equal rights in those Territories; that amongst those rights was the right of the citizens of the different States to emigrate to those Territories with their property of every nature and kind; and, when there, we contended that there was no power under heaven that could drive us out of those Territories, or deprive us therein of the protection of the Constitution and the laws, until the people of the Territory should make a constitution and form a State.

The Senator from Illinois did not agree with us in that. He has been consistent. The Senator from Illinois held that there was a power in the people of a Territory; he believed in Popular Sovereignty; he believed in some inherent right in the people when assembled, even in the original inchoate shape in which they come as emigrants to the Territories, to pass laws to govern themselves; to mold their own Institutions, as he phrased it, and included in that power the right to act against Slavery. We could not agree. Morning after morning we met for the purpose of coming to some understanding upon that very point; and it was finally understood by all, agreed to by all, made the basis of a compromise by all the supporters of that bill, that the Territories should be organized with a delegation by Congress of all the power of Congress in the Territories, and that the extent of the power of Congress should be determined by the courts. Firm in our belief of our rights, conscious that in the Constitution we had guaranty enough; knowing that it was impossible for a judicial tribunal to make other than one decision, we said that we would stand by that decision when made; and if it should be determined by the Supreme Court of the United States that there was a power in this Government to deprive the people of the South of their fair share of the common Territories of the Union, if that power in this Government existed in Congress, and if Congress delegated all its power to the Territories, we would stand by the decision and agree that we asserted a right that found no warrant in the Constitution; and, on the other hand, our brother Democrats of the North, and the Senator from Illinois at their head, agreed that if the Supreme Court of the United States should determine that the Congress of the United States had no power to interfere with Southern rights in the Territories, if, consequently, we had had not the power that we could delegate at all, then the Democrats of the North would join us in showing respect and obedience to that decision, and stand with us on the principle that we advocated as the true one. None of us supposed at the time that the decision would come so quick. None of us knew of the existence of a controversy then pending in the federal courts that would lead almost immediately to the decision of that question. We provided in the Kansas act itself; we introduced an express clause having for its avowed object to bring that question before the courts for decision.

Well, sir, the question did come before the courts, and the Supreme Court of the United States, in the decision in the Dred Scott case, has determined—gentlemen say it is no decision—as doctrine, or as opinion, or in some way has declared that the Congress of the United States has no power so to legislate as to destroy the rights of the people of the South in their slave property in the Territories, and the judges have said as a proposition, so clear that it required no argument, that the Congress possessing no such power, it was plain that it could give none to the Territorial Legislature I do not understand that the gentlemen from the North, the members of the Democratic party, controvert that.

But at a time when we supposed that we all at length stood upon one common platform; that we had at last a guide and a pole star by which the Democratic party could guide the ship of State, a sudden and alarming heresy sprung up in the North, and something was said about the right of the Legislature of the Territories not to destroy Slavery; not to abolish it; not to confiscate by direct legislation the rights of the citizens of the South who might find themselves in the Territories with their property, but, by a side blow, by indirection, and by failure to perform duty, by "unfriendly legislation," to do that which constitutionally they had no power to do by any direct effort of legislative will. Now, sir, the Cincinnati platform, with which the gentleman from North Carolina seems to be so much in love, and which he thinks is sufficient for the constitutional rights of the South, would be sufficient for that purpose, is sufficient for that purpose properly construed; but when the delegates of a great party, assembled together from all portions of the Confederacy, recently met, and the proposition was made to them to adopt the Cincinnati platform, it was made under what circumstances, and with what view? *It was made with a knowledge of every man in that Convention that two distinctly opposite interpretations were put upon that platform—one at the South, and the other at the North.*

Mr. Clingman.—The Senator will allow me to ask him if these two opinions were not upon whether a Territorial Legislature could legislate for or against Slavery? Are those the opinions to which he refers?

Mr. Benjamin.—The opposite constructions are put in several points. One point is, whether the Territorial Legislature has a right to abolish Slavery in the Territories or not, before forming a State Constitution; and another is, whether or not it is the duty of the Federal Government to protect the rights of the people of the South in the Territories. Upon those two points opposite interpretations and opposite principles exist, and were developed in the Charleston Convention.

Mr. Clingman.—I will answer the gentleman when he is through.

Mr. Pugh.—Do I understand the gentleman to say that every member of the Convention agreed that the platform had received two interpretations, or that it was susceptible of it?

Mr. Benjamin.—*I understand that opposite interpretations were plainly and openly given to that platform in Convention, by men whose good faith no man has ever yet disputed to my knowledge.*

Mr. Pugh.—I do not think that was the ground of the difference of opinion at all. I said there never were two interpretations that could be fairly given to it; that the platform purposely, in the language of the Senator from North Carolina, referred that question to judicial tribunals; that the difference of opinion arose upon the judicial question; it did not arise upon the platform; and that consequently it was a false accusation. I say that certainly in no unkind spirit to the Senator; but I say the platform is not susceptible of two interpretations; that it referred a controversy to arbitration. There might be a difference of opinion as to the particular arbitration of it, but there was none as to the terms of submission.

Mr. Benjamin.—I read, Mr. President, with as much attention as I was capable of, everything that occurred in that convention, and I saw the statement over and over again made in the convention, and not controverted, that different opinions were put upon that platform in different parts of the country.

Mr. Pugh.—I certainly controverted it for one. I do not recollect who else may have stated it. It may have been repeated a great many times; but I did controvert it.

Mr. Benjamin.—Now, sir, I say, in relation to that Cincinnati platform, which the Senator from North Carolina seems to think ought to have amply sufficed the South, and to have sufficed the Democratic party, these two opposite interpretations were known to be, intended to be given to it. Further, I say this: I say it was avowed at Charleston, over and over again, that if a construction was given to that platform by which it should be clearly stated that the people of the South were entitled to have their slaves protected in the Territories against any direct interference, either by Congressional or Territorial legislation; if that was avowed; if the doctrine of the party was asserted to be that the Legislature of the Territory, whilst a Territory existed in its inchoate organization, had no right to interfere with Slavery, then it was said, again and again, that no northern State could be carried upon that ground.

Mr. Clingman.—On the question as to whether a Territorial Legislature could legislate against Slavery or for it, I ask the Senator whether that would not necessarily be a question which a court must determine; that if the Legislature legislated or acted in any way, could we, by our opinions, settle it; or is it not, from necessity, a judicial question?

Mr. Benjamin.—The Senator is directing me entirely out of the line of my argument. I must beg him to allow me to proceed in my line. That is not at all what I am at. It has no reference at all to my line of argument.

I say this: I say that distinctly opposite interpretations, or distinctly opposite principles, if you choose, in relation to Southern rights under the Constitution, were avowed at Charleston, by men professing all to be Democrats; and that, in my judgment, it is a brand upon the good faith of the Democratic party, it is an imputation upon their honor, it is unworthy of them, and unworthy of us all, that we should go before the people of this country and ask their votes in favor of one party or another, with the avowed purpose of presenting opposite interpretations or opposite sets of principles in the two sections of the Confederacy, as being the principles of a common party, and forming a common party creed. I say that I will never be a party to any such contest as that. If I go into an electoral contest, I want to know the principles of the party with which I act, and I want, before the people of my State, before the people of the country, to declare those principles, to stand by them, to find them written in letters of light, so that no man can dare misconstrue them, and by them to stand, and with them, if need be, fall.

That I understand to have been the position of the delegation of Louisiana at Charleston. Taking that position, determined that they would not palter to public prejudices by using words in any double sense; that all they did and all they said must go forth to the country incapable of misconstruction; when they found it impossible to have the principles upon which alone they could go into the Presidential contest, stated thus clearly and thus plainly, they withdrew, rightly withdrew, honorably withdrew. I applaud them; I approve them; I stand by them. I think they did as became high-minded and honorable citizens. I think the State will show itself grateful to them for their act. . . . .

Now, the honorable Senator says he is willing to go with Democrats upon almost any platform; that almost any one that we can elect would be preferable to the adversaries against whom we are to be opposed.

Mr. Clingman.—I said any of those proposed. I alluded to those proposed in the Convention.

Mr. Benjamin.—I suppose so. Now, Mr. President, I am not willing to go for any man, I do not care whether his name has been proposed or not, who is not willing to stand upon a platform of principle, of constitutional principle. I am willing to go for any man, whether named or not, who will pledge his honor to stand faithfully and squarely upon a platform of sound principles; and when a platform of sound constitutional principles shall be adopted by a Democratic Convention, satisfactory to me, with my views of constitutional right, and satisfactory to my people—principles satisfactory to my people, I say; I care not for men—then you may put upon that platform any man who can stand upon it honorably, and I will vote for him; I will maintain him; I will canvass my State in his behalf; I will spend all my time and all my breath in his cause, wherever, whenever, and however, I may be asked by his friends. That far, sir, I am willing to go; but I have no stomach for a fight in which I am to have my choice between a man who denies me all my rights openly and fairly and a man who admits my rights but intends to filch them. I have no choice there.

BENJAMIN ON DOUGLAS.

After Mr. Douglas's famous speech of May 15th and 16th, on these resolutions, Mr. Benjamin addressed the Senate again, speaking of Mr. Douglas as follows:

Mr. Benjamin said, when we met here in December, the public mind was greatly disturbed by the irruption of a band of fanatics into a State of the Union, with the avowed intent to liberate the slaves. A large number of resolutions have been offered, all relating to the relation of the General Government to Slavery in the States and Territories. The large number and variety of these resolutions, required that those who professed to belonging to the same party should meet, in order to harmonize and act in concert. A meeting of Democratic Senators was therefore held to accomplish this purpose. The Senator from Illinois, in a speech occupying two days, had presented the extraordinary spectacle of advocating his own claims to the Presidency, and denouncing those who had dared to express their views on subjects before the Senate. The Senator from Illinois assumed that he was the embodiment of the Democratic party, and that all who opposed him were rebels. He arraigned other Senators, and charged them and the representatives of seventeen States at Charleston as being on the high road to disunion. After having thus assailed everybody, he announced that he had only spoken in self-defense, and with princely magnanimity agreed to forgive those who,

as he said, had erred more through ignorance than design. Mr. Benjamin then defended the Democratic Senators from the charge of having undertaken to dictate to the Charleston Convention what sort of platform it should make. When the Kansas bill was before the Senate, the Senator from Illinois called a caucus of Democratic Senators every morning to decide on their action for the day. The late Senatorial caucus had done no more than that. . Yet for this it had been charged with seeking to diminish the Senator's chance for success. Mr. Benjamin next examined Mr. Douglas's charge that seventeen Democratic States had adopted a platform looking to the dissolution of the Union, and had placed themselves under the lead of Mr. Yancey, an avowed disunionist. His State had voted for that platform, and he should vote for the Senate resolutions, and he denied that the Senator from Illinois had correctly stated the meaning of either. Nobody here wanted to make a slave code, a slang term which Mr. Douglas had picked up from the Republicans, nor to force Slavery on an unwilling people. The attacks upon the Democratic Senators were wanton and unprovoked, and he should repel them. The Senator had defended his consistency at great length, which was not the issue between them. The issue was that the Senator from Illinois had made a bargain and had violated it. To prove this he should not go further back than 1857, up to which time the Senator from Illinois was looked upon by the Democratic party with pride and favor. Why was it that a Senator who had thus been treated with favor should now be separated from his former associates? That he had passed over in his speech, and he (Benjamin) would supply the deficiency.

Mr. Benjamin then went into a history of the Kansas act, pointing out the differences between Democrats and Republicans and Douglas Democrats. At that time the Democrats being unable to agree as to the power of the people of the Territories, it was agreed to refer the subject to the Courts and to abide by the decision. He never had attacked the Senator's consistency. It was his consistency that constituted his great crime—adhering still to views which he had agreed to abandon when the Court decided the question, and which the Court had decided against him. This he charged was bad faith. The Senator no longer worshipped at the Democratic shrine, but had wandered forth after strange gods. The Senator from Illinois had admitted that he made this bargain, and yet he had been engaged since 1857 in trying to explain away, in conjunction with the Republicans, the decision of the Court, and to render it useless in case it should be affirmed. He quoted from the Dred Scott decision to show that the principle of right to slave property in the Territories was decided by it. On this point he argued at great length to show that Congress had full power over the Territories within the limits of its constitutional power; that the Constitution forbid the prohibition of Slavery in the Territories by Congress; and as the Territorial Government derived all its powers from Congress, the Territorial Legislature could not do more than Congress could. No sooner was this decision made than it was attacked by the Republicans, and the Chief-Justice assailed as having colluded with the President of the United States. The Senator from Illinois got over his bargain by saying that he did not agree to abide by the decision in the Dred Scott case; but when the case was carried up from the Territorial Courts to the Supreme Court, he would obey that. This was an afterthought, first announced in the canvass of 1858, when pressed by Mr. Lincoln for a seat in the Senate. To save himself from defeat, he introduced his theory as to the power of the people in the Territories. [Mr. Benjamin then read from the discussions between Messrs. Lincoln and Douglas to show that the former was much more candid in his answers than the latter, and he confessed he was not such an ultra Anti-Slavery man as he supposed.] Mr. Douglas told us here that he would abide the decision of the Court, but at home he turns his back on his promise, repudiates his words, and tells his people that he has so arranged the Kansas bill that in spite of the decision the people of the Territories can keep slaves out. To be twice deceived by the same man would be to make them dupes and fools. Even Mr. Lincoln was shocked at his profligacy, and charged him with bad faith. The election came off, and though Mr. Douglas was successful by the arrangement of the Legislative Districts, Mr. Lincoln beat him 4,000 on the popular vote. [Mr. Benjamin next read from Mr. Douglas's Harper's Magazine article, to show that he had absolutely copied Mr. Lincoln's arguments of 1858, and claimed them as discoveries of his own. Mr. Benjamin warned Mr. Douglas that the tendencies of his doctrines were to drive him back, step by step, to the Black Republican camp.] We already find him using the arguments and quoting the language of the Republican party.

On the 24th May, the vote was taken on the first of Mr. Davis's series of resolutions, which was adopted, 36 to 19, the yeas being all Democrats, except Messrs. Crittenden, of Ky., and Kennedy, of Md., Americans. The nays were all Republicans. The second resolution was then read, when Mr. Harlan (Rep., of Iowa) offered to add the following as an amendment:

But the free discussion of the morality and expediency of slavery should never be interfered with by the laws of any State, or of the United States; and the freedom of speech and of the press, on this and every other subject of domestic and national policy, should be maintained inviolate to all the States,

This amendment was rejected, 20 to 36, as follows:

YEAS.—Messrs. Bingham, Chandler, Clark, Collamer, Dixon, Doolittle, Fessenden, Foot, Foster, Grimes, Hale, Hamlin, Harlan, King, Simmons, Sumner, Ten Eyck, Trumbull, Wade, and Wilson—20.
NAYS.—Messrs. Benjamin, Bigler, Bragg, Bright, Brown, Chesnut, Clay, Clingman, Crittenden, Davis, Fitzpatrick, Green, Gwin, Hammond, Hemphill, Hunter, Iverson, Johnson of Arkansas, Johnson of Tennessee, Kennedy, Lane, Latham, Mallory, Mason, Nicholson, Pearce, Polk, Powell, Pugh, Rice, Sebastian, Slidell, Thomson, Toombs, Wigfall, and Yulee—36.

Yeas all Republicans; nays all Democrats, except Crittenden and Kennedy, Americans.

The second resolution was then adopted, 36 to 20, the vote being exactly the reverse of that on Mr. Harlan's amendment.

The third resolution of the series was adopted, 36 to 18, as follows:

YEAS.—Messrs. Benjamin, Bigler, Bragg, Bright, Brown, Chesnut, Clay, Clingman, Crittenden, Davis, Fitzpatrick, Green, Gwin, Hammond, Hemphill, Hunter, Iverson, Johnson of Arkansas, Johnson of Tennessee, Kennedy, Lane, Latham, Mallory, Mason, Nicholson, Pearce, Polk, Powell, Pugh, Rice, Sebastian, Slidell, Thomson, Toombs, Wigfall, and Yulee—36.

NAYS.—Messrs. Bingham, Chandler, Clark, Collamer, Dixon, Doolittle, Fessenden, Foot, Foster, Hale, Hamlin, Harlan, Simmons, Sumner, Ten Eyck, Trumbull, Wade, and Wilson—18.

Yeas all Democrats, except Crittenden and Kennedy; nays all Republicans

The fourth resolution was adopted, 35 to 21, the negatives being all Republicans, except Mr. Pugh, Dem., of Ohio.

Mr. Clingman offered an amendment, in the form of the following resolution, to follow the 4th of Mr. Davis's series:

Resolved, That the exi ting condition of the Territories of the United States does not require the intervention of Congress for the protection of property in slaves.

The amendment was debated at considerable length; but, without taking the question, the Senate adjourned.

On the following day, the amendment was adopted, 26 to 23, as follows:

YEAS.—Messrs. Bigler, Bingham, Bragg, Chandler, Clark, Clingman, Collamer, Crittenden, Dixon, Doolittle, Foot, Grimes, Hale, Hamlin, Harlan, Johnson of Tennessee, Kennedy, Latham, Polk, Pugh, Simmons, Ten Eyck, Toombs, Trumbull, Wade, and Wilson—26.
NAYS.—Messrs. Benjamin, Bright, Brown, Chesnut, Clay, Davis, Fitzpatrick, Green, Hammond, Hunter, Iverson, Lane, Mallory, Mason, Nicholson, Pearce, Powell, Rice, Saulsbury, Sebastian, Slidell, Wigfall, and Yulee—23.

Yeas all Republicans, except Messrs. Bigler, Bragg, Clingman, Crittenden, Johnson (Tenn.), Kennedy, Latham, Polk, Pugh, and Toombs; Nays all Democrats.

The fifth resolution of the series was then adopted, 35 to 2, Hamlin and Trumbull, the Yeas being all Democrats, except Crittenden and Kennedy. The seventh and last of the series was then adopted, 36 to 6, Mr. Ten Eyck, Rep., of New Jersey, voting Yea

---

JUDGE BATES'S PLATFORM.

IMPORTANT CORRESPONDENCE.

LETTER FROM JUDGE BATES ON THE POLITICAL QUESTIONS OF THE DAY.

ST. LOUIS, *March*, 1860.

The HON. EDWARD BATES—*Sir:* As you may have learned from the public prints, the Republicans of Missouri met in Convention, in this city, on Saturday, the 10th instant, to make a declaration of their principles, elect delegates to the National Republican Convention. and complete a State organization. All of this the Convention executed, in a manner wholly satisfactory to its members. It also commended you, by resolution, to the National Republican party, as one well worthy to be the standard-bearer of that party in the coming Presidential election. This fact the undersigned have pride and pleasure in communicating to you, knowing that throughout your life you have carried out, as far as a private citizen might, the sentiments contained in the resolutions adopted on Saturday, and a copy of which we inclose. But as you have voluntarily remained in private life for many years, your political opinions are consequently not so well understood by the Republican party at large as by the Republicans of Missouri.

Inasmuch as the delegation from this State to the Chicago Convention intend to present your name to that body as a candidate for the Presidency, we, in common with many other Republicans of Missouri, desire to procure from you an exposition of your views on the engrossing political questions of the time. We hope that notwithstanding your well-known relucta ce to appear before the public in the light of a Presidential aspirant, you will not refuse to answer the following interrogatories, which, in our judgment, involve all the issues pending between the two political parties of the country.

1st. Are you opposed to the extension of Slavery?
2d. Does the Constitution of the United States carry Slavery into the Territories, and, as subsidiary to this, what is the legal effect of the decision of the Supreme Court in the Dred Scott case?
3d. Are you in favor of the colonization of the free colored population in Central America?
4th. Do you recognize any inequality of rights among citizens of the United States, and do you hold that it is the duty of the Federal Government to protect American citizens at home and abroad in the enjoyment of all their constitutional and legal rights, privileges, and immunities?
5th. Are you in favor of the construction of a railroad from the Valley of the Mississippi to the Pacific Ocean, under the auspices of the General Government?
6th. Are you in favor of the measure known as the Homestead bill?
7th. Are you in favor of the immediate admission of Kansas, under the Constitution adopted at Wyandot?

Yours, respectfully, etc.,

PETER L. FOY,　　CHAS. L. BERNAYS,
HENRY T. BLOW,　　JNO. M. RICHARDSON,
F. A. DICK,　　O. D. FILLEY,
STEPHEN HOYT,　　WM. McKEE,
G. W. FISHBACK,　　BARTON ABLE,
J. B. SITTON.

RESPONSE OF JUDGE BATES.

ST. LOUIS, *March* 17, 1860.

To Messrs. P. L. FOY, Editor of *The Missouri Democrat;* Dr. BERNAYS, Editor of the *Anzeiger;* and other gentlemen:

SIRS: B. Gratz Brown, Esq., as President of the Missouri State Convention, which sat in St. Louis on the tenth of this month, has officially made known to me the proceedings of that body, and by them I am enabled to know some of you as Delegates to the Chicago Convention, representing the Republican party of Missouri.

I have received your letter propounding to me certain questions (seven in number) which you suppose will cover most, if not all, the grounds of controversy, in the approaching Presidential election.

With pleasure I will answer your questions. But before doing so, allow me to glance at the peculiar circumstances in which I am placed, and the strangeness of the fact that I, a mere private man, am called upon to make avowals and explanations, with any view to take me from the shades of private life and place me at the head of the nation. I came to this frontier in my youth, and settled in St. Louis when it was a village. All my manhood has been spent in Missouri, and during all that time I have followed a profession which left my character and conduct open to the observation of society. And while it has been my constant habit freely to express my opinion of public measures and public men, the people of Missouri, of all parties, will bear me witness that I have never obtrusively thrust myself forward in pursuit of official honors. I have held no political office, and sought none, for more than twenty-five years.

Under these circumstances, I confess the gratification which I feel in receiving the recent manifestations of the respect and confidence of my fellow-citizens. First, the Opposition members of the Missouri Legislature declared their preference for me as a candidate; then followed my nomination by a Convention composed of all the elements of the Opposition in this State; and, now, the Republicans of Missouri, in their separate Convention, just held in St. Louis, have reaffirmed the nomination, and proposed, by their delegates, to present me to the National Convention, soon to be held at Chicago, as a candidate for the first office in the nation. These various demonstrations in my own State are doubly gratifying to me, because they afford the strongest proof that my name has been put forward only in a spirit of harmony and peace, and with the hope of preventing all division and controversy among those who, for their own safety and the public good, ought to be united in their action.

For all this I am deeply grateful, and, as far as concerns me personally, I must declare in simple truth, that if the movement go no further and produce no national results, still I am paid and overpaid for a life of labor, and for whatever of zealous effort and patient watching I have been able to bestow in support of a line of governmental policy which I believe to be for the present and permanent good of the country.

And now, gentlemen, I proceed to answer your questions, briefly indeed, but fully, plainly, and with all possible frankness. And I do this the more willingly because I have received from individuals many letters (too many to be separately answered), and have seen in many public journals articles making urgent calls upon me for such a statement of views.

1. Slavery—Its extension in the Territories.

On this subject, in the States and in the Territories, I have no new opinions—no opinions formed in relasion to the present array of parties. I am coeval with the Missouri question of 1819-20, having begun my political life in the midst of that struggle. At that time my position required me to seek all the means of knowledge within my reach, and to study the principles involved with all the powers of my mind; and I arrived at conclusions then which no subsequent events have induced me to change. The existence of negro Slavery in our country had its beginning in the early time of the Colonies, and was imposed by the mother country against the will of most of the colonists. At the time of the Revolution, and long after, it was commonly regarded as an evil, temporary in its nature, and likely to disappear in the course of time, yet, while it continued, a misfortune to the country, socially and politically.

Thus was I taught, by those who made our Government, and neither the new light of modern civilization, nor the discovery of a new system of constitutional law and social philosophy, has enabled me to detect the error of their teaching.

Slavery is "a social relation"—a domestic institution. Within the States, it exists by the local law, and the Federal Government has no control over it there.

The Territories, whether acquired by conquest or peaceable purchase, are subject and subordinate; not sovereign like the States. The nation is supreme over them, and the National Government has power to permit or forbid Slavery, within them. Entertaining these views, I am opposed to the extension of Slavery, and in my opinion, the spirit and policy of the Government ought to be against its extension.

2. Does the Constitution carry Slavery into the Territories?

I answer no. The Constitution of the United States does not carry Slavery into the Territories. With much more show of reason may it be said that it carries Slavery into all the States. But it does not carry Slavery anywhere. It only acts upon it, where it finds it established by the local law.

In connection with this point, I am asked to state my views of the Dred Scott case, and what was really determined by the Supreme Court in that case. It is my opinion, carefully considered, that the Court determined one single point of law only, that is, that Scott, the plaintiff, being a negro of African descent (not necessarily a slave), could not be a citizen of Missouri, and therefore could not sue in the Federal Court; and that for this reason, and this alone, the Circuit Court had no jurisdiction of the cause, and no power to give judgment between the parties. The only jurisdiction which the Supreme Court had of the cause was for the purpose of correcting the error of the Circuit Court, in assuming the power to decide upon the merits of the case. This power the Supreme Court did exercise, by setting aside the judgment of the Circuit Court upon the merits, and by dismissing the suit, without any judgment for or against either party. This is all that the Supreme Court did, and all that it had lawful power to do.

I consider it a great public misfortune that several of the learned judges should have thought that their duty required them to discuss and give opinions upon various questions outside of the case, as the case was actually disposed of by the court. All such opinions are extra judicial and of no authority. But beside this, it appears to me that several of the questions so discussed by the judges are political questions, and therefore beyond the cognizance of the judiciary, and proper only to be considered and disposed of by the political departments. If I am right in this, and it seems to me plain, the precedent is most unfortunate, because it may lead to a dangerous conflict of authority among the coördinate branches of the Government.

3. As to the colonization of the free blacks.

For many years I have been connected with the American Colonization Society, of which the rising young State of Liberia is the first fruit. I consider the object both humane and wise, beneficent alike to the free blacks who emigrate, and to the whites whom they leave behind. But Africa is distant, and presents so many obstacles to rapid settlement, that we cannot indulge the hope of draining off in that direction the growing numbers of our free black population. The tropical regions of America, I think, offer a far better prospect both for us and for them.

4. As to any inequality of rights among American citizens.

I recognize no distinctions among American citizens but such as are expressly laid down in the Constitution. And I hold that our Government is bound to protect all the citizens in the enjoyment of all their rights, everywhere and against all assailants. And as to all these rights, there is no difference between citizens born and citizens made such by law.

5. Am I in favor of the construction of a railroad from the Valley of the Mississippi to the Pacific Ocean, under the auspices of the General Government?

Yes, strongly. I not only believe such a road of vast importance as the means of increasing the population, wealth and power of this great valley, but necessary as the means of national defence, and of preserving the integrity of the Union.

6. Am I in favor of the measure called the Homestead bill?

Yes; I am for guarding the public lands, as well as possible, from the danger of becoming the subject of common trade and speculation—for keeping them for the actual use of the people—and for granting tracts of suitable size to those who will actually inhabit and improve them.

7. Am I in favor of the immediate admission of Kansas under the Wyandot Constitution?

I think that Kansas ought to be admitted without delay, leaving her, like all the other States, the sole judge of her own Constitution.

Thus, gentlemen, I believe I have answered all your inquiries in a plain, intelligible manner, and, I hope, to *your satisfaction.* I have not attempted to support my answers by argument, for that could not be done in a short letter; and, restraining myself from going into general politics, I have confined my remarks to the particular subjects upon which you requested me to write. Your obliged fellow-citizen,

EDWARD BATES.

JUDGE BATES'S LETTER

IN SUPPORT OF LINCOLN.

St. Louis, *June* 11, 1860.

O. H. BROWNING, Esq., Quincy, Ill.

DEAR SIR: When I received your letter of May 22d, I had no thought that the answer would be so long delayed; but, waiving all excuses, I proceed to answer it now.

Under the circumstances of the case it ought not to have been doubted that I would give Mr. Lincoln's nomination a cordial and hearty support. But in declaring my intention to do so, it is due to myself to state some of the facts and reasons which have a controlling influence over my mind, and which I think ought to be persuasive arguments with some other men, whose political opinions and antecedents are, in some important particulars, like my own.

There was no good ground for supposing that I felt any pique or dissatisfaction because the Chicago Convention failed to nominate me. I had no such feeling. On party grounds, I had no right to expect the nomination. I had no claims upon the Republicans as a party, for I have never been a member of any party; so as to be bound by its dogmas, and subject to its discipline, except only the Whig party, which is now broken up, and its materials, for the most part, absorbed in other organizations. And thus I am left, alone and powerless, indeed, but perfectly free to follow the dictates of my own judgment, and to take such part in current politics as my own sense of duty and patriotism may require. Many Republicans, and among them, I think, some of the most moderate and patriotic of that party, honored me with their confidence and desired to make me their candidate. For this favor I was indebted to the fact that between them and me there was a coincidence of opinion upon certain important questions of government. They and I agreed in believing that the National Government has sovereign power over the Territories, and that it would be impolitic and unwise to use that power for the propagation of negro Slavery by planting it in Free Territory. Some of them believed also that my nomination, while it would tend to soften the tone of the Republican party, without any abandonment of its principles, might tend also to generalize its character and attract the friendship and support of many, especially in the border States, who, like me, had never been members of their party, but concurred with them in opinion about the government of the Territories. These are the grounds, and I think the only grounds, upon which I was supported at all at Chicago.

As to the platform put forth by the Chicago Convention, I have little to say, because, whether good or bad, that will not constitute the ground of my support of Mr. Lincoln. I have no great respect for party platforms in general. They are commonly made in times of high excitement, under a pressure of circumstances, and with the view to conciliate present support, rather than to establish a permanent system of principles and line of policy for the future good government of country. The Conventions which form them are transient in their nature; their power and influence are consumed in the using, leaving no continuing obligation upon their respective parties. And hence we need not wonder, that platforms so made are hardly ever acted upon in practice. I shall not discuss their relative merits, but content myself with saying that this Republican platform, though in several particulars it does not conform to my views, is still far better than any published creed, past or present, of the Democrats. And as to the new party, it has not chosen to promulgate any platform at all, except two or three broad generalities which are common to the professions of faith of all parties in the country. No party, indeed, dare ask the confidence of the nation, while openly denying the obligation to support the Union and the Constitution and to enforce the laws. That is a common duty, binding upon every citizen, and the failure to perform it is a crime.

To me it is plain that the approaching contest must be between the Democratic and the Republican parties; and, between them, I prefer the latter.

The Democratic party, by the long possession and abuse of power, has grown wanton and reckless; has corrupted itself and perverted the principles of the Government; has set itself openly against the great home interests of the people, by neglecting to protect their industry, and by refusing to improve and keep in order the highways and depots of commerce; and even now is urging a measure in Congress to abdicate the constitutional power and duty to regulate commerce among the States, and to grant to the States the discretionary power to levy tonnage duties upon all our commerce, under the pretense of improving harbors, rivers, and lakes; has changed the status of the negro slave by making him no longer mere property, but a politician, an antagonist power in the State, a power to which all other powers are required to yield, under penalty of a dissolution of the Union; has directed its energies to the gratification of its lusts of foreign domain, as manifested in its persistent efforts to seize upon tropical regions, not because those countries and their incongruous people are necessary, or even desirable, to be incorporated into our nation, but for the mere purpose of making Slave States, in order to advance the political power of the party in the Senate and in the choice of the President, so as effectually to transfer the chief powers of the Government from the many to the few; has in various instances endangered the equality of the coördinate branches of the Government, by urgent efforts to enlarge the powers of the Executive at the expense of the Legislative department; has attempted to discredit and degrade the Judiciary, by affecting to make it, at first, the arbiter of party quarrels, to become soon and inevitably the passive registrar of a party decree.

In most, if not all these particulars, I understand the Republican party (judging it by its acts and by the known opinions of many of its leading men) to be the exact opposite of the Democratic party; and that is the ground of my preference of the one party over the other. And that alone would be a sufficient reason, if I had no other good reasons, for supporting Mr. Lincoln against any man who may be put forward by the Democratic party, as the exponent of its principles and the agent to work out, in practice, its dangerous policies.

The third party, which, by its formation, has destroyed the organization of the American and Whig parties, has nominated two most excellent men. I know them well, as sound statesmen and true patriots. More than thirty years ago I served with them both in Congress, and from that time to this I have always held them in respect and honor. But what can the third party do toward the election of even such worthy men as these against the two great parties which are now in actual contest for the power to rule the nation? It is made up entirely of portions of the disintegrated elements of the late Whig and American parties—good materials, in the main, I admit, but quite too weak to elect any man or establish any principle. The most it can do is, here and there in particular localities, to make a diversion in favor of the Democrats. In 1856, the Whig and American parties (not forming a *new party*, but united as allies), with entire unanimity and some zeal, supported Mr. Fillmore for the Presidency, and with what results? We made a miserable failure, carrying no State but gallant little Maryland. And, surely, the united Whigs and Americans of that day had a far greater show of strength and far better prospects of success than any which belong to the Constitutional Union party now. In fact, I see no possiblity of success for the third party, except in one contingency—the Destruction of the Democratic party. That is a contigency not likely to happen this year, for, badly as I think of many of the acts and policies of that party, its cup is not yet full—the day has not yet come when it must dissolve in its own corruptions. But the day is coming, and is not far off. The party has made itself entirely sectional; it has concentrated its very being into one single idea; negro Slavery has control of all its faculties, and it can see and hear nothing else—" one stern, tyrannic thought, that makes all other thoughts its slaves!"

But the Democratic party still lives, and while it lives, it and the Republican party are the only real antagonistic powers in the nation, and for the present, I must choose between them. I choose the latter, as wiser, purer, younger and less corrupted by time and self-indulgence.

The candidates nominated at Chicago are both men who, as individuals and politicians, rank with the foremost of the country. I have heard no objection to Mr. Hamlin personally, but only to his geographical position, which is thought to be too far North and East to allow his personal good qualities to exercise their proper influence over the nation at large. But the nomination for the Presidency is the great controlling act. Mr. Lincoln, his character, talents, opinions and history will be criticised by thousands, while the candidate for the Vice-Presidency will be passed over in comparative silence.

Mr. Lincoln's nomination took the public by surprise, because, until just before the event, it was unexpected. But really it ought not to have excited any surprise, for such unforeseen nominations are common in our political history. Polk and Pierce, by the Democrats, and Harrison and Taylor, by the Whigs, were all nominated in this extemporaneous manner—all of them were elected. I have known Mr. Lincoln for more than twenty years, and therefore have a right to speak of him with some confidence. As an individual, he has earned a high reputation for truth, courage, candor, morals, and amiability; so that, as a man, he is most trustworthy. And in this particular, he is more entitled to our esteem than some other men, his equals, who had far better opportunities and aids in early life. His talents, and the will to use them to the best advantage, are unquestionable; and the proof is found in the fact that, in every position in life, from his humble beginning to his present well-earned elevation, he has more than fulfilled the best hopes of his friends. And now, in the full vigor of his manhood, and in the honest pride of having made himself what he is, he is the peer of the first man of the nation, well able to sustain himself and advance his cause, against any adversary, and in any field, where mind and knowledge are the weapons used.

In politics he has but acted out the principle of his own moral and intellectual character. He has not concealed his thoughts nor hidden his light under a bushel. With the boldness of conscious rectitude and the frankness of downright honesty, he has not failed to avow his opinions of public affairs upon all fitting occasions.

This I know may subject him to the carping censure of that class of politicians who mistake cunning for wisdom and falsehood for ingenuity; but such men as Lincoln must act in keeping with their own characters, and hope for success only by advancing the truth prudently and maintaining it bravely. All his old political antecedents are, in my judgment, exactly right, being square up to the old Whig standard. And as to his views about "the pestilent negro question," I am not aware that he has gone one step beyond the doctrines publicly and habitually avowed by the great lights of the Whig party, Clay, Webster, and their fellows, and indeed sustained and carried out by the Democrats themselves, in their wiser and better days.

The following, I suppose, are in brief his opinions upon that subject: 1. Slavery is a domestic institution within the States which choose to have it, and it exists within those States beyond the control of Congress. 2. Congress has supreme legislative power over all the Territories, and may, at its discretion, allow or forbid the existence of Slavery within them. 3. Congress, in wisdom and sound policy, ought not so to exercise its power, directly or indirectly, as to plant and establish Slavery in any Territory theretofore free. 4. And that it is unwise and impolitic in the Government of the United States, to acquire tropical regions for the mere purpose of converting them into Slave States.

These, I believe, are Mr. Lincoln's opinions upon the matter of Slavery in the Territories, and I concur in them. They are no new inventions, made to suit the exigencies of the hour, but have come down to us, as the Declaration of Independence and the Constitution have, sanctioned by the venerable authority of the wise and good men who established our institutions. They are conformable to law, principle and wise policy, and their utility is proven in practice by the as yet unbroken current of our political history. They will prevail, not only because they are right in themselves, but also because a great and still growing majority of the people believe them to be right; and the sooner they are allowed to prevail in peace and harmony, the better for all concerned, as well those who are against them as those who are for them.

I am aware that smalll partisans, in their little warfare against opposing leaders, do sometimes assail them by the trick of tearing from their contexts some particular objectionable phrases, penned, perhaps, in the hurry of composition, or spoken in the heat of oral debate, and holding them up to the public as the leading doctrines of the person assailed, and drawing from them their own uncharitable inferences. That line of attack betrays a little mind conscious of its weakness, for the falsity of its logic is not more apparent than the injustice of its designs. No public man can stand that ordeal, and, however willing men may be to see it applied to their adversaries, all flinch from the torture when applied to themselves. In fact, the man who never said a foolish thing, will hardly be able to prove that he ever said many wise ones.

I consider Mr. Lincoln a sound, safe, national man. He could not be sectional if he tried. His birth, education, the habits of his life, and his geographical position, compel him to be national. All his feelings and interest are identified with the great valley of the Mississippi, near whose centre he has spent his whole life. The valley is not a section, but, conspicuously, the body of the nation, and, large as it is, it is not capable of being divided into sections, for the great river cannot be divided. It is one and indivisible, and the North and the South are alike necessary to its comfort and prosperity. Its people, too, in all their interests and affections, are as broad and general as the regions they inhabit. They are emigrants, a mixed multitude, coming from every State in the Union, and from most countries in Europe; they are unwilling, therefore, to submit to any one petty local standard. They love the nation as a whole, and they love all its parts, for they are bound to them all, not only by a feeling of common interest and mutual dependence, but also by the recollections of childhood and youth, by blood and friendship, and by all those social and domestic charities which sweeten life, and make this world worth living in. The valley is beginning to feel its power, and will soon be strong enough to dictate the law of the land. Whenever that state of things shall come to pass, it will be most fortunate for the nation to find the powers of Government lodged in the hands of men whose habits of thought, whose position and surrounding circumstances, constrain them to use those powers for general and not sectional ends.

I give my opinion freely in favor of Mr. Lincoln, and I hope that for the good of the whole country, he may be elected. But it is not my intention to take any active part in the canvass. For many years past, I have had little to do with public affairs, and have aspired to no political office; and now, in view of the mad excitement which convulses the country, and the general disruption and disorder of parties and the elements which compose them, I am more than ever assured that for me, personally, there is no political future, and I accept the condition with cheerful satisfaction. Still, I cannot discharge myself from the life-long duty to watch the conduct of men in power, and to resist, so far as a mere private man may, the fearful progress of official corruption, which for several years past has sadly marred and defiled the fair fabric of our Government.

If Mr. Lincoln should be elected, coming in as a new man at the head of a young party never before in power, he may render a great service to his country, which no Democrat could render. He can march straight forward in the discharge of his high duties, guided only by his own good judgment and honest purposes, without any necessity to temporize with established abuses, to wink at the delinquencies of old party friends, or to unlearn and discard the bad official habits that have grown up under the misgovernment of his Democratic predecessors. In short, he can be an honest and bold reformer on easier and cheaper terms than any Democratic President can be—for, in proceeding in the good work of cleansing and purifying the administrative departments, he will have no occasion to expose the vices, assail the interests, or thwart the ambition of his political friends.

Begging your pardon for the length of this letter, I remain, with great respect, your friend and obedient servant,

EDWARD BATES.

THE MONROE DOCTRINE.

So much has been wildly said of what is termed the "Monroe Doctrine," in regard to the influence of European Powers on this continent, that we publish exactly what President Monroe said on the subject. We copy from the Seventh Annual Message of Mr. Monroe, dated December 2, 1823:

"It was stated, at the commencement of the last session, that a great effort was then making in Spain and Portugal to improve the condition of the people of those countries, and that it appeared to be conducted with extraordinary moderation. It need scarcely be remarked that the result has been, so far, very different from what was then anticipated. Of events in that quarter of the globe, with which we have so much intercourse, and from which we derive our origin, we have always been anxious and interested spectators. The citizens of the United States cherish sentiments the most friendly in favor of the liberty and happiness of their fellow-men on that side of the Atlantic. In the wars of the European powers, in matters relating to themselves, we have never taken any part, nor does it comport with our policy so to do. It is only when our rights are invaded or seriously menaced, that we resent injuries or make preparation for our defense. With the movements in this hemisphere we are of necessity more immediately connected, and by causes which must be obvious to all enlightened and impartial observers. The political system of the allied powers is essentially different in this respect from that of America. This difference proceeds from that which exists in their respective governments. And to the defense of our own, which has been achieved by the loss of so much blood and treasure, and matured by the wisdom of their most enlightened citizens, and under which we have enjoyed unexampled felicity, this whole nation is devoted. We owe it, therefore, to candor, and to the amicable relations existing between the United States and those powers to declare, that we should consider any attempt on their part to extend their system to any portion of this hemisphere as dangerous to our peace and safety. With the existing colonies or dependencies of any European power we have not interfered, and shall not interfere. But with the governments who have declared their independence, and maintained it, and whose independence we have, on great consideration, and on just principles, acknowledged, we could not view any interposition for the purpose of oppressing them, or controlling in any other manner their destiny, by any European power, in any other light than as the manifestation of an unfriendly disposition toward the United States. In the war between these new governments and Spain, we declared our neutrality at the time of their recognition, and to this we have adhered, and shall continue to adhere, provided no change shall occur, which in the judgment of the competent authorities of this Government, shall make a corresponding change on the part of the United States indispensable to their security.

"The late events in Spain and Portugal show that Europe is still unsettled. Of this important fact no stronger proof can be adduced than that the allied powers should have thought it proper, on a principle satisfactory to themselves, to have interposed by force in the internal concerns of Spain. To what extent such interposition may be carried, on the same principle, is a question to which all independent powers, whose governments differ from theirs, are interested—even those most remote, and surely none more so than the United States. Our policy in regard to. Europe, which was adopted at an early stage of the wars which have so long agitated that quarter of the globe, nevertheless remains the same, which is, not to interfere in the internal concerns of any of its powers; to consider the Government, *de facto*, as the legitimate Government for us; to cultivate friendly relations with it, and to preserve those relations by a frank, firm, and manly policy; meeting, in all instances, the just claims of every power, submitting to injuries from none. But in regard to these continents, circumstances are eminently and conspicuously different. It is impossible that the allied powers should extend their political system to any portion of either continent without endangering our peace and happiness; nor can any one believe that our southern brethren, if left to themselves, would adopt it of their own accord. It is equally impossible, therefore, that we should behold such interposition, in any form, with indifference. If we look to the comparative strength and resources of Spain and those new Governments, and their distance from each other, it must be obvious that she can never subdue them. It is still the true policy of the United States to leave the parties to themselves, in the hope that other powers will pursue the same course."

STATES AND STATESMEN ON THE SLAVERY QUESTION.

WISCONSIN FOR FREE SOIL.

The following resolutions were adopted by the Wisconsin (Democratic) Legislature in 1848, with only three dissenting votes in the Senate and five in the House:

Whereas, Slavery is an evil of the first magnitude, morally and politically, and whatever may be the consequences, it is our duty to prohibit its extension in all cases where such prohibition is allowed by the Constitution: Therefore,

Resolved, By the Senate and Assembly of the State of Wisconsin, that the introduction of Slavery into this country is to be deeply deplored; that its extension ought to be prohibited by every constitutional barrier within the power of Congress; that in the admission of new territory into the Union, there ought to be an inhibitory provision against its introduction, unless clearly and unequivocally admitted by the Constitution—inasmuch as in all cases of doubtful construction, the Rights of Man and the cause of Liberty ought to prevail.

Resolved, That our Senators in Congress be, and they are hereby, instructed, and our Representatives are requested, to use their influence to insert into the organic act for the government of any new territory already acquired or hereafter to be acquired, that is now free, an ordinance forever prohibiting the introduction of Slavery or involuntary servitude into said territory except as a punishment for crime, of which the party shall have been duly convicted according to law.

Resolved, That His Excellency the Governor is hereby requested immediately to forward a copy of the foregoing resolutions to each of our Senators and Representatives, to be by them laid before Congress.

THE DEMOCRACY OF MAINE FOR THE WILMOT PROVISO.

Resolutions adopted by a Convention of the Democratic party of Maine, in June, 1849:

Resolved, That the institution of human Slavery is at variance with the theory of our government, abhorrent to the common sentiments of mankind, and fraught with danger to all who come within the sphere of its influence, that the Federal Government possesses adequate power to inhibit its existence in the Territories of the Union; and that we enjoin upon our Senators and Representatives in Congress to make every exertion and employ all their influence to procure the passage of a law forever excluding Slavery from the Territories of California and New-Mexico.

DELAWARE FOR FREE TERRITORY.

The following preamble and resolution were adopted by the Legislature of Delaware in 1847:

Whereas, A crisis has arrived in the public affairs of the Nation, which requires the free and full expression of the people, through their legal representatives; and *Whereas,* The United States is at war with the Republic of Mexico, occasioned by the Annexation of Texas, with a view to the addition of Slave Territory to our country, and the extending of Slave power in our Union; and *Whereas,* In the opinion of the General Assembly, such acquisitions are hostile to the spirit of our Free Institutions, and contrary to sound morality; therefore be it

Resolved, By the Senate and House of Representatives of the State of Delaware in General Assembly met, That our Senators and Representatives in Congress are hereby requested to vote against the annexation of any Territory to our Union, which shall not thereafter be forever free from Slavery.

MASSACHUSETTS AGAINST SLAVERY.

The following resolution was passed by the Legislature of Massachusetts in 1847, in connection with others on the subject of the Mexican war.

Resolved, That our attention is directed anew to the wrong and "enormity" of Slavery, and to the tyranny and usurpation of the "Slave Power," as displayed in the history of our country, particularly in the annexation of Texas, and the present war with Mexico, and that we are impressed with the unalterable condition, that a regard for the fair fame of our country, for the principle of morals, and for that righteousness that exalteth a nation, sanctions and requires all constitutional efforts for the destruction of the unjust influence of the Slave power, and for the abolition of Slavery within the limits of the United States.

THE WHIGS OF MASSACHUSETTS AGAINST SLAVERY.

The Massachusetts State Convention, held at Springfield, in the latter part of the month of September, 1847, and at which Daniel Webster was nominated as a candidate for the Presidency, passed the following among other resolutions:

Resolved, That the war with Mexico—the predicted, if not the legitimate offspring, of the annexation of Texas—begun in a palpable violation of the Constitution, and the usurpation of the powers of Congress by the President, and carried on in reckless indifference and disregard of the blood and treasure of the Nation—can have no object which can be effected by the acquisition of Mexican territory, under the circumstance of the country—unless under adequate securities for the protection of human liberty—can have no other probable result than the ultimate advancement of the sectional supremacy of the Slave Power.

After recommending "Peace with Mexico, without dismemberment," and "No addition of Mexican Territories to the American Union," the Convention

Resolved, That if this course should be rejected and the war shall be prosecuted to the final subjection or dismemberment of Mexico, the Whigs of Massachusetts now declare, and put this declaration of purpose on record, that Massachusetts will never consent that Mexican Territory, however acquired, shall become a part of the American Union, unless on the unalterable condition that "there shall be neither Slavery nor Involuntary Servitude therein, otherwise than in the punishment of crime."

Resolved, That in making this declaration of her purpose, Massachusetts announces no new principle of action in regard to her sister States, and makes no new application of principles already acknowledged. She merely states the great American principle embodied in our Declaration of Independence—the political equality of persons in the civil state; the principles adopted in the legislation of the States under the Confederation, and sometimes by the Constitution—in the admission of all the new States formed from the only Territory belonging to the Union at the adoption of the Constitution—it is, in short, the imperishable principle set forth in the ever memorable Ordinance of 1787, which has for more than half a century been the fundamental law of human liberty in the great valley of the Lakes, the Ohio, and the Mississippi, with what brilliant success, and with what unparalleled results, let the great and growing States of Ohio, Indiana, Illinois, Michigan, and Wisconsin, answer and declare.

MR. WEBSTER AGAINST SLAVERY EXTENSION.

In the United States Senate, in Aug., 1848. Mr. Webster, in speaking on the bill to organize the Territory of Oregon with a clause prohibiting Slavery, said:

The question now is, whether it is not competent to Congress, in the exercise of a fair and just discretion, to say that, considering that there have been five slave-holding States (Louisiana, Florida, Arkansas, Missouri and Texas) added to the Union out of foreign acquisitions, and as yet only one Free State, whether, under this state of things, it is unreasonable and unjust in the slightest degree to limit their farther extension? That is the question. I see no injustice in it. As to the power of Congress I have nothing to add to what I said the other day. I have said that *I shall consent to no Extension of the area of Slavery on this Continent, nor any increase of Slave Representation in the other House of Congress.*

MILLARD FILLMORE'S VIEWS.

His Buffalo Letter of 1838.

BUFFALO, Oct. 17, 1838.

SIR: Your communication of the 13th inst., as chairman of the committee appointed by "The Anti-Slavery Society of the County of Erie," has just come to hand. You solicit my answer to the following interrogatories:

1st. Do you believe that petitions to Congress, on the subject of Slavery and the Slave-trade, ought to be received, read, and respectfully considered by the representatives of the people?

2d. Are you opposed to the annexation of Texas to this Union under any circumstances, so long as slaves are held therein?

3d. Are you in favor of Congress exercising all the power it possesses to abolish the Internal Slave-trade between the States?

4th. Are you in favor of immediate legislation for the Abolition of Slavery in the District of Columbia?

Answer.—I am much engaged, and have no time to enter into argument, or explain at length my reasons for my opinions. I shall therefore content myself, for the present, by answering all your interrogatories in the affirmative, and leave for some future occasion a more extended discussion on the subject.

I would, however, take this occasion to say, that in thus frankly giving my opinion, I would not desire to have it understood in the nature of a pledge. At the same time that I seek no disguise, but freely give my sentiments on any subject of interest to those for whose suffrages I am a candidate, I am opposed to giving any pledge that shall deprive me hereafter of all discretionary power. My own character must be the guaranty for the general correctness of my legislative deportment. On every important subject I am bound to deliberate before I act, and especially as a legislator, to possess myself of all the information, and listen to every argument that can be adduced by my associates, before I give a final vote. If I stand pledged to a particular course of action, I cease to be a responsible agent, but I become a mere machine. Should subsequent events show, beyond all doubt, that the course I had become pledged to pursue was ruinous to my constituents and disgraceful to myself, I have no alternative, no opportunity for repentance, and there is no power to absolve me from my obligation. Hence the impropriety, not to say absurdity, in my view, of giving a pledge.

I am aware that you have not asked my pledge, and I believe I know your sound judgment and good sense too well to think you desire any such thing. It was, however, to prevent any misrepresentation on the part of others, that I have felt it my duty thus much on this subject.

I am, respectfully, your obedient servant,

MILLARD FILLMORE.

W. Mills, Esq., chairman.

MR. FILLMORE'S ALBANY SPEECH OF 1856.

The following is Mr. Fillmore's speech, delivered at Albany, in July, 1856:

Mr. Mayor and Fellow-Citizens: This overwhelming demonstration of congratulation and welcome almost deprives me of the power of speech. Here, nearly thirty years ago, I commenced my political career. In this building I first saw a legislative body in session; but at that time it never entered into the aspirations of my heart that I ever should receive such a welcome as this in the capital of my native State.

You have been pleased, sir, to allude to my former services and my probable course if I should again be called to the position of Chief Magistrate of the nation. It is not pleasant to speak of one's self, yet I trust that the occasion will justify me in briefly alluding to one or two events connected with my administration. You all know that when I was called to the Executive chair by a bereavement which shrouded a nation in mourning, that the country was unfortunately agitated from one end to the other upon the all-exciting subject of Slavery. It was then, sir, that I felt it my duty to rise above every sectional prejudice, and look to the welfare of the whole nation. I was compelled to a certain extent to overcome long-cherished prejudices, and disregard party claims. But in doing this, sir, I did no more than was done by many abler and better men than myself. I was by no means the sole instrument, under Providence, in harmonizing these difficulties. There were at that time noble, independent, high-souled men in both Houses of Congress, belonging to both the great political parties of the country—Whigs and Democrats—who spurned the dictation of selfish party leaders, and rallied around my administration in support of the great measures which restored peace to an agitated and distracted country. Some of these have gone to their eternal rest, with the blessings of their country on their heads, but others yet survive, deserving the benediction and honors of a grateful people. By the blessings of Divine Providence, our efforts were crowned with signal success, and when I left the Presidential chair, the whole nation was prosperous and contented, and our relations with all foreign nations were of the most amicable kind. The cloud that hung upon the horizon was dissipated. But where are we now? Alas! threatened at home with civil war, and from abroad with a rupture of our peaceful relations. I shall not seek to trace the causes of this change. These are the facts, and it is for you to ponder upon them. Of the present Administration I have nothing to say, for I know and can appreciate the difficulties of administering this government, and if the present Executive and his supporters have with good intentions and honest hearts made a mistake, I hope God may forgive them as I freely do. But, if there be those who have brought these calamities upon the country for selfish or ambitious objects, it is your duty, fellow-citizens, to hold them to a strict responsibility.

The agitation which disturbed the peace of the country in 1850, was unavoidable. It was brought upon us by the acquisition of new territory, for the government of which it was necessary to provide territorial organization. But it is for you to say whether the present agitation, which distracts the country and threatens us with civil war, has not been recklessly and wantonly produced, by the adoption of a measure to aid personal advancement rather than in any public good.

Sir, you have been pleased to say, that I have the Union of these States at heart; this, sir, is most true, for if there be one object dearer to me than any other, it is the unity, prosperity, and glory of this great republic; and I confess frankly, sir, that I fear it is in danger. I say nothing of any particular section, much less of the several candidates before the people. I presume they are all honorable men. But, sir, what do we see? An exasperated feeling between the North and the South, on the most exciting of all topics, resulting in bloodshed and organized military array.

But this is not all, sir. We see a political party presenting candidates for the Presidency and Vice-Presidency, selected for the first time from the Free States alone, with the avowed purpose of electing these candidates by suffrages of one part of the Union only, to rule over the whole United States. Can it be possible that those who are engaged in such a measure can have seriously reflected upon the consequences which must inevitably follow, in case of success? Can they have the madness or the folly to believe that our Southern brethren would submit to be governed by such a Chief Magistrate? Would he be required to follow the same rule prescribed by those who elected him, in making his appointments? If a man living south of Mason and Dixon's line be not worthy to be President or Vice-President, would it be proper to select one from the same quarter as one of his cabinet council or to represent the nation in a foreign country? Or, indeed, to collect the revenue, or administer the laws of the United States? If not, what new rule is the President to adopt in selecting men for office, that the people themselves discard in selecting him? These are serious, but practical questions, and in order to appreciate them fully, it is only necessary to turn the tables upon ourselves. Suppose that the South, having a majority of the electoral votes, should declare that they would only have slaveholders for President and Vice-President, and should elect such by their exclusive suffrages to rule over us at the North. Do you

think we would submit to it? No, not for a moment. And do you believe that your Southern brethren are less sensitive on this subject than you are, or less jealous of their rights? If you do, let me tell you that you are mistaken. And, therefore, you must see that if this sectional party succeeds, it leads inevitably to the destruction of this beautiful fabric reared by our forefathers, cemented by their blood, and bequeathed to us as a priceless inheritance.

I tell you, my friends, that I feel deeply, and therefore I speak earnestly on this subject (cries of "you're right!") for I feel that you are in danger. I am determined to make a clean breast of it. I will wash my hands of the consequences, whatever they may be; and I tell you that we are treading upon the brink of a volcano, that is liable at any moment to burst forth and overwhelm the nation. I might, by soft words, inspire delusive hopes, and thereby win votes. But I can never consent to be one thing to the North and another to the South. I should despise myself, if I could be guilty of such duplicity. For my conscience would exclaim, with the dramatic poet :

> " Is there not some chosen curse,
> Some hidden thunder in the stores of heaven,
> Red with uncommon wrath, to blast the man
> Who owes his greatness to his country's ruin ?"

In the language of the lamented, but immortal Clay : "I had rather be right than be President !"

It seems to me imposs.ble that those engaged in this can have contemplated the awful consequences of success. If it breaks asunder the bonds of our Union, and spreads anarchy and civil war through the land, what is it less than moral treason? Law and common sense hold a man responsible for the natural consequence of his acts, and must not those whose acts tend to the destruction of the Government, be equally held responsible?

And let me also add, that when this Union is dissolved, it will not be divided into two republics, or two monarchies, but be broken into fragments, and at war with each other.

MR. FILLMORE'S LETTER TO A NEW-YORK UNION MEETING IN 1859.

The following is an extract from a letter of Mr. Fillmore, (dated Dec. 16, 1859), in reply to an invitation to attend a Union Meeting at Cooper Institute, New-York.

But it seems to me that if my opinions are of any importance to my countrymen, they now have them in a much more responsible and sat.sfactory form than I could give them by participating in the proceedings of any meeting. My sentiments on this unfortunate question of slavery, and the constitutional rights of the South in regard to it, have not changed since they were made manifest to the whole country by the performance of a painful duty in approving and enforcing the Fugitive Slave Law. What the Constitution gives I would concede at every sacrifice. I would not seek to enjoy its benefits without sharing its burdens and its responsibilities. I know of no other rule of political right or expediency. Those were my sentiments then—they are my sentiments now. I stand by the Constitution of my country at every hazard, and am prepared to maintain it at every sacrifice.

Here I might stop ; but since I have yielded to the impulse to write, I will not hesitate to express, very briefly, my views on one or two events which have occurred since I retired from office, and which, in all probability, have given rise to your meeting. This I cannot do intelligibly, without a brief reference to some events which occurred during my administration.

All must remember that in 1849 and 1850, the country was severely agitated on this disturbing question of Slavery. That contest grew out of the acquisition of new territory from Mexico, and a contest between the North and South as to whether Slavery should be tolerated in any part of that Territory. Mixed up with this, was a claim on the part of the slaveholding States, that the provision of the Constitution for the rendition of fugitives from service should be made available, as the law of 1793 on that subject, which depended chiefly on State officers for its execution, had become inoperative, because State officers were not obliged to perform that duty.

After a severe struggle, which threatened the integrity of the Union, Congress finally passed laws settling these questions ; and the Government and the people for a time seemed to acquiesce in that *compromise* as a final settlement of this exciting question ; and it is exceedingly to be regretted that mistaken ambition or the hope of promoting a party triumph should have tempted any one to raise this question again. But in an evil hour this Pandora's box of Slavery was again opened by what I conceive to be an unjustifiable attempt to force Slavery into Kansas by a repeal of the Missouri Compromise, and the floods of evils now swelling and threatening to overthrow the Constitution, and sweep away the foundation of the Government itself, and deluge this land with fraternal blood, may all be traced to this unfortunate act. Whatever might have been the motive, few acts have ever been so barren of good, and so fruitful of evil.

EDWARD EVERETT'S OPINIONS ON SLAVERY.

The following is an extract of a speech of Mr. Everett, delivered in the House of Representatives, March 9, 1826. (See Benton's Abridgment of Congressional Debates, vol. 8, page 711.)

Having touched upon this point, I ought, perhaps, to add that, if there are any members in this House of that class of politicians to whom the gentleman from North Carolina (Mr. Saunders) alluded, as having the disposition, though not the power, to disturb the compromise contained in the Constitution on this point, I am not of the number. Neither am I one of those citizens of the North, to whom another honorable gentleman referred, in a publication to which his name was subscribed, who would think it immoral and irreligious to join in putting down a servile insurrection at the South: I am no soldier, sir; my habits and education are very unmilitary, but there is no cause in which I would sooner buckle a knapsack to my back, and put a musket on my shoulder, than that. I would cede the whole continent to any one who would take it—to England, to France, to Spain; I would see it sunk in the bottom of the ocean before I would see any part of this fair America converted into a continental Hayti, by that awful process of bloodshed and desolation, by which alone such a catastrophe could be brought on. The great relation of servitude, in some form or other, with greater or less departure from the theoretic equality of man, is inseparable from our nature. I know of no way by which the form of this servitude shall be fixed, but political institution. Domestic Slavery—though, I confess, not that form of servitude which seems to be the most beneficial to the master—certainly not that which is most beneficial to the servant—is not, in my judgment, to be set down as an immoral and irreligious relation. I cannot admit that religion has but one voice to the slave, and that this voice is, "Rise against your Master." No, sir; the New Testament says, "Slaves, obey your Masters;" and, though I know full well that, in the benignant operation of Christianity, which gathered master and slave around the same communion-table, this unfortunate institution disappeared in Europe, yet I cannot admit that, while it subsists, and where it subsists, its duties are not presupposed and sanctioned by religion. I certainly am not called upon to meet the charges brought against this institution, yet truth obliges me to say a word more on the subject. I know the condition of working classes in other countries; I am intimately acquainted with it in some other countries, and I have no hesitation in saying that I believe the slaves in this country are better clothed and fed, and less hardly worked, than the peasantry of some of the most prosperous States of the continent of Europe. Consider the checks on population. What keeps population down? Poverty, want, starvation, disease, and all the ills of life; it is these that check population all over the world. Now, the slave population of the United States increases faster than the white, masters included. What is the inference as to the physical condition of the two classes of society? These are opinions I have long entertained, and long since publicly professed on this subject, and which I here repeat in answer to the intimations to which I have already alluded. But, sir, when Slavery comes to enter into the Constitution as a political element—when it comes to affect the distribution of power amongst the States of the Union, that is a matter of agreement. If I make an agreement on this subject, I will adhere to it like a man; but I will protest against any inferences being made from it like that which was made by the honorable mover of these resolutions. I will protest against popularity, as well as votes, being increased by the ratio of three-fifths of the Slaves.

MR. MITCHELL'S VIEWS.

Mr. Mitchell, of Tennessee.—Sir, I do not go the length of the gentleman from Massachusetts, and hold that the existence of Slavery in this country is almost a blessing. On the contrary, I am firmly settled in the opinion that it is a great curse—one of the greatest evils that could have been interwoven into our system. I, Mr. Chairman, am one of those whom these poor wretches call master; I do not task them; I feed and clothe them well; but yet, alas! sir, they are slaves, and Slavery is a curse in any shape. It is, no doubt, true that there are persons in Europe far more degraded than our slaves, worse fed, worse clothed, etc.; but, sir, this is far from proving that negroes ought to be slaves.

John Randolph, of Virginia.—Sir, I envy neither the head nor heart of that man from the North who rises here to defend Slavery upon principle.

MR. CAMBRELENG'S VIEWS.

Churchill C. Cambreleng, of N. Y., (formerly of N. C.)—The gentleman from Massachusetts has gone too far. He has expressed opinions which ought not to escape without animadversion. I heard them with equal surprise and regret. I was astonished to hear him declare that Slavery—domestic Slavery—say what you will, is a condition of life, as well as any other, to be justified by morality, religion, and international law; and when at the close of his opinion he solemnly declared that this was his confession of faith, I lamented, sincerely lamented, that

> —— "Star-eyed Science should have wandered there
> To bring us back the message of despair."

If, sir, among the wild visions of German philosophy I had ever reached conclusions like this; if in the Aulæ of Gottingen I had ever persuaded myself to adopt a political maxim so hostile to liberal institutions and the rights of mankind, I would have locked it up forever in the darkest chambers of my mind. Or if my zeal had been too ardent for my discretion, this place, at least, should never have been the theatre of my eloquence. No, sir, if such had been my doctrines I would have turned my back forever on my native land. Following the course of "the dark rolling Danube," and cutting my way across the Euxine, I would have visited a well-known market of Constantinople, and there preached my doctrine amidst the rattling chains of the wretched captives. Nay, sir, I would have gone from thence, and laid my forehead upon the footstool of the Sultan, and besought him to set his foot upon my neck, as the recreant citizen of a recreant Republic.

EDWARD EVERETT ON GEOGRAPHICAL PARTIES.

But, sir, I am not prepared to admit that geographical parties are the greatest evil this country has to fear. Party of all kinds, in its excess, is certainly the bane of our institutions; and I will not take up the time of this Committee by disputing which is most deleterious, arsenic or laudanum. It is enough that they are both fatal. The evil of geographical parties is, that they tend to sever the Union. The evil of domestic parties is, that they render the Union not worth having. I remember the time, sir, though I was but a boy, when under the influence of domestic parties, near neighbors did not speak; when old acquaintances glared at each other as they passed in the streets; when you might wreak on a man all the bitterness of your personal and private enmity, and grind him into the dust, if you had the power, and say, he is a Democrat, he is a Federalist; he deserves it. Yes, sir, when party spirit pursued its victim from the halls of legislation, from the forum, from the market-place, to what should be the sanctuary of the fireside, and filled hearts that would have bled to spare each other a pang, with coldness and estrangement. Talk not to me of your geographical parties. There does not live the man, I thank God, on earth, toward whom I have an unkind emotion—one whose rights I would invade, whose feelings I would wound. But if there ever should be a man to whom I should stand in that miserable relation, I pray that mountains may rise, that rivers may roll between us—that he may never cross my path, nor I his, to turn the sweetness of human nature into bitterness and gall in both our bosoms.—*Speech in the House of Representatives*, 1826.—*Benton's Debates, vol. 8, p. 713.*

MR. EVERETT'S VIEWS IN 1837 and 39.

Oct. 14th, 1837, Hon. Wm. Jackson, of Newton, Mass., wrote to Mr. Everett a long letter containing the following questions:

Do justice, humanity, and sound policy, alike require that the slaves of this country should be emancipated?

Is it the right and duty of the citizens of the non-slaveholding States to require of the General Government the abolition of Slavery in the District of Columbia?

Is it just or safe, with regard to our foreign relations and domestic compact, to admit Texas into the Union?

MR. EVERETT'S REPLY.

BOSTON, 31*st October*, 183'.

SIR: I have duly received your communication of the 14th inst., in which you desire to be furnished with my views on certain questions therein propounded. Under other circumstances, I should deem it proper to preface my answer with some preliminary remarks, but my engagements at the present time compel me to reply as concisely as possible.

In answer to the first question, I observe, that Slavery being, by universal admission, a social, political, and moral evil of the first magnitude, it is required by justice, humanity, and sound policy that the slaves should be emancipated by those having constitutionally the power to effect that object, as soon as it can be done peacefully, and in a manner to better the condition of the emancipated. I believe the most considerate portion of the people of the United States, in every quarter, unite in this sentiment; and you are aware that the most eminent Southern names can be cited in its support.

In reply to the second question, I would remark, that all the considerations in favor of emancipation in the States, apply with equal force to the District of Columbia. My opinions on this subject are fully expressed in the resolution adopted by the legislature last winter, with a near approach to unanimity, in the following terms: " Resolved, That Congress having exclusive legislation in the District of Columbia, possesses the right to abolish Slavery in the said District, and that its exercise should only be restrained by regard to the public good.

I know that the slave-trade is carried on to a shocking extent in the District of Columbia. There is no part of the South, where it is reputable to be engaged in this traffic; and no Southern State, I am persuaded, would permit its existence in its own capital, as it exists at the national capital. The South and the North ought to unite in prohibiting it, by act of Congress—which is the local legislature of the District. This has been loudly called for, from the District itself. I have before me a copy of a petition, couched in very strong language, against both Slavery and the slave-trade in the District of Columbia, which was presented to Congress in 1824, signed by nearly seven hundred and fifty names of citizens of Washington, several of whom were known to me to be of the first consideration. I may observe in this connection, that at the same session, I voted in the negative on a motion to lay upon the table the petition of the American Anti-Slavery Society for the abolition of Slavery in the District of Columbia, and on two other motions, intended, in like manner, to deprive this class of petitions of a respectful reception and consideration.

The last question propounded by you refers to the annexation of Texas. It presents the subject of Slavery, in most of its bearings, in a new light. In the States, its introduction was the result of a legislation forced upon the colonies, and in many cases, in despite of acts passed by their legislators, for the prohibition of the slave-trade, and regulated by the crown. Its existence is recognized by the Constitution of the United States. The rights of property growing out of it are in some degree protected by law in the non-slaveholding States (see the opinion of Chief Justice Shaw in the case of the Commonwealth *vs.* Aves—an opinion in the doctrines and principles of which I fully concur); and morality and religion frown on all attempts to put an end to it by violence and bloodshed. But none of these principles countenance a voluntary extension of Slavery; and as the question of annexing Texas is one of voluntary, and almost boundless extension, it presents the subject, as I have said, in a new light. It has been officially stated by the Texan Envoy that the region so called contains two hundred thousand square miles. In other words, it might form twenty-five States as large as Massachusetts. In this vast region, Slavery was prohibited by Mexico; it has been restored, and is rapidly spreading itself under the new government; and no one denies, that if the independence of Texas is sustained, Slavery will be indefinitely extended throughout its ample borders.

The Executive Government of the United States has promptly recognized this independence. and by so doing, has discharged the whole duty that could be required by the law of nations. Whatever step we take toward annexation is gratuitous. This whole subject has been so ably discussed by Dr. Channing, in his recent letter to M. Clay, that it would be superfluous to enlarge upon it. I will only say, that if, at this moment, when an all-important experiment is in train, to abolish Slavery by peaceful and legal means in the British West Indies, the United States, instead of imitating their example, or even awaiting the result, should rush into a policy of g'v'ng an indefinite extension to Slavery over a vast region incorporated into their Union, we should stand condemned before the civilized world. It would be vain to expect to gain credit for any further professions of a willingness to be rid of Slavery as soon as possible. No extenuation of its existence, on the ground of its having been forced upon the country in its colonial state, would any longer avail us. It would be thought, and thought justly, that lust of power and lust of gold had made us deaf to the voice of humanity and justice. We should be self-convicted of the enormous crime of having voluntarily given the greatest possible enlargement to an evil, which, in concert with the rest of mankind, we had affected to deplore, and that at a time when the public sentiment of the civilized world, more than at any former period, is aroused to its magnitude.

There are other objections to the measure drawn from its bearing on our foreign relations; but it is unnecessary to discuss them.

I am, sir, respectfully,
Your obedient servant,
EDWARD EVERETT.

HON. WILLIAM JACKSON.

In 1839, the following questions were put to Mr. Everett by Hon. A. Borden, of Massachusetts:

1. Are you in favor of immediate abolition by law of Slavery in the District of Columbia and of the slave traffic between the States of this Union?

2. Are you opposed to the admission into the Union of any new States the constitutions of which tolerate domestic Slavery?

The following was Mr. Everett's reply:

WASHINGTON, *Oct.* 21, 1839.

DEAR SIR: On Saturday last I only received your letter of the 18th, propounding to me certain interrogatories, and earnestly requesting an early answer. You are aware that several resolves on the subject of these inquiries and their kindred topics, accompanied by a report, were introduced into the Senate of the Commonwealth, year before last, by a joint committee of the two houses, of which the lamented Mr. Alvord was chairman.

Those resolves, after having been somewhat enlarged by amendment, were adopted by the legislature. They appear to cover the whole ground of your two interrogatories. Having cheerfully coöperated in the passage of the resolves, and concurring in the general reasoning by which they are sustained in the powerful report of the chairman of the committee, I respond to both your inquiries in the affirmative.

The first of the three subjects in your inquiry is the only one of them which came before Congress while I was a member. I voted in the negative on the motion to lay upon the table the petition of the American Anti-Slavery Society for the abolition of Slavery in the District of Columbia, and on other motions of the like character introduced to cast off the consideration of this class of petitions.

I am, dear sir, very respectfully, your friend and servant.

EDWARD .EVERETT.

HON. NATHANIEL A. BORDEN.

The " several resolves " to which Mr. Everett refers in the above letter, in the passage of which he " cheerfully coöperated," as Governor of Massachusetts, are as follows:

Resolved, That Congress has, by the Constitution, power to abolish Slavery and the slave-trade in the District of Columbia, and that there is nothing in the terms or circumstances of the acts of cession by Virginia and Maryland, or otherwise, enforcing any legal or moral restraint on its existence.

Resolved, That Congress ought to take measures to effect the abolition of Slavery in the District of Columbia.

Resolved, That the rights of humanity, the claims of justice, and the common good alike, demand the suppression by Congress of the slave-trade carried on in and through the District of Columbia.

Resolved, That Congress has, by the Constitution, power to abolish Slavery in the Territories of the United States.

[For later views of Mr. Everett, see his letter accepting the nomination for the Vice-Presidency in 1860.]

ABRAHAM LINCOLN ON THOMAS JEFFERSON.

Mr. Lincoln having been invited by the Republicans of Boston, to attend a Festival in honor of the anniversary of Jefferson's birthday, on the 13th of April, 1859, replied as follows:

SPRINGFIELD, Ill., *April* 6, 1859.

GENTLEMEN: Your kind note, inviting me to attend a festival in Boston, on the 13th inst., in honor of the birthday of Thomas Jefferson, was duly received. My engagements are such that I cannot attend. Bearing in mind that about seventy years ago two great political parties were first formed in this country; that Thomas Jefferson was the head of one of them and Boston the headquarters of the other, it is both curious and interesting that those supposed to descend politically from the party opposed to Jefferson, should now be celebrating his birthday in their own original seat of empire, while those claiming political descent from him have nearly ceased to breathe his name everywhere.

Remembering, too, that the Jefferson party was formed upon its supposed superior devotion to the *personal* rights of men, holding the rights of *property* to be secondary only, and greatly inferior; and then assuming that the so-called Democracy of to-day are the Jefferson, and their opponents the anti-Jefferson parties, it will be equally interesting to note how completely the two have changed ground as to the principle upon which they were originally supposed to be divided.

The Democracy of to-day hold the *liberty* of one man to be absolutely nothing, when in conflict with another man's right of *property*. Republicans, on the contrary, are both for the *man* and the *dollar*, but in case of conflict the man *before* the dollar.

I remember being once much amused at seeing two partially intoxicated men engaged in a fight with their great-coats on, which fight, after a long and rather harmless contest, ended in each having fought himself out of his own coat and into that of the other. If the two leading parties of this day are really identical with the two in the days of Jefferson and Adams, they have performed the same feat as the two drunken men.

But soberly, it is now no child's play to save the principles of Jefferson from total overthrow in this nation.

One would state with great confidence that he could convince any sane child that the simpler propositions of Euclid are true; but nevertheless, he would fail, with one who should deny the definitions and axioms. The principles of Jefferson are the definitions and axioms of free society. And yet they are denied and evaded, with no small show of success. One dashingly calls them "glittering generalities." Another bluntly styles them "self-evident lies." And others insidiously argue that they apply only to "superior races."

These expressions, differing in form, are identical in object and effect—the supplanting the principles of free government, and restoring those of classification, caste, and legitimacy. They would delight a convocation of crowned heads plotting against the people. They are the vanguard, the sappers and miners, of returning despotism. We must repulse them, or they will subjugate us.

This is a world of compensations; and he who would *be* no slave must consent to *have* no slave. Those who deny freedom to others deserve it not for themselves; and, under a just God, cannot long retain it.

All honor to Jefferson—to the man who, in the concrete pressure of a struggle for national independence by a single people, had the coolness, forecast, and capacity, to introduce into a merely revolutionary document an abstract truth, applicable to all men and all times, and so to embalm it there, that to-day and in all coming days it shall be a rebuke and a stumbling-block to the harbingers of reappearing tyranny and oppression.

Your obedient servant,　　A. LINCOLN.

Messrs. H. L. PIERCE, and others, etc.

ABRAHAM LINCOLN ON NATURALIZATION

SPRINGFIELD, *May* 17, 1859.

DR. THEODOR CANISIUS

DEAR SIR—Your letter, in which you inquire on your own account, and in behalf of certain other German citizens, whether I approve or oppose the constitutional provision in relation to naturalized citizens which was lately enacted in Massachusetts, and whether I favor or oppose

a fusion of the Republicans with the other Opposition elements in the campaign of 1860, has been received.

Massachusetts is a sovereign and independent State, and I have no right to advise her in her policy. Yet, if any one is desirous to draw a conclusion as to what I would do, from what she has done, I may speak without impropriety. I say, then, that so far as I understand the Massachusetts provision, I am against its adoption, not only in Illinois, but in every other place in which I have the right to oppose it. As I understand the spirit of our institutions, it is designed to promote the elevation of men. I am, therefore, hostile to anything that tends to their debasement.

It is well known that I deplore the oppressed condition of the blacks; and it would, therefore, be very inconsistent for me to look with approval upon any measures that infringes upon the inalienable rights of white men, whether or not they are born in another land, or speak a different language from my own.

In respect to a fusion, I am in favor of it whenever it can be effected on Republican principles, but upon *no other condition*. A fusion upon any other platform would be as insane as unprincipled. It would thereby lose the whole North, while the common enemy would still have the support of the entire South. The question in relation to men is different. There are good and patriotic men and able statesmen in the South, whom I would willingly support if they would place themselves on Republican ground; but I shall oppose the lowering of the Republican standard even by a *hair's breadth*.

I have written in haste, but I believe that I have answered your questions substantially.

Respectfully yours,

ABRAHAM LINCOLN.

NEW-YORK FOR THE WILMOT PROVISO.

In January, 1847, Col. Samuel Young introduced the following resolve into the New-York State Senate, and on the 27th of that month it was adopted by a vote of 22 to 6:

Resolved, That if any Territory is hereafter acquired by the United States, or annexed thereto, the act by which such Territory is acquired or annexed, whatever such act may be, should contain an unalterable, fundamental article or provision whereby Slavery or involuntary servitude, except as a punishment for crime, shall be forever excluded from the Territory acquired or annexed.

This resolve subsequently passed the Assembly by a vote which was almost unanimous.

NEW-YORK FOR FREEDOM IN 1858.

The following preamble and resolutions were adopted by the Assembly of the State of New-York on the 10th day of January, 1848, by a vote of 108 to 5, and by the Senate, a few days later, by a majority nearly as emphatic as that of the Assembly:

Whereas, The President of the United States, in his last annual message, has recommended the establishment by Congress of territorial government over the conquered provinces of New Mexico, and the Californias, and the retention thereof as an indemnity, in which said Territories the institution of Slavery does not now exist, therefore

Resolved (if the Senate concur), That our Senators in Congress be instructed, and our Representatives requested, to use their best efforts to insert into any act or ordinance, establishing any or all such provisional or territorial government or governments, a fundamental article or provision, which shall provide, declare, and guaranty, that Slavery or involuntary servitude, except as a punishment for crime, whereof the party shall have been first duly convicted, shall be prohibited therein, so long as the same shall remain a Territory.

Resolved, That the President of the Senate, and the Speaker of the Assembly, be requested to transmit a copy of the foregoing resolutions and preamble to each of the said Senators and Representatives.

NEW-YORK AGAIN FOR FREE TERRITORIES IN 1849.

The following preamble and resolves were introduced into the New-York Senate on the 2d of January, 1849, passed that body by a unanimous vote on the 4th, and were concurred in by the Assembly two days later, on the 6th of January :

Whereas, The people of the State of New-Mexico have petitioned Congress for the establishment of a Territorial Government which shall protect them against the institution of domestic Slavery while they remain a territory of the United States, and have also petitioned Congress for protection against the unfounded claims of the State of Texas to a large portion of their territory lying east of the Rio Grande ; and, *whereas*, it would be unjust to the people of New-Mexico and California, and revolting to the spirit of the age, to permit domestic Slavery—an institution from which they are now free—to be introduced among them : and, *whereas*, since the acquisition of New Mexico by the United States the people thereof have a right to expect the protection of the General Government, and should be secured in the full possession and enjoyment of their Territory : therefore

Resolved, That our Senators and Representatives in Congress be requested to use their best efforts to procure the passage of laws for the establishment of governments for the Territories acquired by the treaty of peace with Mexico, and that by such laws involuntary servitude, except for crime, be excluded from such Territories.

Resolved, That the territory lying between the Nueces and the Rio Grande is the common property of the United States, and that our Senators and Representatives in Congress be requested to use their best efforts to preserve the same as such common property, and protect it from the unfounded claim of the State of Texas, and prohibit the extension over it of the laws of Texas, or the institution of domestic Slavery.

Resolved, That the existence of prisons for the confinement and marts for the sale of slaves, at the seat of the National Government, is viewed by this legislature with deep regret and mortification ; that such prisons and marts ought forthwith to be abolished ; therefore be it further

Resolved, That our Senators and Representatives in Congress be requested to use their strenuous efforts to procure the passage of a law that shall protect slaves from unjust imprisonment, and shall effectually put an end to the slave-trade in the District of Columbia.

R. solved, That the Governor be requested to forward copies of the preceding resolutions to each Senator and Representative in Congress from this State.

MR. DIX FOR SLAVERY PROHIBITION.

These resolutions were presented in the U. S. Senate by the Hon. John A. Dix (now, 1860,) Postmaster of New-York, and defended by him in an elaborate and able speech. On the first resolution, he said :

This resolution was in sentiment, if not in words, identical with those which have been passed by fifteen of the thirty States of the Union. With a single exception, all the non-slaveholding and one of the slaveholding States have declared themselves opposed to the extension of Slavery into territory now free. Sir, I fully concur in the propriety of this declaration. I believe that Congress has the power to prohibit Slavery in California and New Mexico ; that it is our duty to exercise the power, and that it should be exercised now. I am always for acting when the proper time for action has come. I am utterly opposed to any course which shall cast upon others the responsibility which belongs to ourselves. The resolution looks to the exclusion of Slavery from New Mexico and California during their territorial condition only. It does not look beyond that condition with a view to control the people when they shall have come into the Union. It contemplates no invasion of State sovereignty. In this view of the subject, one of the New-York presses which has resisted all interference with Slavery, even in the Territories, pronounced these resolutions conciliatory in their character. I do not know that I should call them either conciliatory or the reverse. They take firmly the ground that New-York has always taken, that Slavery shall by no act of hers be further extended. She believes it to be the ground of principle, of justice, and of right and I do not hesitate to say she will never abandon it—never, never.

THE NEW-YORK WHIGS FOR FREEDOM IN 1847.

At the Whig State Convention held at Syracuse, October 6, 1847, the Hon. James Brooks reported a brief address to the Whigs of the State, which was unanimously adopted. The following are extracts from the address then adopted :

FELLOW-CITIZENS : Hitherto when we have assembled in Convention, there were well known and well recognized bounds to our country, but now that the spirit of conquest has been let loose, who can tell where is his country, whether on the Rio Grande, the Sierra Nevada, the Rio Gila or the Gulf of California, or whether part Spanish, much Indian, and some Negro, Santa Fean or Californian may not be as good an American citizen as himself? Our flag is borne, with fixed bayonets to surround it, and unmuzzled grape-shot to clear the way, in the conquering footsteps of Cortes—by the base of the snowy peaks of Popocatapetl, to the Eternal city of the Aztecs—and Mexicans of every color, and every breed, sprung from commingling Moor and straight-haired African, as well as from Castile and Leon, are made American citizens, or prepared for being made so, by the gentle logic of red-mouthed artillery, thundering from the bristling heights of Cerro Gordo to the bloody plains of Contreras and Churubusco. Wherever that flag is, with its stars and stripes, the emblem of our Nationality, there our hearts are ; but woe ! woe ! to the men, we cry, who have dispatched it upon its mission of Conquest, and what is yet worse, the conversion of a Free into a Slaveholding Territory.

Fellow-citizens, disguise the Mexican war as sophistry may, the great truth cannot be put down, that it exists because of the annexation of Texas ; that from such a cause we predicted such a consequence would follow ; and that, but for that cause, no war would have existed at all. Disguise its intent, purposes and consequences as sophistry may struggle to do, the further great truth cannot be hidden, that its main object is the conquest of a Market for Slaves, and that the flag our victorious legions rally around, fight under, and fall for, is to be desecrated from its holy character of Liberty and Emancipation into an errant of Bondage and Slavery. In obedience to the laws, and in a due and faithful submission to the regularly constituted government of our country, we will rally by and defend our flag on whatever soil or whatever sea it is unfurled ; but before high Heaven we protest against the mission on which it is sent, and we demand its recall to the true and proper bounds of our country, as soon as in honor it can be brought home. We protest, too, in the name of the rights of Man, and of Liberty, against the further extension of Slavery in North America. The curse which our mother country inflicted upon us, in spite of our fathers' remonstrances, we demand shall never blight the virgin soil of the North Pacific. . . . . We will not pour out the blood of our countrymen, if we can help it, to turn a *Free* into a *Slave* soil. We will not spend from fifty to a hundred millions of dollars per year to make a Slave Market for any portion of our countrymen. We will never, for such a purpose, consent to run up an untold National debt, and saddle our posterity with Fund-mongers, Tax-Brokers, Tax-gatherers, laying an excise or an impost on everything they taste, touch or live by. The Union as it is, the *whole* Union, and *nothing but* the Union, we will stand by to the last—but *No More Territory* is our watch-word, unless it be *Free*.

RESOLVES.

Among the *Resolutions* unanimously adopted by this Convention was the following :

Resolved, That while the Whig Freemen of New-York, represented in this Convention, will faithfully adhere to all the compromises of the Constitution, and jealously maintain all the reserved rights of the States, they declare—since the crisis has arrived when the question must be met—their uncompromising hostility to the Extension of Slavery into any Territory now Free, or which may be hereafter acquired by any action of the Government of our Union.

FREE DEMOCRACY OF NEW-YORK CITY AGAINST SLAVERY EXTENSION.

At a Free Democratic Meeting held in the Park at New-York, October 9, 1848, at which Henry Everson presided, and S. J. Tilden, John Van Buren, and John Cochrane spoke, Mr. Cochrane introduced the following Resolves, which were adopted :

Resolved, That the politics of the times indicate precisely to whom remain the principles of the Democracy ; that the absence from the field of discussion of the financial and commercial questions which formerly defined political differences, permits that other party tests than those which, even if demanding attention, still as but questions of expediency, should be, as they have been, postponed to the consideration of that one of vital importance, *the freedom of our land.*

Resolved, that we think contemptuously of the mind which discovers in the extension of the area of Freedom cause for the degradation of the South. Could nature so belie herself that the preservation of their "inalienable rights" to any portion of mankind, must be attended by proportionate violation of those of any other portion, we say, perish those rights dependent on the Slavery of others, rather than one tittle of those be injured that are consistent with the rights of all; that our Constitution and our federal history speak to us through the voices of the Jeffersons, the Pinckneys, the Lees, and the Randolphs of the South, against this miserable, false pretense. It is not so! The success of the free principles for which we contend, will reëstablish the lost equality of the States—lost in the insidious increase of the Slave States from six, their original and constitutional number, to fifteen, the present aggressive and unconstitutional number—lost in the twenty-one voices and votes which Southern chattel slaves possess among the representatives of a free people at Washington—lost in the limited wealth, in the low intelligence, and in the inferior civilization of the South. We would restore this lost equality, and, so far from degrading any portion of the Union, we mean to elevate the whole to the possession of that Freedom which alone should be the National characteristic.

Resolved, That our senses reject the audacious assertion that the Extension of Slave Territory at the South will abate the evil at the North. Aside from the absurdity which it involves, that an evil declines in proportion to and expires with the substance which it procures, experience has taught, and the history of the "Peculiar Institution" itself manifests, that the slaveowner of the "Old Dominion" breeds an increasing gang, and amasses an accumulating hoard, just as the demand for slaves increases with the diffusion of Slavery over free territory at the South. In the year 1790, when Alabama, Mississippi, Louisiana, Arkansas, Missouri, Tennessee, Kentucky, and Florida, were free soil, the slave population was 697,896. In the year 1840, when Slavery had spread over this free soil, it numbered 2,487,355, being an increase in fifty years of 1,787,457 slaves. The extension of Slavery to new territory, instead of abating the evil in Maryland, Virginia, Kentucky, and Missouri, where it numbered in the year 1810, 590,000 slaves, has multiplied them to 775,000, in the year 1840, showing an increase in thirty years of 185,000 slaves. The existence of Slavery depends on its diffusion.

GREENE C. BRONSON'S OPINION IN 1848.

In a letter dated July 15th, 1848, Mr. Bronson, after declining an invitation to attend a political meeting, says :

Slavery cannot exist where there is no positive law to uphold it. It is not necessary that it should be forbidden ; it is enough that it is not specially authorized. If the owner of slaves removes with or sends them into any country, State or Territory, where Slavery does not exist by law, they will from that moment become free men, and will have as good a right to command the master, as he will have to command them. State laws have no extra-territorial authority ; and a law of Virginia which makes a man a slave there, cannot make him a slave in New-York, nor beyond the Rocky Mountains.

Entertaining no doubt upon that question, I can see no occasion for asking Congress to legislate against the extension of Slavery into free territory, and, as a question of policy, I think it had better be let alone. If our Southern brethren wish to carry their slaves to Oregon, New-Mexico or California, they will be under the necessity of asking a law to warrant it ; and it will then be in time for the Free States to resist the measure, as I cannot doubt they would, with unwavering firmness.

I would not needlessly move this question, as it is one of an exciting nature, which tends to sectional division, and may do us harm as a people. I would leave it to the Slaveholding States to decide for themselves, and on their own responsibility, when, if ever, the matter shall be agitated in Congress. It may be that they will act wisely, and never move at all ; especially as it seems pretty generally agreed that neither Oregon, New-Mexico, nor California, are well adapted to slave labor. But if our Southern brethren should make the question, we shall have no choice but to meet it ; and then, whatever consequences may follow, I trust the people of the Free States will give a united voice against allowing Slavery on a single foot of soil where it is not now authorized by law.

I am, very respectfully, your obedient servant,
GREENE C. BRONSON.
To Messrs. J. COCHRANE, and others, Committee.

NEW-HAMPSHIRE FOR THE WILMOT PROVISO.

The legislature (then Democratic) of New-Hampshire, in June, 1847, passed the following resolution :

Resolved, That in all territory which shall hereafter be added to or acquired by the United States, where Slavery does not exist at the time of such addition, or acquirement, neither Slavery or involuntary servitude, except for the punishment of crime, whereof the party has been duly convicted, ought ever to exist, but the same should ever remain free ; and we are opposed to the extension of Slavery over every such Territory—and that we also approve the vote of our Senators and Representatives in Congress in favor of the Wilmot Proviso.

OHIO FOR FREE SOIL.

In the Ohio House of Representatives (session of 1847–8) the following resolution was passed by a vote of 43 to 12 :

Resolved, By the General Assembly of the State of Ohio, that the Senators and Representatives from this State in the Congress of the United States be and they are hereby requested, to procure the passage of measures in the National Legislature, providing for the exclusion of Slavery from the Territory of Oregon, and also from any other Territory that now is, or hereafter may be, annexed to the United States.

ILLINOIS FOR FREE SOIL.

The following Resolutions were adopted by the Senate of Illinois on the 8th of January, 1849, and the House of Representatives on the following day. The Legislature was largely Democratic in both branches at the time :

Resolved by the Senate of the State of Illinois, the House of Representatives concurring, That our Senators in Congress be instructed, and our Representatives requested, to use all honorable means in their power to procure the enactment of such laws by Congress for the government of the countries and territories of the United States acquired by the treaty of peace, friendship, limits and settlement with the Republic of Mexico, concluded February 2, 1848, as shall contain the *express declaration* "*that there shall be neither Slavery nor involuntary servitude in said territories* otherwise than in the punishment of crimes whereof the party shall have been duly convicted."

Resolved by the House of Representatives, the Senate concurring herein, That the Governor be respectfully requested to transmit to each of our Senators and Representatives in Congress a copy of the joint resolution of the Senate, concurred in by the House on the 9th inst., for the exclusion of Slavery from the new territories acquired by our late treaty with the Republic of Mexico.

SOUTH CAROLINA FOR THE FOREIGN SLAVE-TRADE.

In the annual message of Governor Adams, of South Carolina, for the year 1856, he proceeded to argue in favor of the reopening of the slave-trade, as follows :

It is apprehended that the opening of this trade will lessen the value of slaves, and ultimately destroy the institution. It is a sufficient answer to point to the fact that unrestricted immigration has not diminished the value of labor in the northwestern Confederacy. The cry there is the want of labor, notwithstanding capital has the pauperism of the old world to press into the grinding service. If we cannot supply the demand for slave labor we do not want, and which is, from the very nature of things, antagonistic to our institutions. It is much better that our drays should be driven by slaves, that our factories should be worked by slaves, that our hotels should be served by slaves, that our locomotives should be managed by slaves, than that we should be exposed to the introduction from any quarter of a population alien to us by birth, training, and education, and which in the process of time must lead to the conflict between capital and labor, which makes it so difficult to maintain free institutions in all wealthy and civilized nations where such institutions as ours do not exist. In all slaveholding States true policy dictates that the superior race should direct, and the inferior perform all menial service. Competition between the white and black man for this service may not disturb Northern sensibility, but does not exactly suit our latitude.

Irrespective, however, of interest, the act of Congress declaring the slave-trade piracy is a brand upon us which I think it important to remove. If the trade be piracy, the slaves must be plunder, and no ingenuity can avoid the logical necessity of such a conclusion. My hopes and fortunes are indissolubly associated with this form of society. I feel that I would be wanting in duty if I did not urge you to withdraw your assent to an act which is itself a direct condemnation of your institutions. But we have interests to enforce a course of self-respect. I believe, as I have already stated, that more slaves are necessary to a continuance of our monopoly in plantation products. I believe that they are necessary to the full development of our whole round of agricultural and mechanical resources; that they are necessary to the restoration of the South to an equality of power in the Federal Government, perhaps to the very integrity of slave society, disturbed as it has been by causes which have introduced an undue proportion of the ruling race. To us have been committed the fortunes of this peculiar form of society resulting from the union of unequal races. It has vindicated its claim to the approbation of an enlightened humanity; it has civilized and christianized the African; it has exalted the white race to higher hopes and purposes, and it is perhaps of the most sacred obligation that we should give it the means of expansion, and that we should press it forward to a perpetuity of progress.

MR. HAMLIN RENOUNCES THE DEMOCRATIC PARTY.

On the 12th of June, 1856, Mr. Hamlin rose in his place in the Senate, and spoke as follows:

Mr. Hamlin.—Mr. President, I rise for a purpose purely personal, such as I have never before risen for in the Senate. I desire to explain some matters personal to myself and to my own future course in public life.

Several Senators.—Go on.

Mr. Hamlin.—I ask the Senate to excuse me from further service as Chairman of the Committee on Commerce. I do so because I feel that my relations hereafter will be of such a character as to render it proper that I should no longer hold that position. I owe this act to the dominant majority in the Senate. When I cease to harmonize with the majority, or tests are applied by that party with which I have acted to which I cannot submit, I feel that I ought no longer to hold that respectable position. I propose to state briefly the reasons which have brought me to that conclusion.

During nine years of service in the Senate, I have preferred rather to be a working than a talking member; and so I have been almost a silent one. On the subjects which have so much agitated the country, Senators know that I have rarely uttered a word. I love my country more than I love my party. I love my country above my love for any interest that can too deeply agitate or disturb its harmony. I saw, in all the exciting scenes and debates through which we have passed, no particular good that would result from my active intermingling in them. My heart has often been full, and the impulses of that heart have often been felt upon my lips; but I have repressed them there.

Sir, I hold that the repeal of the Missouri Compromise was a gross moral and political wrong, unequaled in the annals of the legislation of this country, and hardly equaled in the annals of any other free country. Still, sir, with a desire to promote harmony and concord and brotherly feeling, I was a quiet man under all the exciting debates which led to that fatal result. I believed it wrong then; I can see that wrong lying broadcast all around us now. As a wrong, I opposed that measure—not, indeed, by my voice, but with consistent and steady and uniform votes. I so resisted it in obedience to the dictates of my own judgment. I did it also cheerfully, in compliance with the instructions of the legislature of Maine, which were passed by a vote almost unanimous. In the House of Representatives of Maine, consisting of one hundred and fifty-one members, only six, I think, dissented; and in the Senate, consisting of thirty-one members, only one member non-concurred.

But the Missouri restriction was abrogated. The portentous evils that were predicted have followed, and are yet following, along in its train. It was done, sir, in violation of the pledges of that party with which I have always acted, and with which I have always voted. It was done in violation of solemn pledges of the President of the United States, made in his Inaugural Address. Still, sir, I was disposed to suffer the wrong, while I should see that no evil results were flowing from it. We were told, by almost every Senator who addressed us upon that occasion, that no evil results would follow; that no practical difference in the settlement of the country, and in the character of the future State, would take place, whether the act were done or not. I have waited calmly and patiently to see the fulfillment of that prediction; and I am grieved, sir, to say now that they have at least been mistaken in their predictions and promises. They have all signally failed.

That Senators might have voted for that measure under the belief then expressed and the predictions to which I have alluded, I can well understand. But how Senators can now defend that measure amid all its evils, which are overwhelming the land, if not threatening it with a conflagration, is what I do not comprehend. The whole of the disturbed state of the country has its rise in, and is attributable to that act alone—nothing else. It lies at the foundation of all our misfortunes and commotions. There would have been no incursions by Missouri borderers into Kansas, either to establish Slavery, or to control elections. There would have been no necessity, either, for others to have gone there partially to aid in preserving the country in its then condition. All would have been peace there. Had it not been done, that repose and quiet which pervaded the public mind then, would hold it in tranquillity to-day. Instead of startling events we should have quiet and peace within our borders, and that fraternal feeling which ought to animate the citizens of every part of the Union toward those of all other sections.

Sir, the events that are taking place around us are indeed startling. They challenge the public mind and appeal to the public judgment; they thrill the public nerve as electricity imparts a tremulous motion to the telegraphic wire. It is a period when all good men should unite in applying the proper remedy to secure peace and harmony to the country. Is this to be done by any of us, by remaining associated with those who have been instrumental in producing these results, and who now justify them? I do not see my duty lying in that direction.

I have, while temporarily acquiescing, stated here and at home, everywhere, uniformly, that when the test of those measures was applied to me as one of party fidelity, I would sunder them as flax is sundered at the touch of fire. I do it now.

The occasion involves a question of moral duty; and self-respect allows me no other line of duty but to follow the dictates of my own judgment and the impulses of my own heart. A just man may cheerfully submit to many enforced humiliations; but a self-degraded man has ceased to be worthy to be deemed a man at all.

Sir, what has the recent Democratic Convention at Cincinnati done? It has indorsed the measure I have condemned, and has sanctioned its destructive and ruinous effects. It has done more—vastly more. That principle or policy of Territorial Sovereignty which once had, and which I suppose now has, its advocates within these walls, is stricken down; and there is an absolute denial of it in the resolutions of the Convention, if I can draw right conclusions—a denial equally to Congress, and even to the people of the Territories, of the right to settle the question of Slavery therein. On the contrary, the Convention has actually incorporated into the platform of the Democratic party that doctrine which, only a few years ago, met nothing but ridicule and contempt here and elsewhere, namely: that the flag of the Federal Union, under the Constitution of the United States, carries Slavery wherever it floats. If this baleful principle be true, then that National Ode which inspires us always as on a battle-field, should be re-written by Drake, and should read thus:

> "Forever float that standard sheet;
> Where breathes the foe but falls before us,
> With *Slavery's* soil beneath our feet,
> And *Slavery's* banner streaming o'er us?"

Now, sir, what is the precise condition in which this matter is left by the Cincinnati Convention? I do not design to trespass many moments on the Senate ; but allow me to read and offer a very few comments upon some portions of the Democratic platform. The first resolution that treats upon the subject is in these words—I read just so much of it as is applicable to my present remarks :

"That Congress has no power under the Constitution to interfere with or control the domestic institutions of the several States, and that all such States are the sole and proper judges of everything appertaining to their own affairs not prohibited by the Constitution."

I take it that this language, thus far, is language which meets a willing and ready response from every Senator here—certainly it does from me. But in the following resolution I find these words :

"*Resolved*, That the foregoing proposition covers, and was intended to embrace, the whole subject of Slavery agitation in Congress."

The first resolution which I read was adopted years ago in Democratic Conventions. The second resolution which I read was adopted in subsequent years, when a different state of things had arisen, and it became necessary to apply an abstract proposition relating to the States, to the Territories. Hence the adoption of the language contained in the second Resolution which I have read.

Now, sir, I deny the position thus assumed by the Cincinnati Convention. In the language of the Senator from Kentucky (Mr. Crittenden), so ably and so appropriately used on Tuesday last, I hold that the entire and unqualified sovereignty of the Territories is in Congress. That is my judgment ; but this resolution brings the Territories precisely within the same limitations which are applied to the States in the resolution which I first read. The two taken together deny to Congress any power of legislation in the Territories.

Follow on, and let us see what remains. Adopted as a part of the present platform, and as necessary to a new state of things, and to meet an emergency now existing, the Convention says :

"The American Democracy recognize and adopt the principles contained in the organic law establishing the Territories of Kansas and Nebraska, as embodying the only sound and safe solution of the Slavery question, upon which the great national idea of the people of this whole country can repose, in its determined conservatism of the Union—non-interference by Congress with Slavery in the States and Territories."

Then follows the last resolution :

"*Resolved*, That we recognize the right of the people of all the Territories, including Kansas and Nebraska, acting through the fairly-expressed will of the majority of actual residents, and whenever the number of their inhabitants justifies it, to form a constitution, with or without domestic Slavery, and be admitted into the Union upon terms of perfect equality with the other States."

Take all these resolutions together, and the deduction which we must necessarily draw from them is a denial to Congress of any power whatever to legislate upon the subject of Slavery. The last resolution denies to the people of the Territories any power over that subject, save when they shall have a sufficient number to form a constitution and become a State, and also denies that Congress has any power over the subject ; and so the resolutions hold that this power is at least in abeyance while the Territory is in a Territorial condition. That is the only conclusion which you can draw from these resolutions. Alas ! for short-lived Territorial Sovereignty ! It came to its death in the house of its friends ; it was buried by the same hands which had given it baptism !

But, sir, I did not rise for the purpose of discussing these resolutions, but only to read them, and state the action which I propose to take in view of them. I may —I probably shall—take some subsequent occasion, when I shall endeavor to present to the Senate and the country a fair account of what is the true issue presented to the people for their consideration and decision.

My object now is to show only that the Cincinnati Convention has indorsed and approved of the repeal of the Missouri Compromise, from which so many evils have already flowed—from which, I fear, more and worse evils must yet be anticipated. It would of course, be expected that the Presidential nominee of that Convention would accept, cordially and cheerfully, the platform prepared for him by his party friends. No person can object to that. There is no equivocation on his part about the matter. I beg leave to read a short extract from a speech of that gentleman, made at his own home, within the last few days. In reply to the Keystone Club, which paid him a visit there, Mr. Buchanan said :

"Gentlemen, two weeks since I should have made you a longer speech ; but now I have been placed on a platform of which I most heartily approve, and that can speak for me. Being the representative of the great Democratic party, and not simply James Buchanan, I must square my conduct according to the platform of the party, and insert no new plank, nor take one from it."

These events leave to me only one unpleasant duty, which is to declare here that I can maintain political associations with no party that insists upon such doctrines ; that I can support no man for President who avows and recognizes them ; and that the little of that power with which God has endowed me shall be employed to battle manfully, firmly, and consistently for his defeat, demanded as it is by the highest interests of the country which owns all my allegiance.

The President.—The question is on the motion of the Senator from Maine to be excused from further service on the Committee on Commerce.

The motion was agreed to.

ACCEPTANCE OF PRESIDENTIAL CANDIDATES.

MESSRS. LINCOLN AND HAMLIN ACCEPT.

The following is the correspondence between the officers of the Republican National Convention and the candidates thereof for President and Vice-President :

CHICAGO, *May* 18, 1860.

To the HON. ABRAHAM LINCOLN, *of Illinois.*

SIR : The representatives of the Republican Party of the United States, assembled in Convention at Chicago, have this day, by a unanimous vote, selected you as the Republican candidate for the office of President of the United States to be supported at the next election ; and the undersigned were appointed a Committee of the Convention to apprise you of this nomination, and respectfully to request that you will accept it. A declaration of the principles and sentiments adopted by the Convention accompanies this communication.

In the performance of this agreeable duty we take leave to add our confident assurance that the nomination of the Chicago Convention will be ratified by the suffrages of the people.

We have the honor to be, with great respect and regard, your friends and fellow-citizens.

GEORGE ASHMUN, of Massachusetts,
President of the Convention.
WM. M. EVARTS, of New-York,
JOEL BURLINGAME, of Oregon,
EPHRAIM MARSH, of New-Jersey,
GIDEON WELLS, of Connecticut,
D. K. CARTER, of Ohio,
CARL SCHURZ, of Wisconsin,
JAMES F. SIMMONS, of Rhode Island,
JOHN W. NORTH, of Minnesota,
GEO. D. BLAKEY, of Kentucky,
PETER T. WASHBURN, of Vermont,
A. C. WILDER, of Kansas,
EDWARD H. ROLLINS, of New-Hampshire,
FRANCIS S. CORKRAN, of Maryland,
NORMAN B. JUDD, of Illinois,
N. B. SMITHERS, of Delaware,
WM. H. McCRILLIS, of Maine,
ALFRED CALDWELL, of Virginia,
CALEB B. SMITH, of Indiana,
AUSTIN BLAIR, of Michigan,
WM. P. CLARKE, of Iowa,
B. GRATZ BROWN, of Missouri,
F. P. TRACY, of California,
E. D. WEBSTER, of Nebraska,
G. A. HALL, of District of Columbia,
JOHN A. ANDREW, of Massachusetts,
A. H. REEDER, of Pennsylvania.

SPRINGFIELD, ILL., *May* 23, 1860.

HON. GEORGE ASHMUN, *President of the Republican National Convention.*

SIR : I accept the nomination tendered me by the Convention over which you presided, and of which I am formally apprised in the letter of yourself and others, acting as a Committee of the Convention for that purpose.

The declaration of principles and sentiments, which accompanies your letter, meets my approval; and it shall be my care not to violate, or disregard it, in any part.

Imploring the assistance of Divine Providence, and with due regard to the views and feelings of all who were represented in the Convention; to the rights of all the States, and Territories, and people of the nation; to the inviolability of the Constitution, and the perpetual union, harmony and prosperity of all, I am most happy to coöperate for the practical success of the principles declared by the Convention.

Your obliged friend and fellow-citizen,
ABRAHAM LINCOLN.

A similar letter was sent to the nominee for the Vice-Presidency, to which the following is the reply.

WASHINGTON, *May* 30, 1860.

GENTLEMEN: Your official communication of the 18th instant, informing me that the representatives of the Republican party of the United States, assembled at Chicago, on that day, had, by a unanimous vote, selected me as their candidate for the office of Vice-President of the United States, has been received, together with the resolutions adopted by the Convention as its declaration of principles.

Those resolutions enunciate clearly and forcibly the principles which unite us, and the objects proposed to be accomplished. They address themselves to all, and there is neither necessity nor propriety in my entering upon a discussion of any of them. They have the approval of my judgment, and in any action of mine will be faithfully and cordially sustained.

I am profoundly grateful to those with whom it is my pride and pleasure politically to coöperate, for the nomination so unexpectedly conferred; and I desire to tender through you, to the members of the Convention, my sincere thanks for the confidence thus reposed in me. Should the nomination, which I now accept, be ratified by the people, and the duties devolve upon me of presiding over the Senate of the United States, it will be my earnest endeavor faithfully to discharge them with a just regard for the rights of all.

It is to be observed, in connection with the doings of the Republican Convention, that a paramount object with us is to preserve the normal condition of our Territorial Domain as homes for Free men. The able advocate and defender of Republican principles, whom you have nominated for the highest place that can gratify the ambition of man, comes from a State which has been made what it is, by special action, in that respect, of the wise and good men who founded our institutions. The rights of free labor have there been vindicated and maintained. The thrift and enterprise which so distinguish Illinois, one of the most flourishing States of the glorious West, we would see secured to all the Territories of the Union; and restore peace and harmony to the whole country, by bringing back the Government to what it was under the wise and patriotic men who created it. If the Republicans shall succeed in that object, as they hope to, they will be held in grateful remembrance by the busy and teeming millions of future ages.

I am, very truly yours,
H. HAMLIN.

The Hon. GEORGE ASHMUN, President of the Convention, and others of the Convention.

MR. BRECKINRIDGE ACCEPTS.

WASHINGTON CITY, *July* 6, 1860.

DEAR SIR: I have your letter of the 23d ultimo, by which I am officially informed of my nomination for the office of President of the United States by the Democratic National Convention lately assembled at Baltimore.

The circumstances of this nomination will justify me in referring to its personal aspect.

I have not sought nor desired to be placed before the country for the office of President. When my name was presented to the Convention at Charleston, it was withdrawn by a friend in obedience to my expressed wishes. My views had not changed when the Convention reassembled at Baltimore, and when I heard of the differences which occurred there, my indisposition to be connected prominently with the canvass was confirmed and expressed to many friends.

Without discussing the occurrences which preceded the nominations, and which are or soon will be well understood by the country, I have only to say that I approved,

as just and necessary to the preservation of the National organization and the sacred right of representation, the action of the Convention over which you continued to preside; and thus approving it, and having resolved to sustain it, I feel that it does not become me to select the position I shall occupy, nor to shrink from the responsibilities of the post to which I have been assigned. Accordingly, I accept the nomination from a sense of public duty, and, as I think, uninfluenced in any degree by the allurements of ambition.

I avail myself of this occasion to say that the confidence in my personal and public character implied by the action of the Convention, will always be gratefully remembered; and it is but just, also, to my own feelings, to express my gratification at the association of my name with that of my friend Gen. Lane, a patriot and a soldier, whose great services in the field and in council entitle him to the gratitude and confidence of his countrymen.

The resolutions adopted by the Convention have my cordial approval. They are just to all parts of the Union, to all our citizens, native and naturalized, and they form a noble policy for any administration.

The questions touching the rights of persons and property, which have of late been much discussed, find in these resolutions a constitutional solution. Our Union is a Confederacy of equal sovereign States, for the purposes enumerated in the Federal Constitution. Whatever the common Government holds in trust for all the States must be enjoyed equally by each. It controls the Territories in trust for all the States. Nothing less than sovereignty can destroy or impair the rights of persons or property. The Territorial Governments are subordinate and temporary, and not sovereign; hence they cannot destroy or impair the rights of persons or property. While they continue to be Territories they are under the control of Congress, but the Constitution nowhere confers on any branch of the Federal Government the power to discriminate against the rights of the States or the property of their citizens in the Territories. It follows that the citizens of all the States may enter the Territories of the Union with their property, of whatever kind, and enjoy it during the territorial condition without let or hindrance, either by Congress or by the subordinate Territorial Governments.

These principles flow directly from the absence of sovereignty in the Territorial Governments, and from the equality of the States. Indeed, they are essential to that equality, which is, and ever has been, the vital principle of our Constitutional Union. They have been settled legislatively—settled judiciously, and are sustained by right reason. They rest on the rock of the Constitution—they will preserve the Union.

It is idle to attempt to smother these great issues, or to misrepresent them by the use of partisan phrases, which are misleading and delusive. The people will look beneath such expressions as "Intervention," "Congressional Slave Code," and the like, and will penetrate to the real questions involved. The friends of Constitutional equality do not and never did demand a "Congressional Slave Code," nor any other code in regard to property in the Territories. They hold the doctrine of non-intervention by Congress, or by a Territorial Legislature, either to establish or prohibit Slavery; but they assert (fortified by the highest judicial tribunal in the Union) the plain duty of the Federal Government, in all its departments, to secure, when necessary, to the citizens of all the States, the enjoyment of their property in the common Territories, as everywhere else within its jurisdiction. The only logical answer to this would seem to be to claim sovereign power for the Territories, or to deny that the Constitution recognizes property in the services of negro slaves, or to deny that such property can exist.

Inexorable logic, which works its steady way through clouds and passion, compels the country to meet the issue. There is no evasive middle ground. Already the signs multiply of a fanatical and growing party, which denies that under the Constitution, or by any other law, slave property can exist; and ultimately the struggle must come between this party and the National Democracy, sustained by all the other conservative elements in the Union.

I think it will be impossible for a candid mind to discover hostility to the Union or a taint of sectionalism in the resolutions adopted by the Convention. The Constitution and the Union repose on the equality of the States, which lies like a broad foundation underneath our whole political structure. As I construe them, the resolutions simply assert this equality. They demand nothing for any State or section that is not cheerfully conceded to all the rest. It is well to remember that the chief disorders which have afflicted our country have grown out of the violation of State equality, and that as long as this great principle has been respected we have been blessed with harmony and peace. Nor will it be easy to persuade the country that resolutions are sectional which command the support of a majority of the States, and are approved by the bone and body of the old Democracy, and by a vast mass of conservative opinion everywhere, without regard to party.

It has been necessary more than once in our history, to pause and solemnly assert the true character of this Government. A memorable instance occurred in the struggle which ended in the civil revolution of 1800. The Republicans of that day, like the Democracy of this, were stigmatized as disunionists, but they nobly conducted the contest under the Constitution, and saved our political system. By a little constitutional struggle it is intended to assert and establish the equality of the States, as the only basis of union and peace. When this object, so national, so constitutional, so just, shall be accomplished, the last cloud will disappear from the American sky, and with common hands and hearts the States and the people will unite to develop the resources of the whole country, to bind it together with the bonds of intercourse and brotherhood, and to impel it onward in its great career.

The Constitution and the Equality of the States! These are symbols of everlasting Union. Let these be the rallying cries of the people.

I trust that this canvass will be conducted without rancor, and that temperate arguments will take the place of hot words and passionate accusations.

Above all, I venture humbly to hope that Divine Providence, to whom we owe our origin, our growth, and all our prosperity, will continue to protect our beloved country against all danger, foreign and domestic.

I am, with great respect, your friend,
JOHN C. BRECKINRIDGE.
The Hon. C. CUSHING, President of the Democratic National Convention.

GEN. LANE'S ACCEPTANCE.

WASHINGTON, *June* 30, 1860.
HON. CALEB CUSHING, PRESIDENT OF THE DEMOCRATIC NATIONAL CONVENTION:

SIR—I have the honor to acknowledge the receipt of the communication you make in behalf of the Democratic National Convention, in which you inform me that, on the 23d inst., I was unanimously nominated by that party for the office of Vice-President of the United States, with the request that I shall accept the nomination.

The platform adopted, and of which you inclose me a copy, meets with my hearty approval, as it embodies what I have been contending for as the only means of stopping sectional agitation, by securing to all equality and constitutional rights, the denial of which has led to the present unhappy condition of public affairs.

Compromises of constitutional principles are ever dangerous, and I am rejoiced that the true Democracy has seen fit to plant a firm foot on the rock of truth, and to give the people an opportunity to vindicate their love of justice and fraternal regard for each other's rights.

Non-intervention on the subject of Slavery, I may emphatically say, is that cardinal maxim of the Democracy—non-intervention by Congress and non-intervention by Territorial Legislatures, as is fully stated in the first resolution of the adopted platform.

In vain should we declare the former without insisting upon the latter; because, to permit Territorial legislatures to prohibit or establish Slavery, or by unfriendly legislation to invalidate property, would be granting powers to the creature or agent, which, it is admitted, do not appertain to the principal, or the power that creates; besides which, it would be fostering an element of agitation in the Territory that must necessarily extend to Congress and the people of all the States.

If the Constitution establishes the right of every citizen to enter the common territory with whatever property he legally possesses, it necessarily devolves on the Federal Government the duty to protect this right of the citizen whenever and wherever assailed or infringed. The Democratic party honestly meets this agitating question, which is threatening to sever and destroy this brotherhood of States. It does not propose to legislate for the extension of Slavery, nor for its restriction, but to give to each State and to every citizen all that our forefathers proposed to give—namely, perfect equality of rights, and then to commit to the people, to climate, and to soil, the determination as to the kind of institution best fitted to their requirements in their constitutional limits, and declaring as a fundamental maxim, that the people of a Territory can only establish or prohibit Slavery when they come to form a constitution, preparatory to their admission as a State into the Union.

If, happily, our principles shall prevail, an era of peace and harmony will be restored to our distracted country,

and no more shall we be troubled with the agitation of this dangerous question, because it will be removed as well from the Territorial legislatures as from the halls of Congress—when we shall be free to turn our attention to more useful issues, promotive of our growth in national greatness.

Our Union must be preserved! But this can only be done by maintaining the Constitution inviolate in all its provisions and guaranties. The Judicial authority, as provided by the Constitution, must be maintained, and its decisions implicitly obeyed, as well in regard to the rights of property in the Territories as in all other matters.

Hoping for success, and trusting in the truth and justice of the principles of our party, and in that Divine Providence that has watched over us and made us one of the great nations of the earth, and that we may continue to merit Divine protection, I cheerfully accept the nomination so unanimously conferred on me, and cordially indorse the platform adopted by the Convention.

I have the honor to be, sir, with much respect,
Your friend and obedient servant,
JOSEPH LANE.

MR. DOUGLAS ACCEPTS.

WASHINGTON, *Friday, June* 29, 1860.

GENTLEMEN: In accordance with the verbal assurance which I gave you when you placed in my hands the authentic evidence of my nomination for the Presidency by the National Convention of the Democratic party, I now send you my formal acceptance. Upon a careful examination of the platform and principles adopted at Charleston and reaffirmed at Baltimore, with an additional resolution which is in perfect harmony with the others, I find it to be a faithful embodiment of the time-honored principles of the Democratic party, as the same were proclaimed and understood by all parties in the Presidential contest of 1848, 1852, and 1856.

Upon looking into the proceedings of the Convention also, I find that the nomination was made with great unanimity, in the presence and with the concurrence of more than two-thirds of the whole number of delegates, and in accordance with the long-established usages of the party. My inflexible purpose not to be a candidate, nor accept the nomination under any contingency, except as the regular nominee of the National Democratic party and in that case only upon the condition that the usages, as well as the principles of the party, should be strictly adhered to, had been proclaimed for a long time and become well known to the country. These conditions having all been complied with by the free and voluntary action of the Democratic masses and their faithful representatives, without any agency, interference, or procurement, on my part, I feel bound in honor and duty to accept the nomination. In taking this step, I am not unmindful of the responsibilities it imposes, but with firm reliance upon Divine Providence I have the faith that the people will comprehend the true nature of the issues involved, and eventually maintain the right.

The peace of the country and the perpetuity of the Union have been put in jeopardy by attempts to interfere with and control the domestic affairs of the people in the Territories, through the agency of the Federal Government. If the power and the duty of Federal interference is to be conceded, two hostile sectional parties must be the inevitable result—the one inflaming the passions and ambitions of the North, the other of the South, and each struggling to use the Federal power and authority for the aggrandizement of its own section, at the expense of the equal rights of the other, and in derogation of those fundamental principles of self-government which were firmly established in this country by the American Revolution, as the basis of our entire republican system.

During the memorable period of our political history, when the advocates of Federal intervention upon the subject of Slavery in the Territories had well-nigh "precipitated the country into revolution," the Northern interventionists demanding the Wilmot Proviso for the prohibition of Slavery, and the Southern interventionists, then few in number, and without a single Representative in either House of Congress, insisting upon Congressional legislation for the protection of Slavery in opposition to the wishes of the people in either case, it will be remembered that it required all the wisdom, power and influence of a Clay and a Webster and a Cass, supported by the conservative and patriotic men of the Whig and Democratic parties of that day, to devise and carry out a line of policy which would restore peace to the country and stability to the Union. The essential living principle of that policy, as applied in the legislation of 1850, was, and now is, *non-intervention by Congress with Slavery in the Territories*. The fair application of this just and equitable principle restored harmony and fraternity to a distracted country. If we now depart from that wise and just policy which produced these happy results, and permit the country to be again distracted; if precipitated into revolution by a sectional contest between Pro-Slavery and Anti-Slavery interventionists, where shall we look for another Clay, another Webster, or another Cass to pilot the ship of State over the breakers into a haven of peace and safety?

The Federal Union must be preserved. The Constitution must be maintained inviolate in all its parts. Every right guaranteed by the Constitution must be protected by law in all cases where legislation is necessary to its enjoyment. The judicial authority, as provided in the Constitution, must be sustained, and its decisions implicitly obeyed and faithfully executed. The laws must be administered and the constituted authorities upheld, and all unlawful resistance to these things must be put down with firmness, impartiality and fidelity, if we expect to enjoy and transmit unimpaired to our posterity, that blessed inheritance which we have received in trust from the patriots and sages of the Revolution.

With sincere thanks for the kind and agreeable manner in which you have made known to me the action of the Convention, I have the honor to be,

Your friend and fellow citizen,
S. A. DOUGLAS.

Hon. WM. H. LUDLOW, of New-York; R. P. DICK, of North Carolina; P. C. WICKLIFF, of Louisiana, and others of Committee.

MR. FITZPATRICK DECLINES.

WASHINGTON, *June 25, 1860.*

GENTLEMEN: Your letter of to-day, informing me that I "have been unanimously nominated by the National Convention of the Democratic party, which met at Charleston on the 23d day of April last, and adjourned to meet at Baltimore on the 18th day of June, as their candidate for the office of Vice-President," was duly received.

Acknowledging with the liveliest sensibility this distinguished mark of your confidence and regard, it is with no ordinary feelings of regret that considerations, the recital of which I will not impose upon you, constrain me to decline the nomination so flatteringly tendered. My designation as a candidate for this high position would have been more gratifying to me if it had proceeded from the united Democracy—united both as to principles and men.

The distracting differences at present existing in the ranks of the Democratic party were strikingly exemplified both at Charleston and at Baltimore, and, in my humble opinion, distinctly admonish me that I should in no way contribute to these unfortunate divisions.

The Black Republicans have harmoniously (at least in Convention) presented their candidates for the Presidency and Vice-Presidency So have the Constitutional Union party (as it is termed). Each party is already engaged in the contest. In the presence of such organizations we still, unfortunately, exhibit a divided camp. What a melancholy spectacle! It is calculated to cause every Democratic citizen who cherishes the Constitution of his country to despond, if not to despair, of the durability of the Union.

Desirous, as far as I am capable of exercising any influence, to remove every obstacle which may prevent a restoration of the peace, harmony, and perfect concord of that glorious old party to which I have been inflexibly devoted from early manhood—a party which, in my deliberate opinion, is the only real and reliable ligament which binds the South, the North, the East, and the West together upon constitutional principles—no alternative was left to me but that which I have herein most respectfully communicated to you.

For the agreeable manner in which you have conveyed to me the action of the Convention, accept my sincere thanks.

Very truly your friend and obedient servant,
B. FITZPATRICK.

To WM. H. LUDLOW, of New-York, and others.

The Democratic National Committee subsequently nominated the Hon. Herschel V. Johnson, of Georgia, who accepted the position.

MR. BELL ACCEPTS.

NASHVILLE, *May 21, 1860.*

DEAR SIR: Official information of my nomination to the Presidency by the National Union Convention, of which you were the presiding officer, was communicated to me by your letter of the 11th inst., at Philadelphia, on the eve of my departure with my family for my place of residence in Tennessee; and diffident as I was of my worthiness, I did not hesitate to signify my intention to accept the position assigned to me by that distinguished and patriotic body. But for convenience, and under a sense of the propriety of acting in so grave a matter with greater deliberation, I concluded, as I informed you at the time by a private note, to defer a formal acceptance until after my arrival at home.

Now that I have had all the leisure I could desire for reflection upon the circumstances under which the nomination was made, the purity of the motives and the lofty spirit of patriotism by which the Convention was animated, as evinced in all its proceedings, I can appreciate more justly the honor done me by the nomination; and, though it might have been more fortunate for the country had it fallen upon some one of the many distinguished statesmen whose names were brought to the notice of the Convention, rather than myself, I accept it, with all its possible responsibilities. Whatever may be the issue of the ensuing canvass, as for myself, I shall ever regard it as a proud distinction—one worth a lifelong effort to attain—to be pronounced worthy to receive the highest office in the Government at such a time as the present, and by such a Convention as that which recently met in Baltimore—a Convention far less imposing by the number of its members, large as it was, than by their high character. In it were men venerable alike for their age and their public services, who could not have been called from their voluntary retirement from public life, but by the strongest sense of patriotic duty; others, though still in the prime of life, ranking with the first men of the country by honors and distinctions already acquired in high official positions, State and national, many of them statesmen worthy to fill the highest office in the government; a still greater number occupying the highest rank in their respective professional pursuits; others distinguished by their intelligence and well-earned influence in various walks of private life, and all animated and united by one spirit and one purpose—the result of a strong conviction that our political system, under the operation of a complication of disorders, is rapidly approaching a crisis when a speedy change must take place, indicating, as in diseases of the physical body, recovery or death.

The Convention, in discarding the use of platforms, exact no pledge from those whom they deem worthy of the highest trusts under the Government; wisely considering that the surest guaranty of a man's future usefulness and fidelity to the great interests of the country, in any official station to which he may be chosen, is to be found in his past history connected with the public service. The pledge implied in my acceptance of the nomination of the National Union Convention is, that should I be elected, I will not depart from the spirit and tenor of my past course; and the obligation to keep this pledge derives a double force from the consideration that none is required from me.

You, sir, in your letter containing the official announcement of my nomination, have been pleased to ascribe to me the merit of moderation and justice in my past public career. You have likewise given me credit for a uniform support of all wise and beneficent measures of legislation, for a firm resistance to all measures calculated to engender sectional discord, and for a lifelong devotion to the Union, harmony, and prosperity of these States. Whether your personal partiality has led you to overstate my merits as a public man or not in your enumeration of them, you have presented a summary—a basis of all sound American statesmanship. It may be objected that nothing is said in this summary, in express terms, of the obligations imposed by the Constitution; but the duty to respect and observe them is clearly implied, for without due observance in the conduct of the Government of the Constitution, its restrictions, and requirements, fairly interpreted in accordance with its spirit and objects, there can be no end to sectional discord—no security for the harmony of the Union.

I have not the vanity to assume that in my past connection with the public service I have exemplified the course of a sound American statesman; but if I have deserved the favorable view taken of it in your letter, I may hope, by a faithful adherence to the maxims by which I have heretofore been guided, not altogether to disappoint the confidence and expectations of those who have placed me in my present relation to the public; and if, under Providence, I should be called to preside over the affairs of this great country as the Executive Chief of the Government, the only further pledge I feel called upon to make is, that the utmost of my ability, and with whatever strength of will I can command, all the powers and influence belonging to my official station, shall be employed and directed for the promotion of all the great objects for which the Government was instituted, but more especially for the maintenance of the Constitution and the Union against all imposing influences and tendencies.

I cannot conclude this letter without expressing my high gratification at the nomination to the second office under the Government, of the eminently-gifted and distinguished statesman of Massachusetts, Edward Everett, a gentlemen held by general consent to be altogether worthy of the first.

Tendering my grateful acknowledgments for the kind and complimentary manner in which you were pleased to accompany the communication of my nomination, I am, dear sir, with the highest respect,

Your obedient servant, JOHN BELL.

To the Hon. WASHINGTON HUNT.

MR. EVERETT'S ACCEPTANCE.

BOSTON, *May* 29, 1860.

MY DEAR SIR: I have duly received your letter of the 11th, in which you inform me officially, that the National Union Convention, recently in session at Baltimore, had done me the honor to nominate me as its candidate for the office of Vice-President of the United States.

I am deeply impressed with this manifestation of the favorable opinion of the Convention, comprising as it did among its members so many persons distinguished for public service, patriotism and intelligence; and fairly representing a considerable portion of the conservative feeling of the country. For the great cordiality with which, as you inform me, my name was proposed and received, my warmest thanks are due.

The grateful acceptance of such a nomination would, under ordinary circumstances, be a matter of course; but it has unavoidably been with me the subject of long and anxious hesitation. The grounds of this hesitation I owe it to the Convention which has honored me with this mark of its confidence, and to myself, to explain; loath as I am to dwell on matters of personal interest of no importance to the public.

It is generally known that I have, for some years past, retired from active participation in political life, not, as I hope I have shown, from indolence or want of sympathy with my fellow-citizens in the pursuit of the great objects of social life. The reasons of my retirement have been more than once publicly stated, and I beg to repeat them here from my speech at the Union meeting in Faneuil Hall last December:

"I did not suppose that anything could occur which would make me think it my duty to appear again on this platform, on any occasion of a political character; and had this meeting been of a party nature, or designed to promote any party purposes, I should not have been here. When compelled, by the prostration of my health, five years ago, to resign the distinguished place which I then filled in the public service, it was with no expectation, no wish, and no intention of ever again mingling in the scenes of public life. I have, accordingly, with the partial restoration of my health, abstained from all participation in political action of any kind; partly because I have found a more congenial, and, as I venture to think, a more useful occupation, in seeking to rally the affections of my countrymen, North and South, to that great name and precious memory which are left almost alone of all the numerous kindly associations which once bound the different sections of the country together, and also because, between the extremes of opinion that have long distracted and now threaten to convulse the country, I find no middle ground of practical usefulness, on which a friend of moderate counsels can stand."

It having been suggested to me, notwithstanding these avowals, that I might be thought of, at the Union Convention, as a candidate for the Presidency, I requested, by telegraphic message and by letter, that my name, if brought forward, might be withdrawn. It is true that in these communications I had only in view a nomination to the Presidency, none other having been suggested to me; but all the reasons above indicated, which led me in advance to decline such a nomination, apply with equal force to the Vice-Presidency. These reasons, of course, still exist in unimpaired force, and I cannot now take an active part in politics without abandoning a deliberately formed purpose, and even exposing myself to the suspicion of insincerity in its persistent avowal.

Without dwelling upon these considerations, of which, however, I am sure the weight will be admitted, I beg leave to advert for a moment to my connection with the movement for the purchase of Mount Vernon, to which your letter alludes in such obliging terms. The favor which has attended my exertions in that cause (if I may without indelicacy say anything on that subject) has been mainly the result of my known and recognized disconnection from party politics. If it could have been even plausibly insinuated that I was, or intended to become, a candidate for high political honors, I should, in my various excursions in aid of that fund, have laid myself open to the imputation of speaking one word for Mount Vernon and two for myself. As it is, the people through out the Union have generously given me credit for hav-

ing a single eye to that meritorious object. As far as the purchase of Mount Vernon is concerned, that object has been effected, under the judicious and efficient management of the Regent and Vice-Regents of the Association, with the aid of their intelligent and active assistants throughout the Union. But a sum of money equal to that already raised is still wanting for the repair of the Mansion, the inclosure of the land purchased, the restoration of the house and grounds, as far as practicable, to their condition in 1800, and the establishment of a permanent fund for their conservation. I own that I am desirous still to enjoy the privilege of coöperating in this noble work, which, however, it will be impossible for me to do to any advantage, whatever may be the result of the present canvass, if I am drawn into the vortex of a strenuously contested election. There are many parts of the country which I have not yet visited. I had promised myself a rich harvest from the patriotic liberality of the States on the Gulf of Mexico, and of those on the Mississippi River (which I have not yet been able to visit, with the exception of Missouri, through often kindly invited), and I confess that it is very painful to me to withdraw from that broad field of congenial labor to tread the thorny and *thankless* paths of politics.

Apart from the pecuniary aspects of the case, which, however, are of considerable importance, I will candidly say that in holding up to the admiring veneration of the American people the peerless name of Washington, (almost the only bond of fraternal sentiment which the bitterness of our sectional controversies has left us), I feel as if I was doing more good, as far as I am able to do any good, and contributing more to revive the kindly feeling which once existed between North and South, and which is now, I grieve to say, nearly extinct, than I could possibly do by engaging in the wretched scramble for office—which is one great source of the dangers that threaten the country.

These considerations, and others of a still more personal nature, have necessarily occasioned me to reflect long and anxiously, before accepting the nomination with which the Union Convention has honored me. In yielding at length to the earnest solicitations which have been addressed to me, from the most respectable sources in almost every part of the Union, I make a painful sacrifice of inclination to what I am led to believe a public duty. It has been urged upon me, and I cannot deny that such is my own feelings, that we have fallen upon times that call upon all good citizens, at whatever cost of personal convenience, to contribute their share, however humble, to the public service.

I suppose it to be the almost universal impression—it is certainly mine—that the existing state of affairs is extremely critical. Our political controversies have substantially assumed an almost purely sectional character— that of a fearful struggle between the North and the South. It would not be difficult to show at length the perilous nature and tendency of this struggle, but I can only say, on this occasion, that, in my opinion, it cannot be much longer kept up, without rending the Union. I do not mean that either of the great parties in the country desires or aims at a separation of the States as a final object, although there are extremists in considerable numbers who have that object in view. While a potent and a baleful influence is exercised by men of this class, in both sections of the Union, a portion of the conservative masses are insensibly and gradually goaded into concurrence with opinions and sentiments with which, in the outset, they had no sympathy. Meantime, almost wholly neglecting the main public interests, our political controversies turn more and more on questions, in reference to which, as abstract formulæ, the great sections of the country differ irreconcilably, though there is nothing practically important at stake which requires the discussion to be kept up. These controversies are carried on with steadily increasing bitterness and exasperation. The passions thus kindled have already led to acts of violence and bloodshed, approaching to civil war in the Territories, and attempted servile insurrection in the States. The great religious and philanthropic associations of the country are sundered, and the kindly social relations of North and South seriously impaired. The national House of Representatives, hovering on the verge of anarchy, requires weeks to effect an organization, which ought to be the work of an hour, and it holds its sessions (many of its members, I am told, armed with concealed weapons), on the crust of a volcano. The candidates for the Presidency representing respectively the dominant sectional ideas, will, at the ensuing election, in all probability, be supported by a purely geographical vote. In other words, we are already brought to a pass, at which North and South cannot and will not coöperate in the periodical reorganization of the Government.

Can such a state of things long continue, especially with the ever-present risk of new causes of exasperation? I own it seems to me impossible, unless some healing course is adopted, that the catastrophe, which the mass of good citizens deprecate, should be much longer delayed. A spirit of patriotic moderation must be called into action throughout the Union, or it will assuredly be broken up. Unless the warfare of inflammatory speeches and incendiary publications is abandoned, and good citizens, as in 1776 and 1787, North and South, will agree to deal with the same elements of discord (for they existed then as now), as our Fathers dealt with them, we shall but for a very few years longer be even nominally brethren of one family. The suggestion that the Union can be maintained by the numerical predominance and military prowess of one section, exerted to coerce the other into submission, is, in my judgment, as self-contradictory as it is dangerous. It comes loaded with the death smell from fields wet with brothers' blood. If the vital principle of all republican government " is the consent of the governed," much more does a union of coequal sovereign States require, as its basis, the harmony of its members and their voluntary coöperation in its organic functions.

Believing, for these reasons, that healing counsels must be listened to, if we are much longer to remain one people, I regard the late National Union Convention as a movement in the right direction. I could wish that it had been earlier assembled; with less exclusive reference to official nominations, and with a more comprehensive representation, if possible, of the conflicting opinions of the country. On general principles and in ordinary times, I admit that third parties are objectionable, but in the existing state of affairs, if there is to be any escape from the present ill-omened conflict, it would seem that a commencement must be made with such a meeting as that of the 9th and 10th, at Baltimore. It was a fair representation of the conservative opinion of the country; and the calmness, gravity and good feeling with which its proceedings were conducted, cannot be too highly praised.

In adopting as its platform the Constitution without note or comment, the Convention, as it seems to me, pursued a wise and patriotic course. No other course was thought of in the earlier days of the Republic. Electioneering platforms are almost without exception equivocal and delusive. It is objected that men differ as to the meaning of the fundamental law; but they differ not less as to any gloss or commentary. The Constitution, in its fair and natural interpretation, is the only basis on which good citizens in every part of the country can now unite; and any attempt to go further will usually have no other effect than to cause those who agree on great practical principles to differ on metaphysical subtleties, or to bring together, by artfully constructed phrases and from selfish motives, those who have nothing else in common.

The candidate for the Presidency, presented by the Union Convention, is every way worthy of confidence and support. I speak from personal knowledge and long association with him in the public service. His distinguished talent, large experience in public affairs, proved integrity and sterling patriotism furnish the amplest pledge for an honest and efficient administration of the government at home and abroad. A citizen of the South, and loyal to her constitutional rights, his impartial and conciliatory course as a public man affords a ground on which he can be supported in either section of the country, without dereliction of principle, and by men of all parties, without a painful sacrifice of former preferences.

Deeply regretting that the Convention has not put it in my power to pay an equally cordial and emphatic tribute to some worthy candidate for the Vice-Presidency, but feeling it a duty to give the desired proof of sympathy with their patriotic efforts to restore the happy days of brotherly concord between the different sections of our beloved country.

I remain, dear sir, sincerely yours,
EDWARD EVERETT.

MR. EVERETT ON SUMNER.

Soon after the brutal assault on Charles Sumner, in 1856, Mr. Everett, in some remarks delivered at Taunton, Mass., referred to the subject as follows:

The civil war, with its horrid train of pillage, fire, and slaughter, carried on, *without the slightest provocation*, against the infant settlements of our brethren on the frontier of the Union; the worse than civil war which has for months raged unrebuked at the Capital of the Union, and has at length, by an act of lawless violence, of which I know no parallel in the history of Constitutional Government, stained the floor of the Senate chamber with the

blood of an unarmed, defenceless man, and he a Senator of Massachusetts: if by laying down my life this hour, I could undo what has been done the last two years (beginning with the disastrous repeal of the Missouri Compromise) to embitter the different parts of the country against each other, and weaken the ties which unite them, I would willingly, cheerfully, make the sacrifice.

In a letter, written subsequently, in explanation of these remarks, Mr. Everett said—

I have condemned from the outset, and still most decidedly condemn the policy of the late Administration towards Kansas. I opposed the Kansas-Nebraska bill in the Territorial Committee, of which I was a member. I voted against the amendment to the bill by which the Missouri Compromise was repealed. I opposed the bill to the best of my ability, in a speech delivered in the Senate on the 8th of February, 1854, of which I send you a copy; and I should have voted against it on its passage (as I stated in my place at the next meeting of the Senate) had not severe illness compelled me, at 8½ o'clock in the morning, to leave the Senate chamber before the vote was taken. I informed my Southern political friends, when the bill was brought in, that it ought to be entitled a bill to " annihilate all conservative feeling in the non-slaveholding States." With these views of the subject, though, as I trust, for reasons higher than any effect on party politics, *I fully concurred in the main line of argument in Mr. Sumner's speech.* Abstaining, however, habitually myself from all personalities in debate, and believing that they always irritate and never persuade nor convince I could not of course bestow my " unqualified approbation" on the manner in which he treated the subject.

GEORGIA ON EVERETT.

On the accession of Gen. Harrison to the Presidency, in 1840, he nominated the Hon. Edward Everett as minister to England, and this nomination was resisted with great pertinacity by the entire force of the Democratic party in the Senate, on the ground of Mr. Everett's Anti-Slavery sentiments, already quoted. The Whigs having a majority in the Senate, the nomination, after a severe struggle, was confirmed. Among those voting for the Confirmation was the Hon. James McPherson Berrien, of Georgia; but his vote on this occasion was so distasteful to the people of Georgia that the legislature of that State adopted the following resolve:

Resolved, That the opinions publicly proclaimed by Edward Everett, now minister to England, of the power and obligation of Congress to abolish Slavery in the District of Columbia, to interdict the slave-trade between the States, and to refuse the admission into the Union of any Territory tolerating Slavery, are unconstitutional in their character, subversive of the rights of the South, and if carried out, will destroy this Union; and that the Hon. John McPherson Berrien, in sustaining for an important appointment, an individual holding such obnoxious sentiments, has omitted a proper occasion to give an efficient check to such sentiments, and in so doing has not truly represented the opinions or wishes of the people of Georgia, of either political party.

The vote of the legislature on the adoption of this resolve was: In the Senate, Ayes 40; Nays 0. In the House, Ayes 101; Nays 40.

JUDGE DOUGLAS ON THE MISSOURI COMPROMISE.

In a speech delivered at Springfield, Ill., in 1849, Senator Douglas, in speaking of the Missouri Compromise, said:

It has received the sanction of all parties in every section of the Union. It had its origin in the hearts of all patriotic men who desired to preserve and perpetuate the blessings of our glorious Union—an origin akin to that of the Constitution of the United States, conceived in the same spirit of fraternal affection, and calculated to remove forever the only danger which seemed to threaten at some distant day to sever the sacred bond of Union. All the evidences of public opinion seem to indicate that this Compromise has become canonized in the hearts of the American people as a sacred thing, which no ruthless hand would be reckless enough to disturb.

POPULAR VOTE FOR PRESIDENT.

MAINE.

COUNTIES.	1856. Republican. John C. Fremont.	1856. Democrat. James Buchanan.	1856. American. Millard Fillmore.	1852. Whig. Winfield Scott.	1852. Democrat. Franklin Pierce.	1852. Free Soil. John P. Hale.	1848. Whig. Zachary Taylor.	1848. Democrat. Lewis Cass.	1848. Free Democrat. Martin Van Buren.	1844. Whig. Henry Clay.	1844. Democrat. James K. Polk.	1844. Abolitionist. James G. Birney.	1840. Whig. Wm. H. Harrison.	1840. Democrat. Martin Van Buren.
Androscoggin...	3388	1699	186	Un	organi	zed.	431	868	106	398	907	24	289	480
Aroostook	837	795	8	724	787	80	431	868	106	398	907	24	289	480
Cumberland ...	8211	5258	605	4471	6504	1379	4797	5989	1744	4483	6367	695	6790	6438
Franklin.......	2529	1358	21	997	1310	596	886	1431	810	1132	1609	392	1848	2058
Hancock	3667	2142	161	1809	2619	214	2075	2318	247	1849	2608	105	2434	2509
Kennebec	7320	2487	340	4489	2703	954	5056	2634	1656	5393	3535	561	6905	3521
Lincoln........	4935	3598	392	5224	5168	563	5316	4670	967	4566	5854	461	6286	5188
Oxford	4364	3116	28	1560	4049	697	1531	3601	1201	1887	4395	397	2932	4800
Penobscot	7861	3798	341	3182	4513	1015	3916	4591	1528	3376	4898	695	4333	4445
Piscataquis	1734	915	97	693	851	381	937	1168	432	1047	1136	228	1275	1136
Sagadahoc	2956	934	397	Un	organi	zed.	2445	2085	1008	2840	2530	435	3684	2597
Somerset	4283	1926	417	2394	2019	457	2445	2085	1008	2840	2530	435	3684	2597
Waldo.........	5159	3138	114	1379	3126	757	1768	3382	1107	1829	4661	816	2694	5069
Washington ...	3299	2867	64	2278	2690	211	2501	2446	449	2329	2605	77	2357	2235
York	6636	5054	154	3393	5270	726	3466	4697	841	3216	5117	453	4785	5725
Total........	67379	39080	3325	32543	41609	8030	35125	39880	12096	34378	45719	4886	46612	46201

Fremont over Buchanan, 28,299; Pierce over Scott, 9,066; Cass over Taylor, 4,755; Polk over Clay, 11,341; Harrison over Van Buren, 411. Mr. James G. Birney received 194 votes in this State, in 1840.

NEW-HAMPSHIRE.

COUNTIES.	Rep. Frem't	Dem. Buc'an	Am. Fill're.	Whig. Scott.	Dem. Pierce.	F. Soil. Hale.	Whig. Taylor.	Dem. Cass.	Free D. Van B.	Whig. Clay.	Dem. Polk.	Abo. Birney.	Whig. Ha'son	Dem. Van B.
Belknap.......	2062	2220	21	737	1837	262	610	1769	334	864	1701	248	Unorg	anized
Carroll	2185	2511	17	491	1825	350	589	1885	625	732	1816	233	Unorg	anized
Cheshire	3910	2269	56	2068	2264	698	1881	2076	945	2358	2070	374	3638	2302
Coos	1200	1508	2	376	1491	167	230	1282	219	348	1364	108	525	1341
Grafton	5029	4620	39	2043	4286	771	1927	4060	1104	2566	4046	631	3691	4978
Hillsboro'	7081	5326	85	2985	4855	1447	2799	4773	1257	3124	4583	675	4084	5072
Merrimac	4949	4730	43	1627	4628	1001	1245	4218	1076	1589	3821	628	2755	5080
Rockingham...	5914	4915	111	2506	4502	1071	2710	3972	982	2830	4007	584	4102	4984
Strafford	3566	2683	20	2003	2250	498	1664	1912	495	1702	1808	330	5280	6755
Sullivan	2449	2007	28	1316	2059	430	1176	1866	523	1553	1944	350	2088	2299
Total	38345	32789	422	16147	29997	6695	14781	27768	7560	17866	27160	4161	26168	32761

Fremont over Buchanan, 5,556; Pierce over Scott, 13,850; Cass over Taylor, 12,982; Polk over Clay, 9,294; Van Buren over Harrison, 6,598. Mr. Birney received 126 votes in 1840.

RHODE ISLAND.

COUNTIES.	Rep. Frem't	Dem. Buc'an	Am. Fill're.	Whig. Scott.	Dem. Pierce.	F. Soil. Hale.	Whig. Taylor.	Dem. Cass.	Free D. Van B.	Whig. Clay.	Dem. Polk.	Abo. Birney.	Whig. Ha'son	Dem. Van B.
Bristol.........	603	337	218	628	367	2	590	131	18	589	109	......	476	136
Kent...........	1260	566	15	839	748	83	690	318	52	786	381	......	669	372
Newport	1258	750	659	1249	1005	48	1207	232	113	1229	473	......	914	417
Providence	6903	4432	331	3888	5529	431	3542	2515	398	3751	3192	......	2482	1711
Washington ...	1443	595	452	1022	1086	80	750	450	149	967	712	......	787	665
Total........	11467	6680	1675	7626	8735	644	6779	3646	730	7322	4867	107	5278	3301

Fremont over Buchanan, 4,787; Pierce over Scott, 1,109; Taylor over Cass, 3,133; Clay over Polk, 2,455; Harrison over Van Buren, 1,977. Mr. Birney received 42 votes in 1840.

MASSACHUSETTS.

COUNTIES.	1856.			1852.			1848.			1844.			1840.	
	Rep. Frem't	Dem. Buc'an	Am. Fill're.	Whig. Scott.	Dem. Pierce.	F. Soil Hale.	Whig. Taylor.	Dem. Cass.	Free D. Van B.	Whig. Clay.	Dem. Polk.	Abo. Birney.	Whig. Ha'son	Dem. Van B.
Barnstable	2667	703	300	1379	892	473	2015	802	516	2290	1415	251	2751	1554
Berkshire	5344	2749	377	3579	2973	631	3549	2387	1549	3656	3885	401	3931	3780
Bristol	8845	2465	936	3827	3267	2091	4840	2170	2832	4872	4903	644	4855	4904
Dukes.........	317	161	122	250	225	48	290	133	81	302	255	24	346	294
Essex	15885	4577	2612	6539	4576	3485	8555	4678	5020	8518	5259	1887	10056	6513
Franklin	4445	1266	260	2552	1726	1218	2133	1542	1645	2725	2047	423	3461	2137
Hampden	5533	2730	631	3445	3458	757	3306	3061	1284	3416	3593	451	3441	3312
Hampshire	5166	832	277	3300	1425	1243	3055	1070	1806	3725	1605	626	4083	1625
Middlesex	17222	7705	4095	8750	8925	5231	9854	6820	5964	9581	9124	1718	9716	8626
Nantucket.....	583	126	73	329	189	189	444	89	159	683	237	41	671	320
Norfolk	8402	3697	2670	3589	3454	2479	4739	2451	3538	5217	4287	888	5404	4238
Plymouth	7228	1772	1496	2993	2080	2440	3568	1847	3189	4449	3315	805	5065	3548
Suffolk	8582	5853	4648	4868	5413	1600	8895	3173	2132	8778	4659	509	7557	4339
Worcester......	17971	4604	1129	7283	5966	7138	5827	5058	8343	9359	7562	2147	11537	6764
Total.	108190	39240	19626	52688	44569	28023	61070	35281	28058	67418	52846	10860	72874	51944

Fremont over Buchanan, 68,950; Scott over Pierce, 8,114; Taylor over Cass, 25,789; Clay over Polk, 14,572; Harrison over Van Buren, 20,930. Mr. Birney received 1,621 votes in 1840.

VERMONT.

COUNTIES.	Rep. Frem't	Dem. Buc'an	Am. Fill're.	Whig. Scott.	Dem. Pierce.	F. Soil. Hale.	Whig. Taylor.	Dem. Cass.	Free D. Van B.	Whig. Clay.	Dem. Polk.	Abo. Birney.	Whig. Ha'son	Dem. Van B
Addison	3362	334	68	2041	378	642	2558	319	1035	2527	772	312	2806	916
Bennington....	2120	785	70	1888	1150	181	1559	1150	616	1656	1450	168	1796	1428
Caledonia	2540	1061	23	1678	1480	487	1367	1158	888	1762	1730	184	2025	1718
Chittenden.....	2844	688	73	1672	803	908	1763	571	1516	1924	1444	386	2286	1381
Essex	622	274	4	467	382	16	370	331	42	392	331	18	448	303
Franklin	2454	870	65	1675	1211	526	1456	691	1204	1872	1438	261	2186	1191
Grand Isle.....	405	92	9	295	186	31	311	130	104	339	165	—	363	162
Lamoille.......	1607	402	13	393	462	689	289	474	754	485	759	411	907	888
Orange........	3207	1364	61	1799	1555	752	1780	1414	1808	2076	1910	412	2874	2216
Orleans	2007	494	6	1199	859	308	1056	562	536	1192	833	245	1294	745
Rutland	4798	831	35	2758	938	773	2911	744	1377	3584	1578	333	4114	1551
Washington....	3821	1359	5	1402	1231	1217	1398	1693	1106	1650	2085	301	2057	1984
Windham......	4068	742	47	2053	881	986	2648	608	1443	2642	1703	385	3472	1715
Windsor.......	5706	1273	66	3358	1528	1105	3656	1103	1908	4669	1843	538	5817	1821
Total.	39561	10569	545	22173	13044	8621	23122	10948	18837	26770	18041	3954	32440	18018

Fremont over Buchanan, 28,992; Scott over Pierce, 9,129; Taylor over Cass, 12,174; Clay over Polk, 8,729; Harrison over Van Buren, 14,422. Mr. Birney received 319 votes in 1840.

NEW-JERSEY.

COUNTIES.	Rep. Frem't	Dem. Buc'an	Am. Fill're.	Whig. Scott.	Dem. Pierce.	F. Soil. Hale.	Whig. Taylor.	Dem. Cass.	Free D. Van B.	Whig. Clay.	Dem. Polk.	Abo. Birney.	Whig. Ha'son	Dem. Van B.
Atlantic........	547	684	160	849	751	—	472	780	—	493	848	......	425	846
Bergen........	436	1548	797	926	1414	—	1004	1262	15	979	1440	......	977	1346
Burlington	3149	3682	1584	3820	3796	114	3898	3014	80	3730	3017	......	3417	2405
Camden	817	1766	2088	1568	1696	27	1967	1236	23	1448	1208	......	Unorg	anized
Cape May.....	177	312	497	604	352	—	657	226	—	780	814	.. ...	696	194
Cumberland ...	642	1574	1231	1371	1312	2	1666	1319	—	1549	1371	......	1497	1190
Essex	4760	6845	4838	6242	5631	85	5997	2824	127	5471	3655	... ..	4636	2832
Gloucester	639	986	1380	1221	1083	55	1297	882	88	1411	902	......	2388	1773
Hudson	1702	2574	1411	1596	1645	29	1484	760	80	1129	703	......	732	501
Hunterdon	1554	3496	1106	2290	3578	—	2191	3220	9	2544	3386	... ..	1830	2783
Mercer.........	2155	2857	1064	2658	2569	13	2631	2058	26	1883	1577	......	2022	1494
Middlesex	1209	2468	1988	2495	2401	—	2469	1807	129	2321	2023	......	2014	1683
Monmouth	1008	3319	1815	1806	3179	5	3119	3450	4	3221	3434	......	2953	2880
Morris	2310	3008	696	2549	2800	25	2889	2424	91	2903	2466	......	2509	2150
Ocean.........	892	660	304	1102	567	—	Un	organi	zed.					
Passaic........	1422	1618	954	1670	1825	—	1749	1804	120	1602	1291	......	1362	962
Salem	432	1769	1516	1724	1783	31	1702	1586	28	1775	1493	......	1582	1302
Somerset	1295	1846	709	1814	1680	1	2028	1617	—	2139	1978	......	1721	1345
Sussex	1601	3054	31	1177	3184	8	1211	3443	46	1295	3490	......	1171	2932
Warren	1596	2877	446	1574	2759	10	1634	2689	13	1645	2899	......	1419	2466
Total	28338	46943	24115	38556	44305	850	40015	36901	819	38318	37495	131	33351	31034

Buchanan over Fremont, 18,605; Pierce over Scott, 5,749; Taylor over Cass, 8,114; Clay over Polk, 823; Harrison over Van Buren, 2,317. Mr. Birney received 69 votes in 1840.

OHIO.

COUNTIES.	1856. Rep. Frem't	1856. Dem. Buc'an	1856. Am. Fill're.	1852. Whig. Scott.	1852. Dem. Pierce	1852. F. Soil. Hale.	1848. Whig. Taylor.	1848. Dem. Cass.	1848. Free D. Van B.	1844. Whig. Clay.	1844. Dem. Polk.	1844. Abo. Birney	1840. Whig. Ha'son	1840. Dem. Van B.
Adams	1407	1790	278	1218	1736	233	1259	1690	196	1252	1611	87	1205	1441
Allen	1415	•1508	94	958	1536	23	728	1070	2	779	1062	9	763	888
Ashland	1912	2089	89	1368	2434	297	Un	organi	zed.					
Ashtabula	5108	975	252	2174	1075	2502	1124	878	2467	3388	1123	537	3738	896
Athens	2299	1350	154	1751	1383	364	1846	1509	320	2050	1425	220	2094	1322
Auglaize	912	1604	88	588	1480	24	Un	organi	zed.					
Belmont	1817	2810	1758	2786	2694	454	2723	2892	543	3140	2821	184	3166	2602
Brown	1785	2700	428	1702	2460	393	1171	2557	403	1798	2342	130	798	1939
Butler	2301	3509	296	2210	3579	122	1959	3536	381	2158	3546	61	2101	3192
Carroll	1750	1255	87	1543	1355	242	1453	1395	345	1701	1584	140	677	1545
Champaign	1995	1711	320	1994	1687	206	1878	1508	330	2069	1409	32	2062	1207
Clark	2641	1539	168	2662	1374	183	2506	1375	208	2477	1155	43	2381	895
Clermont	2188	2741	781	2213	2765	409	2204	2883	404	2189	2627	105	2044	2315
Clinton	2117	1170	240	1424	1063	702	1233	1122	735	1736	1137	172	1847	1006
Columbiana	3516	2497	96	2237	2911	993	1850	2732	865	3416	3743	217	3600	3650
Coshocton	2162	2281	56	1798	2618	73	1814	2422	137	1885	2281	60	1830	2009
Crawford	1685	2154	32	1074	2106	58	952	1678	90	1197	1734	8	009	1206
Cuyahoga	6360	4446	296	2944	3571	2107	1776	2368	2594	3331	2388	312	3102	1814
Darke	2086	1988	209	1719	1797	92	1508	1554	81	1408	1409	25	1303	1071
Defiance	821	895	38	554	896	43	Un	organi	zed.					
Delaware	2367	1649	230	2083	1591	391	1866	1574	268	2548	2017	118	2360	1644
Erie	2258	1377	75	1589	1404	275	1409	999	681	1458	1261	65	1324	1042
Fairfield	1700	3233	711	2117	3311	10	2438	3515	42	2542	3637	15	2463	3318
Fayette	1209	880	378	1221	893	166	1157	946	128	1229	878	67	1132	771
Franklin	3488	3791	574	3498	3652	242	3199	3029	284	2965	2498	72	2886	177
Fulton	1098	772	64	587	727	71	Un	organi	zed.					
Gallia	610	1341	1206	1567	1108	135	1630	1081	95	1484	957	31	1479	725
Geauga	2694	575	58	1147	664	1489	872	922	1373	2274	1101	233	2310	921
Greene	3032	1465	214	2480	1490	500	2085	1256	644	2422	1380	126	2321	1172
Guernsey	2392	1932	210	1941	1809	504	2375	2504	489	2746	2628	218	2606	2186
Hamilton	9345	13051	5680	9252	13435	684	9018	10834	-1986	7201	8983	298	5873	5835
Hancock	1773	1944	37	1076	1617	35	1016	1501	22	907	1247	2	693	1063
Hardin	1091	882	82	882	847	74	596	605	51	510	495	6	431	876
Harrison	2060	1473	110	1723	1462	422	1564	1658	543	2039	1750	195	2008	1739
Henry	587	655	22	325	536	14	217	297	17	229	245	—	191	181
Highland	1810	2140	894	1982	2290	281	2114	2224	342	2148	2164	114	2145	1899
Hocking	1092	1454	115	865	1552	21	856	1319	23	719	1289	2	649	903
Holmes	1285	2103	5	1066	2100	42	1118	2224	45	1142	2317	5	1109	1906
Huron	3468	1709	54	2242	1819	893	1950	1769	876	2564	2136	138	2291	1531
Jackson	938	1383	416	1069	1093	19	987	1108	50	908	1046	13	794	785
Jefferson	2424	1991	259	1995	2169	348	2147	2281	455	2385	2354	95	2300	2218
Knox	2735	2437	124	1874	2692	626	1910	2890	539	2746	3324	134	2441	2789
Lake	2371	628	39	1046	670	1111	777	716	904	1818	901	109	1887	653
Lawrence	743	1150	902	1299	981	15	1164	745	53	1140	658	3	1118	453
Licking	3027	3371	417	2779	3569	582	3030	3468	561	3500	3840	238	3357	3516
Logan	2093	1328	267	2118	1361	191	1652	1147	276	1625	1015	93	1574	845
Lorain	3604	1420	54	1332	1554	1777	647	1473	1616	1956	1793	473	1868	1818
Lucas	1639	1866	486	1238	1271	129	1298	1197	327	1167	881	12	931	526
Madison	997	656	475	1400	655	61	1329	712	80	1269	643	8	1201	571
Mahoning	2323	1937	29	955	1873	1033	Un	organi	zed.					
Marion	1367	1275	4	914	1270	79	1001	1193	55	1425	1480	88	1358	1128
Medina	2635	1572	28	1579	1754	1008	1440	1836	1098	2045	1920	220	1793	1436
Meigs	1998	1603	344	1573	1399	297	1327	1014	305	1341	880	41	1284	649
Mercer	629	1159	114	500	831	11	360	641	16	423	812	4	551	1348
Miami	3171	1988	159	2754	2004	235	2542	1822	272	2572	1657	113	2469	1339
Monroe	1016	2812	413	997	2422	180	999	2574	330	1210	2548	114	1068	2075
Montgomery	4038	4285	391	3886	3744	177	3561	3330	304	3388	3101	83	3427	2951
Morgan	2125	1669	201	2084	1708	220	2320	2448	314	2051	2077	64	1851	1910
Morrow	2031	1667	101	1030	1710	748	Un	organi	zed.					
Muskingum	3172	3391	1092	4228	3500	214	4427	3380	228	4489	3196	86	4367	2772
Noble	1603	1337	154	885	1487	435	Un	organi	zed.					
Ottawa	454	477	1	274	400	2	190	231	45	241	233	9	232	163
Paulding	497	170	5	121	342	5	70	198	—	63	192	—	65	155
Perry	1385	1847	492	1417	2246	17	1488	2192	19	1527	2273	3	1471	2097
Pickaway	1724	2066	382	2175	2041	35	2115	1960	24	2219	2012	10	2201	1187
Pike	523	1175	375	927	1029	16	843	909	33	800	836	16	650	647
Portage	2983	2072	6	1351	2007	1296	1270	2149	1127	2510	2247	244	2524	1968
Preble	2249	1561	278	2253	1633	197	2106	1519	314	2262	1526	70	2299	1331
Putnam	790	1116	4	461	890	61	402	684	8	451	697	2	401	582
Richmond	2726	2909	53	2133	3234	209	2087	3177	188	3443	5574	111	3331	4589
Ross	2436	2681	589	3091	2465	179	3394	2306	174	3321	2380	90	3081	2071
Sandusky	1548	1599	45	1064	1618	88	928	1148	124	997	1214	12	919	917
Scioto	546	634	1321	1804	1424	29	1838	1268	13	1519	1095	—	1472	749
Seneca	2565	2605	103	1972	2809	118	1536	2326	483	1727	2316	41	1483	1616
Shelby	1356	1446	127	1147	1309	54	1021	1129	49	1026	1014	26	955	1027
Starke	3770	3633	29	2740	3634	356	2382	3495	570	2952	3575	76	2701	3106
Summit	3185	1746	74	2336	1965	660	1892	1815	1058	2841	2056	184	2562	1646
Trumbull	4049	1920	18	1968	2039	1739	1364	1951	2075	3837	3544	738	4101	3325
Tuscarawas	3007	2656	18	2659	2685	112	2662	2553	164	2696	2358	85	2338	1787
Union	1431	1055	263	1249	943	255	1080	797	173	1009	710	32	946	577
Van Wert	758	789	32	422	737	6	223	381	—		158	270	—	Unorganized
Vinton	932	1174	51	774	912	95	Un	organi	zed.					
Warren	2688	1776	344	2823	1919	223	2526	1861	402	2822	1795	85	2813	1504

OHIO—(Continued).

COUNTIES.	1856.			1852.			1848.			1844.			1840.	
	Rep. Frem't	Dem. Buc'an	Am. Fill're.	Whig. Scott.	Dem. Pierce.	F. Soil. Hale.	Whig. Taylor.	Dem. Cass.	Free D. Van B.	Whig. Clay.	Dem. Polk.	Abo. Birney	Whig. Ha'son	Dem. an B.
Washington ...	2783	2251	281	2473	2139	333	2079	1930	462	2194	1686	151	2109	1458
Wayne........	2904	2918	47	2288	3143	149	2284	3380	190	2759	3765	75	2798	3321
Williams	1327	1022	49	546	832	160	828	510	154	583	673	—	396	407
Wood	1319	935	143	831	986	20	647	636	29	576	570	1	548	518
Wyandotte	1247	1278	108	990	1290	9	951	1059	46	Un	organi	zed.		
Total.......	187497	170874	28126	152526	169220	31682	138360	154775	85354	155057	149117	8050	148157	124782

Fremont over Buchanan, 16,623; Pierce over Scott, 16,694; Cass over Taylor, 16,415; Clay over Polk, 5,940. Harrison over Van Buren, 23,375. In 1840, Mr. Birney received 903 votes.

NEW-YORK.

COUNTIES.	Rep. Frem't	Dem. Buc'an	Am. Fill're.	Whig. Scott.	Dem. Pierce.	F. Soil. Hale.	Whig. Taylor.	Dem. Cass.	Free D. Van B.	Whig. Clay.	Dem. Polk.	Abo. Birney	Whig. Ha'son	Dem. Van B.
Albany........	5016	7751	5301	7246	8363	133	7068	4002	2407	7109	6916	124	6371	5944
Allegany	6545	1640	856	3670	4009	678	2789	1288	2040	3913	3640	435	4132	3382
Broome	4297	2106	791	2674	3064	347	2490	1959	777	2681	2508	106	2395	2131
Cattaraugus ...	5166	1773	978	3687	3493	561	2604	1677	1236	2743	2634	487	2966	2485
Cayuga	7035	1818	1923	4838	4550	916	4318	1034	3979	4908	5202	376	5164	4864
Chautauqua ...	7037	1847	2017	5612	3708	146	4207	1911	1628	5612	3407	314	5985	3345
Chemung......	2664	1789	766	2326	3189	339	1943	728	2166	1791	2592	106	1693	2296
Chenango	5458	2406	1070	3880	4481	303	3587	2616	1481	4215	4495	243	4386	3995
Columbia......	3818	3020	1981	4142	4455	7	3943	2121	2100	4322	4691	11	4287	4478
Cortland	3596	1181	628	2328	2064	655	1879	946	1803	2378	2858	543	2664	2229
Clinton........	2659	2134	1311	2286	2812	245	1941	1472	1221	1919	2218	410	2023	1828
Delaware......	4367	2107	2009	3289	4052	339	2832	790	2908	3071	4230	205	2988	3847
Dutchess	5512	4039	2013	5495	5600	33	5376	8227	1295	5767	5627	37	5355	5362
Erie...	6901	7536	5520	8023	7033	510	7647	3360	2357	6905	5050	415	6784	8691
Essex	2904	1173	956	2756	1973	174	2629	1002	1119	2612	1998	143	2617	1789
Franklin	1469	1600	1145	1747	2074	130	1353	974	911	1524	1501	93	1440	1110
Fulton	2593	1374	1034	2171	2070	115	1976	380	1602	2107	2192	100	1964	1645
Genesee......	3620	1434	1100	3358	2166	313	2890	1180	1111	3604	2105	298	7057	3809
Greene.	2164	2346	1533	2803	3242	16	2707	1551	1425	2968	3488	30	2991	3258
Hamilton......	149	250	117	126	342			With	Ful	ton.			123	222
Herkimer	5074	1650	1230	2679	4220	555	2430	699	3898	2868	4346	608	3118	4350
Jefferson	8249	3496	1058	5656	6279	757	4841	2445	4342	5576	6291	712	6257	5630
Kings	7846	14174	8647	8487	10621	66	7511	4882	817	5107	4648	77	3293	3157
Lewis	3124	1114	418	1727	2535	303	1223	789	1258	1640	2073	154	1718	1755
Livingston.....	3597	1652	1979	4096	3055	308	3730	889	2100	3773	2709	210	3916	2634
Montgomery...	3076	1485	1713	2995	3373	40	2924	1285	1602	2849	3278	85	2828	3298
Madison......	6312	1861	865	3379	3435	1584	2898	1565	2739	3683	3848	1311	4266	4114
Monroe	7584	4683	3070	7467	6314	775	6589	1443	4671	6873	5611	430	6468	4834
New York	17771	41913	19922	23115	34226	206	29057	18884	5106	26885	28296	117	20958	21935
Niagara........	3906	1864	1985	3413	2862	1056	2828	1318	2080	3100	2589	310	2964	2219
Onondaga	10071	4227	1724	6097	6415	1701	5442	2229	4942	6495	6878	732	6557	6563
Ontario	4551	1642	2189	4402	3347	547	3848	1272	2627	4568	3659	435	4828	3451
Orange	4274	3948	2172	4221	5171	16	4172	3170	1434	4626	5303	37	4371	4845
Oneida........	11172	6386	1601	7831	8636	1033	6032	3535	4816	6983	7717	1144	7156	7768
Oswego........	8246	3683	1175	4375	4973	2148	3655	1134	4254	3771	4382	851	4192	3907
Orleans	3088	1052	1412	2586	2267	605	2402	918	1772	2600	2311	276	2606	2027
Otsego	6373	3595	1229	4454	5486	643	3929	3674	1941	4743	6050	413	4856	5581
Putnam	963	1096	479	826	1521	—	816	996	415	979	1731	—	920	1583
Queens........	1886	2394	2521	2208	2899	12	2444	1310	800	2547	2751	—	2522	2550
Rensselaer.....	5153	4415	4548	6185	6563	218	6241	2685	2930	6360	5618	181	5752	5424
Richmond	736	1550	946	1147	1324	30	1099	860	123	1049	1063	1	903	851
Rockland. ...	668	1526	937	733	1785	—	918	1064	255	794	1679	1	637	1657
St. Lawrence...	9698	1950	1332	4570	5583	1386	3667	613	6023	4672	6008	468	4803	4751
Saratoga	4524	2446	2581	4498	4291	71	4438	2515	1405	4550	4200	119	4416	3873
Schenectady ...	1714	787	1213	1654	1900	—	1716	1069	444	1814	1679	31	1752	1577
Schuyler	2542	981	461	From	Steub	er, Ch	emung	and T	ompki	ns.				
Suffolk	2393	2045	1980	1917	3306	—	2180	1051	1400	2487	3375	14	2415	3482
Seneca	2163	1625	1265	2218	2511	200	1767	1360	1523	2327	2569	124	2466	2472
Schoharie	2376	2837	1630	2958	3846	18	2724	2671	654	2986	3528	111	2895	3345
Sullivan	1690	1583	2037	2054	2681	44	1672	1363	534	1739	1964	80	1475	1679
Steuben	7270	3217	2034	5236	6880	845	4357	1975	3628	4385	5512	243	4081	4820
Tioga	3331	2154	435	2234	2815	197	1782	1683	789	1999	2545	90	1925	2180
Tompkins	4019	1430	1470	3410	3472	862	3003	1270	2648	3845	4013	322	3969	3558
Ulster....	2932	4030	4703	5133	5916	26	4659	1970	2277	4804	4783	12	4491	4280
Washington ...	5174	1632	1848	4230	3174	451	4486	1225	2024	5024	3270	338	5071	3024
Warren	2202	1006	735	1174	1713	119	1270	1019	618	1330	1791	118	1306	1411
Wayne........	5776	1999	1448	4033	4050	941	3567	797	3690	3953	4046	563	4309	3997
Wyoming......	4066	1911	571	3005	2471	727	2881	1337	1630	2754	2102	442	With	Gen'see
Westchester ...	4450	4600	3641	4033	5279	55	4112	2146	1312	4258	4412	19	4083	4354
Yates	2994	915	351	1974	2153	324	1651	862	1483	2056	2110	207	2072	2087
Total	276007	195878	124604	234882	262083	25329	218603	114318	120510	232482	237588	15812	225817	212527

Fremont over Buchanan, 80,129; Pierce over Scott, 27,201; Taylor over Cass, 104,285; Polk over Clay, 5,106; Harrison over Van Buren, 13,290. Mr. Birney received 2,808 votes in 1840. and Gerrit Smith, *Land Reform* and *Abolitionist* received 2,545 votes in 1848.

ILLINOIS.

COUNTIES.	1856.			1852.			1848.			1844.			1840.	
	Rep. Frem't	Dem. Buc'an	Am. Fill're	Whig. Scott.	Dem. Pierce	F. Soil. Hale.	Whig. Taylor.	Dem. Cass.	Free D. Van B.	Whig. Clay.	Dem. Polk.	Abo. Birney	Whig. Ha'son	Dem. Van B.
Adams	2226	3311	662	2236	2635	107	1992	2205	251	1280	1495	149	1617	1852
Alexander	15	401	230	105	296	—	101	212	2	81	188	24	299	424
Bond	153	607	659	494	485	37	391	371	48	564	622	27	513	551
Boone	1748	243	27	551	525	338	414	395	415	375	398	58	220	222
Brown	169	903	433	445	661	—	408	666	20	329	551	—	301	434
Bureau	2603	1234	48	712	670	430	376	306	566	362	878	160	434	279
Calhoun	70	391	163	211	335	—	215	257	3	247	268	—	213	133
Carroll	1161	237	153	499	351	72	426	222	116	221	178	10	244	69
Cass	303	914	438	784	830	—	761	724	11	176	92	—	397	315
Champaign	732	550	236	347	259	—	213	187	—	178	191	—	154	141
Christian	239	884	299	356	426	2	183	254	—	182	216	—	89	147
Clark	709	1318	330	842	966	6	748	759	27	625	756	6	667	611
Clay	29	731	540	284	530	—	207	405	—	186	448	—	218	338
Clinton	161	840	362	375	670	—	351	431	3	334	327	7	326	417
Coles	783	1178	796	997	733	2	877	633	6	776	582	—	1109	695
Cook	9020	5680	342	2089	3767	793	1708	1622	2120	1117	2027	317	1034	1989
Crawford	477	961	244	571	827	11	493	507	—	425	496	—	421	392
Cumberland	246	641	235	293	444	—	108	102	—	191	189	—	Unorganized	
De Kalb	2254	381	75	456	583	355	223	374	427	142	242	131	172	197
De Witt	623	679	878	516	540	20	373	363	20	317	361	3	293	316
Du Page	1387	542	2	381	586	386	313	623	528	372	551	173	428	373
Edgar	952	1342	308	892	924	38	829	816	42	701	884	24	783	720
Edwards	176	283	310	291	162	—	288	113	19	385	185	49	311	212
Effingham	90	784	163	175	527	—	99	380	—	82	364	—	52	207
Fayette	68	947	799	437	678	—	407	452	—	414	653	—	442	645
Franklin	5	1051	251	196	709	—	189	459	—	102	634	—	71	542
Fulton	2021	2724	898	1843	2192	298	1685	1684	371	1484	1537	8	1258	1347
Gallatin	24	764	423	324	592	—	235	537	6	406	1115	—	500	1286
Greene	245	1565	719	864	1297	12	853	1128	86	800	1246	—	870	1175
Grundy	923	618	6	249	388	64	128	207	63	49	91	7	Unorganized	
Hamilton	9	1135	162	223	754	—	125	478	—	125	573	—	126	557
Hancock	1120	2011	999	1286	1466	34	1087	1074	67	747	1399	1	1818	661
Hardin	4	332	229	244	212	—	234	287	—	136	165	—	154	182
Henderson	757	610	158	547	414	84	408	291	65	428	294	—	Unorganized	
Henry	1924	876	47	357	475	91	188	80	228	147	166	—	162	86
Iroquois	750	460	108	378	482	22	268	322	28	204	281	—	154	175
Jackson	14	1056	322	347	531	—	177	248	5	182	347	—	210	337
Jasper	323	679	158	258	461	—	154	228	—	143	276	—	78	178
Jefferson	60	1278	426	395	865	—	280	605	2	227	863	1	210	727
Jersey	387	702	530	651	564	89	530	454	93	555	458	48	517	360
Jo Daviess	2110	1509	44	1481	1425	122	1772	1392	134	1514	1585	14	1079	680
Johnson	2	1144	74	135	751	—	67	290	—	32	882	—	109	440
Kane	3570	912	29	1160	1808	642	855	783	1220	748	1046	299	810	774
Kankakee	1386	258	60	Unorganized.										
Kendall	1622	334	13	515	532	252	392	378	547	357	479	142	Unorganized	
Knox	2851	1490	277	1080	1119	391	830	727	892	746	689	162	740	541
Lake	2347	558	10	697	812	519	321	446	1088	386	620	181	281	267
La Salle	3721	2665	121	1204	1894	552	862	1238	873	427	611	126	1080	1638
Lawrence	89	729	533	510	589	—	464	532	—	427	611	—	676	597
Lee	1804	601	82	478	573	77	300	867	185	244	315	48	241	280
Livingston	585	480	72	164	214	12	82	130	4	66	109	—	85	78
Logan	655	823	484	568	489	—	465	369	4	310	251	—	260	167
Macon	500	821	393	355	486	7	253	323	5	221	328	—	250	377
Macoupin	823	1778	1010	841	1196	74	710	898	96	641	974	6	632	812
Madison	1111	1451	1658	1548	1715	31	1820	1503	162	1657	1496	12	1704	1186
Marion	150	1150	413	285	762	28	227	639	15	182	722	6	174	573
Marshall	1008	834	115	546	579	61	304	322	41	237	263	—	209	183
Mason	267	737	553	561	621	5	391	403	7	255	254	—	Unorganized	
Massac	5	630	251	268	449	—	204	303	—	165	398	—	Unorganized	
M'Donough	590	1370	864	840	838	9	439	416	25	458	493	41	472	427
M'Henry	2869	945	43	5866	1199	645	618	528	1016	493	668	74	846	271
M'Lean	1937	1517	560	256	1058	40	758	626	94	586	477	22	683	531
Menard	109	854	668	644	698	1	605	488	1	397	378	—	434	374
Mercer	1141	769	140	575	498	92	436	315	90	410	321	12	315	198
Monroe	346	900	518	294	1125	—	355	546	—	804	740	—	870	563
Montgomery	162	992	686	415	655	9	382	533	13	355	661	—	311	520
Morgan	963	1656	885	1397	1411	158	1372	1309	139	1443	1421	89	1533	1293
Moultrie	154	432	305	292	263	—	248	191	—	196	204	—	Unorganized	
Ogle	2469	734	289	899	755	294	682	480	418	505	383	95	491	266
Peoria	2082	2459	391	1556	1805	252	1237	1161	368	846	1169	55	744	767
Perry	200	671	433	277	564	59	239	344	44	219	477	22	174	331
Piatt	85	310	350	192	161	—	132	138	—	81	120	—	Unorganized	
Pike	1053	2163	1010	1745	1762	34	1609	1636	159	1411	1456	11	1149	1087
Pope	11	855	214	320	439	—	224	234	—	201	348	—	391	268
Pulaski	21	473	166	112	246	—	84	141	—	90	208	—	Unorganized	
Putnam	532	807	115	300	248	230	266	185	299	237	228	140	259	151
Randolph	709	1222	546	575	814	220	580	689	800	713	771	114	715	817
Richland	39	786	440	174	109	—	321	281	—	289	322	—	Unorganized	
Rock Island	1439	1114	276	764	686	96	583	481	96	466	397	—	426	224
Saline	4	1004	229	209	633	—	122	312	—	Unorganized.				
Sangamon	1174	2475	1612	2125	1606	22	1943	1336	47	1837	1371	—	2000	1249
Schuyler	388	1369	570	844	980	16	807	804	34	610	743	—	732	611
Scott	183	843	536	730	708	8	798	649	15	670	610	7	685	575

ILLINOIS—(Continued).

COUNTIES.	1856.			1852.			1848.			1844.			1840.	
	Rep. Frem't	Dem. Buc'an	Am. Fill're.	Whig. Scott.	Dem. Pierce.	F. Soil. Hale.	Whig. Taylor.	Dem. Cass.	Free D. Van B.	Whig. Clay.	Dem. Polk.	Abo. Birney	Whig. Ha'son	Dem. Van B
Shelby	152	1414	451	446	958	—	337	658	1	815	683	—	408	751
Stark	718	358	152	836	350	82	214	174	84	187	206	33	187	154
St. Clair	1996	1728	973	998	2571	—	1109	2023	63	1042	1945	7	989	1783
Stephenson	1907	1308	50	976	1061	170	780	763	111	488	465	24	371	241
Tazewell	1028	1313	757	1369	869	80	1097	593	96	1011	628	33	1181	661
Union	46	1283	246	169	830	1	108	503	6	94	617	—	78	636
Vermilion	1506	1111	194	997	761	86	942	758	68	869	768	28	1044	587
Wabash	122	481	485	469	355	—	456	303	14	479	315	2	509	254
Warren	1282	1117	307	806	781	158	537	529	140	500	503	35	711	524
Washington	244	1132	283	251	763	28	204	577	27	254	565	8	149	493
Wayne	129	1218	402	359	757	1	318	479	1	265	687	—	205	500
White	27	1062	845	749	782	—	674	513	13	736	748	—	770	639
Whiteside	1902	618	210	554	518	151	391	235	279	384	289	47	375	236
Will	2393	1575	10	1251	1450	820	713	897	540	509	810	209	753	1367
Williamson	10	1419	188	344	799	—	211	575	—	179	766	179	103	578
Winnebago	3636	457	61	1023	820	725	866	240	807	546	368	152	789	321
Woodford	596	747	189	339	635	49	186	309	52	159	322	8	Unorganized	
Total	96189	105348	37444	64934	80597	9966	53047	56300	15774	45528	57920	3570	45537	47476

Buchanan over Fremont, 9,159; Pierce over Scott, 15,663; Cass over Taylor, 3,253; Polk over Clay, 12,392; Van Buren over Harrison, 1,989. In 1840, Mr. Birney received 149 votes.

MICHIGAN.

COUNTIES.	1856.			1852.			1848.			1844.			1840.	
	Rep. rem't	Dem. Buc'an	Am. Fill're.	Whig. Scott.	Dem. Pierce.	F. Soil. Hale.	Whig. Taylor.	Dem. Cass.	Free D. Van B.	Whig. Clay.	Dem. Polk.	Abo. Birney	Whig. Ha'son	Dem. an B.
Allegan	1526	1027	29	547	582	66	274	304	174	328	299	11	257	174
Barry	1495	872	49	478	652	107	243	881	93	228	249	16	128	105
Berrien	1926	1540	182	1017	1234	41	958	1147	108	713	828	85	549	543
Branch	2608	1322	14	1077	1380	202	665	1084	400	644	888	89	543	616
Calhoun	3495	2151	122	1784	1824	440	1254	1487	745	1357	1528	226	1143	1169
Cass	1703	1165	41	987	984	95	788	902	191	760	715	59	670	527
Cheboygan	No return			Unorganized										
Chippewa	No return			No return			51	48	—	54	40	—	22	40
Clinton	1858	1034	14	470	437	146	213	340	131	255	283	19	221	144
Eaton	1888	1228	15	687	786	225	356	546	218	410	376	61	337	229
Emmet	No return			Unorganized										
Genesee	2635	1588	110	1221	1145	301	876	828	315	783	676	188	512	880
Grand Traverse	157	243	2	Unorganized										
Gratiot	388	136	—	Unorganized										
Hillsdale	3446	1408	87	1417	1596	391	1027	1290	482	958	1084	212	843	721
Houghton	201	398	1	No return			Unorganized							
Huron	No return			Unorganized										
Ingham	1849	1534	25	786	992	128	478	692	382	432	441	45	254	261
Ionia	2002	1154	22	659	864	302	379	608	477	418	398	59	266	219
Jackson	2996	2118	46	1727	1840	484	969	1547	1072	1302	1389	475	1504	1121
Kalamazoo	2803	1620	50	1374	1257	411	1010	880	498	982	828	276	954	744
Kent	2931	2516	93	1221	1519	166	652	768	387	476	564	83	319	820
Lapeer	1579	995	31	618	819	142	869	542	205	399	502	88	491	413
Lenawee	4499	2779	167	2419	2857	640	1886	2171	795	2177	2272	228	2118	1865
Livingston	1765	1711	18	931	1419	133	764	1128	280	687	1080	108	700	842
Mackinac	No return			38	292	—	51	127	—	43	100	—		
Macomb	2210	1845	80	1058	1634	509	855	1340	204	963	1359	140	982	1124
Manistee	No return			Unorganized										
Marquette	79	77	20	No return			Unorganized							
Mason	32	12	—	Unorganized										
Midland	169	43	2	Unorganized										
Monroe	1777	1708	34	1112	1582	169	800	1155	398	870	1283	48	939	1023
Montcalm	414	265	7	120	156	6	Unorganized							
Newago	No return			40	104	—	Unorganized							
Oakland	4105	3276	71	2876	3178	552	1942	2781	698	2225	2833	877	2372	2366
Oceana	82	21	—	Unorganized										
Ontonagon	No return			Unorganized										
Ottowa	1392	998	39	863	756	59	142	269	58	42 m		17	81	88
Saginaw	1042	1222	17	867	694	·73	118	183	47	107	104	—	89	100
Sanilac	803	201	1	106	252	—	Unorganized							
Schoolcraft	No return			Unorganized										
Shiawassee	1304	1105	86	519	584	52	281	426	192	300	269	96	283	151
St. Clair	1807	1521	21	852	1110	53	665	818	82	569	617	—	517	446
St. Joseph	2324	1475	12	1164	1259	252	963	1011	418	935	978	84	800	761
Tuscola	442	242	4	80	62	34	Unorganized							
Van Buren	1710	1031	34	613	771	87	353	509	117	273	350	46	182	251
Washtenaw	3570	2833	109	2274	2604	603	2029	2081	917	2347	2549	386	2526	2057
Wayne	5250	5777	205	3407	4680	868	2544	3308	420	2345	2737	192	2246	2237
Total	71762	52136	1660	33859	41842	7237	23940	30687	10389	24337	27759	3632	22933	21131

Fremont over Buchanan, 19,626; Pierce over Scott, 7,983; Cass over Taylor, 6,747; Polk over Clay, 3422; Harrison over Van Buren, 1,802. Mr. Birney received 321 votes in 1840.

INDIANA.

COUNTIES.	1856.			1852.			1848.			1844.			1840.	
	Rep. Frem't	Dem. Buc'an	Am. Fill're	Whig. Scott.	Dem. Pierce.	F. Soil. Hale.	Whig. Taylor.	Dem. Cass.	Free D. Van B.	Whig. Clay.	Dem. Polk.	Abo. Birney.	Whig. Ha'son	Dem. Van B.
Adams	413	847	69	362	672	14	261	398	1	198	296	—	193	153
Allen	1593	3211	145	1225	1964	24	991	1059	13	861	849	—	640	399
Bartholomew	1292	1844	142	1245	1512	26	1011	1167	28	1035	1068	13	982	703
Benton	315	217	8	110	138	19	60	78	3	40	69	1	26	42
Blackford	238	404	47	108	263	15	61	231	28	81	205	8	77	147
Boone	1299	1493	81	936	1161	109	773	916	66	816	871	8	700	686
Brown	148	681	90	102	532	—	70	503	—	59	432	—	50	270
Carroll	1261	1344	22	1075	1256	29	822	1008	76	712	965	8	699	765
Cass	1504	1539	40	1176	1190	50	881	829	55	768	671	18	649	872
Clark	492	1950	1074	1186	1812	24	1200	1510	28	1132	1417	—	1132	1278
Clay	365	1108	296	474	743	8	500	734	29	429	662	—	398	487
Clinton	1261	1364	34	929	1250	75	726	964	87	645	944	12	582	698
Crawford	24	735	509	502	499	—	520	397	—	462	397	—	435	281
Daviess	26	1115	939	726	720	6	735	701	2	807	764	—	738	509
Dearborn	1573	2619	297	1474	2486	89	1378	1801	176	1616	1971	50	1771	1583
Decatur	1718	1689	61	1364	1394	138	1245	1096	143	1275	1091	68	1298	759
De Kalb	1097	1247	75	391	780	164	847	577	45	269	327	6	177	168
Delaware	1736	992	32	1083	937	11	822	694	58	940	732	3	920	532
Dubois	21	1191	236	229	717	—	258	579	1	229	501	—	264	239
Elkhart	1971	1651	18	1068	1343	28	756	1050	142	758	964	1	640	596
Fayette	1189	1002	40	1019	872	80	1040	765	86	1051	908	17	1090	728
Floyd	228	1767	1262	1328	1815	1	1018	1154	17	956	981	—	869	796
Fountain	1606	1588	36	1023	1496	64	900	1343	138	947	1387	—	938	1166
Franklin	1437	2259	41	1473	1956	30	1411	1695	51	1325	1583	8	1188	1115
Fulton	822	835	9	559	581	6	423	404	39	344	308	6	241	108
Gibson	365	1286	766	942	1127	20	860	802	15	796	810	8	788	594
Grant	1395	1035	99	599	836	345	325	623	359	358	423	197	470	364
Greene	379	1129	583	884	944	4	918	921	6	762	909	—	704	634
Hamilton	1748	1185	88	971	901	401	809	805	317	859	766	139	972	688
Hancock	962	1343	24	823	1002	40	665	806	40	719	736	2	721	537
Harrison	873	1681	623	1284	1278	—	1277	1047	1	1252	1144	—	1285	861
Hendricks	1680	1378	74	1252	980	156	1158	775	173	1262	844	26	1190	652
Henry	2741	1229	49	1559	1226	456	1215	1005	455	1458	1005	188	1652	839
Howard	1057	686	83	539	526	165	Unorganized.			277	316	8	143	177
Huntington	1232	1181	58	706	888	88	457	463	46	277	316	8	143	177
Jackson	299	1700	516	614	1188	—	632	1071	7	662	1048		680	737
Jasper	633	548	63	857	847	33	86	190	128	128	175	8	73	95
Jay	883	880	54	875	500	135	276	392	142	331	352	32	283	265
Jefferson	2314	1936	425	2016	2201	286	2075	1609	167	1835	1427	50	1674	1026
Jennings	1293	1159	172	998	1104	59	926	784	96	872	669	4	908	503
Johnson	1095	1608	153	896	1333	20	676	1114	46	659	1150	15	631	948
Knox	557	1512	535	1167	1003	—	1044	741	3	1079	821	1	1077	658
Kosciusko	1662	1075	13	1045	938	26	797	676	64	623	553	5	496	329
La Grange	1406	640	6	667	677	117	629	636	114	590	457	88	391	225
Lake	923	846	8	236	834	58	138	208	189	114	206	5	115	125
Laporte	2532	2239	45	1357	1468	136	1027	877	226	1009	831	53	1069	640
Lawrence	480	1126	660	1054	1113	14	1070	1031	18	1019	1085	3	989	898
Madison	1309	1603	54	1004	1282	83	824	993	55	813	854	20	911	625
Marion	3696	8738	205	2158	2599	110	1877	1789	109	1715	1634	25	1636	1279
Marshall	927	1039	—	843	511	56	305	428	91	199	256	54	154	194
Martin	76	769	850	877	519	5	342	497	7	76	516	—	311	866
Miami	1390	1513	88	994	1196	76	731	770	70	569	517	—	812	244
Monroe	498	1191	892	622	1085	87	780	1084	59	721	1118	12	719	943
Montgomery	1910	2088	142	1559	1852	100	1501	1547	109	1450	1521	8	1413	1222
Morgan	1573	1528	68	1109	1181	132	986	1029	121	1023	1078	24	1012	815
Noble	1257	1198	48	606	807	79	497	618	58	890	438	—	241	228
Ohio	104	505	379	432	455	2	439	459	6	193	168	—	Unorganized	
Orange	49	1207	606	747	1022	3	760	961	6	707	1036	8	708	879
Owen	487	1239	586	901	1060	20	882	953	18	754	888	1	560	221
Parke	1494	1283	192	1312	1084	105	1398	1319	9	1377	1329	12	1360	948
Perry	96	1066	632	684	659	3	599	335	8	564	334	—	560	221
Pike	80	772	574	538	688	1	519	510	1	459	491	—	474	318
Porter	847	614	10	444	527	88	343	401	7	311	305	14	220	194
Posey	306	1819	625	784	1433	26	763	1226	19	678	1154	—	706	965
Pulaski	341	557	27	210	383	1	135	224	1	123	124		51	60
Putnam	1345	1882	423	1712	1466	22	1647	1300	10	1540	1867		1571	1049
Randolph	2042	1253	59	900	993	330	631	787	523	818	809	266	1068	553
Ripley	1425	1661	184	1119	1386	13	1114	988	173	1060	908	89	1000	628
Rush	1644	1685	83	1507	1480	119	1142	1392	87	1580	1362	42	1526	1170
Scott	278	693	264	518	559	11	488	447	16	481	441	1	399	361
Shelby	1510	2075	142	1286	1627	27	1121	1414	18	1107	1342	7	1016	1070
Spencer	235	1260	808	685	710	1	681	471	—	586	496	—	589	824
Starke	112	155	7	66	122	—	Unorganized.							
Steuben	1215	553	19	487	543	90	815	352	194	828	303	42	238	176
St. Joseph	1812	1509	6	998	1052	174	817	667	332	● 863	683	83	809	444
Sullivan	257	1650	397	529	1203	—	465	1142	5	464	1221	1	417	1014
Switzerland	228	1121	1040	1134	1147	7	1093	1106	44	961	1006	8	1023	735
Tippecanoe	2778	2307	45	1918	2446	143	1269	1523	405	1550	1551	37	1508	1200
Tipton	546	738	14	340	461	7	183	235	3	100	119	—	Unorganized	
Union	763	710	19	584	626	149	526	637	208	682	672	60	760	614
Vanderburgh	372	1880	840	945	1817	6	534	667	22	675	556	1	628	370
Vermillion	866	824	80	852	788	4	830	763	—	787	762	—	847	668
Vigo	1165	1808	883	1694	1155	8	1585	852	57	1515	856	—	1511	588

INDIANA—(Continued.)

COUNTIES.	1856.			1852.			1848.			1844.			1840.	
	Rep. Frem't	Dem. Buc'an	Am. Fill're.	Whig. Scott.	Dem. Pierce.	F. Soil. Hale.	Whig. Taylor.	Dem. Cass.	Free D. Van B.	Whig. Clay.	Dem. Polk.	Abo. Birney.	Whig. Ha'son	Dem. Van B.
Wabash	1785	1096	108	1145	959	91	847	739	140	601	575	19	807	198
Warren	1167	767	76	850	552	56	708	460	68	779	470	10	737	347
Warrick	107	1506	480	487	1634	31	457	862	21	394	850	—	355	662
Washington	331	1778	691	1093	1613	11	1126	1643	22	1149	1660	5	1138	1381
Wayne	3688	1958	100	2304	1874	786	2085	1432	839	2321	1436	318	2869	1253
Wells	726	931	16	415	710	23	252	416	18	185	306	3	131	140
White	703	746	42	510	536	13	206	805	84	259	218	—	206	144
Whitley	797	851	57	497	568	11	818	873	21	222	287	2	144	141
Total	94375	118670	22386	80901	95340	6929	69907	74745	8100	67867	70131	2106	65302	51604

Buchanan over Fremont, 24,295; Pierce over Scott, 14,439; Cass over Taylor, 4,838; Polk over Clay, 2,264; Harrison over Van Buren, 13,698.

CONNECTICUT.

COUNTIES.	Rep. Frem't	Dem. Buc'an	Am. Fill're.	Whig. Scott.	Dem. Pierce.	F. Soil. Hale.	Whig. Taylor.	Dem. Cass.	Free D. Van B.	Whig. Clay.	Dem. Polk.	Abo. Birney.	Whig. Ha'son	Dem. Van B.
Fairfield	6233	5589	928	4814	5155	167	5036	4064	462	5368	4599	142	4871	3862
Hartford	8416	7037	309	6329	6639	461	6000	5345	810	6259	5624	287	6216	4496
Litchfield	5481	3986	150	3946	4082	413	3918	3674	800	4668	4335	368	4542	3806
Middlesex	2887	2964	183	2065	2734	238	2136	2152	361	2324	2345	130	2276	2275
New Haven	7976	7315	604	6046	6097	424	5273	4516	806	5546	4726	229	5100	4012
New London	5402	3953	350	3361	4079	637	4020	3421	776	4081	3709	304	3815	3148
Tolland	2407	1953	35	1708	2015	202	1665	1612	191	1964	1950	120	1991	1509
Windham	3913	2248	56	2095	2448	618	2266	2262	799	2620	2544	363	2790	2188
Total	42715	34995	2615	30359	33249	3160	30314	27046	5005	32832	29841	1943	31601	25296

Fremont over Buchanan, 7,720; Pierce over Scott, 2,890; Taylor over Cass, 3,268; Clay over Polk, 2,991; Harrison over Van Buren, 6,305. Mr. Birney received 174 votes in 1840.

PENNSYLVANIA.

COUNTIES.	Rep. Frem't	Dem. Buc'an	Am. Fill're.	Whig. Scott.	Dem. Pierce.	F. Soil. Hale.	Whig. Taylor.	Dem. Cass.	Free D. Van B.	Whig. Clay.	Dem. Polk.	Abo. Birney.	Whig. Ha'son	Dem. Van B
Adams	1120	2637	1249	2725	2018	31	2576	1762	25	2609	1891	6	2453	1628
Allegheny	13671	9062	1488	9615	7226	965	10112	6591	779	8083	5743	435	7619	4573
Armstrong	2963	2680	188	2093	2430	142	2080	2126	141	1453	1983	38	1260	1744
Beaver	2658	1905	236	1805	1943	361	2655	2803	530	2792	2172	270	3143	1710
Bedford	306	2458	1936	2278	2319	—	2836	2816	1	3147	2989	5	2910	2446
Berks	1037	11272	3586	4913	9503	5	5082	9484	51	4000	8674	8	3582	7425
Blair	445	2069	2450	2590	1931	5	2476	1435	4	With	Hunti	ngdon		
Bradford	6938	2314	101	3526	3930	281	3272	1889	1780	3235	3568	63	2631	2844
Bucks	4682	6517	735	4928	5766	58	5140	5364	163	4862	5251	27	4705	4488
Butler	3401	2648	67	2833	2533	166	2505	2247	173	2247	2112	135	2100	1804
Cambria	804	2987	968	1461	2035	15	1233	1386	12	996	1123	2	811	920
Carbon	692	1866	465	749	1311	—	889	1181	1	531	905	—	Unorg	anized
Centre	390	2895	1952	1916	2993	—	1856	2611	4	1860	2425	7	1448	2242
Chester	5308	6333	1448	5700	5520	838	5949	5360	507	6070	5550	106	5642	4882
Clarion	788	2760	950	1218	2642	28	1372	2306	37	814	1883	7	648	1366
Clairfield	718	1978	604	997	1733	24	761	1168	28	544	874	—	499	812
Clinton	618	1485	682	996	1318	2	911	967	1	788	875	—	638	649
Columbia	1239	2889	219	1165	2102	—	2263	3396	29	1738	3370	1	1325	2829
Crawford	5360	3391	45	2775	3427	996	2204	2748	621	2636	3334	189	2469	2908
Cumberland	1472	3427	1579	2878	3188	—	3242	3178	25	3092	3155	5	2791	2695
Dauphin	1615	3094	2439	3673	2675	29	3705	2254	34	3285	2401	16	3124	2187
Delaware	1590	2005	1010	2083	1737	107	2194	1547	84	2090	1466	15	2081	1335
Elk	275	575	52	163	423	14	134	242	16	101	128	9	Unorg	anized
Erie	5156	2584	289	4015	2738	611	3418	2022	357	3621	2226	74	3636	2061
Fayette	2089	3554	1174	3030	3867	—	3045	3441	73	2804	3429	35	2755	3035
Franklin	2446	3469	1233	3904	3358	8	4006	8199	4	3901	3298	—	3586	2892
Fulton	142	970	566	729	831	1	Un	organi	zed.					
Greene	1321	2747	286	1559	2602	30	1476	2379	52	1418	2354	18	1350	2010
Huntingdon	926	2164	1645	2511	2041	2	2590	1922	25	4086	2575	—	3826	2266
Indiana	3612	1762	263	2387	1827	279	2410	1544	204	2200	1448	80	1953	1209
Jefferson	1068	1463	615	1115	1484	22	887	992	19	591	731	5	476	592
Juniata	480	1365	747	559	823	—	850	856	1	1089	1262	—	966	1043
Lancaster	6608	8781	4592	11636	6578	53	11390	6080	163	10295	5943	21	9678	5740
Lawrence	3065	1220	96	1984	1064	514	With	Beav	er and	Merc	er.			
Lebanon	2414	2511	437	3105	2118	1	2996	1862	2	2636	1791	—	2370	1402
Lehigh	3237	4426	122	2993	3493	2	2978	3199	8	2553	2811	—	2405	2450
Luzerne	4850	6791	868	3339	5340	79	3516	3991	176	2699	3950	29	2776	4119
Lycoming	934	3324	1770	2085	2790	5	1992	2244	9	2012	2629	19	1504	2181
McKean	812	526	47	405	597	78	367	418	22	340	419	—	263	276

PENNSYLVANIA—(Continued).

COUNTIES.	1856.			1852.			1848.			1844.			1840.	
	Rep. Frem't	*Dem.* Buc'an	*Am.* Fill're.	*Whig.* Scott.	*Dem.* Pierce.	*F. Soil.* Hale.	*Whig.* Taylor.	*Dem.* Cass.	*Free D.* Van B.	*Whig.* Clay.	*Dem.* Polk.	*Abo.* Birney	*Whig.* Ha'son	*Dem.* Van
Mercer.........	3686	2699	118	2211	2693	769	2977	3094	1080	2840	2869	604	3247	2336
Mifflin.........	216	1491	1050	1392	1620	—	1543	1586	26	1518	1519	9	1226	1269
Monroe	560	2275	69	418	2098	—	518	1830	3	414	1806	1	345	1447
Montgomery ...	2845	7134	2265	4791	5767	160	5040	5627	251	4491	5596	49	4068	4869
Montour	666	1271	149	866	1455	—	With Columbia.							
Northampton ..	1168	5260	1838	2978	4403	16	3191	4203	38	2776	3870	—	2846	3838
Northumberland	566	3059	1340	1619	2451	4	1765	2258	8	1547	2446	7	1351	2187
Perry..........	521	2135	1407	1413	2159	—	1562	2295	5	1370	2321	—	072	1970
Philadelphia....	7993	38222	24084	24566	26022	626	31229	21508	877	23289	18851	228	17844	18077
Pike	270	862	15	202	834	—	216	799	3	151	769	—	135	524
Potter.........	1264	667	6	263	661	325	226	468	248	240	554	50	180	868
Schuylkill	2188	7085	2682	4128	4758	10	4808	3490	35	2571	3404	3	881	2184
Somerset	1458	1763	1405	2986	1203	28	3018	1127	21	2660	1035	6	2501	765
Snyder	443	1255	1064	Unorganized.										
Susquehanna...	8861	2548	51	2035	3046	215	1853	2563	301	1802	2697	93	1560	2022
Sullivan........	309	538	48	177	426	59	129	303	19	Unorganized.				
Tioga	4541	1386	27	1564	2614	79	1264	1344	1039	1159	2193	23	895	1721
Union..........	1429	1092	186	3081	1994	—	3129	1656	25	2788	1765	18	2423	1518
Venango	2041	2157	72	1164	1899	204	1061	1588	164	966	1877	65	855	1276
Warren	2091	1231	49	1138	1433	243	948	1088	136	899	1149	17	827	929
Washington ...	4237	4288	265	3810	4064	370	3898	3820	468	3872	3973	296	4149	3611
Wayne	2172	2259	113	1232	2362	21	997	1642	202	899	1657	15	675	1188
Westmoreland .	4091	5172	299	3203	5509	119	3124	5197	122	2672	4978	71	2778	4704
Wyoming......	1138	1171	74	807	1258	19	861	892	37	814	899	1	Unorganized	
York	511	6876	4301	4700	5585	11	4838	5151	4	4237	5071	1	3792	4382
Total........	147510	230710	82175	179174	198568	8525	185513	171176	11263	161203	167535	8138	144021	143672

Buchanan over Fremont, 83,200; do. over Fremont and Fillmore, 1,025; Pierce over Scott, 19,394; Taylor over Cass, 14,337; Polk over Clay, 6,332 ; Harrison over Van Buren, 349. Mr. Birney received 843 votes in 1840.

MARYLAND.

COUNTIES.	*Am.* Fill're.	*Dem.* Buc'an	*Rep.* Frem't	*Whig.* Scott.	*Dem.* Pierce.	*F. Soil.* Hale.	*Whig.* Taylor.	*Dem.* Cass.	*Free D.* Van B.	*Whig.* Clay.	*Dem.* Polk.	*Abo.* Birney	*Whig.* Ha'son	*Dem.* Van
Alleghany	1938	2248	......	1454	1976	......	1579	1620	......	1424	1491	......	1271	1093
Anne Arundel..	1043	927	......	834	889	......	1693	1486	......	1777	1503	......	604	1384
Baltimore City.	16900	9882	......	9558	14035	......	10474	10995	......	8413	8866	......	7296	7326
Baltimore Co...	3504	3155	......	1946	3001	......	2527	2669	......	2301	2716	......	1941	2626
Calvert........	401	356	......	353	352	......	431	335	......	451	344	......	494	325
Caroline	638	743	......	555	500	......	492	580	......	680	552	......	687	535
Carroll	2346	2099	......	1702	1920	......	1763	1672	......	1784	1694	......	1554	610
Cecil	1884	1845	......	1494	1550	......	1504	1444	......	1527	1504	......	1448	1314
Charles........	461	758	......	657	411	......	769	398	......	785	519	......	841	502
Dorchester	1292	979	......	1239	933	......	1367	820	......	1377	903	......	1381	839
Frederick......	3724	3304	......	3204	3342	......	3158	2983	......	3190	2994	......	2958	2623
Harford	2074	1405	......	1353	1378	......	1521	1253	......	1517	1247	......	1842	1243
Howard	899	683	......	570	625	......	With Anne Arundel.						679	476
Kent...........	833	550	......	662	551	......	645	447	......	728	527	......	679	476
Montgomery...	1208	1126	......	1061	842	......	1057	771	......	1124	852	......	099	665
Prince George..	881	983	......	915	724	......	1051	733	......	1054	666	......	017	609
Queen Anne's..	904	741	......	723	735	......	725	612	......	749	722	......	778	661
Somerset	1593	1321	......	1443	1115	......	1413	1005	......	1449	902	......	1516	844
St. Mary's.....	247	1052	......	681	440	......	788	422	......	783	468	... ...	895	415
Talbot	749	910	......	740	796	......	706	719	......	795	712	......	49	682
Washington ...	2717	2670	......	2669	2728	......	2688	2434	......	2633	2565	......	2484	2290
Worcester	1224	1428	......	1253	1182	......	1351	1130	......	1453	909	......	1494	691
Total	47460	39115	281	35066	40020	54	37702	34528	125	35984	32676	......	33528	28752

Fillmore over Buchanan, 8,345; Pierce over Scott, 4,954; Taylor over Cass, 3,174; Clay over Polk, 3,308; Harrison over Van Buren, 4,776.

DELAWARE.

COUNTIES.	*Rep.* Fill're.	*Dem.* Buc'an	*Am.* Frem't	*Whig.* Scott.	*Dem.* Pierce.	*F. Soil.* Hale.	*Whig.* Taylor.	*Dem.* Cass.	*Free D.* Van B.	*Whig.* Clay.	*Dem.* Polk.	*Abo.* Birney.	*Whig.* Ha'son	*Dem.* Van B.
Kent...........	1580	2083	—	1591	1422	—	1497	1336	1	1578	1416	—	1598	1096
Newcastle	2625	3577	—	2768	3038	62	3090	2717	79	2816	2678	—	2321	2195
Sussex	2020	2344	—	1934	1858	—	1834	1845	—	1869	1877	—	2053	1593
Total........	6175	8004	380	6293	6318	62	6421	5898	80	6258	5971	—	5967	4884

Buchanan over Fillmore, 1,829; Pierce over Scott, 25; Taylor over Cass, 523; Clay over Polk, 287; Harrison over Van Buren, 1,083.

SOUTH CAROLINA CHOOSES ELECTORS BY LEGISLATURE.

GEORGIA.

COUNTIES.	1856. Am. Fillmore.	1856. Dem. Buch'an.	1852. Whig. Scott.	1852. Dem. Pierce.	1848. Whig. Taylor.	1848. Dem. Cass.	1844. Whig. Clay.	1844. Dem. Polk.	1840. Whig. Harrison.	1840. Dem. Van B.
Appling	96	268	13	77	144	108	152	142	98	61
Baker	175	453	101	630	341	634	223	506	182	204
Baldwin	266	800	177	272	382	322	324	307	731	530
Berrien	79	220	Unorganized.							
Bibb	774	959	318	780	705	805	706	862	758	748
Bryan	94	133	60	66	123	60	103	72	80	22
Bulloch	34	460		m. 287	43	877	17	410	25	384
Burke	183	940	15	177	598	215	556	411	593	203
Butts	283	387	11	434	269	420	244	435	185	389
Calhoun	56	251	Unorganized.							
Camden	28	186	31	211	106	220	104	218	166	191
Campbell	448	754	158	338	281	582	205	543	163	427
Carroll	455	1176	185	850	475	834	855	768	276	437
Catoosa	346	365	Unorganized.							
Cass	751	1205	263	654	988	1513	655	1189	561	705
Coffee	16	16	Unorganized.							
Chatham	971	1445	305	1175	843	741	817	835	590	647
Chattahoochee	231	320	Unorganized.							
Chattooga	386	506	114	316	402	398	284	324	186	201
Cherokee	566	1146	81	660	660	983	517	813	869	416
Charlton	38	129	Unorganized.							
Clarke	603	487	139	226	624	495	596	420	617	318
Clay	188	279	Unorganized.							
Clinch	137	171	4	48	Unorganized.					
Cobb	764	1251	307	975	862	1261	658	943	428	658
Colquitt	75	106	Unorganized.							
Columbia	342	456	110	259	519	250	492	807	470	223
Coweta	584	882	215	650	822	662	777	644	792	768
Crawford	228	378	161	367	402	434	377	454	435	458
Decatur	454	396	220	295	498	850	383	346	432	203
De Kalb	458	665	565	1016	799	1097	580	967	665	759
Dade	155	240	65	126	102	258	46	247	38	168
Doherty	197	266	Unorganized.							
Dooley	200	419	175	474	349	571	269	507	226	296
Early	149	299	129	874	200	505	211	419	258	298
Effingham	189	171	18	64	183	99	193	86	158	55
Elbert	854	524	159	107	991	161	999	186	957	105
Emanuel	259	273	5	174	155	207	107	241	80	118
Fannin	152	571	Unorganized.							
Fayette	455	734	267	582	521	717	412	705	837	542
Floyd	812	847	367	494	680	673	850	425	275	267
Forsyth	458	798	106	589	629	747	451	735	348	457
Franklin	183	972	66	435	363	965	376	1058	353	581
Fulton	911	832	Unorganized.							
Gilmer	191	820	116	309	402	855	219	511	127	164
Glynn	91	119	29	40	132	22	92	23	88	14
Gordon	593	890	264	584	Unorganized.					
Greene	576	288	311	172	827	139	780	132	889	126
Gwinnett	749	1092	61	427	745	635	779	763	745	624
Habersham	256	858	98	59	425	778	322	964	290	761
Hall	451	696	64	186	521	664	489	696	445	504
Hancock	427	306	No	Return.	478	283	515	830	481	240
Haralson	66	272	Unorganized.							
Harris	753	528	468	339	870	403	845	463	853	292
Hart	152	610	Unorganized.							
Heard	418	516	258	410	415	473	293	436	815	352
Henry	759	591	428	526	939	824	858	819	931	793
Houston	576	604	273	503	697	674	659	723	667	572
Irwin	80	155	12	192	86	355	21	223	59	121
Jackson	453	773	45	103	561	688	492	664	572	542
Jasper	382	418	132	872	409	512	438	536	495	495
Jefferson	876	353	91	93	607	111	579	108	458	89
Jones	135	808	166	840	404	415	397	455	461	852
Laurens	406	70	67	63	567	25	686	15	556	4
Lee	229	250	189	223	323	181	335	121	304	77
Liberty	133	191	58	133	171	132	179	190	144	78
Lincoln	212	219	18	155	238	120	286	179	317	123
Lowndes	292	443	22	290	507	397	427	362	422	90
Lumpkin	468	736	178	235	652	1097	665	1254	355	786
Macon	385	274	296	386	888	271	831	245	369	808
Madison	215	415	28	69	336	826	347	827	357	286
Marion	495	494	351	425	510	477	517	256	404	193
McIntosh	49	155	16	90	117	98	127	114	119	135
Merriwether	648	703	823	634	717	768	688	926	755	702
Miller	20	153	Unorganized.							
Monroe	656	505	879	631	791	664	798	708	796	675
Montgomery	201	26	14	35	231	24	238	34	167	8
Morgan	268	234	189	286	467	300	442	848	478	280
Murray	240	567	237	323	799	1072	303	669	273	452
Muscogee	933	710	651	875	1330	856	1190	980	1044	811

GEORGIA—(Continued.)

COUNTIES.	Am. Fillmore.	Dem. Buch'an.	Whig. Scott.	Dem. Pierce.	Whig. Taylor.	Dem. Cass.	Whig. Clay.	Dem. Polk.	Whig. Harrison.	Dem. Van B.
Newton	910	844	836	886	1045	502	1025	553	988	851
Oglethorpe	394	451	60	179	636	193	626	241	654	127
Paulding	191	776	44	327	852	420	218	394	227	207
Pike	491	630	184	509	828	892	659	877	560	624
Pickens	198	425	Unorganized.							
Pulaski	240	417	83	231	820	423	247	457	241	275
Putnam	294	353	229	284	399	294	430	351	468	310
Polk	371	259	119	147	Unorganized.					
Rabun	72	407	4	144	55	207	34	253	80	212
Randolph	450	656	362	677	780	724	606	735	509	519
Richmond	1143	890	411	625	908	595	908	647	939	407
Scriven	167	268	8	171	265	223	256	278	180	199
Stewart	598	558	326	491	926	686	892	813	882	639
Sumpter	855	701	325	452	733	587	650	444	449	176
Spaulding	540	545	356	377	Unorganized.					
Talbot	547	442	430	441	819	738	855	912	912	807
Taliaferro	109	238	19	76	388	55	394	67	431	47
Tatnall	186	191	121	55	361	44	338	64	253	28
Telfair	121	110	47	88	160	150	177	198	203	53
Tirrell	313	233	Unorganized.							
Thomas	333	463	89	259	526	250	848	267	426	60
Taylor	312	429	105	264	Unorganized.					
Towns	60	265	Unorganized.							
Troup	1005	412	596	422	1122	384	1055	487	1071	830
Twiggs	178	287	118	267	831	414	889	467	411	373
Union	261	454	97	223	412	641	237	554	107	360
Upson	617	305	355	338	657	344	643	384	632	293
Walker	565	824	372	786	784	965	447	686	387	541
Walton	460	684	111	399	544	741	555	763	516	619
Ware	6	125	1	36	193	161	187	125	215	85
Warren	250	589	25	306	614	360	641	368	552	243
Washington	699	564	236	451	692	626	629	595	593	453
Wayne	39	131	10	65	58	69	138	95	74	51
Webster	263	213	Unorganized.							
Wilkes	279	428	12	193	452	293	430	389	438	352
Wilkinson	282	531	94	502	473	498	387	560	428	474
Whitfield	598	733	293	644	Unorganized.					
Worth	83	227	Unorganized.							
Total	42228	56578	16660	34705	47544	44802	42100	44177	40261	31921

Buchanan over Fillmore, 14,350; Pierce over Scott, 18,045; Taylor over Cass, 2,742; Polk over Clay, 2,077; Harrison over Van Buren, 8,340. In 1852 a Webster Ticket received 5324, and an Independent Pierce Ticket, 5,811.

VIRGINIA.

COUNTIES.	Am. Fillmore.	Dem. Buch'an.	Whig. Scott.	Dem. Pierce.	Whig. Taylor.	Dem. Cass.	Whig. Clay.	Dem. Polk.	Whig. Harrison.	Dem Van B
Accomac	830	821	576	564	544	295	566	472	739	239
Albemarle	1026	1092	1163	1106	833	619	917	702	714	517
Alexandria	946	677	784	577	539	225	Part of	Dist. C.		
Alleghany	183	383	93	206	104	149	114	180	84	171
Amelia	150	276	145	237	163	198	159	274	166	240
Amherst	449	683	450	559	416	418	451	461	372	329
Appomattox	152	431	192	352	190	322	Unorganized.			
Augusta	1904	1499	1664	1388	1354	723	1398	665	1204	4
Barbour	825	938	324	592	287	484	221	468		
Bath	180	258	157	179	152	124	196	250	203	218
Bedford	1044	1015	1189	965	886	534	941	639	919	558
Berkley	846	997	751	924	608	544	663	539	599	372
Boone	113	273	117	212	68	128	Unorganized.			
Botetourt	341	904	421	738	462	683	394	695	407	5
Braxton	494	260	887	290	73 m aj.		186	156	With Lewis.	
Brooke	261	451	281	460	227	276	427	543	350	5
Brunswick	131	566	187	462	213	337	194	408	261	8
Buckingham	320	463	438	530	844	361	548	596	475	5
Cabell	396	598	451	424	287	233	287	846	481	4
Calhoun	27	116	Unorganized.							
Campbell	1065	896	1101	879	794	554	833	656	718	487
Caroline	414	517	443	621	867	425	476	463	899	467
Carroll	260	687	213	488	179	267	121	268	Unorganized.	
Charles City	190	106	176	89	142	58	202	43	173	
Charlotte	247	463	337	369	290	303	337	846	818	8
Chesterfield	850	845	409	854	296	505	838	604	298	5
Clarke	225	404	863	886	209	201	199	220	174	1
Craig	108	850	92	238	Unorganized.					
Culpepper	430	512	447	461	354	818	896	298	351	295
Cumberland	184	274	256	252	235	162	274	207	262	228
Dinwiddie	140	851	819	304	282	228	270	818	302	285

VIRGINIA—(Continued.)

COUNTIES.	1856. Am. Fillmore.	1856. Dem. Buch'an.	1852. Whig. Scott.	1852. Dem. Pierce.	1848. Whig. Taylor.	1848. Dem. Cass.	1844. Whig. Clay.	1844. Dem. Polk.	1840. Whig. Harrison.	1840. Dem. an B.
Doddridge	178	441	86	285 maj.		109	Unorganized.			
Elizabeth City	184	190	156	211	133	120	183	123	141	85
Essex	338	298	273	233	186	135	229	186	241	125
Fairfax	650	727	608	606	489	320	410	391	366	221
Fauquier	884	1081	928	1045	685	503	761	607	683	533
Fayette	318	369	265	243	257	134	249	163	199	183
Floyd	271	483	384	301	271	225	216	297	143	279
Fluvanna	268	309	440	378	271	190	305	244	334	153
Franklin	699	1163	620	802	608	606	619	674	569	515
Frederick	898	1351	1024	1421	795	884	805	887	755	43
Giles	275	439	287	350	274	342	267	350	226	293
Gilmer	127	267	114	324	77	178	Unorganized.			
Gloucester	268	388	267	372	185	197	233	220	247	179
Goochland	198	377	195	396	168	254	165	319	120	333
Grayson	266	562	222	267	193	200	150	331	455	589
Greenbrier	792	658	644	498	658	303	709	351	568	308
Greene	57	472	87	416	63	270	66	300	62	230
Greensville	54	207	67	168	79	130	88	146	110	156
Halifax	329	1173	405	1096	395	848	344	1041	422	964
Hampshire	747	1168	649	1115	581	657	675	694	729	605
Hanover	315	615	450	554	410	427	558	482	450	462
Hancock	190	320	241	849	161	216	Unorganized.			
Hardy	842	637	858	532	525	271	538	272	497	230
Harrison	840	1221	601	992	443	611	479	760	828	1341
Henrico	755	709	646	548	592	393	578	405	445	398
Henry	391	505	330	832	315	251	306	258	311	191
Highland	237	479	170	431	101	288	Unorganized.			
Isle of Wight	142	644	171	645	105	393	93	470	89	583
Jackson	488	605	439	459	239	233	247	304	258	211
James City	122	57	97	45	99	87	103	39	141	9
Jefferson	845	946	958	898	788	594	725	624	667	592
Kanawha	1149	658	1226	776	742	272	983	442	827	324
King George	127	206	182	166	149	112	165	117	168	129
King William	73	274	99	246	93	234	109	337	115	306
King and Queen	168	438	169	349	224	258	250	328	282	305
Lancaster	150	160	136	122	137	107	189	99	170	87
Lee	388	916	403	773	324	521	237	578	275	489
Lewis	299	712	224	566	331	522	329	684	202	109
Logan	60	411	173	308	99	117	123	177	136	189
Loudon	1979	858	1813	788	1453	420	1505	474	1269	881
Louisa	247	632	856	503	307	441	864	535	875	475
Lunenburg	117	486	159	374	169	272	196	333	228	302
Madison	57	750	107	646	69	486	65	512	58	532
Marion	470	1632	560	1197	324	669	286	677	Magnolian	& Har'son.
Marshall	981	981	743	721	558	527	524	554	458	462
Mason	708	561	536	476	349	274	415	363	405	304
Mathews	186	270	177	255	136	189	172	222	180	220
Mecklenburg	271	867	304	680	342	497	276	618	319	561
Mercer	214	492	268	289	191	184	173	177	146	124
Middlesex	128	249	95	157	116	125	131	118	101	123
Monongalia	609	1447	688	1308	434	809	393	780	681	1236
Monroe	731	747	497	499	488	469	425	460	408	420
Montgomery	468	653	501	490	340	306	364	345	338	261
Morgan	329	319	270	259	188	201	183	216	179	145
Nansemond	445	416	500	462	311	280	361	244	383	259
Nelson	520	418	591	444	394	229	443	291	404	237
New Kent	169	193	174	148	167	101	198	177	198	156
Nicholas	366	298	252	167	213	90	170	127	173	120
Norfolk City	787	644	767	792	652	448	634	403	529	298
Norfolk County	1008	1230	921	1224	629	650	627	591	561	478
Northampton	335	256	298	144	170	95	240	116	334	24
Northumberland	249	340	208	279	161	234	185	276	183	300
Nottoway	140	203	122	185	117	143	187	182	132	190
Ohio	1464	1632	1452	1186	977	478	897	402	922	287
Orange	287	437	290	843	296	281	239	288	231	235
Page	57	1034	110	870	69	595	50	628	45	528
Patrick	385	594	489	899	387	272	369	386	342	274
Pendleton	424	500	375	881	285	309	409	552	389	468
Petersburgh	672	836	515	759	392	333	376	336	245	262
Pittsylvania	1227	1355	864	877	884	589	838	635	876	616
Pleasants	178	303	152	237	Unorganized.					
Pocahontas	115	417	116	240	106	212	81	227	107	210
Powhattan	92	244	122	243	154	202	215	210	176	210
Preston	719	1232	647	923	460	527	382	504	396	464
Princess Ann	393	397	409	342	373	299	329	251	402	27
Prince Edward	214	429	227	302	211	253	264	377	268	361
Prince George	74	306	91	282	127	215	139	226	124	237
Prince William	233	709	190	534	207	412	159	457	167	393
Pulaski	200	331	174	223	131	141	166	174	142	161
Putnam	391	396	348	870	192	183	Unorganized.			
Raleigh	228	141	128	63	Unorganized.					
Randolph	218	441	301	337	201	213	207	199	450	321
Rappahannock	351	492	331	436	304	239	359	314	318	300

VIRGINIA—(Continued).

COUNTIES.	Am. Fillmore. (1856)	Dem. Buch'an. (1856)	Whig. Scott. (1852)	Dem. Pierce. (1852)	Whig. Taylor. (1848)	Dem. Cass. (1848)	Whig. Clay. (1844)	Dem. Polk. (1844)	Whig. Harrison. (1840)	Dem. Van B. (1840)
Richmond City	1753	1474	1854	1012	1064	345	847	282	580	176
Richmond County	291	225	234	181	182	148	202	154	177	151
Ritchie	277	506	188	381	124	339	104	254	Unorganized.	
Roane	255	212	Unorganized.							
Roanoke	228	503	208	384	183	249	177	279	159	255
Rockbridge	1036	1124	1031	1084	665	501	697	543	635	528
Rockingham	510	2783	575	2473	895	1655	290	1716	256	1444
Russell	888	755	801	275	482	316	414	416	264	298
Scott	406	810	854	577	296	452	276	531	284	441
Shenandoah	233	2389	291	2094	176	1404	170	1372	102	1218
Smyth	332	572	434	479	826	309	275	371	259	305
Southampton	458	570	498	456	838	807	825	390	878	872
Spottsylvania	448	622	440	565	413	405	488	442	858	868
Stafford	262	539	269	447	230	255	233	346	265	295
Surry	102	230	147	201	94	158	118	168	95	195
Sussex	88	367	107	322	82	273	124	325	109	847
Taylor	432	616	351	383	Unorganized.					
Tazewell	119	1140	243	612	215	548	100	627	113	486
Tucker	16	137	Unorganized.							
Tyler	329	556	340	383	324	290	441	511	325	438
Upshur	295	534	324	439	Unorganized.					
Warren	145	568	169	520	122	285	126	321	110	300
Warwick	51	18	66	14	62	15	67	24	92	8
Washington	644	1115	715	924	485	679	371	723	364	625
Wayne	296	362	225	206	105	110	190	184	Unorganized.	
Westmoreland	439	131	280	83	249	60	305	67	286	81
Wetzel	80	704	102	488	89	318	Unorganized.			
Wirt	191	322	222	288	Unorganized.					
Wise	42	18	Unorganized.							
Williamsburgh	56	57	37	68	47	84	66	50	83	7
Wood	753	875	645	607	430	325	533	330	513	892
Wyoming	81	116	42	29	Unorganized.					
Wythe	531	887	333	615	847	336	309	553	279	47
York	194	114	129	90	118	86	113	109	192	12
Total	60310	89706	58572	73858	45124	46586	43677	49570	42501	43893

Buchanan over Fillmore, 29,396; Pierce over Scott, 15,286; Cass over Taylor, 1,462; Polk over Clay, 5,893; Van Buren over Harrison, 1,392. Fremont received 291 votes in this State, in 1856; and Van Buren 9, in 1840.

ALABAMA.

COUNTIES.	Am. Fillmore. (1856)	Dem. Buch'an. (1856)	Whig. Scott. (1852)	Dem. Pierce. (1852)	Whig. Taylor. (1848)	Dem. Cass. (1848)	Whig. Clay. (1844)	Dem. Polk. (1844)	Whig. Harrison. (1840)	Dem. Van B. (1840)
Autauga	475	621	196	322	553	471	475	633	591	57
Barbour	857	1445	297	809	1205	614	1113	860	1028	64
Benton	443	1687	74	918	566	1272	873	1382	482	124
Bibb	479	539	238	346	474	416	450	596	583	47
Baldwin	219	144	62	72	100	133	149	120	137	11
Blount	87	770	55	422	134	526	84	774	105	72
Butler	792	777	345	251	772	277	666	405	710	27
Covington	288	304	52	117	248	92	148	139	188	6
Chambers	967	1141	668	616	1323	689	1158	936	1039	67
Cherokee	455	1537	242	785	630	921	856	955	377	75
Clark	222	754	98	479	120	327	232	631	230	59
Coosa	802	1167	294	709	626	883	400	796	316	53
Choctaw	404	643	227	334	Unorganized.					
Conecuh	408	425	216	287	426	231	441	277	541	20
Coffee	301	703	118	239	192	174	142	314 }	867	67
Dale	419	945	162	406	368	555	209	616 }		
Dallas	676	831	886	440	860	618	864	722	1024	68
De Kalb	130	900	136	501	257	650	207	700	157	77
Franklin	711	1056	462	993	510	795	498	1079	637	90
Fayette	440	799	81	516	272	841	153	796	203	81
Greene	784	694	694	555	1088	712	1090	819	1366	78
Henry	471	966	94	184	504	496	367	546	325	89
Hancock	14	221	9	65	Unorganized.					
Jackson	97	1790	88	1154	136	1589	87	1751	57	214
Jefferson	196	697	114	339	288	385	264	585	315	58
Lawrence	631	699	512	588	663	656	469	783	649	78
Lauderdale	555	1141	441	803	695	772	474	919	645	98
Limestone	281	790	227	662	874	833	325	965	356	89
Lowndes	703	699	126	186	761	434	710	678	896	52
Marengo	567	789	450	526	739	553	726	634	842	59
Morgan	222	808	208	482	361	335	271	682	358	80
Madison	401	1476	854	1300	465	1385	357	1720	393	198
Monroe	469	604	264	260	479	216	567	359	646	86
Marion	198	700	118	467	193	514	120	638	196	53
Marshall	89	888	111	563	246	708	162	875	142	92

ALABAMA—(Continued.)

COUNTIES.	1856.		1852.		1848.		1844.		1840.	
	Am. Fillmore.	Dem. Buch'an.	Whig. Scott.	Dem. Pierce.	Whig. Taylor.	Dem. Cass.	Whig. Clay.	Dem. Polk.	Whig. Harrison.	Dem. Van B.
itgomery	1158	1100	717	557	1176	669	1016	836	1134	811
ile	1771	1838	1123	1380	1319	1073	1408	1847	1481	1121
on	1239	1039	772	658	1464	532	1087	626	731	338
y	824	808	261	512	826	631	169	849	973	825
	1178	1262	379	703	935	668	862	768	658	627
ens	669	1037	568	752	1044	931	892	967	1062	779
sell	855	994	434	522	970	577	736	624	691	404
dolph	688	1460	90	707	461	770	288	747	279	624
by	468	787	317	315	557	368	511	472	573	407
lair	88	818	44	455	150	456	46	644	42	679
ter	532	703	482	497	820	771	927	1061	1308	1180
aloosa	973	680	527	475	976	694	902	961	1276	938
adega	896	1134	372	672	869	820	633	851	669	788
apoosa	1276	1478	351	845	972	920	728	705	412	486
ker	146	449	54	217	231	383	170	442	244	367
ox	446	813	286	398	639	479	525	629	778	487
hington	152	194	52	65	72	85	273	279	263	277
otal	28552	46739	15038	26881	30482	31363	26084	37740	28471	33991

Buchanan over Fillmore, 18,187; Pierce over Scott, 11,843; Cass over Taylor, 881; Polk over Clay, 11,656; Van Buren over Harrison, 5,520.

MISSISSIPPI.

COUNTIES.	Am. Fillmore.	Dem. Buch'an.	Whig. Scott.	Dem. Pierce.	Whig. Taylor.	Dem. Cass.	Whig. Clay.	Dem. Polk.	Whig. Harrison.	Dem. Van B.
ms	505	380	514	442	643	365	755	452	862	438
ala	501	928	318	673	480	653	276	305	272	306
ité	440	364	325	264	426	809	429	351	500	294
ivar	168	106	67	38	89	49	55	61	62	44
roll	846	938	528	783	885	921	678	742	711	527
lborne	337	387	270	858	464	358	434	429	538	390
homa	226	111	159	115	189	130	143	162	181	109
iah	415	731	272	607	491	587	447	649	571	545
rk	390	522	137	331	211	282	115	853	124	238
octaw	539	1127	332	606	642	743	426	624	388	430
ckasaw	629	861	478	718	846	948	836	632	142	204
ington	88	887	97	303	135	846	98	308	116	233
houn	263	840	216	467	Unorga	nized.				
Soto	709	1159	781	888	836	723	671	709	371	349
nklin	216	342	158	254	226	249	172	220	186	183
ene	No	return.	61	114	184	79	62	175	91	125
ds	1122	751	975	839	1206	822	1199	915	1207	658
mes	500	585	419	484	643	520	578	498	556	318
rrison	182	414	156	276	165	172	108	169	—	—
ncock	109	186	44	112	157	116	57	127	281	107
quena	114	76	48	54	85	58	Unorga	nized.		
wamba	715	1239	402	1014	567	880	368	825	170	894
per	872	599	248	422	343	308	210	403	239	268
kson	60	326	13	213	32	166	17	216	25	172
erson	308	356	202	317	852	290	364	383	412	229
es	70	236	38	114	95	135	72	117	56	106
nper	489	655	317	511	416	450	291	515	326	400
vrence	129	604	97	395	145	438	94	545	123	452
vndes	553	801	499	745	801	780	644	850	620	620
ke	346	615	198	335	328	289	190	285	145	182
iderdale	339	863	310	688	474	667	256	681	239	444
ayette	529	975	401	689	730	760	542	632	382	866
rshall	1250	1465	1078	1304	1306	1344	1035	1184	1006	814
dison	575	541	440	497	614	497	612	486	691	812
nroe	612	1065	467	971	921	1062	549	911	452	487
rion	69	285	48	207	99	162	68	254	136	175
cubee	476	601	377	413	617	667	519	577	514	872
hoba	167	464	51	248	241	254	156	236	113	164
wton	207	427	107	217	184	197	143	270	109	194
ibbeha	268	595	211	344	388	424	241	336	195	219
ry	113	185	94	112	143	69	125	71	110	94
e	279	533	143	412	277	398	232	444	314	376
oia	607	561	427	383	578	344	439	408	832	206
ntotoc	1121	1392	475	1030	757	999	384	709	237	329
nkin	409	546	274	351	356	370	311	406	331	262
flower	120	89	35	48	33	22	7	14	—	—
pson	137	341	159	244	236	264	178	300	201	219
ith	325	433	85	270	210	287	94	249	89	179
tt	66	442	98	247	152	273	112	259	41	108
lahatchie	176	276	143	186	206	219	179	218	186	124
hemingo	983	1862	760	1312	840	1190	480	1004	821	583
nica	44	?	20	34	51	25	36	24	76	58

MISSISSIPPI—(Continued.)

COUNTIES.	1856.		1852.		1848.		1844.		1840.	
	Am. Fillmore.	Dem. Buch'an.	Whig. Scott.	Dem. Pierce.	Whig. Taylor.	Dem. Cass.	Whig. Clay.	Dem. Polk.	Whig. Harrison.	Dem. Van B.
Tippah	816	601	569	1232	981	1236	692	1170	681	584
Wilkinson	872	400	271	865	455	291	441	855	663	148
Wayne	No	return.	71	61	97	52	102	95	94	87
Warren	890	447	723	494	890	478	922	507	1006	422
Washington	148	135	129	90	179	71	209	108	162	64
Winston	301	776	218	448	307	425	201	475	262	288
Yazoo	735	608	453	559	641	497	578	530	561	360
Yallobusha	716	848	549	633	843	846	719	893	739	643
Total	24195	35446	17548	26876	25922	26537	19206	25126	19518	16995

Buchanan over Fillmore, 11,251; Pierce over Scott, 9,328; Cass over Taylor, 615; Polk over Clay, 5,920; Harrison over Van Buren, 2,523.

NORTH CAROLINA.

COUNTIES.	Am. Fillmore.	Dem. Buch'an.	Whig. Scott.	Dem. Pierce.	Whig. Taylor.	Dem. Cass.	Whig. Clay.	Dem. Polk.	Whig. Harrison.	Dem. an B.
Alamance	717	452	With	Orange.	Unorganized.					
Alexander	314	322	219	98	Unorganized.					
Anson	311	723	992	369	1084	359	1012	481	1194	395
Ashe	531	617	558	396	660	358	522	477	578	460
Beaufort	525	796	910	574	923	463	932	527	761	309
Bertie	453	511	498	444	524	302	475	439	496	385
Bladen	463	367	371	582	280	341	280	486	346	414
Brunswick	364	384	352	301	319	237	351	283	350	230
Burke	378	311	761	389	1210	286	1234	228	1628	309
Buncombe	778	731	557	376	996	434	961	412	1436	452
Cabarrus	865	594	642	371	756	377	718	874	891	854
Caldwell	364	374	493	146	503	96	598	219	Fr. Burke	& Wilkes.
Camden	89	474	503	107	493	70	556	101	612	100
Carteret	463	389	414	388	474	317	434	315	454	186
Caswell	917	212	226	931	293	1087	283	1182	276	1169
Catawba	653	168	With	Lincoln.	Unorganized.					
Chatham	761	787	1008	725	1033	519	1136	729	1124	568
Cherokee	443	522	534	290	549	175	390	225	414	113
Chowan	255	212	225	219	295	171	305	166	330	158
Cleveland	796	71	211	494	814	421	366	624	From Lincoln and Rutherford.	
Columbus	527	212	178	857	169	274	135	363	204	315
Craven	595	475	583	694	696	616	682	222	666	540
Cumberland	1257	767	811	1488	812	1191	703	1101	612	950
Currituck	538	128	134	490	198	466	157	551	142	468
Davidson	634	964	1019	497	1087	520	1091	610	1441	390
Davie	279	477	414	259	448	251	529	282	687	225
Duplin	1173	117	186	930	318	939	223	936	253	807
Edgecombe	1581	151	89	1454	143	1335	126	1503	185	1374
Forsyth	1043	772	With	Stokes.	Unorganized.					
Franklin	793	255	363	704	341	658	336	760	374	689
Gaston	597	53	With	Lincoln.	Unorganized.					
Gates	388	305	868	868	879	289	355	355	878	828
Granville	1060	756	991	945	959	831	936	942	933	778
Greene	375	218	325	826	818	237	302	276	297	215
Guilford	413	1515	1552	345	1714	373	2134	515	2300	414
Halifax	683	509	497	424	582	446	592	456	604	856
Haywood	418	191	814	302	418	213	342	267	431	221
Henderson	434	406	493	210	541	116	555	141	In Buncombe.	
Hertford	301	375	290	236	316	144	309	253	396	199
Hyde	248	898	835	227	495	236	318	164	431	89
Iredell	302	1241	909	280	1137	211	1582	830	1780	828
Jackson	404	65	With Haywood.		Unorganized.					
Johnston	958	619	708	870	646	746	595	650	597	549
Jones	211	157	191	201	242	136	203	142	243	182
Lenoir	424	264	282	397	282	334	225	356	No	return.
Lincoln	514	226	621	1418	828	1593	790	1736	1000	1958
Macon	247	308	309	240	427	207	374	224	433	168
Madison	460	182	With	Yancey.	Unorganized.					
Martin	725	311	289	567	361	545	310	580	291	596
Mecklenberg	1031	573	680	1115	775	945	909	1201	1000	1246
McDowell	380	274	With	Burke.	559	161	With	Burke.	Unorganized.	
Montgomery	108	546	620	132	583	82	658	139	1136	105
Moore	440	489	546	484	588	406	540	500	529	495
Nash	1068	61	88	1030	113	798	74	894	78	797
New Hanover	1472	577	383	1400	464	1255	382	1122	293	1042
Northampton	621	466	455	530	493	488	519	364	550	883
Onslow	683	145	175	597	211	686	194	717	143	690
Orange	909	747	1441	1307	1667	1585	1686	1589	1639	1448
Pasquotank	299	532	539	316	570	244	663	232	693	149
Perquimans	254	846	324	270	434	253	440	223	596	134

NORTH CAROLINA—(Continued.)

COUNTIES.	1856.		1852.		1848.		1844.		1840.	
	Am. Fillmore.	Dem. Buch'an.	Whig. Scott.	Dem. Pierce.	Whig. Taylor.	Dem. Cass.	Whig. Clay.	Dem. Polk.	Whig. Harrison.	Dem. Van B.
Person	543	279	263	471	346	518	275	649	214	597
Pitt	730	570	679	602	636	479	634	476	627	391
Polk	156	124	Unorga	nized.						
Randolph	836	1025	1036	277	1196	225	1171	812	1344	269
Richmond	176	500	678	146	699	71	802	117	820	102
Robeson	678	566	660	732	633	545	559	599	579	506
Rockingham	1001	359	342	823	380	766	430	1022	547	905
Rowan	779	865	836	672	859	560	833	586	942	502
Rutherford	576	412	761	301	958	126	1310	296	1802	540
Sampson	927	858	604	867	612	741	583	878	553	741
Stanly	108	731	714	58	725	14	530	48	In Mont	gomery.
Stokes	658	331	1081	1237	1014	912	1084	1153	1212	1061
Surry	706	362	1046	937	1132	852	996	880	1191	812
Tyrrel	92	277	286	87	300	96	283	92	380	83
Union	655	236	With Me	cklenb'g	775	945	Unorga	nized.		
Wake	1472	789	1032	1357	1028	1247	1044	1374	1026	1149
Warren	841	78	167	691	156	667	128	810	105	754
Watauga	148	368	With	Ashe.	Unorga	nized.				
Washington	236	364	302	210	373	149	329	124	432	54
Wayne	1172	208	. 286	1067	258	903	254	911	306	731
Wilkes	380	992	1073	242	1060	121	1208	181	1450	114
Yadkin	483	694	With	Surry.	Unorga	nized.				
Yancy	616	208	236	357	31m	aj.	838	427	415	290
Total	36886	48246	39058	39744	43550	34869	43232	39287	46376	33782

Buchanan over Fillmore, 11,360; Pierce over Scott, 686; Taylor over Cass, 8,681; Clay over Polk, 8,945; Harrison over Van Buren, 12,594. Mr. Hale received 59 votes in this State, in 1852, and Mr. Van Buren 85, in 1848.

TENNESSEE.

COUNTIES.	Am. Fillmore.	Dem. Buch'an.	Whig. Scott.	Dem. Pierce.	Whig. Taylor.	Dem. Cass.	Whig. Clay.	Dem. Polk.	Whig. Harrison.	Dem. Van B.
Anderson	649	348	602	267	602	250	620	325	625	227
Bledsoe	354	271	464	209	508	229	529	259	644	202
Blount	1246	623	827	566	965	663	1046	785	1198	640
Bradley	658	1078	547	778	760	927	572	958	467	791
Bedford	1557	1378	1390	1356	1497	1381	1455	1526	1878	2156
Benton	453	632	340	485	892	459	292	481	259	301
Campbell	345	434	813	252	473	279	337	318	481	328
Carter	728	228	585	140	745	129	739	177	837	99
Cheatham	423	465	Unorga	nized.						
Claiborne	543	785	503	519	700	744	578	857	681	733
Cocke	795	439	743	196	815	189	844	187	917	80
Cannon	428	809	453	727	469	827	318	761	Unorga	nized.
Coffee	307	990	205	722	832	943	280	1000	Unorga	nized.
Carroll	1710	863	1498	649	1493	560	1356	524	1861	852
Cumberland	243	261	Unorga	nized.						
Davidson	3259	2074	2623	2059	2698	1976	2266	1683	1960	1274
De Kalb	554	795	559	588	571	573	488	491	Unorga	nized.
Dickson	382	816	1013	769	386	674	839	706	396	653
Decatur	453	495	400	315	Unorga	nized.				
Dyer	666	599	508	411	883	271	356	272	446	206
Fentress	118	533	153	414	113	432	60	456	140	823
Franklin	331	1427	330	1183	390	1207	358	1123	645	1461
Fayette	1082	1080	1006	1034	1217	1060	1205	1151	1140	902
Granger	1117	736	852	477	1094	489	998	548	1095	449
Greene	880	1852	780	1307	963	1483	1031	1701	1032	1559
Giles	1236	1584	1303	1447	1389	1511	1301	1387	1190	1242
Grundy	28	425	44	327	Unorga	nized.				
Gibson	1832	1284	1570	901	1423	688	1320	611	1272	418
Hawkins	916	1144	778	831	1252	1243	1173	1388	1058	1251
Hamilton	1064	1051	774	648	685	634	644	624	606	473
Hancock	241	525	241	336	Unorga	nized.				
Hardin	748	905	648	808	621	770	505	732	562	581
Hickman	238	1086	241	839	301	988	255	1034	293	952
Humphreys	280	695	263	471	309	482	305	523	191	833
Hardeman	691	1333	716	1024	723	1016	689	1077	676	860
Henderson	1313	805	1193	511	1286	460	1209	492	1318	277
Henry	897	1827	899	1516	860	1349	835	1312	862	1079
Haywood	842	920	790	732	800	672	756	668	807	576
Jefferson	1571	567	1170	312	1468	215	1563	247	1811	131
Johnson	459	178	365	93	382	66	870	79	390	49
Jackson	1261	1180	1118	703	1269	801	1211	807	1302	591
Knox	2551	838	1863	565	2140	439	2015	507	2096	314
Lawrence	514	876	549	583	596	544	489	547	537	372
Lewis	25	242	43	186	Unorga	nized.				
Lincoln	431	2670	606	2297	680	2584	658	2494	831	2581
Lauderdale	395	411	230	277	279	274	286	211	Unorga	nized.
McMinn	970	1059	796	866	960	1024	873	1061	1022	897
Meigs	125	635	141	442	150	534	120	620	119	535

TENNESSEE—(*Continued*).

COUNTIES.	1856. Am. Fillmore.	1856. Dem. Buch'an.	1852. Whig. Scott.	1852. Dem. Pierce.	1848. Whig. Taylor.	1848. Dem. Cass.	1844. Whig. Clay.	1844. Dem. Polk.	1840. Whig. Harrison.	1840. Dem. an B.
Marion	523	444	458	292	562	336	508	381	503	368
Monroe	867	1041	805	847	962	960	859	1086	923	928
Morgan	162	263	240	222	229	187	211	232	211	61
Maury	1316	1823	1324	1799	1516	1970	1292	1988	1497	2025
Montgomery	1368	944	1260	993	1288	969	1271	1029	1101	790
Marshall	649	1278	666	1340	730	1408	635	1398	Unorganized.	
Macon	559	526	616	374	Unorganized.					
McNairy	969	1125	956	967	939	786	773	741	906	477
Madison	1561	981	1426	819	1562	737	1357	768	1312	537
Overton	322	1505	345	1089	467	1112	336	1145	329	988
Obion	533	950	431	644	357	487	282	536	267	357
Polk	402	798	272	470	367	517	260	488	Unorganized.	
Perry	362	525	325	314	433	287	744	513	781	348
Rhea	311	448	300	307	298	324	232	368	209	383
Rhoane	1028	829	820	678	998	671	900	735	1047	545
Robertson	1089	928	1013	769	1236	889	1193	871	1167	650
Rutherford	1469	1368	1495	1313	1754	1439	1730	1500	1706	1475
Sevier	921	164	621	80	787	57	738	78	926	45
Scott	156	224	304	100	Unorganized.					
Sullivan	548	1477	260	1114	436	1375	850	1533	327	1386
Smith	1596	729	1742	520	2380	719	2328	788	2657	688
Stewart	606	895	823	607	574	705	519	704	457	642
Sumner	859	1894	825	1563	922	1994	881	2017	794	1738
Shelby	2114	2044	1824	1628	1828	1607	1625	1352	950	681
Tipton	424	663	357	565	852	482	360	502	573	588
Van Buren	103	265	107	165	130	198	116	190	Unorganized.	
Washington	828	1334	565	853	862	1016	881	1225	892	1083
Warren	411	1130	844	922	407	1161	835	1190	513	1944
Wayne	714	563	666	380	673	386	665	446	760	266
White	808	740	949	518	1064	503	857	468	1201	386
Williamson	1646	775	1583	763	1883	793	1986	859	2017	681
Wilson	2186	1134	2248	923	2517	998	2607	1042	2550	870
Weakley	859	1628	783	1149	669	1080	560	1084	528	723
Total	66178	73638	58898	57018	64705	58419	60080	59917	60391	48289

Buchanan over Fillmore, 7,460; Scott over Pierce, 1,880; Taylor over Cass, 6,286; Clay over Polk, 113; Harrison over Van Buren, 12,102.

LOUISIANA.

COUNTIES.	1856. Am. Fillmore.	1856. Dem. Buch'an.	1852. Whig. Scott.	1852. Dem. Pierce.	1848. Whig. Taylor.	1848. Dem. Cass.	1844. Whig. Clay.	1844. Dem. Polk.	1840. Whig. Harrison.	1840. Dem. an B.
Ascension	276	479	296	360	288	236	239	264	218	218
Assumption	195	837	511	553	469	286	285	279	289	340
Avoyelles	323	584	300	387	299	359	189	364	250	225
Bienville	296	706	172	313	114	189	Unorganized.			
Bossier	202	475	180	248	17	—	59	103	Unorganized.	
Caddo	493	458	344	342	281	300	210	155	With Natchito'es	
Calcasieu	25	296	84	221	41	181	42	128	With Landry	
Caldwell	102	308	54	158	90	149	69	194	No return.	
Claiborne	678	852	330	506	221	323	196	375	No return.	
Carroll	288	441	219	261	268	235	190	221	96	114
Catahoula	411	448	280	310	320	386	243	304	259	231
Concordia	155	135	121	86	188	96	188	95	269	113
De Soto	296	510	241	288	149	217	52	150	Unorganized.	
E. Baton Rouge	540	593	484	485	400	406	325	399	324	308
E. Feliciana	346	464	342	443	349	394	329	419	360	480
Franklin	183	264	110	192	124	162	134	158	Unorganized.	
Iberville	265	517	318	426	429	295	253	235	204	18
Jackson	387	538	174	341	127	193	Unorganized.		252	8
Jefferson	937	122	928	943	717	660	434	403	No return.	
Lafayette	128	453	117	277	108	220	193	399	No return.	
La Fourche	300	753	676	135	739	161	471	187	538	44
Livingston	231	391	159	337	144	243	100	229	127	207
Madison	239	210	171	147	283	192	206	198	147	111
Morehouse	351	332	196	137	178	101	107	81	Unorganized.	
Natchitoches	420	588	289	407	384	495	452	650	667	610
Orleans	5858	2475	4663	4682	5551	4579	3026	2612	2681	1748
Orleans R. B.	194	151	67	161	Unorganized.					
Ouachita	260	390	190	240	168	176	106	206	243	13
Plaquemine	205	248	151	372	187	350	87	1007	40	25
Pt. Coupee	266	521	242	364	288	370	174	175	147	18
Rapides	584	763	401	623	383	543	419	586	475	88
Sabine	189	849	237	251	246	271	255	383	Unorganized.	
St. Bernard	123	122	130	120	124	89	185	84	173	9
St. Landry	807	1108	692	568	754	876	789	406	836	43
St. Helena	309	272	209	246	169	188	154	222	172	28
St. Tammany	304	227	254	208	275	183	169	199	204	8

LOUISIANA—(Continued.)

COUNTIES.	1856.		1852.		1848.		1844.		1840.	
	Am. Fillmore.	*Dem.* Buch'an.	*Whig.* Scott.	*Dem.* Pierce.	*Whig.* Taylor.	*Dem.* Cass.	*Whig.* Clay.	*Dem.* Polk.	*Whig.* Harrison.	*Dem.* Van B.
St. Charles	67	104	101	39	135	85	96	42	69	83
St. James	380	172	321	158	431	117	351	181	379	37
St. John Baptiste	196	217	202	160	228	128	142	113	183	45
St. Mary	449	374	390	243	470	166	352	142	308	87
St. Martin	541	423	479	298	456	240	479	303	463	103
Tensas	157	205	120	107	177	111	157	108	Unorganized.	
Terrebonne	397	382	197	37	353	129	265	164	318	20
Union	545	623	435	465	307	237	206	213	74	76
Vermillion	116	234	136	126	430	52	176	104	Unorganized.	
West Baton Rouge	200	147	220	118	255	109	209	104	183	84
Washington	142	304	125	258	158	190	127	230	150	134
West Feliciana	196	290	190	302	232	261	243	308	253	286
Winn	157	314	57	138	Unorganized.					
Total	20709	22164	17255	18647	18217	15370	13083	13782	11296	7616

Buchanan over Fillmore, 1,455; Pierce over Scott, 1,892; Taylor over Cass, 2,847; Polk over Clay, 699; Harrison over Van Buren, 3,680.

KENTUCKY.

COUNTIES.	*Am.* Fillmore.	*Dem.* Buch'an.	*Whig.* Scott.	*Dem.* Pierce.	*Whig.* Taylor.	*Dem.* Cass.	*Whig.* Clay.	*Dem.* Polk.	*Whig.* Harrison.	*Dem.* Van B.
Adair	455	1033	457	597	568	549	548	639	223	404
Allen	537	718	280	454	423	553	401	635	201	373
Anderson	299	737	292	606	334	547	281	552	181	375
Ballard	323	655	260	328	277	281	282	400	Unorganized.	
Barren	1561	1232	1119	967	1462	1048	1306	1108	787	825
Bath	642	1028	587	785	724	782	611	783	485	470
Boone	937	818	800	769	935	769	888	712	580	468
Bourbon	957	601	978	528	1172	486	1208	521	992	416
Boyle	676	362	603	323	773	347	617	352		
Bracken	876	742	638	517	795	472	753	443	486	275
Breathitt	112	502	96	234	143	151	120	231	Unorganized.	
Breckenridge	1008	628	842	440	1006	422	924	464	755	176
Bullitt	545	561	403	446	499	399	528	436	209	319
Butler	571	451	312	269	349	204	351	290	134	184
Caldwell	463	607	731	874	826	841	780	966	302	497
Calloway	206	1209	189	815	227	664	204	772	99	730
Campbell	906	1219	577	1098	511	814	358	618	484	1026
Carroll	439	511	446	473	433	428	382	370	Unorganized.	
Carter	298	787	180	497	243	510	148	508	Unorganized.	
Casey	601	415	474	230	529	196	468	214	176	220
Christian	1880	1098	973	806	1182	786	1122	825	670	470
Clark	946	418	842	322	1046	319	996	314	838	226
Clay	421	369	278	185	377	125	835	92	202	153
Clinton	261	522	277	848	286	294	262	315	No return.	
Crittenden	506	664	396	486	342	399	284	399		
Cumberland	635	335	501	157	642	153	590	167	304	144
Daviess	954	965	1027	711	986	605	808	622	445	344
Edmonson	161	421	208	218	249	209	174	251	122	144
Estill	474	543	358	322	485	238	392	216	No return.	
Fayette	1404	1006	1376	809	1541	781	1695	824	1266	689
Fleming	949	848	888	698	1159	700	1143	771	898	464
Floyd	85	939	165	222	260	225	190	340	80	549
Franklin	883	794	833	759	926	664	816	634	509	560
Fulton	340	460	152	233	Unorganized.					
Gallatin	310	269	372	411	360	368	348	351	483	525
Garrard	866	423	863	236	1187	191	1128	229	814	218
Grant	639	676	437	572	485	529	396	493	247	225
Graves	475	1380	446	971	468	772	386	884	158	363
Grayson	477	651	433	894	507	845	432	886	268	153
Green	408	639	422	487	517	512	827	1042	274	390
Greenup	866	865	637	660	640	516	593	385	357	265
Hancock	425	407	249	205	304	166	277	213	152	72
Hardin	1226	932	1007	619	1239	631	1095	702	698	526
Harlan	331	264	327	65	350	56	334	75	174	53
Harrison	965	1095	802	947	891	896	859	975	445	714
Hart	509	816	455	578	586	528	579	558	216	387
Henderson	865	767	616	685	731	559	719	638	364	360
Henry	727	1050	744	983	827	1022	708	1044	627	794
Hickman	244	631	155	379	169	353	304	740	198	521
Hopkins	857	1183	737	809	796	766	701	814	403	381
Jefferson	4982	2972	3665	3791	1161	970	1092	1042	610	584
Jessamine	614	553	556	476	682	439	616	469	513	389
Johnson	14	708	64	299	106	214	85	252	Unorganized.	
Kenton	1246	1643	975	1384	985	1228	687	920	Unorganized.	
Knox	588	271	487	164	648	159	589	164	309	95
Larue	546	489	417	348	478	349	382	333		

KENTUCKY—(Continued.)

COUNTIES.	1856.		1852.		1848.		1844.		1840.	
	Am. Fillmore.	Dem. Buch'an.	Whig. Scott.	Dem. Pierce.	Whig. Taylor.	Dem. Cass.	Whig. Clay.	Dem. Polk.	Whig. Harrison.	Dem. an B.
Laurel	408	365	372	187	488	145	384	124	71	00
Lawrence	466	478	385	362	414	318	347	345	68	207
Letcher	79	287	63	78	No	return.	29	161	Unorga	nized.
Lewis	586	631	400	503	521	566	506	543	345	302
Lincoln	796	459	674	338	832	325	769	335	613	317
Livingston	457	372	312	267	403	265	424	327	225	361
Logan	1613	506	1294	384	1402	358	1407	374	902	289
Lyon	253	390	Unorga	nized.						
Madison	1087	832	976	541	1313	564	1202	633	972	420
Marion	418	1154	782	763	765	629	715	737	No	return.
Marshall	104	943	91	425	120	496	94	600		
Mason	1308	994	1337	896	1631	953	1608	799	1231	508
McCracken	660	505	385	416	407	308	256	195	149	106
McLean	404	476	Unorga	nized.						
Meade	714	402	647	230	713	225	650	223	339	123
Mercer	615	1121	594	914	734	1088	557	985	739	938
Montgomery	546	451	518	389	688	548	673	597	522	338
Monroe	561	661	377	350	586	379	451	473	Unorga	nized.
Morgan	289	1068	316	509	413	490	247	512	57	335
Muhlenburg	733	747	814	553	746	437	657	439	344	227
Nelson	793	1041	958	487	1149	464	1326	608	765	425
Nicholas	666	709	592	721	673	704	678	703	428	439
Ohio	813	901	701	624	718	542	601	513	313	247
Oldham	387	528	388	486	476	488	426	625	354	500
Owen	554	1579	505	1186	533	810	485	937	174	649
Owsley	335	401	294	326	330	248	165	129	Unorga	nized.
Pendleton	746	732	262	570	875	599	287	530	133	342
Perry	173	295	130	77	No	return.	113	84	83	172
Pike	161	706	221	194	225	140	251	238	24	213
Powell	167	177	111	133	Unorga	nized.				
Pulaski	956	1336	707	622	947	734	727	708	514	443
Rock Castle	417	184	826	97	497	95	451	73	400	158
Rowan	106	237	Unorga	nized.						
Russell	448	429	437	195	519	180	431	178	226	127
Scott	674	1049	729	888	797	734	803	938	544	993
Shelby	1262	773	1184	753	1434	716	1441	796	1327	586
Simpson	437	537	389	380	448	428	455	418	327	257
Spencer	391	434	331	340	460	351	469	508	292	347
Taylor	817	672	264	527	Unorga	nized.				
Todd	762	573	652	422	808	409	784	406	550	212
Trigg	581	859	560	629	588	632	557	651	271	359
Trimble	275	599	300	491	361	486	268	507	Unorga	nized.
Union	653	925	499	612	501	458	507	584	205	268
Warren	1354	695	982	600	1226	603	1132	687	763	441
Washington	441	1145	637	680	721	678	660	709	253	636
Wayne	515	699	463	342	689	405	535	342	383	349
Whitley	572	338	No	return.	584	93	431	99	269	80
Woodford	672	420	706	410	778	337	750	473	615	325
Total	67416	74642	57068	53806	67141	49720	61255	51988	58489	32616

Buchanan over Fillmore, 7,226; Scott over Pierce, 3,262; Taylor over Cass, 17,421; Clay over Polk, 9,267; Harrison over Van Buren, 25,873.

ARKANSAS.

COUNTIES.	Am. Fillmore.	Dem. Buch'an.	Whig. Scott.	Dem. Pierce.	Whig. Taylor.	Dem. Cass.	Whig. Clay.	Dem. Polk.	Whig. Harrison.	Dem. Van B.
Arkansas	224	226	120	140	80	74	80	93	120	78
Ashley	No	return.	88	146	Unorga	nized.				
Benton	75	753	91	334	90	290	96	351	72	245
Bradley	343	398	188	180	227	124	144	154		
Calhoun	56	291	52	151	Unorga	nized.				
Carroll	184	655	124	333	139	261	No	return.	68	223
Chicot	157	165	85	118	146	110	210	158	191	43
Clark	192	528	136	205	198	223	174	217	119	87
Columbia	504	676	Unorga	nized.						
Conway	147	408	110	259	149	171	167	288	177	201
Crawford	161	871	153	236	345	457	885	565	835	347
Crittenden	No	return.	95	97	104	68	109	129	95	71
Dallas	218	335	150	194	203	265	Unorga	nized.		
Desha	225	334	185	199	208	149	127	55	173	78
Drew	192	377	118	135	198	249	Unorga	nized.		
Franklin	116	449	106	224	Returns	rejected.	146	261	Vote rejected for informality. It was 60 maj. for Van Buren.	
Fulton	51	210	13	77	52	93	No	return.		
Greene	No	return.	94	211	13	46	87	206	18	105
Hempstead	415	610	298	360	875	830	814	359	210	251
Hot Springs	131	478	125	269	141	178	120	237	[illegible]	102

ARKANSAS—(Continued.)

COUNTIES.	1856. Am. Fillmore.	1856. Dem. Buch'an.	1852. Whig. Scott.	1852. Dem. Pierce.	1848. Whig. Taylor.	1848. Dem. Cass.	1844. Whig. Clay.	1844. Dem. Polk.	1840. Whig. Harrison.	1840. Dem. Van B.
Independence	612	860	452	612	422	408	278	835	870	198
Izard	94	495	69	226	No	return.			79	174
Jackson	436	591	292	835	194	235	124	184	107	143
Jefferson	381	515	224	306	195	177	130	147	173	109
Johnson	113	453	193	384	194	850	141	431	160	324
Lafayette	120	176	148	170	85	98	81	70	43	25
Lawrence	282	717	299	417	239	291	112	267	138	214
Madison	79	649	76	274	87	214	63	866	135	253
Marion	126	893	40	187	49	49	No	return.	21	112
Mississippi	121	188	44	88	118	110	No	return.	90	73
Monroe	129	233	57	92	113	98	92	73	124	44
Montgomery	45	353	28	111	Returns	rejected.	With Ho	tspring.		
Newton	32	132	8	79	2	54	16	140		
Ouachita	501	701	452	496	571	428	220	184		
Perry	44	125	15	33	29	30	33	65		
Phillips	464	526	383	873	No	return.	280	276	238	247
Pike	47	296	40	168	67	133	No	return.	23	87
Poinsett	73	248	48	132	44	116	29	171	4	130
Polk	No	return.	17	94	17	59	No	return.		
Pope	163	568	183	825	240	292	241	808	183	263
Prairie	229	893	78	170	41	111	Unorga	nized.		
Pulaski	566	739	285	419	438	455	438	528	606	499
Randolph	67	416	32	95	50	129	59	851	45	252
Saline	213	404	137	277	147	244	130	219	142	135
Scott	98	215	23	83	61	180	85	167	82	112
Searcy	61	803	75	197	No	return.				maj. 50
Sebastian	392	302	180	283						
Sevier	236	523	50	125	103	195	114	801	76	197
St. Francis	308	498	172	307	208	260	99	269	82	246
Union	516	626	384	531	553	635	214	409	124	173
Van Buren	78	805	No	return.	95	186	46	121	28	151
Washington	367	917	826	495	377	480	878	729	422	620
White	201	403	97	139	48	60	95	123	82	46
Yell	147	883	166	325	137	186	80	249		
Total	10787	21910	7404	12173	7588	9300	5504	9546	5160	6766

Buchanan over Fillmore, 11,123; Pierce over Scott, 4,769; Cass over Taylor, 1,712; Polk over Clay, 4,042; Van Buren over Harrison, 1,606.

MISSOURI.

COUNTIES.	Am. Fillmore.	Dem. Buch'an	Whig. Scott.	Dem. Pierce.	Whig. Taylor.	Dem. Cass.	Whig. Clay.	Dem. Polk.	Whig. Harrison.	Dem. Van B.
Adair	283	410	113	201			294	450	Unorga	nized.
Andrew	428	889	466	784	884	689	384	941	Unorga	nized.
Atchison	132	345	106	150	77	136	Unorga	nized.		
Audrain	565	521	200	160	185	166	175	163	132	122
Barry	148	488	72	253	55	217	142	478	98	436
Barton	53	64	Unorga	nized.						
Bates	255	409	104	116	146	186	206	807	Unorga	nized.
Benton	159	467	167	828	208	882	252	664	150	501
Bollinger	199	413	28	112	Unorga	nized.				
Boone	1329	958	1112	613	1102	588	1190	602	1112	500
Buchanan	768	1036	712	857	704	1055	599	1162	840	1128
Butler	84	143	16	26	Unorga	nized.				
Caldwell	237	295	157	209	128	168	129	212	133	154
Calloway	1095	805	670	498	849	631	940	793	881	626
Camden	210	269	67	109	155	282	70	247	Unorga	nized.
Cape Girardeau	664	898	828	487	485	709	518	914	455	764
Carroll	399	659	239	286	266	298	242	311	112	182
Cass	596	561	228	837	No	return.	257	443	Unorga	nized.
Cedar	163	391	65	162	116	271	Unorga	nized.		
Chariton	440	559	848	498	417	577	871	602	246	891
Clark	721	587	825	289	284	242	225	220	240	206
Clay	756	675	626	406	626	418	765	552	457	649
Clinton	406	897	283	290	290	286	310	567	137	268
Cole	259	552	216	462	277	531	418	1122	848	962
Cooper	787	778	645	535	813	633	901	783	778	694
Crawford	460	434	240	278	263	275	237	867	240	264
Dade	833	418	175	276	166	806	255	890	Unorga	nized.
Dallas	132	454	102	844	105	283	76	845	Unorga	nized.
Daviess	880	572	296	851	269	358	816	446	170	264
Dent	77	896	74	96	Unorga	nized.				
De Kalb	172	836	66	167	87	146	Unorga	nized.		
Dunklin	101	147	No	return.	42	42	Unorga	nized.		
Dodge	No	return.	81	35	Unorga	nized.				
Franklin	531	846	277	619	389	680	389	796	855	552
Gasconade	220	403	89	304	87	349	71	826	136	636

MISSOURI—(Continued).

COUNTIES.	1856.		1852.		1848.		1844.		1840.	
	Am. Fillmore.	*Dem.* Buch'an.	*Whig.* Scott.	*Dem.* Pierce.	*Whig.* Taylor.	*Dem.* Cass.	*Whig.* Clay.	*Dem.* Polk.	*Whig.* Harrison.	*Dem.* Van B.
Gentry	396	757	133	233	152	896	Unorga	nized.		
Green	1003	1029	484	920	401	825	851	817	71	432
Grundy	850	335	215	184	225	187	846	365	Unorga	nized.
Harrison	318	495	111	164	63	144	Unorga	nized.		
Henry	402	369	266	245	274	239	280	283	299	421
Hickory	130	333	75	194	98	224	Unorga	nized.	Unorga	nized.
Holt	240	409	189	291	148	248	185	878		
Howard	798	867	675	762	801	888	1013	969	753	901
Jackson	894	1168	728	858	695	954	614	852	457	711
Jasper	294	898	169	355	161	294	115	242	Unorga	nized.
Jefferson	523	387	172	310	246	311	827	349	298	321
Johnson	844	540	360	456	334	451	367	511	225	374
Knox	391	471	210	255	196	197	Unorga	nized.		
Laclede	225	821	71	184	Unorga	nized.				
Lafayette	1293	654	803	532	915	585	820	576	Unorga	nized.
Lawrence	358	574	168	390	170	374	Unorga	nized.		
Lewis	642	761	398	408	479	479	380	403	542	602
Lincoln	572	846	440	587	566	696	578	683	462	543
Linn	383	400	249	282	230	297	269	494	93	235
Livingston	430	501	251	321	195	873	198	851	249	487
McDonald	61	299	63	194	Unorga	nized.				
Macon	435	934	355	473	360	470	327	457	87	500
Madison	355	418	117	259	231	877	183	899	152	275
Maries	67	246	Unorga	nized.						
Marion	1321	727	894	751	1046	797	1017	721	827	534
Mercer	417	450	186	186	144	183	Unorga	nized.		
Miller	108	224	62	279	76	873	74	869	21	317
Mississippi	317	327	117	168	138	181	Unorga	nized.		
Moniteau	387	427	189	853	161	466	Unorga	nized.		
Monroe	1012	762	760	611	807	561	792	578	815	618
Montgomery	603	365	886	265	879	186	359	232	344	262
Morgan	227	403	133	278	167	342	262	544	167	494
New Madrid	295	234	93	32	323	168	298	208	363	194
Newton	236	528	107	323	161	461	189	665	178	660
Nodaway	183	438	61	111	43	148	Unorga	nized.		
Osage	219	412	143	372	92	312	120	434		
Oregon	37	824	11	95	Unorga	nized.				
Ozark	51	149	32	57	69	118	57	208	Unorga	nized.
Pemiscott	111	119	57	34	Unorga	nized.				
Perry	207	586	171	213	822	389	385	463	Unorga	nized.
Pettis	432	319	245	801	230	265	228	319	156	262
Pike	1131	1113	803	758	793	784	861	809	732	746
Platte	1040	1263	910	1060	1102	1494	900	1386	459	968
Polk	412	662	260	504	231	516	273	636	241	860
Pulaski	68	268	39	169	124	241	86	325	196	729
Putnam	257	488	104	121	74	120	Unorga	nized.		
Rolls	534	369	841	278	397	299	422	332	400	835
Randolph	606	595	476	502	607	508	596	571	15	405
Ray	744	874	483	618	509	626	599	734	432	563
Reynolds	82	114	5	98	21	148	Unorga	nized.		
Ripley	41	306	16	83	14	154	81	266	15	325
St. Charles	583	772	878	598	477	569	480	503	586	459
St. Clair	210	347	149	225	148	263	177	842	Unorga	nized.
St. Francois	401	541	250	529	285	274	301	234	221	199
St. Genevieve	308	856	122	165	142	168	193	245	170	222
St. Louis	6834	5534	4298	5826	4827	4778	3688	3329	2515	1874
Saline	853	599	514	443	536	438	591	446	375	822
Schuyler	287	472	177	222	204	192	Unorga	nized.		
Scotland	352	632	216	283	131	240	317	442	Unorga	nized.
Scott	345	222	59	97	147	217	258	480	284	500
Shannon	14	40	—	9	35	54	57	271	Unorga	nized.
Shelby	432	873	207	328	175	263	244	209	233	226
Stoddard	151	815	116	177	97	196	115	823	69	808
Stone	3	137	17	94	Unorga	nized.				
Sullivan	260	553	127	277	154	250	Unorga	nized.		
Taney	34	888	11	168	54	325	86	297	41	258
Texas	91	479	95	167	82	185	Unorga	nized.		
Vernon	172	802	63	153	Unorga	nized.				
Warren	878	869	801	801	851	836	364	341	342	848
Washington	487	578	860	834	473	423	613	588	479	51
Wayne	100	287	—	144	91	245	86	866	57	211
Webster	189	468	Unorga	nized.						
Wright	64	267	95	167	72	181	97	486	Unorga	nized.
Total	48524	58164	29984	38353	32671	40077	31251	41369	22972	29760

Buchanan over Fillmore, 9,640; Pierce over Scott, 8,369; Cass over Taylor, 7,406; Polk over Clay, 10,118; Van Buren over Harrison, 6,788.

IOWA.

COUNTIES.	1856.			1852.			1848.	
	Frem.	Buch.	Fill.	Scott.	Pierce	Hale	Tayl'r	Cass.
Adair	72	27	4	No re	turn.		Uno	rg'd.
Adams	113	78	8	No re	turn.		Uno	rg'd.
Appanoose	191	854	487	247	335	25	44	118
Allamakee	630	500	28	142	123	—	Uno	rg'd.
Audubon	23	31	4	Uno	rg'd.			
Benton	558	426	123	80	89	—	22	43
Black Hawk	566	282	33	No re	turn.		Uno	rg'd.
Boone	203	819	66	40	84	—	Uno	rg'd.
Bremer	327	172	48	Uno	rg'd.			
Butler	223	141	29	Uno	rg'd.			
Buchanan	709	343	21	123	148	—	21	37
Cedar	1016	701	176	338	354	102	205	276
Chickasaw	351	102	32	No re	turn.		Uno	rg'd.
Clarke	346	338	77	20	32	37	Uno	rg'd.
Calhoun	9	14	—	Uno	rg'd.			
Cass	132	84	—	No re	turn.		Uno	rg'd.
Clinton	1245	839	142	278	336	—	168	207
Clayton	1420	754	67	471	461	—	134	188
Cerro G'rdo	101	40	1	Uno	rg'd.			
Crawford	36	8	—	Uno	rg'd.			
Davis	201	1014	752	592	614	12	364	375
Decatur	243	588	133	55	133	—	Uno	rg'd.
Dallas	487	319	20	79	89	—	30	26
Delaware	801	500	149	233	204	18	107	104
Desmoines	1338	1413	522	984	1154	80	955	1070
Dubuque	1322	2427	256	600	1150	6	365	764
Fremont	166	203	103	95	96	—	Uno	rg'd.
Fayette	1043	452	114	167	117	21	Uno	rg'd.
Floyd	224	124	14	No re	turn.		Uno	rg'd.
Franklin	120	33	—	Uno	rg'd.			
Greene	73	117	—	No re	turn.		Uno	rg'd.
Guthrie	196	205	12	7	39	—	Uno	rg'd.
Grundy	65	2	—	Uno	rg'd.			
Hardin	583	195	18	No re	turn.		Uno	rg'd.
Harrison	170	124	9	No re	turn.		Uno	rg'd.
Henry	1767	767	308	832	513	223	655	459
Howard	207	63	—	Uno	rg'd.			
Iowa	492	326	79	112	101	1	25	59
Jackson	1163	1332	276	554	739	12	397	559
Jasper	878	455	33	160	113	3	66	69
Jefferson	1188	1023	206	757	796	97	637	739
Johnson	1215	964	282	415	531	38	286	359
Jones	964	663	10	266	338	22	154	207
Keokuk	895	830	197	326	403	42	231	855
Kossuth	85	12	—	Uno	rg'd.			
Lee	1780	2158	650	1379	1708	201	1189	1614
Linn	1652	971	273	522	592	80	293	383
Louisa	993	642	200	468	368	105	428	286
Lucas	288	855	176	80	85	8	Uno	rg'd.
Menona	41	56	18	No re	turn.		Uno	rg'd.
Marion	No re	turn.		411	489	18	277	306
Madison	580	519	61	103	150	—	Uno	rg'd.
Mahaska	1284	940	268	599	541	39	402	400
Marshall	531	199	104	31	52	—	Uno	rg'd.
Mitchell	314	135	1	No re	turn.		Uno	rg'd.
Monroe	622	603	93	204	295	36	111	195
Montgom'y	68	58	17	No re	turn.		Uno	rg'd.
Mills	287	153	102	42	91	—	Uno	rg'd.
Muscatine	1091	895	32	562	605	30	395	377
Polk	1065	888	91	401	439	13	185	234
Potawato'ie	259	853	84	111	182	—	Uno	rg'd.
Page	100	171	189	29	40	—	Uno	rg'd.
Poweshiek	459	255	87	61	45	2	20	20
Ringgold	92	52	64	Uno	rg'd.			
Shelby	62	19	—	No re	turn.		Uno	rg'd.
Scott	1675	1119	329	517	641	81	335	366
Story	232	272	79	No re	turn.		Uno	rg'd.
Sac	25	35	—	Uno	rg'd.			
Tama	470	296	90	No re	turn.		Uno	rg'd.
Taylor	119	183	31	—	9	—	Uno	rg'd.
Union	102	121	17	No re	turn.		Uno	rg'd.
Van Buren	1092	1396	324	981	1028	48	926	978
Wapello	1093	1175	252	683	762	20	570	584
Warren	855	513	102	95	82	13	Uno	rg'd.
Wayne	133	368	170	63	59	—	Uno	rg'd.
Washington	1188	629	403	473	369	181	340	295
Webster	389	209	31	No re	turn.		Uno	rg'd.
Winneshiek	770	209	13	68	68	—	Uno	rg'd.
Wright	91	24	—	Uno	rg'd.			
Total	43954	36170	9180	15856	17763	1604	11084	12093

Fremont over Buchanan, 7,784; Pierce over Scott, 1,907; Cass over Taylor, 1,009. In 1848, Mr. Van Buren received 1,126 votes in this State.

WISCONSIN.

COUNTIES.	1856.			1852.			1848.	
	Frem.	Buch.	Fill.	Scott.	Pierce	Hale	Tayl'r	Cass.
Adams	1591	625	9	111	86	—	Uno	rg'd.
Bad Ax	597	231	21	No re	turn.		Uno	rg'd.
Brown	499	1004	—	326	515	—	238	309
Buffalo	68	168	—	Uno	rg'd.			
Chippewa	No re	turn.		Uno	rg'd.		With	Cra'f.
Calumet	486	408	1	149	245	—	65	79
Clarke	73	37	—	Uno	rg'd.			
Columbia	2950	1239	7	1133	1233	31	302	145
Crawford	521	429	1	maj.	42		109	215
Dane	3996	3443	6	1004	2138	288	724	757
Dodge	3455	2784	15	1205	2264	429	527	797
Door	No re	turn.		Uno	rg'd.			
Douglas	No re	turn.		Uno	rg'd.			
Dunn	390	119	—	Uno	rg'd.			
Fond du Lac	3292	2511	25	1065	1635	408	446	483
Grant	2809	1419	186	1341	1379	129	1649	1148
Greene	2004	1087	32	659	865	186	479	391
Iowa	1497	1474	27	895	948	—	884	848
Jackson	306	144	6	Uno	rg'd.			
Jefferson	3290	3434	6	1208	1693	859	713	840
Juneau	With	Ada	ms.	Uno	rg'd.			
Kenosha	1508	831	—	483	590	636	Uno	rg'd.
Kewaunee	89	206	—	5	23	—	Uno	rg'd.
La Crosse	987	541	25	260	325	10	Uno	rg'd.
Lafayette	1415	1722	19	850	1389	—	921	1001
Lapointe	No re	turn.		No re	turn.		No re	turn.
Manitowoc	1177	1907	—	209	874	9	77	150
Marathon	269	207	1	No re	turn.		Uno	rg'd.
Marquette	2518	1032	19	maj.	300		214	174
Milwaukee	2798	7188	25	2019	8640	527	1189	2151
Monroe	722	254	6	Uno	rg'd.			
Oconto	No re	turn.		71	101	—	Uno	rg'd.
Ozaukee	360	2032	—	Uno	rg'd.			
Outagamie	602	753	1	145	429	44	Uno	rg'd.
Pierce	414	106	11	Uno	rg'd.			
Polk	95	54	1	Uno	rg'd.			
Portage	680	361	13	No re	turn.		216	225
Racine	2299	1688	6	848	1308	776	907	635
Richland	882	455	37	166	166	—	With	Iowa
Rock	4707	1965	10	1509	1691	923	1300	491
Sauk	2015	993	4	511	595	156	149	158
Shawanaw	68	21	—	Uno	rg'd.			
Sheboygan	1891	1921	15	662	1315	376	372	442
St. Croix	417	252	—	maj.	62		No re	turn.
Trempeleau	190	45	—	Uno	rg'd.			
Walworth	3518	1297	4	965	1141	1433	804	550
Washington	818	2641	7	1156	2350	183	355	1720
Waukesha	2875	2020	8	939	1582	1186	806	961
Waupacca	1636	75	—	No re	turn.		Uno	rg'd.
Waushara	1292	215	6	147	174	116	Uno	rg'd.
Winnebago	2769	1415	20	707	949	575	300	222
Wood	260	95	—	Uno	rg'd.			
Total	66090	52843	579	22240	33658	8814	13747	15001

Fremont over Buchanan, 13,247; Pierce over Scott, 11,418; Cass over Taylor, 1,254. In 1848, Mr. Van Buren received 10,418 votes in this State.

CALIFORNIA.

COUNTIES.	1856.			1852.		
	Frem't.	Buch'n.	Fillm'e.	Scott.	Pierce.	Hale.
Alameda	723	729	213	Uno	rg'd.	
Amador	657	1784	1557	Uno	rg'd.	
Butte	744	2501	1702	1478	1741	
Calaveras	562	2615	1504	2290	2848	
Colusi	18	289	805	225	232	
Contra Costa	188	457	288	413	590	
Del Norte	Uno	rg'd.				
El Dorado	1391	4048	2958	5146	6106	
Fresno	1	218	123	Uno	rg'd.	
Humboldt	103	204	191	Uno	rg'd.	
Klamath	82	832	440	217	210	
Los Angeles	521	721	135	498	574	
Marin	151	850	82	145	137	
Mariposa	165	1254	772	854	1292	
Mendocino	With	Sono	ma.	Uno	rg'd.	
Merced	14	249	124	Uno	rg'd.	
Monterey	220	267	169	54	273	
Napa	157	444	341	208	270	
Nevada	1462	3500	2238	2618	2856	

CALIFORNIA—(Continued.)

COUNTIES.	1856.			1852.		
	Frem't.	Buch'n.	Fillm'e.	Scott.	Pierce.	Hale.
Placer	992	2808	2096	2295	2831	
Plumas	217	1124	865	Uno	rg'd.	
Sacramento	941	3438	3386	3644	3280	
San Bernardi'o	93	814	7	Uno	rg'd.	
San Diego	18	173	38	107	105	
San Francisco	5089	5332	1598	4167	4241	
San Joaquin	548	1285	1040	1159	1198	
San Luis Obispo	107	83	15	112	11	
San Mateo	238	282	113	Uno	rg'd.	
Santa Barbara	183	176	10	78	104	
Santa Clara	809	576	6/3	827	799	
Canta Cruz	196	320	288	186	806	
Shasta	169	1537	1083	757	971	
Sierra	693	2506	2205	1848	1619	
Siskiyou	464	2073	1791	459	492	
Solano	189	799	634	308	365	
Sonoma	882	1515	498	267	474	
Stanislaus	21	436	228	Uno	rg'd.	
Sutter	92	491	347	214	205	
Tehama	44	436	311	Uno	rg'd.	
Trinity	188	1011	882	683	785	
Tulare and Buena Vista	23	248	139	32	40	
Tuolumne	1056	2936	2112	2541	3132	
Yolo	130	553	583	400	350	
Yuba	650	3451	2081	2077	2199	
Total	20691	53365	36165	35407	40626	100

Buchanan over Fremont, 32,674　Pierce over Scott, 5,219.

TEXAS

COUNTIES.	1856.		1852.		1848.	
	Fillm'e.	Buch'n.	Scott.	Pierce.	Taylor.	Cass.
Anderson	825	612	150	412	83	229
Angelina	No re	turn.	28	56	29	52
Atascosa	58	87	Uno	rg'd.		
Austin	120	858	7	22	45	175
Bowie	88	171	Uno	rg'd.		
Bandera	12	9	Uno	rg'd.		
Bastrop	230	403	94	243	42	191
Bell	151	312	26	157	Uno	rg'd.
Bexar	318	747	299	804	189	332
Bosque	20	64	Uno	rg'd.		
Brazoria	74	225	43	143	83	172
Brazos	74	56	9	34	—	33
Brown	Uno	rg'd.				
Burleson	168	261	19	103	9	64
Burnett	76	141	—	21	Uno	rg'd.
Camanche	11	40	Uno	rg'd.		
Cass	352	581	30	75	107	228
Cherokee	514	845	248	696	110	302
Collin	302	564	58	135	43	99
Cooke	—	58	5	14	—	—
Caldwell	196	395	84	235	27	99
Calhoun	maj.	35	94	125	71	76
Cameron	123	492	242	329	⌐	—
Colorado	133	253	30	92	20	68
Comal	26	284	6	112	14	105
Coryell	69	118	Uno	rg'd.		
Dallas	245	603	122	283	57	209
Denton	182	308	—	37	7	46
De Witt	108	253	—	—	16	81
Ellis	176	239	43	90	Uno	rg'd.
El Paso, Earth	maj.	1022	Uno	rg'd.		
Fannin	238	557	68	208	88	245
Falls	74	158	Uno	rg'd.		
Fayette	399	567	165	341	92	175
Fort Bend	136	196	31	86	39	135
Freestone	144	341	8	138	Uno	rg'd.
Galveston	314	431	141	324	71	76
Gillespie	25	115	2	74	—	—
Goliad	135	93	—	—	27	84
Gonzales	363	510	120	209	58	92
Grimes	260	323	53	142	53	186
Guadaloupe	258	359	68	154	81	72
Grayson	182	415	58	198	47	184
Harris	449	645	195	468	289	443
Hays	128	130	21	55	12	43
Hidalgo	—	169	48	119	Uno	rg'd.
Hill	131	175	Uno	rg'd.		

TEXAS—(Continued.)

COUNTIES.	1856.		1852.		1848.	
	Fillm'e.	Buch'n.	Scott.	Pierce.	Taylor.	Cass.
Harrison	505	565	283	402	364	381
Henderson	77	292	23	74	42	62
Hopkins	238	530	29	116	70	227
Houston	170	400	46	125	24	161
Hunt	188	392	19	121	11	66
Jackson	88	93	33	90	13	64
Johnson	79	186	Uno	rg'd.		
Jack	Uno	rg'd.				
Jasper	99	185	30	121	53	113
Jefferson	49	109	Uno	rg'd.		
Kaufman	63	191	Uno	rg'd.		
Karnes	119	103	Uno	rg'd.		
Kerr	Uno	rg'd.				
Kinney	Uno	rg'd.				
Lamar	235	555	57	189	186	358
Lapassas	61	77	Uno	rg'd.		
Lavacca	116	160	33	85	13	84
Leon	235	337	48	124	26	142
Liberty	103	180	40	87	68	144
Limestone	119	101	38	176	40	154
Live Oak	Uno	rg'd.				
Llano	23	55	Uno	rg'd.		
McCullock	Uno	rg'd.				
McLennan	201	293	5	45	Uno	rg'd.
Madison	125	113	Uno	rg'd.		
Matagorda	43	111	30	74	69	79
Maverich	Uno	rg'd.				
Medina	39	136	2	42	—	45
Milam	196	211	56	119	38	119
Montgomery	163	179	74	120	59	163
Nacogdoches	182	557	79	312	97	313
Newton	88	138	16	111	20	56
Navarro	210	300	89	220	44	124
Nueces	maj.	128	21	52	66	56
Orange	60	73	23	39	Uno	rg'd.
Palo Pinto	Uno	rg'd.	—	—	43	194
Panola	185	458	Uno	rg'd.		
Parker	Uno	rg'd.				
Polk	71	285	75	157	56	107
Presideo	No re	turn.	Uno	rg'd.		
Red River	235	288	86	233	177	344
Refugio	37	83	Uno	rg'd.		
Robertson	96	222	53	95	5	57
Rusk	659	1157	242	590	202	455
Sabine	80	118	13	81	38	181
San Augustine	72	182	29	158	70	234
San Patricio	maj.	49	—	30	5	26
San Saba	21	48	Uno	rg'd.		
Shelby	77	309	19	106	99	336
Smith	370	810	—	—	57	144
Starr	17	374	68	76	—	—
Tarrant	92	490	11	61	Uno	rg'd.
Titus	257	502	100	240	123	296
Travis	467	551	118	370	29	219
Trinity	100	161	8	17	Uno	rg'd.
Tyler	No re	turn.	5	52	—	—
Upshur	255	683	137	361	—	—
Uvalde	22	18	Uno	rg'd.		
Van Zandt	48	223	5	43	26	63
Victoria	117	141	9	96	87	80
Walker	343	887	72	228	119	207
Washington	481	654	121	519	123	373
Webb	maj.	382	16	117	Uno	rg'd.
Wharton	40	76	17	59	26	51
Williamson	240	307	62	143	16	41
Wise	11	67	Uno	rg'd.		
Wood	124	385	15	42	Uno	rg'd.
Young	11	89	Uno	rg'd.		
Total	15639	31169	4995	13552	4509	10668

Buchanan over Fillmore, 15,530; Pierce over Scott, 8,557; Cass over Taylor, 6,159.

FLORIDA.

THE vote of this State, in 1856, was: For Fillmore, 4,833; for Buchanan, 6,858; maj. for Buchanan, 1,525. In 1852, Scott received 2,875; Pierce, 4,318; maj. for Pierce, 1,443. In 1848, Taylor received 3,116; Cass, 1,847; maj. for Taylor, 1,269.

POP VOTE FOR PRESI ENT BY STATES

STATES.	1856.			1852.			1848.			1844.			1840.			1836.		1832.		1828.		1824.‡			
	Fremont, Repub'n.	Buchanan, Democrat.	Fillmore, American.	Scott, Whig.	Pierce, Democrat.	Hale, Free Soil.	Taylor, Whig.	Cass, Democrat.	an Buren, Free Dem.	Clay Whig	Polk, Democrat.	Birney, Abolitionist.	Harrison, Whig.	an Buren, Democrat.	Birney, Abol'ist.	Harrison, etc.* Whig.	an Buren, Democrat.	Clay, Nat. Repub.	Jackson, Democrat.	Adams.	Jackson.	Adams.	Jackson.	Crawford.	Clay.
Alabama...	—	46739	28552	15038	26881	—	30482	31363	—	26084	37740	—	28471	33991	—	15637	19068	No op.	J'son.	1938	17188	2416	9443	1680	67
Arkansas...	—	21910	10787	7404	12173	—	7588	9300	—	5504	9546	—	5160	6766	—	1238	2400								
California...	20691	53365	36165	35407	40626	100																			
Connecticut	42715	34995	2615	30357	33249	3160	30314	27046	5005	32832	29841	1943	31601	25296	174	18466	19234	17755	11269	13829	4448	7587	—	1978	—
Delaware...	308	8004	6175	6293	6318	62	6421	5898	80	6278	5996	—	5967	4884	—	4738	4155	4276	4110	4769	4349	By Legislature			
Florida....	—	6358	4833	2875	4318	—	3116	1847	—																
Georgia....	—	56578	42228	16660	34705	—	47544	44802	—	42100	44177	—	40261	31921	—	24930	22126	—	20750	—	18709	By Legislature			
Illinois	96189	105348	37444	64934	80597	9966	53047	56300	15774	45528	57920	3570	45537	47476	149	14983	18097	5429	14147	1581	6763	1542	1901	219	1047
Indiana....	94375	118670	22386	80901	95340	6929	69907	74745	8100	67867	70181	2106	65302	51604	—	41281	32480	15472	31552	17052	22237	3095	7848	—	5815
Iowa......	43954	36170	9180	15856	17763	1604	11084	12093	1126																
Kentucky...	814	74642	67416	57068	53806	—	67141	49720	—	61255	51988	—	58439	32616	—	36955	33435	43396	36247	31172	39084	—	6453	—	16782
Louisiana...	—	22164	20709	17255	18647	—	18217	15870	—	18083	18782	—	11296	7616	—	3383	3653	2528	4049	4097	4605	By Legislature			
Maine......	67379	39080	3325	32543	41609	8030	35125	39880	12096	34378	45719	4836	46612	46201	194	15239	22300	27204	33291	20773	13927	6870	2330	—	—
Maryland...	281	39115	47460	35066	40020	54	37702	34523	125	35984	32676	—	33528	28752	—	25852	22167	19160	19156	25759	24578	14632	14523	3646	695
Massachu's.	108190	39240	19626	52683	44569	28023	61070	35281	38058	67418	52846	10860	72574	51944	1621	41093	33501	33003	14545	29836	6019	30687	—	6616	—
Michigan ..	71762	52136	1660	33859	41842	7237	23940	30687	10389	24337	27759	3632	22933	21131	321	4000	7360								
Mississippi..	—	35446	24195	17548	26876	—	25922	26537	—	19206	25126	—	19518	16995	—	9688	9979	—	5919	1581	6763	1694	8284	119	—
Missouri....	—	58164	48524	29984	38353	—	32671	40077	—	31251	41369	—	22972	29760	—	8337	10995	maj.	5192	3422	8232	311	987	—	1401
New-Hamp.	38345	32789	422	16147	29997	6695	14781	27763	7560	17866	27160	4161	26115	32761	126	6228	18722	19010	25486	24076	20692	4107	648	—	—
New-Jersey	28338	46943	24115	38556	44305	350	40015	36901	829	38318	37495	131	33351	31034	69	26892	26347	23393	23856	23758	21950	9110	10985	1196	—
New-York..	276007	195878	124604	234882	262083	25329	218603	114818	120510	232482	237588	15812	225817	212527	2798	138543	166815	154896	168497	135413	140763	By Legislature			
N. Carolina	—	48246	36886	39058	39744	—	43550	34869	—	43232	39287	—	46376	33782	—	23626	26910	4563	24862	13918	37857	—	20415	15621	—
Ohio	187497	170874	28126	152526	169220	31682	138360	154775	35354	55057	149117	8050	148157	124782	903	105405	96948	76539	81246	63396	67597	12280	18457	—	19255
Pennsylv'a.	147510	230710	82175	179174	198568	8525	185513	171176	11263	61203	167535	8138	144021	143672	343	87111	91475	56716	90983	50848	101652	5440	36100	4206	1609
Rhode Isl'd	11467	6680	1675	7626	8735	644	6779	3646	730	7322	4867	107	5278	3301	42	2710	2964	2810	2126	2754	821	2145	—	200	—
S. Carolina.	Electors Chosen by Legislature.																								
Tennessee..	—	73638	66178	58898	57018	—	64705	58419	—	60030	59917	—	60391	48289	—	35962	26120	1436	28740	2240	44090	216	20197	312	—
Texas	—	31169	15639	4995	13552	—	4509	10668	—																
Vermont...	39561	10569	545	22173	13044	8621	23122	10948	13837	26770	18041	3954	32440	18018	319	20991	14037	11152	7870	24784	8205	By Legislature			
Virginia ...	291	89706	60310	58572	73858	—	45124	46586	9	43677	49570	—	42501	43893	—	23368	30261	11451	33609	12101	26752	3189	2861	8489	416
Wisconsin..	66090	52843	579	22240	33658	8814	13747	15001	10418																
Total....	1341264	1838169	874534	1386580	1601274	155825	1360099	1220544	91263	1299062	1337243	62300	1275011	1122912	7059	786656	761549	530189	687502	509097	647231	105321	155872	44282	46587

Buchanan over Fremont, 496,905 ; Fremont and Fillmore over Buchanan, 877,629 ; Pierce over Scott, 214,694 ; over Scott and Hale, 58,869 ; Taylor over Cass, 189,555 ; Cass and Van Buren over Taylor, 151,708 ; Polk over Clay, 88,181 ; Clay and Birney over Polk, 24,119 ; Harrison over Van Buren, 145,999 ; over Van Buren and Birney, 138,940 ; Van Buren over Harrison and all others, in 1836, 24,893 ; Jackson over Clay, in 1832, 157,313 ; Jackson over Adams, in 1828, 138,134 ; Jackson over Adams, in 1824, 50,551 ; all others over Jackson, 40,818.

* The Opposition vote was divided between Gen. William H. Harrison, of Ohio, Hugh L. White, of Tennessee, Willie P. Mangum, of North Carolina, and Daniel Webster of Massachusetts.

† William Wirt, of Maryland, ran as an Anti-Masonic Candidate, in 1832, receiving a considerable vote in New-England, New-York, and Pennsylvania, which is added to that of Mr. Clay in our Table. Mr. Wirt received the Electoral Vote of Vermont.

‡ Neither Candidate received a majority of the Electoral Vote and the House of Representatives elected Mr. John Quincy Adams.

LATEST ELECTION RETURNS.

Maine—1859.

GOVERNOR.

Counties.	Rep. Morrill.	Dem. Smith.
Androscoggin	3090	2261
Aroostook ...	740	808
Cumberland .	6876	5851
Franklin.....	2331	1949
Hancock.....	2907	1955
Kennebec....	5293	3288
Lincoln......	3868	4180
Oxford	4113	3348
Penobscot ...	6285	4569
Piscataquis .	1488	996
Sagadahoc...	1885	996
Somerset.....	3902	2812
Waldo.......	4429	3141
Washington..	3168	2772
York	6036	5447
Total.	.56361	44373

Maj. for Morrill, 11,988.

New-Hampshire—1859.

By Congressional Districts.

GOVERNOR.

Districts. I.	Rep. Goodwin.	Dem. Cate.
Belknap......	1724	1850
Carroll	2248	2330
Rockingham .	5799	5055
Strafford	3498	2679
Total......	13269	11914

Maj. for Goodwin, 1,355.

II.	Goodwin.	Cate.
Hillsborough..	6476	5461
Merrimac....	4835	4788
Total......	11311	10249

Maj. for Goodwin, 1,062.

III.	Goodwin.	Cate.
Cheshire......	3448	2263
Coos.........	1256	1472
Grafton	4797	4739
Sullivan	2245	2165
Total	11746	10639

Maj. for Goodwin, 1,107.

Vermont—1859.

By Congressional Districts.

GOVERNOR.

Districts. I.	Rep. Hall.	Dem. Saxe.
Addison	3042	543
Bennington..	1866	1253
Rutland	3006	1070
Washington..	2997	1676
Total......	10911	4542

II.	Hall.	Saxe.
Caledonia ...	2217	1337
Orange......	3052	2185
Windham....	3137	950
Windsor......	3428	1330
Total......	11834	5802

III.	Hall.	Saxe.
Chittenden ..	2537	819
Essex	541	428
Franklin.....	2022	1230
Grand Isle...	294	245
Lamoille.....	1513	546
Orleans......	1715	887
Total......	8622	4155
Total State	31367	14499

Maj. for Hall, 16,868.

Massachusetts—1859.

GOVERNOR.

Counties.	Rep. Banks.	Dem. Butler.	Am. Briggs.
Barnstable	1457	760	138
Berkshire.	3276	2605	337
Bristol ...	3360	1831	2017
Dukes....	227	195	94
Essex	8049	4532	1837
Franklin..	2672	1470	200
Hampden.	3303	2646	458
Hampshire	2659	734	886
Middlesex	10688	6488	2609
Nantucket	249	107	93
Norfolk...	4478	2988	1911
Plymouth.	3284	1548	899
Suffolk ...	5473	4434	2165
Worcester.	9605	4999	1221
Total...	58780	35334	14365

Banks over Butler, 23,446.

Connecticut—1860.

By Congressional Districts.

GOVERNOR.

Districts. I.	Rep. Buckingham.	Dem. Seymour.
Hartford	8753	8972
Tolland......	2558	2210
Total ...	11811	11182

Maj. for Buckingham, 129.

II.	Buck.	Sey.
Middlesex ...	2942	3490
New-Haven..	8709	9765
Total......	11651	13255

Maj for Seymour, 1,604.

III.	Buck.	Sey.
New-London .	5672	5102
Windham ...	3700	2586
Total......	9372	7688

Maj. for Buckingham, 1,684.

IV.	Buck.	Sey.
Fairfield.....	6921	7136
Litchfield....	5203	4656
Total...	.12124	11792

Maj. for Buckingham, 332.

Buckingham's majority in the State, 541.

Rhode Island—1860.

GOVERNOR.

Counties.	Rep. Padelford.	Union. Sprague.
Bristol.......	622	644
Kent.........	1012	1460
Newport.....	1547	1542
Providence ..	6007	7237
Washington..	1647	1412
Total......	10835	12295

Maj. for Sprague, 1,460.

The opposition to Mr. Padelford was composed of Democrats, Americans, and disaffected Republicans, calling themselves Conservatives.

Delaware—1858.

GOVERNOR.

Counties.	Opp. Buckmaster.	Dem. Burton.
Kent........	1857	2024
New Castle ..	3457	3416
Sussex	2240	2318
Total......	7554	7758

Burton's maj., 204.

New-York—1859.

COUNTIES.	SEC. STATE. Rep. Leavenworth.	Dem. * Jones.	COMPTROLLER. Rep. * Denniston.	Dem. Church.	PRISON INSP. Rep. Forrest.	Dem. *Elderkin.
Albany	7253	9216	8371	8057	7391	9033
Allegany.....	4771	2133	4886	2022	4766	2136
Broome.......	3491	2915	3597	2811	3489	2916
Cattaraugus..	3973	2900	4044	2796	3970	2888
Cayuga	6180	3541	6410	3311	6072	3631
Chautauqua..	5590	3211	6241	2559	5583	3219
Chemung	2452	2414	2432	2381	2431	2438
Chenango....	4482	3614	4706	3393	4482	3611
Clinton	3252	3184	3332	3104	3228	3206
Columbia	3946	4123	4554	3513	3977	4085
Cortland	3018	2084	3120	1978	3017	2082
Delaware	3600	3484	4143	2934	3604	3476
Dutchess.....	5237	5070	5634	4675	5247	5058
Erie	7466	9416	9666	7204	7582	9332
Essex........	2395	1519	2443	1471	2397	1517
Franklin	2292	2294	2344	2243	2292	2296
Fulton	2669	2446	2732	2374	2672	2437
Genesee	3309	2042	3588	1750	3309	2038
Greene	2500	3253	2691	3058	2500	3250
Hamilton	213	396	213	396	213	396
Herkimer	4426	2661	4510	2572	4433	2648
Jefferson	6860	5004	6902	4948	6859	5006
Kings........	7971	13042	9446	11431	7910	12950
Lewis........	2359	1918	2359	1920	2346	1921
Livingston ...	3215	2676	3591	2299	3220	2668
Madison	4676	2805	4925	2552	4585	2691
Monroe	7065	4793	6970	4882	7108	4742
Montgomery..	2690	3069	3013	2800	2779	3030
New-York ...	18272	38462	22088	34554	18331	38276
Niagara......	3688	3303	4128	2889	3697	3282
Oneida	10288	7306	10400	7209	10322	7284
Onondaga....	8833	6082	9037	5897	8742	6202
Ontario	3571	3104	4377	2298	3571	3098
Orange	4056	4988	4381	4618	4048	4985
Orleans	2848	2230	2859	2196	2914	2160
Oswego	7004	4850	6976	4869	7006	4845
Otsego.......	5469	4912	5502	4879	5472	4903
Putnam......	1018	1210	1088	1141	1029	1198
Queens	1315	3540	1907	2937	1385	3464
Rensselaer ...	5002	7933	7424	5516	4950	7902
Richmond....	678	1659	1002	1300	747	1558
Rockland	749	1751	1051	1429	782	1746
Saratoga	4352	4417	4752	4017	4360	4389
Schenectady .	1779	1780	1981	1577	2244	1811
Schoharie ...	2563	3605	2702	3402	2508	3596
Schuyler	1884	1821	2143	1590	1940	1796
Seneca..	1903	2363	2240	2026	1919	2342
Steuben......	5759	4850	6069	4516	5758	4848
St. Lawence..	7846	3347	8009	3186	7701	3464
Suffolk......	1694	2632	2110	2221	1706	2625
Sullivan	1670	3102	2463	2304	1679	3088
Tioga........	3023	2580	3147	2458	3015	2586
Tompkins....	3280	2514	3501	2296	3284	2512
Ulster	4034	5596	5089	4617	4040	5622
Warren......	2183	1683	2187	1680	2182	1685
Washington...	4735	2974	5135	2569	4737	2969
Wayne	4658	3210	4804	3057	4660	3210
Westchester..	4330	6548	5172	5690	4348	6522
Wyoming	3128	1812	3148	1787	3115	1816
Yates........	2236	1208	2247	1195	2231	1209
Total......	251139	252589	275952	227304	251784	251194

Jones' maj., 1450; Denniston's, 48648; Forrest's, 590.

AGGREGATE VOTE FOR OTHER STATE OFFICERS.

Treasurer...Dersheimer,* 275,587 ; Vanderpoel, 226,755—48,832
Att'y Gen'l..Myers,*......276,792 ; Tremain, ...227,345—49,447
State Eng'r.Storey, ...250,880 ; Richmond,*.252,312— 1,432
Canal Com..Chapin,......251,449 ; Skinner,*...251,777— 328
*Judge of Ap.*Davies,*.....272,275 ; Johnson,...227,171—45,104
*Clerk of Ap.*Hughes,*....275,286 ; Lewis,....227,355—47,931

The above are the actual returns sent from the various counties of the State to the State Department at Albany ; but in consequence of informality in some of the returns, the officially declared result, on a number of candidates, varies from the actual. The vote for Forrest is declared at 243,430 ; Elderkin, 237,579 ; Storey, 246,041 ; Richmond, 250,247 ; Chapin, 245,976 ; Davies, 265,568 ; Johnson, 223,525 ; Lewis, 221,084.

* Nominated and supported by the American, or "Balance of Power" Party.

New-Jersey—1859.

GOVERNOR.

Districts.	Opp. Olden.	Dem. Wright.
I.		
Atlantic.....	853	740
Camden ...	2324	2339
Cape May ..	570	497
Cumberland.	1830	1635
Gloucester..	1477	1206
Salem	2051	1981
Total.....	9105	8398

Majority for Olden, 707.

	Olden.	Wright.
II.		
Burlington..	4748	3392
Mercer	3587	2981
Monmouth..	3005	3451
Ocean......	1341	730
Total....	12681	10561

Maj. for Olden, 2,120.

	Olden.	Wright.
III.		
Hunterdon...	2726	3445
Middlesex ..	3253	2497
Somerset ...	2011	1888
Warren	2116	2842
Total....	10106	10622

Maj. for Wright, 516.

	Olden.	Wright.
IV.		
Bergen	1262	1518
Morris......	3076	3138
Passaic......	2463	1870
Sussex	1842	2528
Total.....	8643	9054

Maj. for Wright, 411.

	Olden.	Wright.
V.		
Essex.......	7883	7454
Hudson	3131	3726
Union	1766	1899
Total.	12780	13079

Maj. for Wright, 299.

TOTAL VOTE OF STATE.

Olden, ... 53,815
Wright, ... 51,714

Maj. for Olden,.. 1,601

Pennsylvania—1858.

CONGRESS.

Districts.	Union. Ryan.	Dem. Florence.
I.		
Ward 1.....	1527	1431
" 2.....	1481	1414
" 3	878	1027
" 4.....	720	1387
" 5 part	312	449
" 7.....	1574	1115
Total.....	6492	6823

Nebinger, *Anti-Lecompton Dem.*, 2,442.
Florence over Ryan, 331.

	Morris.	Martin.
II.		
Ward 5 part	618	687
" 6.....	926	817
" 8.....	1134	878
" 9.....	1162	896
" 10.....	1818	802
Total	5653	4080

Maj. for Morris, 1,623.

	Verree.	Landy.
III.		
Ward 11	987	872
12	1132	831
16	1284	1126
17	934	1336
18	1667	973
19 part	973	696
Total.....	6977	5834

Reed, *Am.*, 52.
Verree over Landy, 1,143.

PENNSYLVANIA.

CONGRESS—(Continued.)

Districts.	Union. Millward.	Dem. Phillips.
IV.		
Ward 13....	1691	846
" 14....	1940	864
" 15....	1976	1328
" 19 part	506	750
" 20 ...	1820	1129
" 21 part	320	240
" 23 part	405	316
" 24....	1091	978
Total.....	9749	6451

Broom, *Am.*, 253.
Millw'd over Phill's, 3,298.

	Wood.	Jones.
V.		
Ward 21 part	923	660
" 22....	1543	777
" 23 part	1203	768
Montg'ry Co.	6032	5004
Total.....	9701	7209

Maj. for Wood, 2,492.

	Broomall.	Manley.
VI.		
Chester.....	2388	4021
Delaware...	2288	1164
Total.....	4676	5185

Hickman, *A. L. D.*, 6,786.
Hick'n over Manley 1,601.

	Longnecker.	Roberts.
VII.		
Bucks	5235	5122
Lehigh	3089	2954
Total.....	8324	8076

Maj. for Longnecker, 248.

	Schwartz.	Jones.
VIII.		
Berks.......	7321	7302

Maj. for Schwartz, 19.

	Stevens.	Hopkins.
IX.		
Lancaster...	9513	6341

Maj. for Stevens, 3,172.

	Killinger.	Weidle.
X.		
Dauphin....	8255	2281
Lebanon ...	2712	1460
Union......	1318	787
North'ld, pt.	160	27
Snyder	1452	1034
Total.....	8897	5589

Maj. for Killinger, 3,308.

	Campbell.	Dewart.
XI.		
Northumb'ld	1602	1825
Schuylkill...	551	3035
Total.....	7153	4860

Coke, *A. L. D.*, 3,141.
Cam'l over Dewart, 2,766.

	Scranton.	McReyn's.
XII.		
Columbia....	1907	1442
Luzerne	6193	3262
Montour....	990	584
Wyoming...	933	898
Total.....	10023	6186

Maj. for Scranton, 3,837.

	Shoemaker.	Dimmick.
XIII.		
Carbon......	1538	1126
Monroe	783	1261
Northampton	2275	2992
Pike........	179	491
Wayne	1791	2139
Total.....	6566	8009

Maj. for Dimmick, 1,443.

	Grow.	Parkhurst.
XIV.		
Bradford....	4774	920
Susquehanna	3180	1859
Tioga	3211	580
Total.....	11165	3359

Maj. for Grow, 7,806.

	Hale.	White.
XV.		
Centre	2551	1911
Clinton......	1870	1294
Lycoming ..	2484	2028
Mifflin......	1471	1139

PENNSYLVANIA.

CONGRESS—(Continued.)

Districts.	Union. Hale.	Dem. White.
XV.		
Sullivan	314	489
Potter......	1048	488
Total.....	9238	7349

Maj. for Hale, 1,889.

	Junkin.	Fisher.
XVI.		
Cumberland	2560	2768
Perry	1948	1483
York........	4138	4349
Total.....	8646	8600

Maj. for Junkin, 46.

	McPherson.	Reilly.
XVII.		
Adams	2295	2169
Bedford	1859	1974
Franklin....	3384	3060
Fulton......	575	713
Juniata.....	1235	1165
Total.....	9348	9081

Maj. for McPherson, 257.

	Blair.	Pershing.
XVIII.		
Blair	2798	1567
Cambria....	1700	2273
Huntingdon.	2115	1261
Somerset ...	2501	1578
Total.. ...	9114	6679

Maj. for Blair, 2,435.

	Covode.	Foster.
XIX.		
Armstrong..	2425	2001
Indiana	3035	1585
Westmorel'd	3797	4629
Total.....	9257	8165

Maj. for Covode, 1,092.

	Knight.	Montgo'y.
XX.		
Fayette	1275	3299
Greene......	731	2156
Washington.	3792	3799
Total.....	5798	9254

Maj. for Montgo'ry, 3,456.

	Moorhead.	Burke.
XXI.		
Allegheny, pt.	6539	4879

Maj. for Moorhead, 1,660.

	McKnight.	Birmin'm.
XXII.		
Allegheny, pt.	2935	217
Butler........	2503	285
Total......	5438	502

Williams, *Anti-Tax*, 3903.
McK. over Wms., 1,535.

	Stewart.	McGuffin.
XXIII.		
Beaver	1871	1126
Lawrence...	1951	615
Mercer	2899	2036
Total.....	6721	3777

Maj. for Stewart, 2,944.

	Hall.	Gillis.
XXIV.		
Clarion......	1558	2019
Clearfield...	1028	1445
Elk	895	479
Forrest.....	No return.	
Jefferson ...	1871	1049
McKean....	835	479
Venango ...	1953	1671
Warren	1765	969
Total.....	8905	8111

Maj. for Hall, 794.

	Babbitt.	Marshall.
XXV.		
Crawford....	3140	2033
Erie	3220	2080
Total.....	6360	4113

Maj. for Babbitt, 2,247.

In 1859, the Opposition, or People's Party Ticket for State officers, was elected by 17,000 to 1,800 majority.

LEGISLATURE—1859–'60.
SENATE .Opp., 21; Dem., 12
HOUSE..Opp., 67; Dem., 33

Maryland—1859.

CONGRESS.

Districts.	Opp. Cox.	Dem. Stewart.
I.		
Caroline.....	814	798
Dorchester ..	1182	1220
Queen Anne's	901	967
Somerset	1500	1426
Talbot.......	709	989
Worcester ...	1278	1534
Total......	6384	6934

Maj. for Stewart, 550.

	Webster.	McHenry.
II.		
Balt. Co., pt..	1690	1760
Carroll.......	2433	2297
Cecil	2044	1970
Harford......	2095	1647
Kent	836	769
Total......	9098	8443

Maj. for Webster, 655.

	Harris.	Preston.
III.		
Balt. City, pt.	8026	2554
Balt. Co., pt..	1591	1672
Total......	9617	4226

Maj. for Harris, 5,391.

	Davis.	Harrison.
IV.		
Balt. City, pt.	10168	2796

Maj. for Davis, 7,372.

	Hoffman.	Kunkel.
V.		
Alleghany ...	2201	2289
Frederick....	3673	3718
Washington .	2842	2842
Total......	8716	8849

Maj. for Kunkel, 133.

	Hagner.	Hughes.
VI.		
Anne Arundel	1107	1082
Calvert......	439	442
Charles......	575	632
Howard	762	843
Montgomery.	1177	1304
Prince Geo.'s	842	985
St. Mary's ...	452	1014
Total......	5354	6302

Maj. for Hughes, 948.

LEGISLATURE—1857.
SENATE..Amer., 15; Dem., 7
HOUSE...Amer., 44; Dem., 29

Virginia—1859.

GOVERNOR.

Districts.	Opp. Goggin.	Dem. Letcher.
I.		
Accomac.....	768	675
Elizabeth City	214	164
Essex	325	270
Gloucester...	383	365
James City ..	111	31
King and Queen	271	429
Lancaster ...	156	107
Matthews....	315	253
Middlesex ...	179	214
New Kent ...	239	132
Northampton.	227	153
Northumber'd	108	194
Richmond Co.	296	261
Warwick	60	31
Westmoreland	444	146
Williamsburg.	40	55
York	171	102
Total......	4307	3582

Maj. for Goggin, 725.

Muscoe H. R. Garnett, *Dem.*, elected to Congress without opposition.

	Goggin.	Letcher.
II.		
Charles City..	245	66
Greensville ..	93	142
Isle of Wight.	148	582
Nansemond..	462	271
Norfolk City..	836	527

VIRGINIA.

GOVERNOR—(Continued.)

Districts. II.	Opp. Goggin.	Dem. Letcher.
Norfolk Co....	591	381
Portsmouth...	678	537
Prince George	187	267
Princess Anne	367	864
Southampton	536	493
Surry	134	167
Sussex	127	291
Total	4404	4088

Maj. for Goggin, 366.

John S. Millson, *Dem.*, elected to Congress without opposition.

III.	Goggin.	Letcher.
Caroline	619	502
Chesterfield..	581	779
Goochland...	234	259
Hanover	572	689
Henrico	1248	850
King William.	148	318
Louisa	496	397
Richm'd City.	2043	1588
Total	5941	5382

Maj. for Goggin, 559.

Daniel C. Dejarnette, *Ind. Dem.*, elected to Congress, over John S. Caskie, regular *Dem.*, by 100 majority.

IV.	Goggin.	Letcher.
Amelia	203	204
Brunswick...	188	482
Charlotte	406	403
Cumberland..	252	204
Dinwiddie....	230	267
Lunenburgh..	179	433
Mecklenburg.	384	606
Nottoway....	195	178
Petersburg...	944	636
Powhattan...	136	132
Pr'ce Edward	271	316
Total	3388	3861

Maj. for Letcher, 473.

William O. Goode, *Dem.*, elected over Flournoy, *Ind. Dem.* Mr. Goode died before taking his seat, and his place was filled by the election of Roger A. Pryor, *Dem.*

V.	Goggin.	Letcher.
Appomattox	263	470
Campbell....	1385	1129
Franklin	1010	884
Halifax	358	758
Henry	576	419
Patrick	503	593
Pittsylvania..	1396	1107
Total	5491	5360

Maj. for Goggin, 131.

Thomas S. Bocock, *Dem.*, reëlected to Congress, without opposition.

VI.	Goggin.	Letcher.
Albemarle	1303	931
Amherst	732	654
Bedford	1386	815
Buckingham.	535	467
Fluvanna....	482	326
Greene	126	387
Madison	132	586
Nelson	739	383
Total	5435	4549

Maj. for Goggin, 886.

Shelton F. Leake, *Ind. Dem.*, elected to Congress by 1,550 maj. over Powell, regular *Dem.*

VII.	Goggin.	Letcher.
Alexandria ..	874	620
Culpeper.....	497	475
Fairfax	69?	717

VIRGINIA.

GOVERNOR—(Continued.)

Districts. VII.	Opp. Goggin.	Dem. Letcher.
Fauquier	931	1020
King George.	205	196
Orange.. ...	426	879
Prince Wm...	251	712
Rappah'nock.	509	463
Spottsylvania	498	588
Stafford	299	507
Total	5181	5677

Shackelford, *Ind. Dem.*, received 430 votes for Congress.

Maj. for Letcher, 496.

Wm. Smith, *Dem.*, elected to Congress by 302 maj.

VIII.	Goggin.	Letcher.
Berkeley	883	1057
Clarke	252	371
Frederick....	888	1124
Hampshire ..	701	1063
Jefferson	857	875
Loudoun	1798	722
Morgan	274	261
Page	130	960
Warren	215	456
Total	5998	6889

Maj. for Letcher, 891.

Alex. R. Boteler, *Opp.*, elected to Congress by 167 majority.

IX.	Goggin.	Letcher.
Augusta	2170	1402
Bath	230	231
Hardy	771	354
Highland	229	478
Pendleton....	383	411
Rockbridge ..	1280	1208
Rockingham .	700	2402
Shenandoah..	273	1912
Total	5986	8398

Maj. for Letcher, 2,412.

John T. Harris, *Ind. Dem.*, elected to Congress, over Skinner, regular *Dem.*, by 931 majority.

X.	Goggin.	Letcher.
Brooke	213	369
Hancock	144	304
Marion	468	1197
Marshall	828	688
Monongalia..	641	975
Ohio	1323	1030
Pleasants....	76	146
Preston	505	810
Taylor	530	551
Tyler	289	460
Wetzel	65	809
Total	5082	7284

Maj. for Letcher, 2,202.

Sherrard Clemens, *Dem.*, reëlected to Congress, without opposition.

XI.	Goggin.	Letcher.
Barbour	426	817
Braxton	349	317
Cabell	413	504
Calhoun	26	277
Doddridge ...	104	609
Gilmer	60	325
Harrison	780	1092
Jackson	388	510
Kanawha....	1138	467
Lewis	259	649
Mason	588	448
Putnam	451	427
Randolph....	226	430
Ritchie	137	422
Roane	302	261
Tucker	17	176
Upshur	292	422

VIRGINIA.

GOVERNOR—(Continued.)

Districts. XI.	Opp. Goggin.	Dem. Letcher.
Wirt	136	302
Wood	836	660
Total	6928	9115

Maj. for Letcher, 2,187.

Elbert G. Jenkins, *Dem.*, elected to Congress by 1,838 majority over Laidley, *Opp.*

XII.	Goggin.	Letcher.
Alleghany	210	355
Boone	150	292
Botetourt	486	714
Clay	90	49
Craig	92	256
Fayette	346	885
Floyd	522	389
Giles	463	352
Greenbrier ..	889	779
Logan	94	480
Mercer	557	429
Monroe	845	672
Montgomery.	615	388
Nicholas	364	303
Pocahontas...	134	419
Raleigh	381	148
Roanoke	283	409
Wayne	269	320
Wyoming....	170	78
Total	6960	7167

Maj. for Letcher, 207.

No opposition to H. A. Edmundson, *Dem.*, for Congress.

XIII.	Goggin.	Letcher.
Buchanan ...	73	164
Carroll	461	344
Grayson	384	497
Lee	688	624
McDowell	115	33
Pulaski	314	239
Russell	751	404
Scott	600	559
Smyth	598	454
Tazewell	541	621
Washington..	966	870
Wise	208	226
Wythe	743	775
Total	6442	5810

Maj. for Goggin, 632.

Elbert S. Martin, *Ind. Dem.*, elected to Congress by 803 majority over Floyd, regular *Dem.*

TOTAL VOTE OF STATE.

Opposition.

Governor..Goggin.. 71,543
Att'y Gen..Preston.. 64,368

Democrats.

Governor..Letcher.. 77,112
Att'y Gen..Tucker.. 73,124

Maj. for Letcher, 5,569; do. for Tucker, 8,756.

North Carolina—1859.

CONGRESS.

Districts. I.	Opp. Smith.	Dem. Shaw.
Bertie	665	506
Camden	538	109
Chowan	294	286
Currituck....	236	658
Gates	452	406
Halifax	562	759
Hertford	479	293
Martin	352	750
Northampton.	599	758
Pasquotank...	569	340
Perquimans..	431	280
Tyrrell	397	131
Washington..	471	255
Total	6045	5531

Maj. for Smith, 514.

NORTH CAROLINA.

CONGRESS—(Continued.)

Districts. II.	Scattering.	Dem. Ruffin.
Beaufort	140	837
Carteret	—	202
Craven	80	875
Edgecomb ...	4	867
Greene	50	285
Hyde	16	183
Jones	59	140
Lenoir	17	81
Onslow	38	397
Pitt	61	509
Wayne	11	827
Total	476	4382

Maj. for Ruffin, 3,906.

III.	*McDuffie.	Winslow.
Bladen	192	383
Brunswick ...	No return.	
Columbus....	92	272
Cumberland..	404	1089
Duplin	67	780
New-Hanover	90	789
Richmond ...	No return.	
Robeson	—	325
Sampson	104	598
Total	949	4186

Maj. for Winslow, 3,237.

* Independent Democrat.

IV.	Sanders.	Branch.
Franklin	232	626
Granville	290	675
Johnson	546	860
Nash	66	879
Orange	572	729
Wake	696	1405
Warren	57	653
Total	2459	5827

Maj. for Branch, 3,368.

V.	Gilmer.	Williams.
Alamance	576	689
Caswell	183	836
Chatham	983	852
Guilford	2047	468
Montgomery..	639	179
Moore	529	559
Person	201	502
Randolph....	1203	427
Total	6361	4512

Maj. for Gilmer, 1,849.

VI.	Leach.	Scales.
Alexander....	539	366
Allegany	147	833
Ashe	739	452
Davidson	1470	793
Davie	681	379
Forsyth	955	1061
Iredell	1583	472
Rockingham..	402	1417
Stokes	517	768
Surry	601	926
Yadkin	932	697
Total	8566	7664

Maj. for Leach, 902.

VII.	Walkup.	Craige.
Anson	765	257
Cabarrus	517	858
Catawba	181	688
Cleveland....	106	729
Gaston	96	703
Lincoln	192	489
Mecklenburg.	411	777
Rowan	756	849
Stanly	771	68
Union	280	627
Total	4075	5495

Maj. for Craige, 1,420.

VIII.	Vance.	Coleman.
Buncombe ...	833	858
Burke	559	414
Caldwell	529	228

NORTH CAROLINA.

CONGRESS—(Continued.)

Districts.	Opp. Vance.	Dem. Coleman.
VIII.		
Cherokee	675	393
Haywood	307	449
Henderson	631	514
Jackson	245	376
Macon	489	339
Madison	334	425
McDowell	476	351
Polk	157	180
Rutherford	767	643
Watauga	321	191
Wilkes	1190	359
Yancy	463	616
Total	8026	6331

Maj. for Vance, 1,695.

TOTAL VOTE OF THE STATE.

Opposition.

Cong., '59 .... Opp.,...36957
Gov'nor, '58...McRae, 39965

Democrats.

Cong., '59 .... Dem.,.. 43928
Gov'nor, '58...Ellis... 56222

Dem. maj. on Congress, 6,971; Ellis, 16,257.

Georgia—1859.

CONGRESS.

Districts.	Opp. McIntyre.	Dem. Love.
I.		
Appling	37	448
Berrien	165	345
Brooks	289	300
Bryan	128	152
Bulloch	21	569
Camden	43	137
Chatham	649	696
Charlton	11	190
Clinch	105	261
Coffee	41	279
Colquitt	84	144
Echols	49	132
Effingham	254	170
Emanuel	131	465
Glynn	41	176
Irwin	9	200
Johnson	146	180
Laurens	187	235
Liberty	115	218
Lowndes	216	236
McIntosh	72	144
Montgomery	259	55
Pierce	19	199
Tattnall	176	291
Telfair	140	192
Thomas	428	477
Ware	44	231
Wayne	22	125
Total	3881	7247

Maj. for Love, 3,366.

Districts.	Douglas.	Crawford.
II.		
Baker	92	207
Calhoun	102	299
Chattahoochee	242	338
Clay	225	253
Decatur	517	511
Dooley	230	544
Dougherty	197	299
Early	93	263
Lee	209	215
Macon	385	284
Marion	318	387
Miller	48	201
Mitchell	97	353
Muscogee	682	749
Pulaski	148	406
Quitman	157	199
Randolph	544	468
Schley	217	218
Stewart	572	557
Sumter	592	507
Terrell	878	274

GEORGIA.

CONGRESS—(Continued.)

Districts.	Douglas.	Crawford.
II.		
Webster	275	216
Wilcox	8	259
Worth	109	272
Total	6437	8279

Bethune, *Ind.*, received 417 votes for Congress.

Crawford over Douglas, 1,842.

Districts.	Hardeman.	Spoor.
III.		
Bibb	908	879
Butts	325	381
Crawford	248	396
Harris	683	453
Houston	534	556
Monroe	633	580
Pike	423	618
Spaulding	445	474
Talbot	564	492
Taylor	320	362
Upson	553	292
Total	5636	5483

Maj. for Hardeman, 153.

Districts.	Wright.	Gartrell.
IV.		
Campbell	889	777
Carroll	443	1169
Clayton	283	357
Cobb	552	1180
Coweta	477	775
De Kalb	363	708
Fayette	315	544
Fulton	899	1221
Heard	337	565
Henry	653	598
Merriwether	592	672
Troup	750	816
Total	6053	8877

Maj. for Gartrell, 2,824.

Districts.	Shackelford.	Underw'd.
V.		
Cass	151	1236
Catoosa	80	628
Chattooga	223	514
Cherokee	109	1121
Dade	13	324
Fannin	339	415
Floyd	127	989
Gilmer	77	982
Gordon	257	740
Haralson	28	366
Milton	132	390
Murray	118	712
Paulding	43	871
Pickens	72	751
Polk	48	431
Walker	190	740
Whitfield	155	1129
Total	2162	12339

Majority for Underwood, 10,177.

Districts.	Lytle.	Jackson.
VI.		
Banks	67	504
Clarke	232	511
Dawson	65	552
Forsyth	293	555
Franklin	65	851
Gwinnett	283	699
Habersham	386	331
Hall	592	587
Hart	73	768
Jackson	380	702
Lumpkin	72	739
Madison	152	465
Rabun	17	541
Towns	19	252
Union	43	637
Walton	416	582
White	96	368
Total	3251	9644

Maj. for Jackson, 6,393.

GEORGIA.

CONGRESS—(Continued.)

Districts.	Opp. Hill.	Dem. Harper.
VII.		
Baldwin	313	385
Greene	629	247
Hancock	391	269
Jasper	449	383
Jones	189	282
Morgan	382	189
Newton	723	745
Putnam	288	332
Twiggs	167	325
Washington	578	639
Wilkinson	393	557
Total	4492	4353

Maj. for Hill, 139.

Districts.	Wright.	Jones.
VIII.		
Burke	351	514
Columbia	417	407
Elbert	413	518
Glascock	64	232
Jefferson	454	339
Lincoln	186	220
Oglethorpe	375	458
Richmond	1103	920
Scriven	259	282
Talliaferro	211	188
Warren	345	442
Wilkes	329	392
Total	4507	4912

Maj. for Jones, 405.

TOTAL VOTE OF THE STATE.

Opposition.

Governor . Akin 42195
Congress . . Opposition 36419

Democrats.

Governor . Brown... 63806
Congress . . Dem.,.... 61184

Majori's.—Brown, 21,611; Congress, 24,715.

Louisiana—1859.

CONGRESS.

Districts.	Opp. Bouligny.	Dem. LaSere.
I.		
Orleans, Rt. Bk.	197	128
" 2d Dist.	999	708
" 3d Dist.	904	493
Plaquemines	67	814
St. Bernard	48	158
Total	2215	1796

Maj. for Bouligny, 419.

Bienvenu received 497 votes for Congress.

Districts.	Nichols.	Taylor.
II.		
Ascension	335	418
Assumption	215	569
Jefferson	410	558
Lafourche	269	693
Orleans, 1st Dis.	1289	999
" 4th Dis.	356	559
St. Charles	65	97
St. James	273	244
St. John Baptiste	175	185
St. Mary	169	501
St. Martin	476	664
Terrebonne	427	421
Total	4459	5908

Maj. for Taylor, 1,449.

Districts.	Cannon.	Davidson.
III.		
Avoyelles	—	654
Carroll	—	753
Catahoula	—	513
Concordia	—	179
E. Baton Rouge	283	675
E. Feliciana	285	450
Iberville	—	404
Livingston	—	437
Madison	11	256
Point Coupee	—	575
St. Helena	Rejected.	
St. Tammany	65	292
Tensas	—	250

LOUISIANA.

CONGRESS—(Continued.)

Districts.	Opp. Cannon.	Dem. Davidson.
III.		
Washington	60	420
W. Baton Rouge	—	162
W. Feliciana	22	268
Total	726	6288

Maj. for Davidson, 5,562.

Districts.	Jones.	Landrum.
IV.		
Bienville	127	799
Bossier	130	584
Caddo	820	822
Calcasieu	Rejected.	
Caldwell	55	198
Claiborne	90	957
De Soto	33	643
Franklin	326	202
Jackson	150	754
Lafayette	3	278
Morehouse	303	412
Nachitoches	440	708
Ouachita	103	429
Rapides	562	889
Sabine	Rejected.	
St. Landry	Rejected.	
Union	392	768
Vermillion	Rejected.	
Winn	186	380
Total	3220	8823

Maj. for Landrum, 5,603.

TOTAL VOTE OF THE STATE.

Opposition.

Governor... Wells... 15587
Lt. Gov. ...Ray 16047
Sec. State..Blake... 15156

Democrats.

Governor...Moore .. 24434
Lt. Gov. ...Hyams.. 24913
Sec. State ..Hardy .. 25142

Texas—1859.

This State elected State Officers and Congressmen in 1859. The Congressional vote was as follows:

CONGRESS.

Districts.	Ind. Ochiltree.	Dem. Reagan.
I.		
Anderson	214	834
Angelina	50	301
Bowie	10	870
Cass	252	756
Chambers	38	99
Cherokee	284	1165
Colin	3	1111
Cooke	24	375
Dallas	70	894
Denton	12	628
Fannin	26	1113
Grayson	25	938
Harrison	No return.	
Henderson	No return.	
Hopkins	53	991
Houston	87	681
Hunt	18	796
Jack	3	115
Jasper	17	335
Jefferson	24	98
Kaufman	91	514
Lamar	25	996
Liberty	52	273
Nacogdoches	226	638
Newton	20	218
Orange	46	109
Panola	74	680
Polk	49	534
Red River	18	835
Rusk	173	1476
Sabine	62	147
San Augustine	13	368
Shelby	50	635
Smith	233	903
Titus	57	956
Trinity	94	874

TEXAS.

CONGRESS—(Continued.)

Districts. I.	Ind. Ochiltree.	Dem. Reagan.
Tyler	30	525
Upshur	162	730
Van Zandt	36	840
Wise	81	239
Wood	76	558
Young	—	93
Total	3464	23977

Maj. for Reagan, 20,513; do. for Houston, independent candidate for Governor, 4,354.

II.	Hamilton.	Waul.
Atascosa	172	90
Austin	355	533
Bandera	18	26
Bastrop	358	424
Bee	No return.	
Bell	818	274
Bexar	766	991
Blanco	118	42
Bosque	127	53
Brazoria	118	309
Brazos	118	82
Brown	27	1
Burleson	373	289
Burnett	285	93
Caldwell	295	302
Calhoun	146	179
Cameron	4	418
Colorado	357	273
Comal	36	89
Comanche	100	25
Coryell	208	101
De Witt	204	281
Ellis	308	271
El Paso	57	207
Earth	209	23
Falls	218	112
Fayette	566	551
Fort Bend	173	172
Freestone	250	305
Galveston	837	400
Gillespie	69	147
Goliad	198	133
Gonzales	450	427
Grimes	419	254
Guadaloupe	229	318
Hamilton	43	7
Harris	836	598
Hays	No return.	
Hidalgo	3	227
Hill	216	170
Jackson	141	57
Johnson	249	134
Karnes	150	81
Kerr	31	32
Lapassas	212	64
Lavacca	329	330
Leon	374	379
Limestone	218	335
Live Oak	86	60
Llano	81	76
McLennan	348	228
Madison	168	93
Mason	No return.	
Matagorda	63	168
Medina	58	199
Milam	317	208
Montague	—	—
Montgomery	262	177
Navarro	370	301
Nueces	225	139
Palo Pinto	151	28
Parker	495	198
Presideo	No return.	
Refugio	No return.	
Robertson	229	185
San Patricio	17	31
San Saba	158	14
Starr	No return.	
Tarrant	448	233
Travis	595	428
Uvalde	No return.	
Victoria	No return.	
Walker	435	345

TEXAS.

CONGRESS—(Continued.)

II.	Hamilton.	Waul.
Washington	641	678
Webb	116	86
Wharton	82	119
Williamson	458	204
Zapata	42	130
Total	17198	16007

Maj. for Hamilton, 1,191; do. for Houston, 4,873.

Hamilton ran as an independent Democrat. Hardin R. Runnells was the regular Democratic Candidate for Governor. Runnells beat Houston, for the same office, two years before, by 9,805 majority.

TOTAL VOTE OF THE STATE.

Independents.

Governor	Houston,	36227
Lt. Gov.	Clark,	31458
C. L'd Office	Crosby	28828
Congress	Indep'nt	20662

Democrats.

Governor	Runnells,	27500
Lt. Gov.	Lubbock,	30325
C. L'd Office	White	33303
Congress	Dem.,	39984

Major's.—Houston, 8,727; Clark, 1,133; White, 4,975;

Tennessee.—1859.

CONGRESS.

Districts. I.	Opp. Nelson.	Dem. Haynes.
Carter	812	342
Cocke	945	587
Greene	1062	2026
Hancock	367	641
Hawkins	—	174
Jefferson	1602	654
Johnson	547	218
Sevier	1058	261
Sullivan	542	1589
Washington	996	1335
Total	7931	7827

Maj. for Nelson, 104.

II.	Maynard.	Ramsay.
Anderson	889	344
Campbell	451	540
Claiborne	775	676
Fentress	No return.	
Grainger	1206	743
Knox	2593	916
Morgan	248	280
Overton	364	1431
Scott	No return.	
Total	6476	4930

Maj. for Maynard, 1,546.

III.	Brabson.	Smith.
Bledsoe	492	330
Blount	1273	723
Bradley	795	1028
Cumberland—with Bledsoe.		
Hamilton	1284	918
Marion	481	393
Meigs	150	610
Monroe	943	1067
McMinn	1054	1094
Polk	379	742
Rhea	348	431
Roane	1044	889
Sequatchie	179	138
Total	8372	8313

Maj. for Brabson, 59.

TENNESSEE.

CONGRESS—(Continued.)

Districts. IV.	Opp. Stokes.	Dem. Savage.
Coffee	447	909
De Kalb	825	753
Grundy	66	885
Jackson	1426	1043
Macon	556	437
Smith	1598	674
Van Buren	153	166
Warren	528	1043
White	1034	750
Total	6633	6160

Maj. for Stokes, 473.

V.	Hatton.	*Ready.
Cannon	520	860
Rutherford	1452	1531
Sumner	810	1642
Williamson	1609	728
Wilson	2328	1083
Total	6719	5844

Maj. for Hatton, 875.

* Independent, supported by the Democrats.

VI.	No Candidate.	Thomas.
Bedford		1450
Franklin		1540
Lincoln		2393
Marshall		1472
Maury		2168
Total		9023

Dem. maj. for Gov., 4,278.

VII.	Gibbs.	Wright.
Benton	29	882
Decatur	229	512
Giles	259	1569
Hardin	389	958
Hickman	89	1119
Humphreys	204	735
Lawrence	258	949
Lewis	5	258
McNairy	831	1170
Perry	208	555
Wayne	210	678
Total	2711	9380

Maj. for Wright, 6,669.

VIII.	Quarles.	Menees.
Cheatham—with Davidson.		
Davidson	3383	2462
Dickson	447	837
Montgomery	1870	1015
Robertson	1243	1120
Stewart	551	802
Total	6994	6236

Maj. for Quarles, 758.

IX.	Etheridge.	Atkins.
Carroll	1720	1023
Dyer	736	665
Gibson	1967	1385
Henry	1019	1844
Henderson	1815	799
Lauderdale	464	419
Obion	682	1072
Tipton	375	607
Weakley	1159	1616
Total	9437	9430

Maj. for Etheridge, 7.

X.	Sneed.	Avery.
Fayette	921	929
Hardeman	600	1108
Haywood	778	903
Madison	1362	876
Shelby	1987	2138
Total	5648	5954

Maj. for Avery, 306.

Currin, *Ind.*, received 236 votes for Congress.

TENNESSEE.

TOTAL VOTE OF THE STATE.

Opposition.

Gov.	Netherland	68218
Cong.	Opposition	60921

Democrats.

Gov.	Harris	76226
Cong.	Democratic	78079

Majorities.—Harris, 8,008; Dem. maj. on Cong., 12,158.

LEGISLATURE—1859.

SENATE...Opp., 11; Dem., 14
HOUSE....Opp., 34; Dem., 41

Kentucky—1859.

CONGRESS.

Districts. I.	Opp. Morrow.	Dem. Burnett.
Ballard	97	718
Caldwell	180	681
Calloway	118	1221
Crittenden	234	753
Fulton	140	442
Graves	277	1429
Hickman	45	671
Hopkins	166	1316
Livingston	251	426
Lyon	48	433
Marshall	34	916
McCracken	217	699
Trigg	123	978
Union	818	857
Total	2248	11540

Maj. for Burnett, 9,292.

II.	Jackson.	Peyton.
Breckinridge	921	708
Butler	509	555
Christian	987	1057
Daviess	1242	1448
Grayson	565	590
Hancock	421	474
Henderson	878	896
McLean	No return.	
Mechlenburg	883	1070
Ohio	793	1141
Total	7199	7989

Maj. for Peyton, 740.

III.	Bristow.	Sale.
Allen	547	709
Barren	1697	1336
Edmonson	No return.	
Hart	459	733
Logan	1453	464
Monroe	663	581
Simpson	407	587
Todd	726	426
Warren	1212	789
Total	7164	5575

Maj. for Bristow, 1,589.

IV.	Anderson.	Chrisman.
Adair	547	1097
Boyle	789	803
Casey	696	448
Clinton	812	578
Cumberland	652	368
Greene	482	681
Lincoln	935	440
Pulaski	1214	1875
Russell	479	482
Taylor	857	648
Wayne	741	831
Total	7204	7201

Maj. for Anderson, 8.

V.	Jewett.	*Brown.
Anderson	594	471
Bullitt	309	509
Hardin	732	965
Larue	493	361
Marion	540	965
Meade	837	500

* Independent Democrat.

KENTUCKY.

CONGRESS—(Continued.)

Districts. V.	Opp. Jewett.	Dem. Brown.
Mercer	358	1168
Nelson	497	999
Spencer	306	380
Washington	900	609
Total	5066	6927

Maj. for Brown, 1,861.

VI.	Adams.	Garrard.
Breathitt	299	394
Clay	418	511
Estill	556	493
Floyd	427	673
Garrard	812	370
Harlan	490	218
Jackson	170	132
Johnson	54	760
Knox	807	314
Laurel	429	874
Letcher	223	227
Madison	1267	943
Owsley	456	314
Perry	265	270
Pike	277	664
Rock Castle	499	246
Whitley	715	343
Total	8164	7241

Maj. for Adams, 923.

VII.	Mallory.	Holt.
Henry	646	1029
Jefferson	4256	3324
Oldham	353	536
Shelby	1161	766
Total	6416	5675

Maj. for Mallory, 741.

VIII.	Harlan.	Simms.
Bourbon	965	684
Fayette	1410	986
Franklin	863	819
Harrison	926	1317
Jessamine	598	587
Nicholas	737	1009
Scott	732	1062
Woodford	634	468
Total	6865	6932

Maj. for Simms, 67.

IX.	L. T. Moore.	J. W. Moore.
Bath	743	1040
Carter	484	832
Clarke	935	412
Fleming	952	928
Greenup	1163	854
Lawrence	809	496
Lewis	664	731
Mason	1274	875
Montgomery	587	502
Morgan	562	1147
Powell	190	166
Rowan	142	244
Total	8505	8227

Maj. for L. T. Moore, 278.

X.	Jones.	Stevenson.
Bracken	754	778
Boone	826	970
Campbell	689	1242
Carroll	366	528
Gallatin	382	492
Grant	663	800
Kenton	950	1706
Owen	415	1439
Pendleton	615	871
Trimble	179	474
Total	5839	9295

Maj. for Stevenson, 3,456.

TOTAL VOTE OF STATE.

Opposition.
Governor..Bell.....67,271
Congress...Opp.,....64,670

Democrats.
Governor..Magoffin 76,187
Congress...Dem.,...76,552

Missouri—1858.

CONGRESS.

Districts. I.	Rep. Blair.	Dem. Barrett.
St. Louis	6681	7057

Breckinridge, *Am.*, 5668.

Barrett over Blair, 426.*

* Contested by Frank Blair, who finally obtained the seat; but resigned and referred the matter back to the People.

Districts. II.	Opp. Henderson.	Dem. Anderson.
Audrain	412	599
Boone	481	1356
Calloway	367	1696
Lincoln	462	1038
Marion	956	1068
Monroe	526	1240
Montgomery	441	601
Pike	1122	1233
Ralls	873	592
St. Charles	659	902
Warren	290	577
Total	6089	10902

Maj. for Anderson, 4,813.

In the Third District, John B. Clark, *Dem.*, was elected without opposition.

IV.	Adams.	Craig.
Andrew	598	1021
Atchison	153	511
Buchanan	780	1997
Caldwell	270	388
Clay	993	826
Clinton	504	545
Daviess	507	843
De Kalb	195	512
Gentry	464	1266
Harrison	594	852
Holt	460	550
Nodaway	162	825
Platte	1128	1412
Ray	1066	891
Total	7824	12439

Maj. for Craig, 4,615.

V.	Reid.	Woodson.
Benton	502	253
Cass	449	617
Cole	744	116
Cooper	727	853
Henry	221	762
Jackson	1447	1075
Johnson	515	850
Lafayette	340	936
Miller	450	176
Moniteau	391	649
Morgan	285	868
Pettis	207	455
Saline	669	832
Total	6947	7942

Smith, *Ind.*, 2,038.

Woodson over Reid, 995.

VI.	Richardson.	Phelps.
Bates	10	826
Barton	59	193
Barry	232	687
Camden	241	242
Cedar	220	628
Dade	218	652
Dallas	462	272
Gasconade	541	245
Greene	1185	1029
Hickory	168	850
Howell	156	97
Jasper	844	434
Laclede	855	878
Lawrence	508	566
Maries	36	472
McDonald	153	346
Newton	410	779
Oregon	137	189
Osage	427	451
Ozark and Douglas	240	878

MISSOURI.

CONGRESS—(Continued.)

Districts. VI.	Opp. Richardson.	Dem. Phelps.
Polk	672	630
Pulaski	118	255
St. Clair	114	721
Stone	118	173
Taney	206	486
Texas	124	573
Vernon	41	409
Webster	526	579
Wright	84	889
Total	8050	13424

Maj. for Phelps, 5,374.

VII.	Zeigler.	Noell.
Bollinger	186	528
Butler	98	211
Cape Girard'u	734	548
Crawford	150	423
Dent	52	468
Dunklin	833	58
Franklin	1012	767
Iron	853	174
Jefferson	864	620
Madison	81	554
Mississippi	126	377
New-Madrid	227	327
Pemiscot	55	268
Perry	150	759
Phelps	71	498
Reynolds	178	187
Ripley	66	412
Scott	298	392
Shannon	12	197
St. Genevieve	278	897
St. Francois	349	608
Stoddard	217	472
Washington	273	702
Wayne	200	458
Total	5808	10404

Maj. for Noell, 4,596.

At the same election a vote was taken for Superintendent of Public Schools, at which Starke, *Dem.*, was chosen over Provines, *Am.*, by 33,384 majority.

Ohio—1859.

GOVERNOR.

Districts. I. & II.	Rep. Dennison.	Dem. Ranney.
Hamilton	18285	14178

Maj. for Ramsey, 893.

III.	Den.	Ran.
Butler	2238	3479
Montgomery	4747	4615
Preble	2261	1496
Total	9246	9590

Maj. for Ranney, 344.

IV.	Den.	Ran.
Allen	1574	1656
Auglaize	696	1277
Darke	2201	2454
Mercer	540	1057
Miami	2722	1839
Shelby	1352	1517
Total	9085	9800

Maj. for Ranney, 715.

V.	Den.	Ran.
Defiance	778	1083
Fulton	1037	707
Hancock	1674	1796
Henry	670	841
Lucas	2225	2073
Paulding	441	326
Putnam	735	1087
Van Wart	837	865
Williams	1191	1013
Wood	1429	1021
Total	11017	10812

Maj. for Dennison, 205.

OHIO.

GOVERNOR—(Continued.)

Districts. VI.	Dennison.	Ranney.
Adams	1405	1753
Brown	1657	2275
Clermont	2689	2988
Highland	2168	2175
Total	7919	9191

Maj. for Ranney, 1,272.

VII.	Den.	Ran.
Clinton	1721	1019
Fayette	1093	761
Greene	2466	1362
Madison	1018	929
Warren	2689	1615
Total	8987	5686

Maj. for Dennison, 3,301.

VIII.	Den.	Ran.
Champaign	1732	1612
Clarke	2249	1574
Delaware	2358	1776
Logan	1650	1238
Union	1241	910
Total	9230	7110

Maj. for Dennison, 2,120.

IX.	Den.	Ran.
Crawford	1550	2258
Hardin	1152	1127
Marion	1388	1391
Ottaway	328	578
Sandusky	1473	1822
Seneca	2461	2661
Wyandotte	1295	1390
Total	9597	11227

Maj. for Ranney, 1,630.

X.	Den.	Ran.
Gallia	1865	1857
Jackson	1198	1289
Lawrence	1450	1246
Pike	669	1085
Ross	2587	2688
Scioto	1608	1424
Total	8877	9089

Maj. for Ranney, 162.

XI.	Den.	Ran.
Athens	1843	1237
Fairfield	1394	2821
Hocking	976	1897
Meigs	1912	1437
Perry	1898	2281
Vinton	979	1049
Total	9002	10222

Maj. for Ranney, 1,220.

XII.	Den.	Ran.
Franklin	3762	4634
Licking	3080	3438
Pickaway	1710	2147
Total	8502	10219

Maj. for Ranney, 1,717.

XIII.	Den.	Ran.
Erie	1983	1535
Huron	2924	1568
Morrow	1919	1770
Richland	2735	2952
Total	9561	7825

Maj. for Dennison, 1,736.

XIV.	Den.	Ran.
Ashland	1834	1914
Lorain	3391	1689
Medina	2413	1457
Wayne	2944	3285
Total	10582	8345

XV.	Den.	Ran.
Coshocton	2198	2461
Holmes	1241	1964
Knox	2603	2533
Tuscarawas	2831	2778
Total	8873	9736

Maj. for Ranney, 863.

OHIO.

GOVERNOR—(Continued.)

Districts. XVI.	Rep. Dennison.	Dem. Ranney.
Morgan	1835	1308
Muskingum	3604	3467
Washington	2198	1781
Total	7637	6556

Maj. for Dennison, 1,081.

XVII.	Den.	Ran.
Belmont	2280	2591
Guernsey	2103	1663
Monroe	757	1585
Noble	1448	1355
Total	6588	7194

Maj. for Ranney, 606.

XVIII.	Den.	Ran.
Portage	2620	2088
Starke	3725	4005
Summit	2560	1734
Total	8905	7777

Maj. for Dennison, 1,128.

XIX.	Den.	Ran.
Cuyahoga	5834	4115
Geauga	1881	529
Lake	1807	538
Total	9522	5182

Maj. for Dennison, 4,340.

XX.	Den.	Ran.
Ashtabula	3737	1049
Mahoning	2424	2041
Trumbull	3143	1791
Total	9304	4881

Maj. for Dennison, 4,423.

XXI.	Den.	Ran.
Carroll	1600	1255
Columbiana	3125	2235
Harrison	1764	1384
Jefferson	2294	1822
Total.	8783	6696

Maj. for Dennison, 2,087.

TOTAL VOTE OF THE STATE.

Dennison, *Rep.*,.... 184,502
Ranney, *Dem.*,.... 171,266

Maj. for Dennison, 13,236

Michigan—1859.

CHIEF JUSTICE.

Districts. I.	Rep. Martin.	Dem. Felch.
Jackson	2702	2321
Livingston	1718	1810
Washtenaw	3231	3088
Wayne	3894	4212
Total	11540	11431

Maj. for Martin, 109.

II.	Martin.	Felch.
Branch	2191	1221
Cass	1518	1276
Hillsdale	2643	1501
Lenawee	3865	2537
Monroe	1714	1850
St. Joseph	1934	1428
Total	13865	9813

Maj. for Martin, 4,052.

III.	Martin.	Felch.
Allagan	1293	1396
Barry	1535	948
Berrien	1816	1941
Calhoun	2915	2063
Clinton	1432	1131
Eaton	1758	1332
Gratiot	449	241
Ionia	1887	1223

MICHIGAN.

CHIEF JUSTICE—(Conti'd.)

Districts. III.	Rep. Martin.	Dem. Felch.
Kalamazoo	2326	1513
Kent	3199	2448
Mason	73	32
Montcalm	469	314
Newago	287	245
Oceana	124	132
Ottawa	1643	1076
Van Buren	1598	1307
Total	22804	17337

Maj. for Martin, 5,467.

IV.	Martin.	Felch.
Alpena	38	—
Bay	145	134
Cheboygan	1	111
Chippewa	40	86
Emmett	21	147
Genesee	2122	1576
Gr'd Traverse	235	187
Houghton .**	152	378
Ingham	1861	1719
Iosco	48	4
Isabella	42	25
Lapeer	1476	1098
Mackinac	27	158
Macomb	1932	1671
Manistee	82	47
Manitou	14	23
Marquette	120	159
Midland	123	16
Oakland	3479	3396
Ontonagon	154	141
Saginaw	989	911
Sanilac	908	317
Shiawasse	1150	1089
St. Clair	1932	1563
Tuscola	621	299
Total	17707	15100

Maj. for Martin, 2,607.

TOTAL VOTE OF THE STATE.

Martin, *Rep.*, ... 65,916
Felch, *Dem.*,....... 53,681

Maj. for Martin, .. 12,235

Indiana—1858.

CONGRESS.

Districts. I.	Rep. *Hovey.	Dem. Niblack.
Daviess	784	1032
Dubois	191	1117
Gibson	1072	1021
Knox	1042	1206
Martin	441	865
Pike	569	612
Posey	1299	1309
Spencer	1210	907
Vanderburgh.	1846	1163
Warrick	542	1097
Total	8946	10329

Maj. for Niblack, 1,383.

II.	Wilson.	English.
Clark	1129	1446
Crawford	533	716
Floyd	1535	1429
Harrison	1367	1493
Orange	611	994
Perry	601	985
Scott	556	708
Washington	1102	1522
Total	7434	9293

Maj. for English, 1,859.

III.	Dunn.	Hughes.
Bartholomew.	1340	1227
Brown	253	548
Jackson	778	1249
Jefferson	2378	1491
Jennings	1323	943

INDIANA.

CONGRESS—(Continued.)

Districts. III.	Rep. Dunn.	Dem. Hughes.
Lawrence	1095	880
Monroe	1075	964
Switzerland	1121	1083
Total	9363	8385

Carr, *A. L. Dem.*, 1,432.
Dunn over Hughes, 978.

IV.	Hackleman.	Holman.
Dearborn	1472	2335
Decatur	1672	1444
Franklin	1264	2185
Ohio	424	492
Ripley	1381	1464
Rush	1643	1555
Total	7856	9425

Maj. for Holman, 1,569.

V.	Kilgore.	Devlin.
Delaware	1293	718
Fayette	1069	933
Henry	1956	912
Randolph	1572	1053
Union	743	640
Wayne	2750	1665
Total	9383	5921

Maj. for Kilgore, 3,462.

VI.	Porter.	Ray.
Hancock	875	1040
Hendricks	1662	1174
Johnson	1114	1415
Marion	3956	3054
Morgan	1590	1402
Shelby	1579	1631
Total	10776	9716

Maj. for Porter, 1060.

VII.	*Davis.	Secrest.
Clay	842	709
Greene	1266	1112
Owen	1190	759
Parke	1795	507
Putnam	1820	1656
Sullivan	1122	1100
Vermillion	907	515
Vigo	1951	1226
Total	10893	7584

Maj. for Davis, 3,309.

VIII.	Wilson.	Blake.
Boone	1500	1380
Carroll	1885	1382
Clinton	1184	1346
Fountain	1580	1626
Montgomery	1936	1989
Tippecanoe	2441	2021
Warren	1002	643
Total	11028	10387

Maj. for Wilson, 641.

IX.	Colfax.	Walker.
Benton	279	204
Cass	1527	1477
Fulton	888	927
Jasper	643	483
Lake	1068	550
Laporte	2789	2224
Marshall	1215	1122
Miami	1551	1519
Porter	1146	1025
Pulaski	420	552
St. Joseph	2067	1586
Starke	144	185
White	809	756
Total	14541	12610

Maj. for Colfax, 1,931.

X.	Case.	Dawson.
Allen	1949	2707
De Kalb	1047	1157
Elkhart	1971	1649
Kosciusco	1584	1057
La Grange	1062	460

INDIANA.

CONGRESS—(Continued.)

Districts. X.	Rep. Case.	Dem. Dawson.
Noble	1278	1080
Steuben	1118	441
Whitley	776	866
Total	10780	9417

Maj. for Case, 1,363.

XI.	Pettit.	Coffroth.
Adams	474	842
Blackford	251	379
Grant	1297	973
Hamilton	1471	1003
Howard	1009	622
Huntington	1218	1395
Jay	847	772
Madison	1209	1451
Tipton	505	627
Wabash	1797	1126
Wells	670	848
Total	10748	10088

Maj. for Pettit, 710.

AGGREGATE VOTE OF STATE.

Republicans.
Sec. State..Peelle...104828
Auditor....Lange...105493
Treasurer..Harper...105416
Att'y Gen.. Otto.....105757
S. Pub. Ins.Young,..105014

Democrats.
Sec. State..McClure,107409
Auditor....Dodd....107242
Treasurer .Cun'g'm.107634
Att'y Gen..McDon'd 107291
S. Pub. Ins.Rugg ...107910

* Anti-Lecompton Democrats.

Illinois—1858.

CONGRESS.

Districts. I.	Rep. Washburne.	Doug. Bright.
Boone	1704	286
Carroll	1137	256
Jo Daviess	1938	1476
Lake	1677	620
McHenry	2224	1081
Ogle	2092	815
Stephenson	2140	1489
Winnebago	2899	484
Total	15811	6457

Jackson, *A.L.D.*, 870.
Washburne over Bright, 9,354.

II.	Farnsworth.	Dyer.
Cook	10108	8278
De Kalb	2067	612
Du Page	1280	496
Kane	3172	1121
Lee	1638	689
Rock Island	1542	1802
Whiteside	1990	700
Total	21797	13198

Blackman, *A.L.D.*, 701.
F'worth over Dyer, 8,599.

III.	Lovejoy.	Armstrong.
Bureau	2546	607
Champaign	1271	900
De Witt	992	755
Grundy	999	715
Iroquois	1199	744
Kankakee	1366	852
Kendall	1423	405
La Salle	4040	3438
Livingston	986	794
M'Lean	2570	2155
Putnam	582	299
Vermillion	1661	1126
Will	2678	2198
Total	22313	14988

Le Roy, *A.L.D.*, 1,828.
L'joy over Armst'g, 7,325.

ILLINOIS.

CONGRESS—(Continued.)

Districts. IV.	Rep. Kellogg.	Dem. Davidson.
Fulton	2980	3224
Henry	2242	1101
Knox	2965	1820
Marshall	1203	1054
Mason	822	1038
Mercer	1419	898
Peoria	2601	2623
Stark	929	584
Tazewell	1783	1960
Warren	1732	1406
Woodford	811	1152
Total	19487	16860

Gale, A.L.D., 553.
Kellogg over D'son, 2,627.

Districts. V.	Grimshaw.	Morris.
Adams	3004	3280
Brown	590	849
Calhoun	171	507
Hancock	2054	2234
Henderson	1001	755
McDonald	177	1944
Pike	1991	2471
Schuyler	1063	1489
Total	11648	13529

Davis, A.L.D., 504.
Morris over G'shaw, 1,881.

Districts. VI.	Matheny.	Harris.
Cass	743	1068
Christian	591	923
Greene	765	1517
Jersey	574	1053
Macoupin	1615	2093
Menard	780	851
Morgan	1789	2054
Montgomery	786	1222
Sangamon	2803	3010
Scott	650	1002
Shelby	550	1394
Total	11646	16193

McConnell, A.L.D., 277.
Harris over Math'y, 4,547.

Districts. VII.	Oglesby.	Robinson.
Clay	424	712
Clark	1976	1405
Coles	1859	1573
Cumberland	488	696
Crawford	693	922
Edgar	1446	431
Effingham	214	803
Fayette	605	842
Jasper	459	619
Lawrence	455	662
Logan	1315	1174
Macon	1168	939
Moultrie	513	570
Piatt	546	480
Richland	499	755
Total	11760	13588

Baldwin, A.L.D., 36.
R'son over Oglesby, 1,828.

Districts. VIII.	Baker.	Fouke.
Bond	731	700
Clinton	377	883
Jefferson	288	1193
Madison	2054	2185
Marion	575	1142
Monroe	569	1149
Randolph	917	1090
St. Clair	2464	2058
Washington	435	1090
Total	8410	11490

Hope, A.L.D., 198.
Fouke over Baker, 3,080.

Districts. IX.	Phillips.	Logan.
Alexander	41	378
Edwards	395	267
Franklin	19	1030
Gallatin	207	815
Hamilton	6	1155

ILLINOIS.

CONGRESS—(Continued.)

Districts. IX.	Rep. Phillips.	Dem. Logan.
Hardin	46	856
Jackson	79	1225
Johnson	7	1157
Massac	15	750
Perry	474	798
Pope	18	774
Pulaski	67	589
Saline	3	1143
Union	65	819
Wabash	396	623
White	611	1250
Williamson	48	1554
Wayne	804	1195
Total	2796	15878

Parish, A.L.D., 144.
Logan over Phillips, 13,082.

For Superin't of Public Instruction, Bateman, *Rep.*, received 124,556 votes; French, *Doug.*, 122,413; Reynolds, *Buch.*, 5,173.

For Treas'r, Miller, *Rep.*, received 125,430; Fondey, *Douglas Dem.*, 121,609; Dougherty, *Buch'n Dem.*, 5,071.

THE VOTE FOR LINCOLN AND DOUGLAS.

At this election, Messrs. Lincoln and Douglas canvassed the State for U. S. Senator, to be chosen by the Legislature then elected; and while Mr. Douglas carried a majority of the Legislature, Mr. Lincoln had the popular vote. The aggregate vote of the State for members of the Legislature was as follows:

Lincoln, *Rep.*,.... 124,698
Douglas, *Dem.*,... 121,190
Buch. Dem. and Scattering, ... 4,683
Lincoln over Douglas, 3,508.

In Five Districts of the State there were no Republican Candidates for the Legislature. In these five Districts, the Republican State Ticket received 577 votes, which, added to the vote of Mr. Lincoln (to which they clearly belong), makes his majority in this State, over Douglas, 4,085.

Wisconsin—1859.

GOVERNOR.

Districts. I.	Rep. Randall.	Dem. Hobart.
Kenosha	1821	906
Milwaukee	2811	6251
Racine	2111	1634
Walworth	3133	1459
Waukesha	2785	2295
Total	12161	12545

Maj. for Hobart, 384.

II.	Randall.	Hobart.
Adams	594	293
Bad Ax	995	619
Buffalo	264	414
Chippewa	156	248
Clarke	71	42
Crawford	619	748
Dane	3727	3880
Douglas	84	60

WISCONSIN.

GOVERNOR—(Continued.)

Districts. II.	Rep. Randall.	Dem. Hobart.
Dunn	192	175
Eau Claire	320	233
Grant	2496	1715
Green	1726	1141
Iowa	1454	1320
Jackson	493	298
Juneau	1060	874
La Crosse	1219	1034
Lafayette	1102	1514
Lapointe	72	109
Marathon	206	509
Monroe	939	578
Pepin	432	255
Pierce	506	805
Polk	161	141
Portage	743	582
Richland	745	647
Rock	4089	1578
St. Croix	516	560
Sauk	1659	799
Trempeleau	366	134
Wood	235	280
Total	27191	21080

Maj. for Randall, 6,111.

III.	Randall.	Hobart.
Brown	423	1066
Calumet	518	678
Columbia	2595	1646
Dodge	3492	3856
Door	72	78
Fond du Lac	3214	2530
Green Lake	1453	662
Jefferson	2327	2512
Kewaunee	167	567
Manitowoc	704	2134
Marquette	586	792
Oconto	852	446
Ozaukee	627	1577
Outagamie	494	733
Shawanaw	105	87
Sheboygan	1772	1889
Washington	684	2106
Waupacca	1167	624
Waushara	1126	380
Winnebago	2235	1570
Total	24110	25883

Maj. for Hobart, 1,770.

TOTAL VOTE OF THE STATE.

Randall, *Rep.*,	63465
Hobart, *Dem.*,	59508
Maj. for Randall,	3957

Oregon—1859.

CONGRESS.

Counties.	Rep. Logan.	Dem. Stout.
Benton	222	422
Clackamas	380	379
Clotsop	54	34
Columbia	63	72
Coos	52	63
Curry	54	37
Douglass	839	495
Jackson	218	663
Josephine	211	411
Lane	532	585
Linn	602	723
Marion	1062	296
Multnomah	563	434
Polk	254	284
Tillamook	10	5
Umpqua	132	43
Wasco	115	255
Washington	356	201
Yamhill	412	318
Total	5631	5670

Maj. for Stout, 39.

Iowa—1859.

GOVERNOR.

Districts. I.	Rep. Kirkwood.	Dem. Dodge.
Adair	120	76
Adams	177	122
Audubon	58	60
Appanoose	627	985
Cass	179	152
Clarke	462	851
Dallas	530	448
Davis	717	1142
Decatur	390	771
Desmoines	1704	1923
Fremont	293	504
Guthrie	257	260
Harrison	297	851
Henry	1596	998
Jasper	946	705
Jefferson	1282	1192
Keokuk	1025	1043
Lee	2159	2392
Louisa	956	679
Lucas	521	457
Madison	651	729
Mahaska	1212	1187
Marion	1256	1438
Mills	262	245
Monroe	749	665
Montgomery	125	115
Page	377	833
Polk	1078	1048
Potawatomie	295	600
Poweshiek	595	411
Ringgold	260	125
Shelby	78	96
Taylor	304	257
Union	151	198
Van Buren	1397	1402
Wapello	1016	1260
Warren	937	609
Washington	1203	946
Wayne	416	535
Total	26663	26755

Maj. for Dodge, 92.

II.	Kirkwood.	Dodge.
Allamakee	743	1025
Benton	914	732
Black Hawk	815	550
Boone	298	413
Bremer	417	438
Buchanan	816	570
Buena Vista	2	6
Butler	474	246
Calhoun	17	17
Carroll	30	30
Cedar	1152	1002
Cerro Gordo	117	72
Cherokee	12	7
Chickasaw	439	808
Clay	3	9
Clayton	1630	1429
Clinton	1605	1521
Crawford	45	55
Delaware	844	894
Dickinson	31	15
Dubuque	2751	8153
Emmet	18	5
Fayette	2102	849
Floyd	495	281
Franklin	201	51
Greene	126	146
Grundy	110	17
Hamilton	192	105
Hancock	19	14
Hardin	645	458
Howard	336	279
Humboldt	49	29
Ida	4	3
Iowa	765	549
Jackson	1273	1477
Johnson	1602	1395
Jones	1161	1153
Kossuth	75	87
Linn	1771	1345
Marshall	795	442
Mitchell	516	204
Monona	105	105
Muscatine	1457	1364

IOWA.

GOVERNOR—(Continued.)

Districts. IL.	Rep. Kirkwood.	Dem. Dodge.
Palo Alto	3	44
Plymouth....	24	11
Pocahontas ..	16	17
Sac	28	37
Scott	2208	1625
Story	395	358
Tama	500	295
Webster	252	333
Winnebago ..	11	24
Winneshiek..	1022	771
Woodbury...	132	163
Worth.......	98	26
Wright	80	52
Total	29741	26556

Maj. for Kirkwood, 3,185.

TOTAL VOTE OF THE STATE.

Kirkwood, *Rep.*, ... 56404
Dodge, *Dem.*,....... 53311

Maj. for Kirkwood, 3093

Minnesota—1859.

GOVERNOR.

Counties.	Rep. Ramsey.	Dem. Becker.
Anoka.......	383	165
Benton	143	94
Blue Earth ..	734	560
Brown	343	300
Carver	473	524
Cass.........	No return.	
Chisago	284	156
Crow Wing...	8	55
Dakota......	1007	1056
Dodge.......	593	444
Farribault ...	210	109
Fillmore.....	1399	1171
Freeborn	438	227
Goodhue.....	1220	706
Hennepin ...	2013	1117
Houston......	675	716
Isanti........	No return.	
Jackson	21	18
Kannabec ...	9	6
Kandiyohi...	19	3
Le Sueur	577	625
Manomin....	No return.	
Martin	18	10
McLeod	197	95
Meeker......	147	108
Mille Lac	No return.	
Monongalia..	47	30
Morrison.....	88	115
Mower	412	488
Nicollett.....	424	227
Olmsted	1119	777
Pine	6	28
Pembina.....	No return.	
Ramsey......	1485	1773
Renville	8	37

MINNESOTA.

GOVERNOR—(Continued.)

Districts.	Rep. Ramsey.	Dem. Becker.
Rice.........	1045	828
Scott	552	917
Sherburne ...	131	68
Sibley	8C8	526
Stearns......	875	660
Steele	448	178
Todd	No return.	
Wabashaw...	793	512
Waseca	359	254
Washington..	953	707
Winona	1209	814
Wright	579	265
Carlton, St. Louis, Lake,	88	119
Total....	21335	17583

Maj. for Ramsey, 3,752.

LEGISLATURE.

SENATE.Rep., 23; Dem., 13; Independent, 1.
HOUSE..Rep., 58; Dem., 22.

California—1859.

GOVERNOR.

Counties.	Rep. Stanford.	Dem. Latham.	A.L.D. Currey.
Alameda..	299	1066	664
Amador...	232	2023	985
Butte.....	854	1915	1666
Calaveras.	35	3275	1391
Colusa ...	15	541	166
Con'a Costa	41	805	378
Del Norte.	18	392	126
El Dorado.	408	3096	2413
Fresno....	1	359	11
Humboldt	83	397	372
Klamath..	1	607	120
Los Ang'ls	220	1916	49
Marin	67	467	75
Mariposa..	8	1462	212
Mendocino	11	730	85
Merced....	1	231	32
Monterey..	46	495	175
Napa.....	14	810	905
Nevada...	581	3185	2534
Placer....	896	3226	1117
Plumas...	193	882	649
Sacram'to.	228	3526	2678
San Bern'o	39	532	6
San Diego.	17	259	1
San Fran'o	3027	4747	2943
San Joa'in	209	1806	878
S. Luis Ob'o	30	284	30
San Mateo	105	420	418
Santa B'ra	35	431	—
Santa Clara	626	1407	367
Santa Cruz	150	499	451
Shasta....	8	1456	432
Sierra	295	2814	1666

CALIFORNIA.

GOVERNOR—(Continued.)

Counties.	Rep. Stanford.	Dem. Latham.	A.L.D. Currey.
Siskiyou ..	43	2159	1308
Solano....	88	1172	827
Sonoma...	64	1981	1148
Stanislaus.	13	389	106
Sutter	87	695	159
Tehama ..	35	770	92
Trinity ...	4	1285	829
Tulare and B'na Vista	11	821	63
Tuolumne	969	3723	737
Yolo......	66	757	568
Yuba.....	437	2442	1471
Total..	10110	62255	31298

Latham over C'rey, 30957; over both, 20847.

AGGREGATE VOTE ON OTHER STATE OFFICERS.

Republicans.
Lt. Gov ....Kennedy, 11148
Congress ..Baker,... 41488
" Sibley,... 301
*Sup. Court.*Shafter.. 11799

Democrats.
Lt. Gov ....Downey,. 59051
Congress ..Burch .. 57665
" Scott 56998
*Sup. Court.*Cope 59397

Anti-Lecompton Democrats.
Lt. Gov ....Conness.. 31051
Congress ..Booker .. 2969
" McKibben 43474
*Sup. Court.*Sprague.. 30978

Baker, *Rep.*, was generally supported by the Anti-Lecompton Democrats, and McKibben by the Republicans.

South Carolina.

There is no opposition to what is termed the Regular Democracy in this State, and no officers are elected by the entire vote of the State, the Governor and State officers, as well as the Presidential Electors, being chosen by the Legislature.

Alabama.

An Election was held in this State in 1859, for Governor, Congressmen and Legislature, in which the opposition to the regular Democracy claimed the suffrages of the people, on the

ALABAMA.

grounds of greater devotion to the interests of the South, but exhibited only a feeble show of strength, Andrew B. Moore, regular Dem., being reëlected Governor over Wm. F. Samford, Independent, by about 20,000 majority. The Regulars also carried the entire Delegation in Congress ; the only close contest being in the Third (Montgomery) Dist., where Clopton, Regular Dem., beat Judge, Independent, by 214 majority.

Mississippi.

An Election was held in this State for Governor, State Officers, and Congressmen, in 1859, which resulted in the success of the Democracy by more than three to one, Pettus, Dem., for Governor, receiving 34,559 votes to 10,308 for Walter, Independent. The Democratic Candidates for other State Officers ran ahead of Mr. Pettus. For Congress there was hardly a show of opposition to the Democratic candidates.

Florida.

The last general Election in this State was for Congress, in 1858, when both candidates were Democrats. Hawkins, the regular Democrat, receiving 6,465 votes, and Westcott, Independent Dem., 4,070.

Arkansas.

There is not sufficient opposition to the Regular Democracy in this State to create the slightest interest in the elections. At the last election for Congressmen (1858) in the First District, Hindman, Dem., received 18,255 votes, to 2,853 for Crosby, Independent ; and, in the Second District, Rust, Dem., received 16,302 to 3,114 for Jones, and 3,452 for Drew, Independent candidates.

Made in the USA
Monee, IL
07 July 2026

56551364R00138